THE IRWIN SERIES IN MANAGEMENT
AND
THE BEHAVIORAL SCIENCES

L. L. CUMMINGS and E. KIRBY WARREN
CONSULTING EDITORS

JOHN F. MEE   ADVISORY EDITOR

International Business and Multinational Enterprises

STEFAN H. ROBOCK
Robert D. Calkins Professor of International Business
Graduate School of Business
Columbia University

KENNETH SIMMONDS
Professor and Chairman of Marketing
London Graduate School of Business Studies

 1973

RICHARD D. IRWIN, INC.   Homewood, Illinois   60430
IRWIN-DORSEY INTERNATIONAL   London, England   WC2H 9NJ
IRWIN-DORSEY LIMITED   Georgetown, Ontario   L7G 4B3

First Printing, June 1973
Second Printing, July 1974
Third Printing, December 1974
Fourth Printing, April 1975
Fifth Printing, October 1975

ISBN 0-256-01472-8
Library of Congress Catalog Card No. 72–98121

Printed in the United States of America

PREFACE

ONE OF the most dramatic and significant world trends of the last two decades has been the rapid and sustained growth of international business. In its traditional form of international trade as well as its newer form of multinational business operations, international business has become massive in scale and come to exercise a major influence over political, economic, and social development throughout the world.

This growth in business activity across national boundaries has brought with it many changes. To begin with, the rise of the multinational enterprise has confronted nation states with local business units that are closely linked with operations lying outside the nations' local jurisdiction. As a result nation states have had to grapple with a wide range of new policy issues that are not satisfactorily covered by the traditional conceptual framework for thinking about the protection of national interests—a framework primarily focused on controlling transfers of goods and money as they cross national borders. The business executive has also been confronted with new management problems. He has had to develop methods for operating simultaneously in many different and differently changing environments, to deal with new elements of risk and conflict, and to give much greater consideration to the role of his firm in influencing social and economic change. The management task has expanded and changed considerably from that faced within purely domestic operations.

It was not until the early 1960s that awareness of the problems that arise when business operations extend across national boundaries began to have any significant impact on business education. By this time there was a growing realization that existing theories, generalizations, principles, methods, and techniques of business management that had been built up largely from business experience within the United States were neither general nor universal. More explicit attention to the international dimension of business began to appear in business curricula. In established fields such as marketing, finance, accounting, and management, more specifically international content was added to existing courses. New international business courses also emerged.

At an early stage the new international business courses frequently consisted only of selected tools and materials culled from the fields of international trade and international economics—a reflection of the newness of the field and the limited development of concepts and research. In these courses there tended to be a bias towards national issues and little direct attempt to develop the special skills demanded by the realities of multinational operations. Other courses simply joined together international aspects of conventional business courses, particularly finance and marketing, with little attempt to develop skills in assessing environmental differences.

With a decade of experimentation and research now behind it, however, international business has evolved into a field of study and research with its own identity. Its central focus is the set of management problems stemming from the movement of goods, human resources, technology, finance, or ownership across national boundaries. As befits a course for business managers, the field has a managerial orientation, and assessment of national issues is placed in this perspective. Furthermore, the field of international business has moved well beyond an applied international economics orientation to draw heavily upon other related fields such as politics, sociology, anthropology, and law where materials from these disciplines are relevant to the tasks of the international manager. It is now widely accepted that international business courses with this focus and integration can provide a basic frame of reference and develop the international dimension of business teaching in a way that other subject areas with their own focus and conceptual approaches are unlikely ever to achieve.

This book grew out of the authors' experience of ten years' teaching of international business courses in the graduate business schools of Indiana, Columbia, Manchester, and London universities. There was a need for a basic introductory text which was both intellectually challenging and had a direct focus on the development of management skills in handling the problems of multinational business. The text is divided into five principle sections. Part I introduces the new field of international business and examines the forces underlying its expansion and the patterns that are emerging from this growth. Part II presents the monetary, trade, and legal frameworks within which international business transactions take place. Part III is concerned with the common interests and conflicts between international firms and nation states, with particular attention to controls that nations exercise over transfers across national boundaries. Part IV deals with the assessment and forecasting of the economic, social, political, and legal aspects of the environment within which the international firm operates, and Part V covers the management of the various functions of the multinational firm, paying particular attention to the issues that are specific to international activity.

Experience in teaching has shown that a course covering topics in the order in which they are presented in the text produces a clear and interesting progression for the student. Students generally benefit from a short grounding in the terminology and concepts covering international monetary and trade transactions and their regulation. From this base the natural progression is to examine first the wider issues of the firm's relationship with different national interests. Decisions taken within individual businesses which have consequences for more than one nation must inevitably be colored by the national objectives and responsibilities of those concerned. It is also wise to examine how such actions will be viewed by the nation states. As a next step, before moving on to examine the detailed structuring of action decisions, there is a strong case for building a more solid foundation of ability in assessing what is going on in the international environment and in forecasting changes that might influence the outcome of a businessman's decisions. The last few years have seen major advances in environmental forecasting methods forged for the specific purpose of international business decision making.

Whatever the course design that is adopted, students clearly appreciate a continual examination of the relevance of the material to the management task. Discussion exercises and questions designed with this in mind have been included at the end of each chapter. Also available at the end of the text is a series of problems and cases that can be drawn upon to support the course design adopted by the instructor. All of these materials are aimed at strengthening practical analysis and decision making skills within international business situations.

The material included in the text has been used successfully with both undergraduate and graduate students and extensive footnotes have been included as an aid to more advanced study of areas in which students may have a special interest. While the book is primarily designed for business readers, it should be useful for government decision makers who must take into account the present and future behavior patterns of international firms in designing national policies. Students of political science who are interested in the role of international business in shaping governmental patterns should also find it of interest.

Many professional colleagues and practitioners have given the authors invaluable assistance in the long and arduous task of preparing a comprehensive book on such a new and dynamic field. Professors Warren J. Keegan, Nathaniel H. Leff, Charles F. Stewart, and James A. F. Stoner at Columbia Business School have made many excellent suggestions while using the material in preliminary form. Professors Henry P. deVries and Willis L. M. Reese of the Columbia Law School were kind enough to review and comment on the legal environment material. Professors J. Boddewyn, Sune Carlson, Richard Farmer, John Fayerweather, and Hans Schollhammer also provided helpful criticisms and suggestions. Peter Mathias, a graduate student at Columbia, made significant contributions as a research assistant and Mr. George Browne provided a highly professional editorial review of the manuscript. It is Shirley Robock to whom we owe most. It was Shirley who reviewed, criticized, edited, and provided research assistance over several years on all of the chapters of the book.

The many versions of the draft manuscript were processed with patience, good cheer, and efficiency by Sonya Whynman, Lynn Kauderer, Cheryll Johnson, Meryl Balchin, and Sue Melkman. A word of acknowledgment is also due to the postal services on both sides of the Atlantic— we cannot understand why they both make losses.

May 1973   STEFAN H. ROBOCK
                                                    KENNETH SIMMONDS

CONTENTS

21. Multinational Management of Human Resources 513

General Policy on International Executives: *Foreign Nationals for Managing Subsidiaries. Headquarters Managers. Criteria for Choosing a Policy.* Problems of Cross-National Transfers: *New Working Relationships. Family and Social Adjustments. Career Patterns.* Recruitment and Selection of International Executives. Training for the International Executive. Compensation Policies. Labor Relations in the Multinational Firms: *Transnational Labor Union Collaboration.*

Part VI
CASES AND PROBLEMS IN
INTERNATIONAL BUSINESS 539

PART I

The Nature and Scope of International Business

1

THE FIELD OF INTERNATIONAL BUSINESS

A DEFINITION OF INTERNATIONAL BUSINESS

INTERNATIONAL BUSINESS as a field of management training and scholarly research deals primarily with business activities that cross national boundaries, whether they be movements of goods, services, capital, personnel, transfers of technology, or even the supervision of employees. International business has recently emerged as a separate branch of management training because of the growing scale and complexity of the international involvement of business firms and because transactions across national boundaries give rise to new and unique problems of management and governmental policy which have received inadequate attention in traditional areas of business and economics.

Business transactions that run between different sovereign political units are not new phenomena on the world economic scene. Some business firms have had foreign direct investments and foreign operations for many years, predominantly but not limited to companies in the fields of mining, petroleum, and agriculture.[1] Foreign trade, moreover, has a venerable history dating back to the emergence of the nation-state. But since the end of World War II a dramatic change has occurred in the patterns of international business activities. Thousands of business firms in many nations have developed into multinational enterprises

---

[1] Mira Wilkins, *The Emergence of Multinational Enterprise: American Business Abroad from the Colonial Era to 1914* (Cambridge, Mass.: Harvard University Press, 1970). This study shows that American direct foreign investment prior to 1914 was not limited to extractive industries and utilities but also included "a surprising number of . . . U.S. headquartered multinational manufacturing companies. . . ." (p. ix).

with ownership control or other links that cross national boundaries. These firms which have begun to take a global view from markets back to resources and to integrate markets and production on a world scale have become predominant. International trade between essentially domestic firms of different nations has continued to grow in absolute value, but its relative importance in the total international business picture has steadily declined.[2]

Issues facing international managers and national governments with respect to their roles in this changing pattern of business activities across national boundaries have become the prime concern of the international business field. The field gives special attention to the advent of the multinational business enterprise—an enterprise based in one country and operating in one or more countries other than the home base country.[3] International business thus encompasses but is not limited to international trade. It not only includes the activities of firms directly engaged in performing international trade services, such as shipping, communications, and international financial transactions, but also comprises the activities of all multinational enterprises, whether of private, government, or mixed ownership. Each business unit has a wide range of choices for adjusting business activity between different nations. Direct exporting from the home-base country is only one of them. Foreign production is a new international business concept used to describe the trend of multinational firms to establish production facilities in countries other than the home-base country in order to supply local demand in foreign countries or export to other markets.[4] Another aspect is portfolio investment across national boundaries involving the purchase of securities without transfer of managerial control.

International Business, Foreign Operations, and Comparative Business

As a new field of study develops, it is natural that ambiguities and differences of opinion will exist in defining the field. In order to clarify the scope of the authors' approach to international business, we should differentiate between international business, foreign business, and com-

---

[2] For an interesting discussion of why investment is displacing trade, see Emile Benoit, "Interdependence on a Small Planet," *Columbia Journal of World Business,* Spring 1966.

[3] David E. Lilienthal, "The Multinational Corporation," in *Management and Corporations 1985* ed. M. H. Anshen and G. L. Bach (New York: McGraw-Hill Book Co., 1960). The term "multinational firm" was probably first used by David E. Lilienthal in a paper delivered at Carnegie Institute of Technology in April 1960.

[4] For example, see Judd Polk, Irene W. Meister, and Lawrence A. Veit, *U.S. Production Abroad and the Balance of Payments* (New York: National Industrial Conference Board, 1966).

parative business. The last two concepts are sometimes used as synonyms
for international business. Foreign business refers to domestic operations
within a foreign country while comparative business studies focus on
similarities and differences among countries and business systems. The
great merit of comparative studies in business, as well as in other fields
such as politics, sociology, and economics, is the new perspective and
better understanding of home institutions and environments that is frequently secured.[5] But as Fayerweather has explained, ". . . They are
not properly part of international business because they focus on business
processes involving only one country at a time."[6]

The three concepts—international business, foreign business, and comparative business—are interrelated and have large overlaps. The manager
of international business operations may benefit greatly from many types
of comparative business studies and from a knowledge of many aspects
of foreign business operations. At the same time, foreign business operations and comparative business as fields of inquiry and training do not
have as their major point of interest the special problems that arise
when business activities cross national boundaries. For example, the vital
question of potential conflicts between the nation state and the multinational firm, which receives major attention in international business
studies, is not likely to be central or even peripheral in foreign operations
and comparative business studies.

An example from the field of accounting will illustrate the principal
boundaries and focus of international business. A manager engaged in
foreign business needs to know only the accounting practices in the
host country. A comparative approach to accounting examines the systems and practices in many countries with the main objective of identifying similarities and differences among countries as well as universal
patterns, if they exist. International business concentrates on the accounting needs for managing a multinational firm doing business across
national boundaries. The accounting problems and techniques for international business operations are related to differences in national accounting systems. In some important respects, the accounting activities
of the multinational firm will be influenced by tax and legal considerations of the specific countries in which the firm is operating. Within
these constraints, however, accounting in international business is primarily concerned with fulfilling the needs of multinational operations
through an effective and uniform accounting system that cuts across
national boundaries.

---

[5] For example, see J. Boddewyn, *Comparative Management and Marketing* (Glenview, Ill.: Scott, Foresman and Co., 1969).

[6] John Fayerweather, *International Business Management* (New York: McGraw-
Hill Book Co., 1969), p. 6.

The Scope of International Business Activities

As international business has evolved from a situation where importing and exporting activities were dominant to the current stage of development in which multinational enterprise plays a large and increasing role, there has been a strong tendency to emphasize the manufacturing activities of multinational firms. In large part, this emphasis results from the use of international direct-investment data to describe the new international business trends. Since manufacturing and other production activities are relatively capital intensive, they tend to show up importantly in investment statistics.

Inter-nation business operations, however, include a wide range of highly significant business activities in fields other than manufacturing. In addition to international trade and foreign production in mining, petroleum, agriculture, and manufacturing, extensive business transactions across national boundaries occur in service fields such as construction, hotels, tourism, business consulting, retailing, and wholesaling; in air and ocean transportation; in financial activities such as commercial and investment banking, securities and mutual funds, and insurance; in communications such as radio, television, telegraph, telephone, magazines and books, newspapers, news services, and movies; in the field of technology through royalty and licensing agreements and research and development institutes.

The Multinational Corporation

The multinational corporation has become well recognized as a key feature of the changing international business pattern. But general agreement on the definition of a multinational corporation does not yet exist.[7] Some of the definitions proposed emphasize structural criteria such as the number of countries in which a firm is doing business, or ownership by persons from many nations, or the nationality composition of top management. Other definitions stress performance characteristics such as the absolute amount—or relative share—of earnings, sales, assets, or employees, derived from or committed to foreign operations. Still other definitions are based on behavioral characteristics of top management such as "thinking internationally."

Another approach has proposed a set of definitions that suggest an evolutionary process of internationalization.[8] In this scheme a firm is classified as international if it engages in foreign business but has made

---

[7] Yair Aharoni, "On the Definition of a Multinational Corporation," *Quarterly Review of Economics and Business,* Autumn 1971, pp. 27–37.

[8] S. Rolfe, *The International Corporation* (Paris: International Chamber of Commerce, 1969), p. 12.

no direct foreign investments. A multinational firm would be one which allocates company resources without regard to national frontiers but is nationally based in terms of ownership and top management. A transnational firm would be a multinational firm managed and owned by persons of different nationalities. A supranational firm would be a transnational firm that is legally denationalized by becoming incorporated through an international agency, when, or if, this possibility exists.

The definitional debate is not simply a matter of semantics. It is important in the sense that it reflects the heterogeneity of the field and the reality that there are a number of different kinds of so-called multinational companies. It is also a reminder that researchers in the field need operational definitions that will permit them to identify which firms are to be included in their studies and which are not. Consequently, the users of research studies and statistics on multinational enterprises must be alert to the specific definitions being used.

In this book, the labels of multinational and international corporations will be used interchangeably. They refer to a cluster of corporations controlled by one headquarters but the operations of which are spread over many countries.

With the growing international involvement of business firms, more and more companies—American, European, Japanese, and others—are finding that a large share of their assets are deployed around the world, that many of their employees are foreign citizens, that a large amount of their earnings are in foreign currencies and that they are operating to an important extent outside the legal jurisdiction of the country in which the parent company is incorporated. In these circumstances, the companies have become multinational corporations, and the nature of their operations has been significantly transformed. They come to be managed as world enterprises, with international considerations dominating their decisions. The world becomes the company's market and sphere of operation, and the home country becomes but one part.

Although many U.S. firms have recently been moving aggressively into international business operations, the multinational corporation is not uniquely nor exclusively an American phenomenon. In fact, if one were looking only two decades ago for examples of multinational firms, the names of European rather than U.S.-based corporations would have come to mind: the British-Dutch companies—Unilever and the Royal Dutch Shell Group—Switzerland's Nestlé, Britain's Imperial Chemical Industries, the Netherlands' Philips Lamps, and Sweden's Ericsson Telephone.

Not all international business is conducted by multinational corporations. Export and import activities, for example, do not require that a company establish and operate overseas branches, affiliates, or other units of the home corporation. The licensing of patents and technology

in foreign countries can be accomplished without a predominantly domestic company becoming multinational. The dividing line to mark the
stage at which a company becomes multinational, however, is difficult
to determine. Many domestic companies go through a gradual evolution
toward making direct investments, first establishing marketing, procurement offices, or warehouses in foreign countries. Even when a business
firm crosses the imaginary and imprecise boundary between domestic
and multinational, its degree of international commitment and internationalization may range over a wide spectrum.

In one sense, the emergence of the multinational corporation reflects
a differential pace in the evolution of political institutions relative to
business organizations. While business activities have become more and
more internationalized, the development of international governmental
organizations has not accompanied business and economic trends. Consequently, business corporations cannot be incorporated and licensed with
an international governmental agency as a world corporation. They still
must be created and exist under the jurisdiction of a specific nation-state.
Yet the multinational firm may have different patterns of ownership
and control. In most cases, in the present stage of evolution, both ownership and control of the multinational corporation reside in the base
country. In other significant cases, ownership and control is divided
between two or more countries even though the enterprise is the legal
creation of a single nation-state. If this trend continues, as it probably
will, other patterns of control will develop.

From the standpoint of business management, multinational operations
raise many problems associated with the need to deal with a wide range
of environmental factors in several different countries. It also raises
new internal issues in organization and operations. From the standpoint
of world-development aspirations, the multinational corporation offers
a nongovernmental vehicle for transferring technology, financial resources, management techniques, and marketing experience among nations at various stages of development.

What Is Different about International Business?

One can recognize the growing international involvement of business
firms and the rapid trend toward multinational enterprises and yet question the need for international business as a separate field of study.
The argument can be made that management principles are universal
and that concepts being taught in the functional fields of marketing,
finance, production, and control are as relevant to business management
in one country as they are, in another. The manager in the world economy, the argument goes, may need only supplementary training in the
traditional fields of international economics and international trade.

Despite these arguments, a rapid trend has emerged to give explicit attention to the international dimension of business and to recognize international business as a separate field in the business area. The trend is supported by the view that earlier theories, generalizations, principles, methods, and techniques, developed in response to norms in the United States where management training has had its greatest flowering, were neither general nor universal. In contrast to purely domestic operations, business activities across national boundaries require considerable familiarity with international means of payments and involve new elements of risk, conflict, environmental adjustments, and influence over social and economic change. At best, only some of these elements are covered in traditional international economics and trade courses, and have been only briefly treated in traditional management courses.

Although unique variables and considerations of business have fostered the development of the field as a separate entity in the business area, not everything concerning international business must be studied separately under that heading. Some aspects of international business may be covered effectively by extending existing fields; others can be better developed as a unified whole rather than as segmented appendages to existing fields. For example, an understanding in depth of cultural differences as they affect international business operations is more likely to develop when the subject is treated as a unified whole, than if the scholars of finance, marketing, production, and management were each to study separately the adjustment of their function to different cultures.

There are four aspects of international business activity around which new types of thinking are beginning to emerge. These four aspects overlap to some degree and do not exhaust the potential for new approaches that may evolve. Each stems from unique problems that develop when business crosses national boundaries, and each gives rise to a new area of study and body of concepts.

International Risk. The special risk elements confronted in international business activity include financial, political, regulatory, and tax risks. They arise from causes such as the existence of different currencies, monetary standards, and national goals, but they are all measurable through their effect on profitability or ownership.

The financial risk elements involve balance-of-payments considerations, varying exchange rates, differential inflation trends among countries, and divergent interest rates. In the political area, the risk of expropriation or lesser harassment directed toward the foreign firm must be considered for many years ahead when heavy capital investments are being contemplated. The regulatory risks arise from different legal systems, overlapping jurisdictions, and dissimilar policies that influence such conditions as the regulation of restrictive business practices and the application of antitrust laws. In the tax field, unforeseen changes in fiscal policies can affect significantly the profitability of the multinational corporation. Furthermore, uncertainty as to application of tax laws frequently creates a risk of double taxation.

International economics provides essential tools for understanding the risks arising from balance-of-payments considerations, foreign exchange regulation, problems of international liquidity, tariff policies, and trade restrictions. Political theory is developing new insights into nationalistic tendencies and the preferences of different societies for varying mixes of public- and private-sector activities. Legal research on international business transactions has been expanding, and a growing amount of international tax research is enlarging the general understanding of different tax systems and practices.

But the coverage in these related fields does not meet many of the major needs of international business, and the extension and application of the materials and concepts to multinational business operations have been slow. The need is becoming recognized for a continuing business intelligence activity of considerable complexity to identify and predict international risks. Ideally, international risks should be analyzed for underlying causal forces, and projections into the future should be formulated in terms of probabilities and quantified in terms of potential costs.

Public policy has been even slower to adopt ideas and analyses that recognize the implications to international business activities of international economic and political variables. The vigorous business and academic criticism of U.S. policies adopted in 1968 to restrict direct foreign private investment in order to improve the balance of payments showed that the international business effects of such policies needed to be better identified in the formulation of governmental policies. In the case of foreign investment controls, the recipient countries need to examine more rigorously the effect of such controls on international business and the question of how much and what kind of outside investment benefits the country.

Multinational Conflicts.   Of major concern to international business are the conflicts that arise because of different national identities of owners, employees, customers, and suppliers and because of divergencies between the interests of sovereign national states and the business goals of multinational corporations.[9] Some of the conflicts occur within the international firm, and others involve the firm's relationship to the external environment.

An extremely troublesome area of external conflict concerns profit-motivated decisions that result in the transfer of funds, production, and employment from one country to another. The results of these decisions may at times run contrary to the national economic policies of one

⁹ Howe Martyn, "Multinational Corporations in a Nationalistic World," *Challenge Magazine*, November–December 1965, pp. 13–16.

or all of the countries involved. For example, extension of credit to foreign subsidiaries at times when the foreign nation is attempting to dampen purchasing power through monetary restrictions and exchange controls can undermine national objectives as well as place local firms at a competitive disadvantage. The list of areas in which conflicts occur also includes such matters as contribution to local exports or reduction of imports, national interests in strengthening local research, and management of the country's international competitive position.[10]

External conflicts frequently arise in decisions concerning a firm's allegiance to national defense policies. An example is the French subsidiary of an American computer manufacturer, which, in deference to American allegiance, did not solicit computer sales from Eastern Europe. Another example resulted from the different national-security policies followed by the United Kingdom and the United States in dealing with Cuba. As a result of this difference, a British subsidiary of an American firm was persuaded to maintain American allegiance and not sell motors that would be installed in passenger busses going to Cuba. Conflicts on national defense matters are likely to increase with the growing numbers of foreign-owned subsidiaries in technically advanced fields.

Within the international corporation, the mixture of national allegiances raises further issues. Home-country nationals tend to dominate top-management echelons of American-based multinational firms, and there is a tendency to retain research and administration functions in the developed countries. Disparities in wage and salary rates have also led to widely practiced discrimination on the basis of nationality. A number of nations have already placed restrictions on the numbers of foreign expatriates they will allow in local operations.

The conflict aspect of international business requires thinking that will relate a multiplicity of interests, each with different objectives and different criteria for evaluating potential outcomes. No other business field covers this successfully. The international businessman, trained to identify each conflicting interest and to think through the possible actions and reactions from each viewpoint, will be better prepared to plot his own best strategy in a complex situation. One of the functions of international business study should be to erase any tendency to make blindly nationalistic decisions or revert to pure economic arguments. To date, efforts to construct an international framework for establishing the legal validity of claims and actions of different parties involved in these conflict situations have been relatively unsuccessful.

Multiple Environments. The most pervasive distinction between international and domestic business lies in the environmental framework. Aside from its relationship to the elements of risk and conflict discussed

---

[10] For example, see Raymond Vernon, "Saints and Sinners in Foreign Investment," *Harvard Business Review,* May–June 1963, p. 157.

above, the multiplicity of environments in international business creates a wide range of operational problems that require new tools, concepts, analytical methods, and types of information. The wider the scope of the firm's international activities, the greater become the environmental diversities and the more crucial becomes the task of identifying, evaluating and predicting environmental variables. The environmental framework must be enlarged to include forces operating at a supranational level—such as the European Common Market—and forces involving relations between pairs of countries as well as variables associated with different national settings.

One important category of environmental variables relates to business activity open to the international business firm and to the form of business organization that must be used. Public utilities, including electric power, communications, and transportation, are not open to private enterprise in many countries. Business activity in natural resources such as petroleum and mining is restricted by many nations to domestic private or public enterprises. In some situations, the options open to international business firms require joint ventures with majority local ownership or joint ventures with government.

A second major category of environmental variables involves the diversity of the institutional settings. Labor unions, for example, are organized on different philosophical foundations and play different roles from country to country. Patterns of national, regional, and local economic planning vary greatly in scope and in their influence over business activity. Capital markets and financial institutions are in different stages of development and, in some cases, are evolving along different paths.

Another broad environmental variable involves cultural differences that affect business management. International business needs to know how cultural differences influence the behavior of customers, suppliers, and employees, and how these influences on behavior will change. This aspect of international business encompasses the full range of communication problems arising out of different languages, customs, and values.

International business has begun to develop its own body of cultural analysis following the functional division of business, with marketing questions receiving most attention. Considerable management literature has focused on the cultural adjustment of expatriate management and on the differences in foreign management and work force that might require adjustment of organization or procedures.[11] While concern for specific problems initially channeled cultural analysis along these func-

---

[11] Richard N. Farmer and Barry M. Richman, *Comparative Management and Economic Progress* (Homewood, Ill.: Richard D. Irwin, Inc., 1965); John Fayerweather, *The Executive Overseas* (Syracuse: Syracuse University Press, 1959); Barry M. Richman and Melvyn R. Copen. *International Management and Economic Development* (New York: McGraw-Hill Book Co., 1972).

tional lines, the common need throughout many business functions to understand cultural factors is for a more unified approach, which might be titled "Cultural Analysis for Business Decisions." Other customary segments of environmental study—educational, political, economic, and legal—might also be more effectively explored in a unified manner.

International Business and Development. International business is frequently a major change agent, a means of transferring technology, and a key force in the economic and social development of a nation. This can be true for developed countries, such as those of Western Europe, as well as for underdeveloped countries. Thus, international business requires new concepts that provide an understanding of what can and what cannot be achieved by the change agent and the potential contributions that international business can make to development.

The need to identify and justify the contribution that a proposed international business activity will make to an underdeveloped country has been forcefully stated by Richard Robinson:

The reason for attempting at least a semi-rigorous analysis of what a firm proposes to do in an underdeveloped country within the context of the national interest of that country lies in the near certainty that the host government will analyze the project in similar terms—if not at first, then later. The Western businessman must be prepared to defend the utility of his local enterprise in terms of sustained economic growth and political modernization.[12]

The large diversified international corporation that has flexibility in its selection of countries and products to offer within those countries is much in need of specialized knowledge on economic development to guide its global operations. Although economists have given some attention to the divergence between social benefit and a firm's profit-maximizing alternative, they have stopped far short of the specific calculations needed by the international business decision maker. Economists have also investigated the costs and benefits to a country from foreign private investment, but they have not yet developed an adequate and objective framework for decision making on such questions by the host countries.

One facet of the contribution of international business to development that requires more attention is its role in encouraging indigenous entrepreneurship. The international firm may create new entrepreneurial opportunities external to the firm for local suppliers and merchants. It may also attract much of the entrepreneurial potential in a country and thereby inhibit the possibilities for development of other national enterprises.

The role of international business in development raises moral and ideological issues. It is frequently true that profit motivation will keep

[12] Richard D. Robinson, *International Business Policy* (New York: Holt, Rinehart & Winston, 1964), p. 100.

a firm away from the less developed markets. Yet the opportunity for the greatest long-term good from the viewpoint of both the corporation's home country and the developing nations may well be to enter the developing country.

Once a corporation has entered a developing market, a whole range of new issues arise. One such issue is the degree to which the firm should become involved in the community and undertake expenditures normally the function of the public sector.[13] As a number of studies have demonstrated, the paternalistic firm, which provides much of the normal functions of the public sector, can foster animosity among the local population.[14]

INTERNATIONAL BUSINESS TRAINING

Some students will study international business as a field of concentration intending to follow a career working in foreign countries or in the headquarters operations of a multinational firm that uses nationals for operating foreign subsidiaries. Others will study international business as a supplement to their concentration in the functional fields of accounting, marketing, finance, and so on. Still others will be interested in international business as a preparation for working in government positions on the development and implementation of policies and programs for assisting and controlling business activities across national boundaries. For all these kinds of clientele, a minimum preparation for dealing effectively with the international dimension of business should include two goals: to develop familiarity with the body of knowledge on international business and to develop in the person special sensitivities, attitudes, flexibility, and tolerance.

The need for personal and emotional training to deal with international business matters deserves particular emphasis in this introduction because such training requires more than textbook reading. Ethnocentrism and personal parochialism can be diluted in a number of ways, some of which can be included within a broad framework of international business training. Student exchange programs can stimulate personal reconditioning through the experience of living and working in a foreign environment. When students from various countries and cultures are studying together, the students can be exposed to other cultures and values through class discussions and through team projects, if the teams are composed of different nationalities.

The international businessman needs training experience that develops

---

[13] Clifton R. Wharton, "Aiding the Community: A New Philosophy for Foreign Operations," *Harvard Business Review*, March–April 1954, pp. 64–72.

[14] Stacy May and Galo Plaza, *The United Fruit Company in Latin America* (Washington, D.C.: National Planning Association, 1958), pp. 240–43.

in him a special kind of personal and emotional radar to alert him to certain situations, where specific values and ways of action that he takes for granted in his own environment are different in other cultures and nations. The successful international businessman needs enough flexibility to understand what underlies these differences and enough tolerance to recognize that types of behavior and sets of values different from his own may be valid for other people. In an operational sense, he must recognize that what are constants for domestic business may be variables in international business.

EXERCISES AND DISCUSSION QUESTIONS

1. "To deny that international business is a valid field for academic effort is to suggest by analogy that such subjects as international politics, international economics, and international law are equally not academically respectable. It is true that international business borrows very heavily from all three, as they borrow from each other, but the core problem in international business is quite different." Discuss.

2. Of the top 50 foreign companies in *Fortune's* list of "300 Largest Industrials Outside the U.S.," which would you consider to be not multinational? Why?

2

THEORETICAL EXPLANATIONS OF INTERNATIONAL BUSINESS

BUSINESS ACTIVITY across national boundaries for many centuries was predominantly in the form of importing and exporting between firms which did not control activities in more than one country. In such a world, international trade and international business were considered synonymous. It was logical to look to international trade theory as a framework for understanding current patterns and anticipating future trends in international business relations.

With the emergence of the multinational firm and the resulting dramatic change in patterns of inter-nation business and in the structure of the world economy, trade theory has proved to be too limited for explaining the current realities of international business. Theoretical and empirical studies of direct private-investment flows have added to our understanding of the role of the international corporation. Yet the development of a theoretical basis, or framework, for explaining and predicting international business patterns is still in an early stage. There has been no movement to discard trade theory. But something more is needed. The task is difficult because it is no longer realistic to neglect the business firm and the way its decisions affect patterns of activity. The macro theories of international economics must be integrated with the micro theories of the behavior of the firm.

This chapter will examine the limitations of traditional theories and summarize the various new theories of international business that have been advanced. It will attempt also to develop a framework for interpreting the quantitative description of international business patterns to be presented in the next chapter.

RELATED THEORIES

International Trade Theory

With its long history and high refinement, international trade theory continues to shape much business thinking and, even more so, the actions of government. For this reason, the international manager needs to be reasonably conversant with it even though trade theory has only limited utility for explaining the modern international business era. Because it still constitutes the rationale for many features of the environment within which the manager must operate, it is reviewed in some detail in Chapter 5 as a key component of the traditional trade framework. At this point, however, the emphasis is on trade theory's limitations for explaining the forces underlying the growth of international business.

The major objective of trade theory is to explain why countries trade, what goods countries will export and import, how gains from trade are divided among trading countries, and how adjustments are brought about when trade patterns are disturbed.[1] In attempting to demonstrate the gains from trade and to explain the commodity composition of trade, classical trade theory assumes that factors of production (labor, natural resources, and capital) are free to move within each country and are immobile between countries.

Within trade theory, the foundation stone for explaining patterns and gains from trade is the *doctrine* or *law of comparative advantage*. The doctrine demonstrates that a country gains by producing more of those goods in which it is relatively more efficient and by exporting these in return for goods in which its absolute advantage is least. One country may have an *absolute advantage*, that is, it may be more efficient in terms of factor inputs per unit of output over another country in the production of every possible commodity. But so long as countries are not equally efficient in every commodity a basis for trade exists. This will be numerically demonstrated in Chapter 5.

By placing stress on relative costs, the doctrine of comparative advantage demonstrates the gains from specialization and trade. If a country specializes in those products in which it has the greatest comparative advantage relative to other nations and trades those products for goods in which it has the greatest comparative disadvantage, the total availability of goods secured by the country with the use of a given amount of resources will be enlarged. It follows, therefore, from the comparative advantage doctrine that free trade will maximize global output from the standpoint of the world as a whole because free trade allocates

---

[1] Charles P. Kindleberger, *International Economics*, 4th ed. (Homewood, Ill.: Richard D. Irwin, Inc., 1968), p. 19.

economic tasks among countries so as to maximize world output and income.

The failure of traditional trade theory to anticipate and explain the growing importance to the world economy of the internationalization of business operations stems partly from the way the question to be answered is posed. Trade theory asks the question, "Why do countries trade?" This is the wrong question. Businessmen trade, and increasingly, they transfer goods across national boundaries for their own business activities without selling them outside their organization. The question should be, "Why are goods and services transferred between countries?"

When this question is answered, it is clear that the decision-making unit is the business enterprise and not the country. To be sure, decisions are heavily influenced by government actions. Nevertheless, business decisions by international corporations—not traditional trade concepts—have become the focal point for explaining most of what happens internationally. Moreover, an explanation of international business actions provides an integrated account of the transfer of investment and working capital as well as the transfer of goods.

The business firm has a number of different ways open to it for supplying market demand in a foreign country. Trading or exporting is only one of the options. Depending on the circumstances, a business firm can supply foreign demand by licensing its product or processes to a foreign firm, or it may establish a production facility in a foreign market in lieu of exporting. Traditional trade theory rules out these options by assuming that investment capital is not mobile between countries and by overlooking the importance of technological know-how, management, and marketing skills as significant factors of production which can form the basis of comparative and competitive advantage.

The failure of traditional trade theory to explain today's world is also partly due to its complete omission of the rationale behind the twentieth-century development of marketing. The Ricardian concept assumes that commodities being sold in an international marketplace are standard, basic, and transferrable—wheat, cotton, and wine, for example. Today's firms, however, are continually adjusting many dimensions of their products against their assessments of customer wants—against the market. There is no simple standard commodity.

More and more firms are putting together marketing strategies against world markets, not just their home markets. Starting from an assessment of world markets, the decision maker tends to identify his market objectives and work backward to arrive at his location of production and distribution pattern. As the markets change, so do the patterns of activity of the international firms, and these patterns loom large in the changes in the international position of individual national economies.

Direct Investment Theories

International economics has devoted considerable attention to international capital movements as well as international commodity flows. In the capital field, issues of importance for understanding international business patterns are being considered under the heading of *direct investment*, that is, investment that carries with it decision-making control by the foreign investor as contrasted to *portfolio investment* which does not.

The general theory of international capital flows suggests that capital will move from one country to another in response to differences in the marginal productivity of capital. In other words, capital will move from where it is abundant to where it is scarce, or from countries where rates of return are low to where they are high. However, in recent years the flows of direct-investment capital have been increasing sizeably and rapidly, and the general theory does not explain the patterns in a satisfactory way. For example, there are substantial two-way flows of direct-investment capital. As we shall see in Chapter 3, American enterprises are making large direct investments in Europe at the same time that European firms are making substantial direct investments in the United States. Furthermore, it has been observed that direct investment often does not involve an international capital movement. Business firms have been increasing their foreign direct investment by borrowing funds in the local country.

To explain direct-investment patterns, international economists have enlarged their framework of international investment theory to recognize the role of the multinational corporation. In effect, this is a beginning step toward integrating the micro theory of the firm with the macro theory of international capital movements.

Various direct-investment theories have been advanced by economists. One view has been that direct investment represents not so much an international capital movement as capital formation undertaken abroad. Another has been the "defensive investment" concept of Alexander Lamfalussy.[2] Direct investment is undertaken where there are large and growing markets regardless of immediate profitability. In this view, where markets exist, profits will be found in the long run. Still another theory explains foreign direct investment as a currency phenomenon brought about by the market's preference for holding assets denominated in selected currencies. As Aliber argues, "If the world were a unified currency area, exchange risk and a currency premium would not exist;

---

[2] Alexander Lamfalussy, *Investment and Growth in Mature Economies* (Oxford, England: Basil Blackwell & Mott, Ltd., 1961).

then the analysis of direct foreign investment would be in terms of the economics of location."[3]

BUSINESS MANAGEMENT STUDIES

The field of business management has long had a predominantly domestic orientation. Several current lines of research in the management studies field, however, contribute to our understanding of international business patterns.

One of the most valuable lines of investigation has been the effort to identify forces likely to enlarge the geographical horizon of the business enterprise. In a utopian world the issue of geographical horizon would not arise because the business firm and business managers would be aware of and prepared to take advantage of attractive business opportunities wherever they exist. The reality is that the business firm is usually born with a geographical horizon limited to a locality, a region, or the home country. Until recently, most business enterprises did not bother to look at the possibilities of investing or establishing operations outside their home country.

As Aharoni has suggested, "Companies do not in practice reject such investment opportunities because the expected profits are not sufficient to compensate for the risks involved; they simply do not bother to devote the time and effort necessary to calculate the rate of return on such investments."[4] Brilliant foreign opportunities may have existed that the enterprise was not aware of, or not interested in, because they were beyond the geographical horizon of the enterprise.

But the horizon of the business firm is not necessarily static or immutable. Geographical horizons can be changed by forces arising within the organization and by exogenous forces stemming from its environment. The decision to "look abroad" or "go international," according to Aharoni is brought about by the interaction of several forces—partly environmental and partly inside the organization. The decision results from a chain of events, incomplete information, activities of different persons both within and outside the firm, and a combination of several motivating forces. The most significant internal forces are those arising from a strong interest by one or more high-ranking executives. The most significant external forces are outside proposals to the company,

---

[3] Robert Z. Aliber, "A Theory of Direct Foreign Investment," in *The International Corporation,* ed. Charles P. Kindleberger (Cambridge, Mass.: The M.I.T. Press, 1970), p. 34.

[4] Yair Aharoni, *The Foreign Investment Decision Process* (Boston, Mass.: Division of Research, Graduate School of Business Administration, Harvard University, 1966), p. 50.

The Product Cycle Model

The product cycle model, associated with the work of Raymond Vernon, has contributed significantly to a better understanding of the evolution of many U.S. multinational enterprises. In explaining direct-investment patterns, the model suggests a sequence of events that are a function of the evolution of a product and emphasizes innovation and oligopoly position as a basis for exports and later direct investment.[10]

In the product cycle model, a firm's international involvement follows sequential stages in the life cycle of the product it innovates. The sequence begins with the *new product stage* in which the product is manufactured in the United States and introduced into foreign markets through exports. In the *mature product stage,* as technology becomes sufficiently routine to be transferred, as a firm's export position becomes threatened, and as foreign demand expands to the point that it can support a production facility of economic size, the enterprise is induced to produce abroad—generally in other advanced countries. In a third stage, the *standardized product stage,* production may shift to low-cost locations in the less developed countries from which goods may be exported back to the home country and other markets.

The home-country location in the first stage is explained by Vernon as the need during the experimental period for having swift communication within the enterprise and with suppliers and customers. Also, when a product is new, profit margins may be high and cost considerations are likely to be less important than at a later stage. The decision to set up foreign manufacturing facilities is explained as a response to a perceived threat to the firm's export position and an effort to retain an oligopolistic advantage. In the final stage, cost considerations become the principal determinant of location.

The product cycle model has been useful for explaining the past history of some U.S.-controlled enterprises, particularly in the manufacturing field.[11] But as Vernon himself has concluded, "Though this may be an efficient way to look at enterprises in the U.S. economy that are on the threshold of developing a foreign business, the model is losing some of its relevance for those enterprises that have long since acquired a global scanning capacity and a global habit of mind."[12]

Another observation that can be made concerning the product cycle

---

[10] Raymond Vernon, "International Investment and International Trade in the Product Cycle," *Quarterly Journal of Economics,* May 1966, pp. 190–207; Vernon, *Sovereignty at Bay* (New York: Basic Books, 1971), pp. 65–112.

[11] For example, see L. T. Wells, Jr., "Test of a Product Cycle Model of International Trade," *Quarterly Journal of Economics* 83 (February 1969): 152–62; R. B. Stobaugh, "The Product Cycle, U.S. Exports and International Investment" (D.B.A. thesis, Harvard Business School, June 1968).

[12] Vernon, *Sovereignty at Bay,* p. 107.

model is the limited use it makes of location economics. The sequence of moving from exports to the establishment of decentralized-producing facilities has been an evolutionary pattern for market-oriented types of industries within the United States. The automobile industry was initially centralized in the Detroit area. As demand increased in specific regions of the United States to a point that justified establishing an economic assembly operation, the economics of location (mainly savings in transport costs of components as compared to assembled automobiles) stimulated the enterprise to make direct domestic investments elsewhere. The decentralization of the rubber tire industry from Akron, Ohio, to virtually all regions of the United States is another example of expanding markets and location economics.[13]

A similar sequence of motivation by location economics has frequently been followed by a firm "going international." It first becomes established in a foreign market through exports. As demand grows in the market, due to sales efforts by the firm and/or the economic expansion of the foreign country, the firm needs to enlarge its productivity capacity. If the locational characteristics of the industry are toward market orientation, the firm is likely to substitute local production for exports. In the international field, savings on import tariffs must be considered in locational decisions as well as other traditional location factors.

The location-economics approach complements the emphasis of the product cycle on innovation and oligopoly threat. In the case of market-oriented types of industries, cost-saving potentials through locating near the market and demand factors exogenous to the firm, such as rapid economic growth in the European Common Market, may be more significant than either the maturing of a product or an oligopoly threat in stimulating a firm to substitute local production for exports. Location economics also explains why some products such as aircraft, industrial machinery, and ball-point pens continue to be exported even when they become a "mature" product, because of limited potentials for savings through a market location. Finally, location economics can resolve the asymmetry dilemma Vernon poses for the product cycle model in the European and Japanese firms have not penetrated the U.S. economy extensively through direct investment.[14] The locational advantage for many Japanese industries, as was true for Volkswagen in its decision against locating a production facility in the United States, is in home-country production and penetration of the U.S. markets through exports. Through cost-reducing innovations in transatlantic-ocean transportation, in the case of Volkswagen, the trade-off in favor of home-country loca-

---

[13] Glenn E. McLaughlin and Stefan Robock, *Why Industry Moves South* (Washington, D.C.: National Planning Association, 1949).

[14] Vernon, *Sovereignty at Bay*, pp. 109–12.

tion prevailed. The Japanese logistical strategy will be discussed further below.

International Transmission of Resources

Probably the most comprehensive framework for explaining international business patterns is that formulated by John Fayerweather around the role of the multinational firm in the transmission of economic resources among nations.[15] Extending the basic philosophy of resource transfers embodied in trade theory, Fayerweather enlarges the concept of resources to include technological, managerial, and entrepreneurial skills, as well as natural resources, capital, and labor. He then argues that differentials in the supply-demand relationship of resources among countries generate basic economic pressures for the inter-nation flow of resources and create opportunities open to the multinational firm. Governmental actions or policies distort or reshape these resource-differential relationships as basically determined by free economic forces into the actual patterns of opportunities open to the firm. In responding to these opportunities, the types of resources transmitted, the selection of countries, and the choice of transmission methods depend on the characteristics and strategy of specific multinational firms. In sum, three groups of factors—resource differentials, governmental actions, and characteristics of the business enterprise—determine the way in which the multinational firm plays a role in the international transmission of resources.

Fayerweather's conceptual framework broadly encompasses economic concepts related to international trade and investment as well as behavioral models of the business enterprise. It recognizes oligopoly elements as a stimulus to foreign investment by including oligopoly advantages within the broad category of skill resources. It assigns a major role to governments in influencing international business patterns through actions that affect resource-differential relationships and the entry conditions for foreign enterprise.

Fayerweather has labeled his contribution as a conceptual framework for international business management. It distinguishes the resource transmission role of the multinational firm from that of the strictly national firm in two ways. Having developed a global horizon, the multinational firm is concerned with resource differentials among countries. It is also critically concerned with the institutional constraints of nations which affect the flow of resources among nations.

As a model for explaining and predicting international business pat-

---

[15] John Fayerweather, "International Transmission of Resources," in *International Business Management: A Conceptual Framework* (New York: McGraw-Hill Book Co., 1969), pp. 15–50.

terns in a world where many business enterprises have developed global horizons, the Fayerweather framework makes a significant contribution. It is general enough so that most dimensions of international management can be incorporated within it. It does not, however, address itself to the process by which essentially domestic firms acquire their global horizons, nor does it attempt to provide a general theory of the evolutionary history of international business expansion. Furthermore, it appears to be predominantly concerned with manufacturing activities and the role of markets in motivating international expansion.

THE EVOLUTION OF INTERNATIONAL BUSINESS: AN HISTORICAL MODEL

Practice has clearly run ahead of theory in the international business field. Yet considerable progress has been made in identifying underlying forces and in formulating conceptual frameworks for understanding and predicting international business activities. In summarizing the present state of knowledge, it is helpful to deal separately with two interrelated components of the complex subject, namely, the historical evolution of international business and the normative behavior of the multinational enterprise.

Turning to the historical model, the forces underlying the recent emergence of international business to a dominant role in the world economy can be conveniently grouped into three categories: environmental forces, technological trends, and the growth process of the business enterprise. The purpose of the model is to explain the timing of international business expansion, the industrial patterns, the nationality of multinational enterprises, and the countries into which expansion has occurred. All of the elements, of course, are part of an interdependent system with feedback interrelationships.

Environmental Forces

An Expansionist World Economy.   The most pervasive force shaping the timing, size, and structure of international business expansion has been the unprecedented and sustained economic growth of the world economy since the early and mid-1950s. The expanding economic environment generated new levels and patterns of demand. It permitted enterprises to mature and grow. And the higher individual incomes that resulted from overall growth have meant more than proportionate increases in consumer demand for manufactured and luxury goods of the type that have created special opportunities for international enterprises.

Increased demands for natural resources stimulated both public and private investment in resource exploration and development. With improved technology for exploration, many new sources of raw materials have been discovered throughout the world.

International business has both contributed to and benefited from accelerated world-growth trends. Most certainly, a return to the worldwide depression environment of the 1930s or to the historical patterns of recurring business cycles would not have encouraged international trade expansion nor the rapid growth of foreign production.

Improved Inter-Nation Framework. Another unique feature of the post-World War II period, was the cooperative efforts of the principal nation-states to improve the international financial system so as to facilitate financial transactions between nations. Most nations supported inter-governmental agreements to reduce trade barriers. The moves to create free trade and common market areas stimulated the expansionist world economy and facilitated the emergence of new patterns of international business activity.

National Economic Environments. National policies of both home and host countries have been generally favorable in recent years toward the growth of international trade and foreign production. Most nations have adopted aggressive and ambitious economic-development goals that assigned a high priority to industrial expansion. In many cases, industrialization goals have been easiest to fulfill by attracting foreign enterprise. In other cases, however, for reasons of national security and public policy, governments have limited certain fields of business activity to domestic enterprises and often to government enterprises.

National Political Environments. Political goals of national governments have long shaped patterns of international trade and investment. During past periods of colonial-expansionist aspirations by many national governments, the phenomenon was referred to as "trade follows the flag." Although colonial relationships have gone out of style, other political goals of nations have fostered the post-World War II expansion of international business. For political reasons, some nations are supporting policies to assist the less developed countries (LDC) by establishing special lending and risk-insurance programs to encourage national firms to undertake business projects in the LDCs. During hot periods in the cold war between the United States and the USSR, the United States provided special incentives for business firms willing to invest in a battleground country like India to meet the Soviet competition of low-interest foreign loans.

Technological Trends

A new era of expanded research and accelerated technological development followed the end of World War II. A deluge of new products and new processes shaped demand patterns and created new business opportunities for technologically dynamic enterprises. New technology, as noted above, stimulated and assisted in the discovery and exploitation of natural resources. Technological developments, particularly in computers, communications, and transportation, spurred and supported the evolution of the business firm from domestic to global horizons.

Trends in technological progress are often associated with national environments. Consequently, they explain a great deal about the nationality of the emerging multinational enterprises. National societies have differential capacities for invention (the creation of a new product or a new process) and innovation (the act of making a new product or process economically viable). The relative position of countries has changed over time. In some cases, such as that of the United Kingdom in the last half of the nineteenth century, nations may have a high capacity for invention but lag behind other nations in innovation.[16] During the mid-twentieth century, the United States became a leader in technological development.

One factor has been the growing influence of national governments in accelerating and influencing the process of invention and innovation. As Kindleberger has observed, ". . . as the creative process changes from the brilliant flash of insight into the systematic canvas of possibilities, . . . the locus of invention may depend more on which country has the biggest defense budget, from which inventions emerge as a by-product, or the largest (or best?) system of technical education."[17] The national defense programs of the United States have been a major force in creating technological advantages which have been exploited internationally by U.S. business firms. The national environment and national policies in Japan emphasized technological adaptation and innovation and supported a growing international involvement by Japanese business firms.

New technology tended to alert business firms to foreign market opportunities and new sources of resource inputs as explained in the product cycle thesis. It provided oligopoly elements that give the foreign enterprise a competitive advantage over local firms. It follows that much of the postwar expansion of international business was in science-based or research-intensive industries in rapid-growth sectors and by U.S. enterprises.

The Growth Process of the Business Enterprise

The evidence is more impressionistic than factual, but it appears that the business enterprise, particularly in the industrialized countries, has

---

[16] John H. Dunning, *American Investment in British Manufacturing Industry* (London: Allen & Unwin, 1958), p. 21.

[17] Kindleberger, *Foreign Trade and the National Economy* (New Haven: Yale University Press, 1962), p. 87.

been accelerating its capabilities rapidly in recent years. For many centuries, the gaps among nations in business capability were not sufficiently large to stimulate a rapid growth in multinational business operations. Business firms were generally small in relation to their national markets, and the nature of business operations was relatively simple. But rapid advances in transportation, communications, and computer technology have made the world smaller and increased tremendously the geographic area within which the enterprise can operate efficiently. Many firms have grown rapidly in size and resources and are no longer small in relation to their national markets, even in the United States.

At the same time, the complexity of business operations and the resource requirements for an optimal-sized enterprise have escalated manifoldly. Business has become more capital intensive. Research, development, and technology have become more sophisticated and more proprietary. Management functions at many levels are requiring highly advanced skills. With such an acceleration in the capability of the business firm and in the requirements for managers and other business employees, disparities among the managers and firms of different nations have widened. The potential for enterprises to have competitive advantages which are sizeable enough to justify taking the additional risks of international operations has increased phenomenally.

As its capability expanded and the opportunities for foreign operations multiplied, the business enterprise became fertile ground for stimuli that extended the firm's horizon beyond its domestic market. For some firms, an international horizon was only an advanced stage on its learning curve, and the evolution to a global strategy was relatively continuous. For many other enterprises, including relatively large companies in the United States, the move to an international horizon involved an abrupt change in behavior and a major transformation in business thinking.

The subject of geographical business horizons involves broad questions of individual and social behavior patterns. The variables are many and complex, yet some order seems to exist. The patterns can be simplified by grouping the motivating forces into two general categories, namely, factors internal to the firm and external forces. The categories are not mutually exclusive because the horizon-extending stimulus may come both from within and from outside of the firm.[18] Some of the principal internal forces for internationalizing horizons have been the influence of a high executive, the development of new technology or products, dependence on foreign sources for raw materials, the desire to find a use for old machinery, the accumulation of excess internally generated investment funds, and the observed need for a larger market. Illustrative of external forces are the influence of customers, the initiative of foreign governments, the pressure and example of competitors, the more general

---

[18] Aharoni, "The Decision to Look Abroad," in *Foreign Investment Decision Process,* pp. 49–75.

social pressure in business circles that leads to the bandwagon effect, the stage of economic development of the home country, the home country's political aspirations, and the occurrence of a dramatic event such as the formation of the European Common Market.

In general, one might expect European business executives to have developed international horizons because the small size of their countries, frequent contacts with citizens of other nations, traditions of speaking several languages, and so forth, would all tend to make the individuals internationally conscious. To some extent, this expectation is confirmed by the long international business tradition of British-Dutch Unilever, the Netherlands' Philips Lamps, and Sweden's Electrolux, Ericsson (LM), SKF, and Stabernack Verpackung Matches (STAB)—companies which began setting up factories around the world before the turn of the century. But the European experience also illustrates that an international or cosmopolitan horizon for business executives is not a sufficient condition. In addition, business firms must have competitive advantages and be aggressively dynamic. Furthermore, for more than a decade after World War II, European and Japanese business enterprises recognized as their primary challenge the reconstruction of their own war ravaged domestic economies.

As business enterprises gradually evolved into transnational institutions, their early motivation for establishing foreign production facilities were generally responses to specific opportunities or threats rather than the implementation of a comprehensive global strategy. In some cases, the firm went international as a "market seeker," expanding the production and sale of present products into new markets. In other cases, the firm's move abroad was primarily as a "raw materials seeker," particularly in petroleum and mining. A third group was the "production-efficiency seeker," looking for lower costs of production through labor costs but sometimes through lower costs of power or another input. Sometimes a search for knowledge was combined with a search for markets, as in the case of some European firms interested in acquiring marketing and product development experience in U.S. markets that could be fed back into other operations.[19] As the firm developed a global horizon, all of these components became an integral part of a total global strategy.

A RATIONAL MODEL FOR THE GLOBAL BUSINESS FIRM

The key element for explaining and predicting international business patterns is the role of the enterprise and its evolution from a predomi-

---

[19] W. Dickerson Hogue, "The Foreign Investment Decision-Making Process," mimeographed (Paper presented to the Association for Education in International Business, 29 December 1967).

nantly domestic firm to one with a global orientation. At the present stage of the world economy, the enterprise with a global horizon and strategy is still far from representative of all firms engaging in international business. Yet the tendency for evolving into a global enterprise appears to be inherent in the process of a firm going international. The rational global model, which forms the foundation for Part V—Managing the Multinational Enterprise, should be introduced at this point as being representative of the behavior patterns of a large and ever-increasing number of enterprises conducting business activities across national boundaries. The assumption is that the rational global model will shortly become the representative model.

In the rational model, the business firm evolves to the stage where it has a world horizon and a global strategy. It attempts to maximize the business goals of the firm by operating wherever the best opportunities exist. Typically, the firm will be incorporated and will owe its legal existence to a nation-state or a political subdivision of a nation-state. As an economic or business creature, the firm may even select the best political jurisdiction for its home base in terms of business advantages to the firm. This is similar to domestic firms in the United States choosing to be incorporated in the state of Delaware because of special business advantages inherent in Delaware incorporation. Nation-states, as the current form of political organization in the world, will continue to be extremely important in controlling the business environment. But for the global firm, national political boundaries are a constraint rather than an absolute limit for seeking out business opportunities.

On the basis of continuing world reconnaissance of opportunities and threats to it competitive position, the firm selects the markets it wants to be in. These decisions are based upon such factors as differential growth rates of markets, the costs of getting into different markets, and the potentials for securing a satisfactory share of specific markets. Working back from its market decisions and following standard location economics criteria, the firm will develop logistic models on a world scale that represent rational patterns for supplying the selected markets. The logistic models will include sources of raw materials, production sites, service and marketing facilities, research activities, and even the supplies of labor, management, and capital. By incorporating the marketing and logistics options into a general programming model, the firm develops its optimal business operations strategy.

On a domestic basis, the rational model is accepted as a normal pattern for doing business within a nation. The global model is basically the same as the more familiar domestic model, except that the global model includes in the decision-making process a new range of variables and risks resulting from the crossing of national boundaries. Important among these are the fragmentation pressures of the diverse national environments to which the multinational firm must relate itself. As Fayerweather has emphasized, the satisfaction of national interests and a reduction of nationalistic emotional resistances favor approaches which are oriented toward localism rather than global unity. This tendency conflicts with a *unification* strategy which may constitute a substantial portion of the basic rationale for the existence of the multinational firm and the source of a considerable part of its competitive advantage.[20]

The growth process of the firm might be visualized as following a path along which business enterprises develop from a completely local to a global orientation. To achieve the global enterprise status, a series of necessary conditions underlying the rationale model must be fulfilled. The firm and its management must have an international horizon and access to resources necessary for global operations. It must have competitive advantages that it can exploit. It must be in product or service fields that are not limited economically or legally to local and national markets. For example, the production of common bricks is not a promising field for international business because technology is relatively simple and transportation costs are high in relation to the value of the product. Nor is the production of enriched uranium a promising field because it is a business activity legally limited to national markets by national security considerations.

To the extent that these and other necessary conditions are fulfilled, enterprises can be classified across a spectrum into earlier or later stages of internationalization, and their behavior patterns can be explained as predictable variations from the rational model. Thus, no simple pattern presently explains all forms of international business activities. Nor can all international transactions be considered as sui generis or unique to the individual case. Instead, our hypothesis is that a number of behavior patterns exist, that each pattern is a partial or incomplete form of the rational model, that enterprises and types of business activity move in a rational manner from one category of behavior pattern to another, and that the components of international business activity—that is, the movement of goods, services, personnel, financial flows, and capital—can be explained by a finite (and relatively small) number of behavior patterns into which the motivating firms and types of business can be grouped.

Summary

The practice of international business has clearly run ahead of the development of a theoretical framework for explaining and predicting

---

[20] Fayerweather, "The Global Business Strategy," in *International Business Management,* pp. 133–67.

international business patterns. The new and more complex patterns of business transactions across national boundaries cannot be satisfactorily explained by traditional economic theories of international trade and international investment. The principal limitation of such theories is that they have not included the business enterprise and its growing influence on inter-nation business relations.

A series of new approaches, evoked by the international business reality, are beginning to provide a theoretical framework for international business. Among these are the explanations for the emergence of the multinational enterprise as a mechanism for the international transmission of resources, as a consequence of the product cycle, and as a means of exploiting oligopoly advantages in foreign areas. The present state of the knowledge can best be summarized by considering as separate but related issues (a) the historical evolution of international business patterns, and (b) a rational model for the global business firm. The first framework helps to explain how present patterns have evolved. The second framework helps to explain and predict international business patterns as globally oriented firms become increasingly dominant in the world economy.

The recent rapid expansion of international business firms can be explained by a combination of environmental forces, technological trends, and the growth process of the business enterprise. Aided and stimulated by an accelerated capability to extend their operations geographically, business enterprises in the industrialized countries perceived and increasingly responded to foreign business opportunities and threats to their oligopoly positions. Technological trends played a major role in providing enterprises, particularly in the advanced countries, with oligopoly elements that gave them a competitive advantage over local enterprises in a host country. Other sources of competitive advantage were product differentiation built on advertising, access to capital, and management skills. Although the business enterprise has been the active force underlying the recent rapid growth of international business, a pervasive and dominant influence was a favorable world environment. This included an expansionist world economy, an improved inter-nation financial and trade framework, and the growth-mindedness of nations that characterized the post-World War II period.

The theoretical framework that is becoming most useful for understanding future patterns is the rational model of the global firm. It has developed a global horizon and continuously scans the world for new opportunities and threats to its position. The global firm has access to adequate financial, human, and organization resources to operate in many countries. It includes in its planning and operations a series of variables and risks that are different in kind and degree from those encountered in operating within a single nation-state. Its operations are heavily influenced by the pressures and policies of diverse national environments.

EXERCISES AND DISCUSSION QUESTIONS

1. As an executive of a predominantly domestic firm that seems unaware of global opportunities or threats, what would you do to expand the horizon of the enterprise and "go international"?
2. What new factors come into play in international plant location decisions that do not affect location decisions solely within a domestic market?
3. Why has the U.S. pharmaceutical industry been internationally minded but the iron and steel industry has not?
4. Which U.S. industries whose production facilities are predominantly in the United States are likely to establish foreign production facilities over the next decade? See Table 2.1 for information on the extent of foreign operations by the largest U.S. industrial corporations.

TABLE 2.1

Extent of Foreign Operations by Largest U.S. Industrial Corporations
(based on data for the 500 largest industrial corporations
as contained in the 1965 *Fortune* summary)

SEC Industry No.	Industry	No. of Companies in Industry Sample*	Median Percentage of Foreign Content of Companies with Foreign Operations†	Median Percentage of Foreign Content of Industry‡ as Represented by Sample
283	Drugs	15	31%	31%
291	Petroleum Refining	29	32	27
352	Farm & Construction Machinery	14	27	27
301	Tires and Inner Tubes	6	27	22
357	Office Machinery & Computers	10	21	21
354	Metalworking Machinery	8	20	20
284	Soaps, Detergents & Cosmetics	7	20	20
355	Special Industry Machinery	6	20	20
371	Motor Vehicle & Parts	22	18	18
208X	Soft Drinks	3	18	18
342	Cutlery, Tools & Hardware	3	18	18
356	General Industry Machinery	8	17	17
383	Optical Instruments	7	17	17
366	Communications Equipment	12	17	16
211	Cigarettes	5	15	15
333	Nonferrous Metals	18	14	13
349	Misc. Fabricated Metal Products	10	18	13
326	Concrete, Gypsum, Asbestos	9	17	13
281	Chemicals, Organic & Inorganic	27	13	12
204	Grain Mill Products	11	15	12
351	Engines and Turbines	4	10	10
374	Railroad Equipment	4	10	10
285	Paints and Varnishes	4	10	10
207	Confectionary Products	3	10	10
361	Electrical Equip. & Apparatus	18	9	9
363	Household Appliances	7	9	8
358	Service Industry Machines	5	8	8
341	Metal Cans	3	8	8
321	Glass & Glass Products	6	10	7
203	Canning Fruits & Vegetables	15	9	7
202	Dairy Products	8	10	7
271	Newspapers and Books	10	8	7
372	Aircrafts and Parts	19	8	6
262	Paper & Allied Products	21	9	6
208	Alcoholic Beverages	8	10	6
365	Radio & Television Sets	6	6	5
241	Lumber & Wood Products	5	7	5
331	Steel Works & Mills	31	6	4
201	Meat Products	12	8	4
231	Apparel	6	7	4
221	Textile Mill Products	18	6	3
314	Footwear, except Rubber	5	5	3
205	Bakery Products	9	15	2

* Percentages for industries represented by less than 10 companies have a low confidence level. Industry group 25. Furniture and Fixtures, which was represented by only one company, was omitted.
† These median percentages represent approximations. They are based on either one or a combination of several of the five measurement criteria (sales, earnings, assets, employment, or production abroad). No adjustment was made for differences in the size of the companies in the sample.
‡ These percentages were obtained by multiplying the percentages in the preceding column with the percent of companies in each industry having foreign operations.
Source: Nicholas K. Bruck and Francis A. Lees, *Foreign Investment, Capital Controls, and the Balance of Payments* (New York: New York University, Institute of Finance, Graduate School of Business Administration, April 1968), pp. 94-6.

3

SIZE AND GROWTH PATTERNS OF INTERNATIONAL BUSINESS

COMPREHENSIVE FACTUAL INFORMATION on the international business phenomenon has become available only in scattered bits and pieces. Although the dramatic change in the pattern of business between nations could easily be seen by the man in the street, yet, without a theory to explain the development, statistical agencies have long ignored it.

The best data available have been on the international private investment of U.S.-based firms, and it has become customary to use the U.S. data to illustrate what is occurring. Observers generally added a caveat that the growth of international business is not exclusively a U.S. phenomenon and noted that such European firms as Shell, Philips, and Unilever were also an important part of the new trend. But in a factual way, the overall picture of the international business phenomenon including non–U.S.-based firms as well as U.S.-based firms has only slowly become available, even in terms of only one dimension—the amount of investment involved.

There is no international agency with central responsibility and authority for the collection of data on the evolution of international business operations. The few efforts to accumulate data have been mainly tied to the orthodox trade and balance-of-payments theory. In the monetary field, the International Monetary Fund has been active in encouraging nations to improve their data collection on balance-of-payments and monetary activities, and other international agencies have pressed for improved and expanded data on trade.

Whatever information is available on international business operations and investment, therefore, must come from the statistical programs of the different nations. These programs vary widely in coverage, in concepts and in quality of statistical information on international business. The United States and the United Kingdom, whose business firms have two of the biggest stakes in international business, have been expanding their statistical coverage of some aspects of international business. The availability of data on Canadian, Swedish, German, and Japanese firms has also been growing. At the other extreme, virtually nothing has been published on the total overseas investment of French, Dutch, and Belgian firms.

IMPORTANCE OF MEASURING INTERNATIONAL BUSINESS

How much difference will it make and to whom whether businessmen have a better picture of the international business phenomenon? The monetary crises and the pressures for monetary reform are a case in point. Much of the diagnosis of the international monetary problem in the early 1970s blamed speculators for placing pressure on weak currencies and bringing about devaluations. Remedies were proposed which were expected to protect the system against the forces that emerged from the diagnosis. On the other hand, the limited and fragmentary data available on international business suggested a different diagnosis. Remedies quite different from those being considered may be necessary for adjusting the monetary system to the changed structure of the international economy.

Foreign direct investment by international firms based in all countries reached an estimated total of $140 billion in 1970 and had been expanding annually at from 10 to 20 percent. A large share of this investment is exposed to the risk of foreign exchange devaluation, and the conservative treasurers of international business firms are developing a great deal of sophistication in forecasting the foreign exchange crises of countries in which their firms are operating and in protecting their foreign assets from foreign exchange risks. They may do this by using local borrowing instead of bringing in outside funds, by accelerating payments for goods and services from outside the country, by advance repatriation of profits, and by a series of other actions and inactions. With such a large foreign investment outstanding, prudent and conservative financial strategies of the international business firms can easily place a pressure equivalent to several billion dollars on a currency when it appears to be weakening. Thus the estimate that devaluation might occur and the consequent business steps taken to protect against devaluation make the forecast a self-fulfilling prophecy.

It is not only international agencies that need data on international business. How can any country develop an effective policy to influence exports and foreign exchange earnings without taking into account the decisions of international business firms and their strategies? Yet policy makers are only beginning to recognize the important role being played by international business. If they want to include international business in their considerations, they will quickly discover that they have not been collecting the necessary factual information.

There are many other uses for figures on international transactions, and figures that best identify the underlying causes of change are likely to produce the best diagnoses and remedial actions. Certainly, there will be added imperfections when the world that officials see reported and against which they form their actions is harnessed to out-of-date theories that do not recognize major causes of change.

WHAT MEASUREMENTS ARE NEEDED?

The objective of the party using the information will, of course, influence the information required. The business firm interested in allocating its efforts over global markets will require different data than the international agency concerned with the overall stability of international transactions. National governments will want still different data for regulating the activities of international business within their individual economies. These differences in objectives, however, should not be taken too far in specifying the information any party would want. The information used by any party capable of influencing the situation will inevitably be significant to the other parties likely to be affected by the action taken. The different requirements for international business information, however, can be satisfied from a limited range of basic statistics covering operations (current accounts) and ownership (capital accounts) of international business. This is just as well, because such statistics will have to be collected from individual firms by the governments holding jurisdiction over them, and they will have to be collected in a form that fits normal accounting procedures.

On the capital side the basic data required will be the size and source of ownership, financing and profits, and location of assets. On the operations side a minimum will be the size, location, and destination of current production. For both capital and current accounts, comparison with past figures will disclose the pattern of change, and comparison with noninternational business will disclose any significant differences.

These are not new statistical concepts. Most countries have been collecting statistics on production, imports, exports, ownership, and investment flows. What is new, however, is the requirement to collect these statistics to show the underlying pattern of international business.

To produce these statistics it would be necessary to start with figures supplied by individual firms—the decision-making units. The following simple table would meet all these requirements if summed separately for international businesses and purely national businesses. Summation across countries for particular industries or product lines would then provide a picture of the international business pattern.

TABLE 3.1

Operations   *(Current a/c)*

Payments to other countries by country of source
  (foreign inputs)
    a. to affiliates
    b.. to other
\+ Local purchases
\+ Local added value
= Total sales value
− Sales to other countries by country of destination
    a. to affiliates
    b. to other
= Local sales value

Ownership   *(Capital a/c)*

Ownership	by country of source
Other financing	by country of source
Assets	by country of location

A few examples of what might be shown by such information will make the proposal more concrete. A national government will be able to see what share of a local market is under the control of international business, what proportion of these sales are represented by value added within the country, and whether there is a significant difference between international firms and national firms in this respect. If the value added locally by international firms is small, the government might consider means of increasing the local components. On the export side, the proportion that exports represent of the ultimate sales of international firms may be deduced from international tabulations by industry. A country with a high level of exports by international firms may in fact discover that further local processing is possible. From a firm's viewpoint the same statistics would be valuable if governments were likely to use them. They would also form a basis for marketing strategy and monitoring competitors' actions. Comparison of the international pattern from year to year would disclose changes in location and destination of production by international competitors.

The simple breakdown of statistics into national and international classifications would thus provide the factual basis for many decisions. There are, however, many definitional difficulties involved in such a classification. This comes through clearly when examining the patchy efforts to date to provide data on international business.

Private Direct Investment

The most common way of measuring international business is to present figures on the size of international direct investment. Although definitions vary greatly from country to country,[1] direct investment generally covers only investment in which the business is controlled from abroad. The U.S. government defines this as an ownership interest in foreign enterprises of at least 10 percent. It is distinguished from portfolio investment, which brings an ownership interest but not managerial involvement. At the borderline, though, the classification becomes rather arbitrary.

Direct private investment is the easiest measure of international business activity to collect from available data. It is usually obtained by totaling annual flows of inbound investment plus profits and deducting annual outflows of capital and dividends. These cumulative totals of historical flows, however, do not show current values of assets owned. Furthermore, financing through borrowing or sale of equities locally may not be recorded. While this does not immediately appear in the traditional balance of payments, such borrowing can affect it and is an important measure of international expansion.

In describing the size of international business, one of the major limitations of direct foreign investment data is its tendency to focus only on the investments of international firms outside their home-base country. If international business encompasses the global investment of multinational firms, then investments in the home country, as well as foreign investments, would have to be included. If Unilever in Holland and IBM in the United States have become truly international firms with global horizons and global strategies, the investment in their home country should be considered as international business investment. In the absence of a system for incorporating with an international agency, each business firm must have a nationality of incorporation. Yet, as a global business firm, it has its own worldwide goals and strategies, which may vary as much from those of the home country as from those of other countries.

If criteria could be established to determine when corporations become international rather than domestic firms, the resulting estimate of the total investment in international business would be many times that

---

[1] The problem of varying national definitions of direct investment is beginning to receive attention. See "Problems of Measuring Private Capital Flows to Less Developed Countries," mimeographed (Paris: Organization for Economic Cooperation and Development, 25 November 1968); "Rapport De La Commission Au Conseil concernant les travaux du 'Groupe d'experts nationaux en statistiques de mouvements de capitaux,'" (Brussels: Commission Des Communautés Européennes, 30 January 1969).

of total foreign direct investment and would probably represent a major share of the total business investment of the noncommunist world. The best criteria would seem to be the horizons and strategy of the company rather than the share of assets or sales outside of the home country. The share of assets or sales criteria would be biased by the size of the home-country economy and market. An international firm based in the Netherlands would tend to have a large share of its assets or sales outside the country because of the small size of the home-country economy. An international firm based in the United States, on the other hand, would probably have a relatively smaller share of assets or sales outside of the United States because the home-country market is so large.

Such an approach—to determine size and trends in the investment of globally oriented business firms including investment in the home-base country—is not merely a matter of academic interest. To the extent that such firms are maximizing international goals, both home-country and foreign investment are relevant to the economic and foreign policies of nations. If *XYZ* company in the United States has a global strategy, it will protect its U.S. assets against a prospective devaluation of the U.S. dollar in the same way that it protects its French assets against a devaluation of the franc.

There are other omissions, too, from the usual figures for foreign direct investment. Aircraft used for international business operations are mobile pieces of capital equipment and are not classified as foreign investment. Another understatement results from special international business techniques such as those used by Japan. Japan has been intimately involved in the financing of minerals and petroleum projects in other countries, but it has made its funds available as loans to be repaid to the Japanese financing groups through the shipment of the raw materials. In recent years, Japanese firms have been financing foreign projects with loan-purchase contracts totaling billions of dollars. The Japanese pattern is not portfolio investment, and it is not direct investment in the sense that the Japanese acquire equity and have management participation. As a hybrid form, the pattern results in making capital available and in preempting a share of the output of the project. It does not fit the standard definitions, but it represents a significant form of international business activity.

The foreign direct investment method of describing the size of international business has still another major limitation. It does not give appropriate recognition or emphasis to important international business activities that are not capital intensive. The international operations of hotel chains, commercial banks and other financial institutions, advertising, accounting, and consulting firms, and many other types of commercial and service enterprises do not involve major capital investment and do not show up as an important element in the direct investment measurements of international business activities.

Foreign Production

More significant than the value of investment is the size of international business operations. The traditional approach for measuring business between nations is through export and import data. Since trade is essentially between business firms (some of which may be government enterprises) rather than nations, it should be recognized that the business enterprise has options in the method it will use to supply demand in foreign markets.

The concept of *international production* has emerged to define a major option for the firm. As introduced by Judd Polk, it describes "the deliveries which one nation makes in the markets of another via the direct expedient of producing there locally, as distinguished from exporting to that market the product of facilities located at home."[2] When used in this way, however, the term is really a misnomer because it excludes home-country production of the international firms and activities that do not produce buyable export commodities. The concept of *foreign production* would appear to be more appropriate for describing the activities of international firms outside of their home country.

Foreign production, as defined here, is the phenomenon of a business enterprise in one country moving management, technology, personnel, and capital across national boundaries to produce goods and services in another country. The goods and services may be exclusively or largely for the local market. Foreign production may also result in exports back to the home country or to a third-country market. Foreign production can be of three general types: (1) market-oriented, (2) resource-oriented, and (3) production-efficiency-oriented. Each of these three types of foreign production is influenced by traditional industrial location economics.

In many situations, the business enterprise substitutes foreign production for exports because foreign market demand has grown sufficiently to justify the establishment of an economic size production unit. The motivation in such cases is frequently to achieve economies from proximity to the market. It is the same motivation as that involved in establishing regional production facilities within the U.S. market when demand in a region grows to a certain level. Foreign production can also replace exports when the foreign country imposes burdensome sanctions on imports through tariffs, taxation, or foreign exchange constraints,

---

[2] Joint Economic Committee, Congress of the United States, *Issues and Objectives of U.S. Foreign Trade Policy* (Washington, D.C.: U.S. Government Printing Office, 1967).

and when prospective production costs in a foreign nation are significantly lower, either because of lower factor costs or special incentives.

Foreign production and exports can also be complementary. Business firms with a global strategy may achieve economies of scale from specialization by producing specific components in one foreign plant and supplying all other plants around the world from the output of this plant. Thus the movement of goods across national boundaries becomes foreign trade and exports even though the goods are only being transferred from one unit of the firm to another unit of the same firm. In some corporations, inter-company foreign exports occur as a result of a vertical logistics strategy for locating stages of production on a global basis. This is true of most international petroleum firms.

A large and growing share of world exports and changes in them are thus accounted for by internal product movements of the international company. The significance of this development is beginning to be noted by national governments as they attempt to formulate trade and tariff policies to achieve national balance-of-payments objectives. Patterns of many types of exports (particularly manufacturers), which are assiduously analyzed and projected by such international agencies as UNCTAD, cannot provide any realistic insights into future export possibilities without taking into account trends in foreign production and the strategies of the global firms.

When governments begin to collect the necessary information, they will discover different logistics strategies for firms of different nationalities and in different industries. Within the automobile industry, for example, the European and Japanese firms have been supplying the U.S. market through exports, whereas the U.S. automobile companies are primarily engaged in foreign production to supply non–U.S. markets.

The transfer of goods across national boundaries, however, is only one component of the international business sector. International business activity also includes transportation, tourism, communications, private finance, services, and the sale of technology. An awareness of the size and structure of business activities being operated on the basis of international business criteria would have to include the full range of internation business activities.

For some purposes, a measurement of value added would be even more appropriate than measurements of either investment or production. The value added within the national boundaries, excluding the import content, is of great significance to governments. Statistics on foreign production would be misleading, for example, if they showed an increase while local value added was in fact decreasing. It is quite clear that the available data and the concepts used for their collection are most inadequate for the sorts of decisions needed to function in a world in which international business is so pervasive.

Size of International Investment

How much can be pieced together from available statistics? Can we begin to answer the question: "How big is international business?" In the world as a whole, the book value of direct foreign private investment totaled a minimum of $140 billion as of the end of 1970, as shown in Table 3.2.[3] The leading home-base country was the United States with 56 percent of the total, followed by the United Kingdom with about 16 percent. However, these countries publish the most complete information. If more complete data were available for the other countries, the United States and United Kingdom shares would be somewhat lower. Other important home countries for international business firms are France, Canada, the Netherlands, West Germany, Switzerland, Italy, Japan, and Sweden. Switzerland is a special case in the sense that many firms from other countries have been using Switzerland as a conduit through which investment outflows are channeled. Thus the data may reflect much more activity than that of truly Swiss firms.

U.S. firms are dominant in the international business field, but they do not monopolize the field. The fact that 44 percent of total direct investment is accounted for by non–U.S. firms may come as a surprise to some. In the case of noncommunist world exports, the U.S. share of 15 percent of the total might be considered somewhat small since the United States has 42 percent of the noncommunist world gross national product (GNP).

Although the $140 billion figure estimated for the book value of direct investment in 1970 represents the equivalent of the total GNP of a country like France it is heavily understated in a number of ways. Book-value estimates are cumulative totals of historical cost or values at the time the investment was made. Including the effects of appreciation in value of fixed assets and inflation, the book-value figures would probably have to be increased by from 50 to 100 percent.

With adjustments for understatement of book values, the exclusion of investments in transportation equipment, incomplete coverage such as the omission of reinvested earnings in the West Germany estimates, and other data deficiencies, a more realistic estimate of total direct foreign investments would probably be at least $250 billion.

---

[3] The OECD has estimated overseas direct investments as of the end of 1966 at $89.6 billion. See *Private Direct Investment in Less Developed Countries: Capital Flows, Assets and Income, DAC* 14 mimeographed (Paris: OECD, 1968). Another estimate indicates the aggregate outstanding investment was a minimum of $85 billion as of 1964. See Jack N. Behrman, "Some Patterns in the Rise of Multi-National Enterprise," (Research Paper 18, Graduate School of Business Administration, University of North Carolina at Chapel Hill, March 1969). Behrman concludes, however, that the total was probably closer to $100 billion after adjusting for deficiencies in the available data. For 1968, he estimates outstanding direct investment "would be on the order of $125 billion."

TABLE 3.2. Foreign Direct Private Investment by Country of Ownership: 1970 (billions of U.S. dollars)

Countries	Total GNP		Exports		Direct Investment	
	Amount	%	Amount	%	Amount	%
United States	$ 974.1	40.2	$ 42.6	15.3	$ 78.1	55.6
European Economic Community (EEC)						
West Germany	187.6	7.7	34.2	12.3	5.3	3.8
France	133.1	5.5	17.7	6.4	6.6	4.7
Italy	93.1	3.8	13.2	4.7	2.4	1.7
Netherlands	31.6	1.1	11.8	4.2	6.2	4.4
Belgium–Luxembourg . . .	25.9	1.3	11.6	4.2	2.4	1.7
EEC Total	$ 471.3	19.4	$ 88.5	31.8	$ 22.9	16.3
European Free Trade Association (EFTA)						
United Kingdom	120.2	5.0	19.3	6.9	21.7	15.5
Sweden	32.7	1.3	6.8	2.4	1.9	1.4
Switzerland	20.4	.8	5.1	1.8	5.5	3.9
Austria	14.4	.6	2.8	1.0	.3	.2
Denmark	14.0	.6	3.4	1.2	.1	.1
Norway	11.4	.5	2.4	.9	.1	.1
Portugal	6.3	.3	.9	.3	n.a.	–
EFTA Total	$ 219.4	9.1	$ 40.7	14.5	$ 29.6	21.2
Japan	198.5	8.2	19.3	6.9	3.6	2.6
Canada	85.3	3.5	16.1	5.8	5.4	3.9
Australia	33.9	1.4	4.6	1.7	.6	.4
Japan, Canada, Australia Total	$ 317.7	13.1	$ 40.0	14.4	$ 9.1	6.9
Other noncommunist countries	$ 442.5	18.2	$ 67.0	24.0	n.a.	n.a.
World Total for Non-communist countries	$2,425.0	100.0	$278.8	100.0	$140.2	100.0

Sources: Total GNP: *Statistical Yearbook, 1970*, (New York: United Nations, 1971), pp. 503–605.
Exports: *Yearbook of International Trade Statistics 1969*, (New York: United Nations, 1971), pp. 13–19, *Monthly Bulletin of Statistics* (New York: United Nations, 1973).
Foreign direct investment: Generally the following source was used extensively—*IMF Balance of Payments Yearbook, 1967–71*, 24, (IMF, Washington, D.C., Australia—Commonwealth Bureau of Census Statistics, *Annual Bulletin Of Overseas Investment;* Belgium–Luxembourg—estimate based on inflows and OECD data on investments in LDCs and National Bank of Belgium, "Report on the Activities of the Year Presented to the General Meeting" (Brussels, 22 February, 1971), p. 42; Canada—*Canada's International Investment Position* (Ottawa: Statistics Canada, December 1971); Denmark—*IMF Balance of Payments Yearbook, 1967–71;* France—estimate based on OECD, *DAC 14*, 23 April 1968, table 1, p. 11; EEC and other OECD COUNTRIES from 1962 through 1966, as reported by the French Ministere de L'Economie et des Finances in News Release no. 1045, French Information Service, New York, 29 February, 1968; *Business Week*, 30 November 1968—estimates French investment at $9 billion; *Statistique Etudes Financieres/Ministere de L'Economie et des Finances*, April 1970; Italy—Italian data are cumulative total of direct investment outflows 1958–66 from "Banco D'Italia Report" for 1966, and for earlier years from "Ufficio dei Cambi" as reported in *European Financing of Latin American Development* (Washington, D.C.: Inter-American Development Bank), p. 203; *Banco D'Italia Abridged Translation of the Report for the Year 1970* (Rome, 1971), p. 69; Japan—Ministry of International Trade and Industry, *Tokyo Keizai Monthly Statistics*, Shinposha, Tokyo, Japan; Netherlands—estimate based largely on inbound investment shown by receiving countries plus OECD estimate of flows to LDCs; Norway—*IMF Balance of Payments Yearbook, 1967–71;* Sweden—Swedish data from Harald Lund, *Swedish Business Investment Abroad, 1960–65*, (Federation of Swedish Industries, December 1967); Sveriges Riksbank, 1970; Switzerland—estimate from *EFTA Bulletin, July–August 1969*, p. 4; United Kingdom—data from *Board of Trade Journal*, 26 January 1968, plus estimates of petroleum investments made from annual reports of Shell and British Petroleum. Banking and insurance investment are not included in official estimate because of "problem of definition"; United States—data from U.S. Department of Commerce, *Survey of Current Business;* West Germany—data (does not include reinvested earnings) from *Deutsche Bundesbank, Monthly Report*.

Size of Production for Foreign Markets

Turning from the size of investment in international business to the size of their operations, the statistics are even fewer. While data on imports and exports are of the best quality of any international statistics, largely because of the pervasive practice of taxing trade, information on foreign production is scanty. As a result, the estimates that can be presented are highly speculative. Allowing for a wide range of error, they suggest that the phenomenon is massive in size and growing much more rapidly than exports.

The movement of goods across national boundaries as exports totaled $279 billion for the noncommunist countries in 1970. Foreign production by international firms in the same year is estimated to have reached a level of about $230 billion (Table 3.3). The value of foreign production,

TABLE 3.3
Product Categories of World Exports and Foreign Production

World Exports* (f.o.b.)	1955	1970	Foreign Production	1970
Food, live animals, etc.	20%	14%	Agriculture, forestry, fishing	2%
Raw materials, excluding fuels	19%	11%	Mining and smelting	5%
Fuels, etc.	11%	9%	Petroleum	23%
Manufactured goods	50%	66%	Manufacturing.	60%
Chemicals	(5%)	(7%)		
Machinery, transportation equipment.	(19%)	(29%)		
Other manufactures	(26%)	(30%)	Other and not classified . . .	10%
Total.	100%	100%	Total.	100%
Total (billions of US dollars) . .	$93	$311	Total (billions of US dollars)	$230

*Excludes Mainland China, Mongolia, North Korea, North Vietnam, and trade between East and West Germany.
    Source: Export data from United Nations, *Monthly Bulletin of Statistics.* Foreign-production estimates based on same sources as for investment data described in footnotes to Table 3.2.

in order of importance, includes manufacturing, petroleum production and refining, mining and smelting, agriculture, and the operation of public utilities.[4]

---

[4] The value of foreign production is available for the manufacturing and mining operations of U.S. firms and for Swedish firms in all fields. The rest of the estimated total has been derived from national data on foreign direct investment using ratios of sales to book value as shown in *U.S. Business Investment in Foreign Countries* (U.S. Department of Commerce, 1960), report of a special 1957 census. The ratios of sales to book value varied with the type of activity; manufacturing 2.2:1, petroleum 1.6:1, mining and smelting 1.0:1, agriculture, forestry, and fishing 1.3:1, and public utilities 0.6:1. Direct investment in trading offices, services, finance, hotels, and other nonproduction activities was not included in arriving at the foreign-production estimate.

Most foreign production was sold within the markets of the nations in which the operations were located. But some of the value of foreign production represented components or raw materials brought in from outside of the producing country and thus were already included as some other country's exports. For example, 32 percent of total U.S. exports went to foreign affiliates of American firms during 1965.[5] Some of the foreign production was exported, thus resulting in another overlap with the export data.

The extent to which foreign production goes into international trade varies greatly with the type of activity. A study of the foreign production of Swedish companies—mainly manufacturing—shows that 85 percent of sales was in local markets and 15 percent was exported.[6] Data for U.S. firms as of 1968 indicated that 78 percent of the sales of manufacturing plants was local and 22 percent entered into international trade.[7] In some cases, foreign manufacturing plants are established to supply the home-country market, and in other situations the foreign plants may be a base for exporting to third-country markets. But data on these important patterns are not available.

A much smaller share of the foreign production of petroleum is for local markets. The 1957 special U.S. census does not separate production and refining, but it shows local sales to be 65 percent of the total. A breakdown between production and refining would undoubtedly show that the bulk of petroleum is exported from the producing area and that most refining output is sold in local markets. In the case of mining and smelting operations, U.S. data show that in 1968 only 22 percent of the output went to local markets, 35 percent was exported to the United States and 43 percent was exported to other countries.[8]

On the basis of these figures, an overlap between exports and foreign production of about $80 billion can be estimated. It is probable that large amounts of the overlap are movements across national boundaries among units of individual international companies.

The joining of the concepts and data of exports and foreign production by international firms begins to outline a real world of inter-nation sales of goods that is far different and more complex than the obsolete image that now underlies much, if not most, of the national decision making on trade policies. The size of sales by business firms outside their home country is much larger than that indicated by traditional

---

[5] Marie T. Bradshaw, "U.S. Exports to Foreign Affiliates of U.S. Firms," *Survey of Current Business,* May 1969, pp. 34–51.

[6] Harald Lund, *Svenska Foretags Investeringer i Utlandet* (Stockholm: Industriforbundets Forlag, 1967).

[7] R. David Belli, "Sales of Foreign Affiliates of U.S. Firms, 1961–65, 1967, and 1968," *Survey of Current Business,* October 1970, pp. 18–20.

[8] Ibid., p. 20.

export data. In 1970, for the noncommunist countries, foreign markets absorbed goods valued at about $500 billion. Probably about half were supplied by exports and half by foreign production, depending on how one handles the overlap.

Size of International Operations

The most dramatic indication of the size of international business comes when the international production concept is used to show a total for international operations. This would include foreign production, home operations of international firms, and intangible services, as well as production of goods.

This concept gains its significance from the proposition that firms in the international category tend to pursue an international strategy that might run contrary to the national objectives of even their home country. Performance objectives would be likely to lead to concentration on the largest and fastest growing markets, production in cost-minimizing locations and avoidance of weakening currencies. If a large proportion of world business is able to adjust its affairs in such ways, even to a small extent, international business will largely determine the international economic situation.

The basis for classifying businesses as international will determine, of course, the size of the estimate. By defining U.S. multinational enterprises as those large enough to be on *Fortune's* 500 list and having manufacturing subsidiaries in six or more countries, Vernon estimated that the total sales of 187 U.S. international companies exceeded $200 billion in 1966 and accounted for between 32 and 39 percent of the total for all U.S. enterprises.[9]

As a less precise estimate and to provide only a rough gauge of the importance to the world economy of all international firms, "international" may be specified as representing all enterprises with a minimum of 10 percent of either sales or production outside their home country. On this basis, international business accounted for about $750 billion of revenues per annum in 1970. This was almost equivalent to 30 percent of the noncommunist world gross national product. Of course, GNP is estimated on a value-added basis and cannot be compared directly to revenues. The 500 largest U.S. industrial firms, which derive more than 50 percent of their revenue from manufacturing and/or mining, had total revenues in 1970 of $463 billion.[10] Of the top 200 corporations

---

[9] Raymond Vernon, *Sovereignty at Bay* (New York: Basic Books, 1971), pp. 13–15.

[10] *Fortune,* May 1971, p. 188.

outside the United States, a majority would also be international. Their combined revenues for 1970 were recorded at $236 billion.[11]

The estimate of $750 billion includes international revenues for services, thus getting away from the myopic concentration on manufacturing fostered by a theory aimed at commodities. As previously mentioned, internationalism is widespread in nonmanufacturing. Commercial banking on an international scale has long engaged the interest of large British and U.S. banks. Many insurance companies have extensive international activities in direct-insurance underwriting and in reinsurance. One study, for example, shows subsidiaries of British insurance companies in the United States as receiving over $1 billion in premiums paid each year. Numerous construction firms of many nationalities operate internationally. Television companies sell reruns of their home-country productions to foreign countries. Hotel and motel chains and retail and wholesale firms have expanded their activities across national boundaries.[12] Transportation and tourism are well entrenched as international activities.[13] The sale of technology through licensing and royalty agreements has also become a substantial source of financial flows between nations.

PROJECTING THE OVERALL PICTURE

The five indicators of international business size that we have discussed give the following picture:

	Estimate for 1970 for all noncommunist countries ($ billion)
World exports	279
Foreign production	230
Production for foreign markets	530
Operations of international units	750
International direct investment	140

Presently available data, generally collected without any sensitivity to the emergence of the international business phenomenon, thus show that international business has become a significant factor in the world economy. But this picture is only a snapshot of one point of time and needs to be supplemented with data on trends.

---

[11] *Fortune*, August 1971, p. 154.

[12] See Stanley C. Hollander, *Multinational Retailing* (East Lansing, Michigan: Michigan State University, 1970).

[13] See H. Peter Gray. *International Travel–International Trade* (Lexington, Mass.: D.C. Heath & Co., 1970); Mahlon R. Strazheim. *The International Airline Industry* (Washington, D.C.: The Brookings Institution, 1969).

International direct investment by firms of all nationalities appears to have been expanding over more than a decade by at least 10 percent annually and more likely at a rate close to 15 percent. Based on these rates, we estimate that foreign production has been expanding at 13 percent annually—an estimate most likely to err on the conservative side because an increasing share of international investment has been in manufacturing, for which the ratio of revenues to investment is highest. In comparison, trade has been expanding less rapidly—at an annual rate of about 10 percent.

Although international business cannot continue indefinitely to grow faster than national economies, if past growth rates continue during the near future, the importance of international business in the world economy will increase dramatically. If we assume that world GNP will continue to increase at 5 percent annually, world trade by 10 percent and international direct investment by 13 percent, then by 1980 foreign trade and foreign production combined would double their 1970 share of world business activity. Although not directly comparable figures, this would be the equivalent of more than 40 percent of noncommunist world GNP. Foreign production would be 22 percent and trade 20 percent. Multinational firms would probably also be conducting the major share of international trade in addition to their foreign production role. Manufacturing has offered the greatest opportunities for expansion of multinational firms and manufacturing also represents a growing share of world exports. A larger portion of this increasing share of world trade should thus come under the control of multinational business.

From this overall picture of international business activity we now turn to a more detailed examination of underlying patterns. Significant changes are occurring in the country and product patterns of international business.

CHANGING COUNTRY PATTERNS FOR INTERNATIONAL BUSINESS

Available data on direct investment suggest that the growth patterns since the end of World War II have progressed in two major phases.[14] The first extended until about 1957 and was characterized by the dominance of investment in petroleum and other raw material extraction projects. The United States, the United Kingdom, and the Netherlands invested heavily in petroleum projects in the Middle East. The United States also embarked upon new mining and petroleum projects in Canada and Latin America—principally in Venezuela. The United Kingdom in-

---

[14] "International Direct Investment by Private Enterprise in Western Europe and North America," *Economic Bulletin for Europe, Part B—Special Studies,* (New York: United Nations, November 1967).

vested in Commonwealth countries in Asia and Oceania. Other European countries concentrated on Africa. During this period, direct investment in manufacturing was relatively small. The United States had a dominant position in the export of manufactures, and strict capital controls hindered investment flows between European countries.

A new phase in international business, which began about 1958, extends up to the present. It was characterized by a steep increase in direct investment in manufacturing and trade, directed increasingly to-. ward Western Europe. The establishment of the EEC and EFTA greatly stimulated trade among the members of the groups and created incentives for outsiders to set up production facilities within the common market and free trade areas to avoid tariff discrimination and to take advantage of the rapid economic expansion in those markets.

The available statistics on direct investment since 1958 are plotted in Figure 3.1 on a logarithmic scale to accent the growth rates. The two largest nations in international business—the United States and the United Kingdom—have not been expanding their foreign investment as fast as the other leading nations. However, the historical series for the United Kingdom understates total investment because the official statistics omit petroleum and other items. While the United Kingdom has been lagging farthest behind, the fastest growth has come in investment from West Germany and Japan. They have recorded rapid rates of expansion, although these are still computed on a small base. Furthermore, the data for West Germany do not include reinvested earnings.

While these trend data must be used with caution, they suggest that the roles of Western European countries and Japan are expanding and that the present leading nations such as the United States, the United Kingdom, and Canada are losing some of their dominance. Of course, much of the rapid growth of investment by EEC countries has been within other EEC countries.

Some historical perspective adds support to the indication in the trend data that new national leadership in international business may be emerging. At the end of World War II, the international private investments of the United States, the United Kingdom, Canada, Sweden, and Switzerland remained relatively intact, except for investments in Eastern Europe and China. In contrast, Germany and Japan lost their overseas investments through wartime expropriation. Other European countries with significant foreign investments, mainly in their colonies, were not completely stripped of these investments as a result of the war, but they did lose a great deal through the independence movements in Africa and Asia.

For more than a decade after World War II, Germany and Japan concentrated on domestic reconstruction. As an aftermath of the war,

FIGURE 3.1
Growth Trends in International Direct Investment: Selected Countries

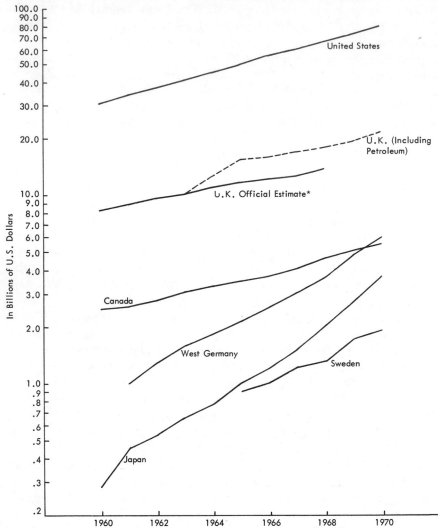

*United Kingdom official estimates do not include investments in oil, banking, and insurance.
Sources: See sources for Table 3.2.

investments by German and Japanese firms were not welcome in many countries. A German observer described the situation:

. . . German private investments abroad are minor as compared with Germany's position in the world economy.

The reasons for Germany's small investments abroad are mainly to be found in the fact that in 1950 the German economy had to begin all over again and during its rehabilitation period had a great deal of home demand for capital and labour. In addition there are the cautious restraints due to the bitter experiences in the past of a twice-repeated loss of German assets abroad and frequently not very inviting investment climate.

Besides, many regions in the world are—partly owing to the former colonial powers' still dominating position—largely unknown to the German entrepreneurs so that for this reason the risk of investment appears to be too high for them.[15]

Turning to the recipient countries, Canada stands out as the country which has absorbed the largest absolute amount of direct investment and has the largest share of total domestic output accounted for by foreign multinational enterprises. According to one authority, foreign corporations in the mid-1960s controlled 60 percent of Canada's manufacturing industry, 75 percent of its petroleum and natural gas industry, and 60 percent of its mining industry.[16] The United States is the second most important recipient of foreign direct investment—$13.2 billion in 1970. But this large amount still represents a relatively small proportion of the country's business activity. If the U.S.-based multinationals, however, are included in an estimate of the share of U.S. domestic output controlled by multinational firms, the comparison with Canada is less dramatic. For other countries, a number of estimates have been made, but they are on varying bases and cannot be compared directly. As one example, at the end of 1966, 18 percent of the equity capital of Italian companies was in foreign hands.[17]

Recipient countries are becoming increasingly concerned with the growing significance of international enterprise in their domestic economies. Studies carried out in those countries with much larger inflows than outflows and at a low stage of development have a flavor of crisis and alarm. Few countries take as unemotional a view toward foreign investment as found in this statement from Sweden, comparing Swedish investment abroad and foreign investment in Sweden:

On the whole, the two sets of trends form a kind of structural rationalization a favourite Swedish expression referring to the rearrangement of industry for more efficiency—on an international scale. If it becomes advantageous for Swedish clothing manufacturers to shift operations to Portugal, this releases workers in Sweden to be employed in more demanding and higher-paying tasks in more capital-intensive, technologically sophisticated, and export-directed industries. . . . As a small but prosperous country, Sweden cannot afford to com-

---

[15] Dr. Wolf Dieter Lindner, "Investment Climate and Private Investments," *Intereconomics*, no. 4 (1968).

[16] Kari Levitt, *Silent Surrender: The American Economic Empire in Canada* (New York: Liverwright, 1971), p. xi.

[17] Banco D'Italia, *Abridged Version of the Report for the Year 1966* (Rome, 1967), p. 57.

TABLE 3.4
International Direct Investment: Some Geographical Patterns

| | Investor Countries | | | | | | | | | |
| | Percentage Distribution | | | | | Annual Growth Rates | | | | |
Host Countries	U.S. (1970)	U.K. (1968)	CAN. (1969)	W. GER. (1970)	JAPAN (1970)	U.S. (64–70)	U.K. (64–68)	CAN. (65–69)	W. GER. (64–70)	JAPAN (66–70)
Grand Total	100.0	100.0	100.0	100.0	100.0	9.8%	5.1%	9.7%	19.6%	31.9%
U.S. $billions	($78.09)	($12.4*)	($5.04)	($5.8)	($3.6)					
A. Industrialized	68%	70.9%	82.6%	75.8%	51.0%	–	–	–	–	25.4
North America	–	–	–	–	–	–	–	–	–	–
Canada	29.2	10.7	–	8.5	–	8.6	3.7	–	18.5	27.2
U.S.	–	12.3	54.8	7.9	–	–	9.2	7.3	29.9	–
Europe	31.3	17.4	21.6	56.9	17.8	12.6	9.6	12.4	21.8	145.4
EEC	15.0	11.3	5.8	30.7	–	13.8	10.9	23.7	24.8	–
Australia–Oceania	4.5	19.8	5.0	1.0	7.8	14.0	5.0	16.3	8.1	137.0
South Africa	1.2	10.5	1.1	0.9	n.a.	10.8	9.1	21.6	15.5	–
Japan	1.9	0.2	n.a.	0.6	–	21.3	14.7	n.a.	7.8	–
B. LDCs	27.5	28.5	17.4	24.2	49.0	6.0	3.4	10.9	15.8	13.9
Latin America	18.8	8.1	14.2	17.4	15.5	8.0	–1.5	14.0	14.0	25.4
Asia (including Middle East)	5.4	7.3	1.0	2.1	30.9	14.5	0.7	4.7	19.7	58.1
Africa	3.3	13.1	2.2	4.8	2.6	–	–	–	–	–
C. Other	4.6	0.6	–	–	–	–	–	–	–	–

*The official United Kingdom estimates do not include investments in oil, banking, and insurance. The amount of these omissions was estimated to total $6.6 billion in 1969 but the geographical distribution of this additional amount is not available.
Sources: See sources for Table 3.2.

pete in every field, and the existence of alternative economic solutions gives a valuable flexibility to the country's basic economic structure.[18]

Although geographical patterns of international business are complex, two clear types of patterns have evolved. (See Table 3.4.) One pattern is that of geographical proximity. The United States and Canada have become closely intertwined in international business. Almost one quarter of U.S. exports and about 30 percent of U.S. direct investment is in Canada. Conversely, the United States accounts for 55 percent of Canadian foreign direct investment and over two thirds of Canadian exports

Similar patterns prevail among the EEC countries. The largest investment flows from West Germany, Italy, Netherlands, and Belgium are to other EEC countries, and French investments in the EEC are probably only second to those in the "franc area." Much of Japan's trade and a growing share of its overseas investments are in Asia. Latin American countries are an exception, trading primarily with the United States, Western Europe, and Japan. This is partly explained by the underdevelopment of transportation and other facilities for trading within the Latin American region.

A second pattern is a close international business relationship continuing between the former colonial powers and their former colonies. British overseas investment and foreign trade is heavily with the Commonwealth countries, which were once British colonies. The French trade and investment relationships are predominantly with the former colonial area, now referred to as the "franc area." The United States is strongly tied in trade and investment to the Philippines.

In general, international business activity among the industrialized or advanced countries is greatest in size and has been growing most rapidly. Sixteen industrial countries with slightly more than one quarter of the population of the noncommunist world, "control" probably 90 percent of multinational business. The remaining noncommunist countries, whose 1.7 billion population represents almost three quarters of the noncommunist world, participate in international business almost exclusively through exports. These countries account for about one quarter of the noncommunist world exports, but over the last two decades even this share has been steadily declining. This phenomenon underlies the pressures being exerted through the United Nations Conference for Trade and Development (UNCTAD) for changes in world-trade policies.

The size and growth rates of the markets of the advanced countries of Western Europe, Canada, the United States, and Japan explain why 64 percent of world exports go to these countries, as compared to 44 percent of exports originating in the areas. (See Table 3.5.) Purchasing

---

[18] *Sweden Now,* March 1968.

TABLE 3.5

Share of World Exports, by Principal Trading Areas

	Exports To			
Exports From	*Advanced Countries*	*Communist Countries*	*Other Countries*	*Total World*
Advanced countries				
1953–58	38.8%	1.6%	20.6%	61.0%
1959–65	43.8	2.3	17.7	63.8
1966–70	54.1	2.8	14.1	71.0
Communist countries				
1953–58	1.8%	7.8%	0.7%	10.3%
1959–65	2.3	8.2	1.6	12.1
1966–70	2.7	6.8	1.5	11.0
Other countries				
1953–58	20.6%	0.7%	7.4%	28.7%
1959–65	16.9	1.3	5.9	24.1
1966–70	13.5	0.8	3.7	18.0
Total World				
1953–58	61.2%	10.1%	28.7%	100.0%
1959–65	63.0	11.8	25.2	100.0
1966–70	70.3	10.4	19.3	100.0

Note: The "advanced countries" include the United States, Canada, Western Europe, and Japan. The "communist countries" include Eastern Europe, the USSR, and Communist China.

Sources: Adapted from *INTERNATIONAL TRADE, 1962*, published by the contracting Parties to the General Agreement on Tariffs and Trade, Geneva, 1963, Table 2; *INTERNATIONAL TRADE, 1965*, Geneva, 1966, Table D; and *Annual Report 1971, World Bank*, (Washington, D.C., 1971), p. 60.

power has also been a major element in attracting international private investment, particularly manufacturing activities most economically located near the market. Foreign investment, though, has expanded less in Japan than in Western Europe because of Japanese governmental policies which have severely restricted the entry of foreign business enterprises. The share of total international investment in less developed countries is small and heavily in the raw materials fields. Until recently, only a small volume of investment has gone to manufacturing for local markets in such countries as Mexico, Brazil, Pakistan, and India.

PRODUCT COMPOSITION OF INTERNATIONAL BUSINESS ACTIVITY

Study of the product composition of international business adds a further dimension to the understanding of international business patterns. Looking first at the static product composition as shown in Table 3.3, it can be seen that manufactured goods represented in 1970 an estimated 60 percent of foreign production and an estimated 66 percent of world exports. The second most important group in exports is food with 14 percent, followed by raw materials and fuels. However, this order is reversed for foreign production.

The leading export items in the food group are (1) fruits and vegetables, (2) coffee, cocoa, and tea, (3) meat and live animals, (4) coarse grains and other feedingstuffs, (5) oilseeds, oils, and fats, and (6) sugar. International business in such food items is primarily through trade. A few international business firms operate tea, fruit, and sugar plantations, mainly as a vestige of the colonial era. But the direct investment and foreign operations role of such international companies is small and probably declining. Raw materials, excluding fuels, involve proportionally smaller foreign production than trade. Products that are important in trade but not in foreign production are timber, pulp, and agricultural raw materials such as natural fibers, hides and skins, and natural rubber. A large share of the world's ore-mining activity, though, is undertaken by international enterprises. While this is sizeable in absolute terms and of dominating importance to specific nations it is relatively small in the total international business picture.

Mineral fuel products, including petroleum, represent about 9 percent of world trade and a much larger share—about 23 percent—of foreign production. In petroleum a small number of international oil giants dominate the field.[19] The seven major oil companies—the "seven sisters," as they were dubbed by Italy's late government oil tycoon, Enrico Mattei—are Standard Oil of New Jersey (now EXXON), Royal Dutch Shell, British Petroleum, Texaco, Standard Oil of California, Gulf, and Mobil. In 1965, these seven companies accounted for 75 percent of free world production outside North America and 60 percent of product sales in those areas.[20]

The share of manufactured goods has been increasing for both international trade and foreign production. Engel's law offers a partial explanation for this growing importance. The law stems from a study into the spending patterns of 153 Belgian households carried out in the late nineteenth century by Ernst Engel, a German statistician, and states that as income grows the demand for food grows at a lesser rate. As world income has grown, there has been a less than proportionate growth in spending on food and a declining share of food products in world trade. On the other hand, price levels for manufactured goods have been rising more rapidly than unit prices for food items and raw materials. Part of the relative gain in manufactured production has thus been caused by price escalation. A corollary to Engel's law is that with rising income the consumer spends increasing proportions on nonfood products—generally manufactured goods. New consumer products such as television,

---

[19] For a history of U.S. multinational raw material ventures, see Vernon, *Sovereignty at Bay*, pp. 26–59.

[20] *Economist*, 10 August 1968, p. 48.

transistor radios, and home appliances have stimulated new demands. Worldwide trends towards industrialization and mechanization have further contributed to the importance of manufactures through the demand for producer goods.

Technological developments have also affected international trade and production patterns through such advances as synthetic substitutes for natural raw materials, improved production processes, and new discovery and exploration techniques for natural resources. In the food category, synthetic materials have been substituting for oils, fats, and sugar. In raw materials, synthetic fibers have been substituting for natural fibers, synthetic rubber for natural rubber, and plastics for metals, and processing improvements have reduced the raw material requirements for a given level of output in numerous cases. Synthetic substitutes are being produced domestically in many countries as a replacement for imports, often by international enterprises. Also, mineral-exporting countries have succeeded in having raw materials further processed in the country before export, with the result that raw material transfers are decreased and manufactures increased.

Although world demand for petroleum and other fuels has been expanding at a significant rate, the share of fuels in world exports has not increased over the last decade. Many countries in Latin America, such as Brazil, Argentina, Bolivia, and Ecuador have been able to substitute expanded local production for imports and the same has been true in Africa. Also, a changing mix of petroleum exports, more crude products and less refined ones, has tended to reduce the gains in the value of petroleum exports. While raw materials producing countries have been pressing to have more processing done within the producer countries, the economics of location has favored the consuming countries in their efforts to have petroleum refineries constructed in the consuming nations.

In the international production of petroleum, the expansion of multinational companies, though, has been slowed to some extent in recent years. A number of producing countries have developed a capacity to exploit their natural resources through domestic companies, owned by the government in some cases, and the share of the seven sisters has declined. Furthermore, producer countries have been pressing for and beginning to receive ownership shares in the projects of the major oil companies.

Concluding Comments

International business activity is large and growing rapidly. Furthermore, when measurement is extended to include all the business that falls under the control of multinational firms, it already represents a significant proportion of total world business.

While it is possible to get an overview of the general size and trends in international business, the estimates and analyses presented in this chapter are of necessity rough. They do not have the precision to answer the specific policy questions of international agencies, governments, or the international businesses themselves. A determined effort to collect figures that depict what is really happening in the world today is urgently needed. A prerequisite for this effort would be a much wider realization that today's world no longer fits the theoretically assumed image of how imports and exports work. Countries do not export, firms do. It is of little use to couch policy making on a fiction.

EXERCISES AND DISCUSSION QUESTIONS

1. Write a report for government officials of a specified country suggesting a program for statistical collection with a view to monitoring and controlling multinational business operations as they affect the country. Explain the concepts you think are relevant and indicate the data requirements as precisely as you can.
2. For a selected minor country make an assessment of the size and roles of multinational business within its economy. Indicate the sources of your information and how you have arrived at your particular estimates.

PART II

The Framework for International Transactions

A NATURAL STARTING POINT for the study of international business is to examine the framework that has grown up over the centuries for dealing with business transactions across national boundaries. This overall framework is made up of three different though interrelated frameworks:

1. The *international financial framework* deals with the means, the recording, and the control of international transfers of monetary claims.
2. The *international trade framework* deals with the means, the recording, and the control of international transfers of goods and services.
3. The *framework of treaties, codes, and agreements* deals with the nature, contents, and limits of arrangements nations have entered into for determining how to treat business rights, obligations, and opportunities that extend across national frontiers.

These three frameworks provide the basic vocabulary for international transactions, and as such introduce many of the terms and concepts necessary for describing international business. They are also the languages of government controls. Controls that governments place on international transactions are largely determined by information collection and reasoning that stems from the conventions of these frameworks. Knowledge of the traditional frameworks is thus important for understanding and predicting the environment within which international business operates.

None of these three frameworks, however, is focused directly on international business. They have been molded by the heritage of international trading between buyers and sellers residing in different countries and acting predominantly as merchants and at arms' length—quite different from the international transactions of large multinational businesses. This has produced a body of knowledge, theories, and controls that concentrate on aggregate flows of goods and finance across a country's boundaries and do not pay direct attention to the objectives and decisions of the businesses that arrange the transactions. The frameworks have limitations given the reality of today's world of multinational firms. Nevertheless, the international businessman must still make international transactions, and these frameworks can provide him with valuable knowledge and perspectives.

An essential similarity in the three frameworks is the absence of a world authority that overrides the jurisdiction of national governments. Each framework is, in effect, a system for relating a particular segment of the economic activities and regulations of different sovereign states. The financial framework is concerned with the way in which the currencies of individual countries are exchanged. With no legal international currency, international transactions must be measured, accounted for and paid for by converting one currency into another. The trade framework is concerned with the relationship of the productive output of one country to that of another. What one country produces for another's markets is subject to a variety of natural and imposed conditions. Finally, the framework of treaties, codes, and agreements provides a system whereby governments agree on how they will align their legal constraints and privileges for activities which carry into more than one jurisdiction.

4

THE INTERNATIONAL
FINANCIAL FRAMEWORK

INTERNATIONAL BUSINESS requires dealing in a number of different national currencies. There is no international money, there are only national currencies. National states regard their monetary units and regulation of their monetary and banking systems as among the most sacred rights of national sovereignty. In a world of more than 100 sovereign nation-states, more than 100 national currencies are involved in transferring purchasing power across national boundaries.

The absence of an international currency would not be particularly significant for international business if all national currencies could be exchanged freely for other currencies and if the rates at which each currency could be exchanged for other currencies remained stable. But the ideal conditions of stable exchange rates and freely convertible currencies do not generally prevail. Relationships between national currencies keep changing. And nation-states frequently impose constraints that restrict the convertibility of their national currencies in international transactions. Although some stability and order has been achieved in inter-nation financial relationships through formal and informal intergovernmental agreements, the international financial framework for international business can only be characterized as complex, highly dynamic, and dominated by national interests.

For the international businessman, changing national policies and changing relationships between currencies generate special financial risks that do not arise in purely domestic business operations. To operate successfully within the international financial framework, the international manager must be able to identify, predict, and insure against these new risk elements. This ability requires a thorough understanding of the structure and operation of the international financial system and the forces which influence national governments to exercise controls over international financial transfers.

THE FOREIGN EXCHANGE MARKET

In a world of national currencies, international transactions require a system whereby one currency can be converted into another. Such transfers of purchasing power from one national currency to another are accomplished through the foreign exchange market and by means of various foreign exchange instruments. The purchase or sale of one currency against another is a foreign exchange transaction. To the American, the Japanese yen is foreign exchange, and to the Japanese, the United States dollar is foreign exchange. Thus *foreign exchange* means the national currency of another country or some form of short-term monetary claim on foreigners or on foreign banks expressed in terms of foreign currencies. The foreign traveler is most familiar with foreign exchange in the form of currencies. The businessman, however, frequently deals with foreign exchange in the form of bills of exchange drawn against foreigners' deposits with foreign banks.

The institutional mechanism through which foreign exchange is bought and sold is called the foreign exchange market.[1] The foreign exchange market permits an American importer, for example, to pay in U.S. dollars and a Japanese exporter to receive his payment for the goods in Japanese yen. The market also provides the mechanism whereby the international business enterprise can convert one currency for another in internal transactions between affiliates and units of the same firm. A Japanese subsidiary may receive new investment funds from U.S. headquarters in the form of U.S. dollars but have to make local payments in Japanese yen. Or the Japanese subsidiary may have to remit some of its profits earned as yen to be used by the parent corporation to pay stockholder dividends in the form of U.S. dollars.

The foreign exchange market has no one formalized structure as do the New York and Tokyo stock exchanges, no centralized meeting place, and no fixed opening or closing time. It embraces banks which have special departments that sell foreign exchange in any currency desired by a customer and purchase any foreign exchange offered to them. It includes exchange brokers and dealers who specialize in certain aspects of the transfer process. These institutional elements of the market cross and recross national boundaries, joining the national markets for the major currencies into a worldwide network.

In practice, the foreign exchange market frequently offsets transac-

---

[1] See Alan Holmes and F. H. Schott, *The New York Foreign Exchange Market* (New York: Federal Reserve Bank of New York, 1965).

tions within countries so that payments between countries may only be necessary for the settlement of net balances. Claims held against foreigners by exporters or creditors are sold to importers or debtors in the same country for settling payments abroad. Even the settlement of net balances between countries may not take place if parties within a country are willing to increase their holdings of foreign currencies. Such a situation has led to the development of the Euro-dollar market whereby Europeans and other foreigners have been willing to hold dollars outside of the United States and use these dollars as an international currency for transactions between each other.

The foreign exchange market performs three main functions. The most important is the transfer of purchasing power from one country to another and from one currency to another. The market also provides credit for foreign trade and other international transactions and facilities for protection against future fluctuations in the exchange value of currencies. This last function is called hedging.

Historically, international transfers were accomplished mainly through foreign bills of exchange. A bill of exchange has been defined as:

an unconditional order in writing addressed by one person to another, signed by the person giving it, requiring the person to whom it is addressed to pay on demand or at a fixed or determinable future time a sum certain in money to order or to bearer. (Uniform Negotiable Instruments Law)

Being a negotiable instrument, the bill of exchange (also referred to as a draft) can be easily transferred, sold, discounted, or otherwise traded. The relative volume of trading in bills of exchange, however, has been reduced in recent years because of the speed and ease with which cable transfers are effected.

Most transactions in the foreign exchange market involve the transfer of a deposit held in a bank abroad. The main device for effecting these transfers is the cable (telegraphic) transfer which is nothing more than an order sent by cable to a foreign bank holding an account for the seller of a particular currency, directing that bank to debit his account and credit the account of the buyer, or some other person designated by the buyer, with a specified amount. The chief advantage of the cable transfer lies in the speed with which it can be effected, thus avoiding the necessity of tying up funds in foreign exchange. The same transfer can also be made by mail.

A third instrument for international exchange transactions is the letter of credit. A letter of credit is a formal document issued by a bank on behalf of an importer customer guaranteeing payment of the exporter's drafts drawn according to the stipulations in his agreement with the importer. It substitutes bank credit for the importer's credit. The letter of credit is a flexible instrument which can be adapted to a great variety of international credit and payment requirements.

The credit function of the foreign exchange market can be provided by bills of exchange as well as by letters of credit. Bills of exchange can be sight drafts, payable immediately on presentation to the drawee or debtor, or time drafts (commonly payable in 90 days after sight) which permit the lapse of a specified amount of time before payments are due. International trade in particular requires credit because of the time it takes to move goods from the seller to the buyer. Banks provide this credit by discounting the bills of exchange, thus giving the exporter his revenue as soon as he dispatches his goods. The amount of discount will be related to prevailing interest rates for loans in the country in which the bank operates, the possibility of fluctuations in the value of the specific currency in which payments are to be made at the time the instrument matures, the credit standing of those for whom the bill is discounted, and the underlying value of the goods involved in the transaction.

In addition to clearing and credit, the foreign exchange market offers facilities for hedging. Hedging is a means of securing protection against the risk of future fluctuations in the value of specific foreign currencies. It is accomplished through the forward market which is similar to the futures markets in commodities. Hedging is accomplished by balancing sales and purchases of an asset so that there is no net open position on the market. Hedging against foreign exchange fluctuations is not restricted to importers and exporters. An even more important use of the forward market has become that of international corporations which may hedge to protect the value of foreign investment if a currency devaluation is anticipated.

An illustration of the use of hedging in international trade may be helpful. Suppose that an American importer must pay a specified sum in British pounds to a British exporter within three months. During the three months the American importer will be what is referred to as "short" on the exchange market, and he stands to lose by an increase in the dollar price of pounds. If the importer buys his pounds immediately, he will not have his funds available over the three-month period for which he is entitled to credit. He can resolve the problem by purchasing the necessary pounds on a 90-day forward contract, which specifies the dollar price he will pay when the pounds are delivered to him. The importer has now offset his short position on "spot" pounds with an equivalent position in "forward" pounds. Regardless of what happens to the spot or current rate of exchange, he will get his pounds at the rate specified in the forward contract. Such protection, of course, involves a cost—as the price of a forward contract is determined by the anticipated risk of a price change. We will return to hedging, particularly as related to protection of foreign investments against devaluations, in the chapter on financial management.

THE EURO-CURRENCY MARKET

A significant change began to occur in the system of international payments and in the importance of the foreign exchange market with the emergence in the late 1950s of the so-called Euro-dollar market. The Euro-dollar market, now becoming labeled "the Euro-currency market," has made it possible for businessmen to deal outside of their country in the currency of the home country. This reduces the need to convert from one currency to another in the foreign exchange market and also insures the businessman to some extent against foreign exchange risk.

The market for Euro-dollars and other Euro-currencies comprises both a commercial banking market for multinational companies, government institutions, individuals, and a wholesale money market among international banks. Euro-dollar deposits have the same monetary value as ordinary U.S. dollars, but the deposit is payable by a banking office located outside the United States, not inside.

The Euro-dollar market emerged as a result of several factors.[2] A principal contributing force has been *Regulation Q* under which the U.S. Federal Reserve System has fixed maximum interest rates that member banks could pay on time deposits. As competition in the United States for funds raised interest rates above the ceilings imposed by the Federal Reserve System, London banks began to bid for the foreign-owned dollar deposits and relend these deposits in Europe and in the United States. Another segment of the supply stemmed from dollar accounts, such as those of the USSR held in European banks to avoid the jurisdiction of American authorities.

The Euro-dollar market grew rapidly during the 1960s with many new sources of supply opening up and with demand for Euro-dollars greatly stimulated by new restrictions on the outflow of direct investment adopted by the United States. The borrowing of Euro-dollars by American multinational firms was not restricted by the U.S. capital-controls program because such financial transactions did not put additional pressure on the U.S. balance-of-payments situation.

By the end of 1972, the size of the Euro-currency market was estimated to have increased to more than U.S. $100 billion. The U.S.-dollar component was estimated at $80 billion. The largest share of the remain-

---

[2] See Milton Friedman, "The Euro-dollar Market: Some First Principles," *Morgan Guaranty Survey,* October 1969, pp. 4–14; Alexander K. Swoboda, *The Euro-Dollar Market,* Essays in International Finance, no. 64 (Princeton, N.J.: Princeton University, 1968); Fred H. Klopstock, *The Euro-Dollar Market: Some Unresolved Issues,* Essays in International Finance, no. 65 (Princeton, N.J.: Princeton University, 1968).

ing currencies traded outside of their domestic markets was in deutsche marks and a lesser share in Swiss francs.[3]

The opportunity to use the Euro-currency market does not directly obviate the risk that a currency will change in value in relation to other currencies but does enlarge the choice of what currency risks the businessman may choose. As the availability of national currencies outside their home country increases, the currency options for both borrowing and lending that are open to the international businessman will become even greater.

FOREIGN EXCHANGE RATES

Exchange rates, the price of one currency in terms of another, are quoted by dealers within a narrow range, depending upon whether they are selling or buying foreign exchange. The rates also vary with the different instruments of exchange. For example, as of July 14, 1972, a major New York bank, quoted the spot price (the price for immediate delivery) of British pound bank notes at U.S. $2.41 for sellers and U.S. $2.52 for buyers. The spot price for bank transfers in the United States for payment abroad was U.S. $2.4605, or below the buying price for bank notes. The price for bank transfers was U.S. $2.4505 and $2.4395 respectively for 30- and 90-day futures reflecting some lack of confidence on that date in the future stability of the British pound.

In countries where foreign exchange controls have been imposed by the government, multiple-exchange rates may exist with different rates prescribed for different categories of exports and imports and different types of international payments. Multiple-rate systems are intended to promote specific national objectives. High rates may be imposed to discourage the import of luxury goods by making such goods more expensive in local currency. Or certain exports may be taxed through a multiple-rate system. In a number of Latin American countries, for example, coffee exporters have to convert their foreign exchange earnings into local currency at a lower rate than prevails for other exports.

To some extent, exchange rates are direct links connecting the cost-price structures of trading countries. But price comparisons between countries based on prevailing exchange rates must always be used with caution.[4]

Foreign exchange rates are basically determined by the supply and demand for foreign exchange. The supply and demand in turn reflect

---

[3] Morgan Guaranty Trust Company, *World Financial Markets,* March 1973, pp. 4–5.

[4] For further discussion of problems involved in using prevailing exchange rates for cross-country comparisons, see Chapter 12.

domestic and foreign prices of goods and services, international capital movements, the judgments of speculators as to the future course of exchange rates, and other factors. Without intervention by governments and monetary authorities, the market would clear itself through the price mechanism. But the possibility would exist for a great deal of fluctuation in the exchange rates. On the supply side, for example, a country may be heavily dependent on exports of a single raw material or a small number of primary products for earning foreign exchange. In a particular year, unfavorable weather conditions may cause Argentina's supply of wheat or Brazil's production of coffee for exports to be abnormally low, thus depressing seriously the flow of foreign exchange from those countries. World prices for copper or tin may drop sharply because of an economic slowdown in the major consuming countries, because new sources of supply become available, or because new synthetic products have been developed that will substitute for the traditional products. Likewise, unusual and unexpected demands for foreign exchange may result from foreign military commitments, domestic political uncertainties, or the need for imports.

Through participation in the International Monetary Fund, most countries committed themselves to exchange rates fixed within narrow limits over which the currencies may fluctuate. When it appeared that the limit points were likely to be exceeded, the monetary authorities of the nations intervened in a number of ways to defend the exchange rate. If the exchange rate could not be maintained within the stated limits, a nation devalued or revalued its exchange rate in terms of other currencies to a new level at which it expected the underlying market forces to be balanced.[5]

Although a system of flexible or freely fluctuating rates has many attractions and has been strongly advocated by many economists, during the early 1970s most governments still preferred a system of fixed exchange rates with periodic adjustments, based on the conviction that apparently stable rates will reduce risk and encourage international trade and international business activity. Furthermore, some authorities felt that freely fluctuating rates are likely to generate anticipations of further movements in the same direction and stimulate a great deal of speculative activity that will accentuate both upward and downward changes in exchange rates.

BALANCE-OF-PAYMENTS ACCOUNTING

The principal guides to the strength or weakness of a currency and its future exchange price are the balance-of-payments accounts of the

---

[5] For a basic economic treatment of this field, see Tibor Scitovsky, *Money and the Balance of Payments* (Chicago: Rand McNally & Co., 1969).

country. Governmental authorities need to keep informed on the international economic position of their country in order to reach decisions on monetary and fiscal policies and on trade and international payments questions. This surveillance is accomplished primarily through balance-of-payments accounting which attempts to record all economic transactions between the residents of a country and residents of foreign countries during a given time period. An understanding of the balance-of-payments accounting system is an essential part of understanding the financial framework for international business. Just as the balance-of-payments accounts indicate the strength or weakness of a country's currency to its government officials, these accounts can also reveal to the international businessman the existence of potential threats to a currency system in which he is interested and provide a basis for the forecasting of exchange rates. Techniques for balance-of-payments forecasting will be discussed in Chapter 12.

Accounting for international transactions is not a rigid science and there are significant variations in definitions, classifications, and accuracy of statistics from country to country.[6] There are millions of separate transactions between citizens, business firms, and the government of a country and their counterparts abroad during a year. A balance-of-payments statement classifies and summarizes the transactions in a way which shows the major sources of receipts and the principal types of payments. Each classification of receipts and payments represents the total of a large number of individual transactions. The main categories for recording transactions, as standardized by the International Monetary Fund are shown in Table 4.1.

The balance-of-payments accounts are built on the double-entry principle with each transaction giving rise to both a debit and credit entry. Generally, credits (or plus signs) are receipts or exports or inflows; debits (or minus signs) are payments or imports or outflows. By definition, the total of debits and credits must add up to zero. In this sense, there is no surplus and no deficit, but equilibrium. Typically, however, all current receipts and payments are not equal. If receipts are larger than payments, the balance of payments shows a surplus. If payments exceed receipts, it shows a deficit. As shown in Table 4.2, total receipts and total payments balance only if settlement items, such as transfers of gold and net changes in foreign assets and liabilities, are included. These balancing items often termed "below the line" accounts are all the transactions listed below the "net liquidity balance" in Table 4.2.

In the below-the-line balancing accounts, the plus and minus signs

---

[6] For more detailed treatment of balance-of-payments accounting and concepts, see Robert W. Stevens, *A Primer on the Dollar in the World Economy* (New York: Random House, 1972), pp. 6–57; Virgil Salera, *Multinational Business* (Boston: Houghton Mifflin Co., 1969), pp. 192–279.

are reversed as an arbitrary accounting device so that the total accounts will balance. For example, a decrease in a country's gold supply is treated as a credit; an increase in the gold supply is a debit. If a country is running a deficit in its balance of trade by importing more than it is exporting, its means of settling this deficit may be giving up some of its gold supply or selling some of its convertible foreign currency. Thus the decrease in a country's supply of gold or foreign currencies would be an offsetting credit and a means of financing the deficit. As will be discussed below, both the size and nature of deficits and the means of financing such deficits are important questions to consider in evaluating the strength and weakness of a country's currency. But at this point, the idea is being introduced that a country can have deficits or surpluses in its international payments while the accounts themselves are balanced—in the sense that debits equal credits.

For the reader who is not familiar with debit and credit concepts in double-entry accounting, it is probably easier to ignore the classification of transactions as debits or credits and view the balance-of-payments accounts as a tabulation of the totals of various international transactions for a period that shows their net effect over the period on the country's external liquidity, that is, its ability to meet the outside world's claims if and when presented. For those who are familiar with accounting, however, a short review of accounting concepts as applied to balance-of-payments accounting should clear up any difficulties in comprehending the classification of balance-of-payments items as debits or credits.

Under the conventions of double-entry accounting the assets of an entity are always recorded as debits and the liabilities as credits. There are two sorts of liability, however, those to outside parties and those to owners of the entity. The liability to owners represents the basic net worth of the entity according to the rules adopted in keeping the accounts and may be expressed as the excess of assets over outside liabilities. Thus the fundamental equation in double-entry accounting is:

$$\text{Assets (debit)} = \text{Liabilities (credit)} + \text{Net Worth (credit)}$$

It is a simple step from this equation to work out the debit and credit entries for any change in assets, liabilities, or net worth. For example, whenever an asset is added (a debit), there must be an increase in liabilities (credit), an increase in net worth (credit), or a decrease in another asset (credit). Conversely, when an asset is reduced (credit), there must be a reduction in a liability (debit), a reduction in net worth (debit), or an increase in another asset (debit). For activities aimed at building net worth, the accounts classification is extended to introduce accounts for costs and revenue. Revenue represents an increase in net

TABLE 4.1
Balance-of-Payments Categories

Categories	Debits	Credits
A. GOODS AND SERVICES		
1. Merchandise	Imports: goods brought in from foreign sources	Exports: goods shipped to foreign destinations
2. Nonmonetary gold	Purchases	Sales
3. Freight and insurance on merchandise	Paid to foreigners on account of international shipments	Received by residents from foreigners on account of international shipments
4. Other transportation	Payments to foreigners for international travel passenger fares, transportation services such as ship repair, stores and supplies, etc.	Receipts by residents from foreigners for international travel passenger fares, transportation services such as ship repair, stores and supplies, etc.
5. Travel	Expenditures by residents to foreigners for goods and services (including internal transportation) when traveling in a foreign country	Receipts by residents for goods and services (including internal transportation) sold to foreigners traveling in reporting country
6. Investment income	Income paid to foreigners on their private investments in reporting country	Income received by residents from private investments abroad
7. Government, not included elsewhere (n.i.e.)	All foreign purchases of central government, not included in items 1–6 and personal expenditures of government personnel, including military in foreign countries where they are stationed	Expenditures by foreign governments, not included in items 1–6, for goods and services and the personal expenditures of foreign civilian and military personnel stationed in reporting country
8. Other services	Payments to foreigners not classified in items 1–7, including management fees, royalties, film rentals, construction activities, etc.	Receipts by residents from foreigners not classified in items 1–7, including management fees, royalties, film rentals, construction activities, etc.
B. TRANSFER PAYMENTS		
9. Private	Payments in cash and kind by residents to foreigners without a quid pro quo such as contributions for missionary, educational, and charitable purposes and gifts by migrants to their families	Receipt in cash and kind by residents from foreign individuals and governments, including pensions received from foreign governments
10. Central government	Transfers by government to foreigners in the form of goods, services, or cash where nothing is received in direct return. Includes pensions, reparations, and grants in support of economic and military-aid purposes	Transfers received by government from foreigners in the form of goods, services, or cash as gifts or grants. Also includes tax receipts from nonresidents

C. CAPITAL AND MONETARY GOLD

Nonmonetary Sectors

Item		
11. Direct investment	Increases in the investment in foreign enterprises effectively controlled by residents or decreases in the investment in domestic enterprises controlled by foreigners, resulting from either short- or long-term transactions	Decreases in the investment in foreign enterprises effectively controlled by residents or increases in the investment in domestic enterprises controlled by foreigners, resulting from either short- or long-term transactions
12. Other private long-term capital (with original maturity of over 12 months)	Increases in foreign assets held by residents or decreases in domestic assets held by foreigners other than direct investment. Long-term items are mainly loans and transactions in securities. Short-term items include currencies, bank deposits, debts to banks and commercial claims	Decreases in foreign assets held by residents, increases in foreign liabilities of residents, decreases in domestic liabilities to foreigners or increases in domestic assets held by foreigners, other than direct investment
13. Other private short-term capital (with original maturity of 12 months or less)		
14. Local government capital	Loans to foreigners, redemption or purchase from foreigners of local or central government securities. Transactions by public enterprises assigned to private sector above and by monetary institutions to monetary sector below	Foreign loan repayments, foreign sales of local or central government securities
15. Central government capital	Foreign loan repayments, foreign sales of local or central government securities	

Monetary Sectors

Item		
16. Private institutions: liabilities	Foreign transactions of deposit money banks and savings banks: Decreased foreign deposits in the country or increased deposits held abroad	Increased foreign deposits in the country or decreased deposits held abroad
17. Private institutions: assets		
18. Central institutions: liabilities	Foreign transactions of central banks which are the monetary authorities that hold official gold and foreign exchange reserves, intervene in the exchange market, issue currency, or create reserve money for deposit money banks:	
19. Central institutions: assets	Increase in holdings of gold and convertible currencies	Decrease in holdings of gold or convertible currencies
20. Errors and omissions	Denotes a net understatement of recorded debts or overstatement of recorded credits because of reporting errors and unrecorded transactions.	Denotes a net understatement of recorded credits or overstatement of recorded debts

Source: International Monetary Fund, *Balance of Payments, Concepts, and Definitions* (Washington, D.C., 1968).

TABLE 4.2
United States Balance of Payments (billions of dollars)

	1969	*1970*	*1971*
Current Account			
Exports	36.4	42.0	42.8
Imports	−35.8	−39.9	45.5
Trade Balance	.6	2.1	−2.7
Military transactions	−3.3	−3.4	−2.9
Travel and transportation	−1.8	−2.0	−2.4
Investment income, net	6.0	6.2	8.0
(U.S. investments abroad)	(10.5)	(11.4)	(12.9)
(Foreign investments in the U.S.)	(−4.5)	(−5.2)	(−4.9)
Other services	.4	.6	.7
Balance on Goods and Services . . . . :	1.9	3.5	.7
Remittances, pensions, etc.	−1.3	−1.4	−1.5
U.S. government grants	−1.6	−1.7	−2.0
Balance on Current Account	−1.0	.4	−2.8
Capital Account			
Private capital—long term	−0.1	−1.4	−4.2
(U.S. direct investment abroad)	(−3.2)	(−4.4)	(−4.8)
(Foreign direct investment in U.S.)	(0.8)	(1.0)	(−0.1)
(Other)	(2.3)	(2.0)	(0.6)
Private capital—short term . . . . ⹁ . .	−.6	−.5	−2.4
U.S. government capital flows	−1.9	−1.2	−1.7
Errors and omissions	−2.5	−1.1	−10.9
Net Liquidity Balance	−6.1	−3.8	−22.0
Liquid private capital flows	8.8	−6.0	−7.8
Official Reserve-Transactions Balance	2.7	−9.8	−29.8
Foreign official agencies	−1.5	7.3	27.4
Gold	−1.0	.8	.9
Special drawing rights (IMF)	—	−.9	−.3
Convertible currencies	0.8	2.2	.4
IMF position	−1.0	.4	1.4

Source: *Survey of Current Business*, U.S. Department of Commerce, Office of Business Economics.

worth and hence is recorded as a credit, while costs, in effect, decrease net worth and are recorded as debits. Hence:

$$\text{Revenues (credit)} - \text{Costs (debit)} = \text{Net Worth (credit)}$$

When costs are incurred (debit), there must be an offsetting credit— either an increased liability or a decreased asset. Likewise, when a revenue earning sale is made, revenue is credited and an asset or a liability account debited. The entry in an asset account might record the cash received or the customer debt for the sale. If the entry is in a liability account it might record a reduction in the amount owing to a creditor.

Applying these double-entry concepts to balance-of-payments accounting, a country's international net worth can be viewed as the difference between the country's external claims against the rest of the world (debit) and the rest of the world's claims against the country's own wealth (credit). This net worth is not a measure of the country's entire wealth, only that portion of it that its residents have channeled through international transactions. When a country exports goods, international net worth is increased by the value of goods channeled into exports (credit), and there is an increase in claims against foreigners to whom the exports are made (debit). Or if a resident pays a foreign account with foreign currency that he obtains from his bank the effect is to reduce the country's foreign liabilities by the amount paid (debit) and to reduce the country's foreign assets by the same amount (credit), that is, foreign currency held by the bank is reduced.

After exporting $1,000 worth of goods and then importing $800 worth of goods, the balance-of-payments accounts for *Country A* would look like this:

Country A	*Balance of Payments*	
	Debit	*Credit*
Exports		1000
Imports	800	
Net merchandise transactions		200
Net short-term claims	200	
	200	200

In this example, only the net change in short-term claims is shown. The country's short-term claims against foreigners were increased by $1,000, and foreigners' short-term claims against the country increased by $800—producing a net increase of $200 in the country's claims against the rest of the world. This method of disclosing only the net movement provides a clue to the way balance-of-payments accounts are compiled in practice.

While presented in the format of double-entry accounting, in fact the total for each category in the balance-of-payments accounts is estimated from whatever sources provide the best estimate—sometimes even readings from small samples. No government could follow a full double-entry procedure of recording complete information on the countless separate transactions by individuals, businesses and government authorities that lie behind a year's change in external net worth. Thus data on imports and exports are usually taken from records of customs authorities, although they might alternatively be based on statistical submissions from the country's banks. Finally, an artificial balancing item, "net errors and omissions" is introduced to balance the accounts. In part, this errors and omissions item will be an adjustment for statistical inaccuracies. In part, it may cover clandestine or other transactions that have gone unrecorded for any reason.

The balance-of-payments accounts are thus basically a balanced list of transactions over a period—usually a year. Just as a list of totals in the accounts recorded in a firm's books can be compiled as a trial balance at any time, so too can the totals of the various categories used in balance-of-payments accounts. Such lists, however, demonstrate little of value until they are arranged and presented in an understandable format. For the firm, a prime distinction is made between items which appear in the revenue, or profit and loss statement, and those which appear in the statement of assets and liabilities, or balance sheet. For the country, a similar distinction is made between current account and capital account. Current account items are those concerned with the country's trading activities in real goods and services and other short-term earnings and expenses. Capital account items are those concerned with the country's transactions in monetary and ownership claims.

There are two categories of accounts which do not fall readily into this classification between current and capital accounts—transfer payments and errors and omissions. Transfer payments cover gifts, donations, and aid. While they may be transfers of capital, they are in many ways similar to the dividends and donations included in the appropriations section of the revenue account of a firm. For a country they are included under the current account heading. Errors and omissions are described in Table 4.1 and are generally shown separately alongside capital account items.

There is one major distinction between balance-of-payments accounting and conventional accounting for a business firm, however. For balance-of-payments accounting, no balances are carried forward from year to year. The practical effect of this is that the net worth account disappears. There is no opening net worth at the beginning of the year, and only the increase or decrease in net worth for the year is shown. This is represented by any balance in the current account which in turn is represented by the net movement in the capital account.

A surplus on current account must always be matched by a debit on capital account, and a deficit by a credit on capital account. A surplus on current account is usually regarded with favor and is sometimes referred to as a "favorable" balance or a "positive" balance. The country's international net worth insofar as it is measured by the accounts will have increased, and, as shown by the offsetting capital account debit, the country must have increased its foreign investments.

Rather than appearing as a balance sheet, the capital account is thus akin to a "Sources and Applications of Funds" statement in conventional business accounting. A sources and applications statement shows the movements in assets and liabilities over the period and is obtained by subtracting the balances in the opening balance sheet from those in the closing balance sheet. The capital account in the balance of payments shows how the deficit or surplus on current account, together with off-setting movements among the various capital accounts, have been distributed among those capital accounts.

The balance-of-payments accounts for the United States for 1969–71 are shown in Table 4.2. This is just one possible way of setting out the basic information, but it shows clearly the distinction between current account and capital account.

Balance and Imbalance in the Balance of Payments

The idea has already been introduced that there can be a deficit or surplus on current account in the balance of payments while the accounts themselves are balanced in the sense that debits equal credits (after allowing for errors and omissions). The balance on current account is a fairly robust indicator of a change in exchange rates, yet it is only one of a number of indicators that are used in analyzing a country's balance of payments.

The balance of trade is used to refer to the relationship between imports and exports. Ordinarily, a country's position is considered to be weakened if it increases its imports and strengthened if it increases its exports. Movements in the balance of trade, however, may be closely linked with changes in other categories in the accounts. Exports, for example, may have resulted from tied aid (that is, foreign-aid grants which require that the funds be spent for purchases from the donor country) or from increased investment overseas, both of which are regarded as weakening a country's international position.

A number of methods are used by the nations of the world to measure and report their international-payments balances.[7] The two most commonly used to represent the balance of payments for the United States are those on the net liquidity basis and on the official reserve-transactions basis (see Table 4.2.) The liquidity balance is intended to be a broad indicator of potential pressures on the dollar and is measured by changes in U.S. official reserve assets and liquid claims and liquid liabilities of all foreigners, either private or government. The official reserve-transactions balance is intended to be an indicator of the immediate market pressures on the dollar during the reporting period resulting from international transactions of the United States. In addition to changes in U.S. official reserve assets, it takes account of changes in liquid and certain nonliquid liabilities to foreign official agencies.

---

[7] For a comprehensive discussion of the methods used and their significance, see David T. Devlin, "The U.S. Balance of Payments: Revised Presentation," *Survey of Current Business,* June 1971, pp. 24–30.

When a nation's international receipts are in excess of payments over a period, the excess or surplus will increase the nation's monetary-exchange reserves. If payments exceed receipts, the resulting deficit will reduce the nation's reserves by an equivalent amount. In a balanced position, a nation can finance all of its international transactions from current receipts and the tendency will be for exchange rates to be stable. But surplus or deficit imbalances which persist over a period of time create pressures for changes in the fixed value of a country's currency in international transactions or for domestic adjustment policies that can restore the international equilibrium.

The causes of the imbalance have a great deal to do with shaping the action that governments must take to restore equilibrium. And the balance-of-payments accounts must be studied and analyzed by businessmen who want to evaluate the degree and strength of a particular country's currency and predict the possible actions that may result.

The potential underlying causes of payment imbalances are myriad and can be reflected in any of the balance-of-payments categories. They include differences in the amplitude and timing of cyclical movements in the economies of the different countries as well as differential price changes, particularly different rates of inflation. Innovations, such as the development of synthetic substitutes for raw materials, changes in consumer tastes, changes in the structure of the domestic economy through induced industrialization, changed patterns of international investment, governmental-aid programs, and private remittances can all be important imbalancing forces. Interventions by governments of other countries in the form of tariffs and controls and the influence of wars can be still others.

Reserves and International Liquidity

While a country's balance-of-payments accounts are the principal guides to the strength of its currency, these accounts only record flows over a period of time. Concentration on deficits or surpluses overlooks the long-term strengths or weaknesses of the country's international position. A full assessment of a country's currency strength requires attention to both the size of its international net worth and its liquidity, as determined by the nature of the assets and liabilities. If the United States runs a deficit of $1 billion in its balance-of-payments accounts as a result of military or foreign-aid grants, decreased exports, or increased imports, the country's international liquidity will probably have been reduced by using up gold or other international reserves to finance the deficit. On the other hand, should a deficit be caused by an increase in U.S. residents' purchases of foreign investments, then, although U.S. liquidity might be reduced in the same way, the long-term strength of the country will not have deteriorated. In the long term the position may even be strengthened by foreign earnings from investments which would not have accrued from the retention of gold reserves.

Measurements of a country's international net worth have not been given the attention that has been accorded to balance-of-payments accounting, and statistics may have to be gathered from a variety of sources. The central authority's holdings of gold, freely convertible currencies, and other foreign currencies are usually published by the central banks and are the prime liquid reserves. The country may have deposited some of these reserves with the International Monetary Fund and have arranged rights to draw these sums and further amounts from the Fund in an emergency. These drawing rights, discussed later in the chapter, increase a country's liquidity without adding to its net worth.

Commercial bank statistics should also be available regularly. The country's commercial banks will usually hold some foreign bank notes, deposits with foreign banks, and a range of short-term claims against foreigners, such as bills of exchange. While these sums are fairly liquid, they will be offset by foreigners' holdings of the country's own bank notes, deposits with the commercial banks, and short-term claims against residents. Commercial banks, moreover, will need some working balance to cover periods of peak demand. Figures on longer-term assets and liabilities are likely to be readily available for transactions with a fixed liability such as government bonds. For other items, however, valuation is a problem as is any measure of liquidity. For both direct and portfolio investment, historical cost is likely to produce a considerable undervaluation.

The international investment position of the United States is published regularly by the Department of Commerce and this statement is shown for 1969, 1970, and 1971 in Table 4.3. It shows, as the balance-of-payments accounts in Table 4.2 do not, that the United States has a substantial international net worth. On the other hand, the country's liquidity is very low, with foreigners' liquid assets and short-term claims exceeding the United States own short-term claims and liquid reserves.

The failure to have a more highly developed accounting for international investment is not due simply to problems of statistical collection. These can be surmounted. The real problem is to change attitudes so that the appropriate measurements for evaluating what an international accounting system really ought to be evaluating will be internationally accepted. The current emphasis on balance of payments became firmly entrenched when trade between independent enterprises of different nations was the dominant form of international business activity.

In a world of trade, persistent deficits meant that the claims of one nation against another were growing. The deficit nation was going further and further into debt to others, with only domestic resources or interna-

TABLE 4.3
United States International Investment Position (billions of dollars)

	1969	1970	1971
United States Assets and Investments Abroad	*151.1*	*166.6*	*181.0*
Private			
long-term—direct	71.0	78.1	86.1
long-term—portfolio	25.3	26.6	29.9
short-term	14.1	15.2	18.9
U.S. government			
long-term	28.2	29.7⎫	34.0
short-term	2.5	2.5⎭	
Gold stock	11.9	11.1	10.2
IMF position	2.3	2.8⎫	1.9
Convertible currencies	2.8	0.6⎭	
Foreign Assets and Investments in United States	*90.8*	*97.5*	*122.5*
U.S. liabilities to private foreigners	71.3	71.1	69.2
(Nonliquid, including direct investments in U.S.)	(42.4)	(48.5)	(53.3)
(Liquid)	(28.9)	(22.6)	(15.9)
U.S. liabilities to foreign official accounts	19.5	26.4	53.2
United States Net International Investment Position	67.2	69.1	58.5

Source: U.S. Department of Commerce, Office of Business Economics.

tional reserves available for eventually settling these debts. Weaknesses in a country's currency reflected mainly the unavailability of goods acceptable to other nations or overpriced goods—in other words, lack of competitiveness or production potential. The relevance of such an accounting system is more limited in a world economy where international private investment and international business activities other than trade have become dominant and where a large share of trade is between affiliates of international corporations rather than between independent firms of different nationalities.[8] Deficits may result from outflows that are used to purchase or establish production facilities or other real assets in foreign countries.

There will undoubtedly be an increased use of international investment measures as traditional attitudes emphasizing balance of payments are changed, but even further developments may be needed to take account of the growing importance of multinational enterprises. Indicators of the ways in which international firms operating on a global scale have affected a country's international position are likely to be necessary as a basis for designing effective controls.

Adjustment Measures for Payments Imbalances

If the deficits are temporary and recognized as such outside of the country, a country can use government reserves or borrowing, for exam-

---

[8] See G. C. Hufbauer and F. M. Adler, *Overseas Manufacturing Investment and the Balance of Payments* (Washington, D.C.: U.S. Treasury Department, 1968).

ple, from the IMF, to meet the deficits. For more serious or persisting deficits, governments have the choice of several lines of action, separately or in combination. Adjustments can be attempted through changes in the exchange rate, through internal economic measures such as better control over domestic inflation, and through quantitative import restrictions and exchange controls.[9]

The most clear-cut adjustment alternative for a government is to devalue its currency, that is, to lower the value of its national currency in relation to gold and other national currencies. The principal hoped-for benefit from devaluation is to encourage exports and discourage imports, thus improving a nation's balance of trade. Exports are stimulated because the price of a nation's goods in foreign currencies has been reduced. Imports are retarded because the domestic cost of imported goods is increased. The strength of these effects will depend upon the magnitude of the devaluation and the price elasticity of demand for exports and imports. If consumers continue to purchase the same quantity of goods even if the price is considerably reduced or significantly raised, the demand for that good is said to be highly price inelastic. But if the consumer varies his purchases with higher or lower prices, price changes can greatly affect foreign exchange earnings of exports or foreign exchange expenditures on imports.

Revaluation is the upward adjustment of the exchange rate to appreciate an undervalued currency. Its effects are the opposite of those of devaluation.

Two major problems exist with the devaluation and revaluation solutions. First, the countries with surpluses whose currencies may have been undervalued or become undervalued due to later events do not feel the same degree of urgency for adjustments as do the countries with deficits. Yet, the best solutions in many cases may be for adjustment action by the surplus countries. Secondly, the United States has not had the degree of freedom that other countries have had for using the devaluation option. In the absence of an international currency and with a slowly growing monetary supply of gold in the world, the U.S. dollar has become almost an international currency. The ramifications of a devaluation of the dollar are extremely great because the United States has financed a large part of its deficit through the willingness of other countries and foreign individuals to hold dollars. Even if the United States changes the relationship of the dollar to gold, as it did in 1972, it cannot improve its competitive position vis-a-vis other currencies unless other countries are willing to revalue their currencies in relation to the dollar.

Adjustments through new or modified domestic policies without alter-

---

[9] For a more detailed discussion of the adjustment problem, see Mordecai E. Kreinin, *International Economics* (New York: Harcourt Brace Jovanovich, 1971), Chapters 4, 5, and 6.

ing exchange rates can be extremely difficult to accomplish for political reasons or because of the unwillingness to place international considerations ahead of domestic goals with which they conflict. For example, a nation can raise international interest rates in order to attract more foreign capital inflows or to discourage capital outflows. Yet, higher interest rates may at the same time slow down domestic expansion because of a higher cost for money. In some circumstances, a nation may wish to reduce purchasing power and the demand for imported goods by slowing down domestic expansion. But a slowdown of domestic expansion may also create unemployment and be politically unacceptable whatever it achieves.

Where domestic inflation is responsible for increasing the price of a nation's goods in foreign markets and producing a decline in export earnings, many of the traditional measures for reversing the decline by controlling inflation clearly lead to economic slowdowns and increased unemployment. In the late 1960s the United States tried to improve its balance-of-payments situation through a wide range of measures including high interest rates, reduced government expenditures, and attempts to control inflation. By subordinating domestic considerations to its international financial balance, however, the United States was attempting to slow the growth of its entire economy with a GNP of over $900 billion, to correct a balance-of-payments deficit ranging from $2 to $6 billion dollars. This sort of reaction raises serious questions about the significance of the accepted balance-of-payments accounting system for signaling strengths and weaknesses in an economy. Better inflation control may be highly desirable for domestic purposes, but when the principal justification for such measures is reduction in the balance-of-payments deficit, the tail may be wagging the dog.

The imposition of quantitative restrictions and exchange controls may well be an easier political path than internal deflation for a country to take. Such controls might accompany internal adjustments or be considered as a solution in themselves. Quantitative or tariff restrictions can reduce imports and improve the balance on goods and services. Restrictions can take many forms. The outright banning of foreign imports is common in less developed countries particularly of so-called luxury goods and goods for which local production is available although at higher prices than imports. Alternatively, imports can be retarded by exorbitant tariffs, which raise the domestic prices to such levels that demand disappears. Exchange controls have a similar effect and can range from the simplest allocation of available foreign exchange among domestic individuals or business firms to controls discriminating against different categories of goods. In some countries different exchange rates have been established which make essential goods less expensive and luxury goods more costly.

Restrictions and controls accompanied by governmental licensing for imports and exports and for foreign exchange remittances generally encourage smuggling, bribery, and other forms of illegal behavior to circumvent the controls. Controls generally do not tackle the basic causes of the payments imbalance. At best, controls may provide some respite from further deterioration of a situation while other more basic remedies are being implemented. Yet, in many cases, restrictions and controls have remained as permanent fixtures.

THE UNITED STATES INTERNATIONAL POSITION

Before moving on to the operation of the international monetary system, an examination of the balance of payments and international investment position of the United States since 1945 (see Table 4.4) provides

TABLE 4.4
United States Balance of Payments and Investment Position 1945–1970
(billions of dollars)

	1945	1950	1955	1960	1965	1970
Balance of Payments						
Trade balance (excl. military	7.2	1.0	2.8	4.9	5.0	2.1
Other goods and services. . . .	−1.5	− .3	− .3	−1.3	− .4	−4.8
Net investment income . . .	.4	1.2	1.9	2.3	4.2	6.2
Unilateral transfers	−7.1	−4.5	−4.8	−4.0	−4.4	−3.1
Balance on Current Account	−1.0	−2.6	− .4	1.9	4.4	0.4
U.S. Assets and Investments						
Private long-term—direct. . . .	8.4	11.8	19.4	31.9	49.5	78.1
Private long-term—portfolio . .	5.3	5.7	7.4	12.6	21.9	26.6
Government long-term	1.6	10.8	12.4	14.1	20.2	29.7
Short-term and liquid claims private and government . . .	1.5	1.8	3.1	7.9	13.4	17.7
Gold stock.	20.0	22.8	21.8	17.8	13.8	11.0
IMF position and SDRs	−	1.4	1.0	1.6	.8	2.8
Foreign Assets and Investments in United States						
Foreign long-term—direct . . .	2.5	3.4	5.1	6.9	8.8	13.2
Foreign long-term—portfolio .	5.5	4.6	8.3	11.5	17.6	31.6
Short-term and liquid claims .	9.1	9.6	14.4	22.8	32.3	58.8
United States Net International Investment Position	19.7	36.7	37.2	44.6	61.4	69.1

Source: U.S. Department of Commerce, Office of Business Economics.

a concrete example of the way in which the situation can change. It also points up the range and varying importance of the forces that contribute to the changes.

Coming out of World War II the United States had a relatively large stock of gold reserves—about $25 billion—with net short-term liabilities of $6.4 billion. During the next decade, U.S. government grants for both economic reconstruction and development and military assistance rose to high levels. These grants, however, were largely offset by trading surpluses due to demands in Western Europe and Asia for reconstructing war-devastated economies. Furthermore, potential competitors for the United States in export markets were busy with domestic reconstruction and their own domestic demands. Remaining deficits were covered by outflows of gold and to an even larger extent by increased holdings of U.S. dollars by foreigners. The deficits and the resulting transfers of gold and the buildup in foreign dollar holdings had little impact on world confidence in the dollar. It was widely accepted that the large gold stocks held by the United States needed to be better distributed among the major countries and an actual dollar shortage existed at the close of the war.

From a peak in 1953, U.S. government grants steadily declined, but direct investment outflows rose steeply in 1956 and 1957 and then continued at a high level, rising sharply again in 1964. Although inflows from earnings and from induced exports of capital goods greatly exceeded direct investment outflows over this period, the rising trend of foreign investment became a focus for concern that deficits would become a permanent fixture. Confidence in the U.S. dollar declined, and there were increased conversions of dollar holdings into gold bullion. The United States remained solvent with its high balance of long-term foreign investments, but its liquidity had declined. At the end of 1964, short-term dollar liabilities were over twice short-term assets.

While the U.S. trade balance rose until 1964, it began to fall off sharply thereafter, raising further questions as to the competitiveness of U.S. goods now that war reconstruction and the formation of the European Common Market and the European Free Trade Area were past history. Exports continued to expand, but imports expanded even more rapidly. A contributing factor was a rise in the U.S. inflation rate attributed to the increased demand stimulated by Vietnam military spending. While the direct foreign exchange costs of the war were partly offset by cuts in other government expenditures overseas, the rising inflation had its effect in increasing imports dramatically. By 1971, the surplus on nonmilitary goods and services, which reached a 1964 high of $6.8 billion, had become a deficit of $2.7 billion. By 1971, however, investment earnings had grown to a net inflow of $8.0 billion, and this growth reflects the tremendous buildup in private long-term assets in foreign countries.

By 1971, it had become generally accepted that the United States would not quickly reverse these trends. There seemed no indication that the United States would gain further comparative advantages from technological or agricultural breakthroughs, nor could it limit price increases any more successfully than its major competitors. Moreover, there were increasing import pressures from developing countries and a growing substitution of foreign production for exports as the overseas projects of American firms matured. With the United States financing deficits by increasing short-term dollar claims, European nations holding the increased dollar claims became less and less prepared to hold additional amounts. The eventual result was the suspension of convertibility of the U.S. dollar on August 15, 1971. Its exchange rate against gold and other currencies was altered in December 1971 and again in 1973.

BACKGROUND TO MULTINATIONAL MONETARY COOPERATION

During the 40 years before World War I, the major countries of the world attempted to secure exchange-rate stability through connecting their currencies to gold. After the war, they continued with a restructured gold standard into the 1930s. Under the gold standard, exchange rates had fixed par values determined by the gold content of the national monetary units. Each country legally defined its standard monetary unit as consisting of a specified quantity of gold. To keep the national currency equivalent in value to the declared gold content, the government stood ready to buy and sell gold in unlimited quantities at the price implied by its relationship to the standard monetary unit. Thus, for example, in 1930 the U.S. dollar was defined as containing 23.22 grains of fine gold, and the British pound was defined as containing approximately 113 grains of fine gold. The U.S. government freely bought and sold gold at the implied price of $20.67 per fine troy ounce, there being 480 grains in a troy ounce.

Under the gold standard, deficits or surpluses in a country's balance-of-payments situation were expected to generate automatic internal adjustments that would correct the situation and restore stability. Classical theory placed primary emphasis on domestic price and income changes which would restore the equilibrium. In effect, it was assumed that countries would subordinate the national economy to the dictates of external economic and monetary relations. But with the world economic crisis of the 1930s, countries became unwilling to undertake domestic policies of price and income deflation and to accept the unemployment that would result from such policies, in order to resolve external balance-of-payments problems. Beginning with Great Britain in 1931, one country after another abandoned the gold standard, despite the fact that the standard had facilitated a vast expansion in world trade up till then. The 1930s saw complete monetary chaos. Currencies of many of the smaller countries fluctuated wildly in the exchange markets propelled by underlying economic forces and waves of speculation.

By the end of World War II, most nation-states were prepared to cooperate in building a new international monetary system. They had learned through painful experience that unilateral actions to influence one nation's currency position relative to other nations could result in retaliatory actions which could vitiate the hoped-for gains. Most nations were willing to recognize that there were opportunities for cooperation through which all parties could gain and that the gains of one nation did not have to be at the expense of another.

The new era in multinational monetary cooperation emerged from the Bretton Woods Conference of 1944 at which the establishment of the International Monetary Fund was agreed. Among the nations that came together at Bretton Woods there was a common fear that, as occurred after World War I, a brief boom would be followed by a disastrous slump. There was also a common dissatisfaction with the paraphernalia of exchange restrictions, multiple rates, and fluctuating currencies that had proliferated during the 1930s. Countries thus shared a common motivation to adopt a code of international conduct that would outlaw competitive depreciation of exchange rates. And they were willing to relinquish some part of national authority in the interests of the international community as a whole.

There were limits to this willingness, however. While the establishment of a world central bank was proposed, the United States, in particular, was not ready for such a step. Governments sought instead to work out new exchange rates by general agreements and to keep them stable once they were fixed. It was anticipated that changes in exchange rates would still have to occur but the preference of governments had changed towards devaluations and against exchange or trade controls as a means of correcting disequilibria.

International Monetary Fund

The initial objectives of the International Monetary Fund are shown in Table 4.5. Member governments, of which there were 125 in 1972, agreed to peg their currencies to gold or to the U.S. dollar, which in turn was pegged to gold. They agreed to make their currencies convertible—to dismantle their exchange controls—after a transition period. And they agreed on rules to police exchange-rate changes. The IMF plan fixed the limits for exchange-rate fluctuations to 1 percent above or below the official parity, with each member government committed to pursue policies to keep its own rates within this narrow range.

The IMF system, sometimes called the system of the adjustable peg, seeks to assure maximum exchange-rate stability, yet to facilitate orderly changes when they are needed and to avoid competitive devaluations like those of the 1930s. A government could alter the par value of its

TABLE 4.5
The Purposes of the International Monetary Fund

(i) To promote international monetary cooperation through a permanent institution which provides the machinery for consultation and collaboration on international monetary problems.
(ii) To facilitate the expansion and balanced growth of international trade, and to contribute thereby to the promotion and maintenance of high levels of employment and real income and to the development of the productive resources of all members as primary objectives of economic policy.
(iii) To promote exchange stability, to maintain orderly exchange arrangements among members, and to avoid competitive exchange depreciation.
(iv) To assist in the establishment of a multilateral system of payments in respect of current transactions between members and in the elimination of foreign exchange restrictions which hamper the growth of world trade.
(v) To give confidence to members by making the Fund's resources available to them under adequate safeguards, thus providing them with opportunity to correct maladjustments in their balance of payments without resorting to measures destructive of national or international prosperity.
(vi) In accordance with the above, to shorten the duration and lessen the degree of disequilibrium in the international balances of payments of members.

Source: Articles of Agreement of the IMF, July 22, 1944.

currency by as much as 10 percent without IMF approval but in consultation with the Fund. Any change exceeding 10 percent required prior approval from the Fund, and such approval was to be granted if the change is designed to correct a fundamental disparity or economic maladjustment.

The IMF's leverage over member countries consists largely of granting or denying access to the Fund's resources in case of financial need. When joining the IMF, member countries pay a subscription quota in gold and U.S. dollars based on certain economic criteria related to size of country, national income, and so forth. Thus, the Fund has gold and convertible currencies that can be made available to the member countries under certain conditions. A member country can exchange its own money for any other member's currency up to a maximum of 25 percent of its quota. Member countries can also negotiate a stand-by agreement with the IMF under which the Fund agrees in advance to make aid available should the need arise. The agreements have the effect of reducing uncertainties from holding or dealing in another country's currency. Member countries can also borrow from the IMF for emergency purposes.

In the 25 years under the IMF system from 1944 to 1969, a number of important exchange-rate changes occurred. In 1949, for example, Britain devalued the pound from $4.03 to $2.80 and in November 1967, again devalued from $2.80 to $2.40. There was a subsequent revaluation to $2.60 in 1971. Then in June 1972 sterling was floated. France devalued the franc in 1957 and again in 1969. Germany and the Netherlands raised their parities in 1961. Exchange-rate devaluations were particularly frequent in the case of many of the less developed countries, which have had great difficulty maintaining price stability while seeking to promote rapid economic growth.

For the first 20 years of this period, the leading nations of the world were fairly well satisfied with the functioning of the international financial system. Trade and international investment flourished. Business and economic relations among countries expanded much more rapidly than national rates of economic growth. Nevertheless, beginning in the mid-1960s, international financial difficulties began to increase in frequency and in intensity, and pressures were generated for reappraising and reforming the system built almost a quarter of a century before for a different kind of world.

Contemporary Problems and Reform Proposals

It has been argued that the only permanent solution to international monetary problems is nothing less than an international currency. The contemporary international system has no central authority, no central bank, and no central currency. Only an unprecedented financial crisis, however, would make an international currency politically feasible. It would involve a sacrifice of national sovereignty, with cooperating nations forgoing the power to regulate their economies through the use of monetary controls.

Short of agreement on one central currency, the growing frequency and intensity of international financial crises have produced an extensive debate on the underlying problems of a multicurrency system and the practicality of different reforms.[10] Leading financial and monetary experts have identified the principal problems with the existing framework as:

1. a shortage of international liquidity
2. lack of flexibility in exchange rates
3. inadequate processes for adjusting to balance of payments disequilibrium.

The liquidity problem arises out of a concern that the expansion of international financial reserves has been lagging too far behind the growing volume of international trade and investment. As the volume of transactions increases, according to the monetary experts, the need for reserves grows, though not necessarily at the same rate. International reserves are needed for net settlements between countries and to cover

---

[10] One classic proposal for reform was put forward in Robert Triffin, *Gold and the Dollar Crisis* (New Haven: Yale University Press, 1960). For a more recent proposal, see Maxwell Stamp, "The Reform of the International Monetary System," *Moorgate and Wall Street,* Autumn 1972.

deficits until adjustment measures take effect. Given the time it takes for a nation to introduce measures to restore equilibrium in its balance of payments, current reserves are said to provide an inadequate cushion so that countries overreact and often are forced to resort to exchange-rate adjustment when internal economic adjustments would be most appropriate.

In assessing the adequacy of international liquidity, major emphasis is placed on official monetary reserves rather than the foreign assets in the hands of private residents of a country. Official reserves comprise the gold and foreign exchange holdings of monetary authorities, plus such additional means of payment as may be available to them through international and bilateral credit facilities. Additions over time to the monetary reserves of gold depend upon new gold production, part of which is used for industrial purposes and only part of which is purchased by nations as monetary reserves. But gold production depends on the relationship between the market price and the cost of mining. Thus, there is no necessary connection between the need for additional monetary reserves and the supply of gold.

A major reform adopted in 1969 and intended to increase liquidity was the creation of Special Drawing Rights or SDRs by the International Monetary Fund. SDRs are the equivalent of gold because all member countries have agreed to accept SDRs for settlement of international transactions. SDRs are made available to member nations in proportion to their IMF quotas. As of January 1, 1971, a total of SDR 9.3 billion had been allocated to IMF participants. There has been disagreement, however, on how much of a supply should be created and on how freely this additional international reserve should be made available to countries. Some countries are concerned that the greater availability of international reserves will cause nations to be less vigorous in undertaking domestic policies necessary for correcting balance-of-payments disequilibria. In other words, greater reserves can become an excuse for postponing necessary, but politically difficult, domestic actions.

The problem of greater flexibility in exchange rates relates back to the rules of the IMF under which member countries pledged to allow their currencies to fluctuate no more than 1 percent above or below the fixed par values. In times of heavy market pressures or financial crises, a currency may press toward its prescribed floor or ceiling, forcing central banks to step into the picture. If a nation's currency threatens to fall below its lower limit, that country's central bank must buy up its currency and furnish dollars or other major currencies. If the pressures are toward the ceiling, the country is obligated to sell its currency and accept other national currencies.

The belief has been growing that the limits are too narrow to allow for problems which are likely to arise and that nations could better weather temporary market pressures on their currencies without having to resort to devaluations or increased valuations if the "pegs" were widened. As a result, the Group of Ten (see below) adopted in December 1971 such a widened band—2¼ percent either side of parity, versus the former 1 percent. Some experts favor a combination of widening the bands and providing a "crawling peg" system of gradual changes in parities. Exchange market forces would point the direction of the crawl—up if a currency is scarce, down if it is plentiful. The amount of the crawl would be limited by agreement. By combining wider bands with a crawling peg, the adjustment process would become more automatic. Speculators would know which way a currency was moving, but with a slow enough rate of crawl the potential for profit would not be enough to spur dangerous speculation.

Others go even further and advocate abandoning fixed rates altogether to let the rates float freely. When there are no controls imposed to regulate a market, whether it be for buttons, housing, or foreign exchange, there is no deficit or surplus and a rate emerges that equates the supply and demand. Balance-of-payments and liquidity problems would disappear. The proponents of floating rates argue that countries would be able to concentrate on the internal economic situation without worrying about the implications for liquidity or fixed exchange rates.

One argument advanced against freely fluctuating rates is that when fluctuations occur, speculators accentuate price swings. So long as an efficient forward market existed, however, speculators might actually damp down fluctuations. If they expected the rate to go up, they would buy low to resell later at a profit, but their buying would itself increase the current demand and force the rate up. Their selling would force the future rate down. International business would have difficulties, though, if currencies did not have adequate forward markets, which is generally the case for small countries. Also, some sorts of risk cannot be avoided, even with the opportunity to cover ahead. An importer who buys goods and covers himself for the amount he will later have to pay for them may find that if the rate falls, those who did not cover would be in a position to undersell him.

Evolving Framework for Further Cooperation

Prior to the 1971 international financial crisis, lacking radical changes in the multicurrency IMF system, there emerged a number of new institutional connections for greater harmonization of national actions to adjust the position of individual currencies. The activities of the Group of Ten and the OECD are particularly noticeable in this category.

The Group of Ten (G-10) was formed in the early 1960s by the ten leading financial countries of the world, other than Switzerland.

It includes Belgium, Canada, France, Germany, Italy, Japan, Netherlands, Sweden, United Kingdom, and the United States. G-10 had study groups working on proposed modifications of the monetary system, particularly the creation of new international reserve units. It tried to promote agreement among major financial powers on IMF reforms as a preliminary step toward reaching agreement among the more than 100 members of the IMF. G-10 met during periods of financial crisis to work out emergency financial support for member countries. In one crisis period during 1968, a subgroup conceived and implemented a two-tier gold system which maintained a fixed price for monetary gold and permitted the price of gold in private markets to be determined by the forces of supply and demand without official intervention. It also took the lead during the 1971 dollar-devaluation crisis. The general arrangement is informal and more confidential than public. It has been a major step toward improved communications and greatly expanded cooperation in national policies affecting international finance. The third world of the poorer nations, however, has demanded representation, and they have been included in the Group of Twenty formed in 1972 as a committee of the IMF to negotiate international monetary reform.

The Organization for Economic Cooperation and Development (OECD), headquartered in Paris, is a successor to the Organization for European Economic Cooperation (OEEC), an agency originally created after World War II to supervise the administration of the Marshall Plan for European recovery. It has become, in effect, an organization of the industrialized or highly developed countries of the world. The agency provides a framework for consultation and cooperation in many fields including that of development assistance programs to the less developed countries. It also brings together the principal industrialized countries on a regular basis in Working Party No. 2 to submit the monetary and fiscal policies of each country to the scrutiny of the group. Through such multilateral surveillance, national policies are influenced and changes are suggested that limit the possibilities for any one country to benefit for long at the expense of the others. The OECD has limited authority, if any, to force countries to change their national policies. In practice, however, the process of communication, review, and discussion appears to exert considerable pressure toward harmonization of national policies in the interest of an improved international financial environment.

Another regional movement of great potential significance to the international financial framework has been occurring in the European Common Market, officially called the European Economic Community (EEC).[11] After a long period of extensive study and many proposals,

---

[11] For a more detailed treatment of regional economic-integration movements, see Chapter 5.

the EEC agreed in early 1971 to proceed with the creation of an economic and monetary union. A principal objective of this move is to unify the currencies of the member countries. The initial step has been modest, involving only action to narrow the exchange-rate variations among the currencies of the member countries. The ultimate goal, however, is the complete elimination of variations in exchange rates among the national currencies of the enlarged European Community.

The achievement of a European Monetary Union, if it occurs, will have far-reaching implications both for the future of Europe and for the international monetary system, including the role of the dollar. A Europe with one money would mean a Europe of one economic and monetary policy. And a European currency will both challenge the dollar as an international currency and make possible closer monetary cooperation between both sides of the Atlantic.[12]

SOURCES OF FINANCE FOR INTERNATIONAL BUSINESS

Another aspect of the international financial framework is the provision of finance specifically for international business. Most nations have special programs for export-credit financing. In addition, some countries have sources uniquely available for medium- and long-term financing of foreign projects. In the United States, for example, such special sources have been the government foreign-aid program, the government-owned Export-Import Bank and Edge Act companies. Edge Act companies are affiliates of U.S. commercial banks chartered to engage exclusively in foreign operations. They provide both loans and equity capital to international business concerns. In Germany, the German Development Company (Deutsche Entwicklugsgesellschaft—DEG) provides finance for international ventures by German firms. These special government sources generally operate in support of some national policy such as encouraging exports or providing development assistance to the less developed countries. In some countries, U.S. firms have access to special sources of local financing, such as Cooley loans. Such funds became available through the U.S. food-aid program which sold surplus food products to the less developed countries and accepted payment in local currencies.

In addition to the domestic capital market of the parent company and the national capital market of the subsidiary, multinational enterprises have been increasingly looking to a third source, namely international institutions and the international capital market.[13] During certain

---

[12] See Richard D. Cooper, "Monetary Unification in Europe: When and How?" *Morgan Guaranty Survey,* May 1972, pp. 4–11.

[13] For a more detailed discussion of short-term foreign money markets and the long-term Euro-bond Market, see Salera, *Multinational Business,* pp. 283–302.

periods in the past, the United Kingdom and the United States were free international capital markets. Foreign companies and foreign governments were able to sell securities and raise capital in these countries without any limits on where the capital was used. In recent years, the United States has discouraged foreign borrowing in the United States through the device of an interest equalization tax which raises significantly the cost of borrowing. And for some time, the United Kingdom has restricted foreign access to its capital market. The principal international capital market has become the Euro-currency market for short-term funds and the Euro-bond market for long-term borrowing which, so far, have managed to operate beyond national jurisdictions and escape national controls.

The World Bank Group, a United Nations agency, is the major international institutional source of financing. The World Bank proper, officially named the International Bank for Reconstruction and Development (IBRD), was spawned by the Bretton Woods agreement along with the International Monetary Fund. The Bank functions mainly in the field of long-term loans for specific reconstruction or development projects. It lends to member governments for private projects when the government endorses and guarantees the loan. After World War II, much of the lending was to European countries for reconstruction. More recently, virtually all of the lending is to the less developed countries, mainly for infrastructure projects such as electric power and transportation development. Loans are also made for agriculture, industry, and, lately, in the field of education. The World Bank is important to international business more as a general force for stimulating economic development than as a direct source for business financing. However, the Bank began to expand its industrial lending activities in the late 1960s.

A subsidiary of the World Bank, the International Finance Corporation (IFC), finances business projects of private enterprises either through loans or equity participation and without the requirement of official government endorsement or guarantee.[14] The IFC provides a multinational source for financing international enterprise but has not attempted to play a broad role in influencing the international business environment. Another subsidiary of the World Bank is the International Development Association (IDA), which makes soft loans, that is, loans with long maturity, relatively low rates of interest, and easy repayment terms. Such loans are available to member governments exclusively for development purposes.

A wide variety of both private and public financing agencies operate on a regional basis. The European Common Market (EEC) has its European Investment Bank, which can be a source of capital for projects

---

[14] James C. Baker, *The International Finance Corporation* (New York: Praeger Publishers, Inc., 1968).

within the Market and in the EEC-affiliated African countries. The Central American Common Market operates a development bank for financing projects within the CACM. Other official inter-governmental agencies are the Inter-American Development Bank, the Asian Development Bank, and the African Development Bank, all of which limit their financing to their respective regions. A relatively new innovation has been the creation of private regional-financing agencies, namely, the Atlantic Development Group for Latin America (ADELA) and the Private Investment Company for Asia (PICA), which provide loans and equity financing to both national and international business enterprises in their regions. The stockholders of ADELA and PICA are mainly large, private banks and industrial companies in Europe, the United States, Canada, and Japan.

The origin of the Euro-currency market was described briefly earlier. It is a truly international market, undisturbed by the rules and restrictions of any national authority. The market is used heavily for short-term credit, and through Euro-bond financing it has become a major source for long-term debt financing. To a minor extent, the Euro-currency market has been used for equity financing. In the beginning, the Euro-bond market was dominated by issues from public or quasi-public borrowers. But from the mid 1960s on, multinational business firms emerged as the most important class of borrowers. U.S. firms became particularly active because Euro-bond borrowing was permitted under the U.S. investment-controls program because it would not have a detrimental impact on the U.S. balance-of-payments situation.

Short- and medium-term Euro-currency financing is arranged through commercial banks and in the normal pattern for such loans. For long-term financing, a commercial bank, merchant bank, or investment bank may assume the underwriting function and form an international syndicate or consortium of banks and other financial institutions for the sale of Euro-bonds. It is normally the parent company rather than the subsidiary that finances in the Euro-currency market. A typical example of a Euro-bond transaction would be an issue of dollar-denominated debentures by a Dutch corporation managed by a consortium of British merchant bankers, a large Dutch bank, and the overseas affiliate of an American investment-banking house, whereby a portion of the issue would be sold to Italian investors who maintain investment accounts in Swiss banks. In the peak year of 1968, the equivalent of more than $3 billion dollars in Euro-bonds was floated for private corporations, about 70 percent of which was for U.S. companies.

The future of the Euro-currency market may be affected negatively by reforms in the international monetary system. It has been argued, however, that the Euro-bond market would survive such changes because of the great advantage it offers in the choice of currencies.

INTERNATIONAL BUSINESS AS A FORCE FOR CHANGE

From the standpoint of international business, the principal focus of the inter-governmental agreements has been on improving the environment for financial flows involved in current transactions. Reform proposals have had little to say about freeing the world of capital controls, creating world capital markets, or the need to reexamine the relevance of traditional balance-of-payments accounting systems. Some changes have been occurrring in the formal structures, but these have been less important than the growth of a patchwork of informal and complex agreements to run the system by closer national cooperation in policy making and in resolving crises.

A countervailing force that may prevail over nationalism in moving toward a truly international financial system is the growing internationalization of business. Already the size of the international business sector is sufficiently large that the actions of financial managers to protect assets against devaluation losses can create decisive pressures on weak currencies. The conservative treasures of international corporations might conceivably, though inaccurately, be labeled currency speculators. Their task, however, is to preserve the value of foreign assets rather than to profit by betting on anticipated currency changes. A wide variety of techniques, including hedging and leads and lags in financial movements into and out of the country, can be used for protection against devaluation risk. If a currency appears to be weak, well-managed international firms will take advantage of these techniques, thus putting even more pressure on a currency and making a prediction a self-fulfilling prophecy.

Whether wider bands and crawling pegs can provide enough new flexibility in the system to reduce the risk of large-scale pressures by international firms against weak currencies is uncertain. They may help. But the basic character of the international financial framework remains dominated by national interests and national criteria while business activities are becoming more and more international. The size of operations of international business may be the force which eventually molds a truly international monetary system to accommodate its needs.

EXERCISES AND DISCUSSION QUESTIONS

1. In economic terms, explain the effects of a devaluation on a country's economy and balance-of-payments situation.

2. Frazer Manufacturing Company established in 1960 a manufacturing and assembling subsidiary in France (as a joint venture with Hooker of the United Kingdom) to supply the European market and for exports to Africa

and the Middle East. It is anticipated that the French franc will shortly be revalued by 10 percent in relation to the U.S. dollar.

You are the manager of the French subsidiary. The home office in Columbus, Ohio, has asked you to prepare a report advising:

   a. How will the revaluation affect the operations of your subsidiary and its profitability to Frazer?

   b. How should the revaluation influence future expansion plans for serving the growing demand in Europe for flexible couplings?

3. Show in double-entry format the entries that would be made in the United States balance-of-payments accounts for the following transactions. Use this sort of format:

    Imports—debit $2 million

    Private short-term capital—credit $2 million

  1. A Japanese company sells electronic equipment to RCA in the United States for $2 million. Freight ($3,000) and insurance ($2,000) are arranged in the United States and paid for by RCA. Payment to the Japanese company is made by a check drawn on the Bank of America in New York.

  2. A U.S. company decides to establish a new plant in Hong Kong to take advantage of cheap labor. The cost of setting up a plant during the year totaled $8.6 million. Half of this was paid out of an account held in Hong Kong. The rest from a U.S. account.

  3. A U.S. company exports $400,000 worth of agricultural equipment to New Zealand and accepts $200,000 worth of shares in the local distributor as part payment. The rest is paid in New Zealand dollars.

  4. Charles L. Hangover went on a trip to the Pacific Islands. He paid for his airfare of $2,000 in the United States but half the travel was done on Quantas (Australian)—the rest on Pan American. The fare was divided between the airlines accordingly. He spent a further $1,500 in the islands.

  5. The U.S. government extends a loan to Israel to purchase military equipment. The loan is for $500 million. It is all spent on fighter aircraft bought from U.S. firms.

  6. An investment trust in the United States buys 200,000 £1 shares in Unilever for $9 each and pays for them from its U.S. account.

  7. Unilever directors declare a dividend of 6 percent and this is paid into the trust's U.S. account.

  8. The United States spends $1.5 million on military exercises in the Pacific. Of this, $.9 million is paid to foreign countries for the use of docking and airport facilities.

  9. The United States extends a $10 million loan to Italy to assist the development of its manufacturing industries. However, Italy spends it on equipment purchased from British companies.

  10. The United States temporarily draws on the IMF for $12 million (which is within its Gold Tranche Position). This money is used to finance imports from Brazil.

4. Explain how a move to floating exchange rates might change the way a government manages a country's economy.

5. How would the formation of a European Monetary Union affect the interests of (a) an American multinational enterprise; (b) a European multinational enterprise?

6. Would you be in favor of an international currency? Give your reasons for and against.

7. What kind of reform plan for the international monetary system would be most beneficial to multinational business?

5

THE TRADITIONAL
TRADE FRAMEWORK

INTERNATIONAL TRADE THEORY continues to shape much business and government thinking, as was pointed out in Chapter 2, even though it has limited value in explaining the changing pattern of international transactions in today's world. The international manager, therefore, should be reasonably conversant with trade theory. Such knowledge will give him a better basis for understanding, analyzing, and predicting government policies with respect to international transactions. It will also help him in preparing his own submissions to government. When a belief in trade theory underlies a government's actions, arguments couched in terms of the theory are more likely to be effective than those that would appear to be irrelevant to decisions based on the theory.

This chapter goes beyond an introduction to the theory of international trade to examine the traditional ways in which governments have acted to influence trade. The patterns and institutions of cooperation between nations as they have attempted to regulate trade are also introduced. Knowledge of these facts is still very important to the manager in today's international economy.

THE BASIS FOR TRADE

Businessmen do not usually go to the expense of transferring goods from one country to another if they can obtain the goods as cheaply without doing so. Thus trade takes place where the prices of goods, or what would be their prices without trade, normally reflect differences in the costs of the inputs that go to make the product. However, the fact that at current exchange rates many things may cost less in one country than in another does not provide an adequate long-term explanation of why trade continues to take place. If one country's costs are lower than the costs ruling in the others then demand for its cheaper goods would force up the exchange rate. There would be a greater demand for its currency as outsiders sought to buy more of its goods than its own citizens sought to buy overseas. High continued demand for the cheaper products might also lead to an increase in the prices of the resources needed to produce the goods. When the price level and the exchange rate finally settled down, there might still be some trade, but it could no longer be said that at the ruling exchange rates cost levels were lower and hence the cause of the trade. On the other hand, when exchange rates are fixed it may be valid to argue that a country is involved in a lot of trade because at that exchange rate its costs are lower. Such an exchange rate undervalues the country's currency and would probably lead to a surplus in the balance of payments.

Instead of absolute cost differences between countries, economists have long placed emphasis on the differences in the relative costs of resources from country to country as the basis for sustained trade. The idea was first introduced by David Ricardo early in the nineteenth century and is known as the *doctrine of comparative advantage.* It starts from the observation that there are differences in the relative abundance of different resources as between countries and that without trade the costs of the specific resources will differ from country to country. The doctrine then goes on to assert that countries will export those products which they make at lowest relative cost and import those for which their costs are relatively high. *Country A* with large and fertile land resources and few people may produce wheat relatively cheaply as against *Country B* with little land and an educated urban population. *Country B* in turn may produce advanced technological goods relatively cheaply. *Country A* would then export wheat and import technological manufactures while *Country B* would export technological goods and import foods.

The traditional economist would begin to explain the pattern of a country's trade by identifying the resources within the country which were in greatest abundance relative to other countries.[1] In the simplest application of the doctrine of comparative advantage resources would be classified as land, labor, or capital. For a more advanced analysis, distinctions should be drawn among different types of labor or management skills, the specific production and distribution facilities that have been built up in the past, and the abundance of particular types of natural resources—minerals, rainfall, or agricultural land.

---

[1] A classic work in Bertil Ohlin, *Interregional and International Trade* (Cambridge, Mass.: Harvard University Press, 1933). For an overall view of trade theory, see Gottfried Haberler, *A Survey of International Trade Theory* (Princeton, N.J.: International Finance Section, Department of Economics, Princeton University, 1961).

A simple arithmetic example of the production and trade between two countries each making two products illustrates how differences in the relative abundance of resources can lead to trade. Imagine the two countries as Australia and Belgium each able to produce only wheat and cloth. The output of each product will differ according to the proportion of a country's resources devoted to it and for a range of production alternatives. These outputs are shown in Table 5.1. If the entire resources

TABLE 5.1
Production Alternatives for Australia and Belgium

		Production			
Percentage of Resources Devoted to:		*Australia*		*Belgium*	
Wheat (%)	*Cloth (%)*	*Wheat (million bushels)*	*Cloth (million yards)*	*Wheat (million bushels)*	*Cloth (million yards)*
100	—	100	0	40	—
75	25	75	20	30	15
50	50	50	40	20	30
25	75	25	60	10	45
0	100	0	80	0	60

of Australia were devoted to the production of wheat, the output would be 100 million bushels. If, instead, these resources were directed to cloth production, the output would be 80 million yards. For combinations of the two products, Australia would have to forgo 1.25 bushels of wheat for every yard of cloth produced.

Thus, if the Australian population could not trade with the rest of the world and were to want 20 million yards of cloth, it would cost the Australians the alternative of 25 million bushels of wheat. This would be the opportunity cost, or price, for obtaining the cloth.

For Belgium, the extreme production alternatives are 40 million bushels of wheat or 60 million yards of cloth. In this case, only .67 bushels of wheat would be given up for each 10 yards of cloth, and if the population wished to have 30 million yards of cloth it would cost them the alternative of 20 million bushels of wheat.

So long as the two countries remain isolated and without trade, cloth will be exchanged for wheat at the rate of one yard for 1.25 bushels in Australia and one yard for .67 bushels in Belgium. These ratios are easily derived from Table 5.1 which is so constructed that the ratios remain constant for all production combinations of wheat and cloth. If we assume that there is perfect competition in the two countries, then we can argue that the prices of wheat and cloth in each must settle at these rates. If the prices were in any different ratio, businessmen would switch resources so as to get greater revenue from the added output than from the output forgone, and they would keep on doing this until prices changed to bring production back in line with demand. We can also argue that the perfect competition will reduce prices to their incremental costs of production. Thus for each country:

$$\frac{\text{Price of 1 yard of cloth}}{\text{Price of 1 bushel of wheat}} = \frac{\text{Resources cost of 1 yard of cloth}}{\text{Resources cost of 1 bushel of wheat}}$$

So prices in Australia and Belgium will differ, given our simplifying assumptions, and there will be opportunity and incentive for trade.

Trade under Constant Opportunity Costs

Continuing our example, what happens when trade takes place? The opportunity for trade creates a single market for the two countries, and if we overlook transport costs, a single price for cloth and for wheat will emerge. This new price will probably lie somewhere between the national prices under isolated conditions. It will be less than the Australian price of 1.25 bushels of wheat for a yard of cloth and higher than the Belgian price of .67 bushels of wheat for a yard. By producing more wheat which it then trades for cloth, Australia would receive more cloth than Belgium by using the same resources directly for its own cloth production. Conversely, Belgium could obtain more wheat for every further yard of cloth it produced than the .67 bushels of wheat it could have produced itself.

Australia will thus tend to specialize in wheat and Belgium in cloth. Together the countries end up with greater production than if they tried to satisfy their individual needs. With trade, they no longer lose output through having to allocate resources to a product which another country could produce comparatively more cheaply.

Note that the emphasis is on the comparative strength of the country in producing an item—not on its absolute strength. In our example, assuming Australia and Belgium have a similar quantity of resources, Australia has an absolute advantage in producing both wheat and cloth. It could produce more of either with a given quantity of resources than could Belgium. Australia's comparative advantage, however, is in wheat and Belgium's in cloth.

The gains that result from trade show clearly from a continuation of the example. Let us suppose that Australians and Belgians each demand 30 million yards of cloth for consumption and that the trade price between Australia and Belgium is set at one bushel of wheat for one yard of cloth. This exchange rate lies between the rates at which wheat can be transformed into cloth. Through reallocating resources in either country, the introduction of trade enables wheat production to increase from 82 to 100 while still maintaining the cloth requirements as shown in Table 5.2. Without trade, each country would produce its

TABLE 5.2
Gains from Trade

	Australia		Belgium		Total	
	Wheat (million bushels)	Cloth (million yards)	Wheat (million bushels)	Cloth (million yards)	Wheat (million bushels)	Cloth (million yards)
Without Trade						
Production and consumption	62	30	20	30	82	60
With Trade						
Production	100	–	–	60	100	60
Exports (–)	–30			–30	–30	–30
Imports (+)		+30	+30		+30	+30
Consumption	70	30	30	30	100	60

own requirements of cloth. With trade, Belgium would concentrate on cloth and Australia on wheat, and they would exchange 30 wheat for 30 cloth. Both end up with a larger supply of wheat than before.

Each country does not have to limit itself to only one product. Had the total demand for cloth been 50 million yards and not 60 million, then Belgium would have produced some wheat as well. Nor does it necessarily follow that both countries benefit from trade. If the exchange price for trade settled at one of the prices existing before trade in either country, the other country would gain all the benefits from the trade. The country whose prices were retained would have to produce as much of one product to obtain the other as it had to produce without trade.

The concept of gains from trade can also be illustrated graphically. Figure 5.1 graphs the production possibilities for Australia and Belgium, with the slope of the curves representing the relative prices of the products in each country and the position of the curves representing the absolute levels of production in the country. When the slopes differ, as they do in this case, there is an opportunity to gain from trade.

In Figure 5.2 the possibility of gains from trade for Belgium is graphed. Alongside the production possibility curve, the rate of product transformation existing in Australia is plotted. This can be obtained very simply by moving the Australian production possibility curve in Figure 5.1 to the left until it coincides with the Belgium curve on the cloth axis, or the slope can be calculated arithmetically and plotted. Point *A* indicates Belgium production without trade. Point *B* represents

FIGURE 5.1
Production Possibilities with Constant Costs

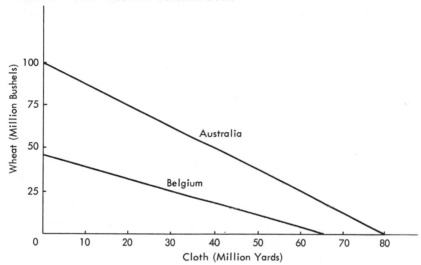

FIGURE 5.2
Gains from Trade under Constant Costs

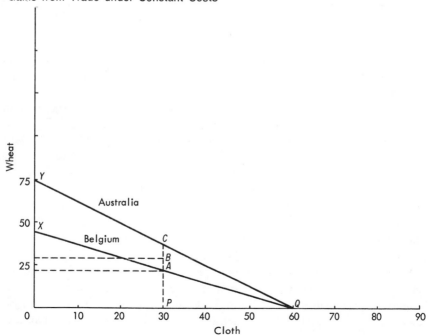

any point lying between the two transformation rates and can always be reached by specializing production and trading with Australia at a rate that would be advantageous to that country. By producing OQ cloth Belgium can export PQ in exchange for PB wheat. Australia would have had to give up PC wheat in order to produce P cloth itself so it gains BC in wheat.

Trade with Monetary Costs and Exchange Rates

Up to this point the discussion has been presented with barter prices measured by the opportunity cost of the alternative output possible. The example becomes more realistic if production is measured in terms of monetary cost, and exchange rates are introduced. Let us suppose that each 1 percent of a country's resources equals a million labor hours, that the wage rates are $2 per hour in Australia and 100 francs per hour in Belgium, and that the rate of exchange has been fixed at 50 Belgian francs for 1 Australian dollar.

Before trade, the costs and prices both locally and in their foreign exchange equivalent are as follows:

	Australian Prices		Belgium Prices	
	$	(Fr.)	Fr.	($)
Wheat (cost per bushel)	2.00	(100)	250	(5.00)
Cloth (cost per yard)	2.50	(125)	167	(3.33)

Australia's absolute advantage shows clearly in that its costs, and therefore its prices, in dollars or francs are below the Belgium prices for both wheat and cloth.

Earlier, we suggested that with trade the international prices might settle so that a bushel of wheat sold for the same price as a yard of cloth, say, a price of 200 francs. A Belgium importer could buy a bushel of Australian wheat for 200 francs and an Australian importer spending 200 francs could buy a yard of cloth. It would then pay Australian firms to switch resources from cloth to wheat. For every yard of cloth, they would give up 200 francs revenue to get 250 francs revenue from 1.25 bushels of wheat. It would also pay Belgium firms to switch to cloth because for every bushel of wheat given up, they could get 1.5 yards of cloth, or an additional 100 francs.

In the real world, however, the process by which the international price level is reached will be much more complicated. For instance the Belgium prices before trade in our example are both higher than the Australian prices at the fixed exchange rate. This may mean that once trade is possible, Belgians endeavor to buy only imported goods with consequent unemployment in Belgium. The strain on the Belgian balance of payments and the need to create work might then lead to a devaluation to, say, 75 francs = $1, so that Belgian cloth became cheaper than Australian cloth, that is, $2.22. Alternatively, it could be that Australian labor pressured for higher wage rates. Australia's output is certainly higher than Belgium's. If the Australian wage rate rose to $3.50 per hour then international prices of 200 francs would look quite realistic. The cost of Australian wheat would be 175 francs and of Belgian cloth 167 francs.

Whether international prices are reached via changes in wage rates or exchange rates, the effect is to change the relative rewards to Belgian and Australian labor. This illustrates a general theme in international economics that over time and on a global front factor inputs into production that face international competition tend to be rewarded in proportion to their actual output. If rewards are too high in one country, prices are likely to rise, exports fall, and imports increase. Pressure on the exchange rate might then lead to devaluation and bring the rewards back into line with the real output.

Trade under Increasing Costs

The example used up to this point has assumed constant opportunity costs. For a country as a whole, however, it is more likely that there will be increasing costs. The more that is produced of one product the greater the decrease needed in the other in order to obtain a further increment. As land and labor are shifted from wheat to cloth production, for example, it seems reasonable that increasingly those resources better suited for wheat will be used up. Naturally, the initial transfers would be arranged to decrease wheat production as little as possible for any given increment in cloth production. But eventually, increasing quantities of wheat would have to be given up.

The gains from trade with increasing costs are illustrated graphically in Figure 5.3. The production possibilities under increasing costs are now represented by curves XX' for Belgium and YY' for Australia instead of the straight lines that appeared in Figure 5.2. Point A again indicates Belgian production before trade, with a resulting output of PA wheat and OP cloth. The internal Belgian price is indicated by the slope of the tangent, which touches the XX' curve at A. The slope of the curve at that point indicates the amount of wheat that would be given up for a given increase in cloth output.

When trade is introduced, the two countries will begin to shift resources towards the product in which they have a comparative advantage in response to traders seeking out the cheaper source. This process will

FIGURE 5.3
Gains from Trade under Increasing Costs

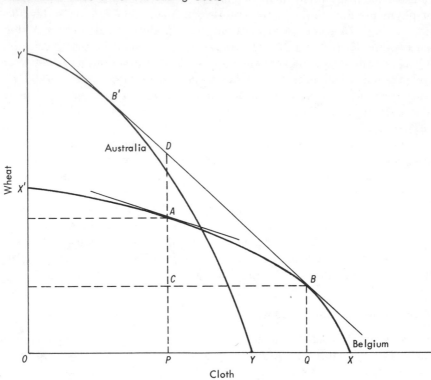

continue until prices in the two countries are equal. In the terms of this increasing cost model, this will occur for Belgium at Point B where the BB' price line is tangent also to the Australian YY' production possibility curve. Belgian production would then move to point B with a production of PC wheat and OQ cloth. If Belgians then want no more cloth than before trade opened up they could trade PQ cloth (the same as CB) for CD wheat, given the international BB' exchange rate. This would place them at a higher consumption level (Point D) than the Belgian production possibility curve would enable them to achieve on their own.

Trade under Decreasing Costs

Even though there are likely to be increasing costs ultimately for a country as a whole, there may well be decreasing costs for individual products or industries. The traditional analysis of cost-volume-profit relationships for an operating firm is usually presented to show economies of scale and hence decreasing unit costs as volume increases. There are also external economies as the size of an industry grows. Specialization may be increased, service facilities sharpened, and risks spread more widely. In industries such as chemicals and electronics, the economies of scale continue up to the largest outputs. Furthermore, for countries in which resources are not fully utilized, the opportunity cost of the other output forgone in order to expand production may be very low and may increase very little, even for considerable expansion of one industry.

When a situation in which a country that is producing under decreasing costs is opened to international trade, it pays the country to move out of the range of production possibilities over which decreasing costs occur. Suppose the XX' curve in Figure 5.4 represented Belgium's produc-

FIGURE 5.4
Gains from Trade under Decreasing Costs

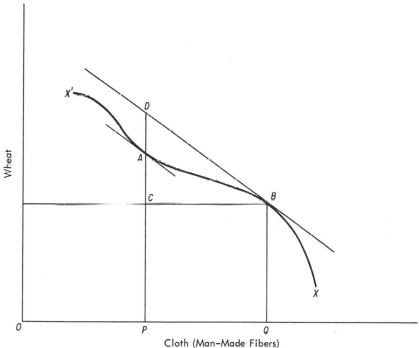

tion possibilities for wheat and man-made fibers for which there are likely to be decreasing costs. Before trade, suppose also that production settles at Point A and that when trade is opened there is no change in the relative prices of wheat and cloth. It will immediately pay the country to move to Point B where it could trade PQ cloth for CD wheat to reach the higher consumption at Point D.

Free Trade versus Trade Restrictions

It should now be clear to the reader that gains can result from trade under conditions of constant, increasing, or decreasing costs—at least in terms of the simple two-product, two-country model. These gains come about because countries specialize in the products that they can produce to comparative advantage. With trade, every country can go beyond the limits of its resource endowment to consume a collection of commodities that exceed any output combination it could produce on its own. With more complicated models involving several countries and several products this general principle still holds.

It is a simple step in any trade model to show that any barrier hampering trade so that an optimum combination of products cannot be reached causes a decrease in the total output and consumption. In other words, free trade maximizes world output.

It may be, however, that an individual country could benefit from restricting trade even though the total output is reduced. By so doing, it might be able to raise employment, bring the country a higher proportion of the gains from trade, or build new industries to a point where they might exist without such protection. In industries where there are decreasing costs, for example, it may be that individual firms do not see the advantages of moving to the higher production levels or are not prepared to bear the risk involved. In order to start the industry moving along the decreasing cost curve, some protection against competition or some form of direct incentive might be considered desirable.[2]

A more detailed analysis of the advantages and disadvantages of trade restriction from the viewpoint of an individual country is left to Chapter 8. When each country independently introduces barriers without anticipating the reactions of others, however, the reduction in trade can be costly to all countries. Thus it is not surprising that on an international level governments are continually pressing for reductions in trade barriers. First, let us examine the nature of these barriers.

Tariff Barriers.   The most common method of restricting trade is the tariff. A tariff is a tax, or duty, levied on a commodity when it crosses the boundary of a customs area. Usually a customs area coincides with national political boundaries. Sometimes it includes colonies or territories of the country. A customs area may also include several independent nation-states, as in the case of the European Common Market.

---

[2] For a fuller treatment of trade theory under constant, increasing, and decreasing costs, and the case for free trade, see Charles P. Kindleberger, *International Economics,* 4th ed. (Homewood, Ill.: Richard D. Irwin, Inc., 1968).

Tariffs may be levied on commodities leaving an area (export duties), or on merchandise entering an area (import duties). As most nations are anxious to increase their foreign exchange earnings through exports, export duties are much less common than import duties.

Nations differ greatly in their tariff systems. When a country offers equal treatment to all commodities of one class, regardless of the country of origin, it is said to have a *unilinear* or *single column* tariff. Another type of tariff system is the *general-conventional* tariff, in which the general column applies to all countries except those with which tariff treaties or conventions have been made. The lower rates granted by these conventions constitute the conventional column. The principal advantages of the general-conventional system is its flexibility for tariff bargaining. A number of countries have tariff systems which provide maximum and minimum rates for like commodities. The maximum rates apply to all countries except those with which reductions have been negotiated.

An important feature of tariff treaties or agreements is what is known as most-favored-nation (MFN) treatment. This provides that the products of a country assured MFN treatment will in each case enter at rates of duty no less favorable than those applied to like products of any third country. A nation which enters into unconditional most-favored-nation tariff treaties is compelled to grant equal treatment to all signatories when it grants tariff concessions to any country. The purpose of such provisions is to simplify tariff bargaining, increasing the likelihood of tariff reductions.

Import duties may be either *specific* or *ad valorem*, or a combination of the two—*compound* duties. Specific duties are levied on the basis of some physical unit such as dollars per bushel, ton, or yard. Ad valorem duties are calculated on the basis of the value of the goods. The term *drawback* refers to a duty which has been paid on imported goods and which is refunded by the government if the goods are reexported.

In the case of ad valorem duties, special problems may arise in selecting the basis for determining the value of the goods. Normally the value is determined by the invoice of sale or by a customs appraiser on the basis of the landed cost in the country—cost plus insurance and freight (CIF). Special provisions may be adopted, however, such as the American Selling Price (ASP) basis of valuation adopted for certain chemical imports into the United States. The ASP law provides that prices prevailing in the U.S. market should be the base for calculating duty rather than the normally lower cost at which foreigners are selling in order to compete in the U.S. market. A number of countries specify the basis of valuation for duty calculation in terms of the wholesale price level in the importing country. This has the effect of raising the height of the tariff and avoiding a duty reduction to the cut price supplier.

Tariffs have the advantage that there is a minimum of administrative discretion in their application and they can be selectively levied in terms of products and with differential rates. Thus it is possible to achieve rather precise objectives with tariffs while at the same time increasing government revenues. On the other hand, tariffs usually increase the cost to the consumer and are generally difficult to change because of the political pressures of groups benefited by the tariff. This may limit a nation's flexibility in bargaining with other nations, particularly where the tariffs are established by statute and a change of law would be necessary to implement any change.

Nontariff Barriers. Among the nontariff barriers to trade, quantitative restrictions or quotas are the most widespread form. A quota establishes the maximum quantity of a commodity that might be imported (or exported) during a given period of time. The limits may be set in physical or in value terms. Quotas may be on a country basis or global quotas with the total limit specified without reference to countries of origin. They may be imposed unilaterally, as in the case of sugar imports into the United States, or they can be negotiated on a so-called voluntary basis as has occurred in the case of textile imports into the United States. Obviously, exporting countries do not readily agree to limit their sales, so the voluntary label generally means that the quotas have been negotiated with threats that even worse restrictions may be imposed by the importing country if voluntary cooperation is not forthcoming.

To the country desiring to restrict imports, quotas have the advantage of being more certain and precise instruments than tariffs, providing greater flexibility in bargaining, and permitting more flexibility in administration. An import duty that is not so high as to prohibit imports does not set a specific limit on the volume of goods imported. A quota system limits with certainty the extent to which foreign producers can compete on the domestic market.

The administration of quotas usually requires a licensing system and raises the problem of deciding which domestic parties shall receive what share of the quota. If the quotas are relatively small in relation to the domestic market, domestic market prices are likely to be higher than imported prices and the recipients of quotas will receive windfall profits. The government could capture these windfall profits by auctioning off the import licenses to the highest bidders, but the more general case is that the profits go to private parties. Inequities and corruption can occur in the allocation of quotas, and with the greater degree of administrative discretion implicit in the system, business firms may find quotas arbitrary and uncertain. Quotas also encourage firms to manipulate the system. Firms may use all of an allocated quota, for example, to import only one section of the class of commodities included under the quota, hoping to force the issue of a further quota to overcome the scarcity of the remaining items. Perhaps the greatest disadvantage of quotas, however, is that unlike tariffs they exert no pressure to keep the level of domestic prices down.

There is a long list of other restrictions that governments can place on trade. It is quite common for regulations ostensibly introduced for other purposes to be applied so as to restrict trade. Thus there may be a restricting application of rules as to required product standards, imposed for safety or standardization reasons; rules as to purity or processing of food products, imposed for health purposes; or rules as to labeling, applied for consumer protection. Government policies of preferring local suppliers for their purchases and of limiting the export of goods for security reasons, also restrict trade.

MULTINATIONAL TRADE COOPERATION

The post–World War II movement toward a new era of international cooperation included plans to create an International Trade Organization (ITO). The ITO was expected to provide an organizational mechanism for negotiating reductions in the levels of tariffs and to work toward the freeing of international trade from quantitative controls and discriminatory practices.

An International Conference on Trade and Employment under the sponsorship of the United Nations was held in Havana, Cuba, late in 1947 to draft a charter for the new organization. In early 1948, the conference completed what became known as the Havana Charter. When ratified, the charter would create the proposed International Trade Or ganization (ITO). It contained a code, or set of rules of conduct, and policies concerning international trade which were to be observed by members of the organization.

The ITO never came into being. Although the United States had taken the lead in proposing the organization, the U.S. Congress never ratified the charter. The scope of the charter was considered by many to be too broad and an interference with national sovereignty. The important commercial policy provisions of the charter, however, are embodied in the General Agreement on Tariffs and Trade, commonly known as GATT, in substantially identical language.

While the meetings for drafting the charter were underway, tariff negotiation sessions were started under the temporary GATT agreement. The temporary arrangement was to be replaced by the ITO when the ITO became operational. U.S. participation in GATT did not require approval of the Congress because GATT was a trade agreement rather than a treaty. Designed as a temporary agreement, Gatt developed into an important institution in place of the aborted ITO.[4]

---

[4] See Raymond Vernon, *American Foreign Trade Policy and the GATT* (Princeton, N.J.: Princeton University Press, 1954).

GATT included only 19 member countries when it began operations 1948. Its membership expanded to 80 nations by 1971, including all the important trading nations outside of the noncommunist world, as well as Cuba, Czechoslovakia, Rumania, and Yugoslavia. The goal of GATT is to achieve a broad, multilateral, and relatively free system of trading, and it sets down principles and rules of conduct directed to this end. The goal is to be achieved through gradual reduction in tariffs and import licensing restraints, adoption of the principle of nondiscrimination—equal treatment with respect to customs duties and procedures—and the provision of an organization for settlement of trade disputes. The agreement endeavors also to abolish the use of quantitative restrictions of trade. Preferential tariff systems existing at the time, such as Commonwealth preferences or the Benelux arrangement, are allowed as exceptions. In spite of provisions regarding nondiscrimination, members may form customs unions or free trade areas, provided there is no net overall increase in barriers to outsiders. A wide range of other exceptions are also allowed under which restrictive policies could continue or be adopted temporarily by a country with aggravated trade or financial problems.

The principal accomplishment of GATT has been sponsoring six major bargaining sessions from 1947 through 1967 which resulted in substantial tariff reductions. The record on trade liberalization resulting from the six GATT rounds of negotiations among the member countries is shown in Table 5.3 as they affected U.S. tariffs.[5] The result is that world tariffs were reduced to the point that they are no longer a major barrier in most cases to world trade.

The advanced countries have gone a long way toward dismantling their extensive systems of import-licensing restrictions on nonagricultural products. But GATT's endeavors to reduce import licensing have been weakened by the exceptions permitted countries (a) in balance-of-payments difficulties, (b) with special domestic agricultural programs, or (c) attempting to industrialize through providing protection to infant industries.

Thus, the vision of a postwar trading system free of the hampering and distorting effects of tariffs, quotas, and discriminatory practices has been only partially achieved. Protectionist sentiment still remains strong when domestic vested interests are threatened. The waivers granted in the field of agriculture leave this area fully planted with restrictions. The exception for countries forming a customs union has encouraged the formation of economic (and political) blocs instead of an integrated world economy. Increased difficulties in the functioning of the interna-

---

[5] For a fuller picture, see Thomas B. Curtis and John Robert Vastine, *The Kennedy Round and the Future of American Trade* (New York: Praeger Publishers, 1971).

TABLE 5.3

Six GATT Rounds Compared

GATT Round	Scope of U.S. Tariff Cutting*	Depth of U.S. Tariff Cuts†
1947	44%	35%
1949	3	35
1951	9	27
1956	11	15
1962	14	20
1967	64	35

*Value of U.S. dutiable imports on which tariff reductions were made or agreed in the year shown, expressed as a percentage of the value of total U.S. dutiable imports in the same year.

†Average percentage reduction in U.S. duties (considering only items whose duties were reduced), weighted by the value of U.S. imports of those items in the year shown.

Sources: U.S. Tariff Commission; U.S. Department of Commerce; Office of the Special Representative for Trade Negotiations; *First National City Bank Monthly Letter*, September 1967.

tional financial system have become an important constraint on trade liberalization. The less developed countries, which now constitute a majority of the membership of GATT, have questioned the value of GATT objectives as related to their development aspirations. Other new problems have arisen with the increased participation of the communist-bloc countries, which by and large have internal state-controlled systems for international trade.

A dramatic feature of the post–World War II world was the awakened desire of the less developed countries for accelerated growth and economic modernization. The free trade ideology, which assumed a static economic structure of nations, did not fit the needs and aspirations of the less developed countries. They adopted protectionist policies to encourage infant industries. They became convinced that they should not continue to rely so heavily on specialization in traditional agricultural and raw material exports but should diversify into product fields such as manufactures, where world demand was expanding more rapidly. In fact, the development philosophy that emerged, heavily influenced by the Economic Commission of Latin America, had little in common with the trade liberalization goals of GATT. And the less developed countries, most of whom were not members of GATT, became gradually convinced that GATT did not and could not represent their trade interests.

In response to this sentiment, a United Nations Conference on Trade and Development (UNCTAD) was convened in 1964 and attended by representatives of 119 nations.[6] The result of the conference was to establish UNCTAD as a permanent United Nations agency which, given its origins and structure, has come to represent the interests of the less developed countries. In the trade field, UNCTAD has been promoting additional international commodity agreements. But the major push has been to persuade the advanced countries to grant tariff concessions to the LDCs, on a nonreciprocal basis, that will permit the LDCs to expand their exports of manufactured goods to the developed countries. As less developed countries had few substantial industries that could survive with less protection they were not in a position to seek such tariff reductions through reciprocal bargaining with the more developed areas. While UNCTAD has wrung some unilateral concessions from the developed countries, they are not major.

Regional Economic Integration Movements

Regional groupings for the purpose of freeing trade between two or more countries have a considerable historical background. The German Zollverein, formed in 1834, was the most important regional grouping of the pre–World War I period and a forerunner of modern Germany.

When GATT was created in 1948, it appeared that nations were prepared to move toward global organizations rather than regional trading groups. However, the general agreement allowed for regional groupings as an exception, with the proviso that such groups should not result in increased discrimination against nonmembers. The desire by neighboring countries to pool political and economic strength against outsiders was a powerful force despite the existence of global trade agreements. And the establishment of regional common markets and free trade areas, referred to under the general label of regional economic integration, began to occur.[7]

The most ambitious of the regional integration movements has been the European Common Market, officially called the European Economic Community (EEC). Other important regional integration projects have been the European Free Trade Area (EFTA), Latin American Free Trade Area (LAFTA), the Central American Common Market (CACM),

---

[6] The report by Raul Prebisch, Secretary General of UNCTAD, *Towards a New Trade Policy For Development* (United Nations, 1964) presented a set of recommendations for promoting the development of the less developed countries through changes in the trade policies of the developed countries which largely shaped the work of the first conference and subsequent UNCTAD activities. See also Harry G. Johnson, *Economic Policies Toward Less Developed Countries* (Washington, D.C.: The Brookings Institution, 1967).

[7] A clear introduction to the theory of economic integration is contained in Tibor Scitovsky, *Economic Theory and Western European Integration* (London: Allen & Unwin, 1958); and in Bela Balassa, *The Theory of Economic Integration* (Homewood, Ill.: Richard D. Irwin, Inc., 1961).

the East African Common Market (which included Kenya, Uganda, and Tanzania), and the Central African Economic Union (which included Cameroon, Congo (Brassaville), Gabon, Chad, and the Central African Republic). Even the Soviet-bloc countries have followed the regional economic integration path through the formation of the Council for Mutual Economic Assistance (COMECON) for coordinating planning, trade, and economic development among the East European nations. Some of the features of the principal regional integration projects are shown in Table 5.4.

TABLE 5.4
Comparative Analysis of Common Markets and Free Trade Areas

	EEC	EFTA	LAFTA	CACM
Date initiated:	March 25, 1957 Rome Treaty	May, 1960 Stockholm Convention	Eff. June 1, 1961 Montevideo	June 3, 1961– July 3, 1962 Costa Rica
Participants:	1. Belgium 2. Denmark 3. France 4. Germany 5. Ireland 6. Italy 7. Luxembourg 8. Netherlands 9. United Kingdom	1. Austria 2. Finland 3. Iceland 4. Norway 5. Portugal 6. Sweden 7. Switzerland	1. Argentina 2. Bolivia 3. Brazil 4. Chile 5. Colombia 6. Ecuador 7. Mexico 8. Paraguay 9. Peru 10. Uruguay 11. Venezuela	1. Costa Rica 2. El Salvador 3. Guatemala 4. Honduras 5. Nicaragua
Associates:	35 countries*	–	–	–
Economic features:†				
Population (millions):	253.4	17.2	243.5	15.2
Total GNP (billions):	$626.5	$94.2	$129.0	$5.0
Income per capita:	$2,475	$1,996	$530	$330
Total exports (billions):	$112.4	$20.6	$12.8	$1.1
Intrazonal	54.2	2.2	1.2	0.3
External	58.2	18.4	11.6	0.8

*See Figure 5.5.
†1970 data.
Sources: 1. *EFTA Reporter* (Washington D.C.: EFTA Information Office, 10 March 1972).
2. Bank mees and N. V. Hope, *The Common Market in Figures.*
3. *Socio Economic Progress in Latin America* (Washington, D.C.: Inter-American Development Bank, 1971).

There are various forms and degrees of economic integration. The loosest and least intensive form is the free trade area. In a free trade area all artificial restrictions on the movement of goods and services among the participating countries are removed, but each country may retain its own tariffs, quotas, or other restrictive devices on trade with nonparticipating countries. The customs union is one degree further along the scale. In addition to the complete elimination of tariffs and quotas on internal trade, a common external tariff is established on goods entering the union from outside. A common market represents the next higher degree of economic integration. Besides (a) eliminating internal trade barriers and (b) establishing a common external tariff, a common market also (c) removes national restrictions on the movement of labor and capital among participating countries, and on the right of establishment for business firms.

From an economic standpoint the chief benefit of economic integration is the trade creation effect. With the removal of protective tariffs, lower cost foreign supplies are likely to substitute for higher cost domestic production. The consumer benefits from the lower prices and domestic resources previously used to produce the newly imported goods can be shifted to more efficient uses.

However, the removal of tariffs on a regional basis, accompanied by the erection of a common external tariff, may lead to trade diversion instead of trade creation.[8] Prior to the formation of the European Common Market, for example, the lowest cost source of supply of a specific product consumer in France may have been the United States. But after the common market was formed, a higher cost producer in Germany may have substituted for the U.S. source of supply because the tariffs facing the German producer were abolished while external tariffs still faced the U.S. producer.

Judgments on the relative magnitudes of trade creation and trade diversion in the case of the European Common Market vary between a negligible difference to a significant net balance in favor of trade creation, but the effects of regional integration movements extend far beyond trade creation or trade diversion possibilities. One of the less tangible but most pervasive benefits of economic integration is the more efficient market structure that results from the encouragement of increased competition.[9]

Of prime significance to international business is the enlargement of the market area that can be supplied by a producing unit without encountering trade restrictions. This permits the enterprise to take advantage of internal economies of scale and thereby reduce the costs of producing in the market area. An expansion in the size of markets can also provide gains to business firms and the economy by creating new opportunities for external economies of scale. The expansion of one industry may lead to the creation of service industries, manpower training

---

[8] See M. E. Kreinin, "On the Dynamic Effects of a Customs Union," *The Journal of Political Economy,* April 1964, pp. 193–95.

[9] See Kindleberger, *International Economics,* 4th ed., pp. 183–201.

facilities, research institutions, and so forth, which become part of the economy's pool of resources available to be drawn upon by other industries. Also, the freeing of the movement of labor and capital within a common market area can contribute greatly to more efficient business operations.[10]

The European Community. The most advanced regional integration movement, the European Community, joined together the countries of Belgium, France, Germany, Italy, Luxembourg, and the Netherlands. The European Community has three parts. It now includes the European Coal and Steel Community (ECSC) set up under the Paris Treaty in 1952 to create a common market in coal, steel, iron ore, and scrap resources. The European Economic Community (EEC), whose institutions were established under the Rome Treaty at the beginning of 1958, goes beyond the Coal and Steel Community and is gradually integrating the six nations' other economic resources. The European Atomic Energy Community (Euratom), also set up at the beginning of 1958 under a second Rome Treaty, is the overseeing authority for nuclear energy developments in the six nations.

The European Community evolved out of a series of post–World War II moves toward economic and political union in Western Europe. Countries other than the six were initially invited to join but did not choose to do so. A strong motivation in the beginning was to form the basis for a United States of Europe, but the commitment toward political union within the new organization was more in spirit than in fact.

The ECSC, EEC, and Euratom share the same institutional framework which consists of a full range of executive, quasi-legislative, and judicial agencies. In addition to the major Community institutions, a number of consultative bodies such as the Economic and Social Committee participate in the Community's work.

Under the customs union agreed to in the Rome Treaty, all customs duties and restrictions on trade in industrial goods within the Community were to be abolished in three stages of four years each. By July 1, 1968, in 10½ years instead of 12, the complete removal of internal trade barriers was accomplished. By the same date, the Community also achieved a common external tariff, generally by averaging the tariffs applied by the individual countries. The free movement of workers anywhere in the Community has been virtually achieved, and restrictions on capital movements from one member country to another are being gradually removed. The Common Market Treaty provides for "freedom of establishment" of firms, branches, agencies, and individuals and "freedom to supply services" (building, banking, insurance, the exercise of

---

[10] For a fuller description, see Finn B. Jensen and Ingo Walter, *The Common Market: Economic Integration in Europe* (Philadelphia: J. B. Lippincott Co., 1965).

the liberal professions, and so forth) anywhere in the Community. Member states must ensure that nationals of other Community countries enjoy equal rights with their own citizens.

The Common Market is not just a customs union. The Common Market Treaty contains provisions for steps which will eventually lead to full economic union. To achieve this, it stipulates that common rules be applied to ensure fair competition, and that common policies be put into effect for agriculture, transport, and foreign trade. In addition, the Community has taken major steps toward common economic, monetary, regional, and social policies on which regular consultation takes place among the member governments.

Under the Rome Treaty, association with the Community is open to all countries. However, the Treaty does not prescribe a precise form for association and the Community has dealt with each application pragmatically. Various association agreements have been negotiated with Greece, Turkey, Israel, and the north African countries of Algeria, Tunisia, and Morocco, after they became independent of France. Also, the Rome Treaty provided for links between the European Community and the former colonies of the Community members. As a result, under the Yaoundé Convention signed in 1963, 18 former colonies in Africa received "associate status," whereby all products of the associated states enter the Community duty free, although the associated states are still able to impose or maintain duties on goods from the Six in order to protect their infant industries. Under various arrangements, a total of 35 countries had negotiated preference agreements with the EEC as of 1972. (See Figure 5.5.)

The economic progress of the Community has been impressive. The countries have sustained rapid growth rates. Trade between the member countries has increased spectacularly, and trade with the rest of the world has continued to expand, though at a lesser rate than internal trade. The harmonization of policies has moved along rapidly on many fronts, the most difficult of which has been the development of a common agricultural policy. Other European countries, originally reluctant to make the necessary sacrifices or concessions to join the Community, have made overtures to join the Common Market. In particular, the United Kingdom was very anxious to join, and after repeated negotiations, agreement was finally reached for formal entry on January 1, 1973. Along with the United Kingdom, membership for Ireland and Denmark brings the Common Market membership to nine countries, and by 1975 associated countries under one or another form of agreement are expected to number 50, including many British Commonwealth countries. The terms for the U.K.'s entry involved a five-year transition period with five successive 20 percent tariff cuts to reach zero tariffs on July 1, 1977. By that date, the EEC and its associates will present a trading

FIGURE 5.5
Who Gets Common Market Preferences?

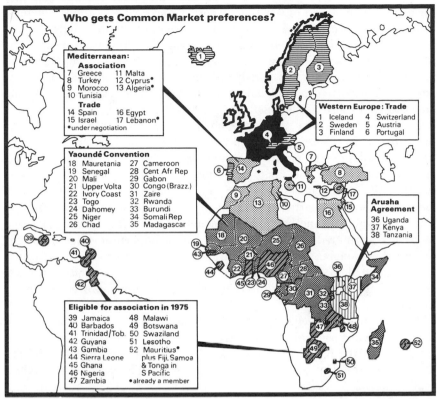

Source: *Economist*, 6 May 1972.

block that stretches from Finland in the north to the border of South Africa.

EFTA. The formation of the European Free Trade Area was inspired by a strong concern about the possible effects of the European Economic Community on the trade patterns of other Western European Countries, who had a variety of reasons for not joining the EEC. The United Kingdom, for instance, had long-standing relationships and tariff arrangements with the rest of the British Commonwealth that presented difficulties. Austria, Sweden, and Switzerland were anxious to avoid any commitment that might be considered to compromise their neutral status.

After prolonged negotiations, the seven countries of Austria, Denmark, Norway, Portugal, Sweden, Switzerland, and the United Kingdom joined in another regional economic integration movement under the Stockholm Convention of 1960. They were later joined by Finland and Iceland. EFTA was less ambitious than the EEC and had no overtones of a political union. The member countries agreed to remove internal tariffs on nonagricultural products in several steps and achieved this goal by the end of 1966, ahead of schedule. Another move was to abolish quantitative import quotas. The convention also contained provisions dealing with deflections of trade, the elimination of the protective element in revenue duties and internal taxes, drawbacks (that is, repayment of import duties on materials which are subsequently reexported or incorporated in exported goods), and the elimination of export duties and quantitative export restrictions.

As a free trade area, there was no provision for a common external tariff for EFTA. Consequently, rules as to origin and location of production were adopted to ensure that only goods which originated in the area benefited from the tariff reductions. Goods originating wholly or substantially from outside the area could not receive EFTA treatment merely by being imported into a member country with low tariffs and then reexported to another member country with high tariffs. In order to receive tariff reduction benefits, the most important rules of origin require that nonarea materials used at any stage of production account for not more than 50 percent of the export price of the goods produced or that the goods were produced by certain specified processes within the area.

EFTA's major achievement was a spectacular increase in intra-EFTA trade. The expansion of external trade was not impressive, mainly because the United Kingdom usually accounted for about half of all EFTA totals, and the United Kingdom experienced difficulties in expanding exports, during the 1960's.

The United Kingdom's successful application for entry into the Common Market in 1973 brought to an end EFTA's role as a significant trade grouping. Although Austria, Finland, Iceland, Norway, Portugal, Sweden, and Switzerland did not join the EEC, their EFTA membership did bring them free trade area treatment with the EEC.

The Less Developed Countries. The EEC and EFTA projects of the advanced Western European countries have been the most successful regional economic integration movements. Among the less developed countries, various groups have moved toward regional integration but with only limited success. In the case of the LDCs, the major objective has been to support industrialization efforts through enlarging markets and intra-regional competition. The hope is that an enlarged market and greater internal competition will permit more efficient producing units over time. So the major aim is to switch purchases away from the rest of the world to member countries, with trade-diversion effects rather than trade-creating effects.

The major integration project in the less developed countries, the Latin American Free Trade Area (LAFTA), took form in 1961 with the ratification of the Montevideo Treaty by seven nations—Argentina, Brazil, Chile, Mexico, Paraguay, Peru, and Uruguay. With the subsequent joining of Bolivia, Colombia, Ecuador, and Venezuela, the 11 LAFTA countries account for about 90 percent of production and trade within the area.

The stated objective in the treaty was "the expansion of present national markets through gradual elimination of barriers to intra-regional trade . . ." The method for achieving the objective was to engage in annual and triennial tariff reduction negotiations with a general commitment to eliminate duties and other restriction on 75 percent of the trade among the countries within nine years. There is no commitment to automatic reductions and the targets were to be met through item by item negotiations.

LAFTA members have had great difficulty agreeing on tariff reductions after the easy cases were negotiated in the early stages. The countries vary greatly in size and stage of development and the small countries have been concerned that reductions in internal tariffs will benefit mostly the large countries. Furthermore, historically the Latin American countries have been trading with outside nations more than among themselves, and in a number of cases, such as coffee from Brazil and Colombia, the member countries are specializing in similar export products.

The principal accomplishments of LAFTA are that the share of intrazonal imports in total LAFTA member country imports increased from 6 percent in 1961 to almost 12 percent in 1970. In addition, nineteen complementation agreements, designed to further industrial integration and diversification by providing for the coordination of investment and for immediate free trade for a specific product or products, have been concluded.[11]

Disillusioned by the lack of progress toward forming a large free trade area, new initiatives were taken to transform LAFTA into a common market where tariff reductions become automatic at specified times in the future and where an institutional framework for greater economic cooperation would be established. The chiefs of state of the Latin American countries agreed at a 1967 Punta Del Este Summit conference to take action beginning in 1970 to establish progressively the Latin American Common Market, which was to be substantially in operation within 15 years. These commitments of the Summit Conference have not yet been implemented.

A more modest Andean subregional common market has been a recent outgrowth of LAFTA. The six participating countries in the Andean

---

[11] Latin American Free Trade Association, *Newsletter,* No. 13, August 1972, p. 4. (Published in Montevideo, Uruguay.) See also Joseph Grunwald, Miguel S. Wionczek, and Martin Carnoy, *Latin American Economic Integration and U.S. Policy* (Washington, D.C.: Brookings Institution, 1972).

group are Bolivia, Chile, Columbia, Ecuador, Peru, and Venezuela. The Andean countries are aiming at a full-fledged economic community in which free trade will be achieved by 1980 and in which individual national interests will be balanced off and common development aspirations pursued through a concerted effort at regionwide industrial planning and rationalization.[12]

The most successful regional integration project in the less developed countries has been the Central American Common Market which included the five nations of Costa Rica, El Salvador, Honduras, Nicaragua, and Guatemala.[13] Internal tariffs have been virtually eliminated on an automatic schedule agreed upon in the treaty and intrazonal trade expanded by over 500 percent from 1961 to 1967. The gradual elimination of internal trade barriers has increased the size of the domestic market and led not only to better utilization of productive capacity, but to expanded investment into new and more complex product lines. A common external tariff has been established, and a full implement of regional institutions has been created. But the total area and population and income of CACM is small.

The Caribbean Free Trade Agreement (CARIFTA) entered into effect in May 1968 and has been joined by virtually all English-speaking countries in the Caribbean. The agreement established free trade among members except for certain products on which restrictions are permitted for from 5 to 10 years.

Significance to International Business.   Given the dramatic success of the EEC, regional economic integration movements are certain to continue as a significant and expanding feature of the international business environment. And regional integration movements can have vital significance for international business operations. Some of the major effects are as follows:

a.   Competitive conditions are changed as between internal and external producers. Firms previously exporting to the area may find it necessary to jump the trade barrier and establish local producing units. Firms located within the market can become more competitive through larger-scale producing units, if economies of scale are important to the industry.

b.   The general attractiveness of markets in countries joining integration movements can increase when growth rates are stimulated by trade creation effects, more vigorous competition and other related forces.

---

[12] Ralph A. Diaz, "The Andean Common Market—Challenge to Foreign Investors, and Harold C. Petersen, "ANCOM: An Andean Paradox," *Columbia Journal of World Business,* July–August 1971.

[13] See Ingo Walter and Hans C. Vitzhum, "The Central American Common Market," *The Bulletin,* no. 44, Institute of Finance, New York University, May 1967.

c. International firms established in common market or free trade areas can become more competitive in third country markets if the increased level of production secured within the home market permits reduced costs for exported goods.

d. Integration movements generally incorporate measures or policies that favor business enterprises from the area as against international enterprises of other nationalities. The EEC, for example, has promoted mergers of European firms as a defensive measure against the expansion of American companies in the Common Market area.

e. Changes in the rules of competition, such as adopting area-wide anti-trust policies, can cause problems for multinational firms that have previously given exclusive rights in specific member countries to subsidiaries or licensees.

For these and other business reasons, one of the challenging issues for the international manager is to be able to predict the establishment, the probable success, and future development patterns of specific integration movements. A growing body of research on optimum and necessary conditions for regional integration success can be of assistance in this respect.[14]

BILATERAL TRADING AGREEMENTS

Despite the restrictions imposed by participation in international trade agreements there are still numerous instances of countries making separate bilateral trading agreements for their mutual advantage. Among such bilateral agreements, the U.S.–Canada Automotive Products Agreement concluded in 1965 deserves special mention.[15] It may serve as a model for creating broader markets to obtain the benefits of specialization and large-scale production for industries in both contracting countries.

The agreement dismantles tariffs and other barriers in the automotive field and permits the integration of Canadian production of both automotive parts and vehicles with that of the United States. It permits production units in each country to produce at efficient levels and for specific products to move between the countries without duty. The selection of products and plants in each country benefited by the agreement has been made within a general objective of maintaining an equitable trade balance between the countries in the automotive field. Automotive

---

[14] For example, see Ardy Stoutjesdijk, "LDC Regional Markets: Do They Work?" *Columbia Journal of World Business,* September–October, 1970.

[15] See *Canadian Automobile Agreement: Second Annual Report of the President to the Congress on the Operation of the Automobile Products Trade Act of 1965,* U.S. Senate Committee on Finance, 21 May 1968 (Washington, D.C.: Government Printing Office, 1968).

trade has increased and automobile prices in Canada have declined because of the increased efficiency that has been permitted by creating a single North American market in automotive products.

Bilateral trading agreements are also common among nonmarket, or socialist countries and between these and the western world. The socialist countries differ in the way they organize themselves for foreign trade, but the common pattern is for the government, through a ministry of trade, to exercise complete control over exports and imports. Foreign traders deal with such a ministry rather than directly with the customer or local vendor of the goods and services. With most economic activities owned by the governments and operated in accordance with national economic plans, foreign trade is also managed according to national plans rather than market-determined commercial opportunities. Political as well as economic considerations can be decisive. Where economic factors prevail, the yardstick is the needs of the total plan rather than the benefits and costs to the individual state enterprise. Under such conditions, tariffs and subsidies for controlling or stimulating trade are unnecessary and not used. World prices are normally the guide for international transactions, and import or export prices may have no relationship to domestic prices. Nor are the planners necessarily constrained by cost-price relationships.

In addition to this centralized control of trade, there is no arrangement for free convertibility of the currencies of socialist countries, so that trade is frequently arranged on a barter basis or with clearing systems whereby sales are balanced with purchases from another country.[16] This system has led to numerous bilateral trading arrangements with specific trading partners under which attempts are usually made to identify the goods each country will trade and set overall trade limits which the parties will attempt to achieve.

INTERNATIONAL COMMODITY AGREEMENTS AND OTHER PRODUCER COOPERATION

There are strong incentives for major producers and exporters of primary products to attempt to stabilize price levels through international commodity agreements and to maximize foreign exchange earnings through bargaining with the principal consumers. Many countries, particularly the LDCs, are heavily dependent on the earnings from exports of agricultural products and raw materials to finance national development programs. And wide fluctuations in international demand and in free market prices can be quite disastrous to the producers and consumers.

---

[16] See Samuel Pisar, *Coexistence and Commerce, Guidelines for Transactions Between East and West* (New York: McGraw-Hill Book Co., 1970).

With the support of UNCTAD and other major international agencies, the move to expand the use of agreements involving both buyers and sellers to stabilize commodity trade has gathered considerable momentum in recent years. Yet, as of 1970 only five international commodity agreements were in force—wheat, coffee, sugar, tin, and olive oil. Each product had a long history of stabilization attempts and not all were functioning to the satisfaction of the producers.[17]

The form of the commodity agreement varies greatly. Under the International Grains Agreements, importers of wheat have agreed to buy only a specified percentage of their commercial imports from individual exporting countries as long as prices moved within a stipulated range. But the agreement provides for no export or production controls, nor for any central accumulation, of stocks. The International Coffee Agreement uses adjustable quota restrictions on exports and includes a program for attacking the long-term problem of overproduction. The International Tin Agreement, which deals with a durable rather than a perishable commodity, utilizes buffer stocks to keep prices within target ranges. A central agency of the tin-producing countries holds a stock of tin and sells or buys tin in order to keep the market price within agreed upon limits.

The international commodity agreements are difficult to negotiate. Where the cooperation of the consuming countries is necessary as is required under UN sponsored agreements, the consuming countries have to be willing to pay higher prices. Increasingly, the consuming countries have agreed to do so as a form of development assistance or for other political objectives. But even when negotiated, the agreements have many weaknesses. They can break down when certain producers see opportunities to get special gains by operating outside the agreement. If the agreements do not regulate the long-run supply, they may more and more misallocate resources into fields where demand is not growing rapidly.

International commodity agreements are a prime issue in the development strategies of less developed countries and in the development assistance policies of the industrialized countries. As compared to direct foreign aid, commodity agreements may be a less efficient way of transferring resources from the developed to the less developed, but most producer countries prefer to have international agreements to stabilize their export earnings rather than be dependent upon foreign countries for direct aid.

Another form of cooperation is producer agreements such as have

---

[17] For a good survey of these agreements, see M. A. G. van Meerhaeghe, *International Economic Institutions* (London: Longmans, Green & Co., Ltd., 1966), and John W. Rowe, *Primary Commodities in International Trade* (London: Cambridge University Press, 1966).

developed in the petroleum field. In 1960, the Organization of the Petroleum Exporting Countries (OPEC) was formed by the major oil-exporting countries (Algeria, Libya, Abu Dhabi, Iran, Iraq, Kuwait, Qatar, Saudi Arabia, Indonesia, Nigeria, and Venezuela) to achieve results similar to those of commodity agreements. OPEC has been well financed and expertly staffed by the member countries. It has devoted its principal attention to group bargaining with the international oil companies on oil concession terms and related matters. And OPEC has been highly successful in increasing the share of oil revenue accruing to the exporting countries. The number of major exporting countries is relatively small, and through OPEC they have succeeded in bargaining as a group and in preventing the international firms from playing one country off against another.

Commodity agreements and cooperation among producers will continue to be important to international business firms operating in selected fields. As a result, important decisions affecting the international transfer of goods will be determined by bargaining and agreement rather than directly by the market. The strategy alternatives available to international business firms, as in the case of petroleum, can be greatly reduced by such intergovernmental agreements.

EXERCISES AND DISCUSSION QUESTIONS

1. Explain the difference between comparative advantage and absolute advantage.

2. In a recent hearing before a senate committee investigating the need for further trade legislation, a labor union official testified as follows:

   "Free trade policies are based on traditional trade theory which is no longer valid in a world dominated by international investment and multinational companies. When the American business firm is faced with severe foreign competition, it can move abroad and meet this competition by producing in a foreign location for the U.S. market. The capitalists can adjust. The American workers cannot.

   "Furthermore, is it in the United States interest for American companies to invest abroad as rapidly as they are doing? U.S. advances in technology, often financed by government tax dollars, are being shipped abroad. The production overseas for foreign markets substitutes for U.S. production. We lose the foreign exchange that might be earned by exports. We lose American jobs, tax revenues, and so forth. Does the United States lose or benefit from multinationalism? What's good for international business is not necessarily what is good for the United States.

   "We want protection while the United States works out a program to control international business. Quotas should be placed on imports into the United States of those goods and product-lines that are displacing significant percentages of U.S. production and employment in order to slow down the disruptive impacts on American society and help to provide an orderly expansion of trade."

You are adviser to a U.S. senator and he has asked you to evaluate this testimony. He would also like your own reasoning as to how the best level of textile quotas, if any, should be determined for the United States.

3. Explain why the protection granted local labor by the imposition of tariffs may not be directly proportional to the heights of the individual tariff rates.

4. Discuss the following claim: "The longer-run effect of the United Kingdom joining the European Common Market will be trade diversion, not trade creation."

5. Are the benefits to producer countries from international commodity agreements significant, or just an illusion?

6. Would you recommend that advanced industrial countries support moves for further commodity agreements? Why or why not?

6

TREATIES, CODES, AND AGREEMENTS

VIRTUALLY ALL NATIONS agree on the desirability of permitting and encouraging international trade. As a result, they have cooperated to construct an international framework that facilitates the transfer of goods and money—two essential ingredients of trade—across national boundaries. Their commitment, however, has limits, so the framework they have created reserves for individual nations the right to impose certain controls over inter-nation flows of goods and money. Nations also agree on the need to facilitate communications and travel between nations. They have cooperated, therefore, through international agreements to create institutions and rules that provide an infrastructure for international communications and travel.

But the international framework that serves reasonably well for a world of trade does not adequately serve the growing sector of the international economy represented by multinational business operations. In addition to transfers of goods and money, international enterprises are concerned with such inter-nation issues as the right to establish businesses in foreign countries, the extension of patent rights and trademarks granted by one nation to another nation, the increased possibilities of double-tax liability and the fair treatment and protection of foreign private investment. Ideally, these ingredients of multinational business operations would be governed by an international legal system. But in the absence of a worldwide legal system, a subject that will be considered in greater depth in Chapter 14, a patchwork system of treaties, codes, and agreements has evolved as a substitute—or wistfully as a forerunner—of an international legal framework for multinational business operations.

Given the inevitable time lag between the identification of a need and the successful negotiation of a bilateral or multilateral international agreement to fill the need, the framework is incomplete and fragmentary—both as to substance and participants. With negotiations among independent sovereign states as the process for constructing the framework, the agreements naturally include only those matters or policies which all the parties can accept as being in their own national interest.

According to modern diplomatic usage, the more important international agreements are referred to as treaties. Those of lesser importance are called conventions, agreements, protocols, and acts. All of these forms are agreements among two or more nations which normally become legally enforceable through the courts of the participating countries. Such key elements of the international framework for trade and financial transactions as the IMF, GATT, and the EEC were created by treaties. Until an effective international legal system evolves for governing private international transactions, the growing number of treaties covering commercial matters will remain as the nearest approximation to international private law that the international firm will encounter.

INFRASTRUCTURE TREATIES AND CONVENTIONS

Most of the infrastructure treaties and conventions of importance to international business have led to organizations currently related to the United Nations. The drafters of the United Nations Charter believed that many areas of economic cooperation, while requiring an intergovernmental approach, could be more effectively covered by relatively autonomous functional organizations. Most of these organizations were to be brought—and have been—into relation with the United Nations as UN Specialized Agencies.

The significance to the international firm of the many infrastructure agencies varies with its fields of business activity. All international business firms are aided through the activities and agreements in the fields of communications and transportation, whereas only those in the pharmaceutical business, for instance, will be directly concerned with the activities of World Health Organization.[1]

The International Civil Aviation Organization (ICAO) fosters the development of safe, regular, and efficient international civil aviation through developing international specifications for air traffic, airports, telecommunications, charts, operations, airworthiness, and personnel, that are adopted and observed by member countries. The International Telecommunications Union (ITU) controls and allocates radio frequencies and facilitates international telegraph and telephone communications.

---

[1] See *United Nations and the Business World* (New York: Business International, 1967).

The Universal Postal Union, initially based on a convention of 1874 and presently a specialized agency of the United Nations, has established compulsory provisions for member countries governing international postal service and operates as a clearinghouse in the settlement of certain accounts. The International Labor Organization (ILO) has adopted conventions on trade union rights and on the protection of the right of workers to organize and bargain collectively. The World Health Organization (WHO) works to improve health conditions and has various international duties relative to the standardization of drugs, epidemic control, and quarantine measures.

As new technologies are developed and new issues become of critical concern to nations, nations are stimulated to create new infrastructure agreements or institutions. Such has been the case with the development of the communications satellite which led to the formation of the international consortium Intelsat. Intelsat facilitates and regulates the international transmission of television broadcasts and other newly feasible means of international communications. The same has been true in the field of environmental control. In the early 1970s, when awareness of the critical need for protecting the environment through international cooperation became universal, a special international conference on the environment was convened in Sweden which led to an agreement to establish a new international agency in this field.

COMMERCIAL TREATIES AND THE RIGHT OF ESTABLISHMENT

Through bilateral commercial treaties, many governments seek to enlarge the opportunity for their nationals to transact business in foreign countries on a nondiscriminatory basis. Commercial treaties between states encompass an extensive variety of subjects. Specific provisions frequently cover such matters as immigration and emigration, conditions of residence, travel, employment and trade, imposition of taxes, navigation, harbor and quarantine regulations, industrial property rights, and tariffs and customs laws pertinent to import and export trade. In addition, commercial treaties frequently contain a most-favored-nation clause which has great importance in assuring nondiscriminatory treatment in commercial relations.

The privilege of doing business in a foreign country and the conditions under which it is formally granted are the substance of a series of treaties known in the United States as Treaties of Friendship, Commerce, and Navigation. The objective of such commercial treaties is to secure for foreigners the right to trade, invest, or establish and operate a business in a country on a nondiscriminatory basis. The fundamental point underlying commercial treaties is that engaging in business transactions in a country other than one's own is a privilege and not a right. Usually, this privilege and the delineation of its conditions are worked out by negotiation between governments.

The United States has entered into over 130 such treaties, tracing back to the eighteenth century. Twelve were negotiated between the world wars and more than 20 were concluded since 1945. The signatories include most of the European countries, Japan, and a small selection of less developed countries. The treaties have changed in form and content over the years. Their emphasis is increasingly on investment and the right of establishment, with consular, tariff, and income tax issues being left to other agreements.[2]

Such treaties, of course, are not always observed. In the early 1960s, for example, the French government under de Gaulle became greatly concerned because American firms were attempting to take over a number of French companies, including France's largest manufacturer of computers (Machines Bull). The French response was to discontinue granting approval for American applications for direct investment in France. The new policy was in the form of a delaying action backed up by requests to firms to withdraw their applications. There were a few outright refusals, but most applicants simply gave up the struggle. Although these restrictions violated France's Treaty of Establishment with the United States, the U.S. government never formally protested and apparently was not asked to do so by U.S. firms that were refused. However, the French ban on new direct investment did not last long because other Common Market countries were anxious and willing to receive the U.S. Companies.[3]

THE PROTECTION OF INDUSTRIAL PROPERTY RIGHTS

Most countries of the world protect industrial property rights, a term which included patents, know-how, and trademarks. But patents are granted and trademarks requested by national governments and they are valid only within the territorial jurisdiction of the granting government. Consequently, foreign exploitation of a patent or trademark requires a parallel grant by foreign governments. The burden of having to file a patent application in every country where the patent is to be used is illustrated by this comment: "Of some 62,000 inventions made in this country (the United States) for which patent applications were filed in the U.S. Patent Office during a single year, foreign protection was sought for 23,000 of them by the filing of 115,000 applications in other countries. . . The president of one large corporation tells us that

---

[2] Henry Steiner and Detlev F. Vagts, *Transnational Legal Problems* (Mineola, N.Y.: The Foundation Press, 1968), pp. 498–500.

[3] Christopher Layton, *Transatlantic Investments,* (Boulogne-su-Seine, France: The Atlantic Institute, 1966), pp. 36–44.

under the present system the cost of obtaining foreign patents is now running close to $2 million for his company."[4] As another example, 10 percent of the money spent on developing the British Hovercraft, a vehicle for rapid transportation over water, went for securing patents around the world.[5]

The hardship of having to file foreign patent applications is alleviated somewhat by the Convention of Paris, executed in 1883 and periodically revised since that date, which established the International Bureau for the Protection of Industrial Property (BIRPI). Under this convention, once an investor has filed for a patent in one country, he has 12 months' priority in applying for the same patent in all other countries that have signed the Paris Convention. The Convention also provides for national treatment as regards the protection of industrial property, that is, each country belonging to the union grants to nationals of other member countries the same rights as it affords its own nationals. About 80 countries on all continents are members, including the Soviet Union which joined in 1965.

The United States is also a party to the Inter-American Convention of 1910 on Inventions, Patents, Designs, and Models to which 13 Latin American countries are parties. In addition, the United States has concluded a number of bilateral arrangements with some countries not members of the above conventions under which U.S. citizens receive national treatment, that is, the same protection extended to their own nationals, and other protection against discriminatory practices in acquiring and maintaining patent rights.

The burdensome necessity of having to file patents in each country governed by different patent laws has generated various proposals to simplify the international framework. A major step forward was achieved in 1972 when 21 European countries agreed by convention to establish a European Patent Office that could make one grant for all of the member countries under a single European patent law. The new European Patents Organization will also be responsible for deciding on appeals lodged against European patents. A new world patent treaty to simplify the operations of the Paris Union has also been in negotiation for a number of years.

INTERGOVERNMENTAL AGREEMENTS ON TAXATION

In a world of separate taxing authorities, problems arise because the entity being taxed, or parts of it, may fall under the jurisdiction of

---

[4] W. O. Quesenberry, Director, Office of International Patent and Trademark Affairs, U.S. Patent Office, in an address before the Joint Symposium of Patent, Trademark and Copyright Section, American Bar Association, Philadelphia, Pa., August 6, 1968.

[5] *Economist,* 17 June 1967.

more than one taxing authority. An enterprise may have its legal residence in one country, do business in another country, and have headquarters in still another country. How is the enterprise to be taxed and how can it avoid paying taxes on the same base to more than one of the taxing jurisdictions? The solution to this problem must recognize both the right of the enterprise to be free from excessive taxation and the right of the different authorities to tax revenues.

The right to levy and collect taxes is one of the most sacred rights of national sovereignty, but there is no clear nor universally accepted theory of tax jurisdiction. Nor is there an international law that specifies who has the right to tax and sets limits to the reach of any country's tax jurisdiction. Business transactions across national boundaries, therefore, can be greatly influenced in both positive and negative ways by the problems or opportunities resulting from varying taxation policies of overlapping national tax jurisdictions.

The tax systems employed by different countries differ significantly in the treatment of who is taxed—that is, in concepts of residence of the firm or individual—and what sources of income are taxed.[6] The most general practice is for nations to tax all income earned within the country, foreign-earned income when remitted and, in some cases, foreign-earned income on an imputed basis even though not remitted. Credit is normally given for taxes paid to foreign governments. In certain cases, tax credits are allowed for foreign taxes that have been waived, such as through tax-incentive programs of less developed countries trying to attract foreign investment.

The probability that two taxing jurisdictions may claim the right to tax the same property or income has stimulated governments to take unilateral actions in their own tax laws to provide credits for taxes paid abroad and to negotiate bilateral treaties with other countries to share the taxes imposed on business conducted in the territory of one country by nationals of another country.

Treaties for relief from double taxation are common and exist between many of the major countries of the world, especially capital-exporting countries, and between them and certain of the less developed countries.[7] Many European countries have signed 10 or more treaties dealing with the subject. The United Kingdom, with about 70 such treaties, has the highest number. The less developed countries generally have only a few such treaties. Venezuela has none. No multilateral treaties on double taxation have been realized as yet, but a draft convention drawn up by the Organization for Economic Cooperation and Development

---

[6] For example, see *Pocket Guide to European Corporate Taxes,* 2nd ed. (New York: Arthur Anderson and Co., 1972).

[7] For further details on the taxation of international business, see Harold J. Heck, *The International Business Environment* (New York: American Management Association, 1969), pp. 125–41.

(OECD) in 1963 has been influential as a guide to countries when they negotiate bilaterally.

As of 1972, the United States had treaties with 30 countries pertaining to the taxation of U.S. business interests in other countries and foreign business interests in the United States. The network of tax treaties among European countries and the United States are shown in Figure 6.1. The

FIGURE 6.1
Chart of Tax Treaties*

	Austria	Belgium	Denmark	Finland	France	Germany	Greece	Ireland	Italy	Luxembourg	Netherlands	Norway	Portugal	Spain	Sweden	Switzerland	United Kingdom	U.S.A.
Belgium		■	T	T	T	T	T	R	T	T	T	T	T	R	T		T	T
Denmark	T	T	■	T	T	T		T	T		T	T			T	T	T	T
France	T	T	T	T	■	T	T	T	T	T	T	T	R	T	T	T	T	T
Germany	T	T	T	T	T	■		T	T	T	T	T	N	T	T	T	T	T
Greece	T	T			T	T	■		T						T		T	T
Ireland	T	R	T	T	T	T		■		T	T				T	T	T	T
Italy	T	T	T		T	T	T		■	T	T		R	T		T	T	T
Luxembourg	T	T			T	T			T	■	T					T	T	T
Netherlands	T	T	T	T	T	T		T	T	T	■	T		R	T	T	T	T
Norway	T	T	T	T	T	T		T	T		T	■	T	T	T	T	T	T
Spain	T	R		T	T	T		R		R	T	T		■	T	T	N	N
Sweden	T	T	T	T	T	T	T	T	T		T	T	R	T	■	T	T	T
Switzerland	T		T	T	T	T		T			T	T		T	T	■	T	T
United Kingdom	T	T	T	T	T	T	T	T	T	T	T	T	T	N	T	T	■	T

* T—Treaty in force.
  R—Treaty awaiting ratification.
  N—Treaty being negotiated.

Source: *Pocket Guide to European Corporate Taxes, April 1972*, p. 85.

conventions to which the United States subscribes are not uniform. They were negotiated under different circumstances at different times and with countries whose taxation structures differ widely. They usually specify, however, how the taxes will be imposed and the persons or types of persons to receive benefits.

The international business firm, as will be discussed in Chapter 20 on financial management, is anxious to maximize profits by minimizing its tax liabilities. It wants to earn profits in the lowest tax jurisdictions whenever possible and to benefit from tax inducements by one country that are not negated by the failure of another country to provide credits for tax waivers. Each country, on the other hand, wants to maximize its share of tax income without making taxes so burdensome that they restrict the expansion of business activity.

The trend in tax treaties appears to be for the host countries of international business firms to impose taxes up to the rates imposed by the home countries of the international business firm. Such a policy can maximize the share received by the host country without increasing the total tax burden on a company. Another trend is for nations to use tax exemptions or low taxes as an attraction for international business activities. But the effectiveness of such government policy depends upon the willingness of the home governments of the international business firms to grant "tax sparing," that is, allow tax credits as if full taxes were paid. The United States, for example, does not grant tax credit for taxes spared abroad and the advantage to U.S. firms of tax inducements in foreign countries may be offset by home-country taxation on the higher foreign profits resulting from the tax concessions.

Some of the principal items included in the OECD draft treaty on double taxation which is having considerable influence in shaping bilateral treaties are as follows:

1. Determination of fiscal domicile.
2. Definition of permanent establishment, that is, what constitutes a permanent establishment for purposes of doing business in a country.
3. Tax jurisdiction of profits from ships and aircraft operating internationally. The treaty proposes that they be taxable only in the country where the effective management of the enterprise is situated.
4. Allocation of income for tax purposes when arising from nonarm's length arrangements between related companies.
5. Dividends—generally taxable in the country of the recipient.
6. Interest—generally taxable in the country of the recipient but the country of source may impose a tax of 10 percent.
7. Royalties—taxable only in the country of the recipient.
8. Capital gains—taxable only in the country where the property is situated.

The networks of bilateral conventions, and especially the drafting of model tax treaties, can remove many conflicts and stabilize the conditions under which international business operates. Conventions can also be a significant factor in decisions regarding the types of business organizations to be established.

INVESTMENT CODES AND THE SETTLEMENT OF INVESTMENT DISPUTES

A major area in which the international framework is still deficient relates to the settlement of investment disputes between parties of different nationalities. The International Court of Justice (See Chapter 14) hears only disputes between nations and is not available to private parties unless their cause is espoused by their respective government. Various codes of fair treatment for international investment and conventions on the responsibility of states for injuries to aliens have been drafted and discussed, but never widely adopted.

The most recent and most promising intergovernmental agreement in this field is the International Center for Settlement of Investment Disputes (ICSID), sponsored by the World Bank. By January 1, 1972, the ICSID Convention had been signed by 66 governments and ratified by 62 of them. This number does not include any of the Latin American countries, all of whom view ICSID as an infringement on national sovereignty.

The convention was designed to encourage the flow of private foreign investment to the less developed countries by creating the possibility, subject to the consent of both parties, for a Contracting State and a foreign investor who is a national of another Contracting State to settle any legal dispute that might arise out of such an investment by conciliation and/or arbitration before an impartial, international forum. The Center came into being in 1967 but had to wait until January 1972 to receive its first request for assistance in the settlement of an investment dispute. The first dispute involved Holiday Inns, S.A. (a Swiss company), and Occidental Petroleum Corporation (a California corporation) on the one side, and the Government of Morocco, on the other.

The FCN treaties concluded by the United States since World War II contain specific guarantees against the taking by one treaty partner of property of the nations of the other treaty partner except for a public interest and for just compensation. The earlier treaties as a rule have no specific guarantees against expropriation and speak more in terms of most-favored-nation treatment than in terms of national treatment.[8] National treatment is treatment toward foreigners no less favorable than treatment accorded nationals in like situations. Most-favored-nation treatment is treatment no less favorable than that accorded in like situations to nationals, companies, and products of any third country. As will be discussed in Chapter 14, because of escape clauses and other weaknesses in FCN treaties, many legal authorities have concluded that such treaties offer only limited protection to international business firms.

Of growing importance in the area of investment disputes are the investment protection agreements that investor countries have negotiated in connection with their investment-guaranty programs. In these cases, investment guarantees such as political risk insurance are provided only

---

[8] *Rights of Businessmen Abroad Under Trade Agreements and Commercial Treaties* (New York: U.S. Council of the International Chamber of Commerce, 1960), p. 11.

for investments in countries that have signed such agreements. One of the main purposes of these agreements is to secure protection for foreign investors against discriminatory legal and administrative actions by host countries.

The agreements do not, as a rule, provide full and automatic protection against nationalization, but the host country usually agrees to provide fair compensation without undue delay. Agreements can be detailed agreements of substance, as in the case of Germany which has negotiated about 40 agreements dealing with such issues as guarantees, financial transfers, entry permission for foreign personnel, and so forth. Other agreements, such as the almost 90 agreements negotiated by the United States, are limited to more procedural matters in the event that investments should be endangered.

An Evaluation

The conduct of multinational business has many ingredients in addition to the transfer of goods and money across national boundaries that ideally would be governed and facilitated by an effective world government and international legal system. In the absence of such a system treaties, codes, and agreements negotiated by nations on a bilateral or multilateral basis have been the principal tool for building a substitute framework. Normally, treaties are obeyed and agreements adhered to. In any event, they serve as an important guide for predicting the behavior of national governments.

The weakness of the structure of international commitments through treaties, codes, and agreements is its inadequate coverage for many ingredients of business operations that have grown in importance with the internationalization of business. Furthermore, the number of countries participating in particular agreements may be limited in comparison with the global horizon of the multinational enterprise. In matters such as the legal forms of business organizations, the regulation of restrictive business practice and the granting of industrial property rights, the international firm still has to function within a multiplicity of different and often conflicting national frameworks.

An international framework constructed through agreements among nations is necessarily limited by divergent national interests and the natural tendency of participating governments to bargain for their own ends. Where national interests differ radically, as between industrialized investor nations and less developed recipients of investment, agreements are difficult, if not impossible, to achieve. Thus many gaps exist in the international framework of treaties, codes, and agreements and are likely to remain.

The framework has been expanding as the frequency and importance of problems generate the necessary willingness on the part of nations to seek new agreements. Nations, however, can be influenced by the multinational enterprise working through its home government, as well as through the governments of other countries in which it is operating. By representing an international rather than strictly national view, the multinational enterprise may be able to accelerate the process of modernizing the international framework to fit the new patterns of international business activity. Some of the likely future developments are discussed in Chapter 14 which deals in more detail with the legal environment.

EXERCISES AND DISCUSSION QUESTIONS

1. Why do you think many of the less developed countries have been reluctant to sign FCN treaties and the ICSID convention while other LDCs have readily become parties to these types of agreements?

2. As the manager of a multinational enterprise, what strategies would you follow to improve the international framework for the transfer of industrial property rights and for expanding the network of tax treaties? Remember that your firm is operating in a number of countries and must appeal to the national interests of all governments.

PART III

International Business and the Nation-State

As BUSINESS ENTERPRISES have internationalized and steadily enlarged the geographic span of their operations, the world's governmental structure has not moved along a similar path. Despite some sentiment for creating a world government and some actual progress in regional political integration, the dominant units of government remain sovereign nation-states.

With the decline of colonialism and separatist movements in many parts of the world, the number of sovereign units of government has increased significantly since the end of World War II. Some observers argue that the nation-state is old fashioned and not well adapted to serve the needs of the modern complex world. Yet nation-states persist as the principal governmental unit with which the international enterprise must coexist.

Each sovereign nation-state has its own nationalistic spirit and set of national interests. The multinational enterprise consisting of many units of diverse nationalities pursues its own business goals on a global basis. In large part, the interests of the nation-state and the multinational enterprise overlap and are in harmony. But to a significant extent, the goals of the enterprise inherently conflict with the goals of one or more nation-states. Chapter 7 provides an overview of the common interests and potential conflict areas between international business and national governments. The subject is a central issue that pervades all aspects of international business operations.

In the traditional fields of international business, nation-states have long recognized the need to control the transfer of goods and money flows across national boundaries in order to harmonize such economic activities with national objectives and to increase national benefits. The patterns of such traditional controls and the underlying national motivations are presented in Chapter 8. As nations have become increasingly aware of the influence that multinational enterprises can exert on national interests, they have been responding by establishing control programs over the operations of multinational enterprises within their national boundaries. These nascent responses and the objectives which nation-states are attempting to achieve with such controls are the subject of Chapter 9. The multinational enterprise is not without its own resources for reacting to control efforts. Its countervailing power is considered in Chapter 10.

7

COMMON INTERESTS
AND CONFLICT AREAS

IN ALL BUSINESS OPERATIONS, the enterprise has common interests and potential areas of conflict with governments and must recognize governmental policies and actions as constraints in business decision making. The nation as a sovereign power sets the rules for governing business transactions within and across its national boundaries. Through such controls, it endeavors to increase national benefits, protect the public interest, and resolve conflicts between business and government. In dealing with predominantly domestic business enterprises, governments normally feel competent to achieve their goals and do not consider their sovereignty threatened. The domestic businessman, of course, has to recognize, forecast, and adjust to the governmental environment. But he has to be concerned only with the constraints imposed by the national interests of the one sovereign state to which he belongs. As long as international business consisted mainly of arms-length transactions between independent parties in different countries, nation-states felt reasonably competent to protect their national interests and were sensitive to few conflicts of interests with international business.

But the rise of the multinational enterprise has tremendously sensitized and dramatically changed business-government relations in international business. In its nature, the multinational enterprise attempts to direct a corporate family of diverse nationalities under its control toward supranational, or global, goals. The parent and each member of the family have a nationality, having been granted their corporate existence by the authority of a specific sovereign nation. But through bonds of common ownership and common strategy that cut across national boundaries, the family group operates as a transnational system that rationalizes its business operations and maximizes its business goals on a global basis. Such goals may be in harmony or in conflict with the goals of one or more nation-states. Each nation-state tries to maximize its own national goals. Each multinational enterprise tries to maximize its own goals on a supranational level. Inevitably, therefore, an inherent conflict potential exists between the multinational enterprise and the nation-state, whether it be the home country of the parent or the host countries within which affiliates are located.

The natural setting, however, is not simply a two-sided situation of inherent conflicts in the goals of the multinational enterprise and the nation in which it is operating. Any member of the multinational family is subject to the commands of the sovereign state within which it operates. Unlike purely domestic firms, it also responds to outside commands emanating from the parent, other family members, or even indirectly from other sovereign states. Furthermore, the local subsidiary can rely for support on the economic power of the entire system and at times on the political power of other sovereigns. Thus, in addition to conflict issues, the presence within a nation of an appendage of a powerful multinational system may also generate local tensions and appear to be a threat to national sovereignty.

The potential conflicts, tensions, and threats to sovereignty have little to do with good or bad intentions on the part of either international business firms or nation-states. The potential for divergent interests is an ineluctable result of the internationalization of business in a world of sovereign states. No multinational governmental organization exists that matches effectively the geographical reach of the multinational business enterprise and that represents the combined interest of the countries in which the enterprise operates. Thus, each of the nation-states has begun to exercise its sovereign power to influence the behavior of the multinational enterprise as the inherent differences in goals have become apparent. One level of national response has been protective or harmonizing—to reduce or reshape perceived threats to national economic, political, and cultural goals. Another level of national response has been less one of reducing conflict than one of trying to capture for a specific nation as large a share as possible of the total global benefits generated by the multinational enterprise. In the latter respect, nation-states are competing against other nation-states.

The phenomenal recent expansion of international business is impressive evidence that the mutuality of interests between the nation-state and the multinational enterprise heavily outweighs the divergent interests. Not surprisingly, international business firms are keenly aware of and emphasize the benefits nations derive from their operations. Yet, international managers must be equally familiar with the conflict potentials either perceived or present in their operations, so as to anticipate and deal with the complex governmental environment of many sovereign nation-states.

A WORLD OF NATION-STATES

The most significant characteristics of the nation-state from the standpoint of international business are that (a) it is sovereign or supreme in authority over its constituents within its borders, and (b) its people are bound together by an emotional or spiritual sense of nationalism which sharply differentiates between the interests of the groups that are part of the nation and external elements. Ideally speaking, the nation-state has both internal supremacy and external independence. The existence of internal government supremacy does not mean that it is constantly being exercised. In some circumstances, sovereign power may be latent and excised only as new situations arise.

External independence or freedom from outside control is never absolute. In practice, the nation-state must be guided by the impact of its decisions on other sovereign nation-states. Many nations have voluntarily accepted limitations on their sovereignty by joining regional groupings such as free trade areas and common markets or international agencies such as the International Monetary Fund. Numerous initiatives have been taken to create larger governmental units on a regional or world basis which would be more in harmony with the growing interdependence of the world. Most of these efforts have failed, and others are having only limited success. Political systems will keep changing, to be sure, but the international businessman can expect to be facing a world system of nation-states for some time to come.

The emotional or spiritual feeling of nationalism associated with the system of nation-states is particularly crucial for international business. Nationalism did not emerge until large groups of the populace in countries began to develop a spirit of unity and common interest. The external aspect of nationalism is a sense of distinctness between "we" on the inside and "they" on the outside. Nationalism supports policies which benefit a nation's own people as against the well-being of others. Nationalism is especially strong in attitudes toward international business, chiefly because of the heavy influence foreign business has exerted historically on the internal social and political affairs of many nations, particularly in the less developed countries.

The international enterprise, when conducting business activities within the territory of a specific nation-state, is subject to its sovereign power and affected by its nationalism, whether it be the home-base country of a multinational corporation or the host country of a foreign subsidiary. Each nation has its own goals and national interests which are continually in process of change. They may be economic, social, or political. They may be emotional, spiritual, or rational. They may be in harmony, or in conflict, with the goals of another nation-state. They may be in harmony, or in conflict, with the goals of the international enterprise. They may be complicated by the fact that a nation-state is both a host country and a home-base country for international enterprises.

Where the international enterprise encounters conflicts, it can rarely look to a higher world tribunal for harmonizing or resolving differences between sovereign nation-states or between the enterprise and a specific nation-state. In theory, the divine right of sovereignty can always prevail over the "divine right of capital." In practice, as we shall see, the international enterprise does have defenses and does not have to be a helpless victim of sovereignty and nationalism.

COMMON INTERESTS WITHIN A BENEFIT-COST FRAMEWORK

The common interest between business activities and the broader society was cited by Adam Smith more than two centuries ago in support of a *laissez faire* government policy. He argued that the "annual revenue of the society" will be maximized when the individual (and presumably the business enterprise) is permitted to employ his capital so as to produce what is of greatest value to the individual. Although the degree of regulation exercised by governments is generally greater than that envisaged by Adam Smith, the basic principle—that the interests of the nation can be maximized by permitting individuals and business firms to maximize their own goals—still persists as the guiding philosophy of the market economies of the world vis-a-vis domestic business activities.

For business activities that cross national boundaries, the principle of common interest enunciated by Adam Smith may not be appropriate. In domestic business, the nation expects to capture somewhere within its boundaries the total net contribution of the enterprise. In the case of international business, however, a specific nation may not receive what it considers to be its legitimate share of the total global benefits. In traditional international trade, nations generally accept the free trade argument that world output from a given set of resources will be increased by international specialization and trade among nations. Yet they are primarily concerned with the separate issue of how the gains are distributed among specific nations. Likewise, most nations might agree in principle that the free movement of multinational enterprises across national boundaries can stimulate the movement of productive resources from areas of lesser relative opportunity to areas of greater relative opportunity and improve overall economic efficiency on a world basis.[1] But here again, the priority interest of the nation is in the distribution of the gains among the many nations.

At a practical level, therefore, the matter of common interests becomes a question of national benefits rather than world benefits. The measuring stick for calculating national benefits can differ sharply from the gauge used to sum up world benefits. Weighing heavily as world benefits will be greater production efficiency and accelerating economic growth. From the specific nation's point of view, many other items are measured such as the effect on national balance of payments, national employment, and so forth. Also, national benefits from *international* business must not be confused with national benefits from business per se. Only the net contribution over what might have been available from domestically controlled business activities really counts to the nation. Furthermore, the nation must compare net benefits to net costs. And the surplus of benefits over costs for multinational enterprises must be greater than that for other alternatives available to the nation in order for significant common interests to exist between the enterprise and a specific nation-state.

The concept of comparative benefit-cost ratios, widely used by governments for decision making on public investments, is gradually being applied in the international business field. Both host and home countries are increasingly examining international business activities in terms of national interests and within the context of comparative benefit-cost appraisals. The international enterprise must be prepared to justify its operations in such terms to each specific nation-state it affects. To date, host countries have shown a high degree of receptivity to international business in many fields because domestic alternatives frequently are not available or, where domestic alternatives exist, the international enterprise has significant competitive advantages.

In home-base nations, multinational enterprises have only recently been scrutinized from a benefit-cost point of view. For many years home countries tended to consider their international business enterprises as national firms with important but not dominant foreign operations. Because the principal international enterprises had their home bases in the industrialized countries with large domestic economies, the sum total of all foreign operations radiating from a specific country were small

---

[1] See Stephen Hymer, "The Efficiency (Contradictions) of Multinational Corporations," *American Economic Review,* May 1970, pp. 441–48. It should be noted that unanimous agreement does not exist on the inevitability of greater global benefits arising from multinational business operations. As Hymer has argued, direct foreign investment "is an instrument which allows business firms to transfer capital, technology, and organizational skill from one country to another. *It is also an instrument for restraining competition between firms of different nations.* (emphasis supplied)." It cannot be presumed, therefore, that multinational business operations invariably contribute to greater efficiency because of the anticompetitive effect inherently associated with it.

enough relative to the total economy to be inconspicuous or not troublesome.

The situation, however, is changing rapidly. International business is becoming ever larger in relation to national economies. The value of international trade, foreign production, and other types of international business operations has been expanding more rapidly than the gross domestic product of the principal home-base countries. Even more important has been the evolution from primarily domestic firms with foreign operations to multinational enterprises with global horizons, operating goals, and strategies. An ever-increasing share of international trade consists of movements within and among multinational enterprises rather than transactions between independent domestic firms located in different nations.

With the trend toward global operations, the enterprise continues to recognize the national interests of the home country as a major environmental constraint, but such considerations must necessarily lose their weight in decision making. In a continuing world environment of sovereign nation-states it appears inevitable that the areas of mutual interest and conflict between the home country and the international business enterprise will be subject to ever-increasing scrutiny and analysis by the home country. As in the case of host countries, the international enterprise will have to relate its activities to the economic and political goals of the home country.

The conceptual framework used by nations for either implicit or explicit evaluations of national benefits and costs is relatively easy to describe. It includes political, social, and psychological considerations, as well as economic effects. The mix of items included in any evaluation will vary from nation to nation, reflecting differences in national priorities. The items will change over time as national interests change. The same item will be given different weights by different nations. And even though one component is evaluated as having a net negative effect, the perceived gains in other components may be sufficiently positive to result in an overall favorable balance.

In practice, the quantification of costs and benefits remains a highly ambiguous subject, even in the economic area, because of both methodological and data limitations. How does a nation measure the value of a transfer of technological and managerial know-how to nationals of that country? What is the value of a foreign enterprise's contribution to national goals of economic and social modernization, or what are the costs of having cultural values changed that are prized by the country? How much is it worth to have more competition injected into an economy or for indigenous entrepreneurship to be stimulated (or stunted) by the entry into a country of foreign firms? For the home as well as the host country, the quantification problem is equally formidable.

Raymond Vernon made the following observation to the President's Commission on International Trade and Investment Policy, which was considering the benefits and costs of U.S. international enterprises to the United States:

There are no economic models as yet sufficiently subtle and dynamic to capture the medium-term and long-term consequences of creating an overseas subsidiary. In the end the decision on whether to support or retard this kind of development on the part of U.S. enterprises must be made by what amounts to an intuitive leap.[2]

Yet, implicitly more often than explicitly, each nation-state makes such calculations, or intuitive leaps, in establishing and exercising controls over international business. Some of the economic benefit-cost issues, however, are more or less amenable to quantification, as we will see below.

With each nation requiring a surplus of benefits over costs from the operations of multinational enterprise, it might appear that the international firm is in the middle of an impossible situation. In order for one nation to have net gains, does another nation have to have net losses? Fortunately, two characteristics of the situation make the multinational enterprise a viable phenomenon in a world of nation-states. One saving feature is that the cost and benefit items have different values for different nations. A loss of jobs to a full-employment German economy because of the establishment of overseas production facilities by a German multinational enterprise will be valued much less as a cost to Germany than the same employment would be valued as a benefit by a host country with a high degree of unemployment which receives a new subsidiary. The second saving feature is that international business activity is not necessarily a zero-sum game in which one nation has to lose in order for another nation to gain. If multinational business results in a more efficient use of world resources, all parties can secure increased benefits. Because the pie to be divided is larger, each nation can have a larger slice.

THE POSITIVE SIDE OF NATIONAL BENEFITS

Before concluding with the general discussion of common interests, it will be useful to summarize the national benefits from international business, even though they are widely appreciated and have been frequently mentioned. Nations probably have the clearest picture of the benefits from importing and exporting activities. Imports make available within a nation goods or materials not produced domestically or which

---

[2] Raymond Vernon, as cited in *U.S. International Economic Policy in an Interdependent World* (Washington, D.C.: U.S. Government Printing Office, July 1971), p. 312.

can be sold at lower prices than domestic production. Imports can help to meet national-security goals by providing stockpiles of critical materials. Imports can be an important competitive and anti-inflationary force in the domestic market. Imports of raw materials and semimanufactured goods can support local efforts to industrialize. And imports can be a significant source of government tax revenue.

The economic contribution of exports has also been well recognized. Exports increase domestic output. With higher levels of output, economies of larger-scale production can also decrease the cost of goods for the domestic market. Exports earn foreign exchange needed to support industrialization and import programs. Exports can generate tax revenues through export, value added, income, or other types of taxes, but tax benefits are becoming less clear with the growing importance of trade between units of the same multinational enterprise. The possibilities for concentrating profits in low tax jurisdictions through transfer-pricing policies may lead enterprises to actions that reduce tax liabilities.

But exports and imports involve costs as well as benefits. Heavy dependence on exports may make a country's domestic welfare critically dependent on the economic situation in foreign countries. In periods of weak foreign demand, domestic employment and national economic growth may suffer. In periods of accelerating foreign demand, export activities can generate domestic inflationary pressures. The costs of imports may be in the form of losses in domestic employment or in outflows of foreign exchange. Imports may also threaten infant domestic industries and stunt national efforts to industrialize. These and many other negative impacts provide the rationalization for national protectionist policies and for the control programs over international transfers discussed in the next chapter.

The positive contributions to a host country of international business operations can be extensive. The multinational enterprise can mobilize external capital, management skills, and technological know-how, and bring these elements into a country. It can supply one or more missing factors that can be combined with locally available human and physical resources. Thus, it can accelerate economic growth both by a transfer of resources and by the multiplier effect of providing an opportunity for locally available resources to become more fully utilized. Multinational firms can provide business experience for nationals that enlarges the entrepreneurial capacity of a country and can supply training for local management, technical, supervisory, and operating personnel. They may open up access to new foreign markets and train nationals in marketing management.

International business may stimulate competition in domestic markets, and competition can be a mighty force for change and development. Linkage effects—the opening up of new opportunities for firms to become suppliers, further manufacturers, and sellers of the product of the foreign-financed venture—can be another type of contribution to economic growth. In sum, economic contributions can be transfers of resources and technology, more rapid national growth, increased employment, new sources of foreign exchange earnings, and a stimulating effect on other types of business activity.

International business can also contribute to the nationalistic goals of a country. It can help to satisfy the national desire to have a modern business and industrial sector and to have high technology prestige products produced within the country. It can help to meet national-security goals by making certain technology available or by creating domestic production facilities for high-priority defense needs.

The influence of international business on social development goals may be intangible and dispersed, yet real. In a broad sense, the multinational enterprise can be a strong force for modernization within a country. It can contribute directly to better education, improved health conditions, and housing.

What are the benefits of multinational enterprise to the home country of the enterprise? Foreign investments can develop sources of natural resources or products which are unavailable—or not available in sufficient quantity—in the home country, or which are cheaper sources of supply. The establishment of foreign-producing facilities may stimulate demand for home country exports of components or raw materials and, in turn, increase home-country employment. Multinational enterprises can generate return flows of income on foreign investment and contribute to the home countrys' balance of payments. The greater total profits likely to accrue to the multinational enterprise through exploiting the potential efficiencies of global operations can mean greater home-country tax revenues on increased profits. The sale of technology and of technical and management services to foreign licensees can also generate income, foreign exchange, and tax revenues for the home country.

Areas of common interest between the political goals of the home country and the activities of the international business firm can also be significant. Trade expansion is generally regarded as a contribution toward better understanding and peace among nations. International business can satisfy home-country nationalistic goals of prestige and national security. And international business can support foreign policies of the home country that are aimed at stimulating the economic growth of less developed countries or at assisting the reconstruction efforts of war-devastated areas.

Simply by focusing on benefits, an enumeration of the potential contributions of international business operations to the goals of specific nations is overpoweringly impressive. Multinational enterprises, quite naturally, emphasize these benefits most forcefully as proof of their common interests with nation-states. But the relationship between international business and national interests of the nation-states also has a negative, or conflict, side which exists at two levels. At the more general level, nations often perceive the total multinational business phenomenon as a source of national tensions and as a threat to both economic and political sovereignty. At the specific level, individual projects involve costs as well as benefits, both of which must be evaluated in determining whether the *net* result of such activities is positive or negative.

Nations' general attitudes toward international business are built from their evaluations of individual business activities. Yet, the threats to sovereignty reflect considerations over and above the sum of the net benefits or costs of individual international business activities. As a result, any specific international business project may become subordinated to the broader issues and not be evaluated as an independent event. Therefore, we will examine the more general nationalistic concerns over loss of sovereign powers before proceeding with a review of available benefit-cost investigations. As Vernon has dramatically characterized the broader question, "Suddenly, it seems, the sovereign states are feeling naked. Concepts such as national sovereignty and national economic strength appear curiously drained of meaning."[3]

THE THREAT OF ECONOMIC DOMINATION

In any individual case, the activities of a multinational firm may offer sizeable net benefits to a nation in which it is operating. But when a dominant share of the domestic economy comes under foreign ownership and control, the merits of the individual case become subordinated to a nation's broader concern for maintaining its economic independence. Over many decades, the new jobs and other benefits generated by foreign investment in Canada were sufficiently appealing to quiet national fears of foreign economic domination. But when 60 percent of Canada's manufacturing industry, 75 percent of her petroleum and natural gas industry, and 60 percent of her mining industry came under control of foreign corporations by the mid-1960s, national sovereignty tolerance levels were breached. As one Canadian scholar has expressed this concern, "Once the most dynamic sectors of our economy have been lost, once most of the savings and investment is taking place in the hands of foreign capitalists, then the best prediction is a steady drift toward foreign control of the Canadian economy with the only certain upper limit being 100 percent."[4]

---

[3] Raymond Vernon, *Sovereignty At Bay* (New York: Basic Books, 1971), p. 3.

[4] Mel Watkins in the preface to Kari Levitt, *Silent Surrender: The American Economic Empire in Canada* (New York: Liveright, 1971), p. xi.

The Canadian example illustrates a nation's concern because of the total share of the national economy that is foreign owned. Nations also become agitated when foreign enterprises dominate a number of key growth industries. Writing in 1901, a British author observed, "The most serious aspect of the American industrial invasion lies in the fact that these incomers have acquired control of almost every new industry created during the past fifteen years."[5] Referring to the British, he concludes, "We are becoming the hewers of wood and the drawers of water, while the most skilled, most profitable, and the easiest trades are becoming American."[6] More than a half century later, a similar manifesto combining nationalistic fears of both sectoral and overall economic domination by foreign enterprise, written by the Frenchman Jean-Jacques Servan-Schreiber, became a best seller throughout much of the world. It warned Europeans that *American industry in Europe* was likely to be the world's third-greatest industrial power within 15 years—just after the United States and Russia.[7] The fear of foreign economic domination has not been exclusively a reaction to U.S. multinational enterprises. As Japanese companies have expanded rapidly in Southeast Asia, they also have evoked nationalistic fears of foreign economic domination.

Ironical as it may be, some of the necessary conditions for successful international business expansion are also the sources for creating national tensions. Foreign firms must have something to offer over and above what is available from domestic enterprise in order to have reasonable prospects for success. This means that expansion opportunities are best in nations where indigenous enterprise and management skills are weak and in industries requiring advanced technology or in ones based on new products where the foreign enterprise has an oligopoly advantage. Multinational enterprises have little to offer in the production of low technology and standardized products for local markets. Bricks are an example of such products. But in sophisticated technology and rapid-growth areas such as computers, international firms have a competitive-advantage basis for entering foreign areas. Thus arises the national fear of becoming technologically dependent upon foreigners.

The multinational threat to national economic autonomy is perceived in many dimensions. As host nations may complain, the decision centers which control the future of many of their key economic sectors are outside of the country and less subject to national controls. The multinational enterprise can shift resources within the system and thus reduce the effectiveness of national programs to control inflation, improve the balance of payments, or expand employment. The research centers for

---

[5] Fred A. McKenzie, *The American Invaders* (New York: Street and Smith, 1901), p. 31.

[6] Ibid., p. 157.

[7] J. J. Servan-Schreiber, *The American Challenge* (New York: Atheneum, 1968).

multinational enterprises are likely to remain in the home country, with the result that a host country becomes technologically dependent on outsiders. Foreign enterprises which command mammoth resources and have a head start in key growth areas are viewed as slowing the emergence of local entrepreneurship in these fields.

The less developed countries which can benefit most from the transfers of resources, management skills, and technology of the multinational enterprise are especially sensitive to the economic domination issue. Some of them characterize the issue as economic neocolonialism, particularly at intermediate stages of development. Foreign investment, as they see it, can change over time from a development stimulant to a retarding influence. As Hirschman has articulated the case, ". . . foreign investment can be at its creative best by bringing in 'missing' factors of production, complementary to those available locally, in the early stages of development of a poor country. The possibility that it will play a stunting role arises later on, when the poor country has begun to generate . . . its own entrepreneurs, technicians, and savers and could do even more along these lines. . . ." The increased domestic capacity for supplying missing factors may in large part be the contribution of multinational enterprise. But, as Hirschman argues, institutional inertia makes for continued importing of so-called scarce factors even when they become locally available. This line of thinking has resulted in proposals that foreign enterprises should be forced to withdraw, or disinvest, at the stage when the "bundle" of factors brought in by the multinational enterprise are no longer complementary to local factors, but become competitive with them and prevent their growth.[8]

It is in the host countries primarily where tensions are generated because of the threat of multinational enterprise to national economic autonomy. Some dimensions of international business operations create similar types of concern in the home countries. The ability of a home country to implement successfully programs for improving its balance of payments, increasing domestic employment, or reducing inflationary pressures can be weakened by the standard operating practices of multinational enterprise to limit foreign exchange risks, to make use of foreign sources of financing, or to expand in the most profitable location which turns out to be a foreign area rather than the home country.

This type of conflict, however, may not arouse the level of nationalistic tensions in the home country that it does in host nations. The home countries are generally advanced industrial countries where the international business sector represents a relatively small, though absolutely large, share of the total economy. Thus, although international firms

---

[8] Albert O. Hirschman, *How to Divest in Latin America, and Why,* Princeton Essays in International Finance, no. 76 (Princeton, N.J.: International Finance Section, Department of Economics, Princeton University, November 1969).

are maximizing their goals on a global basis and at times at the cost of the home-country economic goals, they are not yet viewed as a major threat to home-country economic sovereignty.

THE POLITICAL CHALLENGE

The history of foreign investment during the nineteenth and early twentieth century contains many examples of foreign firms, particularly in the extractive industries, exercising their power to influence political events and political decisions in host countries. Probably the best known cases of political intervention are the activities of United Fruit in Central America and the international oil companies in the Middle East.[9] However, such political buccaneering behavior by business enterprises, characteristic of past eras, has steadily declined and been replaced by more subtle political problems in which the multinational enterprise is frequently a passive instrument caught between different political goals of separate nation-states.

To the host country, the local subsidiary of a multinational enterprise can be perceived as a political arm of the home-country government. Through its control over the parent company, home governments can and have interfered in the political affairs of another, or host country. Over certain periods, for example, the U.S. government has placed partial or complete embargoes on exports of goods and transfers of technology to certain countries such as Mainland China, Cuba, and the Soviet-bloc countries. American subsidiaries in Canada have been criticized for following U.S. policies banning trade with Mainland China, even though Canadian policies permit such trade. American subsidiaries in England and in Europe have been coerced into turning away business from Cuba and Soviet-bloc countries, even though the nations in which the subsidiaries are located have different policies.[10]

Other conflicts with host countries have occurred in the area of extraterritorial jurisdiction. This topic will be discussed in greater detail in Chapter 14—The Legal Environment. The problem is that the application of domestic laws to the operations of a multinational enterprise in one country can influence operations of the same company in another country. The best known example is the enforcement of U.S. antitrust laws, which has had the effect of banning activities in another country which are not against the law of that country. The transnational reach

---

[9] See Stacy May and Galo Plaza, *The United Fruit Company in Latin America* (Washington, D.C.: National Planning Association, 1958), pp. 1–23; Robert Engler, *The Politics of Oil* (New York: Macmillan Co., 1961).

[10] See Jack N. Behrman, "Export and Technology Controls," *National Interests and the Multinational Enterprise* (Englewood Cliffs, New Jersey: Prentice-Hall, 1959), pp. 101–13.

of one country's domestic laws through international business firms conflicts with the sovereignty and political autonomy of another state.

Still another type of political challenge to a host country occurs when the home country of the multinational parent assumes political responsibility for protecting the foreign interests of its citizens. Although foreign subsidiaries are normally incorporated within the countries in which they are operating and subject to national laws as a national corporation, home-country governments are not always willing to accept the results of expropriation under local law. In 1971, Algeria moved to take over majority ownership in all French oil subsidiaries in that country, one of which was owned by the French government. Among official retaliatory actions taken by the French government was a move to block international loans to Algeria for a natural gas plant.[11] The well-known Hickenlooper Amendment to the Foreign Assistance Act of 1961 legally requires the U.S. government, under specified conditions, to use certain governmental powers to protect the interests of its foreign investors. Thus, in dealing with local subsidiaries of foreign enterprises a nation-state can have its political sovereign power threatened when home countries feel forced to intervene—either at the political, economic, or even military level—without the strictly political interests of the home country being at stake.

But the political challenge of the multinational enterprise is not limited to its relations with host countries. It may also be a source of political conflict and a challenge to political autonomy in the home country. The interests of the multinational enterprise and those of the home country are not identical, and the use of home-country political power to intervene in the relations between foreign subsidiaries and host governments often becomes a controversial political issue in the home country. Such intervention can be at the expense of other political interests of the home country. For this reason, the Nixon administration failed to apply the Hickenlooper Amendment to Peru in 1969, when the International Petroleum Company was expropriated.

In the continuing formulation and implementation of its foreign policies, the home country may have its options restricted because of the amount and type of foreign private investment by its citizens located in specific countries. The foreign policy options for the United States toward Middle Eastern countries have undoubtedly been narrowed by the existence of massive American oil investments in the region. The large amount of U.S. foreign investment in Cuba most certainly has been a crucial constraint in U.S. foreign policy relations with that country. Where host countries closely identify multinational enterprises with home-country governments, the home country may see its political rela-

---

[11] *Wall Street Journal,* 1 March 1971.

tions complicated by types of behavior on the part of international business enterprises which are resented by host countries.

The general political-conflict problem that has been emerging in home countries is the extent to which the level and allocation of foreign operations by nationally incorporated firms can be left to the dictates of the market, *if* the home country must assume political responsibility for the enterprises. Some home governments attempt to guide foreign private investment, through incentives or controls, in ways that might minimize the potential sources of political conflict.

The multinational enterprise faces a complex and ambiguous situation in the political conflict area. It has little, if any, capability for reducing the political challenge it represents to host countries when it is used as a political arm of the home government and in cases involving extra-territoriality. It does not relish its role as a carrier of controls. At best, it can urge the conflicting nation-states to undertake bilateral negotiations or participate in inter-governmental programs to harmonize laws or mediate disputes. This path is being followed to resolve jurisdictional conflicts.

In their relations with home countries, international companies have mixed and, at times, ambivalent views. Some companies would like to be independent of the political interests of a home country. Some have even expressed the desire to have an island somewhere in international waters as their home base. Other firms place a high value on having a home-country government that will protect their operations in a foreign country and represent their interests in inter-governmental negotiations on such matters as tariffs and trade policies. In still other cases, multinational enterprises would like to be politically free from their home country on certain matters and still be able to call for its political muscle on other issues.

THE TRANSFER OF RESOURCES

Nation-states find the multinational enterprise difficult to live with because of its threat to national autonomy in economic and political matters and the tensions it generates. At the same time, they find it more unpleasant to live without the multinational enterprise so long as the national benefits from its local operations add significantly to national power and national welfare. One important component in the trade-off between sovereignty and national benefits is the extent to which the multinational enterprise increases the availability of resources and the supply of productive facilities in the countries where it establishes operations.

In an industrialized country like Canada, where national growth has been constrained by inadequate domestic savings and a shortage of skilled manpower, even nationalistic opponents of foreign enterprise agree that such firms have made net additions to the nation's supply of these factors. In other industrialized countries, the important resource transfers have been identified, with little local disagreement, as the fields of technology, management, and skilled technical manpower.

In the less developed countries, the range of resource transfers has generally been much broader. Outside capital has often been a major contribution. Where foreign exchange is a major constraint on growth, foreign capital can help to break this bottleneck. The transfer of technology and the import of management, marketing, and production skills may be valued even more highly than in the more advanced countries. To the extent that the inflow of resources consists of "missing factors," they may complement and effectively "increase" the supply of local factors heretofore idle or less productively used. Thus, the resource transfer effect may be both the net addition from the outside as well as the net increase in the effective value of domestic resources.

Resource transfers have a cost as well as a benefit side. The multinational enterprise may use local resources that are scarce rather than in excess supply. Although local management skills may be in short supply, the foreign enterprise is frequently under pressure to hire nationals. It is then likely to be charged with the opportunity cost of preempting managers who otherwise would be available to initiate and direct indigenous enterprises. Or enterprises may be required by national policies to form joint ventures by enlisting local capital and may be charged on the cost side with preempting scarce local capital which should be available for local enterprises.

Whether such opportunity costs are valid costs in calculating national benefits becomes a complex and multifaceted problem of evaluation. The entrepreneurial function of conceiving, establishing, and taking the risk inherent in a new enterprise is generally recognized as a human skill separate from that required for business managers. In other words, hiring managers is not the same as employing entrepreneurs. Yet in many cases, the unique experience a local manager gains by working with a multinational enterprise may give him the additional knowledge, confidence, and resources that transform a manager into an entrepreneur. Similarly, by using local capital foreign enterprises may enlarge rather than reduce the total supply of that resource. In countries that are attempting to strengthen local capital markets, the selling of stock locally by a well-known and presumably financially secure and profitable international firm can provide a confidence element essential for developing such institutions and thereby help in attracting more savings to capital markets for equity investment.

The profits earned by foreign enterprises can be considered an offsetting cost by a nation. To the extent that a multinational firm transfers profits out of the country, there is a foreign exchange cost. The foreign exchange question will be considered separately below. If it reinvests profits within the country, the cost to the nation may be that a larger amount of the national patrimony comes under foreign ownership. What is frequently overlooked by antagonists to foreign investment is that such profits come out of newly created increments to domestic GNP generated by the multinational enterprise, and that the profits are generally a small share of the total increment. Here again, we have the nonzero-sums game characteristic of international business. Both parties gain. The firm gains profits. The nation gains an even greater increment in GNP and employment.

Turning to a question posed earlier, if the host countries are gaining resources, aren't the home countries losing? This possibility exists, of course. Capital outflows for foreign investment may reduce the supply and/or increase the cost of capital for domestic expansion. They may also reduce the availability of foreign exchange. Sending skilled managers and workers to man foreign subsidiaries will reduce the supply of such skills in the home country. The normal situation seems to be, however, that resources are being transferred from countries in which they are in relatively abundant supply to areas where such factors are in relatively short supply and that the opportunity cost of such resource outflows may be low. Offsetting these home-country costs are a flow of benefits such as repatriated profits, payments to the parent company for royalties and management services, increased exports to overseas subsidiaries, increased exports as an indirect result of expanding world output, and even return flows of technology.

It should be noted, however, that the resource-transfer capability of the multinational enterprise extends far beyond that of bilateral transfers between home and host country. Operating with a global strategy, the firm can transfer resources among any of the nations in which it is operating. Where the enterprise does its financing outside the home country, the home country can benefit by repatriated profits and other payments to the parent company without any cost in capital or foreign exchange outflows.

Under most circumstances, in order to welcome international firms a nation must feel that the net value of resource transfers from such operations is positive. There may be some cases where a net cost, rather than a net benefit, is acceptable because of other compensating national gains. One such situation may be where an international business activity generates large indirect or linkage benefits. The establishment of an agricultural processing plant by a foreign firm may not in itself result in a net transfer of resources, but the stimulus of this plant to agricultural employment and farm output may be a more than offsetting benefit. Another type of situation is the interesting case of the French multinational aluminum producer, Pechiney, entering the U.S. market by acquiring a controlling interest in Howmet, an American producer, and by financing this acquisition mainly from U.S. capital sources. Where is the resource transfer? Pechiney would claim that it has transferred advanced technology to the United States. But, even taking the technology transfer into account, with such giant American companies as Alcoa, Reynolds, Kaiser, and others prepared to meet domestic U.S. demand for aluminum, it would appear difficult to demonstrate net resource-transfer benefits to the United States. Yet, such expansions by foreign firms in the United States have not provoked concerns about national benefits simply because any obstruction by the United States to such incoming projects might easily result in retaliation against U.S. firms overseas.

Resource transfers, of course, have a time dimension. When a direct-investment project is initiated, benefits are greatest and certainly most spectacular. In the initial stages, capital flows in, plants are built, local workers are hired and trained, and local supply contracts are let. After a new project has been started, or a new product or process introduced, a steady decline in benefits is likely to set in. The benefits may never phase out completely. Yet, over time they may lose much of their value to a nation.

The longer the enterprise operates on its original technological, organizational, and other resource-transfer base, the smaller is the value placed on the original benefits by the host country. In many, if not most, cases stimulated by opportunity or pushed by local pressures, enterprises have responded by continually adding to or upgrading their initial technological, organizational, or product contributions. Where firms do not continue adding, the question is likely to be raised by the host country as to whether payments to the foreign investor should continue indefinitely since his net contribution to the nation has declined and may even cease over time.[12]

BALANCE-OF-PAYMENTS EFFECTS

The impact of international business on a nation's balance of payments has long been a sensitive and controversial issue in the less developed countries, where foreign exchange is generally in chronic shortage and a persistent limitation on growth. Although Japan and most European nations have resolved the long-continued balance-of-payments crisis that followed World War II, periodic crises in the industrialized nations have provoked similar concerns but not as a steady diet. The exceptions

---

[12] Peter P. Gabriel, "The Investment in the LDC: Asset With a Fixed Maturity," *Columbia Journal of World Business,* Summer 1966, pp. 109–19.

among the industrialized countries have been, interestingly enough, the two principal investor countries—the United States and the United Kingdom—where the balance-of-payments effects of foreign investment have persisted for some time as a matter of national concern.

The relative abundance of statistical information on balance-of-payments transactions has led to a growing number of scholarly studies which have attempted to resolve controversy in this area. Still, considerable uncertainty prevails as to the complete and precise impact on either investor or host countries because neither the data nor the measuring techniques have been sufficiently comprehensive to trace through the total effects. Even if the methodological and data difficulties were surmounted, the ultimate conclusions would depend primarily on what assumptions are made to what would have happened if the foreign investment had not been made.

In many of the less developed countries, the prevailing view is that international business operations result in a net foreign exchange cost to the host country. The factual support for this belief comes from a simple comparison of annual net capital outflows from the investor countries, generally the United States, and net annual inflows of repatriated earnings. For example, over the 10 year period from 1960 through 1969, the net capital outflows from the United States to the less developed countries averaged about $650 million per year. Over the same period, U.S. companies returned to the United States as repatriated earnings an average of about $2,500 million per year. By including the foreign exchange payments of the subsidiaries to the parent company as royalties and fees, the outflow from the host countries would be increased significantly. From these data, the simple conclusion can be drawn that the less developed countries have been suffering a substantial net loss in foreign exchange from the operations of U.S. multinational enterprises in their countries.

This type of calculation, widely used and popularly accepted by opponents of foreign enterprise, is accurate as to the capital accounts but misleading as to the total balance-of-payments effect of multinational enterprises. Inflows in the form of new capital and outflows of repatriated earnings represent some of the impact. Outflows in the form of royalty fees and payments to headquarters for sharing company overhead are also important. But in a quantitative sense, the capital flows are generally overshadowed by the effects on the trade accounts—exports and imports.

A special study sponsored by an organization of American multinational companies dramatically reveals how the opposite conclusion can be supported, namely, that American multinational enterprises make a large and positive foreign exchange contribution to the Latin American countries by including the trade as well as the capital effects.[13] The study estimates that during the 1965–68 period, U.S. affiliates were responsible for annual foreign exchange earnings by host countries through exports of about $4.5 billion and foreign exchange savings through substitutions for imports averaging at least $4.8 billion, or an average annual total balance-of-payments contribution of $9.3 billion on trade accounts alone. Over the same period, the annual amount of new capital invested in Latin America averaged about $700 million. Repatriated earnings on the accumulated investments were at a level of about $1,440 million annually. Thus, the annual deficit in the capital account of $740 million annually was overshadowed by an annual surplus of $9.3 billion on the trade accounts. The study contains some debatable calculations such as valuing import substitution effects at local prices, whereby imported goods might be available at significantly lower prices. Yet, even with some downward revision in benefits, the net foreign exchange gains to the host countries would be sizeable if the assumption is reasonable that the expanded exports or the import savings would not have been achieved without the foreign enterprise.

If host countries are persuaded to give attention to the trade accounts in evaluating foreign exchange benefits and costs, they naturally begin to focus on the prices paid for import substitution production and whether multinational enterprises improve or make more difficult their possibilities for exporting. The automobile industry in Latin America is an example—probably at the extreme end of the spectrum—of the high cost in domestic resources countries have been paying for the prestige of having nationally produced automobiles and for saving foreign exchange. As a consequence of the uneconomic scale and fragmentation of production facilities, in 1967 a light truck, produced in Mexico with 63 percent local content, cost 1.6 times the imported equivalent. In Argentina, with 83 percent of the value of the finished vehicle produced locally, the same light truck ran 2.5 times import costs.[14] The import substitution example suggests that a complete appraisal of balance-of-payments effects may have to extend even beyond the trade accounts and include costs in local resources incurred in securing foreign exchange gains.

The role of the multinational enterprise in expanding export earnings may be either positive or negative, depending on the particular case. The multinational enterprise following a global strategy will parcel out its world markets to the various subsidiaries and attempt to supply

[13] Herbert K. May, *The Contributions of U.S. Private Investment to Latin America's Growth*—A Report for the Council of the Americas (New York: January 1970).

[14] Jack Baranson, *Automotive Industries in Developing Countries* (Baltimore: The Johns Hopkins Press, 1969), pp. 35–42.

its export demand from areas of lowest cost, or where excess capacity exists or where national pressures or incentives for exporting are most effective. Thus, the subsidiary in any specific country may have a better or a worse chance, but not a free chance, of competing for all export markets. As an independent local company, the same operation would have a free, but probably worse, chance of expanding exports. With its ties to other affiliates in the multinational enterprise system, a local subsidiary may bring to a country special export advantages because the system provides an easy conduit to sales in other countries. But many different possibilities exist and the conclusion will depend upon the specific case being considered. On the whole, the various studies available suggest that the multinational enterprise has been a means of expanding, rather than constraining, exports.[15]

Most certainly, foreign investments in raw materials industries are a major source of increased exports. But here again the evaluation of net foreign exchange benefits from international enterprises depends on whether these products would be produced and exported in the absence of foreign investment and at what price. Until recent years, it seems reasonably clear that many African, Middle Eastern, and Latin American countries would not have been able to supply the necessary capital, technology, and marketing skills from local sources so as to earn the large amounts of foreign exchange from their sales of petroleum and minerals. For those periods, the assumption that local production would not have taken place without foreign enterprise was most likely a realistic assumption. But more recently, particularly as a result of the technology transfers and the opportunity to accumulate capital that has followed from multinational business operations, a more reasonable assumption for many of these countries may be that local production and export can take place without foreign investment. Also, host countries may have alternatives in between these two polar positions, such as hiring foreign technology and management on service contracts rather than permitting direct foreign investment, which change the balance-of-payments effects. Service contracts will limit the foreign exchange costs in amount and over time. Direct investment requires a continuing outflow of repatriated profits.

Other questions that should be included in a comprehensive evaluation of balance-of-payments effects have to do with the pricing of goods for exports and the longer run effect of foreign investment on productivity and prices within the host country.[16] Will the multinational enterprise

---

[15] *Foreign Ownership and the Structure of Canadian Industry*—Report of the Task Force on the Structure of Canadian Industry (Ottawa: Queen's Printer, 1968), pp. 203–7.

[16] These subjects are explored in greater detail in "Chapter 5—National Economic Consequences," in Vernon's *Sovereignty at Bay*, pp. 151–71.

reduce a country's foreign exchange earnings by selling its goods to another unit in the multinational system at a price below the fair market value? Will foreign enterprise increase the efficiency of other producers within the host country over time and contribute to increased exports indirectly because export prices can be reduced? Still another effect might be that foreign enterprises indirectly raise imports as a result of increased incomes in the host country to which the foreign enterprise has contributed. Comprehensive studies that incorporate all of these elements are not available so that the issue of balance-of-payments effects on host countries still remains a frequently disputed conflict issue.

The most complete and technically sophisticated studies of balance-of-payments effects have been made in response to the controversy in investor countries over the impact of outbound foreign investment. Such studies have attempted to include the trade effects as well as the capital accounts, and they have considered the immediate as well as the long-run effects.[17] As in the case of host-country studies, whether the home countries have foreign exchange benefits or costs from the operations of multinational enterprises based in these countries is overwhelmingly influenced by the assumptions on alternatives. If an enterprise can effectively compete in foreign markets through exports from the home country, the establishment of foreign subsidiaries results in foreign exchange losses from export substitution. In the case of foreign production, the home country receives only that share of total profits that is repatriated. The magnitude of profit remissions is obviously minor, compared to total revenues.

If foreign production is for export back to the home country and substitutes for goods previously manufactured in the home country, there is a foreign exchange cost. If domestic producers have been losing the local market anyway to foreign producers, foreign production by a home country enterprise may result in a net benefit because there is no loss on the current account, and the repatriated profits are likely to more than compensate for the initial investment outflow on the capital account. Furthermore, in many cases the multinational enterprise raises some or all of its capital for foreign investment outside of the home country. When the analyst assumes that products sold in foreign markets will shortly be produced in a foreign location, either because a local or other foreign competitor will find such a market location advantageous or

[17] See W. B. Reddaway et al., *Effects of U.K. Direct Investment Overseas: Final Report* (London: Cambridge University Press, 1968); G. C. Hufbauer and F. M. Adler, *Overseas Manufacturing and the Balance of Payments* (Washington, D.C.: U.S. Treasury Department, 1968); Judd Polk, Irene W. Meister, and Lawrence A. Veit, *U.S. Production Abroad and the Balance of Payments* (New York: The Conference Board, 1966); *Implications of Multinational Firms for World Trade and Investment and for U.S. Trade and Labor* (Report to the Committee on Finance of the United States Senate, 93d Congress, 1st sess.) (Washington, D.C.: U.S. Government Printing Office, 1973).

because the country has established formidable quota or tariff barriers to force the establishment of local import substituting industries, the balance-of-payments effects on the investor country will be positive, but paltry, compared to the benefits on trade accounts to the host country.

An unfortunate feature of the controversy over balance-of-payments effects is that even if host and home countries enlarge the scope of their benefit-cost evaluations of the foreign exchange impact of multinational enterprises, and even if agreement can be reached on the alternatives against which specific projects or business operations should be measured, still another major aspect of the question remains that is only beginning to be considered. As will be discussed in Chapter 20—International Financial Management—multinational enterprises have become highly skilled in forecasting foreign exchange risk and in protecting their assets against losses when balance-of-payments difficulties cause a country to devalue. They reduce foreign exchange risks by using local borrowing instead of bringing in outside funds, by accelerating payments for goods and services outside the country, by advance repatriation of profits, and by a series of other actions and inactions. In countries where multinational operations are large, the prudent financial strategies of such enterprises can easily place a critical amount of pressure on either a home- or host-country currency when it appears to be weakening. As the share of international business activity controlled by sophisticated multinational enterprises continues to increase, it is a safe bet that the financial-management impact of such enterprises on a nation's balance of payments will begin to overshadow the long-term capital and trade-account impacts that currently are receiving almost exclusive attention.

Employment and Other Home-Country Effects

As home countries of multinational enterprises became increasingly aware that the private global interests of the enterprise can diverge from the public national interests of the nation, the three principal conflict areas on which they have focused attention have been balance of payments, sharing tax revenues,[18] and the broader issues of international politics and international relations. In time, other latent areas of potential conflicts have also begun to come to the fore. The mix of national interests which shape a government's actions varies with the changing concerns and influence of different groups within the country. At certain times and on certain issues, a specific region within the nation may

---

[18] For a discussion on tax conflict issues, see Michael G. Duerr, *Tax Allocations and International Business* (New York: The Conference Board, 1972); and *Economic Implications of Proposed Changes In the Taxation of U.S. Investments Abroad* (New York: National Foreign Trade Council, June 1972).

be a strong force in determining national interests. At other times and on other issues, the private goals of strong or well-organized business interests or labor unions may be dominant in defining the national interests.

Writing in 1968, on the interest of U.S. labor unions in the overseas expansion of American business, Professor Kindleberger made the following prescient observation:

> One must put the limited nature of the reaction of labor against capital exports down as something of a puzzle and in the future keep an eye on this possible source of support for those interests abroad which also oppose direct investment from the United States.[19]

The puzzle was solved in 1971, during a year of economic stagnation and increasing levels of unemployment, when the U.S. labor movement launched an attack on multinational enterprises for harming the national interest through exporting jobs.[20]

In response to labor union pressures, the U.S. government commissioned several studies to determine whether the spread of multinational business had reduced U.S. employment. However, a Tariff Commission study undertaken for the U.S. Senate concluded that the question could not be answered definitively because "both the analysis and the answer must depend on crucial assumptions" about the extent to which foreign markets would have been lost if foreign production facilities had not been established. Under a "pessimistic" set of assumptions, a net loss of 1.3 million U.S. jobs in manufacturing was identified. Under a so-called "realistic" set of assumptions, net employment in manufacturing increased by roughly a half million jobs.[21]

Another study commissioned by the U.S. Department of Commerce examined in depth nine actual foreign investment decisions distributed among nine manufacturing industries.[22] The industry fields of the case studies were food products, paper and allied products, chemicals, petroleum, rubber products, primary and fabricated metals, electrical machinery, nonelectrical machinery, and transportation equipment. Of the nine cases, four were projects in the less developed countries, two were in Canada, two in Europe, and one in Japan.

---

[19] Charles P. Kindleberger, *American Business Abroad* (New Haven: Yale University Press), p. 70.

[20] Industrial Union Department, AFL–CIO, "New Breed of International Cat," *Viewpoint* (Washington, D.C.: Summer 1971), pp. 10–15.

[21] *Implications of Multinational Firms for World Trade and Investment and for U.S. Trade and Labor,* pp. 6–7.

[22] Robert B. Stobaugh and Associates, *U.S. Multinational Enterprises and the U.S. Economy* (Boston, Mass.: Harvard Business School, January 1972).

The study concluded that although American firms have a preference for operating in the United States, in most cases of foreign investment they do not have the alternative of continuing to serve their relevant market from their U.S. plants. In each of the nine cases investigated, the researchers concluded that the companies were forced to invest to preserve their markets. The foreign investments, therefore, did not result in an export of jobs from the United States because the alternative of producing domestically did not exist or would not have existed within a relatively short period of time. On the positive side, the study concludes that "U.S. foreign direct investment provides jobs for production workers manufacturing components for further processing or assembling in foreign plants, goods for resale abroad or for sale on a commission basis that would otherwise not be sold abroad (so-called associated exports), and capital equipment for use in the foreign plants. Further jobs are provided for white-collar workers in the home office providing services for the foreign plants, technical personnel providing engineering and similar services, and research and development activities that could not be justified without the possibility of gaining income from foreign plants."[23]

As the Tariff Commission emphasized, the conclusions as to home-country employment effects of outbound investment depend on the assumptions as to alternatives. In many, if not most, cases of manufacturing operations the enterprise may actually be forced to establish foreign production facilities to defend its markets. In any event, multinational enterprises would tend to stress this view when forced to demonstrate their common interests with the home country. But in some cases, the foreign investment may be desirable from the standpoint of increasing profits, rather than necessary for avoiding losses. In such cases, the national interests of the home country might be better served by a trade-off of more local employment as against greater business profits. Most certainly, nine case studies will not resolve the controversy.

As usually happens when private interest groups try to make a strong case in support of their view, the labor unions have omitted some important employment considerations in their attack on multinational enterprise. The United States is both a home and a host country for multinational enterprise. As such, it receives employment benefits from non-U.S. international companies that are operating and have been expanding their operations within the United States.

To complete the discussion of home-country conflicts, the potential role of the multinational enterprise in frustrating domestic economic policies should be mentioned. It is the same issue faced by host countries. A nation may be attempting to reduce domestic inflation by reducing

---

[23] Ibid., p. 30.

the supply of money and credit. If there are no controls on short-term financial inflows, as has been true in the United States, multinational enterprises can supply their credit needs through foreign sources of financing, as was done through Euro-dollar borrowing in the late 1960s, and reduce the effectiveness of national economic policies.

Summary

International business operates across and within the boundaries of many discrete sovereign nation-states. The business firm has its private goals that it pursues within a geographical area of its own choosing, which include the sovereign domains of several or many national governments. Governments have their public purposes, some of which are in harmony with and others which may run counter to the private global goals of international corporations. Where conflicts arise, governments will try to use their sovereign power to direct activities toward their national interests. The multinational enterprise will try to thread its way through the multiple and often conflicting claims of many governments with the minimum sacrifice to its goals.

This matrix of common interests and potential conflicts in goals makes for a love-hate relationship between international corporations and nation-states. The countries love the benefits but hate the costs and the national tensions that accompany the benefits. Furthermore, the benefits may be greatest at the time of the wedding and steadily decline thereafter. On balance, the trade-off to both host and home countries appears to have been generally in favor of the benefits, as evidenced by the continued rapid expansion of international business activities. Nevertheless, national governments have long used controls over traditional international transfers of goods, money flows, and persons to increase their share of national benefits from such international transactions. Such controls are now being extended by nations to increase a nation's share of the global benefits generated by multinational enterprises and to reduce the negative effects, such as the threat of economic domination and challenges to economic and political autonomy.

The need to identify its common interests and potential areas of conflict with many different nation-states is a continuing and never-ending operating requirement for international enterprises. The diversity and dynamic nature of these relations does not permit easy generalizations, nor is a general understanding adequate background for the international manager. He must deal with specific business situations in relation to specific national environments. A specific type of business activity may face one kind of response in *Country A* and a completely different type of response in *Country B* and *Country C*. The only certainties are that the situation will constantly be changing and that, in order to maintain its tenure, the international enterprise must be ever ready to justify to a nation-state not only its entry but its continued presence.

EXERCISES AND DISCUSSION QUESTIONS

1. "Prime Minister Pierre Trudeau for the first time said publicly the Canadian government plans to set up an agency to screen foreign investment in Canada." (*Wall Street Journal*, 10 January 1972).

   As an experienced international manager and expert in international business, you have been hired to advise the Canadian government on the implementation of this decision. Prime Minister Trudeau's only advice is that you be realistic and take into consideration the attitudes, motivations, and likely reactions of multinational enterprises. What specific guidelines or criteria do you recommend that Canada adopt to screen inbound investment? What are the reasons for your recommendations?

2. "To control the export of American technology, much of which was financed by public funds and the export of American jobs, the government should regulate, supervise, and curb the export of technology and the substantial outflows of American capital for the investments of U.S. companies in foreign operations." Would you agree or disagree with this statement?

3. "It is characteristic of direct-investment projects that their first order benefits are greatest, certainly most spectacular, in the initial stages of the undertaking. On the other hand, the explicit costs of the foreign investment to the host economy generally behave in an opposite fashion." Explain what the writer meant by this statement and evaluate its validity.

4. Under what circumstances can an acquisition of an existing domestic business operation by a foreign multinational enterprise be justified as contributing national benefits to a country? Under what circumstances would it be difficult to justify an acquisition?

8

NATIONAL POLICIES OVER INTERNATIONAL TRANSFERS

NATION-STATES HAVE FOLLOWED several separate but interrelated paths in their desire to protect national interests and increase national benefits from international business relations. The traditional path since the rise of the nation-states has been to control or stimulate the international transfer of goods. Transfer policies have been extended to include transfers of money, personnel, technology, and legal rights across national boundaries. A second path has been to participate in inter-governmental agreements and multinational agencies that endeavor to shape certain dimensions of the international business environment. Most recently, nations have begun to develop policies and programs specifically directed toward multinational business operations.

The business firm with international activities that are principally importing and exporting will be most affected by national policies over international transfers. The multinational enterprise has to consider national policies over both transfers and multinational business activities in making investment decisions and in conducting its operations. For its guidance the most convenient approach might be to focus on the various dimensions of multinational operations such as the investment decision, marketing, and so forth, and relate the various national influences to each of the phases of international management they affect. This is the approach in Part V. But at this stage, the focus is on understanding what nations have in mind.

The policy making of most nation-states has not yet evolved to the point of considering as interrelated issues their policies toward transfers, inter-governmental agreements and multinational activities, and foreign investment. Much national policy making is still based on a concept of international trade being the dominant form of inter-nation business activity. Consequently, we will consider separately the activities of national governments in each of these categories, even though such a division has become obsolete, and even though government policy making as related to international business is almost certain to become integrated over time. Increasingly nations are becoming aware that they are not achieving their intended results by developing national policies for the international transfer of resources separately from those for guiding international business operations.

The concept of international transfers as used in international business is broad and comprehensive. It includes the physical transfer of goods through importing and exporting. It includes financial flows in the form of direct-investment capital, portfolio investments, profit repatriation, and other money flows induced by international business operations; the transfer of personnel either in support of business activities or directly as a form of international business, that is, tourism; the transfer of technology across national boundaries through licensing and technical-assistance agreements; and the transfer of legal rights such as patent protection or governmental concessions to exploit certain natural resources. The international businessman must be aware of international transfers in such a broad sense because his global operations are likely to be influenced across the full range of transfer activities.

NATIONAL MOTIVATIONS FOR INFLUENCING INTERNATIONAL TRANSFERS

Nation-states attempt to influence international transfers in order to achieve national goals of an economic, political, social, or national-security nature. Generally, national motivations are broadly based and extend far beyond the issues directly related to international business.

Economic Goals

Revenue. Some nations rely upon international transfers as a major source of government revenue. They secure revenue through government trading monopolies, through tariffs, and through exchange controls. Trading monopolies which generate significant amounts of government revenues may exist for either the import or export of specific commodities. Italy and France, for example, have a complete government monopoly over the import of tobacco. Ghana had a state trading agency that monopolizes the export of cocoa beans and provides an important source of government revenue.

Many tariffs were originally imposed primarily for revenue purposes, and some countries still rely on tariffs as the principal source of government revenue. From a practical point of view, governments have found the administrative problem of collecting tariffs much easier than that of collecting income or sales taxes because the import and export of goods is usually concentrated at a relatively small number of locations such as ports. A tariff imposed entirely for revenue purposes, however, would be applied to different products and have different rates from that of a protective tariff. Tariff levels must be moderate, for a tariff which is too high may keep goods from entering or leaving a country or encourage smuggling and evasion and yield no revenue.

Still another way for governments to use international transfers as a source of revenue is through exchange controls. In Brazil, for example, the government appropriates part of the foreign exchange earned from coffee exports. The coffee exporter is required to turn over his foreign exchange to the government and receives payment in local currency at a special rate below the free market rate.

Protectionism.   The most pervasive motivation for national controls over transfers comes under the heading of protectionism. Since the end of World War II, most nations have moved away from protectionism toward freer trade. But in certain fields, national governments continue to be strongly motivated by this goal. In fact, the posture of most nations is contradictory. At a general and theoretical level, they embrace the free trade ideology and its virtues. Yet in many specific instances they impose and implement protectionist measures. In terms of economic goals the contradiction can be explained by the theoretical shortcomings of the free trade ideology. As has already been noted, free trade may maximize on a worldwide basis the levels of output achieved from a given set of resources. But free trade policies provide no guarantee that any one nation will get what it considers to be its fair share of the gains.

The arguments for and against protection are of sufficient importance to be treated separately below. They involve national security and domestic political considerations as well as economic issues. From the economic side the strongest domestic pressures for protection against foreign competition arise where established economic activities become threatened by new competitive forces. Two recent examples in the United States are the steel and textile industries. Both industries employ a large number of workers and are major contributors to national output. As imports have increasingly threatened the position of these industries in domestic markets, the representatives of both industry and the labor unions have pressed for tariffs and other nontariff restrictions to protect the industries against "low wage" foreign industries.

Development Goals.   Tariffs, quotas, and other restrictions on imports may be adopted to implement economic-development goals and to encourage the establishment of new economic activities. Here we have

the venerable infant industry argument which is directed toward changing the structure of a nation's economy and accelerating economic
growth. The argument is that late-comer countries must provide a period
of protection to infant industries for the time-consuming learning process
and for expanding to an efficient scale of production. It assumes that
new industries have a potential for becoming economically viable without protection after the learning period and after reaching a feasible
scale of operations. To encourage such infant industries, nations ban
or restrict imports through tariffs, foreign exchange controls, import
quotas, and similar measures. It is interesting to note that, in his Report
on Manufactures submitted in 1791 to the U.S. House of Representatives, Alexander Hamilton elaborated most persuasively the infant industry argument as the central justification for U.S. policies to encourage
manufacturing.[1]

Development goals may be the justification for governmental actions
that provide special incentives for foreign direct investment and special
tax or foreign exchange incentives to encourage exports. In other situations and during different time periods, development goals may also
be the reason for removing tariffs and moving toward free trade policies
which are expected to stimulate greater efficiency and higher levels of
output from domestic industry.

Balance of Payments.   Within the category of economic goals, the
entire range of issues related to balance-of-payments equilibrium should
be included along with the protection of existing economic activity and
the encouragement of new types of economic activity. As discussed in
Chapter 4, nations are constantly under pressure to achieve equilibrium
in their international transactions and to maintain relatively stable exchange rates. Controls over financial flows and international transfers
of goods and services are frequently adopted on a temporary or indefinite
basis to assist in the resolution of balance-of-payments problems.

Domestic Policies.   Still another economic motivation for controlling
international transfers is to implement high-priority domestic policies.
For example, during a period when strong inflationary pressures are
operating in an economy, a nation may want to control the inflow of
foreign funds through the banking system. During 1969, the United
States was attempting to tighten domestic credit conditions. Commercial
banks, however, were increasing the availability of loanable funds
through borrowing in the Euro-dollar market and thereby weakening
the impact of governmental policies. Thus, in order to implement its
domestic monetary policy, the U.S. government felt it necessary to impose restraints on Euro-dollar transfers.

The desire to protect domestic workers from foreign competition can

---

[1] See Alexander Hamilton, *Papers on Public Credit, Commerce, and Finance,*
ed. Samuel McKee, Jr. (New York: Columbia University Press, 1934), pp. 204–5.

also be a reason for controlling international transfers, particularly through immigration policies and constraints over the movement of people from one nation to another. Other motivations such as political and security considerations may also shape immigration policies. A major U.S. objective for many years has been to protect American workers from the undercutting influence of uncontrolled influxes of workers from less prosperous areas who might be willing to work for less money.

In summary, a nation's economic motivations for using either controls or incentives to influence international transfers may be protection of existing economic activities within the country, encouragement of new types of domestic expansion, restoration of equilibrium in a nation's balance of payments, the use of international transfers as a source of revenue, and the implementation of broad, domestic economic policies. The principal control tools have been tariffs, nontariff restrictions, and capital and foreign exchange controls. The principal incentive tools have been subsidies, special tax provisions, risk insurance, government guarantees, and technical assistance. The tools change over time as new devices are conceived.

Political Goals

Political goals may be the justification for controls or incentives over the transfer of goods, technology, and people. For example, the United States imposed controls for a long period of time over East–West trade, that is, trade with the Soviet-bloc countries. In some cases, trade was completely forbidden with countries like Cuba and Mainland China, with whom the United States was not enjoying friendly relations, on the grounds that trade helps potential enemies to be stronger and eventually works to the political disadvantage of the United States.

Politically motivated national policies have also been adopted to give trade preferences to selected nations, such as the trade preference arrangement that prevailed among the British Commonwealth group of nations. The United States has a quota system which regulates sugar imports into the American market. Although the system had its genesis in the desire to protect domestic beet-sugar producers from the competition of lower cost cane sugar produced in tropical countries, the allocation of import quotas among exporting countries has been based on political considerations. Cuba was the largest seller in the United States under the quota system until Castro came to power in 1959. The subsequent deterioration of political relations with the United States caused Cuba's sugar quota to be suspended.

The Arab countries have attempted to impose transfer constraints on foreign firms that do business with Israel. Mainland China has barred international trade with companies that deal with Taiwan. The United

States created special trading preferences for the Philippines after that country emerged from 50 years of colonial status to become an independent nation. France maintained special relationships with its former colonies after the colonies secured independence. These special concessions have since been assumed by the European Common Market countries as a group.

National policies over international transfers have long been used to reward political friends and to oppose political enemies. To be sure, national controls or special incentives may have highly significant economic effects. Yet in many cases, political considerations are the dominant motivation.

Health Protection

Nations frequently restrict the import of certain commodities, generally agricultural or animal products, to protect the health of their citizens. Such restrictions which attempt to keep out agricultural pests and diseases may be temporary or permanent and generally are applied to commodities from specific infected areas. From time to time, beef products from Argentina could not be imported into the United States because of the danger of spreading hoof-and-mouth disease. A more recent case has been restrictions on the sale in the United States of Peruvian fish-meal products for human consumption. However, sanitary regulations are sometimes used, it is charged, to limit competition rather than to protect against disease.

National Security

National policies to influence international transfers are frequently motivated by national security or military preparedness considerations. Some policies are intended to increase a nation's military strength and to limit the potential military strength of unfriendly nations. As in the case of sanitary regulation, special-interest groups in a country have used national-security arguments to limit competition rather than to achieve sound national-security goals. Often there is no general agreement in a country as to what are valid national-security considerations.

With the ascendancy of nuclear arms on the world military scene, control over nuclear raw materials, such as uranium and thorium, and control over nuclear technology have become key national-security issues. As a result, national policies have emerged for controlling international transfers in nuclear raw materials and technology which are guided by national-security criteria rather than normal commercial business considerations. The fact that nuclear technology has peaceful as well as military uses and that a vast commercial industry in nuclear electric power plants has developed means that special national-security constraints and government participation in the sale of nuclear power equipment has become a part of the civilian business scene.[2] The national interest is to maximize the commercial benefits to a country and, at the same time, to limit the possibility that nuclear power equipment and technology can be used for unfriendly military purposes.

Nuclear power is a new but major aspect of national-security constraints. The more traditional manifestations have been to protect high-cost domestic industries such as in the minerals and petroleum field so that supplies of critical materials are more likely to be domestically available in the case of war. Another type of national policy has been to build up stockpiles of critical materials, frequently through direct purchasing of imports by the government. As a deviation from national defense considerations, such stockpiles have been used to keep domestic prices of imported materials down through government sales from the stockpiles.

At times, bitter controversies arise between different interest groups in a nation as to what kind of protection is justified on national security grounds and as to the best way of achieving national security. For example, the United States established quota restrictions on foreign petroleum imports with the justification that the high cost domestic petroleum industry should be kept operating in the event of a national emergency. The result is that prices to the consumer are significantly higher than they would be if lower cost foreign petroleum could be freely imported. The recipients of quotas for low-price imports that can be sold at relatively high supported domestic prices get a windfall profit, as do domestic producers.

Opponents of many specific controls over international transfers argue that the national-security policies on which these controls are based assume an obsolete type of warfare. In a nuclear war, they say, victories or defeats will be decided quickly, and the availability of petroleum after the initiation of such warfare will no longer be of critical importance. Another argument against protection is that by allowing more imports, domestic resources will be conserved for national defense emergencies rather than rapidly consumed.

THE PROS AND CONS OF PROTECTIONISM

Protectionism is a mildly pejorative label attached to national policies that shelter certain domestic activities from foreign competition by pre-

---

[2] See Lee C. Nehrt, *International Marketing of Nuclear Power Plants* (Bloomington, Indiana: Indiana University Press, 1966).

venting imports in these fields or making them excessively expensive. Protection benefits directly the domestic producers engaged in such activities who generally attempt to identify their private gains as contributing to the national interests. Such national interests may be infant-industry protection, national security, the need to maintain domestic employment and income and reduce foreign exchange outflows by controlling import competition from goods produced by low-wage labor in foreign countries, and the desirability of diversifying the domestic economy to improve economic stability and stimulate growth. Normally, domestic pressures for protection are resolved by political considerations and in favor of the domestic parties with the most political muscle. Yet, the political debate invariably revolves around economic arguments, some of which have qualified validity while others are highly questionable from the standpoint of national interests.[3]

Protectionist measures generally favor one group in a country and at the same time have a negative impact on other sectors of the economy. Therefore, nations have to evaluate the trade-offs involved in protectionist policies and determine the net benefits or costs to the country. If the American steel industry, for example, is given protection against foreign steel imports and domestic prices remain higher than they might otherwise be, the steel companies and the workers in the industry may directly benefit. The first-round effects may result in foreign exchange savings to the United States. On the cost side, other U.S. industries that use steel to produce machinery for export are certain to become less competitive in foreign markets. Their profits, their workers, and their foreign exchange earnings for the country are likely to suffer. Domestic consumers of steel products will have to pay higher prices and, in effect, subsidize the protected industry. Furthermore, foreign countries are likely to retaliate with their own protectionist measures, which could reduce exports, profits, and employment in other U.S. industries. Both the positive and negative effects will have different weights depending upon the economic situation of the country. Even where the net economic impact is negative, a nation may be willing to pay this price to satisfy long-run or noneconomic goals.

The infant-industry argument for protection can be a valid argument, particularly in the less developed countries, if the industry being protected has realistic possibilities of maturing into an adult that no longer requires protection. This justification has been used, however, for initiating types of business activities that are more likely to remain infants and require what amounts to a permanent subsidy. National security can also be a reasonable justification for protection and worth the cost

---

[3] For a comprehensive discussion of the arguments for protection, see Franklin R. Root, Roland L. Kramer, and Maurice Y. d'Arlin, *International Trade and Finance,* 2nd ed. (Cincinnati: South-Western Publishing Co., 1966), pp. 298–316.

to a country if the national-security goals to be served are consistent with a sound, modern security strategy. Likewise, protectionist measures which encourage the diversification of the domestic economy may provide substantial long-term gains to a country that more than offset short-term costs.

Most of the other arguments for protection are questionable or invalid from an economic standpoint, even though they may have great emotional appeal that garners strong political support. Most common among these is the highly plausible but generally fallacious cheap-labor argument, which both industry and labor use to demand protection against "unfair" competition from low-wage workers in foreign countries. The fundamental shortcoming of the argument is the confusion of wage rates with unit labor costs. Labor costs depend on labor productivity as well as wage rates. Productivity depends in turn on the other factors of production such as capital, management, and technology that are combined with labor in the process of producing goods and services. Assuming that all other factors are constant, low wages will mean lower labor costs. But in reality all other factors, including the skills of the workers themselves, are not constant, and high-wage industries in one country can, in fact, produce goods with lower labor costs per unit of output than competing industries in countries where wage costs are low.

The low-wage argument for protection also assumes that the only important cost involved in the ability of businesses to be competitive is the cost of labor. Labor costs vary greatly from industry to industry as a share of total costs per unit of output. In some industries such as shoe manufacturing or textile manufacturing, labor costs will be relatively important. In other highly capital-intensive industries such as petroleum refining or chemicals, labor costs will be a small share of total costs. Therefore, even if labor costs (not wage rates) are lower in certain countries, the competitive advantage in terms of total costs of a product or service may be minor compared to variations among nations in other production or distribution costs. The cost of electric power, for example, is much more significant in the production of aluminum than labor costs. One nation may have comparative advantages in large supplies of low-cost labor. Other nations may have their comparative advantages in low costs of raw materials, transportation, borrowing of money, or electric power. The relative importance of the cost components depends on an industry's production function. Labor costs are not the only, nor the most important, competitive consideration for all types of economic activity.

Some proponents of protection broaden the low-wage argument to a general plea for equalizing all production costs between foreign and domestic producers on the grounds of "fair competition." Such a policy would violate whatever validity there is in the argument that a country should specialize in those fields in which it has a comparative advantage due to differences in resource endowments and trade with others. It would be just as valid or invalid for Japanese steel manufacturers to ask for protection against the lower prices that U.S. firms are able to pay for coking coal because the United States happens to have favorable resource endowments in these fields. In fact, if the arguments for protection to equalize differences in costs of production were accepted, there would be no basis whatever for trade taking place.

RECENT TRENDS IN CONTROLLING THE TRANSFER OF GOODS

Commercial or trade policies are the conventional labels for national efforts to influence the import and export of goods across national boundaries. As previously noted, such policies have usually assumed that international trade is still predominantly in the traditional form of transfers of goods between independent buyers and sellers in different countries. The structural change underway in the international economy whereby a large and growing share of international transfers of goods are between units of the same multinational enterprise has thus far been only dimly recognized by government policy makers.

In the market economy countries of the world, nations have long used tariffs as a principal governmental tool for influencing the international transfer of goods. During the depression years of the 1930s, the world trend was away from liberal multilateral trade policies and toward autarky, or national policies of self-sufficiency. High national tariffs were the rule. But, beginning in the mid-1930s and particularly since the end of World War II, there have been steady and vigorous moves toward liberalizing international trade, and the extent and levels of tariff restraints on international transfers have been reduced dramatically. Yet, tariffs still represent an important restraint, though not a bar, to international transfers. They are difficult to compare among nations because they have become extremely detailed and complex after years of adaptation to the pressures of special interests. When sufficiently high, tariffs after a period can become an effective bar to imports.

With the steady worldwide reduction in tariffs, attention has shifted to the wide range of nontariff restrictions on the international transfer of goods. Such controls include quantitative restrictions, voluntary and involuntary quotas, licensing of imports and exports frequently as a counterpart to balance-of-payments controls, policies which give preference to domestic suppliers such as the "Buy American" policies for governmental purchases, discriminatory taxes, and special restrictions such as requiring that certain exports or imports be transported on ships of the specific nation.[4] In certain fields the noncommunist countries also impose state monopolies on international trade.

Nations would like to impose such restrictions on trade as would be likely to achieve their national interests, but in practice they have to be constrained to some extent by the effects of such restrictions on others. Unilateral actions harmful to the interests of other countries may provoke retaliation that can more than cancel out the expected national gains. As a result, the kinds of intergovernmental agreements discussed in Chapter 5 have set limits on the freedom of action by individual nations.

In the post–World War II period, the rich countries made major progress in dismantling tariff barriers and import quotas against each other. Negotiations to this end were carried out under the auspices of GATT following a general principle of reciprocity. Each major trading country aimed to yield no more in concessions than it gained from others. Under the most-favored-nation principle (MFN), benefits granted to any one country were extended automatically to all other countries. The series of postwar multilateral negotiations culminated in the Kennedy round of trade negotiations completed in June 1967. That round brought about general cuts in tariffs averaging nearly one third. The steady and sizeable postwar decline in tariffs is illustrated by the trend of U.S. tariff levels shown in Table 8.1.

TABLE 8.1

General Level of U.S. Tariffs: Imports for Consumption

		Ratio of Duties to Values	
Tariff Acts	*Yearly Average*	*Dutiable Imports (percent)*	*Total Imports (percent)*
Hawley Smoot Tariff (1930)	1930–33	53	18
Trade Agreements Act (1934).	1936–40	38	15
Extensions of Trade Agreements Act	1946–50	16	7
Extensions of Trade Agreements Act	1956–60	11	7
Trade Expansion Act (1962)	1966–70	11	7

Source: *Statistical Abstract of the United States, 1971*, table 1251 (Washington, D.C.: U.S. Government Printing Office, 1972).

The less developed countries did not participate actively in the postwar movement to negotiate tariff reductions. With small markets, they

[4] See Harry G. Johnson, *Economic Policies Toward Less Developed Countries* (New York: Praeger Publishers, Inc., 1967), pp. 104–7; Robert E. Baldwin, *Nontariff Distortions of International Trade* (Washington, D.C.: The Brookings Institution, 1970).

have little to offer in reciprocal negotiations as concessions of interest to others. They are rarely staffed well enough to sustain tough, persistent, sophisticated negotiation positions against the developed countries. Also products of special interest to the less developed countries often get left aside when tariffs are cut more generally.[5] As a result, the LDCs have come to focus more and more on securing preferential tariff arrangements with the advanced countries on a nonreciprocal basis working through UNCTAD.

Another inter-governmental constraint on national policies has been the postwar expansion of regional trading areas. The formation of the European Economic Community, the Latin American Free Trade Area, and other regional integration movements was stimulated by the desire of nations to increase their national benefits from international trade. By participating in such inter-governmental arrangements, nations have given up in varying degrees their authority to exert controls over the transfer of goods within the trading area of which they are a part.

In evaluating a country's degree of tariff protection, average tariff levels are not very informative. Tariff levels vary tremendously from product to product. Furthermore, nominal tariffs as they appear in government tariff schedules, that is, the rate of duty expressed as a percentage of the total value of the imported product, are not really a measure of the full effect of the tariff. If import protection on the raw material is zero, but 10 percent on a processed form of the product, the effective protection against imports of the product in processed form is much higher than the apparent, or nominal rate of 10 percent.

The distinction between nominal and effective rates can be illustrated by the case of textiles. Fabric may enter at a duty of 20 percent and yarn at 10 percent. Suppose that $250 of yarn is required to produce $500 of fabric. The duty on $250 of yarn will be $25. The value added to the yarn by weaving would be $250. If the fabric were imported at 20 percent duty, the total duty on $500 worth of fabric would be $100. Thus, the difference in the duty between the yarn and the fabric, or the duty on the value added by weaving ($250), is $75. The net duty difference as a percentage of value added is the effective, as opposed to the nominal, tariff rate. This gives an effective rate of 30 percent, as compared with the nominal rate of 20 percent.

Generalizations about tariff patterns must necessarily be subject to many exceptions. Nevertheless, the general pattern seems to be as follows:

1. Low tariffs on raw materials which a country does not produce—to encourage domestic processing industries; high tariffs on semifinished

---

[5] Harold B. Malmgrem, *Trade for Development* (Washington, D.C.: Overseas Development Council, 1971), pp. 15–17.

products easily produced in many countries—to protect local workers.
2. High tariffs on agricultural products and minerals where local production is noncompetitive with imports and does not completely fill local demand.
3. Low tariffs on products of advanced technology where producing nations have been successful in reciprocal bargaining and where local production may not be feasible.

Since tariffs normally escalate with each stage of manufacture, the effective rate on value added often exceeds the nominal rate by a substantial amount.

The ideal world for the global enterprises would be one free of tariffs and other controls over the international transfer of goods. In such a world, global operations could be organized on the basis of economic considerations to achieve the potential economic efficiencies of multinational operations. For this reason, managers of multinational enterprises are generally less protectionist than are managers of domestic enterprises. But within the multinational enterprise, the vested interest of different groups may come into conflict. Reductions in tariffs on finished goods or on components, as in the case of sewing machines or radio and television components imported into the United States, may permit a firm to improve its competitive position in a national market through overseas sourcing. At the same time, workers for the multinational enterprise are likely to oppose tariff reductions that might eliminate their jobs.

Export Promotion

Nations adopt programs for encouraging as well as restricting the international transfer of goods. The less developed countries in particular have become greatly concerned about the need to earn foreign exchange through expanding exports. And the United States itself, with a steadily disappearing balance-of-trade surplus in the late 1960s, established programs for export promotion.

Governmental action to promote exports may even include assuming responsibility for normal business functions, such as sponsoring market research on foreign sales opportunities and establishing trade promotion offices in foreign countries. At the more traditional level, the government may offer tax incentives such as exemption from certain domestic taxes if goods are exported, direct bonus payments or subsidies through administration of exchange controls, special credit for exporters, and insurance programs under which the government assumes varying degrees of political and commercial risk.

The United States has its Export-Import Bank which promotes U.S. exports by providing medium- and long-term financing to foreign buyers. Under the Webb-Pomerene Act of 1918, American companies are exempted from the prohibitions of the Sherman Antitrust Act when they join with other companies, who might be competitors, in an export trade association. Another means of promoting exports is the special tax arrangement offered since 1942 of a 14-point reduction in the U.S. tax due by companies that can qualify as a Western Hemisphere Trade Corporation. To qualify for this benefit, an American company must do all of its business in the Western Hemisphere, derive 95 percent of its gross income from the active conduct of trade or a business, and receive 95 percent of its gross income from sources outside of the United States.

Since 1962, export credit insurance has been offered to U.S. exporters by the private Foreign Credit Insurance Association, in partnership with the Export-Import Bank. As incentives for expanding exports, the association offers low-cost blanket insurance policies covering both commercial and political risks in selling abroad on credit. Most big exporting countries have a similar institution which provides exporters with cover against risk. Britain, for example, has its Export Credit Guarantee Department which performs this function. The most recent innovation in this field by the United States was the Domestic International Sales Corporation (DISC), permitted under the Revenue Act of 1971, which grants unlimited deferral on export profits to this new type of corporation. To qualify as a DISC, a domestic corporation must derive 95 percent or more of its gross receipts from exports and related income and 95 percent or more of its assets must be used in export activities.

The issue of unfair competition frequently arises in connection with incentive programs for encouraging exports. Importing countries may interpret these incentives as encouraging dumping or unfair competition. From the standpoint of international business, such incentive programs may be significant, but they may also create potentials for conflicts with importing countries.

INTERNATIONAL TRANSFERS OF MONEY

Nations influence the international transfers of money through foreign exchange controls, capital controls, policies of tied aid, through supervision of the foreign operations of domestic banks and other financial institutions, and through taxation. Many economists and some businessmen argue against any kind of national control over money transfers. They prefer freely fluctuating exchange rates determined by the market forces, which will provide automatic adjustments for balance-of-payments disequilibrium. The principal merit of a hands-off policy to those who advocate it is the greater likelihood of achieving necessary adjustments. In addition, it is argued that many misallocations of resources through exchange controls can be avoided. In recent years, the preference of central bankers and government officials for a system of stable exchange rates has prevailed, and the normal pattern has been for nations to make frequent and extensive use of controls over financial transfers.[6]

Foreign Exchange Controls. As mentioned in Chapter 4 in the discussion of adjustment measures for payments imbalances, nations frequently resort to direct controls over all foreign exchange transactions. In effect, with such controls a nation's currency becomes inconvertible, that is, it is not freely transferable into another national currency. Persons are not permitted to buy or sell foreign currencies freely. There can be degrees of inconvertibility depending on the nature and extent of the exchange controls. The government normally requires that all receipts of foreign exchange be turned over to the central bank or some other designated government agency. Exchange can be bought only for specified purposes and in amounts determined by the government. A license is therefore required for the purchase of foreign exchange. Exchange controls can be limited to import and export transactions, or they can also cover transfer payments such as profit remittances and capital flows.

Under a system of exchange controls, the government must decide on priorities and quotas for the allocation of foreign exchange. Thus exchange-control systems can become extremely complex and even arbitrary. Above all, effective functioning of a control system requires an accurate ability to anticipate the future supplies of foreign exchange likely to be available. Some countries establish overall quotas in several categories with multiple exchange rates which permit the import of high-priority goods at the lowest rates and imports of goods determined to be nonessential or luxury goods at prohibitive rates. In some exchange-control systems, quotas of foreign exchange have been allocated to the different categories and then auctioned off to the highest bidders.

The overall objective is to reduce the demand for foreign exchange through increasing the cost to foreign exchange buyers. Higher rates are one technique. Others may include requiring importers to make substantial deposits when they secure importing licenses. The deposit requirement ties up funds which might otherwise be earning a return and thereby increases the cost of importing. Invariably, exchange controls require some form of import licensing.

Effective functioning of an exchange-control system requires not only that all foreign exchange purchases be regulated but that all foreign exchange receipts by individuals, businesses, and government agencies

---

[6] The International Monetary Fund's *Annual Report on Exchange Restrictions* describes current policies and practices of each member country of IMF and is a valuable reference for international managers.

be captured and directed into a central pool. Consequently, an export licensing and policing system is generally designed to assure that foreign exchange receipts are turned over to the government in exchange for local currency at fixed rates. At times, a so-called free market is allowed to operate alongside exchange controls, but only limited types of transactions are legal in the free market. Frequently, exporters may be allowed to keep a share of their export earnings, which they can sell at the higher rates prevailing in the free market. Generally, the free market is used by tourists for securing local currency but at rates higher than would prevail without exchange controls.

One of the major problems constantly confronting exchange-control authorities is the black market, where exchange is bought and sold in disregard of official regulations. Depending upon the severity of the exchange controls and the administrative capacity of government agencies, black-market activities in foreign exchange and import licenses can be extensive. In the case of one less developed country, the black market became so highly developed that future sales of import licenses were even being quoted. When the official rates are far below what would be a free rate, the opportunities for earning illicit profits are great, and extensive graft and corruption are almost certain to emerge.

Exchange controls may have great advantages in buying time while basic adjustments are undertaken to secure balance-of-payments equilibria or to implement development programs. However, the more serious the imbalance between supply and demand for local currency, the more difficult such a system is to administer effectively. Under all circumstances a government needs a high degree of knowledge concerning a nation's economy and its future prospects along with an honest and highly skilled administrative capacity. If exchange controls are substituted for other difficult but essential policies necessary for correcting underlying imbalances or are maintained over long periods of time, graft, corruption, and illicit operations are inevitable with their detrimental influence on levels of morality and the effectiveness of the controls.

From the standpoint of the international businessman, exchange controls will complicate and burden international money transfers by adding to costs. They can be beneficial, however, to certain types of operations when used to encourage investment inflows or exports of particular goods. The financial management problem is increased in some ways but may be reduced in other ways, if, for example, such controls avoid major devaluations. The extent to which they hinder or help business operations thus has to be evaluated for specific situations.

Tied Loans and Aid. A relatively new but significant form of national policy for influencing money transfers has emerged in recent years in the form of so-called tied loans, or tied aid. Under this system, a country making foreign loans or granting foreign aid, requires that the funds be restricted to purchasing goods or services from the granting country. In theory, at least, the increased supply of a country's currency that is made available to foreigners will not weaken the country's balance-of-payments position because the outflow of funds is offset by a comparable sale of goods or services.

The United States, in particular, has adopted an extensive policy of tying loans and direct military and development-assistance grants. The objective has been to try to implement its programs of foreign assistance while at the same time minimizing or neutralizing the effect of such programs on its national goal of reducing its balance-of-payments deficit. In trying to implement two national goals which can be and have been in conflict in the case of the United States, the country has tried to have its cake and eat it at the same time.

Tied aid is not always effective from a balance-of-payments standpoint, and it can at the same time defeat the development-aid objectives. A nation receiving tied loans or aid may be able to shift its foreign purchases so that the granting country may sell the equivalent of its loan or grant in goods or services but lose other foreign exchange earning possibilities that normally were available to the granting country.

The disadvantage in terms of development objectives is that the aid or loans may force the receiving country to make purchases where costs are not lowest and thereby create less than optimum cost conditions for new facilities. In addition, the tying of aid or loans, unless by pure chance the granting country is the lowest cost source of supply, can generate a great deal of dissatisfaction and bad will on the part of the recipient.

Capital Controls.   Flows of short-term and long-term capital can be influenced by traditional exchange-control programs, but it is more common for nations to adopt special capital controls. Like foreign exchange controls, capital controls normally require licensing by governmental authorities for international transfers of funds.

Most countries have had some form of capital controls since the end of World War II. The motivation for capital controls has most frequently been to support policies for maintaining equilibrium in a nation's balance of payments. Capital controls have also been used as a means of implementing development priorities, for influencing the patterns and size of international business operations in a country (this will be discussed further in Chapter 9), and to support through incentives or to implement through embargos varied foreign policy objectives.

From the end of World War II until the late 1960s, the United States had a minimum of controls over capital flows. The only formal direct controls were on capital flows to selected communist countries considered to be unfriendly. Otherwise, either residents or nonresidents were free to transfer funds in or out of the United States. In fact, the United

States served as a capital market for many foreign enterprises and governments, and the funds secured through the sales of securities were freely transferred for use out of the country. In the mid-1960s, the United States began to become concerned about its persistent balance-of-payments deficit and initiated statutory and voluntary controls. An interest equalization tax was established in 1964 of up to 15 percent payable by American purchasers of foreign securities issued in the United States by most borrowers from developed countries in order to reduce the outflow of U.S. capital. Later, voluntary and then statutory restraints on outflows of direct private investment were adopted,[7] and additional restrictions were placed on the foreign financial activities of U.S. banks.

Capital controls represented a direct reversal of previous national policies which encouraged capital outflows for private investment through favorable tax treatment and through special governmental insurance and guaranty programs directed toward reducing the risks of foreign investment. But the United States and a few other countries were exceptions to the general rule because most countries have long had a variety of capital controls in force.

Capital controls generally treat residents and nonresidents differently. For example, in 1971 West Germany had no restraints on the import or export of capital by residents or nonresidents, except for payments and transfers to Rhodesia. But nonresidents were required to secure a license in order to buy commercial paper or fixed interest-bearing securities in the German market. Japan, on the other hand, followed a policy of requiring approval for capital transfers, whether by residents or nonresidents. Sometimes, controls differentiate between portfolio investment, or the purchase of securities without management control, and direct investment.

The importance of capital controls will vary from country to country depending upon the size of capital movements in relation to the country's balance of payments. Administration may be simpler than a full-fledged exchange-controls program, with fewer parties involved in either capital inflows or outflows. Furthermore, such controls generally allow governmental authorities a great deal of discretion to meet changing circumstances. The disadvantage of capital controls, however, may be that short-term benefits in improving the balance-of-payments situation are secured at the expense of even greater long-term gains. Profitable direct investment, for example, can generate a continuing stream of return flows in the form of repatriated profits.

Other Controls. A number of new types of national controls over financial transfers are emerging in response to the growing size and

---

[7] For an example of the domestic debate over U.S. controls, see F. Michael Adler and G. C. Hufbauer, "Foreign Investment Controls: Objective-Removal," *Columbia Journal of World Business,* May–June 1969, pp. 29–37.

importance of international business activities in commercial banking and investment securities. The home governments of multinational banking firms, particularly the United States, are showing increased interest in foreign banking activities as they affect domestic policies. An example already cited is the expansion of loanable funds in the United States through Euro-dollar borrowings abroad. The growth of mutual investment funds outside of the United States, which have been selling shares to local citizens in many countries and investing in foreign security markets, has been so dramatic that countries in which the mutual funds were operating began to establish regulations over such activities. The regulations are motivated both by the desire to control international transfers of funds and to provide protection to local investors.

Taxation laws are used in many ways to influence international financial transfers. National policies governing transfer pricing of transactions between affiliates of the multinational firm and home-country tax liability for income earned abroad are only two examples of national policies which can greatly influence the amount and pattern of financial flows generated by multinational corporations.

INTERNATIONAL MOVEMENT OF PERSONS

Nations have numerous policies affecting the movement of persons across national boundaries which are important to international business. The temporary movement of persons, as tourism, has itself become a major international business activity and a major source of foreign exchange earnings for many nations. International trade depends to a large extent on the ability of businessmen to move from nation to nation. The identification and exploitation of direct-investment business opportunities requires that business executives be free to travel internationally. International business operations may be dependent upon the ability of management personnel or production workers to move across national boundaries. The transfer of technology through the transfer of persons can be significantly influenced by national policies toward the international movement of persons.

National policies for controlling the entry and exit of persons from a country generally are not motivated primarily by a national desire to encourage or discourage international business activities. Broader political, economic, and social considerations invariably underlie such policies, which generally distinguish between persons entering a country for a temporary stay such as tourists or, at the other end of the spectrum, persons who want to enter a country on a permanent basis. In between are persons who want to stay in a country for a reasonably long period without intending to seek employment in the country, such as students.

Still another in-between category would be foreigners who enter for a definite tour of duty or period of employment but who do not intend to become permanent residents of the country.

The basic means for controlling the international movement of persons is through passports and visas. Passports are issued to persons by the country of which they are a citizen or permanent resident. The issuing country can restrict movements by not authorizing passport holders to enter specified countries, as the United States has forbidden its citizens to travel in Cuba. Visas are issued by the country into which persons desire to travel. Political considerations can be grounds either for refusing citizens a passport or for denying visas.

Most countries, anxious to expand their tourist industry, impose minimum restrictions on the movement of persons on temporary visits. In many countries of the world, visas are not even required for tourists from most other countries or are issued as a formality. But even in the case of tourists, special restraints of a political nature may be imposed.

The most restrictive policies are applied to persons who wish to seek employment in a foreign country or become permanent residents. During certain periods of history, such as the late nineteenth and early twentieth centuries, countries like the United States encouraged immigration. Up till 1940, the United States received millions of immigrants from Europe. Australia and Canada aggressively encouraged and even promoted immigration during periods when they were trying to develop their vast countries. Argentina and Brazil have also had periods of relatively open immigration. But the general world pattern, except for parts of western Europe, has become one of selective and limited immigration. The United States has become one of the toughest on matters of immigration, even making it difficult, until recently, for foreign companies established in the United States to bring in their own management personnel to work in the States.

In Western Europe, since about 1955, there has been greatly increased movement of workers across national borders. A basic feature in the European Common Market treaty was to permit the free movement of labor within the Community. The major movements have been northward, especially to Switzerland, Belgium, France and Germany, first by Italians and then by Greeks, Spaniards, Portuguese, and Turks. The mobility of workers in Europe has tended to limit wage-rate variations and has greatly improved the functioning of the European labor market.

From the standpoint of international business, the complex and even discriminatory national regulation of the international movement of persons is more likely to be burdensome than prohibitive. Yet, there may be specific cases where persons important to the international operations of an enterprise may be restricted from entering a country in which the enterprise would like to have the person work.

INTERNATIONAL TRANSFER OF TECHNOLOGY

The concept of technology encompasses technical and managerial know-how which is embodied in physical and human capital and in published documents and is transmitted across national boundaries in various ways. Traditional trade theory, by limiting its horizons to land, labor, and capital, did not direct the attention of economists and government officials toward technology as a key production factor. But the situation has been changing rapidly, and governments have become keenly concerned about encouraging inflows of technology as a major means of achieving national goals for economic and social development. At the same time, nations have become active in trying to minimize foreign exchange costs to a country and maximize national benefits through policies for influencing the amount, type, and the conditions under which transfer of technology occurs.

Technology may be transferred in many ways including (a) flows of books, journals, and other scientific and technical publications; (b) the movement of people including the inflow of technical, scientific, and management personnel, and the outflow of nationals on foreign educational, training, and observation assignments; (c) the direct importation of machinery and equipment; (d) direct foreign investment accompanied by equipment and personnel; (e) licensing, patents, and know-how agreements; and (f) technical-assistance programs of governments, either on a bilateral or multilateral basis. The means of transfer are not mutually exclusive.

National policies in many different fields have a direct or indirect influence on international transfers of technology. Policies that influence the transfer of persons and goods, already discussed, have important implications for the transfer of technology. The same is true of national policies toward direct investment and the operations of international business firms to be discussed in Chapter 9. At this stage, we will limit our attention to independent transfers, as contrasted to transfers accompanying flows of capital, goods, and persons, which relate to the functioning of the patent system and the use of agreements for licensing, providing know-how, and supplying technical assistance.

In the industrially advanced countries, the prevailing philosophy is that rapid technological progress is encouraged through a patent system that gives the established owner of certain new technology a monopoly over the use of the technology during a fixed number of years—17 years in the case of the United States. In the less advanced countries which have relatively dim prospects for promoting domestic research and invention, the issue of giving monopoly protection to technology rights looks quite different. To them the question is whether the adoption of a patent system will help or hinder the country's access to foreign technology on acceptable terms.

Consequently, national patent systems for protection of rights over technology do not universally exist, and where such systems exist the rights of foreigners to use the protection varies greatly. Considerable work is underway by such groups as the International Bureau for the Protection of Industrial Property (commonly referred to as BIRPI) to promote model laws and international agreements that will regularize the flow of technology under terms that protect the national interests of both the developed and less developed countries. But for some time to come, the national and international environment for governing technology flows is likely to be complex and instable.

Many countries attempt to influence technology transfers by requiring that all agreements be registered and approved by governmental agencies. Through such controls, the receiving countries try to minimize their cost, particularly in foreign exchange, under licensing and know-how agreements. A second common objective is to minimize the restraints in such agreements, such as limiting the markets in which the licensee can sell. Licensing agreements may restrict the licensee to the domestic market so that the licensor will not have to compete in third country or home-country markets against his licensee. A third and related objective is to reduce the monopoly effects of technology-transfer agreements even in the domestic market.

INTERNATIONAL TRANSFER OF RIGHTS

The international transfer of rights is closely related to the subject of national policies for influencing international business operations and direct foreign investment. Many types of international business activity require that a foreign corporation be able to secure certain rights in a country. Many countries make distinctions between foreign and domestic firms in the granting of these rights. Concessions for mining radioactive minerals, such as uranium or thorium, are restricted in some countries to domestic enterprises and even in some cases to government domestic enterprises only. The ownership of agricultural land or forestry rights cannot be transferred to foreigners in other situations. In general, national policies restricting the transfer of ownership, concession rights, and similar access are most common in the fields of natural resources.

Other fields in which national controls are likely to be encountered are public utility and communications fields. The motivation behind such limitations and controls are generally labeled as national-security considerations.

Summary

The transformation of the world economy from a dominance of trade to a flourishing of international business will gradually move governmental and business thinking out of the traditional framework of national controls over trade and international payments. International business depends upon a much wider range of international transfers than those of goods and money. Even within the field of money and goods transfers, the concern of nations for influencing these flows has broadened considerably from the traditional patterns designed for a world of trade.

In principle, international business firms prefer a minimum of national interference over transfers of goods, money, persons, technology, and rights across national boundaries. They support their position by traditional free trade theory which argues that economic output for the world as a whole can be maximized under conditions of free international flows. In practice, international enterprises can benefit as well as be hindered by such national policies.

The nation-states give lip service to the venerable concepts of the virtues of free trade, but in practice they have chosen not to let free market forces prevail. One of the most basic reasons, generally more implicit than explicit, motivating nations to influence international transfers is the fact that maximizing output for the world as a whole does not necessarily mean that each country will share these benefits in a proportion satisfactory to the country. Thus, many controls and incentives to influence transfers have been designed by nations to attempt to increase their shares of the benefits.

Another broad category of motivations for influencing national transfers is the priority given to noneconomic national goals over economic considerations, such as trying to implement national-security goals, to satisfy political pressures of certain domestic groups, and to minimize foreign influences in a country. In other cases economic considerations may be dominant, such as in the national desire to accelerate economic development or secure economic diversification.

EXERCISES AND DISCUSSION QUESTIONS

1. U.S. Oil-Import Quotas:
    Substantial Changes in Oil-Import Controls May Result From Hearings Opening Today*
    "Oil-import controls are rooted in considerations of national security, an all-purpose concept that is usually interpreted as meaning the U.S. government should assure itself of ample long-term fuel supplies by maintaining a healthy domestic industry, while keeping trade channels open for friendly foreign nations. Faced with a rising tide of imports, President Eisenhower

launched a voluntary oil-import program in 1957. It applied only to crude oil, and caused a sharp increase in imports of refined products. Two years later, Mr. Eisenhower decreed mandatory controls restricting foreign crude and various oil products.

"The rival domestic coal industry claims that removal of controls on residual fuel oil would be an economic disaster for the coal-rich Appalachian area. East Coast users of fuel oil want controls removed as a step to lower fuel costs and they are supported by major suppliers such as Standard Oil Co. of New Jersey.

"Government officials assert that in most cases petroleum products cost the Pentagon at least twice as much in this country as overseas. In any event, they note, about 85 percent of these overseas purchases are from U.S. international companies which return substantial amounts of their overseas revenue to this country. Hence, the resulting balance-of-payments drain under current policy is less acute than might appear at first glance."* (*Wall Street Journal*, 10 March 1965.)

*Justice Department Favors Oil-Import Curbs Ending or Easing**

"The Justice Department recommended that oil-import quotas either be eliminated or replaced by milder restraints. Current quotas on foreign crude oil impose serious costs on the economy which aren't necessary to the attainment of any reasonable national-security goals.

"Current quotas stifle competition from foreign oil companies, resulting in higher prices to U.S. consumers. The import quotas themselves do nothing to preserve this country's domestic oil for use in national emergencies.

"If some restraints are needed, a small protective tariff would be preferable to quotas. Such a tariff might help finance government subsidies to the oil industry as an incentive to explore for new reserves, the report said."* (*Wall Street Journal*, 14 August 1969.)

*Oil Firms' Objections**

"A Mobil Oil Corp. spokesman stated that the health of the domestic oil industry and the national economy as a whole would be seriously affected if import controls were completely removed. Domestic oil exploration would fall off drastically, natural gas production would be unable to meet demand after 1973, the oil industry's contribution to the U.S. balance of payments would be reversed, and the economies of oil-producing states would be severely hit.

"A Shell Oil Co. spokesman said it wouldn't make any comment until it has a copy of the Justice Department recommendations."* (*Wall Street Journal*, 14 August 1969.)

a. As an adviser to a U.S. Senator from a state that does not produce oil, evaluate the opposing arguments and recommend the policy you think the U.S. government should follow.

b. As an official of Shell Oil Co., the U.S. subsidiary of the Anglo-Dutch multinational oil company, what position would you take on U.S. oil-import quotas? In what way might it differ, if any, from the position of Mobil Oil Corp.?

2. What policies do you think that the United States should follow with regard to East-West Trade? To what extent should the United States use pressure to influence policies of other western nations with regard to trade with the socialist countries? Should most-favored-nation treatment be extended by the United States to other socialist countries as has been done for Yugoslavia?

3. "President Luis Echevarria has sent to the Mexican Congress proposed legislation that would require government approval for all contracts in Mexico relative to foreign technology, patents, and brand names.

"Under the legislation, all companies using foreign technology or acquiring new or additional technology abroad would be required to submit complete details to the National Registry, which, in turn, would have power to decide whether it is applicable in Mexico and whether a fair price is being charged for the foreign technology being used." (*Wall Street Journal*, 7 November 1972.)

As a Mexican manufacturer with experience as a licensee of foreign technology, you have been asked by the National Registry to suggest further guidelines to be used by the registry in administering the new law. What do you recommend and why?

4. What are the principal objectives of exchange-control systems and how do exchange controls serve these objectives?

5. "To place capital controls on outflows of direct private investment is to kill the goose that lays the golden eggs." Discuss.

9

NATIONAL CONTROLS OVER MULTINATIONAL BUSINESS

As NATIONS have become increasingly aware of the nature and growing importance of multinational enterprises with global horizons, they have been responding with new national policies to deal with this modern phenomenon. One response has been an extension of traditional transfer controls to influence the activities of foreign-owned subsidiaries in host countries and parent companies in home countries. Capital controls, for example, previously used mainly in support of balance-of-payments goals have been broadened to regulate entry conditions for foreign enterprise. But with a growing conviction that something more was needed, most nations have adopted additional piecemeal measures specifically directed toward multinational business. Slowly, but inevitably, nations have been moving from piecemeal measures toward a general and coordinated national policy in this area.

The responses of host and home countries have not been uniform, either in timing or in substance. The levels of sensitivity to multinational enterprises have varied greatly among countries. Even where levels of sensitivity are similar, responses have differed depending upon country characteristics and national goals. Thus, a description of prevailing policies in the many individual countries would be burdensomely detailed and soon out-of-date. Furthermore, several standard reference sources are available to the international manager for securing such detailed information on a current basis.[1]

---

[1] One such source is *Obstacles and Incentives to Private Foreign Investment, 1967–1968*—Studies in Business Policy, no. 130, 2 vols. (New York: The Conference Board, 1969); other sources are the information guides published periodically by accounting firms such as Price Waterhouse & Co. and Arthur Anderson & Co.; *Investment Laws of the World* (Dobbs Ferry, N.Y.: Oceana) a loose-leaf service prepared by the International Centre for Settlement of Investment Disputes.

But country responses do have a general pattern and an underlying rationale. An understanding of both the patterns and the rationale can prepare the international manager for anticipating where and how national controls are likely to affect the operations of an international enterprise. Such knowledge also provides the base for forecasting the national-control environment, a subject to be covered in Chapter 16. The need for forecasting is clear where business firms make long-range international business commitments, because future control policies are certain to be much more important than those prevailing at the time of the commitment.

The label *controls* is used here in a particular sense to cover anything done by a government directly or indirectly to influence or regulate international business, whether through its operations, ownership, or existence. Controls in this sense may be negative curbs or restraints. They may also be direct incentives. In many cases what are usually referred to as incentives are relaxations of restrictions with corresponding savings to business enterprises. Tax concessions, tariff reductions, remittance guarantees, and increased depreciation allowances are examples.

The topic of national controls over multinational business should be differentiated from the related issue of investment climate. National-control policies can be an important element in the investment climate facing the international enterprise. But the concept of investment climate, as generally used by business firms, normally includes many other factors such as economic growth trends, general economic policies of a country, political patterns and trends, and a range of other business attractions or deterrents not uniquely related to international enterprises.

Also, it should be noted that multinational business operations and foreign direct investment are not synonymous. Strictly speaking, foreign direct investment refers to capital flows, whereas multinational business operations may be based on local financing instead of, or in addition to, foreign direct-investment flows. Furthermore, the impact on either a host or home country of multinational business operations is much broader than the issue of capital flows.

A GENERAL FRAMEWORK

In a world of many nation-states, the diversity and dynamic nature of national controls over multinational business does not permit easy generalizations. Nevertheless, several broad guidelines can be identified that provide a general framework for a more detailed discussion of national controls.

1. *Basic motivations.* Prompted by a mixture of economic, political and social considerations, nations impose controls to (a) reduce the threats to their sovereignty and economic independence and (b) to

gain more national benefits. The desire to increase national benefits has a qualitative as well as a quantitative dimension, as reflected in policies to favor types of business activities that best fit national development goals.

2. *A nation's position as predominantly a host or a home country.* If a nation is the home of many firms with foreign operations, its control policies are certain to be constrained by the possibility of retaliation. For example, if the United States broadens its controls over the domestic operations of non-U.S. companies or the foreign operations of U.S. companies, other countries are likely to react by creating similar or more burdensome controls over the foreign operations of American companies.[2]

3. *Foreign enterprise—a second-best alternative.* In few, if any, cases would countries prefer foreign enterprise, if capital, management, and technology could be secured on reasonable terms through domestic enterprise. The bias in favor of domestic enterprise, usually private but sometimes public, emerges from a conviction that the activities of local firms will be more harmonious with the economic, political, and social interests of the nation than those of foreign enterprises.

4. *Receptivity determinants.* In addition to benefit-cost evaluations of specific projects, the receptivity of host countries to foreign enterprise will vary with types of business activities, with the extent to which the total economy or particular industrial sectors are dominated by foreign firms, and by the nationality mix of foreign enterprises already operating in the country.

5. *Benefit-cost evaluations.* The explicit or implicit evaluations of the national benefits to be derived from multinational business have an important time dimension, depend upon real or imagined alternatives, vary with a country's characteristics such as stage of development, country size, and resource endowment, are shaped by the state of knowledge as to appropriate evaluation methodologies and availability of data. In the last analysis, the evaluations depend significantly on the culture bias, political views, and the business, economic, and political sophistication of the individuals in both government and business circles who are given the evaluation responsibility.

6. *Bargaining power.* National-control policies will reflect the respective bargaining power of the specific country and multinational firms

---

[2] Donald T. Brash, "Australia as Host to the International Corporation," in *The International Corporation,* ed. Charles P. Kindleberger (Cambridge, Mass.: The M.I.T. Press, 1970), p. 304. As Brash reports, "the decisive factor" in the 1968 decision of the Australian government to restrict the freedom of foreign enterprises to borrow on the Australian market "was the introduction of the U.S. 'guidelines' policy" restricting the export of capital from the United States by American companies.

and the changes over time in bargaining power. Nations compete against other nations for multinational enterprises, and such competition may reduce sharply a nation's bargaining power. If one country goes much further than others in its restrictive controls, it lowers its ranking in the eyes of all international firms and ultimately surrenders more than it gains. On the other hand, the bargaining power of nations can be greatly increased by national coalitions, as in the case of the oil-producing countries. A nation with a low level of income and a modest growth rate will have little bargaining power in attracting market-oriented foreign firms as contrasted to a high income and rapidly expanding country.

This general framework for understanding country strategies has been integrated with the strategies of business firms into a loose game theory format in Chapter 16 for predicting the changing patterns of national controls. At this stage, however, several of the country features require some additional elaboration.

The concepts and availability of data for measuring the impact of multinational enterprises, as emphasized in previous chapters, are still in an early stage of development. As better concepts emerge and more relevant data are collected, the factual bases on which nations base their control policies will gradually change. However, technical progress in evaluation techniques and an improved understanding of the complex impact of multinational business will not necessarily reduce conflict potentials between nations and multinational enterprises nor result in fewer and less burdensome controls. But such progress may result in more objective, more orderly, and more predictable processes in the formulation and implementation of national controls.

The relationship between a country's stages of development and its receptivity to foreign enterprise also deserves further mention. At an early stage of development, when a nation has low levels of income and modest or nonexistent manufacturing, mining, or other modern business sectors, the nation may be so anxious to move ahead that it values highly any type or amount of foreign private investment. At an intermediate stage of development in which an indigenous business sector has begun to emerge, a nation may assign lower values to the benefits and higher values to the cost elements of foreign business projects or operations, thus presenting a lower level of receptivity to foreign enterprise. The local business sector may be another force for resisting expansion by foreign enterprise. Also, the nation may begin to feel that it has a larger range of alternatives that will permit it to reduce the country's dependence on outside forces.

In countries at a relatively advanced stage of development, receptivity to foreign enterprise may rise again to a high level, particularly if domestic enterprise has expanded rapidly enough so that major foreign business projects still represent a relatively small part of the total national economy and of a particular sector. The greater the relative share of the total economy or selected sectors controlled by foreign interests, the more difficult it is for government officials in a host country to welcome foreign investment. Also, the advanced countries are likely to be the home base for important multinational firms and thereby be constrained from adopting restrictive policies.

The relationship between a country's stage of development and its receptivity to foreign enterprise might be described as a U-shaped curve, as shown in Figure 9.1, with the level of receptivity plotted on the

FIGURE 9.1

National Receptivity to Foreign Enterprise: The U-Curve Hypothesis

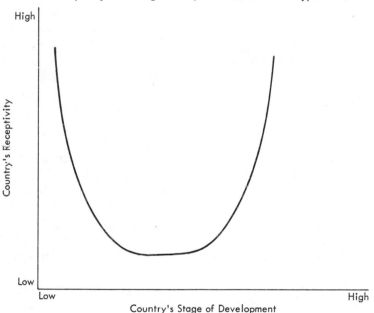

vertical scale and the stage of development represented on the horizontal axis. The U-curve hypothesis can also explain changing receptivity attitudes toward foreign enterprise in specific sectors of business activity. In the early stage of development of a high priority field of business activity, such as in the case of computers during the 1960s, foreign enterprise may be warmly encouraged when a country has no local enterprises in the field. At a later stage, foreign firms may be less welcome as indigenous potential for growth emerges and national concern grows over having a strategic economic activity controlled too heavily from outside the country. If a stage is reached where the field of business activity has grown large and domestic enterprise has become sizeable or dominant, receptivity to foreign firms may again reach a high level.

For any specific nation, the national control environment may include both incentives and restrictions directed toward multinational business. But in order to focus on types of control measures and the motivations underlying the various strategies, we will consider incentives and restrictions separately for both host and home countries, recognizing that any specific nation can be both a host and a home country.

INVESTOR OR HOME-BASE COUNTRIES: INCENTIVE PROGRAMS

Over many decades, for political as well as economic reasons, the colonial powers in the world encouraged their business firms to expand in the colonies. This trend became past history after World War II with the rapid move of the colonies toward independence and with the shift in national priorities by many of the former colonial powers toward domestic recuperation from the ravages of war. Furthermore, as an aftermath of the war, German and Japanese firms had little interest in foreign investments due to the bitter experience of losing their assets abroad through wartime expropriations of alien property and because they were not welcome in many countries.

As of the 1970s, the principal home-base countries for international firms were the United States, the United Kingdom, France, Canada, Italy, Germany, Japan, Netherlands, Switzerland, Belgium, and Sweden. Among this group, only the United States encouraged the foreign expansion of its international firms during most of the post-World War II period. This situation began to change in the late 1960s. The United States introduced some restrictive controls at about the same time West Germany and Japan began to encourage the foreign expansion of international enterprises based in their countries.

After World War II, the United States was anxious to assist in the reconstruction and revitalization of Western Europe and Japan and to help the less developed countries achieve their aspirations for accelerated economic growth. One of the measures adopted to implement these goals was to encourage foreign direct investments by American business enterprises. As an aside, it should be noted that the Allies declared a moratorium on new private investment in Germany in 1945 until reconstruction had proceeded far enough to enable fair valuations to be established. As Kindleberger reports, "The basic theme was that a Germany which had sold out its industrial assets at fire-sale prices would not be ready for democratization."[3] Foreign private investment was emphasized in

---

[3] Charles P. Kindleberger, *American Business Abroad* (New Haven, Conn.: Yale University Press, 1969), p. 39.

development-assistance programs because international business could transfer technology as well as capital to the less developed countries.

The adoption of incentive programs in the late 1960s by West Germany and Japan was motivated in part by highly favorable balance-of-payments situations. Both countries encouraged private investment outflows as an alternative to revaluation. Also, both countries had made spectacular recoveries from the effects of World War II and were anxious to resume the important international business role they had played in the period prior to the war.

Home-country inducements vary in detail among the countries. But the general types of inducements are as follows:

Taxes. Bilateral tax treaties to prevent double taxation of foreign income. Lower tax rates, tax deferrals, or special write-offs on income earned abroad.

Foreign risk insurance. All investor nations now have insurance programs to cover major types of foreign investment risks. The key features of each country's investment guaranty programs is presented in Table 9.1. All of the programs except those of the United States and Japan were only recently initiated. The geographic coverage varies from worldwide in the case of Canada to investments in 11 selected countries in the case of Sweden. The types of risks generally insurable are those of expropriation, war losses, and inability to transfer profits.

Capital assistance. Special loan programs to industry through government banks or development corporations, loans by the United States of local currency available in certain countries from the sale of agricultural "surpluses" under Public Law 480, and even equity participation by government (West Germany) in specific projects in developing countries.

Development assistance. The United Kingdom, for example, will provide aid to developing countries for basic infrastructure projects, such as a road or power facilities essential to a British private investment project.

Investment promotion. Subsidies or cost sharing for conducting investment feasibility studies. Programs to collect and disseminate data on foreign markets, economic trends, and investment opportunities.

Political support. Some investor nations (Belgium) do not in specific cases defend their nationals who invest abroad. The United States, through the Hickenlooper amendment to the 1962 Foreign Assistance Act, is committed to economic retaliation if U.S. private investment is expropriated without prompt action for compensation.

Political representation. Investor countries have used their political influence to persuade host countries to relax their restrictions over inbound foreign business investment. For example, in recent years the

TABLE 9.1
Investment Guaranty Schemes (generally covering expropriation, war, and transfer risks)

Country	Date Established	Geographic Coverage	Investment Coverage	Premium Rate per Year (in percent)	Amount Outstanding (end of 1971, in millions)
Australia	1966	Worldwide	All types	0.75	$ 49.0
Belgium	1971	Worldwide*	Equity and loan	n.a.	n.a.
Canada	1969	Less developed countries	All types	0.3–0.9	$ 3.6
Denmark	1966	Less developed countries	Equity and loan, if controlling interest	0.5	$ 11.7
France	1971	Selected less developed countries	Mainly loans	0.8	n.a.
Germany	1960	Countries having signed bilateral agreements (39)	All types	0.5	$341.0
Japan	1956/57	Worldwide	All types	0.55–0.70	$171.0
Netherlands	1969	Less developed countries	All types	0.8	$ 17.0
Norway	1964	Worldwide	Equity plus loans, if equity present	0.5	$ 16.6
Sweden	1968	11 selected countries	Equity and loan if controlling interest	0.7	n.a.
Switzerland	1970	Less developed countries	All types	†	$ 11.0 (March 1972)
United Kingdom . .	1972	Worldwide	All types	1.0	n.a.
United States	1948	Countries having signed bilateral agreements (92)	All types	0.25–0.90	$ 99.0 (June 1972)

* Limited to countries having signed bilateral agreements.
† Normal rates: principal—1.25%, profits—4% of expected profits.
Source: *Investing in Developing Countries* (Paris: OECD, 1972), pp. 12–14.

United States has been pressuring Japan directly and through the OECD to liberalize its stringent limitations on foreign investment.[4]

Support programs are comparable to incentives in the sense that they increase the attractiveness of foreign investment. For example, as part of their investment-guarantee programs, such countries as the United States, Germany, Switzerland, and Sweden have negotiated bilateral investment agreements with a number of host countries intended to protect investors from arbitrary actions by governments.

By the end of 1971 the German government had concluded bilateral agreements with 39 developing countries for the protection and promotion of German direct investment, and the United States had signed investment-guarantee agreements with 92 countries. The German experience has been that the developing countries have been careful to avoid even minor breaches of the agreements. The German agreements provide for an arbitration procedure. If a country is condemned under the arbitration procedure, it may lose international standing which may lead to a loss of credit-worthiness. Thus, in a not so subtle sense, insured investments carry with them an implicit hint that investor countries will be concerned about the imposition of controls and the adoption of policies that will require insurance payments. It should be noted, however, that investment-guarantee programs normally are not available for all types of foreign investment and in all geographic areas.

In general, investor countries have provided more extensive inducements for international business expansion in the less developed countries than in the industrialized countries. International business firms have generally favored such inducements and have frequently urged the expansion and improvement of incentive programs. The effectiveness of such programs in influencing business decisions is not clear. In some cases, the availability of inducements may be minor.

With the growing recognition in investor countries that the interests of the international firm and its home country are not identical and as conflict potentials between the international firm and its home country become more apparent, incentive programs of investor countries are likely to be heavily complemented by control programs such as those discussed below.

INVESTOR OR HOME-BASE COUNTRIES: CONTROL PROGRAMS

For a long period after World War II, most Western European countries and Japan imposed capital controls on outbound foreign investment

[4] M. Y. Yoshino, "Japan as Host to the International Corporation," in *The International Corporation,* ed. Charles P. Kindleberger (Cambridge, Mass.: The M.I.T. Press, 1970), p. 371.

in favor of their domestic reconstruction programs. The United Kingdom with its Commonwealth ties and France with its colonial and later *franc area* relations exempted capital movements within these areas from controls because such investments did not seriously affect the sterling area or franc area balance of payments. But in other areas France and the United Kingdom followed the practice of other European countries and controlled or licensed capital outflows. Such control programs were generally inspired by international monetary considerations rather than by explicit policy decisions related to international business.

After the Western European countries and Japan succeeded in restoring the convertibility of their currency, many of the capital controls were relaxed. The situation in the early 1970s included a broad spectrum of degrees of control. Canada and West Germany had no capital or foreign exchange controls restricting outflows of foreign private investment, except for special restrictions by West Germany on transactions involving Rhodesia. Denmark and the Netherlands required that firms wishing to invest abroad seek permission from the government but such permission was normally granted. France and the United Kingdom also required government approval for capital flows outside the sterling and French franc areas. Italy had extensive regulations affecting Italian investments abroad. It required that special licenses be granted in certain situations and that all residents register with the government their participation in firms whose registered offices were outside of Italy. The United States, long the citadel of no controls, was enforcing specific upper limits on investment outflows but did not have a comprehensive review and licensing policy. Japan required that all foreign investments above a certain modest limit be reviewed in detail and approved by the government. But because of its continuing strong balance-of-payments situation, Japan was shifting from a restrictive stance to a policy of encouraging foreign investments.

In addition to capital controls, investor countries influence multinational business operations through national-security policies and enforcement of antitrust laws. National-security policies are invoked to limit licensing and direct foreign investment in the fields of nuclear energy and military equipment. Normally, the production of national-defense materials and equipment is restricted to the home country. Antitrust laws have been used by the United States to prevent the foreign expansion of multinational business firms through acquisitions. For example, the acquisition in 1968 of Braun, A.G., in Germany by the Gillette Company of the United States was opposed by the U.S. government under the antitrust laws—on the grounds that the acquisition would reduce potential competition in the United States because among its many products, Braun made safety razors and blades.

In the field of licensing, investor countries have not exerted much control in the past. A special exception is the U.S. program to supervise and restrain trade and other business relations with the communist countries. This control area, however, has been receiving increased attention. In the United States, the labor unions have urged the government to regulate, supervise, and control the export of American technology, by regulating the foreign license and patent arrangements of American companies.[5] The Burke-Hartke bill introduced in the U.S. Congress in 1971 provides that the foreign licensing of patents should be prohibited when in the judgment of the President of the United States "such prohibition will contribute to increased employment in the United States."[6] The demand for controlling or prohibiting foreign licensing has also been urged on the grounds that the American taxpayer, through U.S. government financing of research and development, has often paid for the new technology that is being exported to the competitive disadvantage of the United States.

Another emerging control issue in investor countries is related to foreign policy considerations. The Japanese became concerned in the early 1970s about rising resentment, particularly in some Southeast Asia countries, toward Japanese business expansion as neocolonialism. Japan's response has been to include some review of political-impact considerations in its comprehensive control system over outbound investment. Japan has also considered the possibility of establishing rules of conduct for the behavior of its international firms that would reduce nationalistic tensions in host countries.

In the United States, the question of imposing controls that might reduce the foreign policy impact on the United States of overseas operations by American multinational companies came to the fore in the late 1960s and early 1970s because of expropriations by Peru and Chile of U.S. subsidiaries in the natural resources fields.

Through such measures as the Hickenlooper amendment, the United States has assumed a great deal of responsibility for using its governmental influence to protect the interests of international business firms with U.S. nationality. In 1969 the government of Peru expropriated the assets and operations of the International Petroleum Company, a Canadian company whose shares were almost completely owned by Standard Oil of New Jersey.[7] In 1971 a new Marxist government in Chile expropriated the local subsidiaries of major U.S. copper companies. In

---

[5] Testimony of AFL–CIO President George Meany before the Subcommittee on International Trade of the U.S. Senate Finance Committee, May 18, 1971.

[6] S. 2592, 92d Congress, 1st session, September 28, 1971, Sec. 602(a).

[7] See Richard N. Goodwin, "Letter from Peru," *New Yorker,* May 1969, pp. 41–46.

both cases, for reasons of foreign policy and political relations with Latin America the United States backed away from a hard-line position and did not impose the retaliatory actions called for by law.

The question raised by these cases is whether an investor country which assumes responsibility for representing the interests of its international business firms in foreign areas should also assume the responsibility for screening the expansion plans of international firms so as to minimize the potential damage that controversies over international business interests can have on the foreign policy interests of the investor country. The political problem was bluntly raised as far back as 1962 by then Secretary of State Dean Rusk, in testimony before the Foreign Relations Committee on the hearings of the Foreign Assistance Act of 1962:

I don't believe that the U.S. can afford to stake its interests in other countries on a particular private investment in a particular situation, because someone has to live with the results anyhow . . . I do think that such a provision would create very severe complications in our relations with other governments . . . If we are to tie American policy by law to the private investor overseas, then I think that we, of necessity, must reassure ourselves as to the operations, the conduct, the financial structure, and other aspects of those private investors . . .[8]

As the absolute and relative importance of international business increases, the potential for conflicts with the foreign policy of the major investor countries seems to increase almost geometrically. One alternative for investor countries is a comprehensive screening program as used by Japan. Another alternative is to screen only those projects which apply for government risk insurance. Still another alternative is for the home country to be neutral and require international business firms of its nationality to assume all of the risks of dealing with foreign governments. The latter alternative may be feasible if the foreign interests of national firms are small. But for countries like the United States, international firms are powerful domestic political forces. Many of them expect their government to give them protection. Furthermore, the activities of international firms may have significant repercussions for an investor country, even though such a nation is not anxious to assume responsibility for its international firms. Disputes may cause difficulties for the home country whether it likes it or not.

In summary, control programs over multinational enterprises by home-base countries are still in an incipient stage. Certain traditional

---

[8] *Foreign Assistance Act of 1962, Hearings Before the Committee on Foreign Relations,* U.S. Senate, 87th Congress, 2nd Session (Washington, D.C.: Government Printing Office, 1962), p. 31.

control programs adopted for national-security reasons, for balance-of-payments considerations, and in support of domestic antitrust philosophies have been applied to international business operations and other types of international economic relations. But control programs inspired by the international business phenomenon per se are only in an early stage of evolution. Potential conflicts between international business operations and the foreign policy goals of the investor countries; pressures by home-country labor unions for controls over international enterprise on the grounds that the export of production facilities and jobs is to the detriment of domestic employment;[9] and concern over the possible negative effects on the international competitiveness and economic strength of investor countries by the export of technology—financed to a substantial degree by government research expenditures—are some of the emerging issues likely to influence future patterns of investor-country controls over international business operations.

HOST COUNTRIES: INCENTIVE PROGRAMS

For obvious reasons, the less developed countries and the less developed regions within an economically advanced country are most likely to be offering incentives to encourage the establishment and expansion of business enterprises. But as suggested by the U-curve hypothesis, a country may offer attractive incentives at an early stage of development, later reduce its incentives, and even impose restraints. Or it may have a mixture of inducements for some fields and restraints in others. Normally, the incentives are available to either domestic or foreign firms—such as Italy's long standing effort to accelerate development of its poorer Southern region. But in the case of many of the newly industrializing nations, where indigenous enterprise is weak or nonexistent, incentive programs are intended primarily to attract foreign business firms.

Incentives are usually authorized by special laws that leave considerable bargaining discretion for government administrators. Many small, newly independent countries with little local industry may offer a broad range of incentives that are not selective as to type of business activity. On the other hand, the semi-industrialized or even industrialized countries may direct their incentives to specific types of new activities. For example, Brazil decided in the middle 1950s to develop a domestic automobile industry and established a series of attractive incentives specially designed to persuade new investors to enter this field.[10] Japan has made

---

[9] See Elizabeth Jager, "Multinationalism and Labor," *Columbia Journal of World Business*, January–February 1970.

[10] Lincoln Gordon and Englebert Grommers, *United States Manufacturing Investment in Brazil* (Boston: Harvard Business School, 1962), pp. 46–64.

special concessions in selected cases where the expansion of specific types of international business activity was given a high national priority.

In brief, incentive program reflect a nation's stage of economic development, its specific development priorities and its need to compensate for such business limitations as small local markets in order to attract new industries. A few examples can illustrate the many ways incentives vary with the particular objectives of a country. Ethopia, Malaysia, and Nigeria offer tax incentives that are more generous for larger amounts of invested capital. Germany and South Africa place a premium on investments in particular locations where economic development is sought. The Ivory Coast and El Salvador programs differentiate among industries, granting more liberal concessions to the types they consider more desirable. Germany encourages both housing and research and development expenditures by allowing their amortization for tax purposes. Lebanon increases its incentives on the basis of the employment contribution of a foreign investment, and India places a premium on the number of shifts worked. Many countries, including Malaysia, Israel, and the Philippines, have special incentives to encourage projects that will increase the nation's exports.[11] In some cases, usually through administrative discretion rather than published regulations, countries try to encourage a mix of nationalities for inbound investment so as to reduce the appearance or reality of foreign economic domination by one country.

An important force in shaping incentive programs has been the competition among host countries, or the alternative locations available to the international enterprise. This has been particularly important in relation to regional integration movements. With the elimination of internal tariff walls within the European Common Market, a foreign firm locating in any of the member countries has free access to the markets of the others. Consequently, competition has developed among the countries in attracting foreign investment. Some of the smaller member countries, in particular, have been offering strong inducements to foreign industry interested in the Common Market. If agreement can be reached among the countries to harmonize their policies on foreign investment, special incentives may be eliminated or reduced in their appeal.

For the future, it should be noted that investment promotion efforts are not limited to the nonsocialist countries. Several Eastern European socialist countries have taken special steps to permit and encourage foreign private companies to make direct investments in their countries. The investment promotion measures being used illustrate the reciprocal nature of inducements and restrictions because reductions in restrictions

---

[11] The Conference Board report on *Obstacles and Incentives to Private Foreign Investment, 1967–68,* 1 (New York, 1969), contains official profiles from 60 countries of the incentives, assurances, and guarantees they offer.

have operated as incentives. An early technique was to permit co-production agreements whereby a Western private company provides technology and machinery to build or reequip a plant in a communist country and takes part of the production in payment.[12] In 1967 Yugoslavia went further and passed new foreign investment legislation which reinterpreted its concept of *social ownership* to permit joint industrial ventures with foreign capitalist companies under a *pooling-of-funds contract.*[13] Still another technique has been to encourage arrangements whereby a Western company and a communist state enterprise incorporate a fifty-fifty joint venture in a third country—capitalist. The new entity then engages in business in both the East and West and splits the profits.[14]

The usual types of incentives being offered generally fall into the following categories:

Tariff protection. Potential import competition is reduced or eliminated by special high tariffs or through import controls.

Duty-free imports. Equipment and sometimes future supplies of raw materials or components are allowed to enter the country duty-free or on special concessionary terms.

Financial assistance. Short- and long-term loans, generally from government agencies, may be available at special low-interest rates.

Tax concessions. Tax reductions, deferrals and even 10-year tax holidays are being offered in certain countries.

Foreign exchange guarantees. Specific governmental guarantees that foreign exchange will be granted for profit remittances and capital repatriation.

Other governmental assistance. The government may assist in assembling parcels of land or agree to build roads or other public facilities needed to complement a project, or even provide subsidies for training personnel.

The establishment of a free port or a border industry program can effectively attract foreign investment by using a combination of incentives. In both types of programs, the industry is permitted to import materials and components duty free, employ local labor to assemble them, and export the products paying a duty only on the value added. Mexico's National Frontier Program, adopted in 1966, attracted within six years 280 U.S. plants employing an estimated 40,000 Mexican workers to a 12-mile zone along Mexico's border with the United States.[15] The

[12] Emile Benoit, "Business Partnerships With Communist Enterprises," *Worldwide P & I Planning,* November–December 1967, pp. 18–24.

[13] Miodrag Sukijasovic, "Foreign Investment in Yugoslavia," in *Foreign Investment: The Experience of Host Countries,* ed. Isaiah A. Litvak and Christopher J. Maule, (New York: Praeger Publishers, Inc., 1970), pp. 385–406.

[14] *Business Week,* 16 January 1971, p. 41.

[15] See Donald W. Baerresen, *The Border Industrialization Program of Mexico* (Lexington, Mass.: D.C. Heath & Co., 1971).

sites are generally leased in order to circumvent Mexico's prohibition against foreign ownership of land along the border.

The effectiveness of incentives in implementing host country policies and aspirations varies greatly. In countries where the ingredients necessary for making an international business project viable and profitable are not present, even the most attractive incentives will not yield the desired results. On the other hand, in a case such as Brazil's effort to develop quickly a major automobile industry, the special incentives almost certainly were a major factor in the decisions of the foreign firms to establish automobile assembly and components plants. The size of the market was large, and many other conditions appeared to be favorable. The incentives provided a significant reduction in the risk element.

HOST COUNTRIES: CONTROL PROGRAMS

Host countries are at many different stages in devising policies and programs for controlling multinational business. A small but growing number of nations, having addressed themselves directly to the issue, have formulated a comprehensive set of policies and devised a coordinated set of control instruments. The more usual situation has been for countries to follow an evolutionary case-by-case approach in responding to the novel and complex multinational business phenomenon.[16] Nevertheless, the apparently piecemeal evolution of control policies has followed, in various mixtures, four principal themes: (1) protect political independence, (2) reduce economic dependency on foreigners, (3) increase the national presence in the decision making of multinational corporations, and (4) maximize national benefits from foreign enterprise.

Given the variations in national goals, national-control programs differ in the aspects of multinational business on which they focus and the tools used to achieve national objectives. Tax measures, foreign exchange controls, and legal restrictions are used in varying proportions. A growing tendency has been to supplement restrictive measures over multinational firms with affirmative policies to strengthen domestic industries—through mergers, financial assistance for research and development, and other means—and thus hope to limit the competitive opportunity for foreign enterprises.

Some control policies are established by specific laws or as provisions of the nation's constitution. Other policies may be periodically formulated as part of national economic planning. The various Indian Five Year Plans, for example, have specified which fields are to be open

---

[16] See Isaiah A. Litvak and Christopher J. Maule, eds., *Foreign Investment: The Experience of Host Countries* (New York: Praeger Publishers, Inc., 1970) for essays on the control policies in the developed countries of Australia, Belgium, Canada, France, Japan, Norway, South Africa, and the United Kingdom, and in the less developed countries of Argentina, India, Tunisia, and Yugoslavia.

to foreign enterprises over the plan period. In addition to, and sometimes instead of, specific laws and plans relating to foreign enterprise, host countries may have one or more government agencies with responsibility for screening, coordinating, and bargaining with foreign direct investors, and the granting of government permission for entry.

Any firm wishing to invest in France must apply to the Ministry of Finance for permission. In Japan, the Foreign Investment Council makes the final decision on whether an inflow of investment or technology (licensing agreements) should be allowed after receiving the recommendations of a subcommittee on which various ministries are present. India has a Foreign Investment Board that is responsible for coordinating and expediting all matters related to foreign private investments and collaborations, but decision-making authority on separate features of a foreign investment project is decentralized. Where government authority is widely dispersed, where guidelines are vague, where strict ethical standards do not prevail, the process of controlling the entry of foreign projects may involve crude or highly sophisticated forms of bribery and corruption.

Many governments have encountered difficulties in designing systematic approaches to the issue of international business because several government agencies with varying time perspectives and different government responsibilities are involved. For example, in countries where the treasury, the ministry of finance, or the central bank have been the government agencies most concerned with foreign capital, policies have often been shaped to an excessive extent from a foreign exchange perspective and in a short-run horizon. Also, policy makers have tended to focus upon new foreign enterprises and projects, thereby neglecting established international business activities which may be having an even greater impact on host country goals and objectives.

Activities Reserved for Nationals

In a number of countries, foreigners are excluded from certain business fields. They are excluded from the tobacco and mining industries in Sweden; from development of certain natural resources in Brazil, Finland, and Morocco; from retail trade in the Philippines; from Norway's textile and shipping industries; from holding mining rights in Italy; from oil exploration and development in Brazil, Chile, and Mexico. In a number of African and Asian nation-states, agricultural activity is reserved for nationals. Moreover, in some African nation-states the marketing of certain export products can be handled only by state-owned companies.

Mexico is an interesting example of the degree and kinds of entry restrictions that can be faced by foreign firms. The Mexican constitution prohibits foreign ownership of land within 31 miles of the coastlines or 62 miles of the borders with other countries. Mexican companies permitting foreign shareholders are not allowed to own land in the restricted zones. In accordance with the constitution, the petroleum industry, the generation and distribution of electric power, railroads, and telegraphic communications are legally reserved for the government. Private enterprise, whether domestic or foreign, is therefore restricted from these fields. Foreigners, except as minority investors, are not permitted to invest in Mexican banks or other credit institutions, and in insurance companies. Recent administrations have also required, but not retroactively, either 100 percent ownership or a majority of Mexican ownership in a wide range of industries, including radio and television broadcasting; production, distribution, and exhibition of motion pictures; all phases of the soft-drink industry; advertising and publishing; and fishing and packing of marine products. The specific industries covered by administrative restrictions have changed from time to time and, under certain circumstances, exceptions may be approved by the government.

The general pattern of restricted areas for foreigners is as follows: the public-utility fields are generally restricted, either because of ideological preferences for public enterprise or because the activities are considered to be indispensable for national development. Governments generally reserve the communication fields such as television, radio, and news publications to domestic firms or the government for protection of vital national interests. As a Canadian government report explains, "Communications media lie at the heart of the technostructure of modern societies. Canadian ownership and control facilitate the expression of Canadian points of view."[17] Protecting national interests is also the rationale for prohibiting foreign ownership in the banking, insurance, and other financial fields. To quote the Canadian report again, "Financial institutions, because of their pervasiveness and their potential as bases for influence and control, constitute the commanding heights of the economy. Canadian ownership and control facilitate the exercise of Canadian economic policies."[18]

Restrictions in the fields of natural resource arise out of a political philosophy common in many countries of the world, and frequently spelled out in their legal systems, that natural resources should be the property of all the people, and that all citizens should share in the benefit from these resources. Certain other restrictions, such as the prohibition against ownership of land by foreigners near a country's borders, can be explained by national-defense considerations.

---

[17] "Foreign Ownership and Structure of Canadian Industry," *Report of the Task Force on the Structure of Canadian Industry* (Ottawa: Queen's Printer, 1968), p. 389.

[18] Ibid., p. 389.

Minimizing Foreign Economic Power

The policies to minimize foreign economic power are two-pronged. They can be designed to strengthen domestic enterprise or weaken the power of foreign firms. Sometimes, both objectives are accomplished in single actions. The Japanese government has long had a strict policy of encouraging licensing rather than direct foreign investment. Such a policy can be effective if a country is extremely attractive to international business firms, and if the domestic-industry sector is strong and has potential and resources for fully utilizing the technology part of the foreign business package without the accompanying investment and management resources.

Governments also attempt to minimize foreign domination by opposing or prohibiting the acquisition of domestic firms by international enterprises. Even though Machines Bull, France's largest manufacturer of computers, was in financial difficulties in 1963, and General Electric was willing to provide urgently needed additional capital in exchange for minority participation, the French government agreed to the GE-Bull partnership only after trying to keep Bull viable with French capital and other assistance. With the same objective of favoring domestic firms, the French government has limited the import quotas of foreign oil companies operating in France more severely than those of French companies. France has also followed the strategy of promoting and encouraging mergers on the assumption that larger and presumably more competitive domestic firms will reduce the competitive advantages of foreign firms and restrict the inflow of foreign investment. For example, two of France's biggest companies—steelmaker Pont-a-Mousson and glassmaker Saint-Gobain—joined together in 1969 to create the country's biggest industrial corporation, in line with governmental policies to make French firms more competitive in domestic and foreign markets.

Other policies aimed at reducing foreign control are generally directed toward having nationals share in the ownership and control of foreign business projects. Most countries favor joint ventures, that is, a partnership between the foreign firm and a local business firm or group, or preferably the sharing of the ownership with nationals through public sale of equity within the country. Japan followed a policy for many years of limiting foreigners to 49 percent ownership in joint ventures, although exceptions were made when highly desired industries could not be secured on these terms.[19] Mexico, which along with Japan has been an attractive area for foreign investment, has also taken a hard line on having Mexicans share in the ownership of Mexican affiliates or sub-

---

[19] See Noritake Kobayashi, "Foreign Investment in Japan" in *Foreign Investment,* ed. Litvak and Maule, p. 150. In 1967, 58 companies in Japan were owned 100 percent by foreign investors.

sidiaries of international business firms. Its so-called Mexicanization policy is promoted through bargaining when permission is granted for foreign firms to establish businesses in the country and through policies that limit certain tax exemptions or export permits to companies at least 51 percent owned by Mexican nationals. In other cases, countries may discriminate in taxes, the granting of import permits, and in government purchasing in favor of firms which have a large or majority share owned by nationals. Some countries such as Sweden require that the directors of a Swedish joint stock company be resident Swedish subjects. However, the Swedish Board of Commerce can grant exemptions allowing up to one third of the Board to consist of foreign nationals.

Under pressure from the OECD countries and the United States, Japan liberalized its policies toward foreign investment in 1967. The new policy allowed foreign companies to invest up to 100 percent in 17 specifically identified industries. But, the fields opened up more widely to foreign investment were fields in which Japanese firms had become all but impregnable—such as beer, steel, motorcycles, some textile spinning, and moderate-scale shipbuilding.

Maximizing National Benefits

Every nation-state is anxious to secure for itself and its citizens a maximum share of the benefits created by international business enterprises. In furtherance of national economic development and foreign exchange goals, some governments have developed what are called *local-content* policies. Prospective investors are asked to commit themselves to a schedule of increasing the locally produced content of the final product over a stated period of time. Such local content policies have been widely applied to automobile manufacturers who have expanded in Latin America, with the hope that the development impetus of new types of activity will continue over time and be extended into other related areas of activity. As mentioned previously, countries may have to pay a high price for having local content when local markets are not large enough to permit economic scale production for many parts and components.

Another way of increasing local benefits is through employment policies imposed on international enterprises. The labor law of Mexico provides that at least 90 percent of a foreign company's employees must be Mexican citizens. Executives are generally excluded in calculating this percentage. The immigration of foreigners for managerial and other positions is permitted only if qualified Mexicans are not available. Some countries, such as the Central American nations, also establish limits in relation to the total payroll. Interestingly, each firm may exclude two administrators from the above computation.

In the area of foreign exchange, many techniques are used to maximize national benefits. Countries are becoming increasingly sensitive to export strategies of international business firms which do not allow each subsidiary or affiliate to compete freely for export markets. Through negotiations nation-states try to ensure that new enterprises located in their country are free to export and to earn foreign exchange. Other common policies are to set limits or establish continuing control over remission of profits, repatriation of capital, and royalty payments to the home office of the foreign enterprises. Outflows of foreign exchange can be increased or decreased through the transfer-pricing policies for goods and services moving among units of the international enterprise. Consequently, governments are becoming sensitive and beginning to formulate policies to regulate transfer pricing.

Still another area for maximizing national benefits is through tax policies. Because international enterprises are subject to taxation in the home country for profits earned abroad and generally receive credit for foreign taxes, many countries are raising their tax rates to a level comparable to that in the United States, the principal home country of the international enterprises. The business firm will not have to pay extra taxes, but the host government rather than the home government will get the revenue.

In the natural resource industries, some host countries have succeeded in increasing national benefits through agreements with other major producing nations to follow common strategies in negotiating with multinational enterprises. The Organization of Petroleum Exporting Countries (OPEC), created in 1960, includes most of the principal oil-producing countries and has been the outstanding example of inter-nation cooperation to reduce potential competition between host countries. An analogous organization has been formed among copper producing countries, and additional groups have been proposed in other minerals fields.

A somewhat similar effort to have a common policy for handling foreign investments has been the Andean Pact, negotiated in 1971 by the five-country trading group—Bolivia, Chile, Colombia, Ecuador, and Peru. The Andean Pact takes a hard line toward foreign investments, limiting the degree of foreign ownership, and generally requiring that foreign firms agree to fadeout, or divest their ownership into national hands over a fixed period of time. Such a common policy can reduce competition among the Andean countries, but the net result may be a loss in bargaining power if the tough rules discourage foreign investment. OPEC has a quasi-monopoly position because it includes almost all the principal countries available as sources of supply for the multinational oil companies. The Andean countries do not have this kind of muscle on their side.

Natural Resources and Concession Agreements

Host-country policies controlling international business activity in natural resource fields have a special ideological and even emotional flavor. In most countries of the world, subsurface mineral rights and often forestry resources are reserved by law as the *property of the Crown,* or of the nation as a whole. This legal pattern results from the belief that resources provided by nature should be used for public benefit rather than private profit. Thus, the international business firm operating in the natural resource field is frequently dealing directly with government officials rather than with private owners of property, and with an issue that is of public rather than private concern. The situation is further complicated when the natural resource being exploited is exhaustible, and the nation cannot expect the project to continue indefinitely making its contribution to the national economy and public welfare.

The issue of controls over foreign firms does not arise, obviously, where countries restrict the exploitation of certain natural resources to government or domestic enterprises. But where foreign firms are allowed to operate, special controls or policies are generally imposed.[20] The standard arrangement has been for a foreign company to purchase a concession giving it exclusive rights to explore in a particular area and to develop and produce the minerals or the petroleum found in that area for a stated number of years. The host government receives royalties on the materials extracted and income taxes on the net earnings of the concessionaire. The production of petroleum and minerals is generally for export, frequently to other foreign affiliates of the producing companies. The bulk of international business activity in resource exploitation is located in the less developed countries, and in these countries the resource industries are likely to be major sources of foreign exchange earnings, domestic employment, and economic growth. Consequently, host countries are especially anxious to secure a maximum share of the benefits by extending national controls over production, pricing, and marketing.

Specially negotiated concession agreements are intended to spell out the conditions under which foreign enterprises can operate. But in many of the countries, governments have changed with great frequency, and the new government may endeavor to alter or renegotiate the agreements. In fact, the renegotiation of concession agreements is almost certain where foreign enterprises have secured unusually favorable arrangements and when the respective bargaining power of the two parties changes.

---

[20] See R. F. Mikesell, ed., *Foreign Investment in the Petroleum and Mineral Industries: Case Studies on Investor-Host Relations* (Baltimore: The Johns Hopkins Press, 1971); Raymond Vernon, "The Raw Material Ventures," in *Sovereignty at Bay* (New York: Basic Books, 1971), pp. 26–59.

New control measures may be invoked when a nation feels that the foreign firm has not made sufficiently vigorous efforts to find new reserves in its concession areas. In April 1965, the Mexican government suspended all sulphur shipments by the Pan-American Sulphur Company, a U.S. firm which produced the bulk of Mexico's sulphur. The government charged that the company had made little effort to discover and develop new reserves of sulphur and that reserves were being depleted at too rapid a rate. Export quotas were then established with provision for upward adjustment as new reserves were discovered.

Host countries usually want the foreign enterprise to hire mainly local personnel and purchase as many local commodities and services as possible. Frequently, host countries also require the foreign firm to provide services for employees such as education and housing, or even highways and railroads required for the project, which are normally the responsibility of the government. Pressures are also great for joint ventures either with the national government and/or domestic private interests. And in some cases, such as Venezuela, new foreign involvements are limited to oil-service contracts which keep ownership of the oil in government hands and make the state oil company a partner of the oil contractor.

Over time, the degree of ownership and control by foreign firms is likely to decline because the unique contributions that the foreign firm makes to the domestic resource industries are also likely to decline. The bargaining power of the foreign firm is ultimately based on the degree to which its capital, technical skills, managerial ability, and marketing knowledge are needed by a foreign country. As the foreign enterprise earns profits for the country and trains local technical and operating personnel, it undercuts its own bargaining power by making less scarce the unique contributions that it had to offer initially.

Rules of Conduct

Canada has been in the vanguard of thinking and debate on host-country policies toward international business. It is unique among the industrialized nations in the extent of foreign ownership of Canadian industry. The only key sectors of the economy largely immune from foreign control are agriculture, banking, and the communications media—the last two of which Canada has tried to reserve for nationals. Canada's posture has been to welcome foreign investment but to try to harmonize the activities of multinational firms with Canadian interests and policies. The proposals being debated in the early 1970s are likely to be the foundation for a comprehensive national policy toward international business and may well be the harbinger of more widespread national policies that international business will encounter in the future in countries where the general view is favorable toward inflows of foreign private investment.

In early 1966, Canada's minister of trade and commerce sent to all foreign subsidiaries a set of 12 "Guiding Principles of Good Corporate Behavior in Canada." The list (See Table 9.2) implicitly suggests the kinds of reform which ministers of both Conservative and Liberal governments in Canada have been urging upon subsidiaries and U.S.-parent companies, although it has not yet been the basis for specific regulatory actions by the government.[21] In 1967, a new Minister of Finance, Walter L. Gordon, pressed for a stiff policy on foreign subsidiaries and persuaded the cabinet to appoint a task force of eight academic economists to advise the government on the whole issue of the economics and politics of foreign ownership. By the time the report was released in February 1968, other political issues had come to the fore and the report was released as representing the view of the task force members rather than official government policy.[22]

Among the proposals of the Watkins Report (named after Professor Melville H. Watkins, head of the task force) are the following:

1. A special agency should be created to coordinate policies with respect to multinational enterprises and administer the "Guiding Principles" program.
2. Both Canadian-owned and foreign-owned corporations should be required to provide the government with a large amount of additional information required for policy making in the international business field.
3. The Canadian anti-combines legislation should be revised and applied more vigorously. The maximization of the net economic benefit for Canadians requires increased action to maintain competition.
4. Economic efficiency. The size of the net economic benefit from foreign direct investment depends critically on whether factors of production are used efficiently in Canada. The government should provide more leadership and planning in rationalizing Canadian industries.
5. Extraterritoriality. Positive steps should be taken to block the intrusion into Canada of United States laws and policy applicable to American-owned subsidiaries with respect to freedom to export to communist countries, antitrust law and policy, and balance-of-payments policy.

Another task force prepared a report on the regulation of foreign investment for the Trudeau government in 1971. Although it was not officially released, the report was the basis for new official regulatory actions that were expected to be adopted.

---

[21] David J. Ashton, "U.S. Investments in Canada: Will the Other Shoe Drop?" *Worldwide P & I Planning,* September–October 1968, pp. 50–58.

[22] *Foreign Ownership and the Structure of Canadian Industry,* Report of the Task Force on the Structure of Canadian Industry (Ottawa: Queen's Printer, 1967).

TABLE 9.2

Canada's 12 Good Corporate Behavior Principles (as they relate to alleged objectionable U.S. subsidiary practices)

Guiding Principle Summary	*Alleged Objectionable Practice*
1. Full realization of the company's growth and operating potential in Canada.	1. U.S.-based corporate planners institute expansion and cutback plans without regard for Canada's plans and aspirations.
2. Make Canadian subsidiary self-contained, vertically-integrated entity with total responsibility for at least one productive function.	2. The Canadian subsidiary is primarily an assembler of imported parts or distributor of goods produced elsewhere so operations can be easily shut down or transferred.
3. Maximum development of export markets from Canada.	3. Filling export orders to third-country markets from the U.S. country stocks, earns credits for U.S. balance of payments rather than Canada's.
4. Extend processing of Canada's raw materials through maximum number of stages.	4. Have as few materials-processing stages as possible in Canada to minimize political leverage.
5. Equitable pricing policies for international and intracompany sales.	5. Negotiated or spurious prices by Canadian-U.S. subsidiaries are designed to get around Canadian income taxes.
6. Develop sources of supply in Canada.	6. Preference for United States or third-country sources for purposes of corporate convenience or political leverage.
7. Inclusion of R&D and product development.	7. The concentration of R&D and product design in the United States means Canada can never develop these capabilities.
8. Retain substantial earnings for growth.	8. Profits earned in Canada do not stay to finance Canadian expansion.
9. Appointment of Canadian officers and directors.	9. Use of U.S. officers and directors to prevent development of local outlook in planning and execution.
10. Equity participation by Canadian investing public.	10. Creation of wholly owned subsidiaries denies policy determination and earnings to Canadians.
11. Publication of financial reports	11. Consolidation of Canadian operating results into parent company statements or failure to publish any relevant information.
12. Support of Canadian cultural and charitable institutions.	12. Failure locally to support such causes as the United Appeal where parent corporations give generously to comparable U.S. campaigns.

Source: David J. Ashton, "U.S. Investments in Canada: Will the Other Shoe Drop?" *Worldwide P & I Planning*, September–October 1968, p. 57.

The Need for a Predictive Theory of Controls

Nation-states are generally in an early stage of formulating national policies toward international business operations—in large part because of the newness of the phenomenon. But the situation is highly dynamic because international business activity has grown at a rapid rate, both absolutely and in relation to the total size of national economies. The actions of home-base countries and host countries can modify investment returns and the attractiveness of global opportunities being considered by the multinational firm. Thus, international enterprises are finding it increasingly justified to devote major attention to a careful prediction of the controls to which their activities will become subject within different countries. The framework for a predictive theory will be presented in Chapter 16.

EXERCISES AND DISCUSSION QUESTIONS

1. "Investment-guaranty insurance merely encourages both investing companies and host governments to behave more irresponsibly, knowing that the investing company's government would bail the company out. Safeguards should be written into such schemes that would prevent a company claiming on the guarantee scheme if it had somehow provoked the host government into nationalization, for instance by bad labor practices or disguised political activity locally." Discuss.

2. What are the advantages and disadvantages of varying the cost and availability of investment-guaranty insurance for different types of business activities and for different host countries as against charging a standard risk premium for all projects and all areas?

3. The United States has a vital national-security interest in securing dependable foreign sources of critical minerals at a reasonable cost. Therefore, it should give maximum support and protection to the foreign direct investments of U.S. international resource industries in such fields as petroleum and copper, where U.S. domestic production is insufficient for U.S. needs. Discuss.

4. You have been retained by an industrialized country, such as France, to recommend a strategy and policies for regulating the entry and continuing operations of foreign multinational companies in that country. What are the two or three most important issues that you would have to resolve? What information would you need to complete your assignment? In what ways would the key problems and the nature of your recommendations be different if you were working for a less developed country, namely, a small, newly independent country in Africa?

5. Host-country policies that require multinational companies to share ownership with nationals are frequently used to minimize the economic power of foreign interests. But such policies will also reduce the amount of foreign

capital transfers to the host country and reduce the supply of local capital for domestic entrepreneurs. Why do you think so many host countries are insisting that foreign firms share ownership with locals?

6. Under what circumstances would you as a host country prohibit foreign companies from acquiring domestic companies?

7. In formulating an investment promotion program to attract foreign direct investment to a less developed country, which incentives do you think would be most effective and why?

10

THE COUNTERVAILING POWER OF INTERNATIONAL BUSINESS

INTERNATIONAL BUSINESS is not without its own power for countering the impact of national controls. There is a landmark English legal case in which Lord Justice Tomlin ruled that every man is entitled to order his affairs so as to minimize the tax for which he would be liable (Inland Revenue Commissioners v. Duke of Westminster—1936). A similar concept applies to the international enterprise. It is under no obligation not to use the legal means available to it to avoid controls that may hinder attainment of its legitimate global-business objectives.

The experienced international enterprise goes even further. It will plan to avoid future controls. It will examine the existing strategies of relevant countries toward multinational business and international transfers, project the likely pattern of change, and adapt its own strategy accordingly. The firm is not an unprotected, misused pawn of omnipotent nations. In many ways the firm is the more powerful player in the international business game.

This chapter will introduce some of the means at the command of international firms for adjusting to controls and for exerting countervailing power. The focus will be on the ways in which the business enterprise can act to mitigate the effects of national controls. The decision-making procedures by which businessmen choose an appropriate mix of these adjustments is the subject of Part V of the book.

REFUSAL TO INVEST

The simplest and most direct form of countervailing power available to the international enterprise is to refuse to make new investments, or even to discontinue existing operations, in countries where national controls have made the business environment unattractive. From a nation's point of view, its optimum strategy is to set each of its controls at a level which maximizes net national benefits. This control optimum must recognize the opportunity loss of benefits from investments not made and business activities that would have come or remained if such controls had not been imposed. With nationalistic enthusiasm, nations have frequently exceeded the control optimum and been forced to relax or abandon controls when they became aware of what they were losing in potential new investments or expansions.

In both developed and less developed countries, the loss of future foreign investments has operated as a constraint on national-control policies. In the case of France, for example, during the period between 1963 and 1968 when strong de Gaullist policies restricted foreign investment inflows, U.S. investment increased by 141 percent in Holland, 113 percent in West Germany, 175 percent in Belgium, and only 55 percent in France. The trend did not coincide with President Pompidou's view of France's national interests. Shortly after he was elected in mid-1969, national-control policies were sharply altered, even to the point where the ministry of industry opened an office in New York to stimulate U.S. investment.[1]

In contrast to France's previous refusal to allow General Motors to build a major plant in the Strasbourg area, French officials in 1970 began aggressively to solicit another major American automobile manufacturer, the Ford Motor Company, to invest in France.[2]

Uganda offers a similar example from a less developed country. In May 1970, the government adopted a policy requiring the government to have a majority equity participation in foreign companies engaged in manufacturing, mining, plantation, insurance, and banking activities. Within less than a year's time, a new government canceled the policy "so as to secure the confidence of foreign investors."[3]

A change in national controls may alter the optimum locational pattern for the operations of an international firm and the ranking of its alternatives on its investment schedule, as will be discussed in Chapter 16. In some cases, the firm will choose an alternative country in which to expand. In other situations, a prospective expansion may be deferred or abandoned because expected profits no longer fall within the investment limits of the firm. It seems, clearly enough, that the refusal to invest can be a defensive move against either home-country or host-country controls.

---

[1] *Business Week*, 5 September 1970.

[2] *Economist*, 28 February 1970.

[3] *Economic Times* (Bombay), 12 March 1971.

HOME-COUNTRY SUPPORT

Although investor countries vary in their willingness to lend official support to assist the foreign operations of their international enterprises, the possibility of support merits inclusion in an examination of the countervailing power of international business. In some cases, home countries have been enticed to support the purely private interests of its citizens in foreign situations. The more common situation in recent years is for the investor country to undertake certain actions because it sees that its national interests are at stake.

By having foreign projects covered by home-country investment-guarantee schemes, the international enterprise may secure home-country support as well as risk insurance. Such programs, however, do not explicitly guarantee that the home country will intervene on behalf of the international enterprise.

In 1963, the United States threatened to withhold government economic assistance from Indonesia in order to get Indonesia to improve its settlement terms for the takeover of U.S. oil-company properties. The U.S. Export-Import Bank has refused to make loans to Chile for the purchase of American jet aircraft after Chile's expropriation of U.S. copper companies, and the U.S. government has used its influence in international agencies such as the World Bank and the Inter-American Bank to deny financing to countries that have taken undesirable action against U.S. companies.

But the United States is not alone in lending its official support to counter host-country measures against multinational enterprises. In a countermove following Algeria's seizure in 1971 of 51 percent of French oil interests, the French government officially requested the U.S. Export-Import Bank to deny a $150 million loan that Algeria was seeking for a natural gas plant. France also threatened to discontinue the sizeable financial and technical assistance help it was giving to Algeria in order to negotiate a better settlement on the oil expropriations. When Libya expropriated the oil assets of British Petroleum in 1971, the British foreign office is reported to have approached other oil importing nations, "expressing concern for BP's rights."[4]

In some situations, home-country support can be more direct. The United States and other countries have pressured the Japanese to reduce their restrictions on the entry of foreign investment. The United States in particular has mentioned the possibility of retaliation through increased restrictions on Japanese business access to the U.S. market. As a result of these official efforts, in 1971 American automobile manufacturers were allowed to make their first direct-investment entry into the

---

[4] *Wall Street Journal,* 31 December 1971.

Japanese market through minority joint-venture arrangements with Japanese companies.

Still another way in which the home country can give support to its multinational enterprises is through legal actions in the World Court, as discussed in Chapter 14. But such support through World Court litigation has not been an effective source of countervailing power.

MEASURES TO INCREASE HOST-COUNTRY RECEPTIVITY TO FOREIGN INVESTMENT

Stimulating Local Enterprise

If the international firm accepts the U-Curve hypothesis that a host country's receptivity varies inversely with the share of the total economy or of key sectors controlled by foreign interests, it can take steps to increase receptivity and decrease controls by stimulating the growth of indigenous enterprise. It can, for example, plan and implement aggressive programs for encouraging independent local firms to become suppliers, processors, further manufacturers, and sellers of the product of the foreign-financed venture. The development-linkages benefits are much heralded by proponents of foreign investment but, too frequently, the linkage opportunities are left to slow natural forces or are realized not by domestic business but by other foreign investors.

More by necessity than by design, Sears Roebuck de Mexico demonstrated two decades ago the effectiveness of policies to stimulate local enterprise in increasing host-country receptivity without prohibitive costs. In establishing its first large, modern department store in Mexico, Sears had assumed that it would import about 70 percent of its merchandise from the United States. But in late 1947, less than a year after opening its first store, the company had to face a drastic change in the Mexican economic situation. Due to foreign exchange difficulties, Mexico placed an embargo on a wide range of consumer imports. To meet this unexpected challenge, Sears responded by a mammoth program of encouraging new local enterprises as sources of supply. Within six years, and through cooperation with 1,300 local firms, Sears was able to buy in Mexico 80 percent of the merchandise it sells there.[5]

Developing Local Allies

Another interesting example of measures to increase national receptivity is the case of Firestone's rubber-growing operations in Liberia. As

---
[5] Richardson Wood and Virginia Keyser, *Sears Roebuck de Mexico, S.A.* (Washington, D.C.: National Planning Association, 1953).

a planned rather than unanticipated program, Firestone initiated a rubber-growers assistance program designed to help Liberians grow rubber on their own farms. As reported in another NPA study,

> Firestone provides not only free trees but also free technical services. It will survey the planter's farm and draw up a planting program for him. When the trees reach tapping age, the Company will prepare a complete management plan, which includes a detailed map of the tree stands, their division into tasks and the marking of each tree with its task designation, and a tapping schedule best suited to the needs and capabilities of the farm. At the farmer's request, the Company will periodically inspect his rubber trees and advise him on improved care, cultivation, and tapping. It will set up his bookkeeping and records systems and teach him how to keep them current. It will provide free biological services in the event of tree disease, storm damage, or other difficulties, Firestone will sell him at cost and on interest-free credit terms all of the plantation equipment and supplies he needs both initially and subsequently.
>
> Finally, the Company will market his production and will transport it to the Harbel and Cavalla plantations if the farmer has no suitable vehicle of his own.[6]

Through assisting local enterprises, a number of which happen to be owned by political leaders and government officials, Firestone increased its supply of rubber while reducing its relative share of the local rubber-growing industry. It was also protecting itself against adverse governmental controls by helping many nationals secure a vested interest in favorable governmental actions toward rubber growing.

Sharing Ownership through Joint Ventures

Probably the best-known means of increasing host country receptivity is through sharing ownership in local subsidiaries with nationals. Although the decision to engage in joint ventures involves many considerations other than a defensive move against national controls, this strategy can have the multiple effect of reducing the apparent threat of foreign domination, securing local allies, and enlarging the role of indigenous enterprise in the local economy.[7] Complete ownership of local subsidiaries gives the multinational enterprise greatest flexibility in such areas as organization, inter-company pricing, and dividend policy. Yet, many firms find that divestment of some of the equity can provide more than offsetting benefits through protection against controls. The greater the proportion of ownership that is divested, the greater the gain in protec-

---

[6] Wayne Chatfield Taylor, *The Firestone Operations in Liberia* (Washington, D.C.: National Planning Association, 1956), p. 94.

[7] For example, see Lawrence G. Franko, "Joint Venture Divorce in the Multinational Company," *Columbia Journal of World Business* May–June 1971, pp. 13–22.

tion and the greater the loss of parent-company control. The distribution as well as the share of the local ownership can be important. The advantage of having local ownership in the hands of a small number of local partners with significant holdings is that such partners are likely to take an active interest in protecting the profitability of their investment from erosion by government controls. The advantage of a wide dispersion of local ownership is that the international firm may be able to retain a degree of control greatly in excess of its ownership share.

Under the pressure of necessity, the predominantly negative attitudes of most multinational enterprises toward local sharing of ownership have been changing. A common objection expressed by many companies has been that host-country security markets are not sufficiently developed to absorb any significant amounts of stocks. Even though this may have been true in the past, the situation appears to be changing. In 1968, for example, when General Electric made a public offering of 10 percent of the total stock in its Mexican subsidiary, the issue was quickly over-subscribed.[8] In the mid-1960s a joint venture of the Cummins Engine Company in India offered 24½ percent of its shares to the public through the Bombay stock exchange and the purchase orders received totaled more than 50 times the number of shares being offered.[9]

At one time partnership with national governments was almost completely avoided by international corporations. It was regarded by many American executives as next door to communism. Realization of some of the advantages, however, has made this sort of arrangement more common. In 1970, as one example, U.S. Steel entered into a joint venture with the government of Brazil whereby it had a 49 percent interest in a new iron-ore mining project estimated to cost $300 million to $400 million. With the local government as a partner, there is a negative incentive for controls or harrassment—and in some cases an incentive for positive advantages. Moreover, a government usually has ample funds for desirable expansion, is less interested in profit distribution than in growth, and generally uninterested in taking over the business itself or undertaking day-to-day management. Private partners frequently produce problems on each of these counts.

Selective Ownership Divestment

Another ownership strategy is to separate the parts of the activity requiring physical assets from the commercial or technical sides and to arrange heavy local ownership in the physical side. Less can be expropriated if it is already owned locally, and the local investors may

---

[8] *Wall Street Journal*, 5 July 1968.

[9] Personal interview with Cummins' officials, 1965.

find it entirely in their interests to retain the pattern and not to become involved in a wider range of activity with which they are unfamiliar. United Fruit, a favorite leftist target in Latin America, has divested itself over the last decade and a half of the majority of its Latin American landholdings and has focused more heavily on its marketing and transportation activities in the banana business.[10]

Conversely, some international businesses may find that retention of commercial activity by local entrepreneurs is advantageous. In many countries, for example, the importer-distributor is a powerful political force. Working through such an outlet may ensure continued access to the market, even though the international company would be able to carry out much more effective distribution on its own account.

Multiple Nationality for International Business Projects

In some countries, the domination of the foreign business sector by firms of a single nationality may be an important stimulus for stronger national controls. One response to this fear of economic domination is for multinational enterprises to acquire multiple nationality or to undertake projects together with firms of other nations. Both Royal Dutch Shell and Unilever have carefully nurtured the dual Dutch-British nationality of the parents because they have found the ambiguity to be useful. When Indonesia's Sukarno was being unfriendly to the Dutch, these enterprises emphasized their British identity. Where antagonism emerges against the British, it is the Dutch identity that comes to the fore.

Consortia of international business firms of different nationalities, such as the Iranian consortium of Western companies, have been common in the field of petroleum. A similar pattern has been followed more recently in the field of mining. Some examples are the Fria bauxite project in Guinea, the Freeport nickel project in Indonesia, and iron-ore mining projects in Australia.

Changing Nationality

For the future, it is conceivable that multinational enterprises may change their nationality in order to be better received by host countries and/or to avoid home-country controls. With the expansion of the European Common Market and the accompanying preferences being displayed toward international companies of common market nationality, some American multinational firms have already been considering a change in the nationality of their parent firm.

---

[10] *Business Week,* 22 November 1969.

ENTRY AND OPERATING STRATEGIES

A wide range of defensive measures for avoiding national controls can be grouped under the rubric of entry and operating strategies. These defenses make use of the inherent flexibility and total enterprise capability of the multinational firm. They permit a company to adjust or re-arrange its patterns of location, its logistics, and its operating policies so as to have activities take place where the costly effects of national controls are minimized. Some of the options, as discussed below, are the choice of business activity, selection of products, location of production sites, location of intangible assets, sourcing and movement of funds and profits, ownership divestment of certain assets, and control of distribution and markets.

The Choice of Business Activity

One of the most obvious ways for a firm to avoid controls is to change the type of activity engaged in. Gone are the days when a maker of buggy whips limited his activity to making and trading in nothing but buggy whips. Confronted with restrictions concerning one area of business, the firm can quickly move to others. For many international corporations this is particularly easy. Most have many facets to their business and can develop those in which controls do not hamper achievement of the firm's objectives. When ITT's telephone company was bought out by the government of Peru in the late 1960s, the company shifted its Peruvian activities into more acceptable company lines, such as the construction of a Sheraton hotel (ITT subsidiary) and the manufacturing of electrical equipment. Union Miniere, S.A.—the Belgian company described as "a mining company without any mines" after its vast copper mines were expropriated in the Congo in 1967—began investing in chemical and industrial concerns and became active in data processing, nuclear research, engineering, and metallurgy.[11]

Where the compensation terms for the sale or expropriation of a company's assets require reinvestment for a period of time in the same country, such as in the case of ITT, the choice of new business activity will be influenced by the locational restriction. In other situations, such as the Union Miniere case, the company can scan the global environment for opportunities, thus placing all interested nations that might possibly receive the investment in competition with each other.

The prime criteria in the search and selection of expansion opportunities will almost certainly be growth, risk, and return on capital. Whatever the emphasis in any individual case, these criteria will favor expansion

---

[11] *Wall Street Journal,* 28 December 1970.

where capital and profits look least vulnerable to erosion by government controls or by political risk. Variations in the vulnerability of different types of business activities will be discussed in Chapter 15 on political risk. A few decades ago, foreign investment in public utilities were politically and economically popular with both host countries and investors. But styles have changed and public utilities presently have the highest degree of vulnerability to expropriation and national controls and are generally avoided for new investments. The extractive industries, particularly petroleum and mining, also have a high degree of risk. By using a high-risk factor in evaluating such investments, international firms weigh them less favorably as attractive choices of business activity.

Lower vulnerability is likely to occur in intermediate production which buys from and sells to local entrepreneurs. Both supplier and customer can act as buffers against imposition of controls. In many cases the intermediate type of production is likely to be essential to the customer's output, and to require technological expertise which neither supplier nor customer could or would want to provide for itself.

Location of Production

Some national controls are directed toward increasing production levels of local subsidiaries by forcing such foreign resident firms to export, or at least to maximize the proportion of local production in their local sales. Firms, however, have other objectives than maximizing production in any one location, and these may lead them to locate their production so as to gain economies of scale or lower transportation and tariff costs. The extent to which a firm can adopt a cost-minimizing plant location plan can be limited by the actions of competing firms. Nevertheless, a firm normally has sufficient locational flexibility for many countries to be restrained in their imposition of controls. As soon as a nation's controls are raised above those of alternative locations, the country becomes a less likely location for new investments or expansions of existing facilities by international firms. Conversely, when it reduces its control level, as did France after General Motors built its major plant in Antwerp, Belgium, rather than in Strasbourg, France, a country is more likely to be a recipient of future investment.

An interesting case of using location to avoid what the company considered unacceptable pollution controls was the decision of Hoechst AG to locate a new steel plant in Dortmund, West Germany, when Dutch authorities raised antipollution objections to a planned Hoechst plant near Rotterdam. The Rotterdam plant was to be a joint project with the Hoogovens of Holland.[12]

---

[12] *Wall Street Journal,* 6 July 1971.

In some industries, firms have been known to maintain reserve production potential in several countries as a deterrent to individual nations imposing added controls. In the 1950s, for example, United Fruit kept large amounts of improved land prepared for banana planting but unplanted. The stated company objective was to have land reserves in case its plantations were exposed to diseases or other natural hazards. Another obvious advantage was the possibility of shifting the location of production as a defense against national controls. The international oil companies have been accused of stockpiling oil reserves in some countries as an implicit threat to oil-producing countries that there are limits to the extent to which national demands can be met and output still maintained.

Strength can be built against both home and host countries by setting up directly competing units within the same organization but located in different countries. Such an arrangement can be particularly effective in limiting national controls if the subsidiaries directly compete with each other for the same export markets. Any restraining controls applied locally might give the competing subsidiary an export advantage.

Yet another defense available to the multinational enterprise lies in adoption of a truly international production network in which each plant specializes in some part of the total process. This means that most subsidiaries will contribute export income to the country of residence. Any insistence by the local government on further local production could be demonstrated by the international corporation as likely to jeopardize exports to units elsewhere in the network.

Location of Intangible Assets

A powerful source of strength for international firms in combating national controls is their ability to control the location of intangible business assets. These include research and development ability, technical, marketing, and management know-how. When the firm controls essential technical know-how, the extent to which any host country can move against it is severely circumscribed. If the activity requires continual injections of up-dated research output, expropriation of purely production facilities could be self-defeating. More gradual attempts at creeping controls, such as limitation of profit remittances or permission to expand, could be offset by the firm through withholding new developments as a bargaining gambit. The same situation prevails when the international firm retains the production, marketing, and management expertise through the use of expatriate personnel rather than training nationals. This suggests, unfortunately, that countries perceived to be high-risk control areas are less likely to maximize the technology-transfer benefits from multinational enterprises.

Control of Distribution and Markets

When production or extraction is located in one country and the consumer in another, the international firm can build a strong position through control of the access to the market. If the firm owns the channels of distribution or has built an unassailable market position, controls imposed over production must not take the costs beyond those the marketing organization could obtain elsewhere. So long as no supplying country is in a monopoly position and supplying countries do not act in unison, any action by one will be checked by the failure of the others to act likewise. In some cases, international corporations have built themselves into virtually single-buyer positions from competing suppliers.

But just as a nation's bargaining position can be undercut by the availability of other sources of supply, so can the bargaining strength of an international enterprise be sapped when other companies are willing to do the marketing. In 1971 Guyana nationalized its bauxite mines owned by Alcan. Given a world oversupply of bauxite, Alcan was unlikely to have trouble finding other sources of supply. In the closely knit world of a small number of aluminum producers, it appeared that Guyana was going to have serious difficulty in selling its bauxite. But to Guyana's rescue (and Alcan's dismay) came a London metal-brokerage company that apparently saw market possibilities in Eastern Europe and Japan. As the *Economist* observed, the brokerage firm "has been rather rude to the world's major aluminum companies, which will not make its task easier."[13] To be sure, the London firm encountered marketing difficulties. Shortly thereafter, Alcan was able to arrive at a mutually acceptable settlement, which included acting as the marketing agent for Guyana.

Even within one country, an international business firm likely to be hampered by creeping controls may build a stronger position by retaining dominance of the market. Some of the U.S. manufacturers of branded consumer goods in Japan, for example, seem to have adopted a policy of purchasing supplies from a range of local suppliers while retaining all the marketing in their own hands. This limits the amount of investment required, and at the same time builds added protection against controls. Small producers without experience in marketing branded consumer products should act as a buffer against Japanese government interference, being in a position to make growing production profits and not at all keen to take over the marketing themselves. There would be no incentive to expropriate locally owned operations and a great deal of difficulty in expropriating marketing know-how.

---

[13] *Economist,* 3 July 1971.

Sourcing and Movement of Funds and Profits

When governments place controls on financial remittance or the use of local funds for balance-of-payments reasons, to implement domestic economic policies, or to avoid excessive profit taking, the multinational firm is in a particularly strong position to avoid much of the intent behind these controls. Using a variety of legal forms of incorporation, it can generally arrange to allocate the ownership control of its assets and activities to a preferred pattern of jurisdictions. It can use assets in one nation to support borrowing in another, obtain funds from outside a nation for inward remittances at a time when local firms would find great difficulty obtaining further capital, or adopt a range of other financial management policies discussed in Chapter 20. This strength has been used frequently in both home and host countries in times of inflation and tight monetary controls to build up a larger market share at a lower cost than would be the case were local competitors on the same footing.

The international movement of funds can also be carried out through a range of internal transactions that are difficult to police. Charges for royalties, interest, travel, training, research and development, corporate overheads, machinery, advice, use of overseas facilities, and so on endlessly, can be arranged in such a way that no government could prevent significant transfers of funds without stopping all business transactions. Then there are the more controllable, but still quite effective, possibilities of altering the transfer prices for components, raw materials, part assemblies, or finished goods.

All these actions affect the location of profit. They are thus equally employable for arranging the place at which profit is taken so that taxation is minimized. In some cases, however, the arrangement that would minimize taxation is not that which would locate the funds in the way the business would find optimal. In such cases, the avoidance of taxation tends to dominate the other motives.

TRADE-OFF DEALS

The use of trade-offs and bargaining as a countervailing power to national-control policies can be illustrated by the case of Merck Sharp & Dome in India. During the 1950s, Merck had developed a solid market in India for drugs through exporting and some local packaging. In 1955 and 1956, the Indian government made it clear that it was moving in the direction of producing more antibiotics in its fully owned company, Hindustan Antibiotics (Private) Limited. In support of this plan, India received technical assistance from the USSR in developing a master plan for expanding government production in the pharmaceutical field and an offer of a large loan at extremely low rates of interest.

At the time these plans became known, representatives of MSD International were in India negotiating to establish a plant on quite different terms. Because of the preeminence of MSDs technological know-how, the Indian government suggested a partnership with a government corporation. It also suggested as an alternative that MSD provide technical assistance and train personnel to help Hindustan Antibiotics establish a plant for manufacturing streptomycin. After a period of bargaining, a compromise plan was agreed to. MSD was permitted to join forces with a privately owned Indian firm to manufacture a wide range of products in return for providing technical assistance to the state-owned company for the production of streptomycin. MSD agreed to prepare the plans for the government plant, train Indian personnel, and make its know-how in this field available for a modest fee.

As a key official of MSD explained, "We ended up not on our initial terms but not on theirs either. It was a period of often tough bargaining, but never chiseling. A basic understanding was reached by the willingness to appreciate each other's philosophy, motivation, objectives, and problems. Should we have adopted the attitude that she would do business with us on our terms or not at all? Should we have surrendered the field to Russia by default? I hardly think anyone would seriously advocate that course."[14]

The key source of MSDs bargaining power was its superior technical know-how. With this as a starting point and a willingness to bargain and consider trade-offs, it was able to bend a government policy that was rapidly moving in the direction of precluding private and foreign enterprise from an important business field.

LEGAL AND OTHER DEFENSES

The local subsidiaries of multinational firms generally have the option of contesting national-control actions in the local courts. When Venezuela passed a new law in 1971 which appeared to give the government reversion rights at the end of a concession period to local investments by the oil companies other than those directly connected with oil production, the major oil producers in Venezuela contested the constitutionality of the law before the Venezuela supreme court. Two American copper companies, whose properties were nationalized by Chile in 1971, appealed the terms of settlement offered by the government to a special tribunal created by the constitutional reform that permitted the nationalization of these properties. Although such appeals will take some time to be

---

[14] Dr. Antonie Knoppers in a speech to the Pharmaceutical Manufacturers Association, New York, December 8, 1958.

decided and although the international companies are uncertain about success, in the judgment of the companies such resort to legal defense in local courts appears to warrant the effort.

Another related strategy has been to undertake legal action in the courts of nations other than the host country. One of the American copper companies expropriated in Chile brought suit in a U.S. federal court in New York to block Chile's use of assets in the United States pending resolution of the copper company's claim for compensation. Subsequently, Chile agreed to pay the copper company for a loan it made to its Chilean subsidiary for developing a copper mine in Chile. As reported by an American newspaper, "There was some speculation that President Allende cleared payment to unfreeze the government's assets in the U.S."[15] Indeed, after Chile consented to make the payments, the copper company agreed before the New York court to give 36 hours notice before trying to attach the assets of LAN-Chile Airlines, the Chilean national carrier, which had temporarily suspended flights to the United States.

Where the output of multinational firms is exported from the host countries, international firms have used boycotts as an effective means of countervailing power. When Libya nationalized the local assets of British Petroleum in 1971, BP advertised in more than 100 newspapers around the world advising potential purchasers that the company reserves its rights with regard to Libyan oil. Although both BP and the British government denied that they had organized a formal boycott of Libyan oil, other petroleum companies and oil-importing nations began to shun the purchase of crude oil from the expropriated properties. In 1951, when foreign oil properties were nationalized by Iran, BP and other oil companies successfully used the boycott technique to block oil sales by Iran for three years. Iran eventually invited BP back as a 40 percent interest holder in a Western consortium.

Direct Influence over Governments

A review of the countervailing power of international companies must include the possibility of influencing governmental authorities through direct lobbying. In a political world it would be unusual if the business firm could not find some basis for exerting influence. For an international enterprise there may always be some local interest that would identify with it and be prepared to lobby accordingly. The larger the involvement, the stronger the incentive for those interests locally identifying with it. In some countries it is usual for particular interest groups to exercise influence disproportionate to the importance of their claims. It would

---

[15] *Wall Street Journal,* 28 February 1972.

not be too much to claim that international firms have found direct influence so effective that on many occasions they have decided not to use it simply because they know that the arrangement they would be able to make would be so inequitable in their favor that a later backlash would be very likely.

COMPETITION BETWEEN COUNTRIES

The encouragement of competition between different countries is also an option open to the international firm if the nature of its business permits a number of alternative locations. Auction markets for internationally traded commodities ensure this competition, for example. For the international investment, it is just as feasible to move from requesting permission to carry on business in a particular country to a solicitation of what amounts to bids from competing countries. In some cases, the weakest countries will be adding taxation holidays, dividend-remittance guarantees, and many other incentives in order to attract investment away from countries in which location is initially more attractive to the international investor.

Whenever a business has something of value that can be offered to several nations, the power to control can be eroded by competition between countries. And the limits on the exercise of this power are set by the weakest of the nations concerned. No other nation can impose on a firm a higher cost in terms of controls unless that cost is offset in some other way by higher profitability.

Summary

This chapter has shown that indeed the international enterprise is not without protection against the nation-state. In fact, its countervailing power is much greater than the picture of sovereign nations and their control programs and policies would indicate. The next section of this book is concerned in part with how firms decide what cards they will play in this international game.

EXERCISES AND DISCUSSION QUESTIONS

1. "The management of a multinational firm should in no way take it upon itself to decide what different contributions the firm will make to the various societies in which it operates. Within the external pressures and constraints surrounding the firm, mangement's first task is to ensure the firm's survival, and beyond that to pursue the balanced interests of its owners, employees, and customers." If you do not agree with this statement what guidelines would you give to the management of multinational firms?

2. Discuss the following proposals: The chief executive of a multinational corporation *should not:*
   a. accept any politically motivated direction from the government of the corporation's home country that would limit the performance of a foreign subsidiary.
   b. seek partnership with a foreign government in order to gain privilege or protection for its operations.
   c. use power stemming from its domestic operation to lobby the home government to intercede on the firm's behalf with foreign governments under whose jurisdiction the firm's subsidiaries operate.
   d. select expatriates for the top management of foreign subsidiaries because they can be trusted to place the firm's interests ahead of the local environment.

3. "In order to protect their traditional international business operations some multinational firms monopolize distribution channels and effectively deny small producers in developing countries reasonable access to international markets. Such action is against the principles underlying U.S. commercial law and should not be permitted under U.S. law simply because those harmed fall outside its jurisdiction." Comment on this statement. Can you identify any firms to which you think this statement might apply?

4. It has been argued that one way a multinational firm should use its strength is to ensure that countries know they are really in direct competition for its new investment. If you agree, how would you suggest the firm go about ensuring this awareness and what risks do you see?

5. What are the distinguishing characteristics of product areas that will in general have low vulnerability to government controls in less developed countries and what reasons do you have for your expectations?

PART IV

Assessing and Forecasting the International Business Environment

THE MOST PERVASIVE DISTINCTION between international and domestic business lies in the environmental framework. The multiplicity and diversity of environments create a wide range of demands on the international enterprise and the international manager for new tools, concepts, analytical methods, and types of information. In essence, many dimensions of business decision making which have been constants in domestic business become environmental variables.

This part focuses on both assessments and forecasting. Assessment means identifying the environmental factors relevant to a particular business activity that may vary among nations. This process can be illustrated by legal transactions. Where contract law differs among nations, the legal transactions of an international business firm must recognize and take into account such differences when legal agreements are consummated.

But assessment of environmental differences is not enough. The enterprise must constantly be forecasting the environmental situation for at least two reasons. One reason is that environments are dynamic and constantly changing. The other reason is that the international enterprise is generally making long-term commitments where future conditions may be far more important than the present situation.

Emphasizing the need for forecasting raises all of the well-known objections to forecasting. There is no agreed usage of the term. What we have in mind is not an exercise in predicting the future with near-certain accuracy, but identifying probable future outcomes with varying ranges of confidence. Although no completely scientific method of probing the future has yet been invented, the reality is that every decision maker is a forecaster, regardless of whether his forecasts are implicit, explicit, subconscious, or conscious. The question is whether the enterprise tries to make use of scientific analysis as an aid to decision making or leaves the task to intuition alone.

The subsystems of the environment selected for examination are the economic, cultural, legal, and political environments. Although the identification and evaluation of markets is essentially a matter of business operations, this subject has been included in the environment section because it follows closely on the assessment of the general economic environment. National-control forecasting has also been included in this section as a major task in environmental forecasting.

The chapters which follow examine separately the major subsystems of the international business environment, although the many components of the environment are causally intertwined and present in varying mixtures when a specific management responsibility must be undertaken, as is recognized in Part V.

11

CULTURAL DIFFERENCES
AND CULTURE CHANGE

CROSSING NATIONAL BOUNDARIES involves a step into different social and cultural environments. And the problems faced by the enterprise that does business in one language and one culture are quite different from those that arise when dealing with two, three, four—or perhaps fifty languages and cultures. Groups of people, or societies, differ in their values and beliefs, in their aspirations and motivations, and in the ways they satisfy their desires. Such cultural differences pervasively influence all dimensions of international business activity.

THE MEANING OF CULTURE

By culture we mean the whole set of social norms and responses that condition a population's behavior. It is these that make one social environment different from another and give each a shape of its own. The basic discipline that is most relevant here is cultural anthropology. Cultural anthropologists have devoted a great deal of time and effort to definitions of culture, arguing what should or should not be included.[1]

Basic to all is the idea that culture is acquired and inculcated. It is the set of rules and behavior patterns that an individual learns but does not inherit at birth. For every society these norms and behavioral responses develop into a different cultural pattern which gets passed down through the generations with continual embellishment and adaptation; but with its own focus on aspects that are most highly developed.

[1] See A. L. Kroeber and Clyde Kluckhohn, "Culture: A Critical Review of Concepts and Definitions," (Papers of the Peabody Museum of American Archaeology and Ethnology, Harvard University, Cambridge, Mass., 47, no. 1, 1952), pp. 1–223.

For much cultural conditioning, the individual is unaware of the learning. The subtle process of inculcating culture through example and reward or punishment is generally much more powerful than direct instruction, and the individual unwittingly adopts the cultural norm. This process of learning a cultural pattern, called enculturation, conditions the individual so that a large proportion of his behavior fits the requirements of his culture and yet is determined below his level of conscious thought.[2] To the individual his cultural conditioning is like an iceberg—he is unaware of nine tenths of it.

The concept of culture is so broad that it gives little guidance to anyone wishing to study or compare cultures. Some classification of the elements of a culture is needed as a basic framework for grasping the cultural pattern. One such approach was proposed by George P. Murdock in the form of an elaborate list of more than 70 cultural universals which he argued occur in every culture known to history or ethnography. Arranged in alphabetical order to emphasize their variety, these are listed in Table 11.1. While a one-dimensional check list such

TABLE 11.1
Cultural Universals

age grading	food taboos	music
athletic sports	funeral rites	mythology
bodily adornment	games	numerals
calendar	gestures	obstetrics
cleanliness training	gift giving	penal sanctions
community organization	government	personal names
cooking	greetings	population policy
cooperative labor	hair styles	postnatal care
cosmology	hospitality	pregnancy usages
courtship	housing hygiene	property rights
dancing	incest taboos	propitiation of
decorative art	inheritance rules	supernatural beings
divination	joking	puberty customs
division of labor	kingroups	religious rituals
dream interpretation	kinship nomenclature	residence rules
education	language	sexual restrictions
eschatology	law	soul concepts
ethics	luck superstitions	status differentiation
ethnobotany	magic	surgery
etiquette	marriage	tool making
faith healing	mealtimes	trade
family	medicine	visiting
feasting	modesty concerning	weaning
fire making	natural functions	weather control
folklore	mourning	

Source: George P. Murdock, "The Common Denominator of Cultures" in *The Science of Man in the World Crises*, ed. Ralph Linton (New York: Columbia University Press, 1945), pp. 123–42.

[2] Melville J. Herskovits, *Cultural Anthropology* (New York: Alfred A. Knopf, Inc., 1963), p. 326.

as this has major limitations it can nevertheless be of considerable value. The international manager of a firm selling razors and razor blades, for example, must be aware that he is dealing with the puberty customs of different cultures. Moreover, as most razors are given as gifts he is also dealing with gift giving, courtship and family patterns. An examination of cultural patterns under each of these headings will certainly suggest differences in marketing strategy from country to country.

A sensitivity to the elements of culture and the ways in which they differ brings with it an ability to analyze any happening from its cultural perspective. What on the surface may look like a similar happening in different cultures may well be composed of many different cultural elements. The apparently simple phenomenon of a family meal, for instance, could be viewed as an extensive set of different rules concerning the time the meal is eaten, the seating arrangements, the roles played by each in initiating or ending conversation and in interrupting or changing the subject, the comments regarded as humorous, the facial expressions used, the values placed on different foods, the attitudes towards age, and so on. Moreover, the shape and size of the table will differ, as will the utensils, the way they are used, and how the people eat.

CULTURE AND COMMUNICATION

Knowledge of cultural differences is particularly important in understanding the communication problems that arise, both within the international firm and in its relationships with the external world. Cultural bias is a constant risk in the transmission of ideas and in the management-decision process.

A language is inextricably linked with all aspects of a culture, and each culture reflects in its language what is of value to the people. Culture is largely inculcated through language—spoken or written. Very little of what man learns is actually learned from his individual experience. Language, then, becomes the embodiment of culture. It may even condition what we look for and therefore see. One anthropologist comparing the structure of languages pointed out that Eskimo languages have several different words for types of snow, while the English language has one, and Aztec uses the same basic word stem for snow, ice, and cold. With only one word for snow we tend to identify only the broad classification.[3]

When communication involves translation from one language into another, the problems of ascertaining meaning that arise within one culture are multiplied many times. Translation is not simply a matching of words with identical meanings. It involves interpretation of the cul-

---

[3] Paul Henle, *Language, Thought, and Culture* (Ann Arbor: University of Michigan Press, 1958).

tural patterns and concepts of one country in terms of the patterns and concepts of another. Awareness of the difficulties of translation is particularly important for legal agreements. As a distinguished international lawyer has noted, "When contracts cross national borders, they may alter in character as well as language."[4]

Communication does not always take the form of language. All behavior communicates, and as Edward Hall has so clearly pointed out, each culture may be different in the way it experiences and uses time, space, relationships, and a variety of other aspects of culture.[5] The use of time in one culture may convey a set of meanings quite different from the meanings for a similar use of time in another culture. To be 30 minutes late for an appointment with a business associate may be the height of rudeness in *Culture A* but in *Culture B* it may be early and unexpectedly reliable. Different messages may be conveyed by the amount of notice given for a meeting, the time of departure, invitations to future commitments, or the way in which a party agrees to the order of discussion at the meeting. In some cultures a delay in answering a communication is interpreted by the other party as a lack of interest. In other cultures the more important a matter the more time is taken to respond.

In a similar way, the use of space conveys different meanings. The distance one person stands away from another indicates the degree of relationship or interest and can dramatically influence what is said. For a given type of interaction, different cultures have different norms for the appropriate distance. Middle Easterners and Latin Americans, for example, stand much closer than Western Europeans. The size of an office in relation to other offices conveys a great deal about the status of an American businessman. In the Arab world, the size and location of an office are poor indicators of the importance of the man who occupies it.

THE NEED FOR CULTURAL SENSITIVITY
IN INTERNATIONAL BUSINESS

Any business operating within a single country must adjust to the culture within which it operates, but the need for cultural sensitivity and adjustment is much greater for the international firm. The local firm may introduce an innovation in the form of a new product or new business practice only infrequently. For the international firm, in comparison, cross-national transfer of any one of its old products or

---

[4] Henry P. deVries, "The Language Barriers," *Columbia Journal of World Business,* July–August 1969, p. 79.

[5] Edward T. Hall, *The Silent Language* (New York: Doubleday & Company, 1959).

conventional practices may represent an innovation. When a firm has an existence outside a culture, many of its actions will introduce something new. There are many ways in which a firm may be an unwitting agent for transplanting aspects of one culture into another. The assessment of cultural differences is thus of primary importance to international business. This need for cultural assessment is further underlined by the fact that most international businessmen will be steeped in the norms of one culture and find it difficult to appreciate the complex cultural patterns of different societies.

Cultural differences which can affect international business operations arise in all aspects of business activity and have their impact within each of the traditional functions. Differences in the behavior of customers must be taken into account in product policies and marketing strategies. The German housewife values convenience and can be rather easily persuaded to buy packaged soup. The French housewife prefers homemade soup because it fulfills her image of herself as the mother. Many aspects of a product such as packaging, color, and advertising message, can be easily changed to fit the local culture without changing the product's basic nature.

Differences in behavior and values of employees can have a major impact on the effectiveness of production-management policies. The African factory worker, for example, may find paternalism a desirable practice because it helps him replace security feelings that he loses when he leaves his traditional group. The American factory worker, on the other hand, tends to feel that paternalistic management is outdated because it restricts his current need to express his individuality.

The external relations of the international firm can also be strongly influenced by cultural variables. In dealing with local business firms in a specific national environment, the international enterprise may have to recognize that agreements and accommodations among potential competitors, rather than aggressive competition, are the accepted norm. Bribery may be the traditional means of influencing official actions in some countries and unacceptable in others. In raising money from local banks or security markets, personal reputation may be the key requirement in one environment whereas a high degree of financial disclosure may be the more important element in another.

KEY CULTURAL DIFFERENCES FOR INTERNATIONAL BUSINESS

The international manager may never become an expert anthropologist, sociologist, and social psychologist in addition to his role as a management specialist. But he should become generally familiar with key cultural elements that are likely to influence international business activities. The brief survey that follows will serve as an introduction to some of these elements and the ways in which they affect international business.

Assumptions and Attitudes

One of the principal differences among cultures is in assumptions and attitudes relating to man's ability to influence the future. For example, an assumption that people can substantially influence the future underlies much of U.S. management philosophy. This belief in self-determination contrasts sharply with a fatalistic viewpoint in some Moslem cultures that the future is not in man's hands. It differs also from a mystical view that events are likely to be determined by the capricious influence of spirits that must be appeased.[6] Whatever the explanation for varying attitudes, the critical issue for business operations is whether a person believes that events will occur regardless of what he does, or whether he believes that he can help shape future events.

The self-determination or "master of destiny" attitude is generally qualified by the accompanying view that future aspirations must be realistic and that hard work is necessary to achieve future goals. With these qualifications, the self-determination assumption has profoundly shaped U.S. management practices. As only one illustration, long-range planning becomes a worthwhile investment because of confidence that planning can influence what is to happen. Obviously, in cultures where the fatalistic or mystical attitudes prevail, management practices based on other assumptions are not likely to be effective.

Variations among cultures in attitudes toward time have already been noted as an aspect of communications. Many misunderstandings can occur because of different concepts of time. Operating difficulties can arise when workers from an agrarian peasant society are required to accept the kind of scheduling of time and routine essential for efficient industrial operations. In most agrarian societies, work is not equated with time and is not regularly and precisely scheduled. Instead, work is geared to seasonal emergencies, climatic threats, or sporadic exhaustion of supplies or resources.[7] Thus, setting time schedules or deadlines will evoke a positive response in certain cultures and a negative response in others.

An interesting learning experience for dealing with varying national attitudes toward time is to arrange a social event for participants from different countries. What time should be placed on each invitation to make sure that most of the guests will be present together? Fortunately

---

[6] William H. Newman, "Is Management Exportable?" *Columbia Journal of World Business,* January–February 1970, pp. 7–8.

[7] Conrad M. Arensberg and Arthur M. Niehoff, *Introducing Social Change: A Manual for Americans Overseas* (Chicago: Aldine Publishing Co., 1964), p. 164.

for hostesses, most guests respond on the basis of time concepts in the country in which such events take place rather than time attitudes in their native culture.

Personal Beliefs, Aspirations, and Motivations

Personal beliefs and aspirations shape the factors that motivate individuals. The dominant view in a society toward wealth and material gain can have a significant bearing on the types, qualities, and numbers of individuals who pursue entrepreneurial and management careers as well as on the way workers respond to material incentives.[8] In most countries in the world, wealth tends to be considered as desirable and the prospect of material gain operates as a significant motivation. But there are still some traditional societies where a worker will be on the job until he earns a certain amount of money and then be absent until these earnings are exhausted. There are affluent societies where many young people have become more interested in job satisfaction per se, or the opportunities in a prospective job for involvement in public welfare activities, than in traditional financial rewards.

Variations among cultures in the dominant views toward achievement and work, which can be a vital determinant of management performance and productive efficiency, have been the subject of considerable research by David McClelland and his associates under the rubric of "achievement motivation."[9] The achievement motivation of an individual refers to a basic attitude toward life, namely, the willingness to commit oneself to the accomplishment of tasks considered by the person to be worthwhile and difficult. An achievement-motivated person makes accomplishment an end in itself. He does not reject tangible rewards, but they are not essential.

Measures of achievement motivation have been devised, and the desire for achievement by business managers and others have been studied cross culturally. The views toward achievement in a country appear to be closely associated with rates of economic development. Countries where individuals show a high-achievement motivation tend to have rapid rates of growth. McClelland maintains that achievement motivation is the prime factor in managerial success. He suggests that the best place to recruit managers in a number of countries is from the middle and lower classes because these people are more apt to have a high-achievement need than if they come from either upper- or lower-class background. Most recently, experiments have been undertaken in

---

[8] Richard N. Farmer and Barry M. Richman, *Comparative Management and Economic Progress* (Homewood, Ill.: Richard D. Irwin, Inc., 1965), pp. 177–89.

[9] David C. McClelland, *The Achieving Society,* (Princeton, N.J.: D. Van Nostrand Co., 1961).

various countries on the possibilities and the techniques for changing patterns of achievement motivation.

The extent to which objective analysis is used for decision making varies greatly among cultures. There is a strong cultural belief underlying U.S. management practices that decisions should be based on objective analyses of facts and that all persons who can contribute relevant information should be consulted. Such objective analyses require large inputs of data and the development of impersonal decision-making techniques.

Decision making on a factual and rational basis is not the standard pattern in some societies. The personal judgment of a senior executive may be the accepted basis for a decision, and a request that the executive explain or give the rationale for his decision would be interpreted as a lack of confidence in the executive's judgment. Furthermore, it may be considered inappropriate for a senior executive to seek facts and consult others—especially his juniors—on matters on which he is already presumed to be wise. In such cultures, traditional, emotional, and mystical considerations, rather than objective analyses, are dominant.

Misunderstandings have frequently occurred between North Americans and South Americans because of the Latin use of rhetorical speech in discussions. North Americans want to get down to business, to deal directly with the issues, and to eliminate the flowery talk. The Latins are likely to oppose such pressure. Traditionally, such directness has not been the way they reach decisions.

Interpersonal Relations

The importance of cultural variables in interpersonal relations can be illustrated by different views of authority, or family responsibilities, and of tolerance for personal criticism. The dominant view of authority in a society may range from an autocratic system at one extreme to a democratic-participative system at the other extreme. If authority is looked upon as an absolute natural right of management or of other types of formal leaders, the effect on managerial behavior would typically be a high degree of centralization and little delegation of authority. At the other extreme, managerial authority would be shared with subordinates and workers, and considerable decentralization in decision making would be typical of business enterprises.

It is not possible to say which forms of managerial authority along the continuum are best in terms of efficiency or in achieving other business goals. The forms vary greatly from Japan to West Germany and from the United States to Yugoslavia. Yet, each of these countries have had impressive records of business performance and economic growth in recent years. Whatever authority system prevails in a given country, the international enterprise will have to relate its management patterns to the expectations and traditions of local employees.

Authority systems are highly relevant to aspects of business operations other than management. In marketing, it is important to know whether decision making within customer organizations with respect to purchases is typically decentralized or reserved to the top-echelon executives. In negotiating with governments, the international businessman will have to know whether decision authority resides with low-level bureaucrats or must be handled at the highest levels of government bureaucracy.

Another cultural variable that influences interpersonal relationships is the pattern of family ties. Some version of the extended family still prevails in many countries. Under this pattern large numbers of near as well as quite distant relatives are encompassed in a system of shared rights and obligations. All members of this group are interdependent, and it is the responsibility of the leaders to see that economic resources are available to satisfy the needs of each member of the group. The extended family pattern is still strong in a country like India. In contrast, the more limited nuclear family which only includes the mother, father, and children is the significant unit of many of the advanced countries.

Strong and extended family ties can result in what has been characterized as patrimonial management.[10] Ownership and key positions in a business enterprise are held by family members. Nepotism is generally dominant in the full range of employment decisions, and business goals are oriented toward family interests and aspirations. Such patrimonial management has the advantages of encouraging teamwork, loyalty, and mutual interest. Family codes can enforce morality in financial and other matters, and family loyalty attracts and holds managers in situations where the supply of qualified managers is limited. But the extended family situation also has drawbacks. It emphasizes nepotism rather than competence. It can vitiate the will to work by limiting personal incentives. Family business may be run like an authoritarian household with little concern for considerations other than family goals. And family enterprises may suffer from a lack of invigorating ideas and innovations which can come from outsiders.

Family patterns can be extremely important from the standpoint of marketing as well as general management. In Western societies, the husband and wife typically share decision making on family purchases, with children and other members of the family having a secondary vote. In the extended family, the family patriarch holds the key decision-making position, although this is declining with the monetization of the economy, the demise of family enterprises, and an increase in geographic and social mobility. Notwithstanding these changes, the international manager must understand the different family patterns that presently prevail.

---

[10] Frederick Harbison and Charles A. Myers, *Management in the Industrial World* (New York: McGraw-Hill Book Co., 1959), pp. 69–73.

Another cultural element that affects interpersonal relations is the difference among societies in frankness of expression and tolerance for personal differences. In Far Eastern cultures it is traditional to value politeness over blunt truth. The Japanese businessman finds it inappropriate to say "no" in many situations. In dealing with an American, the Japanese may make all kinds of barely favorable noises and then maybe say that he'll think about the matter. He has actually told the American "no," but it is entirely possible that the American thinks he has said "yes," and the American later imagines that he has somehow been deceived.

In many Latin American countries frankly expressed differences in views do not easily fit the culture. If a person expresses criticisms of a policy in order to improve the quality of decision making, such statements are likely to be interpreted as personal attacks. If a subordinate disagrees with his boss, the boss will most certainly feel insulted. Persons in subordinate positions are expected to present information or judgments which support the ideas of senior officials or be silent.

Social Structure

A final category of cultural elements can be grouped under the general heading of social structure. It includes such variables as inter-class mobility, determinants of status, and patterns of education.

Few societies in the world assume that all men are equal. Instead, societies have traditional systems of ranking individuals and groups. Relative positions in the social hierarchy are based on ethnic, cultural, educational, and linguistic differences, as well as on economic position. Sometimes traditional social structures are fairly rigid such as the caste system of India. Sometimes the distinctions are more fluid and considerable inter-class mobility is the rule. In most countries of the world there is a distinction between the elite, who have political and economic control of the country, and the relatively underprivileged peasant groups.[11]

Two aspects of social structure are of special concern to the international enterprise—inter-class mobility and the status assigned by a society to individuals who engage in business occupations. If a rigid social structure prevents a substantial number of individuals from moving into the ranks of management or other responsible business positions, managerial effectiveness is likely to be constrained in many, if not most, business activities. If the status assigned to business pursuits is low in the social structure, it will be difficult to attract adequate numbers of competent persons to business positions.

Even the United States, which is widely regarded as a rather open

---

[11] Arensberg and Niehoff, *Introducing Social Change,* p. 41.

society with few class distinctions, has extensive class barriers to individual mobility. Many business firms have excluded from executive positions virtually all minority groups, including, Blacks, Jews, Mexicans, Orientals, American Indians, and many others. Such barriers have been breaking down, yet it is still true that social barriers may be serious obstacles for many highly qualified and competent persons in the United States. In most other countries, social barriers are likely to be even greater hindrances to individual mobility. The British social system, although much more flexible than it was a few decades ago, still assigns great importance to family and university background when individuals are being considered for high level positions in government and business.[12]

In many countries of the world much higher status tends to be associated with land ownership or government positions, or professional or intellectual activity than is enjoyed by the businessman, engineer, mechanic, agronomist, or some other person concerned directly with production.[13] There is probably no country in the world where businessmen have the highest status. Even in the United States such occupations as supreme court justice, medical doctor, professor, and physical scientist have outranked corporation executives in surveys of high school students. Yet in many countries such as the United States, Japan, and even the USSR, managers of business enterprises have sufficiently high social status to enable business enterprises to attract large quantities of capable recruits.

Educational patterns generally reflect and reinforce patterns of class mobility and status. Where class mobility is high and status depends upon merit rather than family or caste, the educational system is likely to be open to students on the basis of their performance, and training in technical and management fields is available. Most commonly throughout the world, higher education has been restricted to the elite and upper classes and the patterns of education have emphasized the liberal arts and preparation for living the good life. Thus, the supply of trained people may be relatively small and the kinds of training available not closely related to business.

THREE PRECAUTIONS FOR CULTURAL ASSESSMENT

In examining cultural patterns the manager should be aware of similarities as well as differences. Cross-cultural analysis for international

---

[12] For example see David J. Hall and Gilles Amado-Fischgrund, "Chief Executives in Britain," *European Business*, January 1969; David Granick, *The European Executive* (London: Weidenfeld and Nicolson, 1962), Chapter 7.

[13] UNESCO, *Report of the World Social Situation* (Paris: 9 March 1961), p. 79.

business tends to emphasize differences because they are likely to create business problems. But to err by perceiving more differences than actually exist can also cause serious difficulties. Take the matter of managerial preferences for risk taking. The American executive may see the Japanese as different, whereas recent cross-cultural studies suggest that they are alike.[14] An American might find himself needlessly overexplaining his position, trying to convince the Japanese to be more adventuresome.

Another general caveat is that observed cultural patterns may be representative of a national group yet not applicable to everyone in the group. What is usually being discussed is a modal pattern, and considerable variation from the mode will exist within a group or a subset of the group. In fact, for some cultural characteristics there may be a wider range within a given society than between societies. The businessman should be careful always to define the limits of the group he is interested in and still be prepared to allow for individual differences.

Finally, the manager should endeavor to recognize his own cultural biases. Every person unwittingly tends to bias his view of other cultures by his unconscious acceptance of his own cultural conditioning. It takes a great deal of discipline to force the mind to see things that one's own culture ignores or places of low value. Then again, the closer to the culture the observer is, the more difficult he finds it to see accurately the changes that are taking place in it.

OVERALL APPROACHES TO CULTURAL ASSESSMENT

The international businessman may never have the time nor the need to build a comprehensive picture of a particular culture. He will usually be concerned with individual elements of culture that have a direct bearing on his managerial decision making. On the other hand, a familiarity with one or two ways in which an overall culture can be conceptualized will give him a framework on which to draw. At the least it will provide him with a mental check list of elements that may be important to his particular problem. Two such overall approaches which have been utilized in the international business literature, both two-dimensional, will be briefly outlined here. The first is that developed by Edward T. Hall[15] and the second an attempt by Richard N. Farmer and Barry M. Richman to develop a cultural framework specifically related to business decision making.[16]

---

[14] Bernard M. Bass, *The American Adviser Abroad,* Technical Report 27, Management Research Center of the College of Business Administration, (Rochester, N.Y.: University of Rochester, August 1969), p. 12.

[15] Hall, *The Silent Language,* especially Chapter 3.

[16] Farmer and Richman, *Comparative Management.*

Hall presents his map of culture as a two-dimensional matrix composed of 10 aspects of human activity which he calls Primary Message Systems. These are shown in Table 11.2. While each aspect can be ex-

TABLE 11.2
Primary Message Systems of Edward Hall's *Silent Language*

Primary Message System	*Depicts Attitudes and Cultural Rules for:*
1. Interaction	The ordering of man's interaction with those around him, through language, touch, noise, gesture, and so forth.
2. Association	The organization (grouping) and structuring of society and its components.
3. Subsistence	The ordering of man's activities in feeding, working, and making a living.
4. Bisexuality	The differentiation of roles, activities, and function along sex lines.
5. Territoriality	The possession, use, and defense of space and territory.
6. Temporality	The use, allocation, and division of time.
7. Learning	The adaptive process of learning and instruction.
8. Play	Relaxation, humor, recreation, and enjoyment.
9. Defense	Protection against man's environment, including medicine, warfare, and law.
10. Exploitation	Turning the environment to man's use through technology, construction, and extraction of materials.

Adapted from Edward K. Hall, *The Silent Language*, (Garden City, N.Y.: Doubleday & Company, Inc., 1959), pp. 61–81.

amined alone, Hall shows how a grasp of the complex interrelationships of a culture can be obtained by commencing with any of the 10 aspects and studying its intersection with each of the others. In a matrix there will be two intersections of each pair of aspects. If we were to start examination of a culture through the learning aspect, it would first intersect with the interaction aspect to raise questions about interaction in learning and the learning of interaction. We might want to examine the pattern that teachers and learners adopt for communicating with each other or what rules and knowledge gets passed on within the culture concerning the ways people should interact. Again, the matrix provides two intersections of bisexuality and learning. Under these we could study the differences in how and what the sexes are taught and, on the other hand, what is taught about sexual roles in society. Both aspects will differ from culture to culture.

For a more direct application of Hall's matrix to international business, take the example of a large manufacturer of toys and games assessing opportunities in a new country. The firm will be directly engaged in the play aspect of the new culture, and it is certain that the cultural patterns with respect to play will differ from those the firm is currently dealing with. Use of Hall's matrix would raise 18 categories of questions about play patterns in the new culture. Stemming from the intersection of "play" with the remaining "primary message systems," the first two categories would ask about interaction in play and about play in interaction, the second two would ask about the associations—that is, organizations involved in play and about games involving associations, and so on. Questions raised within the 18 categories are illustrated in Table 11.3 but it must be clear that the map does not magically produce the right answers or even the right questions. This is simply one structured approach to investigating how a new culture may differ. The reader who rejects a structured approach, however, should be sure in his own mind that his ad hoc alternative does develop an adequate sensitivity to the important cultural differences.

Farmer and Richman also use a matrix approach. They propose a list of critical environmental constraints, or cultural elements, from which the 15 shown in Table 11.4 are taken. Against this, they set another listing of 77 critical elements in the managerial process. The general categories for the critical elements are planning and innovation, control, organization, staffing, direction, leadership and motivation, marketing policies, production and procurement, research and development, finance, and public and external relations. Farmer and Richman contend that managerial effectiveness is largely determined by the pattern of external constraints. As the environment changes, so too must the pattern of management. What might be effective in producing results in one culture may be completely ineffectual in another. By examining the managerial alternatives against the background of external constraints managers will move towards a pattern of business practice most appropriate to the situation, and away from absolute rules imposed without regard for the situation. In a very simple application, for example, the internal procedures and organization structure should change radically where the bulk of the workers do not accept the idea of cause and effect, that is, the scientific method. Fewer rational requests and guiding principles will be called for and more direct rules and internal checking procedures will be required.

This type of matrix approach can be readily adapted to any business situation. On the vertical axis would appear relevant cultural variables and along the horizontal axis the dependent variables of interest to management. The body of the matrix would show the nature of the relationship between cultural variables and each management variable.

TABLE 11.3
A Business Application of Edward Hall's Map of Culture

Intersections of Play and Other Primary Message Systems	*Sample Questions Concerning Cultural Patterns Significant for Marketing Toys and Games*
1. Interaction/play	How do people interact during play as regards competitiveness, instigation, or leadership?
2. Play/interaction	What games are played involving acting, role playing, or other aspects of real world interaction?
3. Association/play	Who organizes play and how do the organization patterns differ?
4. Play/association	What games are played about organization; for example, team competitions and games involving kings, judges, or leader-developed rules and penalties?
5. Subsistence/play	What are the significant factors regarding people such as distributors, teachers, coaches, or publishers who make their livelihood from games?
6. Play/subsistence	What games are played about work roles in society such as doctors, nurses, firemen?
7. Bisexuality/play	What are the significant differences between the sexes in the sports, games, and toys enjoyed?
8. Play/bisexuality	What games and toys involve bisexuality; for example, dolls, dressing up, dancing?
9. Territoriality/play	Where are games played and what are the limits observed in houses, parks, streets, schools, and so forth?
10. Play/territoriality	What games are played about space and ownership; for example, Monopoly?
11. Temporality/play	At what ages and what times of the day and year are different games played?
12. Play/temporality	What games are played about and involving time; for example, clocks, speed tests?
13. Learning/play	What patterns of coaching, tuition, and training exist for learning games?
14. Play/learning	What games are played about and involving learning and knowledge; for example, quizzes?
15. Defense/play	What are the safety rules for games, equipment, and toys?
16. Play/defense	What war and defense games and toys are utilized?
17. Exploitation/play	What resources and technology are permitted or utilized for games and sport; for example, hunting and fishing rules, use of parks, cameras, vehicles, and so forth?
18. Play/exploitation	What games and toys about technology or exploitation are used; for example, scouting, chemical sets, microscopes?

TABLE 11.4
Critical Environmental Constraints

Educational-Cultural Variables

1. *Literacy level:* The percentage of the total population and those presently employed in industry who can read, write, and do simple arithmetic calculations, and the average years of schooling of adults.
2. *Specialized vocational and technical training and general secondary education:* Extent, types, and quality of education and training of this kind not directly under the control or direction of industrial enterprises; the type, quantity, and quality of persons obtaining such education or training and the proportion of those employed in industry who have such education and training.
3. *Higher education:* The percentage of the total population and those employed in industry with post-high school education, plus the types and quality of such education; the types of persons obtaining higher education.
4. *Special management-development programs:* The extent and quality of management-development programs which are not run internally by productive enterprises and which are aimed at improving the skills and abilities of managers and/or potential managers of different types and levels attending or having completed such programs.
5. *Attitude toward education:* The general or dominant cultural attitude toward education and the acquisition of knowledge, in terms of their presumed desirability; the general attitude toward different types of education.
6. *Educational match with requirements:* The extent and degree to which the types of formal education and training available in a given country fit the needs of productive enterprises on all levels of skill and achievement. This is essentially a summary category; depending on the type of job involved, different educational constraints indicated above would be more important.

Sociological-Cultural Variables

1. *Attitude toward industrial managers and management:* The general or dominant social attitude toward industrial and business managers of all sorts, and the way that such managers tend to view their managerial jobs.
2. *View of authority and subordinates:* The general or dominant cultural attitude toward authority and persons in subordinate positions, and the way that industrial managers tend to view their authority and their subordinates.
3. *Interorganizational cooperation:* Extent and degree to which business enterprises, government agencies, labor unions, educational institutions, and other relevant organizations cooperate with one another in ways conducive to industrial efficiency and general economic progress.
4. *Attitude toward achievement and work:* The general or dominant cultural attitude toward individual or collective achievement and productive work in industry.
5. *Class structure and individual mobility:* The extent of opportunities for social class and individual mobility, both vertical and horizontal, in a given country, and the means by which it can be achieved.
6. *Attitude toward wealth and material gain:* Whether or not the acquisition of wealth from different sources is generally considered socially desirable, and the way that persons employed in industry tend to view material gain.
7. *Attitude toward scientific method:* The general social and dominant individual attitude toward the use of rational, predictive techniques in solving various types of business, technical, economic, and social problems.
8. *Attitude toward risk taking:* Whether or not the taking of various types of personal, collective, or national risks is generally considered acceptable, as well as the dominant view toward specific types of risk taking in business and industry; the degree and extent to which risk taking tends to be a rational process in a particular country.
9. *Attitude toward change:* The general cultural attitude toward social changes of all types which bears directly on industrial performance in a given country, and the dominant attitude among persons employed in industry toward all types of significant changes in enterprise operations.

Source: Richard N. Farmer and Barry M. Richman, *Comparative Management and Economic Progress* (Homewood, Ill.: Richard D. Irwin, Inc., 1965), p. 29.

CULTURE CHANGE AND RESISTANCE TO CHANGE

A characteristic of human culture is that change does occur. Attitudes, values, beliefs, and behavior are constantly changing, although change may not be occurring rapidly or without resistance. The manager and the enterprise operating cross culturally, therefore, cannot rely upon a static understanding of cultural elements. Business performance can be very sensitive to changes in cultural patterns through their effects on both customer demand and the internal operations of the firm. Furthermore, successful marketing is very largely a matter of correct timing and strategy in the development of innovations, the adoption of which imply a receptive culture. Of greatest interest to the international businessman will be an understanding of what aspects of a culture will resist change and how those will differ among cultures, how the process of change takes place in different cultures, and what the speed of change will be.

There are two seemingly contradictory forces within cultures. On the one hand, people attempt to protect and preserve their culture with an elaborate set of sanctions and laws invoked against those who deviate from their norms. On the other hand, the environment within which a culture exists is continually changing, and a culture must change in order to ensure its own continuity.[17] Where a culture comes into contact with other cultures this same dichotomy exists. On the one hand, there is an ingrained belief, called ethnocentrism, that the ways of one's own culture are superior to those of other cultures, and on the other hand, a realization that a culture must be competitive if it is to retain its own identity.

These conflicting forces operate to make some elements of culture highly resistant to change, while others immediately fall to innovations. Yet other elements may give an impression that they are immutable but then change suddenly. How can these elements be differentiated?

Edward Hall's classification of cultural aspects into formal, informal, and technical, provides a valuable insight here. The distinction between these classes is based primarily on differences in the way the cultural norm is learned, the culture's level of awareness of the norm, and the response to a deviation from the norm.

Formal aspects are at the core of the culture and really determine its essence. They are taught through example and admonition as rules for which there is either right or wrong, with clear indication of when a mistake has been made. There is a formal awareness of what the norm is and a great deal of emotion if the norm is violated. In most societies it has been a formal rule, for example, that there should be no enjoyment from hurting others physically or from seeing them hurt.

---

[17] Arensberg and Niehoff, *Introducing Social Change*, p. 99.

The rule is that hurting people is not fun, and from early childhood this will be made very clear, with penalties for breaking it.

Informal rules are not taught so directly. Usually the learner picks them up by imitation and is unaware of learning them. The society is generally unconscious of the rules, and if one is violated, there would only be an expression of anxiety, or some informally learned reaction. The average child does not receive direct instruction in how to play. He is left to observe others and to do likewise. If the child attempts to dominate his playmates, for example, they will very likely develop ways of excluding him, but it would be unlikely for him to receive direct instruction on how to behave in groups.

Technical rules are usually taught in an instructional sense with logical and coherent reasoning attached to them. These are at the highest level of awareness as they are verbalized, reasoned, and explicit. There are few emotions attached to the violation of a technical rule. Breaking a rule by adopting a different training approach for an athletic sport, for example, would occasion intellectual interest but little emotion.

The aspects falling into each category differ from culture to culture. If we continue with a sporting example, for instance, we might find that the English regard acceptance of the referee's rulings as a fundamental principle of sportsmanship—a formal rule which would produce an emotional response from most of the population if they were confronted with a direct violation. On the other hand, the Germans may have a clear set of technical rules for when and how to object to rulings, while Americans adopt an informal approach that objections should be made as and when justified. Any aspect of culture could be compared between cultures in this way, and it is possible on an overall comparison probably incorporating a great deal of selective perception to argue that England has a formal culture, Germany a technical culture and the United States an informal culture. The reason for introducing the distinction, however, is not to produce comparisons but rather to produce a first classification of cultural aspects that indicates the likelihood of resistance to change.

Attitudes towards change clearly differ for each of the three classes. Formal rules would be held with great tenacity, change very slowly, and be particularly resistant to any attempt to force change from outside. Informal rules can change more easily. There is room for more deviation by individuals and imitation can be selective in one direction or another. Change comes most easily with technical rules, because they are readily observed, talked about, transmitted, and accepted at a more or less rational level.

While early conditioning in the rules of a culture gives it stability, later enculturation gives it the opportunity to change. Such changes are most likely to take the form of learning from real experience or from conscious comparison of alternatives on the technical level, with discussions among mature individuals as to the advantages of change, and eventual consensus.[18] Thus, the key to culture change seems to lie in the informal system. In a complex and changing environment, imitation of others will not be perfect. When some of the variants that emerge seem to work better than others, they are copied and eventually develop as technical rules. As such, they are brought up to the conscious level and communicated as worthwhile.

Technical changes are most likely to deal with details of an activity—for example, the use of a new fertilizer, or the introduction of a new type of motor. But the piling up of many minor variations that are initially consonant with the existing formal system can open the way for more fundamental changes in the formal and informal systems. A series of technical changes in this way creates a "cultural drift."[19] Technical and informal rules seem to surround each part of the formal system, and when these supports are removed, formal rules may eventually give way. This may explain why some parts of a culture reject change persistently only to collapse suddenly later on. Hall illustrates this sort of phenomena with the change in attitude towards premarital chastity in the United States.[20] Changes in women's social life, education, career patterns, and dress habits, and the widespread use of the private car removed many technical supports to the formal rule. After resisting change for many years, the rule eventually changed very rapidly.

The interrelationship of the elements of culture fuels the change process. Each change may affect others with which it is in association. An extreme variant introduced at the technical level may produce a dynamic reaction throughout the entire culture. The introduction of the motor vehicle would be an example here.

Not all the new elements that evolve from within a culture, or are introduced from outside, are adopted by the culture. They have to fall on fertile ground in the sense that there is a perception of the need for the change and a broad acceptance of it. The social structure of the society and those who introduce the change or are aware of it will thus be important factors in its acceptance. These are examined more fully in the next section. Anthropologists, however, have noted that cultures tend to develop a particular interest in some parts of their system—called a cultural focus. One culture may build up a very elaborate set of rules concerned with family life, another may focus on agriculture, technology, or religion, and so on. Where this happens the culture is more likely to develop and adopt changes in those areas on which it places this emphasis. Conversely, less important areas will change less

---

[18] Herskovits, *Cultural Anthropology*, p. 453.

[19] Ibid., p. 506.

[20] Hall, *Silent Language*, p. 113.

and there will be lower tolerance for change in them. The Arabs, for example, have regarded the "fellahin" engaged in agriculture as of very low status and have adopted few agricultural innovations in comparison with the Israelis who accord agriculture high status and reward successful agricultural innovation with almost national fame.

For the international businessman, then, it seems that he would have most success in introducing change in those parts of the culture that are treated technically and that are considered important. The greatest opportunities for business, though, may lie in identifying those areas where informal adaptations seem to be most successful and then acting as the agent in making a broader section of the population aware of them.

SOCIAL DYNAMICS OF CULTURAL CHANGE

It is as important for the international businessman to identify the roles different people will play in the change process as it is to identify what cultural aspects will resist change. When we talk of cultural change, we are really talking of changes in the pattern of behavior of the individuals adhering to that culture. The order in which persons with different characteristics adopt an innovation and the influences that affect their decision are thus of particular importance. The field of diffusion studies has a great deal to say about these.

Adopters of any innovation are conventionally classified into five groups according to the order in which they adopt the innovation, as follows:[21]

Adopter Category	
Innovators	first 2.5%
Early adopters	next 13.5%
Early majority	next 34%
Late majority	next 34%
Laggards	remaining 16%

The idea behind this classification is that common characteristics may be identified for the adopters of each stage. It has been observed that adopter distributions for a wide range of innovations follow a bell-shaped curve over time that tends towards normality. Hence, the standard adopter classification divides innovations into those within one, two, or three standard deviations of the mean on a time basis. The rate

---

[21] Everett M. Rogers, *Diffusion of Innovations* (New York: The Free Press of Glencoe, 1962). Chapter 6 provides the references for most of the research generalizations that follow in this section.

of adoption refers to the time scale for the diffusion through the relevant population. A great deal of research has gone into identifying the characteristics of an innovation that will determine its rate. For example, the more advantageous an innovation, the faster its rate of adoption. Similarly, the faster the rate the more compatible the new idea is with the culture, and the greater its communicability.

An individual's innovativeness has been shown to vary directly with the norms of his social system, but there are fairly general findings that innovators are regarded by themselves and by others as deviants from the norms of their culture or subculture. They tend to have a characteristic venturesomeness and to have seen more of other cultures than later adopters. One study of firms commencing export activity showed almost all the innovators to have international backgrounds.[22]

Early adopters tend to have a higher position in the social hierarchy than innovators and to rate high as opinion leaders. They may have a considerable influence on later adopters. The dominant characteristic of the people who make up the early majority seems to be their capacity for deliberation. They do not adopt until other respected persons have done so, seldom emerging as leaders. Contrasted with this, the dominant value of the people who make up the late majority is skepticism. They tend to wait until the weight of public opinion must definitely favor the innovation before they proceed. Laggards have a dominant value of tradition. They tend to be older, to be suspicious of innovations, and to take the past as their point of reference.

Associated with the study of diffusion, and particularly relevant for cultural change, is the concept of an adoption process. This is conceived of as a set of five mental stages through which an individual passes from first hearing about an innovation until he finally adopts it. These are (1) awareness, (2) interest, (3) evaluation, (4) trial, and (5) adoption. Studies of each of these stages and the information and influence sources important at each stage have provided some significant generalizations about adoptions. It has been found that impersonal sources of information tend to be most influential at the awareness stage, and personal sources tend to be most influential at the evaluation stage. Commercial change agents, that is, advertising and selling, seem to be more important at the trial stage than at any other stage. In the earlier stages of the process nonlocal sources of information tend to be most important. But in the later stages local sources take the command position. These findings may be very significant for firms planning the introduction of products into new cultural environments.

It has been found that the period from awareness to trial is shorter for earlier adopters than for later adopters. Thus, awareness spreads

---

[22] Kenneth Simmonds and Helen Smith, "The First Export Order: A Marketing Innovation," *British Journal of Marketing,* Summer 1968.

faster than the adoption of an innovation. It is not surprising, therefore, that over the diffusion cycle, commercial-change agents tend to become less important and personal influence to become more important.

In the marketing field it has been shown many times that when buying new or important products, buyers consult or copy other users.[23] These are frequently called reference groups,[24] but may be reference individuals.[25] They may be groups to which the customer aspires or belongs, or possibly to which he wants to avoid belonging. In some cases these reference groups will be the ones who have already adopted the innovation and in other cases merely the ones whose opinion is sought.

Opinion leaders can play an important part in the introduction of an innovation and many studies have examined the "two step flow of communication" in which opinions are sought, weighted, and discussed and then finally a decision made.[26] Early adopters are most likely to be opinion leaders and as against their followers have a higher social status and financial position, have more social participation, and use more impersonal and technically accurate sources of information, with a wider geographical spread.[27]

Social-class identification by groups within a culture can also affect the diffusion of an innovation. A social class, however defined, is likely to exhibit some common variants of the overall national culture, particularly if its members are grouped in the same living environment. One landmark study suggests that the cultural norms of a social class at the particular time was of significant factor in the acceptance or rejection of a particular innovation.[28] The pattern of interaction and influence that leads to adoption or rejection may also be largely carried on within one social class.[29] Changes may thus not trickle down the social scale with each class striving to copy classes above it. The international businessman must be prepared, therefore, to observe what happens within social groups as well as across a society as a whole.

---

[23] For example see Eva Mueller, "The Sample Survey," in *Consumer Behavior,* vol. 1, *The Dynamics of Consumer Reaction,* ed. Lincoln H. Clark (New York: New York University Press, 1954), p. 45.

[24] Tamotsu Shibutani, "Reference Groups and Social Controls," in *Human Behavior and Social Processes,* ed. Arnold M. Rose (Boston: Houghton Mifflin Co., 1962), p. 128–47.

[25] Herbert Hyman, "Reflections on Reference Groups," *Public Opinion Quarterly,* Fall 1960.

[26] Elihu Katz and Paul Lazarsfeld, *Personal Influence* (Glencoe: Illinois Press, 1955).

[27] Rogers, *Diffusion of Innovations,* Chapter 8.

[28] Graham Saxon, "Class and Conservatism in the Adoption of Innovations," *Human Relations,* 9, no. 1 (1956): 91–100.

[29] Charles W. King, "Fashion Adoption: A Rebuttal of the 'Trickle Down Theory,'" in *Toward Scientific Marketing,* ed. Stephen A. Greyser (Chicago: American Marketing Association, 1963), pp. 108–25.

METHODS OF CULTURAL ASSESSMENT
FOR BUSINESS DECISIONS

There is no one method for firms to adopt in making cultural assessments as a basis for specific business decisions. Business problems can cover such a wide range that the methods employed may extend from a narrow depth study of receptivity to a new management practice, through to broad assessment of a society's attitudes to spending. In all cases involving cross-cultural management, however, there will be a common problem of the cultural bias of either the researcher or the manager, or both.

Cultural bias can be reduced by using researchers from the culture to be studied, and through the development of culturally sensitive management (see Chapter 21). Specific attempts to eliminate what Lee has called the "self-reference criterion" (SRC), however, can be built into the research approach.[30] Lee suggests that problems be first defined in terms of the cultural traits, habits, or norms of the home society then redefined, without value judgments, in terms of the foreign cultural traits, habits and norms. The difference between these two specifications indicates the likely cultural bias, or SRC effect, which can then be isolated and carefully examined to see how it influences the concept of the problem. Following this examination, the problem is redefined with the bias removed. Lee has illustrated how such an approach can be used for a wide variety of business problems. Its value lies in forcing the researcher or manager posing the problem to make very specific his assumptions about the cultural elements affecting the problem and to question whether they hold for another culture.

The introduction to patterns of cultural change earlier in this chapter also suggests methodological approaches that may be helpful in assessing cultural environments as a basis for business decisions involving cultural change. The first is a mapping of the way any change is expected to diffuse through the culture. The second is a mapping of the decision making and influence process for the key individuals to be affected by the change at each stage. Such mappings make quite explicit the assumptions that are held about the change process and frequently provide a necessary framework against which to specify actual research questions. Without some mapping of these two processes any quantification on which to base a decision to introduce the change could hardly be soundly based.

An interesting summary of research, which finally achieved a verbal presentation of these two processes after a tortuous research process, has been used as a case study in many business schools over the last

---

[30] James A. Lee, "Cultural Analysis in Overseas Operations," *Harvard Business Review,* March–April 1966, pp. 106–14.

decade.[31] Failing to gain adequate penetration of the French market for its packaged soups, an international company commissioned a motivational research study into the attitudes of French housewives towards soup. After research involving 60 nonguided interviews, 4 group discussions, 200 localized semiguided interviews, 2,000 general interviews, and 400 supplementary interviews, the research group identifies the characteristics of housewives with different attitudes towards the purchase of packaged soup. The reader is then left to discuss the problems of measuring the numbers of housewives in each category and building an appropriate promotional campaign.

The concept of the rate of adoption can also be employed in projecting the demand for new products. The rate of adoption in this early stage of diffusion is simply projected ahead on the assumption that the adoption will follow a normal curve in the later stages. Bass and King have attempted this with a minor degree of success for a range of products.[32]

Adjusting to Cultural Differences

For the multinational enterprise the impact of cultural variables affects management at two levels, the national and the multinational. The issues at the national level might be characterized as bicultural. The distinction is essentially the same as that made in Chapter 1 between foreign operations and international business. At the national level, the situation is largely of a "we and they" type. The manager of a subsidiary must be aware of possible conflicts between local conditions and the cultural assumptions underlying the business practices being imported. Essentially these problems are two-sided and management personnel of subsidiaries must be the bridge between the local situation and the international enterprise.

At the multinational level, or more specifically at the global or regional headquarters of the international enterprise, the task is to coordinate and integrate business activities that are operating in many different cultural environments. Managers must deal with many languages and across many cultures. The problems are both horizontal—across many cultures—and vertical—between each subsidiary and headquarters. And the organizational structure and policies of the global enterprise must facilitate communications and the implementation of policies across many cultures in order to achieve global goals.

To the extent possible, the experienced international enterprise will

---

[31] *The Chardon Company,* a case prepared by L'Institute pour l'Etude des Methodes de Direction de l'Enterprise (IMEDE), Lausanne, Switzerland, 1960.

[32] Frank M. Bass and Charles W. King, "The Theory of First Purchase of New Products," in *A New Measure of Responsibility for Marketing,* ed. Keith Cox and Ben M. Enis (Chicago: American Marketing Association, 1968).

try to accept the values of local culture patterns and seek to work within the limits of the accepted behavior patterns and customary goals that underly these beliefs. In all circumstances, local traditions and habits are given respect and, as often as is possible in foreign operations, local concepts are permitted to continue in preference to substituting those of another culture pattern. As a general rule, foreign firms find it wise to adjust to local standards with less deviation than is permitted native companies because of nationalistic sensitivity to foreign influences.

Lee suggests that three general classes of business adaptation are important—product, individual, and institutional—and that the degree of necessary adjustment ranges from none, or token, to comprehensive.[33] Adaptation is defined as the achievement of business goals with a minimum of problems and setbacks due to the various manifestations of cultural conflict.

Adaptation in product policies, which includes marketing strategies, can be illustrated by the experience of the Singer Sewing Machine Company in meeting different requirements of cultural patterns in the various markets it sells.[34] In Moslem countries, the women's position has been a secluded and protected one, particularly with strangers. The practice of purdah, or wearing a veil so as to be screened from the sight of strangers, reflects this cultural pattern. The success of sewing-machine sales has been through sewing classes which Moslem women would not ordinarily be permitted to attend. In fact, at least one sewing-machine salesman was sent to jail in Sudan for trying to encourage the wives to attend sewing classes. Singer was able to overcome this problem by selling the husbands first on how much additional work the women could do with sewing machines after taking sewing lessons. This was accomplished by having demonstration classes for the men who became convinced of the advantages and then ordered the wives to attend.

Individual adjustment is required of managers, and in the case of overseas personnel, the wives and families are also faced with the need to adjust to cultural differences. An expatriate manager who wishes to motivate natives in a host nation, not merely order them around, must first make some changes in himself. He may have to make adjustments in his personal manner of dealing with people. He should learn the local language. He should understand different attitudes toward time and adapt his behavior to local norms where such adaptation does not prejudice the achievement of business goals. Individual adjustments may be required to deal with other businessmen and government officials, as well as with employees and colleagues.

Institutional adaptation relates to changes in organizational structure

---

[33] Lee, *Cultural Analysis,* p. 107.

[34] "How to Attract the Ladies Without Starting a Riot," *Forbes,* 15 October 1964, p. 22.

and organizational policies to fit cultural differences. Institutional adaptation may be required at either the national or international level, or more commonly at both levels. The Syntex Corporation with headquarters in Mexico City, its research center in California, and operations in at least 10 countries other than Mexico and the United States, chose to approach its adaptation problems through emphasis on organizational change. The company's philosophy is that the organization's culture must be changed in order for employees to change and develop most effectively. As a result, considerable attention has been devoted to an organization model and the establishment of guidelines for creating the projected type of organization.[35]

International enterprises will have to face adaptation issues related to the home environment as well as to the cultural patterns of foreign countries. Adaptation may be required in governmental-relations policies, in patterns of dealing with other business enterprises, and in internal operating policies. Hiring practices used in the United States may overlook class distinctions and assume that people from different areas and factions will work well together. A company operating in Bangladesh may encounter serious difficulties by hiring Bihari refugees from India to work side by side with native Bengalis.

The general approach for cultural adaptation is to become explicitly aware of the cultural traits, habits, or norms of both the international enterprise and the foreign environment as they affect particular business problems. Then it is possible to examine how the culture bias of the enterprise complicates or prejudices an optimum solution of the problem. Where the effect of the culture bias is significant, adaptations of a product, institutional or individual nature may be required by the enterprise. In many cases, as we will discuss below, part or all of the solution may be to try to change local cultural patterns.

Promoting Cultural Change

Promoting change in the buying patterns of consumers and in the working behavior of employees is a common challenge facing the business enterprise, whether domestically or internationally oriented. And guidelines developed for inducing change are generally applicable to both domestic and international business operations. Additional complications at the international level are the significantly larger number of cultural variables, unfamiliarity and lack of experience with many new situations, and the limitations of culture conditioning on the manager or the enterprise trying to induce change.

Some of the guidelines for promoting change that have been developed by the anthropologists for cross-cultural situations are as follows:

---

[35] Harold M. Rush, *Behavioral Science: Concepts and Management Applications* (New York: National Industrial Conference Board, 1969), pp. 130–38.

The New and the Old. Unless they produce dramatic benefits, the easiest way to have innovations accepted is not to have them present an open conflict with traditional values and customs but rather to graft on to them. Medicine is one field in which this problem has often occurred. In societies which have continued to rely on folk-medical practices, it has frequently been effective to relate new Western medical products to irrational traditional beliefs.

Prestige. Individuals may change because of a desire for prestige, in emulation of people with more status than themselves. The acceptance of a foreign-made product over a domestic one frequently occurs because of such a status motivation for change.

Timing and Introduction. A well-conceived project can fail because the right time was not chosen to initiate it. For many years the principal department stores in Mexico City were of an elegant type, catering to the upper classes. By the time Sears, Roebuck opened their first store in Mexico City in 1947, a growing middle class was emerging which demanded different goods and service. The timing for Sears entry into Mexico was most certainly a major factor in the company's success.[36]

The examples cited from the anthropological literature have been related primarily to the marketing side of international operations. There are also many ways of introducing the change essential for achieving managerial goals. Most frequently, change is introduced through formal authority. Another important way is to expose employees to new experiences through expertly designed training programs. Also, rational arguments and theoretical explanations have been used to convince others. Incentives can be developed that reward changed behavior such as increased output. Participation and group discussions may also stimulate persons to recognize the need for change and initiate it.

The success of induced change in other cultures will invariably depend upon success in closing a communications gap between the innovators and the people to be motivated. And one of the key gap problems in management is cultural differences in the understanding of the concept of productivity. Another major need is to set up various measures to protect employees from economic loss or from decreases in status and personal dignity. Furthermore, where a great deal of change is desired, people should not be worn out with trivial changes. The capacity to accept change in a given cultural setting should be saved for only large and crucial issues.

The international enterprise may promote change, but it is the members of the foreign culture who have to accept change. The general strategy, therefore, must be to discover the ways and incentives characteristic of the culture that are likely to result in acceptance. The comparative business literature is replete with examples of unsuccessful attempts to

---

[36] Richardson Wood and Virginia Keyser, *Sears, Roebuck de Mexico, S.A.* (Washington, D.C.: National Planning Association, 1953).

induce cultural change. Yet, the success stories are numerous also and provide considerable encouragement for the likely success of well-designed and well-informed efforts to promote cultural change.

INTERNATIONAL BUSINESS AS A CHANGE AGENT

A final topic related to the cultural components of the international business environment is the role of international business as a change agent. Here we are referring to the cultural fallout as well as the deliberately promoted cultural changes. The concept of international business as a change agent invariably has a favorable connotation in business circles and refers to such benefits as the transfer of technology and management skills, the training of workers, and the social and economic modernization effects in the host country. All of these features of international business are generally assumed to be positive and desirable contributions to the countries in which international business activity takes place. But as the social scientists have observed, cultural change can have both positive and negative aspects for the members of a given society.

A case study of the International Basic Economy Corporation (IBEC) provides some interesting examples of cultural change being pushed too fast with resulting negative backlash. IBEC was founded shortly after World War II by Nelson Rockefeller and other members of his family as a pioneering business venture to demonstrate the beneficial role that private enterprise could play in the less developed countries. The early operations of the company were primarily in Brazil and Venezuela. In appraising this early experience, Broehl concludes:

> Cultural difference and resistance to change were greater than had been anticipated in both countries. . . . The laborers on the IBEC farms were expected quickly to adopt new methods, the Venezuelan fishermen were to be taught better methods by the U.S. fishermen. The consumer was counted on to accept a new concept of food marketing in the supermarket. Some of these concepts were proved not as sound as the ostensibly outmoded ways, but even those that were manifestly "better"—in the sense of being more efficient and less costly—were often not quickly adopted. . . .
>
> Early attacks in Venezuela against "the Rockefeller interests" can, in part, be explained by this resistance to change. For such resistance is bred of fear of the change, and brings an almost conditioned reflex of retaliation.[37]

Some of the cultural changes for which the international enterprise can claim credit are consistent with the goals of national leaders who are anxious to modernize and industrialize their society. The nature or the pace of other changes, such as in the case of IBEC, can provoke

---

[37] Wayne G. Broehl, Jr., *The International Basic Economy Corporation* (Washington, D.C.: National Planning Association, 1968), p. 79.

negative reactions to the international enterprise by government leaders or groups in the society. Because it is an agent of change, whether or not the change is intentional, the international enterprise should attempt to anticipate the changes for which it might be held responsible and the full chain of results from changes it is promoting.

Where the changes are perceived as beneficial by local interests, the bargaining position of the enterprise is strengthened. Where the expected changes are likely to appear dysfunctional and be negatively received, the international enterprise may want to modify its operational patterns or prepare to meet local antagonism, for a while at least.

Summary

When the business firm crosses national boundaries and begins to operate in a number of countries, it is faced with a wide range of cultural differences that can significantly affect the achievement of business objectives. The problem of identifying cultural differences is difficult because of the natural tendency for people to observe and evaluate behavior of others in terms of the cultural conditioning of their own country. Furthermore, cultural patterns are not static but constantly changing. The problems faced in the cultural field involve much more than an intellectual appreciation that differences exist. International managers must develop cultural sensitivity, frequently through living experience in cross-cultural situations. With cultural sensitivity, the enterprise will be aware of the need to identify cultural variables and to adjust its organization and its operations to cultural differences. In many situations, the enterprise will have to promote cultural change in order to achieve its business goals. In a broader sense, the international enterprise itself is a powerful cultural-change agent. It must anticipate the changes that it causes and the reception that such changes will receive in host countries.

APPENDIX

The International Research Groups on Management (IRGOM)[38]

Since the middle 1960s, the International Research Groups on Management (IRGOM) have been gathering a bank of data and understanding relevant in the search for normative cross-cultural similarities and differences. IRGOM has studied how Americans and nationals from else-

---

[38] Bernard M. Bass, *The American Advisor Abroad,* Technical Report no. 27, Management Research Center of the College of Business Administration, The University of Rochester, August 1969.

where react to the same standardized simulations of personnel, interpersonal, and organizational phenomena. The program encompasses 25 countries in the Americas, Europe, Asia, and Africa, and the subjects of study are mainly middle and senior managers—mainly from industry, but some from government and the military as well.

The simulations consist of 14 basic exercises which cover areas such as company objectives, compensation, managers' life goals, supervision, planning, and negotiation. In general, the exercises are constructed so that the manager-trainee first makes individual decisions about some important management issue. Subsequently, he meets in a small group to discuss the situation, and a group action, that is, a group plan or opinion or decision is usually taken—or some task is completed. Decisions, attitudes, and performance results are assembled for all trainees in the group and compared to the responses from trainee groups in other parallel study groups in the same training session.

As of late 1969, more than 60,000 exercises had been distributed from which 20,000 individual cases have been obtained and stored in the IRGOM data bank.

EXERCISES AND DISCUSSION QUESTIONS

1. "Cultural anthropology has certainly spawned a lot of empirical research, but as far as theory is concerned it is barren. The few tested theories that are available, moreover, have to be stretched a long way to reach anything of value to inter-cultural business." Discuss.

2. Give your own definition of culture.

3. Some multinational firms issue a standard corporate manual for international use containing set organizational definitions and rules, personnel policies, and budget and accounting instructions. What limits on the types of standardized instructions would you recommend that a firm with operations in many countries adopt?

4. From whatever sources are available to you, build a comparison of the family decision-making process for a major consumer purchase in two different cultures. Specify the roles played by the different family members, the pattern over time of interaction among the family with respect to the purchase, the weighting placed upon different product characteristics by each family member, and the rules by which a consensus is finally arrived at.

5. Select one of the aspects of a culture—(1) the status ranking of different occupations, (2) the roles of the sexes, (3) the times of life with which different activities are associated, (4) the exercise of organizational authority, or (5) courtship patterns—in which you are aware of a change in the cultural norms and carry out the following activities:
    a. Describe the nature of the change.
    b. Give your opinion as to whether the culture regarded it formally, informally, or technically.

c. Identify some distinguishing characteristics of the innovators and early adopters.

d. Describe any role you think business played in stimulating the change.

e. Describe the business significance of the changes for any foreign firm operating within the culture.

6. "The prime function of most executive development courses is not knowledge transmission but rather the transfer of a set of norms which conform with organizational objectives." Do you think it is acceptable for a U.S. top executive of a multinational firm to use executive-development courses to transfer to the management of foreign subsidiaries the norms that he has chosen?

12

THE ECONOMIC
ENVIRONMENT

MODERN BUSINESS ENTERPRISES have long recognized the continuing
need for assessing and forecasting the economic environment within
which they operate. It has become standard operating practice for the
business manager to keep informed, either through in-house staffs or
outside sources, on trends in the overall economy, in specific sectors,
and in consumer-buying patterns. Thus, assessing and forecasting the
economic environment, unlike the parallel task for the cultural environment, will not require the international firm to initiate a new type of
activity. Instead, its task will normally be one of extending the scope
of on-going programs.

As the firm moves from domestic to international forecasting of the
economic environment, changes are needed. First, it must evaluate a
number of national economies instead of just one. It must develop an
understanding of widely varying economic patterns and institutional
settings, particularly in the less developed countries. It must forecast
the balance-of-payments outlook for specific countries. It must be prepared to handle special problems which arise when cross-national comparisons are needed or when national data must be consolidated on a
regional or international level. Furthermore, it must incorporate into
its assessments and forecasts of national economies likely changes in
the international framework for international transfers—the subject
of Chapters 4 and 5, as well as the economic impact of anticipated
expansions in a country by the international enterprise itself.

THE NEEDS OF THE INTERNATIONAL ENTERPRISE

For the business firm newly venturing into international activities,
the task of analyzing the economic environment in many nations of

widely varying characteristics will appear formidable. Nevertheless, even at its early stage of internationalization, the firm can reduce the task to manageable proportions. First, it must be selective and focus on those aspects of the environment that are of special importance to its field of business activity and its specific interest in a country; that is, is it interested in a particular country as a market seeker, resource seeker, or production-efficiency seeker? Second, the firm can obtain much of the needed information from data and reports published by national and international agencies. And third, short-cut techniques are available for a preliminary scanning of the economic environment in many countries so as to reduce the number of situations where in-depth analysis is required.

As the enterprise becomes multinational, the task of assessing and forecasting the economic environment will be decentralized and shared among the various units of the system. The foreign subsidiaries will assume primary responsibility for economic and market studies in their areas of operations. Headquarters staff can then limit its responsibilities to making cross-national comparisons, integrating national forecasts into an enterprise-wide forecast against which global policy decisions can be made, and assessing the international financial framework and trends in inter-nation relationships.

Much of the environmental-forecasting activity of the subsidiaries will be to guide local operating decisions. In this sense it will not differ significantly from what is required by a purely domestic enterprise. But as part of a multinational system, the subsidiary will have to fulfill two additional requirements. First, it will have to follow a sufficiently standardized approach so that headquarters can make cross-country comparisons and combine individual country results into a broader mosaic. Second, each subsidiary will have to include sufficient information in its assessment and forecast on the country's international economic relations, such as balance-of-payments forecasts, so that the links can be made between the economic environment of the subsidiary and the rest of the multinational system.

At the headquarters level, the assessments of national economic environments and of the international framework for inter-nation transfers are needed as inputs for capital-budgeting decisions, for guiding operating decisions, for formulating system-wide policies, and for exercising a review function. When the firm expands into new countries where there is no subsidiary, headquarters will have to assume full responsibility for economic environmental analysis.

The technical responsibility for assessing and forecasting will usually be handled by specialists. But in order to use such forecasts, the international manager will need to have considerable familiarity with techniques and limitations. He must be aware of statistical perils, the problems of accurate perception, and the difficulties inherent in making cross-national comparisons or in joining economic information based on different data bases into broader mosaics. He should be generally familiar with the process of appraising overall growth prospects of different countries. He should comprehend the need for and the limitations of balance-of-payments forecasting. In dealing with the less developed countries, the manager should have an understanding of the development process, international development-assistance programs, and the importance of national-development priorities. In dealing with host and home governments, he will need to understand the conceptual and measurement difficulties involved in the economic analyses of the impact of his enterprise.

International managers may have to adjust to new and unfamiliar patterns in economic institutions and policies. For example, when undertaking international responsibilities, a manager from the United States may have his first contact with national economic planning and government enterprises as major features of a foreign nation's economic environment. In such a situation, he will have to enlarge his background to understand why such patterns exist and what role they are expected to play. He may also be required to revise some ethnocentric biases coming out of his American cultural conditioning.

As a business firm moves toward becoming a global enterprise, one of its forward-planning activities will be to scan the world horizon continuously for expansion opportunities. In particular, it will want to identify promising market areas, and it will develop a reconnaissance system that will survey all countries for attractive market opportunities. But in a world of almost 200 separate countries, is it feasible in terms of personnel and costs for any but the international giants to undertake such a continuing and comprehensive global search?

Fortunately, by following a sequential process and by making use of general economic data available from international agencies, even a small firm can keep globally informed. In a first step, through macro-economic scanning or the use of selected general economic indicators, a preliminary list of countries can be selected as attractive possibilities for further investigation. A second cut can then be made in the number of areas through sectoral analyses or studies of specific components of a country's economy. After the enterprise has reduced its opportunity list to manageable proportions, it can then afford to undertake a limited number of detailed and in-depth market-demand investigations along the lines discussed in Chapter 13.

STATISTICAL PERILS

In appraising economic environments, the likelihood of inaccurate perceptions of economic environments is always high because of variations in the concepts, coverage, and quality of national statistics, and because of statistical biases correlated with a country's stage of economic development. Bias frequently exists, for example, in the widely used measure of economic levels, trends, and market potentials—per capita gross national product (GNP). GNP is the money measure of the overall annual flow of final goods and services in an economy, and per capita GNP is derived by dividing total GNP by total population. Although most nations use the same general concept, the extent to which the statistical estimates reflect the actual situation in different countries can vary significantly.[1]

In less developed countries there is a bias toward understating levels of economic activity. Statistical coverage becomes increasingly comprehensive as economic levels rise and the availability and the quality of data improve as a country becomes more affluent and develops more complex institutions and improved record keeping. Moreover, as an economy develops, an increasing share of economic activity passes through the marketplace and is counted as national output. For example, housewives purchase bread instead of baking it themselves.

Another statistical peril involves variations in official definitions from country to country. The label "manufacturing activity" is an example. French statistics, unlike those of most other nations, include fishing and the quarrying of building materials as manufacturing, whereas wine production is classified as agriculture. Iran includes the extraction of crude petroleum as manufacturing, whereas most countries report petroleum production as mining activity.[2] Another example arises with differences in the measurement of the labor force. United States data use 16 years of age as a lower limit as contrasted to 14 years for many other countries.

Even where definitions and statistical coverage are similar, statistics can vary greatly in quality, or in margins of error. Statistical quality varies among nations, among different items in the same country, and among different statistical observations for the same item in a country. The collection and processing of economic data require considerable expertness and large expenditures. Affluent countries can make the necessary investment without great strain on available resources. The less developed countries generally do not have adequate resources and their economic statistics are likely to have large gaps and wide margins of error.

One keen observer has noted a close correlation between the efficiency of a nation's tax-collection system and the quality of statistical data.

---

[1] See T. P. Hill, *The Measurement of Real Product* (Paris: OECD, February 1971). This study examines growth rates of gross domestic product for all OECD member countries and for many individual industries from the standpoint of the different types of measurement used and the margin of error attached to each.

[2] United Nations, *Statistical Yearbook 1970* (New York, 1971), pp. 221–31.

The logic behind this generalization is that business firms and others will keep good records if forced to do so by an efficient tax-enforcement scheme. But if tax evasion is chronic, accurate record keeping may not be customary. Or if accurate records exist, they are not likely to be used for reporting to official government agencies.

Variations among economic sectors in statistical quality result in large part from the greater difficulty of collecting data in one area as against another. For example, data on imports and exports are usually the best, while data on agricultural production are the weakest. The high quality of foreign trade statistics results from the fact that imports and exports generally flow through a limited number of ports of entry and involve some government surveillance for tax or control purposes. Contrast this situation with the problem of collecting agricultural data from hundreds of thousands (or millions) of reporting units widely separated geographically and from an agrarian social group which frequently has low levels of education and record-keeping experience.

Because of statistical defects and differences such as those noted, it is not uncommon for statisticians whose principal experience has been acquired in such data-rich environments as that of the United States to deprecate excessively the value of foreign statistical data. Such ethnocentric reactions may perform a disservice to the efforts of the international enterprise to make accurate perceptions. The statistician has his own professional bias. He is likely to be most concerned with the extent to which statistics accurately measure a given reality. Such professionalism naturally results in small tolerances for errors.

For the international manager, the degree of error that can be tolerated depends upon the decision being made. In many situations, a wide margin of error would not seriously affect a decision. For example, national product estimates for a country may understate the economic reality. Yet, if the statistical bias is rather consistent from year to year, the business firm can draw a reasonable conclusion as to whether a country is expanding and even as to the rate of expansion. Likewise, cost-of-living data for a given country may be based on observations in only one or two principal cities but they may provide a reasonable indicator over time of general trends in price levels.

Macro-Economic Scanning

Macro-economic scanning makes use of such general economic indicators as the economic size of countries, levels of income, and recent growth trends. These data are published on a regular basis by such international agencies as the United Nations, the World Bank, the International Monetary Fund, and the Organization for Economic Cooperation and

Development (OECD).[3] A firm's minimum criterion for identifying opportunity areas will vary, of course, with the type of product for which it is seeking markets and with the economic or minimum size of production unit required. A prospective producer of automobiles, for example, will be looking for areas of larger economic size and higher-income levels than a prospective manufacturer of bicycles. A seller and maker of refrigerators or washing machines will be interested only in countries with relatively large economies and relatively high-income levels, whereas a soft drinks company can find opportunities in countries of smaller economic size with relatively low levels of income. In all cases, the firm will give priority attention to rapid growth situations and be less interested in countries where the economy has not been expanding.

Economic Size. The economic size of a nation is measured by its total GNP. Recent estimates by the World Bank of the GNP for 134 countries are shown in Table 12.1. The same data are also portrayed graphically in Figure 12.1 which has the size of each country scaled in proportion to its total GNP. At the top of the economic ladder is the United States with a GNP of more than $700 billion (expressed in 1964 dollars). At the bottom of the scale are small African countries such as Botswana, Gabon, Lesotho, Mauritania, Somalia, and Swaziland, as well as the Pacific islands of Fiji with total GNPs of $100 million or less.

The attraction of the industrialized countries on the basis of economic size is highlighted by several comparisons. Italy's GNP is equivalent to that of Mainland China, even though China has 14 times the population of Italy. Canada has about the same GNP as India, although India has 25 times as many people. Switzerland's total GNP is superior to that of Indonesia, even though Indonesia's population is almost 20 times as large.

Income Levels. GNP per capita is a synthetic figure—total GNP divided by total population—and it does not describe patterns of income distribution. Yet, despite its many limitations,[4] per capital GNP can

---

[3] The OECD is a particularly valuable source of published information on the industrialized countries. Its 23 member countries, which account for 70 percent of world trade, are Australia, Austria, Belgium, Canada, Denmark, Finland, France, Germany, Greece, Iceland, Ireland, Italy, Japan, Luxembourg, the Netherlands, Norway, Portugal, Spain, Sweden, Switzerland, Turkey, United Kingdom, and the United States. New Zealand and Yugoslavia have special-status relationship with the OECD but are not full members. Of particular importance for macro-economic scanning is the monthly OECD publication, *Main Economic Indicators,* which is designed to provide a picture of recent changes in the economies of member countries. Every two years, the monthly historical statistics over the last decade are published as a companion volume to *Main Economic Indicators.*

[4] For example, see Everett E. Hagen, *The Economics of Development* (Homewood, Ill.: Richard D. Irwin, Inc., 1968), pp. 7–16.

TABLE 12.1

Gross National Product by Country, 1969 (at factor cost in billions of 1964 U.S. dollars)

	Country	GNP		Country	GNP		Country	GNP		Country	GNP
AFRICA				Sudan	1.3[2]		Uruguay	1.4		Cyprus	0.5
1	Algeria	2.9	36	Sudan	1.3[2]	68	Uruguay	1.4	100	Cyprus	0.5
2	Angola	1.0[1]	37	Swaziland	0.1[2]	69	Venezuela	8.5	101	Czechoslovakia	16.5
3	Botswana	0.1	38	Tanzania	0.9		**ASIA and OCEANIA**		102	Denmark	9.6
4	Burundi	0.2	39	Togo	0.2	70	Afghanistan	1.0	103	Finland	7.9
5	Cameroon	0.7	40	Tunisia	0.9	71	Australia	22.8	104	France	105.2
6	Central African Republic	0.2	41	Uganda	1.1	72	Burma	1.7	105	Germany (East)	22.8
7	Chad	0.2	42	Upper Volta	0.3	73	Ceylon	2.0	106	Germany (Fed. Rep. of)	113.3
8	Congo (Brazzaville)	0.2	43	Zambia	1.0	74	China (Mainland)	58.6[2]	107	Greece	6.3
9	Congo (Dem. Rep. of)	1.3		**NORTH and CENTRAL AMERICA**		75	China (Republic of)	3.5	108	Hungary	9.5
10	Dahomey	0.2	44	Canada	47.6	76	Fiji	0.1	109	Iceland	0.3
11	Egypt, Arab Republic of	4.4	45	Costa Rica	0.7	77	Hong Kong	2.9	110	Iran	8.3
12	Ethiopia	1.4	46	Cuba	2.3[2]	78	India	49.3	111	Iraq	2.4
13	Gabon	0.1	47	Dominican Republic	0.9	79	Indonesia	11.1	112	Ireland	2.7
14	Ghana	1.3	48	El Salvador	0.8	80	Japan	124.7	113	Israel	3.8
15	Guinea	0.3	49	Guatemala	1.5	81	Khmer Republic	0.8	114	Italy	63.3
16	Ivory Coast	1.0	50	Haiti	0.3[2]	82	Korea (North)	2.9[2]	115	Jordan	0.5[3]
17	Kenya	1.2	51	Honduras	0.5	83	Korea (Republic of)	5.6	116	Kuwait	1.8
18	Lesotho	0.1[2]	52	Jamaica	0.9	84	Laos	0.3[2]	117	Lebanon	1.3
19	Liberia	0.2	53	Mexico	24.2	85	Malaysia	3.1	118	Luxembourg	0.7
20	Libya, Arab Rep. of	2.4	54	Nicaragua	0.6	86	Mongolia	0.5	119	Malta	0.2
21	Malagasy Rep.	0.6[2]	55	Panama	0.8	87	Nepal	0.7	120	Netherlands	19.2
22	Malawi	0.2	56	Puerto Rico	3.3	88	New Zealand	5.3	121	Norway	7.1
23	Mali	0.4	57	United States	732.3	89	Pakistan	11.3	122	Poland	26.1
24	Mauritania	0.1		**SOUTH AMERICA**		90	Papua New Guinea	0.4[2]	123	Portugal	4.1
25	Mauritius	0.2	58	Argentina	18.6	91	Philippines	6.3	124	Rumania	14.7
26	Morocco	2.9	59	Bolivia	0.7	92	Singapore	1.4	125	Saudi Arabia	2.3
27	Mozambique	1.3[2]	60	Brazil	21.1	93	Thailand	4.9	126	Spain	22.9
28	Niger	0.3	61	Chile	4.1	94	Viet-Nam (North)	1.6[2]	127	Sweden	19.6
29	Nigeria	4.6	62	Colombia	5.1	95	Viet-Nam (South)	2.0[2]	128	Switzerland	14.3
30	Rhodesia	1.0	63	Ecuador	1.2		**EUROPE, U.S.S.R. and MIDDLE EAST**		129	Syria, Arab Rep. of	1.3
31	Rwanda	0.2	64	Guyana	0.2	96	Albania	0.7[2]	130	Turkey	10.1
32	Senegal	0.7	65	Paraguay	0.5	97	Austria	9.2	131	U.S.S.R.	245.5
33	Sierra Leone	0.3	66	Peru	3.7	98	Belgium	16.5	132	United Kingdom	89.4
34	Somalia	0.1	67	Surinam	0.2[2]	99	Bulgaria	6.1	133	Yemen, Arab Rep. of	0.4[2]
35	South Africa	12.4							134	Yugoslavia	9.9

[1] Figures are for 1967.   [2] Figures are for 1966.   [3] Figures are for 1968.

Source: International Bank for Reconstruction and Development, *Trends In Developing Countries* (Washington, D.C., 1971).

FIGURE 12.1*

Gross National Product by Country, 1969 (in billions of 1964 U.S. dollars)

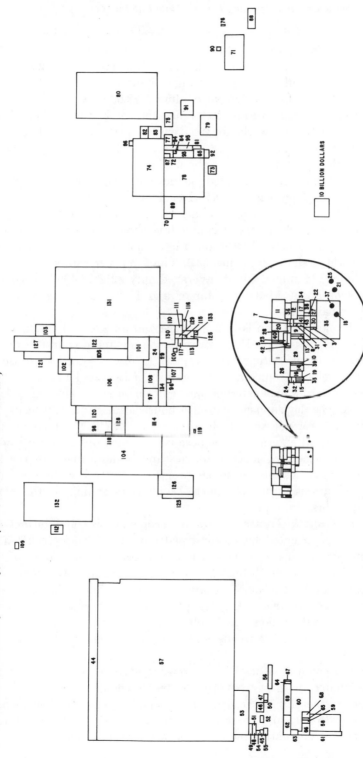

* See Table 12.1 for identification of countries.
Source: International Bank for Reconstruction and Development, *Trends in Developing Countries* (Washington, D.C., 1971).

be used as a rough guide to income levels. Recent estimates by the World Bank for more than 100 countries with populations of 1 million or more are shown in Table 12.2. The United States ranks again at the top of the ladder with an average of more than $4,000 per person in 1969, followed by Sweden with almost $3,000. Oil-rich Kuwait, excluded from the table because its population totalled only about 700,000, ranked second in the world in 1969 with a per capita GNP of $3,320. At the bottom of the economic scale are countries like India and Indonesia with per capita GNPs of about $100.

Countries are often classified as developed or developing countries based on average per capita GNP. Developing countries are also referred to as LDCs (less developed countries). Although there is no general agreement as to where the dividing line should be, one representation of the gap between the LDCs and the economically advanced countries of the world is shown in Table 12.3. The GNP per capita for 80 LDCs, not including Mainland China, averaged only $218 in 1969, as compared to levels of about $1,400 for Japan and Italy and more than $4,000 for the United States.

The development gap is both a cause and an effect of the more rapid expansion of international enterprise in the advanced countries of North America, Western Europe, and Japan. It explains the aspirations of the less developed countries for a greatly accelerated rate of economic progress, toward which international enterprise can make valuable contributions. The development gap also nourishes nationalistic feelings and defensive control policies which often make the LDCs unattractive to the international enterprise. Yet because so much of the world's population is in the less developed countries and because many of the LDCs are making remarkable economic progress, they are certain to receive continuing attention in the macro-economic scanning of the globally oriented business enterprise.

Recent Growth Trends.   Data on economic size and income levels must be supplemented by recent trend data in order to secure a more dynamic picture of a country's economic attractiveness. *Country A* may have high income levels but be relatively stagnant. *Country B* may have lower levels of income but have more attraction to the international enterprise because the country is growing rapidly. Such trend data for per capita GNP is shown in Table 12.2. Per capita GNP growth rates reflect both total GNP trends and the population growth rates shown in Table 12.4.

Because population has been increasing at rates of only about 1 percent annually in most Western European countries, per capita gains have been generally above 3 percent annually. Japan's phenomenal per capita growth rate of 10 percent for the decade of the 1960s also reflects a low rate of population increase—only 1 percent annually. In contrast,

TABLE 12.2
Gross National Product Per Capita, 1969 and Average Annual Growth Rate, 1960–69*

Country	GNP per Capita (US dollars)	Growth Rate (per-cent)	Country	GNP per Capita (US dollars)	Growth Rate (per-cent)
United States	4,240	3.2	Uruguay	560	-0.8
Sweden	2,920	3.4	Jamaica	550	3.0
Switzerland	2,700	2.6	Chile	510	1.7
Canada	2,650	2.8	Costa Rica	510	2.9
France	2,460	4.8	Portugal	510	4.9
Denmark	2,310	3.7	Mongolia ‖	460	1.0
Australia	2,300	2.9	Albania ‖	430	4.9
New Zealand	2,230	2.0	Nicaragua	380	2.8
Germany, Fed. Rep. of	2,190	3.7	Saudi Arabia	380	7.1
Norway	2,160	4.0	Guatemala	350	1.9
Belgium	2,010	3.5	Iran	350	4.9
Finland	1,980	3.9	Turkey	350	3.4
United Kingdom	1,890	1.8	Malaysia	340	3.8
Netherlands	1,760	3.1	Peru	330	1.4
Germany (East) ‖	1,570	4.1	Iraq	310	3.0
Israel	1,570	5.3	China, Rep. of	300	6.3
Libya, Arab Rep. of	1,510	21.7	Colombia	290	1.5
Austria	1,470	3.9	El Salvador	290	1.9
Japan	1,430	10.0	Zambia	290	5.4
Puerto Rico	1,410	6.0	Cuba ‖	280	-3.2
Italy	1,400	4.7	Dominican Republic	280	0.4
Czechoslovakia ‖	1,370	3.9	Jordan §	280	4.7
USSR ‖	1,200	5.6	Korea (North) ‖	280	5.9
Ireland	1,110	3.5	Brazil	270	1.4
Hungary ‖	1,100	5.5	Algeria	260	
Argentina	1,060	2.6	Honduras	260	1.1
Venezuela	1,000	2.5	Syria, Arab Rep. of	260	4.7
Poland ‖	940	5.1	Ecuador	240	1.2
Trinidad and Tobago	890	3.8	Ivory Coast	240	4.7
Bulgaria ‖	860	6.7	Paraguay	240	1.0
Romania ‖	860	7.5	Rhodesia	240	0.4
Hong Kong	850	8.7	Tunisia	230	2.1
Greece	840	6.2	Angola	210	1.4
Spain	820	6.5	Korea, Rep. of	210	6.4
Singapore	800	4.5	Mozambique	210	3.3
South Africa †	710	3.8	Papua New Guinea	210	2.0
Panama	660	4.8	Philippines	210	1.9
Lebanon	580	2.1	Liberia	200	1.3
Mexico	580	3.4	Senegal	200	-0.1
Yugoslavia	580	4.6	Ceylon	190	2.1

TABLE 12.2—continued

Country	GNP per Capita (US dollars)	Growth Rate (percent)	Country	GNP per Capita (US dollars)	Growth Rate (percent)
Ghana	190	0.0	Afghanistan	–	0.3
Morocco	190	3.4	Burma	–	1.8
Sierre Leone	170	1.2	Burundi §	–	0.0
Bolivia	160	2.4	Chad	–	–1.3
Egypt, Arab Rep. of	160	1.2			
			China (Mainland)‖	–	0.8
Thailand	160	4.7	Congo, Dem. Rep. of	–	0.2
Cameroon	150	2.0	Dahomey	–	0.9
Mauritania §	140	4.6	Ethiopia	–	2.3
Viet-Nam (South)	140	1.8	Guinea	–	2.6
Central Africa Rep.	130	0.0			
			Haiti	–	–1.0
Kenya	130	1.5	Malawi	–	1.0
Khmer Rep.	130	0.5	Mali	–	1.2
Yemen, People's Dem.			Nepal	–	0.4
Rep. of	120	–4.6			
India	110	1.1	Niger	–	–0.9
Laos §	110	0.2			
			Nigeria	–	–0.3
Malagasy Rep.	110	0.0	Rwanda	–	–0.8
Pakistan	110	2.9	Somalia §	–	1.5
Sudan	110	0.6	Tanzania ‡	–	1.6
Uganda	110	1.7	Upper Volta	–	0.1
Indonesia	100	0.8			
			Viet-Nam (North)‖	–	3.2
Togo	100	0.0	Yemen, Arab Rep. of §	–	2.3

* Countries with populations of 1 million or more.
† Including Namibia.
‡ Mainland Tanzania.
§ Estimates of GNP per capita and its growth rate are tentative.
‖ Estimates of GNP per capita and its growth rate have a wide margin of error mainly because of the problems in deriving the GNP at factor cost from net material product and in converting the GNP estimate into US dollars.
Source: *Finance and Development*, 9, no. 1. (March 1972): 51. (In view of the usual errors inherent in this type of data and to avoid a misleading impression of accuracy, the figures for GNP per capita have been rounded to the nearest $10.)

population has been expanding at between 2.5 and 3.5 percent annually in most Latin American countries, and higher total GNP growth rates have been required to match the per capita gains of other areas where population is expanding less rapidly.

Historically, as a nation's income levels rise and urbanization increases, the rate of population increase slows down. Population control as an affirmative development measure is being adopted to some degree in the less developed countries, but whether or not rapid population increases burden economic-development efforts is still a controversial question in many countries. Yet the arithmetic is clear. The faster popu-

TABLE 12.3

Gross National Product per Capita of Developing
and Selected Developed Countries, 1960 and
1969 (GNP at factor cost in 1969 U.S. dollars)

Region	1960	1969
Developing Countries*	173	218
Japan	606	1,434
Italy	928	1,401
United Kingdom	1,610	1,894
Germany, Fed. Rep. of	1,578	2,192
Canada	2,065	2,654
United States	3,200	4,241

NOTE: Estimates for the following developing
countries are included in this table:
Africa: Algeria, Cameroon, Central African Republic,
Chad, Congo (Brazzaville), Congo (Dem. Rep. of),
Dahomey, Egypt, Arab Rep. of, Ethiopia, Gabon,
Gambia, Ghana, Guinea, Ivory Coast, Kenya, Li-
beria, Libya. Arab. Rep. of. Malawi, Mali. Mauri-
tania, Mauritius, Morocco, Nigeria, Rhodesia,
Senegal, Sierra Leone, Togo, Tunisia, Uganda,
Upper Volta, and Zambia.
Asia: Afghanistan, Burma, Ceylon, China (Rep. of),
Fiji, Hong Kong, India, Indonesia, Khmer Rep.,
Korea (Rep. of), Malaysia, Pakistan, Philippines,
Singapore, and Thailand.
Southern Europe: Cyprus, Greece, Malta, Portugal,
Spain, Turkey, and Yugoslavia.
Latin America: Argentina, Bolivia, Brazil, Chile, Co-
lombia, Costa Rica, Dominican Republic, Ecuador.
El Salvador, Guatemala, Guyana, Honduras, Ja-
maica, Mexico, Nicaragua, Panama, Paraguay, Peru,
Trinidad and Tobago, Uruguay, and Venezuela.
Middle East: Iran, Iraq, Israel, Lebanon, Saudi Arabia
and Syria, Arab. Rep. of.
    Source: International Bank for Reconstruction and
Development *Trends in Developing Countries* (Wash
ington, D.C., 1971).

lation expands, the larger the overall rate of growth required to achieve
per capita increases. Countries with rapid population growth normally
have a large share of their population in the lower-age groups. As a
result, the potential labor force will be a relatively small share of total
population. Expenditures required for education will be disproportion-
ately large, and the heavy educational costs have to be borne by the
relatively small share of the population that is productively employed.

    An Illustration. The macro-scanning process can be illustrated for
an international firm that produces consumer durable goods requiring
a reasonably large total market as well as relatively substantial income
levels. By scanning the economic size of Latin American countries, the
enterprise would be likely to focus attention on both Argentina, with
total GNP in 1964 U.S. dollars of almost $20 billion, and Mexico, with
$24 billion. Moving on to income levels, Argentina with average GNP
per capita of $1,060 would at first appear more attractive than Mexico

TABLE 12.4
Population (mid-1969) and Average Annual Growth Rate (1960–69)*

Country	Popu- lation (thou- sands)	Growth Rate (per- cent)	Country	Popu- lation (thou- sands)	Growth Rate (per- cent)
China (Mainland)	740,000	1.5	Korea (North)	13,300	2.6
India	526,043	2.3	Peru	13,172	3.1
USSR	240,333	1.3	Netherlands	12,873	1.3
United States	203,213	1.3	Tanzania‡	12,557	2.6
Pakistan	126,740	2.7	Australia	12,296	2.0
Indonesia	116,600	2.4	Ceylon	12,244	2.4
Japan	102,322	1.0	Kenya	10,890	3.1
Brazil	92,282	3.2	Nepal	10,845	1.8
Nigeria	64,560	2.6	Malaysia	10,600	3.0
Germany, Fed. Rep. of	60,842	1.0	Hungary	10,295	0.3
United Kingdom	55,534	0.7	Venezuela	10,035	3.5
Italy	53,170	0.8	Belgium	9,646	0.6
France	50,330	1.1	Chile	9,566	2.5
Mexico	48,933	3.5	Portugal	9,560	0.9
Philippines	35,900	3.1	Uganda	9,500	3.0
Thailand	35,128	3.1	Iraq	9,350	3.5
Turkey	34,450	2.5	Greece	8,835	0.7
Spain	32,949	0.9	Cuba	8,513	2.5
Poland	32,555	1.0	Bulgaria	8,440	0.8
Egypt, Arab Rep. of	32,501	2.5	Ghana	8,341	2.5
Korea, Rep. of	31,139	2.6	Sweden	7,968	0.7
Iran	28,475	3.0	Mozambique	7,539	1.8
Burma	26,980	2.1	Austria	7,371	0.5
Ethiopia	24,769	2.0	Khmer Rep.	7,284	3.3
Argentina	23,983	1.6	Saudi Arabia	7,235	1.7
Viet-Nam (North)	21,340	3.2	Malagasy Republic	6,656	2.4
Canada	21,089	1.8	Switzerland	6,230	1.7
Colombia	20,463	3.2	Ecuador	5,890	3.4
Yugoslavia	20,351	1.1	Syria, Arab Rep. of	5,866	2.8
South Africa†	20,218	2.3	Cameroon	5,736	2.1
Romania	20,010	0.9	Yemen, Arab Rep. of	5,556	2.1
Congo, Dem. Rep. of	17,900	2.1	Angola	5,430	1.3
Viet-Nam (South)	17,867	2.7	Upper Volta	5,278	2.2
Germany (East)	17,096	–0.1	Rhodesia	5,090	3.2
Sudan	15,186	2.9	Guatemala	5,014	3.1
Morocco	15,050	2.9	Ivory Coast	4,942	2.8
Czechoslovakia	14,418	0.6	Tunisia	4,919	3.0
Afghanistan	13,975	2.0	Denmark	4,891	0.7
China, Rep. of	13,800	3.0	Mali	4,881	2.1
Algeria	13,349	2.4	Bolivia	4,804	2.6

TABLE 12.4—continued

Country	Popu- lation (thou- sands)	Growth Rate (per- cent)	Country	Popu- lation (thou- sands)	Growth Rate (per- cent)
Haiti	4,768	2.0	Lebanon	2,645	2.5
Finland	4,703	0.7	Dahomey	2,640	2.9
Malawi	4,398	2.6	Sierra Leone	2,510	2.0
Zambia	4,020	2.6	Honduras	2,495	3.4
Hong Kong	3,990	2.9			
			Papua New Guinea	2,363	2.4
Dominican Republic	3,951	3.0	Paraguay	2,314	3.1
Niger	3,909	3.0	Jordan	2,242	3.2
Guinea	3,890	2.7	Albania	2,075	2.9
Norway	3,851	0.8	Singapore	2,017	2.4
Senegal	3,790	2.2			
			Nicaragua	1,915	3.5
Rwanda	3,650	3.1	Togo	1,896	2.6
Chad	3,510	1.5	Libya, Arab Rep. of	1,869	3.7
Burundi	3,475	2.0	Jamaica	1,863	1.5
El Salvador	3,390	3.7	Costa Rica	1,680	3.3
Ireland	2,921	0.3			
			Central African Republic	1,518	2.4
Laos	2,893	2.4	Liberia	1,480	2.8
Uruguay	2,852	1.3	Panama	1,417	3.3
Israel	2,822	3.3	Mongolia	1,251	3.1
New Zealand	2,777	1.8	Yemen, People's Dem.		
Puerto Rico	2,739	1.7	Rep. of	1,220	2.2
			Mauritania	1,136	2.2
Somalia	2,730	2.5	Trinidad and Tobago	1,040	2.5

*Countries with populations of 1 million or more.
†Including Namibia.
‡Mainland Tanzania.
Source: *Finance and Development*, vol. 9, no. 1 (March 1972): 50.

with $580. But the picture changes when recent trend data are examined. Mexico's average per capita growth rate over the last decade, 3.4 percent, compares to 2.6 percent for Argentina despite the fact that population has been expanding at 3.5 percent in Mexico as compared to 1.6 percent in Argentina. The Mexican market has been expanding more rapidly than the Argentinian market in terms of both income and number of consumers and almost certainly warrants priority attention.

A Second "Cut"

Sectoral Trends. After opportunity areas have been identified in a preliminary way, the firm will want to examine the economic structure and sectoral trends in the selected countries. This step will provide overviews of the size and trend of the agricultural sector for firms whose markets are in agricultural production, or of the mining and manufacturing sectors for firms whose interests are in those areas. For most countries, these detailed data can be secured from United Nations sources[5] or from OECD publications.[6]

Structural data can also provide clues as to future-growth prospects. In general, growth potentials are less for countries where agriculture comprises a large share of national output. More than in other sectors, growth in agriculture is constrained by low-income elasticities in the demand for foodstuffs and by the rate at which new production techniques can be adopted. As industry approaches agriculture in size, countries become capable of more rapid growth, particularly during the period in which domestic manufacturing is substituting for imported goods. Empirical studies have shown a regular pattern of change in economic structure associated with rising levels of income. As income increases, the shares spent by consumers for necessities decrease while the shares for luxury goods, service, recreation, and other goods produced by the manufacturing (secondary) sector and the trade and services (tertiary) sectors increase. As shown in Table 12.5, the average pattern, based

TABLE 12.5
Normal Variations in Economic Structure with Level of Development

Level of GNP per Capita (in 1964 US $)	*Output Composition (percentage share of total)*				
	Primary (agriculture, fishing, and forestry)	Industry (manufacturing and mining)	Services	Utilities	Total*
$50	58.1	7.3	29.9	4.6	100
$100	46.4	13.5	34.6	5.7	100
$200	36.0	19.6	37.9	7.0	100
$300	30.4	23.1	39.2	7.7	100
$400	26.7	25.5	39.9	8.3	100
$600	21.8	29.0	40.4	9.1	100
$800	18.6	31.4	40.5	9.7	100
$1,000	16.3	33.2	40.4	10.2	100
$2,000	9.8	38.9	39.3	11.7	100

*May not total 100 percent because of rounding off.
Source: Hollis B. Chenery, "Targets for Development," in *The Widening Gap*, ed. Barbara Ward, et al., (New York: Columbia University Press, 1971), table 1, pp. 30–31. All values are computed from multiple regressions for a sample of about 100 countries over the period 1950–65. The values shown apply to a country of 10 million population in the year 1960.

[5] For example, see table 2 in the standard tables for each country, "Industrial Origin of Gross Domestic Product," in *United Nations Yearbook of National Account Statistics 1969* (New York, 1970).

[6] See *National Accounts of OECD Countries 1953–1969* (Paris: OECD, July 1971).

on a study of about 100 countries, is for industry (including mining) to account for only 7 percent of total output in countries with $50 per capita GNP. Industry's share rises to 39 percent of total output for countries with $2,000 per capita GNP. Agriculture follows a reverse trend of a declining share in total output as income rises.

Structural changes within sectors generally accompany the changes in the relative importance of the sectors and again follow a regular pattern. For example, the manufacturing sector of low-income countries is likely to have a predominance of textile and food processing industries, whereas high-income countries have a heavy concentration in the manufacture of machinery and other technologically sophisticated products. Although the development pattern of a specific country will deviate in varying degrees from the normal pattern deduced from the growing number of empirical studies, the normal patterns are still extremely useful in forecasting the growth prospects for industries or products closely related to the sectoral structure of a country.[7]

Inflation. Another feature of the economic environment that must be assessed by the international enterprise is inflationary price pressures. High rates of inflation may be the prelude to foreign exchange devaluation, and an inflationary environment requires special business strategies and knowledge.

The traditional view toward inflation that has long prevailed in many of the advanced countries, including the United States, is that countries with high rates of inflation are unattractive for business operations. One reason is that high inflation rates are believed to be associated with low rates of economic growth. Another reason relates to the assumed difficulties of having profitable operations in an inflationary environment. Most experienced international enterprises, however, have abandoned these traditional views. Empirical evidence has shown that inflation is not a good indicator of either slow or rapid economic growth. Some countries have achieved rapid growth with inflation. Conversely, other countries have had poor success in accelerating growth, even though price levels have remained stable. Furthermore, international managers have developed appropriate operating policies for operating profitably in inflationary situations.

In assessing countries from the standpoint of inflation, the international manager should be particularly interested in whether a country is experiencing wide variations in inflation rates and whether the country has adopted measures to minimize or neutralize the effects of inflation.[8]

---

[7] See *Sectoral Aspects of Projections for the World Economy,* 3 vols. Papers delivered at Elsinore, Denmark, 14–27 August 1966 (New York: United Nations, 1969).

[8] A standard source for price-trend data is the monthly *International Statistics* published by the International Monetary Fund, Washington, D.C.

A country can adjust to high rates of inflation if there is reasonable certainty about the rate to expect. If expectations are not disturbed by wide variations in the rate of inflation from year to year, business activity need hardly be impaired.

In many countries, both developed and less developed, policies and techniques have been adopted to offset the effects of inflation in selected areas of economic activity or even across the board. Loans, savings accounts, pensions, or other fixed obligations, as well as wages and salaries, can include provisions for cost-of-living adjustments. Brazil has probably the most comprehensive policies where fiscal correction is applied to virtually all incomes, long-term debt obligations—both private and government—and even to delinquent taxes. With such a policy Brazil was able to achieve real growth from 1968–71 of between 9 and 11 percent annually, despite the persistence of a 20 percent rate of inflation.

External Dependence and Economic Integration. The degree to which a country's economy is dependent upon external forces can be another important factor in the economic environment. A nation that is a closed or relatively self-sufficient economy has maximum control over its economic future, and the forces influencing such trends will be predominantly domestic. Over many decades, the USSR was largely a closed economy and until recently Mainland China had reduced its external dependence to a minimum. At the other extreme, foreign trade of the Netherlands is the equivalent of 32 percent of its gross national product.

The ratio of foreign trade to gross national product indicates the vulnerability of a national economy to fluctuations in international trade. Thus the Netherlands depends to a high degree on economic-expansion trends in the countries to which it is exporting. At the other extreme, the United States with exports representing only 4 percent of GNP is less affected by fluctuations in other countries.

External dependence is related to the availability of foreign exchange as well as domestic growth trends. A high degree of external dependence may mean a high foreign exchange earning capacity and an ability to secure a great deal of external stimulation to internal growth. Thus, external dependence is not "good" or "bad" per se, but high external dependency means that a careful analysis of external forces must be included in the assessment and forecasting of a country's future prospects.

Another form of external dependence is a country's obligations to service and repay foreign loans. External debt and interest obligations can be compared to foreign exchange earnings as a measure of the capacity to repay. For many less developed countries, annual public debt service and investment-income payments have risen to a level of more than 10 percent, and, in a few cases, above 25 percent of foreign exchange earnings.[9] But a high ratio of debt service to foreign exchange earnings is not necessarily an indication of a crisis situation. The capital inflow may have been invested so as to increase future capacity to repay through increased exports or import substitution.

For a growing number of nations, an important type of external dependence comes from participation in a regional economic-integration movement. If a high degree of coordination is achieved by such groups as the European Common Market and the Andean subregional integration movement in Latin America, the task of assessing national economic environments may become easier for the international enterprise. An assessment or forecast for a regional grouping may be substituted for similar studies of a number of separate countries.

CROSS-NATIONAL COMPARISONS
AND MULTICOUNTRY COMPOSITES

Special problems arise when the multinational enterprise has to make inter-country comparisons and when a composite picture of several national economies must be constructed. Not only are national differences involved, but financial data expressed in national currencies must be converted to a common unit for inter-country comparisons. Most commonly, current exchange rates are used to translate measures in local currencies to a common currency unit such as the U.S. dollar or the currency of the enterprise's home country.

Ideally, for purposes of inter-country comparisons, translations to a common currency should be derived from national currency figures on the basis of purchasing power parities or through direct real-product comparisons. However, such comparative data are available for only a limited number of countries and generally relate to different periods of time.

The use of exchange rates can result in a considerable overstatement of economic differences among countries, especially those in the highest and lowest income categories. A study carried out for India, for example, indicates that U.S. per capita product in 1959 exceeded that in India by a ratio of 30:1 when the comparison was based on exchange rates. But a comparison based on a purchasing power parity calculation resulted in a ratio of about 12:1.[10] Another study for Latin America produced similar results when purchasing power equivalents were used for

---

[9] *Partners in Development,* Report of the Commission on International Development (New York: Praeger Publishers, Inc., 1969), table 11, p. 373.

[10] See "Technical Note" in *World Bank Atlas* (Washington, D.C.: International Bank for Reconstruction and Development, 1971).

inter-country comparisons of real income.[11] Expressed in U.S. dollars, 1960 per capita GNP in Argentina was $561 when pesos were converted by exchange rates as compared to $868 on the basis of purchasing power equivalents. The difference for Uruguay was even greater—from $477 to $853. For the Latin American region the per capita product increases from $337 to $431, or from 12 percent of U.S. per capita GNP to almost 16 percent.

The reason for such different results lies primarily in the divergent price and product structures of different countries. Exchange rates, even when they approximate balance-of-payments equilibrium rates, equate at best only the prices of internationally traded goods and services. They may bear little relationship to the prices of goods and services not internationally traded, which in most countries form the large bulk of the total national product. Specifically, the prices of farm products and of services in less developed countries are in most cases considerably lower, relative to industrial prices, than in the more developed countries. Moreover, agricultural output generally accounts for the major part of overall national output in the LDCs, while the opposite is true in developed countries. As a result, the internal purchasing power of the currency of a low-income country will generally be greater than indicated by the exchange rate.

The use of exchange rates for converting national currency data into a common currency is further complicated by the fact that official or par value rates do not always constitute equilibrium rates. Economic history provides countless instances where a given exchange rate has been maintained for a lengthy period of time, even though the internal price level has long since fallen out of line with prices in other parts of the world. A straight conversion on the basis of the overvalued rates would overstate both absolute levels and changes over time. An additional problem arises when no single or unique rate of exchange exists. The international enterprise wishing to express national data in a selected currency is given the choice of free rates, controlled rates, preferential, basic, auction, nonpreferential rates and so forth depending on prevailing national policies.

No easy solution exists for the problem of inter-country comparisons. To the extent that nations follow flexible exchange-rate policies, the problems of multiple and nonequilibrium rates are reduced. A partial solution is to rely on the statistical reports of international agencies, such as the *International Financial Statistics* publication of the International Monetary Fund, which attempt, so far as possible, to present data from the various countries that are comparable. Where comparable data are not available, the business firm will have to make its own

---

[11] "Measurement of Latin American Real Income in U.S. Dollars," *Economic Bulletin for Latin America,* 12, no. 2, (United Nations: New York, 1968): 107–42.

judgments, keeping in mind the consistent downward bias in converting the figures from the less developed countries into a common currency.

FORECASTING ECONOMIC-GROWTH PROSPECTS

By macro-economic scanning and further in-depth investigations, the global enterprise may have identified a number of countries which appear to offer attractive business opportunities. As a next step, the firm will want to evaluate the future economic prospects of the countries. Here it becomes involved in the familiar and difficult problem of forecasting. Although there is no agreed usage of the term, forecasting is used here in a loose way referring to anticipations about the future. In a more precise technical sense, forecasting might be defined as probabilistic statements at particular confidence levels as contrasted to predictions— nonprobabilistic statements on a near-absolute confidence level.[12]

Fortunately, evaluations of future economic-growth prospects can frequently rely on available comprehensive long-range planning studies. To be sure, such planning studies vary immensely in quality and in validity. Still, many are highly useful and reasonable guides to future prospects and future growth patterns. Such planning studies may be for the nation as a whole, for regions, and for sectors of the economy. For the less developed countries, extensive planning studies are frequently available from national agencies and from international organizations. The World Bank, in particular, has sent economic survey missions to most of the less developed countries, and many of the mission reports are publicly available. For the industrialized countries, future outlook studies may be available from the OECD and from government and nongovernment sources within the country.

Two recent studies for Sweden and Switzerland illustrate the kind of long-term forecasting analysis that is available. The government of Sweden publishes once every five years a long-term forecast prepared by the Secretariat for Economic Planning. The study published in 1970, for example, covers in detail the development outlook through 1975 and examines prospective trends up to 1990 in a more general way.[13] For the 1970–75 period, total GNP is forecast to increase at an annual rate of 3.8 percent. The most rapid growth in the Swedish economy is expected to take place in the petroleum industry with an annual average growth rate of 10 percent, followed by chemicals (8 percent), converted paper

[12] For a general discussion of forecasting, see Michael Young, ed., *Forecasting and the Social Sciences* (London: Heinemann, 1968). The OECD publication, *Techniques of Economic Forecasting* (Paris, March 1965), describes the methods of short-term economic forecasting used by the governments of Canada, France, the Netherlands, Sweden, the United Kingdom, and the United States.

[13] Secretariat for Economic Planning, Ministry of Finance, *The Swedish Economy 1971–1975 and the General Outlook up to 1990* (Stockholm, 1971).

goods (7 percent), metal-working products (6 percent), mining (6 percent), and paper and pulp (5.5 percent). For the 1980–90 decade, a number of alternative development paths are charted, depending on such variations as overall growth rate and growth in public consumption.

The Swiss Federal Government recently commissioned a study on "Development Perspectives of the Swiss National Economy up to the Year 2000."[14] The work is not one of actual prognosis, but rather an attempt to project forward from the development trends in the Swiss economy and thus to illuminate the problems which may face Switzerland in the near future. Although such a study is intended primarily as an aid for government policy making, the analysis provides business firms with useful insights as to an economy's growth outlook. According to this study Swiss population growth, which has averaged 1.5 percent during the past two decades, should drop to about 0.6 percent in the future, giving Switzerland a total population of about 7.5 million by the year 2000. Total GNP in real terms, that is, adjusting for price inflation, is projected to increase by 3.2 percent annually and GNP per capita by 2.6 percent. In addition to examining population and production trends, the planning study also examines the restructuring trends within the Swiss economy.

With the development of computers and econometric models, economic forecasting has become highly technical, complex, and at times very expensive. Yet the general types of forecasting are relatively few and do not require special knowledge to comprehend.[15] From a methodological point of view, the simplest type is a statistical extrapolation of historical trends. The statistical method assumes that existing patterns will continue into the future. This assumption is more likely to be correct over the short term than over the long term and for relatively static rather than for dynamic economies. A second method is to rely on qualitative techniques such as a canvas of expert opinions or of advance plans and commitments by groups within an economy. This method, often relied upon when little quantitative or historical data are available, is frequently used in the new technology and new product area. The third method is quantitative model building, which in practice makes use of the previous two methods.

Quantitative model building has a number of advantages.[16] It is comprehensive and requires the forecaster to consider the total business

[14] F. Kneschaurek, *Entwicklungsperspektiven der Schweizerischen Volkswirtschaft bis zum Jahre 2000,* Hochschule St. Gallen für Wirtschafts—und Sozialwissenschaften, Zentrum für Zukunftsforschung, Teil I-VI, (St. Gallen) March 1969–April 1972.

[15] See John C. Chambers, Satinder K. Mullick, and Donald D. Smith, "How to Choose the Right Forecasting Technique," *Harvard Business Review,* July–August 1971, pp. 45–74.

[16] See John P. Lewis and Robert C. Turner, *Business Conditions Analysis,* 2nd ed. (New York: McGraw-Hill Book Co., 1967), pp. 363–91.

situation and all sectors of the economy, including the external sector. More so than the others, it is analytical and requires the forecaster to reason from identified causes to predictable results on the basis of a theoretical framework. Another characteristic is the essentially quantitative nature of the forecast generally using national-income accounting as the basic statistical vocabulary. Furthermore, quantification requires that magnitudes as well as directions be expressed. Finally, model building can be flexible and take into account institutional changes and alternative assumptions. But the international manager should be constantly aware that forecasting models generate no knowledge about the future that is not fed into them. Their results can be no better than the assumptions, the choice of data, and the judgments that compose the analysis. It is critically important, therefore, that the underlying assumptions be made explicit so that the forecasts can be adjusted as uncertain future events reveal themselves. It is customary, also, to make such forecasts within a range that emphasizes the probability character of trying to look into the future.

A survey undertaken almost a decade ago of the extent to which large econometric models were being used for national-economic planning and forecasting identified more than 30 countries with such work underway by either governmental or private groups. Most of the models were for the national economy as a whole, but a few also have regional subdivisions. This work has become increasingly refined and efforts were underway in the early 1970s to link national models together.[17]

To illustrate the nature and use of economic forecasts, let us take the case of an international company interested in the future demand for food in specific nations. In this case, the firm could make use of the projections for 1980 made by the Food and Agriculture Organization (FAO) of the United Nations.[18] The FAO study made projections for 130 individual countries and about 50 commodities. The projections for food demand were based on estimates of future population and assumptions as to expected growth in per capita gross domestic product.[19] The assumptions as to GDP growth rates were based on historical trends,

---

[17] Richard Stone and Colin Leicester, "The Methodology of Planning Models," in *National Economic Planning* ed. Max F. Millikan (New York: National Bureau of Economic Research, 1967), pp. 15–38; R. J. Ball, ed., *The International Linkage of National Economic Models* (New York: American Elsevier, 1972).

[18] Food and Agricultural Organization of the United Nations, *Agricultural Commodity Projections,* 2 vols. (Rome, 1971).

[19] William J. Abraham, *National Income and Economic Accounting* (Englewood Cliffs, N.J.: Prentice-Hall, 1969), p. 21. Gross domestic product (GDP) and gross national product (GNP) should be differentiated, although the distinction is not of great importance for most countries. GDP measures the value of goods and services produced in a country and does not take account of the nationality of those supplying the labor or capital. When factor income from abroad is added and factor income paid abroad is deducted the result is national product or income.

studies done by international agencies for some countries, expert advice, and national economic plans where available.

Given the projections of population and per capita GDP, the estimates of food demand were made by projecting historical patterns on the basis of income elasticities of the demand for each of the commodities. The income elasticities, or the changes in demand as income rises, were based on numerous household surveys and analyses of the relationship between consumption of different commodities and disposable income. These background studies and additional statistical analyses provided the basis for selecting the value of the income-elasticity coefficients and the most appropriate functions for the various countries and commodities. The results of the FAO study show, as one example, that the total demand for milk and milk products in Spain is projected to reach 6.44 million tons in 1980 as compared to 5.02 million tons in 1970.

Balance-of-Payments Forecasting

In assessing and forecasting the inter-nation dimensions of the economic environment, the multinational enterprise will need to anticipate structural changes in the international financial framework, as discussed in Chapter 4, and to forecast the possibility of devaluations or revaluations and foreign exchange controls for the countries in which it is operating or which it is considering for operations. The use of balance-of-payment forecasts in capital budgeting and financial-management decisions is considered in Chapter 20.

Forecasting the probability, timing, and amount of foreign exchange devaluations or revaluations is really part and parcel of the forecasting of foreign exchange controls.[20] Controls are possible reactions to balance-of-payments difficulties just as are devaluations or revaluations. No country changes the value of its currency without reason and the reasons can become apparent by studying the country's balance of payments, inflation, international reserves, and external public and private debt situation. But while economic analysis can suggest what an exchange rate should be at any point of time and whether a country should change its parity, the main difficulty in short-term forecasting is that the actual decision to change an exchange rate is ultimately political.

Balance-of-payments forecasting first estimates the probable size of a devaluation or revaluation based on changes in the value of a country's currency in relation to other countries in its international trade network. Next, it forecasts the probability of a devaluation or revaluation taking

---

[20] For more detailed discussions of balance-of-payments forecasting techniques, see David B. Zenoff and Jack Zwick, *International Financial Management* (Englewood Cliffs, N.J.: Prentice-Hall, 1969), pp. 68–88; R. B. Shulman, "Are Foreign Exchange Risks Measurable?" *Columbia Journal of World Business,* May–June 1970, pp. 55–60.

place within a forecast period. In addition, it should also supply the international manager with a probable error of the forecast.

Inflation Trends. In forecasting currency changes and controls, the attention paid to inflation assumes that countries will modify the external relationship of their currency with that of related countries in order to maintain purchasing power parity. For the country being studied, major trading links—suppliers, customers, and competitors—must be identified and the relative rates of inflation compared among the network countries. To forecast future changes in relative inflation rates, the analyst must be aware of directions of change in monetary and fiscal policy, probable rates of change in labor costs, in productivity, and in other determinants of domestic inflation in each of the network countries.

A change in purchasing power relative to partner countries, however, may be offset by other factors. The availability of adequate international reserves, for example, may permit a country to tolerate balance-of-payments deficits without having to devalue its currency. Thus, inflationary analysis should be complemented by an examination of external assets and obligations and prospects for future foreign exchange earnings.

Foreign Exchange Earnings Prospects. Future supplies of foreign exchange will depend upon exports of goods, sale of services (including tourism), unilateral transfers, and both short- and long-term capital inflows. Forecasting future export prospects involves conventional supply and demand analysis of a country's principal export products and prospective new exports. In the case of traditional exports, an examination of recent trends in both quantity and price of specific exports and growth trends in the principal buyer countries can provide considerable insight into future prospects. Additional considerations will be a country's capacity for increasing the supply of export goods, possible variations in supply conditions due to weather and related conditions, the price and income elasticity of demand for specific products, the competitive position of countries that are alternative sources of supply, and the possibilities for changes in tariff and quota regulations imposed by buyer countries.

Fortunately for the international businessman many official agencies, both national and international, undertake and publish on a continuing basis studies of the future international trade prospects for a wide range of products. FAO undertakes many studies in the agricultural area. In the field of manufactured goods, the U.N. Conference on Trade and Development (UNCTAD) has been studying many products to identify new export possibilities for the less developed countries. In the field of minerals, the U.S. Bureau of Mines is an important source for research on future world demand and supply conditions.

Many countries, particularly the less developed countries, have been trying to change the composition of their exports from heavy reliance on primary products from agriculture and mining to increased exports of manufactured and semimanufactured goods. In support of this effort, UNCTAD has been pressing the advanced countries to grant unilateral tariff concessions for manufactured exports from the LDCs. In addition, individual countries have established trade-promotion programs and special incentives for the export of manufactured goods and, in a number of cases, achieved significant results. The forecast of future export prospects of many LDCs will have to include an evaluation of the possibility of achieving success in such trade-diversification programs.

Unilateral transfers can be either from foreign governments or from individuals. Foreign exchange inflows as development-assistance grants can be sizeable in the case of certain countries and the prospects of future flows will depend heavily on political and security policies of donor governments and the availability of resources for international development agencies. Private unilateral transfers are significant for some countries such as Israel, which has received sizeable foreign donations, the Philippines, where many Filipinos receive veterans payments having served in the U.S. armed forces, or some southern European countries where nationals have migrated to work in other countries and are sending regular remittances to families remaining at home.

Capital inflows will depend on the interest of foreign firms in making direct investments and on the policies of the country toward encouraging or controlling foreign investment. Future prospects for inflows of portfolio investment, loan funds, and short-term deposits attracted by high-interest rates must also be analyzed.

Foreign Exchange Needs. Set off against the forecast of future foreign exchange availability will be an estimate of foreign exchange needs for imports, for purchases of foreign services, and for servicing foreign debt and the capital accounts. The forecast of import requirements can begin with an analysis and a projection of recent trends in both quantities and prices of principal import items. The projections should then be modified to reflect significant future changes likely to occur. Such a change might be the discovery of new resources that will substitute for imports, for example, petroleum, or a one-time need for large imports of capital goods to initiate a major industrialization project, or a high demand for kinds of goods not being produced within the country stimulated by rapidly rising consumer incomes.

Forecasting the foreign exchange requirements of the capital accounts involves mainly government debt service, private dividend outflows and foreign debt service, profit remittances by foreign business firms, and related business outflows such as licensing and royalty payments. Data on government and private debt obligations are normally published by the central bank or some other financial agency of a country. Such data are frequently incomplete and should be supplemented by information from international financial agencies or multinational banks. Information on past private remittances will have to be supplemented by data on inflow trends of direct private investment and by prospective changes in remittance patterns. For example, when local expansion prospects for foreign firms become less promising, as in the case of countries which have discontinued granting new exploration concessions to oil companies, profit remittances are likely to be only as high as permitted by local authorities.

The leads and lags in each country between policy change and effect on the economies must also be considered. The analysis of inflation, together with expected changes in capital flows, becomes a basis for forecasting the balance of payments. The outcome of changes in the balance of payments will be reflected in the country's international reserve position. The sufficiency of reserves thus becomes of major significance in forecasting foreign exchange controls and the probability and timing of devaluation or revaluation.

Political and Personality Considerations. The economic forecasting task can be quantitative and scientific. But personality characteristics of the decision maker and political considerations, which are more difficult to forecast, are also crucial components of currency change decisions. The political decision maker has a string of temporizing alternatives to devaluation which he will normally exhaust before he is willing to take the more drastic devaluation step. He can use import controls, exchange controls, foreign short-term borrowings from abroad, export incentives, selective taxes, and so forth. A similar range of alternatives to avoid or postpone revaluations are available. Consequently, for short-term forecasting, the analyst must become familiar with the background, education, training, and past behavior of the politician with decision responsibility to anticipate whether he will lean toward controls or toward free-market solutions for his balance-of-payments problems, and the analyst must follow progress through the temporizing alternatives to the currency change that may be inevitable. Such surveillance is essential for forecasting the timing. And timing is extremely important because of the cost over time of hedging against foreign exchange risk.

Forecasting National Institutional Environments

For countries where economic forecasts and market-demand studies have revealed attractive business opportunities, the international firm will want to extend its investigation into those aspects of the institutional environment that are of special importance for the activity being considered. The firm may need to know about local banking and other financial institutions, as well as the extent to which local capital markets operate effectively. Other significant issues may be the role of labor unions and patterns of labor-management relations, the importance of government enterprises and the business fields in which they are operating, the influence of economic-planning agencies, the types of business regulation that will be encountered, and patterns of social-welfare programs.

In some situations, an assessment of the institutional environment may heavily influence the firm's decision to invest or initiate operations. For example, the prospective business opportunity may be in a field where government enterprises are likely to extend their activities and where future expansion possibilities for a private foreign company may be restricted by institutional patterns rather than by economic-growth prospects. In other situations, assessing the institutional environment may not be critical for the investment decision but of primary importance in shaping the business project and in providing guidance for future operations. For example, if local capital markets are poorly developed and promise to remain so, the firm that would prefer to do local financing through a public offering of shares in the subsidiary might still proceed with its project but change its financing plans in favor of other strategies.

Both of the examples cited underline the dynamic nature of the institutional environment and the need for forecasting future trends. Where government enterprises might have a key impact on contemplated operations, it is not enough to know the fields in which government enterprise is currently operating. The foreign firm must make some judgments or forecasts as to future expansion trends of public enterprises. Or in the case of capital markets, the important question may not be how capital markets currently perform but whether presently underdeveloped capital markets are likely to expand sufficiently in the future to become a significant source of local financing.

In securing the information it needs on current patterns, the firm is not likely to encounter serious problems. But where rapidly changing dimensions of the institutional environment have to be projected into the future, the forecasting task can be difficult. Economic forecasting, with all its limitations and uncertainties, has become a relatively well-developed technical field. But the need for forecasting the institutional environment has not yet become well recognized and techniques are still in an incipient stage. Furthermore, unlike the situation in economic forecasting, the international firm can not yet look to international and national governmental and research organizations for a large flow of institutional forecasting studies.

Yet the situation is far from hopeless. In some cases, such as antitrust laws, many countries appear to be moving toward a harmonization of substantive laws,[21] and separate forecasting for specific nations may

---

[21] Seymour J. Rubin, "The International Firm and the National Jurisdiction," in *The International Corporation,* ed. Charles P. Kindleberger (Cambridge, Mass.: The M.I.T. Press, 1970), p. 193.

become part of a broader forecast of the legal environment. In other areas, forecasting can be done by an analogy technique whereby patterns in one country can be projected on the bases of patterns in another country at a higher stage of development. For example, if the less developed capital markets in Western Europe appear to be evolving toward the more developed patterns in the United Kingdom or the United States, the United Kingdom or United States patterns can provide important clues as to future trends in Western European countries. The analogy approach, also relied upon in the sectoral projections discussed above, assumes that the economic structure of low-income countries will generally follow the path already traveled by the higher-income countries.

But where institutional patterns are clearly following different evolutionary paths in different countries, forecasting will have to be based on more speculative techniques. For example, the role played by labor unions and patterns of labor-management relations appears to be following independent patterns in Italy, Japan, and the United States.[22] Consequently, it is unlikely that the role of labor unions in Italy will eventually become similar to present U.S. patterns when the Italian economy achieves present U.S. levels of income. In such situations, the forecasting approach will have to identify in each country the particular factors that have been shaping institutional patterns and then attempt to forecast trends in the underlying factors. Italian labor unions generally have a political affiliation and play an important, direct political role in the country. Furthermore, many of the issues that are normally resolved in the United States through collective bargaining, such as vacations and pensions, are resolved in Italy through governmental legislation. Consequently, a forecast of labor union patterns in Italy would require that considerable attention be given to the political situation and political trends. Japanese labor union patterns are deeply rooted in cultural characteristics of that country, and any forecast would have to give major attention to cultural factors.

Many dimensions of the institutional environment will be considered in subsequent chapters. Some aspects of business regulation form part of the legal environment. Capital markets and financial institutions are an important aspect of international financial management. The labor-management patterns are essential information for managing human resources. At this stage, however, two general features of the institutional environment can be examined to illustrate in greater detail the importance of institutional dimensions and how judgments might be made in those areas as to future trends. The role of government enterprise and national economic planning have been selected because these are

---

[22] See Paul T. Hartman and Arthur M. Ross, *Changing Patterns of Industrial Conflict* (New York: Wiley, 1960); Everett M. Kassalow, *Trade Unions and Industrial Relations: An International Comparison* (New York: Random House, 1969).

likely to be unfamiliar features of the institutional environment for business managers and enterprises of American nationality.

Government Enterprise. Most governments, including those of the so-called capitalistic countries, influence the national economic environment through direct participation in business activities.[23] Enterprises may be completely owned and operated by the government, or may be organized as mixed corporations with the government as the major stockholder and in effective management control. Increasingly, governments have been forming joint ventures with foreign enterprise. Government enterprises have been of major importance in most of the advanced industrial countries, as well as in the less developed countries. In Italy, for example, through such holding companies as National Hydrocarbon Agency (ENI) and the Institute for Industrial Reconstruction (IRI), the government is a significant and frequently majority stockholder in enterprises producing motor vehicles, machinery, iron and steel, shipbuilding, and chemicals. In 1971, the IRI Group included more than 130 different companies employing 353,000 workers. It had annual sales of over $5,440 million and an investment capacity of $1,600 million a year.[24]

Aside from preempting fields of business activity, government enterprises can exert a wide range of influences on the economic environment. Any attempt to forecast economic growth in Argentina during the middle 1960s would have had to take into account the extraordinary deficit of the government-owned railways. To meet the deficit, the government diverted resources from programs designed to stimulate economic expansion and contributed greatly to inflationary forces by increasing the supply of money in circulation. Government enterprises can exert an inhibiting influence on the development of capital markets. Government enterprises frequently secure new capital directly from governmental financial institutions or taxes thereby reducing the potential size of private capital markets for business financing. Where government enterprise is strong, labor costs and labor-management relations can be strongly influenced by the patterns of public enterprises which can be subjected directly to political pressures. And finally, the costs of certain materials and services may be determined by social policies implemented by government enterprises in the fields of transportation and electric power rather than on the basis of normal business criteria.

In order to assess and forecast the role of government enterprises in the business environment, the forces which have stimulated the estab-

---

[23] See A. H. Hanson, *Public Enterprise and Economic Development,* 2nd ed. (London: Routledge and K. Paul, 1965); W. Friedmann and J. F. Garner, eds., *Government Enterprise: A Comparative Study* (New York: Columbia University Press, 1970).

[24] Italian Institute for International Trade as reported in the *Wall Street Journal,* 15 October 1971.

lishment and expansion of government enterprise can be identified and grouped into eight categories.

1. *National attitudes toward natural resources.* As previously discussed, where natural resources are the legal property of the state, one way of trying to share the benefits of these resources with all of the people in a country is through government enterprise.

2. *Social-welfare goals.* Where public aims are considered to prevail over private-profit goals, government enterprise is one of the ways to achieve such aims. In public-utility fields, such as transportation, public-welfare possibilities are important and some government enterprises are actually run at a loss in order to achieve social goals.

3. *Absence of private enterprise as a feasible alternative for achieving priority development goals.* The establishment of government steel plants in many LDCs has been justified by the felt national need for a steel industry and by the absence of private business interest in such projects because of large capital requirements or other considerations.

4. *Involuntary nationalizations.* The nationalization of the coal-mining industry in Britain and passenger railways in the United States are examples of situations where private industries were operating with great difficulties. The government took over to rationalize operation and to save businesses considered vital to the national interest.

5. *Revenue purposes.* Governments have assumed monopolies of such business activities as tobacco and liquor (state governments in the United States) simply for the purpose of capturing profits for public revenue.

6. *Competition.* Government enterprises have been established to operate as competitive yardsticks in fields in which private enterprises also exist, such as the electric power operations of the Tennessee Valley Authority in the United States.

7. *Historical accidents.* A prime case in this category is the Renault automobile company of France. During World War II, the private owners of Renault collaborated with the enemy. In retaliation, the French government expropriated the company immediately after the war.

8. *Ideological forces.* Government ownership has sometimes had its origins in a moral crusade to wrest the commanding heights of the economy from self-seeking capitalists or, in its more modern version, from foreign interests. Ideological forces have been important in both advanced and less developed countries. In the less developed countries, indigenous private enterprise may be extremely weak and, where nationalistic forces want to reduce the role of foreign enterprise, government enterprises are created to substitute for foreign business.

For any specific country, the total public enterprise sector may have evolved as a consequence of a mix of the various underlying forces. In order to speculate about future trends, the several types of business activities will have to be analyzed separately. In the natural resource fields, for example, where the motivation for public enterprises comes from a philosophy that the benefits of these resources should be public rather than private, future trends are likely to be in the direction of more public enterprise, particularly in the less developed countries where local private capital and entrepreneurship is not a feasible alternative. The main determinant of momentum will be the speed with which nationals acquire the skills and experience to operate such enterprises. Similar trends should be expected in the fields of public utilities such as electric power, telephones, and railroads because of the underlying social-welfare motivation.

Although private enterprisers may feel that there is a strong and immutable trend toward an increasing role for government enterprises, numerous instances exist where enterprises once owned and operated by the government have moved into the private sector. In the Philippines, the government established textile plants as pioneering projects to demonstrate the viability of a type of manufacturing activity that had been given priority in development planning and which had been neglected by private enterprise. Although the government projects were not outstanding commercial successes, they were sufficiently successful to attract private enterprise to the field, and the government withdrew. A similar strategy was followed by Puerto Rico in its "Operation Bootstrap" development program. Still another example of denationalization when certain government goals were achieved is the case of Volkswagen in Germany. The company was government owned after World War II because the private sector was in disarray. But as reconstruction progressed, Germany reverted to its ideological preference for private enterprise and sold shares in the company.[25]

National Economic Planning.   In recent years, with the notable exception of the United States, economic plans and national economic planning have become a common feature of country environments. For non-U.S. multinational enterprises, economic planning is a familiar environmental factor but the same is not likely to be true for most enterprises of U.S. nationality.

Many forces explain the spread of economic planning. During World War II, the industrialized countries resorted to planning to ensure that scarce materials and other resources were used for high priority production goals. The success of wartime planning and the requirement under

---

[25] Volkswagenwerk, G.M.B.H. was transformed in July 1960 into Volkswagenwerk, A.G. whereby the Federal Republic of Germany and the state of Lower Saxony each retained 20 percent of the share capital. The remaining 60 percent was sold to qualified residents of Germany. See *Moody's Industrial Manual: 1972* (New York: Moody's Investor Services, 1972), p. 3814.

the Marshall Plan for European recovery—that each participating European nation prepare comprehensive plans as a condition for receiving aid—gave impetus to permanent economic-planning agencies. In the less developed countries, development planning was stimulated by the achievement of the USSR in this field, by the encouragement and assistance of international development agencies, and by the requirement of foreign-aid donor countries for long-term plans as a prerequisite for receiving development assistance.

Economic planning is a difficult term to define since it has been applied in so many different ways. Certainly the type of comprehensive economic-planning practices in the USSR, sometimes referred to an imperative planning, or planning with controls, differs sharply from the kinds used in Western Europe. The best known of the European planning styles is the indicative planning of France in which discriminatory taxation and financing facilities, rather than direct controls, are used to persuade private firms to accept the plan targets. The less developed countries have chosen forms of economic planning which lie somewhere in between.[26]

Across the spectrum, economic planning rejects the efficiency of laissez faire as the guiding force. It substitutes governmental planning and controls or incentives for the marketplace as a preferred method of allocating scarce resources to projects or activities considered to be priority goals for the economy. The justification for substituting government action for the marketplace in making economic decisions may be that markets are weak, or that they do not function satisfactorily when resources are scarce in relation to needs and when structural changes have to be achieved in the local economy.

Among the Western European countries, France, the Netherlands, Norway, and Sweden have practiced economic planning the longest. Norway has sought to rationalize and coordinate investment and economic policy through a system of annual and intermediate range national budgets which represent the action program of the government. The Netherlands prepares long-term development plans, but the plans do not carry official sanction. In Sweden, economic planning is closer to economic forecasts than to plans for action. The Dutch and Swedish plans are drawn up with the help of the private sector, while in Norway there are no such consultations.

French indicative planning embraces the entire economy but operates through indirect rather than direct controls. The effectiveness of French planning is furthered by a close degree of cooperation between leading

---

[26] Albert Waterson, *Development Planning: Lessons of Experience* (Baltimore, Md.: The Johns Hopkins Press, 1965).

industrialists and their counterparts in the nationalized industries.[27] Discriminatory treatment in taxation and financing is applied to those firms which conform to planning guides and carry out specific targets. The chief financial institutions are under government control and tend to discriminate in favor of firms and industries adhering to the plan. The significance of this financial leverage can be seen in the fact that during the Third Plan Period (1958–61) one half of the fixed investment which took place in the private sector was financed through government-controlled institutions.

Planning is quite different in the less developed countries. Many of them have adopted plans which are much more extensive than in the developed countries of Western Europe and Japan. But their plans have often been much less successful in terms of what they hoped to accomplish. This unfavorable situation reflects problems characteristics of less developed countries—inadequate administrative and technical skills, overambitious demands for development, lack of statistical data, high degree of sensitivity to agricultural changes, and often unstable political conditions.

Although considerable disillusionment has set in for national economic planning as a development panacea, revised forms of planning which are more sophisticated and less ambitious are likely to continue for some time as part of the international business environment. The implications of this to the international business enterprise are several.

Foreign private enterprise has generally been subjected to more restrictive attention than national business firms. In India, for example, national plans have established overall limits for the total participation of foreign enterprise and have delineated the specific areas in which foreign investment would be permitted.

National planning attempts to establish priorities for sectors and for specific targets in sectors, and international enterprises will have to fit their plans within these priorities in order to be well received. Even when projects fall within priority sectors, projects are likely to be evaluated by detailed criteria as a means of determining the contribution and the cost in relation to scarce resources being allocated or goals being sought. For example, the foreign exchange earning (or saving in case of import substitution projects) and the foreign exchange costs will be closely scrutinized where foreign exchange constraints are significant. Criteria may exist with regard to choice of technology and the amount of employment that will be created. And where the geographical distribution of new projects is given high importance, the pro-

---

[27] For two contrasting views on the impact of French planning on business decision making, see Hans Schollhammer, "National Economic Planning and Business Decision Making: The French Experience," *California Management Review*, Winter 1969, pp. 74–88; John McArthur and Bruce R. Scott, *Industrial Planning In France* (Boston: Harvard University, Graduate School of Business Administration, 1969).

posed location of the new project will be important. Expansions that can be located in the depressed regions of countries are generally given special preference.

In assessing and forecasting the economic environment, the international enterprise will have to become familiar with the planning activities and the plans. It will also have to appraise the degree of commitment to planning and plans that actually exists. It is easier to prepare plans than to implement them. In many countries, for a variety of reasons, government actions may not follow published plans. In some cases, international enterprise will be able to participate in the planning process and make important contributions. In all cases, the planning dimension of the environment is dynamic, and forecasting will be required.

THE DEVELOPMENT PROCESS AND THE LDCs

As a group, the less developed countries (LDCs) have become known as the "Third World," the "First World" being the economically advanced nonsocialist countries, and the "Second World" being the socialist or centrally planned economies. In the Third World countries, many features of the national economic environment differ only in degree from the environment in the advanced countries. But in other important respects, economic patterns in Third World countries are sufficiently unique to warrant special attention. In particular, the LDCs have almost universally given top priority to the achievement of rapid economic and social development, with a great intensity and comprehensiveness to their commitment.

Of direct interest to international business firms are the numerous external programs initiated to assist in development efforts. The advanced countries and the international agencies have recognized the development gap between the LDCs and the advanced countries as a critical world problem and have established a wide range of governmental programs to transfer financial and technological resources of the LDCs. In addition, many investor countries provide special incentives to encourage private investment in the LDCs. Such external assistance programs must be included in the international enterprise's assessment of the economic environment in Third World countries and may also be viewed as directly creating business opportunities for many firms.

Another reason for giving special attention to the Third World is that the challenge of trying to raise economic levels for such a large share of the world's population has stimulated a tremendous amount of research and technical studies on the development process. This growing body of technical knowledge is being widely applied in the LDCs to accelerate development. In order to assess the economic environment in the LDCs, their economic institutions, their policies, and their future prospects, the international enterprise needs at least a minimum familiarity with the prevailing body of technical knowledge on the development process.

Most multinational enterprises are based in the high-income industrialized countries. Most of the recent expansion by multinational enterprises has been in the advanced countries. And most international managers have acquired their international experience in dealing with economic environment issues in the advanced countries. It is quite likely, therefore, that the reservoir of experience and knowledge available to many, if not most, international firms may not be adequate for assessing and forecasting the significantly different economic environments in the LDCs.

To be sure, some business firms have long been active in the LDCs as resource seekers for supplies of petroleum, minerals, and tropical agricultural products such as tea, cane sugar, and bananas. More recently, some production-efficiency seekers have been establishing feeder plants in the LDCs to produce textiles and electronic components for export to the advanced countries. But as market seekers, international enter-prises have been showing only modest interest in the LDCs because of their small markets, low-income levels, and perceived political risk. Yet, a large share of the world's population is in the Third World, and many of the LDCs are achieving relatively high growth rates. As incomes rise, effective demand rises even faster for the kinds of advanced products that can be supplied by international firms. It is a reasonably safe forecast that the LDCs will have a much greater business attraction for the multinational enterprise in the future than they have had in the recent past.

Many of the newly independent and low-income countries are highly concerned about foreign economic domination and have been reluctantly receptive at best to foreign enterprise. Even where countries are receptive, they frequently impose many entry conditions. At the same time, many multinational firms have shown little enthusiasm for establishing operations in the LDCs because of company biases against sharing ownership locally, accepting invitations for joint ventures with government enterprises, and sacrificing efficiency by conforming to local content requirements. Yet, the barriers on both sides are likely to be relaxed. The countries invariably rank industrialization as a high-priority goal, and this is the area in which international enterprise has tremendous potential for contributing to national goals. As markets in the LDCs continue to expand at rapid rates, business operations in these countries can contribute in a major way to the goals of the enterprise.

The economic environment in the LDCs has been much influenced by the evolution of theoretical explanations of the development process. Many different theories have been advanced to account for low levels of economic activity in certain countries, ranging from climate and natural resources endowment to cultural and social factors.[28] The principal differences among the many development theories stem from different assumptions as to the facts and from questions of emphasis. The various theories, however, are more complementary than contradictory and are gradually evolving toward a complex explanation that recognizes the need to move on many fronts in order to accelerate economic growth.

In terms of general strategy, the early approach of most nations was to emphasize capital as the prime mover. Increasing savings and stimulating capital formation through domestic or foreign means was seen as the principal need for accelerating economic growth. As experience and understanding increased, development strategies became broader and more complex. Capital continues to be recognized as a crucial bottleneck but not necessarily the only one. Other issues are emphasized such as increasing the absorptive capacity of a country for capital flows, the elimination of institutional blocks, the need to invest in human resources, and the importance of encouraging technology transfers from more advanced countries. Foreign exchange as a constraint has also received considerable attention leading to an emphasis in many nations on expanding exports and attracting more public and private transfers of capital. In virtually all cases, heavy reliance has been placed on national economic planning and on government enterprise as a source of entrepreneurship.

The development process requires much more than preparing economic blueprints or injecting more capital into a system. Many preconditions for investment must be established in order to secure significant results. Such preconditions may be a mixture of increasing the skills of people, improving the administrative capacity of private and public institutions, creating new technologies, and securing greater efficiency in the operations of political institutions and political decision making in a country. The detailed requirements for a specific country will vary, depending upon resources, the present state of the economic infrastructure such as transportation and communications facilities, soundness of economic policies, and so forth.

In most cases, development-minded countries give great emphasis to industrialization as a means of expanding national productivity and creating new employment. Industrialization strategies will vary greatly. In many less developed countries, industrialization policies are first directed toward opportunities for further processing of raw materials normally exported from the country. Import substitution industries will

---

[28] The theoretical literature on economic development is vast. For a survey and synthesis, see Gerald M. Meier, *Leading Issues in Economic Development,* 2nd ed. (New York: Oxford University Press, 1970); Everett E. Hagen, *The Economics of Development* (Homewood, Ill.: Richard D. Irwin, Inc., 1968).

also be encouraged as an easy means of stimulating the industrialization process, because a domestic market will already be available, and because such industries hold the promise of saving foreign exchange. More recently, attention has shifted to encouraging export industries because the growth possibilities for import substitution industries appears to decline after a first initial period.[29]

The agricultural sector traditionally receives a great deal of development attention because it is generally the largest sector in the LDCs and because productivity is generally low. Land reform proposals to increase output generally face major opposition in this sector.

Conflicts among economic, political, and social goals is a general phenomenon. Most countries have less developed regions such as the South of Italy or the Northeast of Brazil where, for political reasons, development will have to receive special incentives. Geographical distribution to satisfy political goals may conflict with achieving rapid-growth rates. From the social-welfare viewpoint, the issue invariably arises as to how increased economic gains should be distributed as between increased consumption or increased investment. On the one hand, there is widespread desire for economic growth to be reflected quickly in improved living conditions. On the other hand, increased consumption generally means the reduced availability of savings for new investment in further growth.

Within many sectoral programs, particularly industry and agriculture, conflicts frequently arise concerning the use of capital-intensive rather than labor-intensive technologies. Most of the less developed countries have serious problems of unemployment and underemployment. Thus the preference is for adopting new technologies that will create maximum employment. But in many situations, the only technology options available are capital-intensive ones developed in the advanced countries to fit the needs in such countries. In other cases where the labor-intensive technology option is available, its adoption may make the enterprise less competitive than if capital-intensive technology is used.

Even these brief comments should suffice to demonstrate the complexity of the development process, and the need for considerable expertise on the part of the international enterprise in forecasting the economic environment. Fortunately, many national and international agencies will be forecasting trends in the developing countries, and such technical studies can be used by the international manager as his familiarity with development issues increases.

---

[29] See Albert O. Hirschman, "The Political Economy of Import-Substituting Industrialization in Latin America," *Quarterly Journal of Economics,* February 1968, pp. 1–12; Stefan H. Robock, "Industrialization Through Import-Substitution or Export Industries: A False Dichotomy," in *Industrial Organization and Development,* ed. J. W. Markham and G. F. Papanek (Boston: Houghton Mifflin Co., 1970), pp. 350–65.

The worldwide surge of interest in development that followed World War II spawned a variety of development-assistance programs that have become an important part of the economic environment. The Marshall Plan program of the United States made sizeable resources and technical assistance available for the reconstruction of Europe. Still on a bilateral basis, the United States extended capital and technical assistance to the less developed countries beginning in the early 1950s. The USSR and other socialist countries have also initiated development-assistance programs. After reconstruction was well advanced, the countries of Western Europe and Japan joined in the move of the advanced countries to provide governmental assistance to the less developed areas of the world.

A major share of the activities of the United Nations is concentrated on development assistance. The International Bank for Reconstruction and Development, established at the end of World War II as part of the Bretton Woods Agreement, has become a major multilateral source of development assistance. Many regional development banks such as the Asian Development Bank and the Inter-American Development Bank have also been created as multilateral agencies to support the development efforts of the poor countries.

The specific content and the size of bilateral and multilateral development-assistance programs changes as a result of political forces and experience. Yet their importance to the international enterprise should continue. Development-assistance programs can play a key role in determining future economic trends in specific countries and must be taken into account in environmental forecasting. They can also be a source of financial resources and other types of support for a wide range of international business projects. The special development role that can be played by international enterprise has been fully recognized by development-assistance agencies, both bilateral and multilateral. Thus many development-assistance programs have designed specific measures to encourage the expansion of international business activities and considerable attention has been devoted to finding ways to expand the flow of foreign private investment in ways that are acceptable to the host countries.

Summary

Modern business enterprises, whether domestic or international in their orientation, have developed considerable sophistication for analyzing and forecasting economic trends. Through in-house staffs or outside consulting services, the domestic manager keeps abreast of national economic trends and future prospects in gross national product, in specific sectors of the economy, and in product fields of special interest. An extension of known techniques and domestic experience is much more feasible in forecasting the economic components of the international business environment than in the cultural and political dimensions.

For countries which engage in national economic planning, the international enterprise can use national-planning studies as a principal source for its forecasts. Such studies will have to be evaluated in terms of their possible real impact on governmental policies and actions. They should also be examined to identify crucial development bottlenecks and constraints.

The forecasting of structural changes, which can be of major significance for a specific type of international business activity, is also frequently a part of the national-planning exercises. Input-output matrices which incorporate the interrelationships of different sectors of the economy are sometimes used as a tool in forecasting future structural patterns. Analogies with other countries at a higher stage of development are another basis for structural forecasting. As the economic structure of national economies is certain to change with economic growth, an extrapolation of past trends would be almost certain to give misleading forecasts for the future.

To the extent that a national economy is dependent upon external economic considerations such as foreign markets or inflows of private investment of external development assistance, the economic forecasts will have to examine carefully such external forces and external future prospects.

Forecasting the economic environment will have to include estimates and projections of institutional features of national economics such as the role of economic planning and of government enterprise. Although the possibilities of using quantitative tools for such forecasting are limited, other methodologies are available.

All the conventional limitations of forecasting the future that exist in domestic economic forecasting carry over to the task of forecasting the economic dimensions of the international business environment. In addition, the great variations in national patterns and crucial domestic variables plus the influence of the inter-nation economic framework make the international task more complex and more difficult. Although forecasting results must be qualified by statements of degree of probability, the forecasting exercise is an important way to become familiar with the critical variables likely to influence future environmental trends in specific countries. As the future unfolds and the content of the key variables become more certain, necessary adjustments and revisions can be more easily made in the available forecasts.

EXERCISES AND DISCUSSION QUESTIONS

1. As an exercise in macro-economic scanning, rank the first five African nations with a population of 1 million or more in terms of the total size of their

economy. In terms of growth rates in per capita GNP, what are the five fastest growing of the Asian economies with a population of 1 million or more?

2. According to the normal pattern, what would you expect industry's contribution to total GNP to be in France, Malaysia, and Brazil? How do these expected patterns compare with the actual structure?

3. Would you consider establishing operations in a country like Brazil that has been experiencing annual rates of inflation of about 20 percent per year from 1967 to 1971? Why or why not? (Note: Over the 1967–71 period, Brazil's GNP expanded from 9 to 11 percent annually, in real terms.)

4. "International executives of big pharmaceutical companies with a stake in Italy are so concerned about the outlook for the country's enticing but volatile $1 billion drug market that they are ready to reach for their tranquilizers. The immediate cause of their jitters is a combination of rising labor costs and the government's desire to hold down drug prices. Way in the distance, like a creeping Excedrin headache, is the specter of a state-owned pharmaceutical company to manufacture and sell drugs on the open market." (*Business Week*, 15 May 1971, p. 62.) As an official of an international pharmaceutical company, how would you assess this speculation that government enterprise might become a competitor of yours in Italy?

5. Under what circumstances, if any, would you be in favor of comprehensive national economic planning in India? The United Kingdom? Mexico? The United States?

6. "A country may have a trade surplus, but still have an increasingly serious balance-of-payments deficit because of capital outflows or rising remittances. Careful assessment must be made of short-term v. long-term outflows." Discuss.

7. "Whatever the causes, rapid increases in prices mean a currency is depreciating internally—and an external depreciation may become necessary." Discuss. Under what circumstances would domestic inflation *not* lead to devaluation?

13

MARKET-DEMAND FORECASTING

WHEN MR. SMITH became president of a relatively small but rapidly growing pharmaceutical company in midwestern United States, he was keenly aware that his company was one of the few American pharmaceutical companies without international operations. He also realized that domestic demand for one of the company's best selling products was no longer growing as rapidly as in the past. An obvious possibility for maintaining the company's growth pattern, therefore, appeared to be that of following the company's competitors by "going international."

He asked his small planning staff to recommend quickly one or two promising markets where the company might establish foreign operations. In the absence of international experience and information on foreign markets, and with the need to take action quickly, the staff hurriedly developed its first foreign investment proposal by a relatively simple method. It selected a country where a principal competitor had recently established operations, on the assumption that this internationally experienced firm must have made a favorable assessment of growth possibilities for the country and promising market prospects for its products. However, a marketing man from the company did visit the country that had been selected to interview a number of retail pharmacies in the two principal cities as a check on recent sales patterns.

With this simple approach to market-demand forecasting, the company made its first international move. Fortunately, the project eventually became profitable, and the company later expanded into a number of other areas. But neither Smith nor other chief executives of business enterprises have recommended this strategy for securing the market-demand forecasts needed for investment decisions. Especially when a company becomes globally oriented, the approach must be broadened from one-market-at-a-time to a system that supplies continuing appraisals of global market opportunities against which the company can develop and implement a global strategy.

SPECIAL INTERNATIONAL ELEMENTS

How does the global firm assess the market demand for the type of product or services it can supply in a large number of foreign markets? Even after the search has been narrowed to countries which are potentially attractive because of their economic size and growth trends, the number of promising opportunities is still likely to be too large. But is the principal difference between domestic and international market-demand forecasting mainly one of a greatly increased number of market areas to be assessed?

In large part, market-demand forecasting is the same activity and requires the same skills and techniques whether it is directed to domestic markets or foreign markets.[1] But there are differences.

The environments in which the tools and techniques are applied are different, and the variations among countries in the availability and quality of the needed data may also require less familiar and less sophisticated techniques than are customary for domestic market research. The multinational enterprise with a global strategy will want the market-demand studies for different countries to be sufficiently standardized so that cross-country comparisons can be made. From the standpoint of cost, relatively inexpensive techniques may be needed so that a large number of potentially interesting market opportunities can be appraised. A final difference may be in the time period used for domestic as against international market-demand forecasts. Where foreign opportunities involve initiating new operations, require a large commitment of resources, and where a high degree of risk is perceived because of limited familiarity with operations in a new country, the firm may want to have a longer-range forecast than would normally be required for guiding domestic decisions.

The American firm "going international" will have to make an especially large adjustment in its market-demand forecasting activity. Not only is the United States outstanding in the availability of data from government, trade associations, and other sources, but it has also accumulated an impressive stock of market research studies, market research organizations and skilled personnel. Furthermore, the flowering of market research in the United States has been aided by a cultural

---

[1] For a standard reference on market research, see Harper W. Boyd, Jr. and Ralph Westfall, *Marketing Research,* 3rd ed. (Homewood, Ill.: Richard D. Irwin, Inc., 1972).

variable that favors considerable openness concerning economic and business information as contrasted to the attitudes of secrecy prevailing in many other countries.

In Western Europe and Japan, local interest in market research has grown rapidly in recent years. National and international efforts have markedly improved the availability and the quality of data that can be used for market research. Thus in a growing number of foreign countries, techniques used in the United States can be applied with relatively few modifications.[2] The main requirements will be knowledge of a foreign language and some awareness of statistical perils resulting in different definitions. In one important respect, the task may be even easier than in the United States because many national economic-planning studies are available in foreign countries, whereas national economic planning has not been part of the recent U.S. environment.

In some respects, the problem of market-demand forecasting may be easier for European and Japanese international companies. Traditionally, non-U.S. firms have been more active in international trade, because of the relatively small size of their domestic markets compared to American companies. Through their export activities such firms may already be familiar with foreign markets. In the U.S. market they will of course encounter a data-rich situation to which their market research personnel should be able to adjust easily.

The special international activity to which this chapter is addressed is market-demand forecasting for countries where the availability of data and planning studies is limited and where different and relatively inexpensive techniques may have to be used. In particular, when analyzing the small and fragmented markets of the numerous countries of the Third World, techniques are needed that provide useful demand estimates from a minimum of data and at a modest expense. The resulting market demand forecasts may be less authoritative than desired but still of reasonable quality for business decision making.

THE GENERAL APPROACH

Market-demand forecasting can be based either on past experience in the country being studied or on analogous experience in another country. Forecasts can be made directly, by extending actual sales data into the future, or indirectly on the basis of an established relationship between demand for the product or service and independent variables such as economic or demographic characteristics of the country. All market-demand forecasting represents some blend of these approaches.

In many countries, particularly the less developed nations, the data

---

[2] See Robert J. Alsegg, *Researching the European Markets,* AMA Research Study 95 (New York: American Management Association, Inc., 1969).

problems limiting market-demand forecasting are likely to be threefold. First, actual sales data may not be available. Second, data may not be available on some of the important variables that influence future demand, with the consequence that forecasts will have to be based on fewer variables than would be desired. Third, some or all of the bare minimum of data required are not available for the country being studied, with the consequence that data and relationships used for forecasting will have to be based on the experience in other countries.

A number of techniques have been used successfully for analyzing country markets where data sources are limited. Historical-demand patterns can be extrapolated by using trade and production data as a substitute for actual sales information. The relationship between demand and an independent variable can be analyzed through the use of income elasticities or regression analysis. In some cases, more complex econometric models and input-output studies can be used.[3] These techniques are discussed separately below, but all of them are different versions of the general approach of forecasting on the basis of relationships.

Extrapolating Historical-Demand Patterns

Where sales rates are not available for a country, the most common approach is to use trade and production data as a proxy for market-demand patterns. These data are relatively easy to secure from national and international publications. Through the adoption of a uniform tariff classification by many countries, the comparability of trade data among countries has been improved. The United Nations now publishes import-export data in great detail for most countries.[4] Market demand, also called apparent consumption, is estimated by combining local production and imports, and then making adjustments for exports and fluctuations in inventory levels.

A major problem in relying on published statistics is the time lag before publication. Another complication is that inventory data generally are not available in countries with underdeveloped statistical systems. One way to compensate for short-term inventory and other fluctuations is to use longer time periods and calculate an annual average or a moving average. The disadvantage of this adjustment is that the estimate may not indicate current sales rates.

Forecasts of future market demand can be made by extrapolating historical patterns of apparent consumption. Where imports supply a large share of local market demand, an extrapolation of historical trends

---

[3] Most of these techniques are discussed in greater detail in Reed Moyer, "International Market Analysis," *Journal of Marketing Research,* 5 (November 1968): 353–60.

[4] United Nations, *Yearbook of International Trade Statistics.*

may understate future demand if imports have been controlled. Furthermore, when local production replaces imports, domestic demand may increase faster than suggested by import trends, assuming that domestic prices remain constant, merely because local facilities can provide quicker and more flexible service to customers. Characteristically, too, import substitution industries expand rapidly during an early stage when an established market already exists and domestic production is substituting for previously imported goods. After the substitution stage, the growth rate in production tends to slow down to the normal pace of growth in domestic demand.

Having developed an historical series on apparent consumption, the crucial question becomes the appropriate pattern for projection. A straight extrapolation is most valid for a short time period and for a relatively mature economy. But it assumes that future trends will follow the patterns of the historical past. This assumption is precarious for a low-income country that is expanding rapidly and undergoing structural changes.

One basis for modifying extrapolations may be the industrial growth patterns already experienced by other countries of the world. The typical patterns of growth in manufacturing industries based on trends in 7 to 10 countries are shown in Figure 13.1. Within the manufacturing sector, the chart relates the percentage of total manufacturing production accounted for by major industrial groups to gross domestic product per capita. Although the typical pattern does not necessarily describe the actual development pattern to be followed by any given country, it suggests that the share of income spent on textiles, as one example, should be extrapolated at a declining rather than constant rate, whereas the demand for metal products can be expected to increase at a rate faster than gains in per capita GDP.[5]

Extrapolation of apparent consumption can be based on per capita as well as total consumption. For example, a straight-line extrapolation of per capita aluminum consumption in Latin America over the period from 1950 to 1963 shows a gain from .44 kilograms per capita in 1963 to 1.85 in 1975. The per capita projection when joined with population forecasts translates into an increase in total market demand from 93,000 metric tons in 1963 to 580,000 metric tons in 1975. In the case of aluminum, after experimenting with several types of projection techniques, the straight-line extrapolation with some slight adjustments was evaluated as the best forecast.[6]

---

[5] For further details see Alfred Maizels, *Industrial Growth and World Trade* (Cambridge, England: Cambridge University Press, 1963); H. B. Chenery, "Patterns of Industrial Growth," *American Economic Review*, September 1960.

[6] Joseph L. Fisher, "Global Projections for the Mining Sector," *Sectoral Aspects of Projections for the World Economy*, 2 (New York: United Nations, 1969): 54, 113.

FIGURE 13.1

Typical Patterns of Growth in Manufacturing Industries†

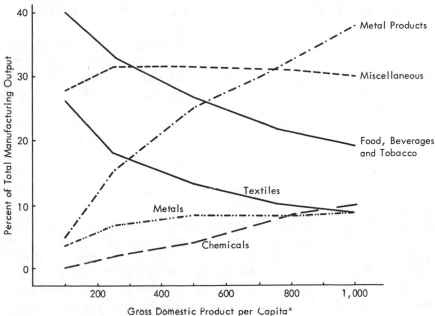

* Dollars at 1955 prices.
† Based on time-series analysis for selected years, 1899–1957.
  Source: Alfred Maizels, *Industrial Growth and World Trade* (Cambridge, England· Cambridge University Press, 1963), p. 55.

Forecasting with Income Elasticities

In many situations, market-demand forecasting can be partially or wholly based on income elasticities. The concept of income-elasticity measures the relationship between the change in demand for a product and changes in income.

Symbolically the formula below measures the income elasticity for commodity A where Q represents the quantity demanded, Y is the income and Δ refers to quantity changes.

$$\frac{\dfrac{\Delta QA}{QA}}{\dfrac{\Delta Y}{Y}}$$

If demand increases at the same rate as income, a product would have an income elasticity of one. If demand increases only half as fast as income, the income elasticity of a product would be 0.5. Goods with values of more than one are income elastic. Goods with values of less than one are income-inelastic. Income elasticities have been calculated for individual or family incomes and separately for various levels of income. Where detailed data on family and personal income distribution are not available, as in many LDCs, income elasticities have been calculated for a country as a whole in relation to average per capita income for the country. In the absence of better market information, the latter form of income elasticities can be a reasonably satisfactory approach to market-demand forecasting.

Market-demand forecasting by the income-elasticities method requires four steps. First, current levels of demand are determined. Second, average per capita income is forecast for the selected future period. Third, income elasticities are determined either from a country's own historical experience or from the experience of other countries. Finally, future market demand is estimated as current demand times a factor derived by multiplying the projected increase in per capita income and the income elasticity for the commodity. If per capita income is expected to increase by 50 percent in the forecast period and the income elasticity of the product is 1.5, total demand should increase by 75 percent.

Income elasticities are widely used by economic planners for establishing development targets for a country. Consequently, a considerable amount of information has been developed on income elasticities.[7] In general, the empirical information follows the patterns suggested by Engel's law. The income elasticities for food and other necessities are generally less than one and for luxury goods more than one. The results of several income-elasticity studies that cover both consumer and industrial products and some services are shown in Table 13.1. The data are averages and may not apply equally to all income groups. Also note the differences that can result by calculating the elasticities through cross-sectional analysis—comparing a number of countries at different levels of income for the same time period, and through times series, that is, comparing patterns over time for the same country.

The Agricultural Commodities Projections study of the FAO, referred to in Chapter 12, was heavily based on income-elasticity data for food and other agricultural commodities.[8] The coefficients used in the study were determined from a collection and analysis of more than 100 household surveys undertaken in the FAO member countries. Based on these

---

[7] See United Nations, *Industrialization and Productivity, Bulletin 9* (New York: 1965), "Analysis and Projections of Consumption Demand: Methodological Notes," pp. 49–81.

[8] *Agricultural Commodity Projections, 1970–1980,* 2 (Rome: Food and Agricultural Organization of the United Nations, 1971) presents a comprehensive statement on the scope and methodology of the study. Research Working Paper No. 1 on the subject of "Income Elasticities of Demand for Agricultural Products" is available as a separate release from the official report.

TABLE 13.1
Income Elasticity Measurements

Commodity	Cross Section	Time Series
Food and beverage, excluding alcoholic beverages	0.54,† 0.53‡	0.8*
Alcoholic beverages	0.77†	—
Tobacco	0.88†	—
Clothing	0.8,* 0.9,*	0.7,* 0.8*
	0.84,† 0.89*	
Textiles	0.5*	0.8*
Household and personal services	1.19†	—
Communication services	2.03†	—'
Recreation.	1.15†	—
Health	1.80†	-
Durable consumer goods.	—	2.7*
Furniture	1.61‡	—
Appliances.	1.40‡	—
Metals	1.52‡	—
Chemicals	—	2.1*
Machinery and transportation equipment, except		
passenger cars.	—	2.1*

*Source is Meritt L. Kastens, "Organizing, Planning, and Staffing Market Research Activities in an International Operations," *Market Research in International Operations*, Management Report no. 53 (New York: American Management Association, 1960), p. 42.
†Source is Milton Gilbert and Associates, *Comparative National Products and Price Levels* (Paris, France: OECD, 1958), p. 66.
‡From author's calculations.
Source: Reed Moyer, "International Market Analysis," *Journal of Marketing Research*, table 2, 5 (November 1968): 356.

and other studies, income-elasticity coefficients and demand functions were selected for each of the numerous products covered by the study.

Several cautions in the use of income elasticities should be noted. A high income elasticity for a product does not necessarily mean a high-volume market. It merely indicates that demand will increase rapidly as incomes rise. In terms of volume, the large markets for some time to come in most countries will be in necessities, even though the growth in these markets may be relatively slow. Furthermore, income elasticities indicate a constant relationship between demand changes and income changes. For specific products, it is likely though that after income reaches a certain level, the demand will increase at an increasing rate. This is particularly noticeable for consumer durables. Prices also affect the elasticities in several ways. If prices in a country for the products of a new industry are relatively high, and if such prices fall as the industries become more mature, demand for such products will increase from a combination of price and income factors. As between countries, prices can vary greatly because of taxes, subsidies, and other factors. Such differences must be taken into account in using income elasticities. Thus, income elasticities are useful guides but not a substitute for more comprehensive market research.

Estimating by Analogy

Forecasting by analogy has already been referred to as a technique that can be used to anticipate future changes in the institutional environment and to predict structural changes in national economies.[9] The same approach is commonly used for market-demand forecasting. This technique assumes that product usage moves along a normal path as a country's stage of development advances. Thus, prevailing patterns of demand in more advanced countries can be used to estimate future market demand in a late-developing economy as incomes rise. The use of cross-sectional income elasticities is essentially estimation by analogy, and the use of typical patterns of growth in manufacturing industries as a guide for market demand extrapolations is another example.

An example of using the analogy method for estimating a country's future demand for copper is shown in Figure 13.2. Per capita consumption of copper over the 1959–63 period was calculated for 24 countries and 6 regions and plotted on a double logarithmic chart in relation to average per capita GDP for each of the countries and regions. For example, Mexico with per capita GDP of about $350 (1960 dollars) consumed about 0.6 kilograms of copper per capita. If we assume that Mexico is following a development pattern similar to that of Argentina, we can estimate that copper use will approximate 0.9 kilograms as per capita GDP approaches $600. If the South African pattern is more analogous, Mexican copper use will rise more sharply to about 1.4 kilograms when per capita GDP rises to $480.

The analogy method can also be used for verifying the reasonableness of market-demand forecasts based on other techniques. Figure 13.3 was actually used in this way for testing forecasts of the demand for electricity in South Central Brazil based on a wide range of separate studies and varied techniques.[10] The average per capita consumption and per capita GDP were calculated for a four year period for 55 countries and then plotted on a double logarithmic chart. A regression line (see below) was then calculated for all the observations and plotted. The forecasts for South Central Brazil for 1970, 1975, and 1980 all fell above the line, implying a higher than average per capita use of electricity in relation to per capita GDP. This result was consistent with the actual patterns in the past and could be explained by a number of special characteristics of the area for which the forecast was made. Consequently, the analogy technique supported the reasonableness of the forecasts.

---

[9] See Chapter 12.

[10] Antonio Dias Leite, Stefan H. Robock, and Leonid Hassilev, *Methodology for Long-Term Forecasting and Application to South Central Brazil,* (Paper delivered at the World Power Conference, Tokyo, Japan, 1966, no. 75).

FIGURE 13.2
Per Capita Copper Use and GDP (1959–63)

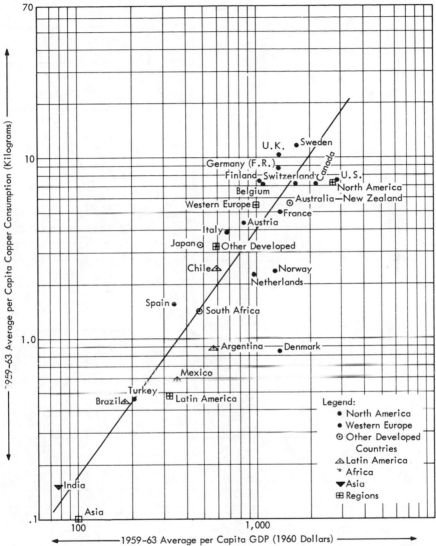

Source: *Sectoral Aspects of Projections for the World Economy*, vol 2. Papers delivered at Elsinore, Denmark, 14–27 August 1966 (New York: United Nations, 1969), p. 87.

FIGURE 13.3

Per Capita Consumption of Electricity and per Capita GDP

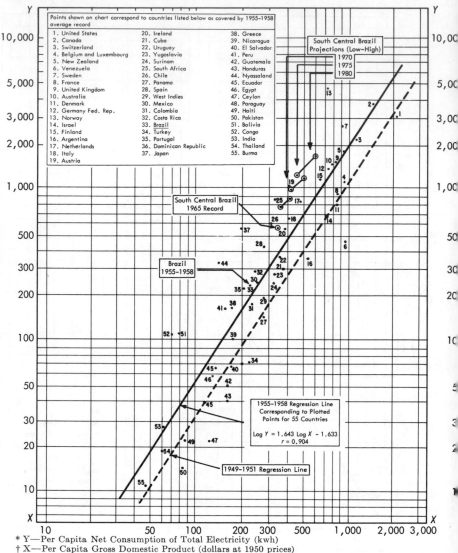

* Y—Per Capita Net Consumption of Total Electricity (kwh)
† X—Per Capita Gross Domestic Product (dollars at 1950 prices)
Source: *NACIONES UNIDAS—Estudios Sobre la Electricided en America Latina*, 1 (Mexico, D. F., October 1962): 75.

Blind reliance on the analogy technique can result in erroneous estimates in a number of situations. Differences in culture, tastes, and habits that dictate consumption patterns may limit the validity of analogies. Technical factors such as new inventions or substitute products may cause future consumption patterns of the late-developed countries to change sharply from the patterns of presently advanced countries. Price differences among countries, because of import tariffs for example, or over time, can also cause errors. Nevertheless, used with caution, the method can be extremely useful where data are limited.

Regression Analysis

Regression analysis can be a powerful tool in forecasting market demand, especially for countries where data on current demand are scarce. And even where estimates are made by income elasticities or by analogy, regression analysis provides a basis for refinement and testing the reasonableness of estimates.

Regression analysis is simply a statistical technique for determining the relationship between two or more variables. A regression equation can express the quantitative relationship between the demand for a specific product and a gross economic indicator. In a technical sense, demand would be called the dependent variable and the indicator (or several indicators) would be the independent variable. This relationship can be determined for *Country B,* or a number of countries, and then applied to *Country A* in which the firm is interested even though information is not available in *Country A* on current market demand for the product. In such a case, the market demand estimate is based on both regression analysis and on analogy, as the relationship discovered for other countries is assumed to be applicable for the country in which the business firm is interested. Regression analysis can also be used when data on current consumption is available for *Country A* to compare market-demand patterns in *Country A* with the experience in other countries so that future forecasts can be verified or modified.

Some regression results that relate the consumption of various commodities to a gross economic indicator are summarized in Table 13.2. A linear regression model ($y = a + bx$) was used with y as the amount of a product in use per thousand of population and x as per capita

TABLE 13.2
Regression of Consumption on Gross National Product (various products)

Product	Number of Observations	Regression Equation	Unadjusted R^2
Autos.	37	−21.071 + .101x	.759
Radio sets	42	8.325 + .275x	.784
TV sets.	31	−16.501 + .074x	.503
Refrigerators.	24	−21.330 + .102x	.743
Washing machines.	22	−15.623 + .094x	.736

Source: Reed Moyer, "International Marketing Analysis," *Journal of Marketing Research,* table 4, 5 (November 1968): 358, based on United Nations, *Statistical Yearbook,* 1962; Alfred Maizels, *Industrial Growth and World Trade* (Cambridge, England: Cambridge University Press, 1963), pp. 308–9.

GNP. The equations explain from 50 to 78 percent of the variation in the dependent variable as shown by R.[2] Actually these regression results are an example of using a proxy for demand data because they are actually based on the amount of each product in use per capita rather than on sales.

The regression results in Table 13.2 show that an increase of $100 in per capita GNP will result, on the average, in an increase of 10 automobiles, 10 refrigerators, 9 washing machines, 7 television sets, and 27 radio sets per 1,000 population. This, however, is a very simple way of predicting demand for consumer durables. More advanced techniques that allow for saturation of the market, life of the product, and replacement rates are common.[11]

Another example of regression analysis was shown in Figure 13.3 which analyzes the demand for electric power in relation to per capita GDP. The relationship for all the 55 countries is expressed in the regression line, and the positive r of .9 indicates that there is a very high correlation between GDP per capita and the demand for electric power.

Regression analysis may not give reliable results for some products where the relationship of demand to other variables is highly complex and data are not available on all the essential variables. For example, demand forecasts may require data on many variables other than income (or GNP) such as prices, government expenditures, availability of consumer credit, advertising and promotion for a new product, and so forth. Fortunately, however, the consumption of many products can be estimated reasonably accurately by knowing only the per capita income (or GNP) in the countries being studied.

MORE ADVANCED MODELS

More complex and more costly multiple regression models are in use by major multinational firms where they can obtain projections for a variety of indicators that will affect sales. The expertize involved in developing these models falls within the field of econometrics and will not be compressed into this chapter. Instead, we will simply illustrate the field through one example—the use of an econometric model to measure the sales for still cameras, as developed by Armstrong.[12] His econometric model was based on the following conceptual model:

$$S_{i,t} = f(M_{i,t}; A_{i,t}; N_{i,t})$$

---

[11] For example, see Erwin E. Nemmers, *Managerial Economics,* part 2 (New York: John Wiley and Sons, Inc., 1962).

[12] J. Scott Armstrong, "An Application of Econometric Methods to International Marketing," *Journal of Marketing Research,* 7 (May 1970): 190–98.

where

S = camera sales per year by country
M = market size (i.e. number of potential buyers)
A = ability to buy
N = consumer needs and
    i refers to the country and t to the year.

Trade and production data were used to estimate sales by country for 30 countries. The model assumes that camera sales depend in each country on some relationship to market size, ability to buy, and consumer needs. In turn, market size was estimated on the basis of total population, literacy rates, proportion of the population age 15 to 64, and share of the population that was in nonagricultural employment.

Ability to buy was estimated on the basis of an index-of-living standard, an estimate of rate of change in the ability to buy, and information on camera prices. Various measures were used for consumer needs, such as households per adult, rainfall, and proportion of children in the population.

On the basis of this conceptual model and subsequent analysis, a predictive model was developed. The forecasting model was tested by backcasting, that is, estimating camera sales for an earlier period, from 1953–55, on the basis of data from 1960–65. The results were reasonably good.

As is apparent from even this brief description, the data-collection task for developing and for using more complex regression models is substantial. The selection of the minimum number of variables to include in the model requires considerable testing and judgment. If the necessary investment in time and resources can be justified, market-demand forecasting with an econometric model can have the additional benefit of producing a substantial amount of information that can be used for guiding marketing and other operations, once a project is established in the country being studied. For firms such as Xerox, Kodak, and Singer, a solidly developed quantitative estimate of the potential in each market can form the basis for controlling subsidiary performance and for longer-range commitments to production facilities.

Input-Output Analysis

Input-output or inter-industry analysis has been used for number of years to describe the economic structure of a country and as a basis for national economic planning.[13] More recently, market researchers have

---

[13] United Nations Statistical Office, *Problems of Input-Output Tables and Analysis* (New York, 1966).

recognized the value of input-output tables, where available, for market-demand forecasting, particularly for industrial products where much of the demand will be derived from the growth of other industries.[14] Input-output tables have been published for many of the developed countries, such as Japan and the Netherlands, and for a large number of underdeveloped countries. An inter-industry model used for Japanese sectoral planning divided the total economy into 60 productive sectors, resulting in what is called a 60 by 60 matrix. However, many of the tables break down the entire economy into only a small number of broad industry groups and cannot provide much detail on specific products.

Conceptually, input-output tables recognize the interrelationships of each sector in an economy to all others. (See Table 13.3.) The total output of one sector reading across the rows in the transaction table, for example agriculture, becomes the input of all sectors (including the agricultural sector itself). At the same time, reading down each column, each sector receives its inputs from the other sectors. The input-output and output relationships of each sector, including households and foreign trade, to all the others are quantitatively expressed by coefficients.

Where input-output tables are sufficiently detailed, one can trace the direct and indirect impact on the demand for one product of changes in demand for the products of other industries. The tables can show the extent to which sales are made to final users or consumed as intermediate goods. Also, input-output tables can provide information on the number of sectors that are users of the products from another sector.

Input-output tables were used as a tool for the sectoral planning phase of Japan's Medium-Term Economic Plan covering the period from 1964 to 1968.[15] By applying known input-output relationships to projections of the general magnitude and direction of the economy's growth, as one example, gross output of pulp, paper, and related products was estimated to increase over the period at an annual rate of 16.1 percent. The plan also revealed the projected increases in the various components of gross output such as intermediate demand, final demand, exports, and government purchases.[16]

Input-output analysis also has its limitations. A tremendous amount of data and analysis is required to construct tables that can provide

[14] Jack G. Faucett, "Input-Output Analysis as a Tool of International Market Research," *Market Research in International Operations,* Management Report no. 53 (New York: American Management Association, 1960), pp. 41–59; Roger K. Chisholm and Gilbert R. Whitaker, Jr., *Forecasting Methods* (Homewood, Ill.: Richard D. Irwin, Inc., 1971), pp. 62–95.

[15] Economic Planning Agency, *Medium-Term Economic Plan, 1964–1968* (Tokyo, 1965).

[16] Shuntaro Shishido, "A Multisectoral Projection Model for a Developed Economy—An Experience with Japanese Sectoral Planning," *Sectoral Aspects of Projections for the World Economy,* 3 (New York: United Nations, 1969): 184–85.

detailed industry or product information. Consequently, as has been suggested, data limitations and the lack of resources have often resulted in tables that are too general or too incomplete to be of great value for specific market-demand forecasting. Also, input-output tables normally used fixed technical coefficients. This means that future changes in production processes, the effects of changes in production levels, and other dynamic factors are not taken into account by forecasts based on the tables.

Despite these limitations, input-output analyses can be useful. Many countries have been devoting sizeable resources toward the improvement of input-output tables for their countries, and considerable effort is being made by technicians to resolve the problems of fixed coefficients and inadequate data. The principal motivation and justification for such efforts is the value of input-output tables for governmental planning and policy making.

INFRASTRUCTURE REQUIREMENTS AND SERVICES

The market demand for many products and services that can be supplied by international enterprises results directly or indirectly from governmental programs to expand infrastructure facilities and services such as transportation, electricity, education, housing, and health. Because of the government's direct responsibility for infrastructure and its need to provide financing, wholly or in part, for such facilities, a considerable amount of governmental planning work is likely to be available. From these data the business firm can obtain excellent guidelines to future market demand. Where the less developed countries are soliciting international financing from agencies like the World Bank, market studies must normally be prepared as a component of the project proposal submitted for financing.

The types of planning studies usually undertaken for the planning of future infrastructure needs vary greatly among the particular fields.[17] In the case of electric power, future needs are derived from growth targets for the total economy and the planned expansion of specific types of industrial and other productive activity. Such planning studies have a high degree of probability that they will be implemented. Electric-power projects are revenue producing and thus can provide some of their financing. Electric power must also be available in order that other growth targets can be reached. In the case of housing, education, and health, the implementation of official plans is likely to be more uncertain because social-welfare plans are generally limited by the future

---

[17] See Richard Cibotti, "Projections of Infrastructure Requirements and Services," *Sectoral Aspects of Projections for the World Economy*, 2 (New York: United Nations, 1969): 148–205.

TABLE 13.3
Input-Output Tables: a Simplified Illustration

COUNTRY A—TRANSACTIONS, 1960

							Final Demand					
	Agric.	Food Proc.	Coal	Electric Energy	Plastic Products	Apparel	Consumer Expenditures	Government Operations	Exports	Investment	Total Final Demand	Total Output
Agriculture	–	50	–	–	–	–	100	–	50	–	150	200
Food processing	25	–	–	–	–	–	150	–	25	–	175	200
Coal	–	10	–	50	10	5	15	5	–	5	25	100
Electric energy	10	30	5	–	25	5	35	10	–	30	75	150
Plastic products	–	10	–	5	–	5	10	–	220	–	230	250
Apparel	–	–	–	–	–	–	50	–	150	–	200	200
Wages and salaries	80	50	40	30	100	70	–	20	–	100	120	490
Imports (total)	35	20	15	25	40	75	150	10	–	175	335	545
Agricultural chemicals	20	–	–	–	–	–	–	–	–	–	–	–
Paint & varnishes	5	–	–	5	10	–	5	–	–	15	–	–
Textiles	5	–	5	5	–	60	15	–	–	–	–	–
Iron castings	5	–	10	5	30	–	–	–	–	10	–	–
Other	–	20	10	15	30	15	130	10	–	150	–	–
Profits, interest, dep'n, taxes	50	30	40	40	75	40	–	–	–	50	50	325
Total Output	200	200	100	150	250	200	510	45	445	360	1,360	1,360

COUNTRY A—PRODUCTION COEFFICIENTS, 1960

	Agric.	Food Proc.	Coal	Electric Energy	Plastic Products	Apparel
Agriculture	–	.250	–	–	–	–
Food processing	.125	–	–	–	–	–
Coal	–	.050	–	.333	.040	.025
Electric energy	.050	.150	.050	–	.100	.025
Plastic products	–	.050	–	.033	–	.025
Apparel	–	–	–	–	–	–
Wages & salaries	.400	.250	.400	.200	.400	.350
Imports (total)	.175	.100	.150	.167	.160	.375
Agricultural chemicals	.100	–	–	–	–	–
Paints & varnishes	.025	–	–	.033	.040	–
Textiles	.025	–	–	–	–	.300
Iron castings	.025	–	.050	.033	–	–
Other	–	.100	.100	.100	.120	.075
Profits, interest, dep'n, taxes	.250	.150	.400	.267	.300	.200
Total Output	1.000	1.000	1.000	1.000	1.000	1.000

Source: Reprinted by permission of the publishers from AMA Management Report no. 53, *Market Research in International Operations.* © 1960 by the American Management Association, Inc.

availability of government revenues. For political and welfare reasons, it is common for governments to establish ambitious targets in these fields which may not be realistic.

AVAILABLE MARKET SURVEYS

As a part of their export promotion programs, some governments undertake substantial programs of foreign market research at government expense. For example, as of July 1971, the U.S. Department of Commerce was offering on a loan basis to American business firms about 400 foreign market surveys that had been prepared on a contract basis by private research organizations or by Commerce Department market research officers abroad.[18] Such studies ranged from the market for graphic art equipment in Argentina to the market for electronics production equipment in West Germany. The emphasis in such studies is likely to be on products for export rather than for foreign production.

Summary

After screening the global horizon and making a preliminary identification of countries that appear to have attractive economic situations, the globally oriented firm will want to examine the market-demand prospects for its products in countries that appear promising. In a growing number of countries, government planning reports or available market research studies can supply the international firm with sufficient information on which it can decide whether or not it will undertake a detailed business opportunity analysis for the country. In other situations, particularly in the less developed countries, the firm will need to make its own market-demand studies, using techniques that are not too costly and that can produce reasonable results where the availability of data is limited. A number of such techniques have been suggested. In general, they make use of analogies and methods that relate the market demand for a product to one or more general economic or demographic indicators. As a subsequent step, in-depth field surveys will be required to examine the competitive and operating environment that the international firm will encounter in the promising markets.

EXERCISES AND DISCUSSION QUESTIONS

1. Compile a list of sources of economic and market data for a specified African nation other than South Africa.

---

[18] U.S. Department of Commerce, *Cumulative Index to Foreign Market Surveys, December 1968–July 1971* (Washington, D.C.: U.S. Government Printing Office, 1971).

2. *Country A's* GNP rose from $6 billion by a further $550 million during 1972 and its steel consumption, all imported, rose by 400,000 tons to 3.8 million tons. Population also increased from 10 million to 10.4 million. What is the income elasticity of demand for steel? Do you think this would provide a very accurate indicator for predicting steel usage over the ensuing five years?

3. Select a less developed country and for either textiles or metal manufactures. Determine the forecasting methods you think would have been most appropriate for forecasting demand at each of two dates within the last 20 years, separated by at least five years.

4. "It may be true that all European countries are traveling the same road towards what has been called 'salvation through industrialization' and it may be possible, therefore, to forecast some of the probable changes in living habits as the process continues. Even so, there are still great differences between one place and another, between one nation and another, and in the rates at which they change. These differences reveal themselves in a great diversity of what people will buy. Economic development is certainly affecting culture and customs, habits and attitudes, traditions and mentality; but these, in turn, are reacting on what is going on in the economy—in production, consumption, and distribution. You may detect the general trend; but look around Western Europe and you will discover all sorts of subtle variations in the speed and character of the change. Here the emancipation of women may be moving more slowly. There peasant and aristocratic attitudes may persist."

   In the light of this extract, what types of products would you expect to follow dissimilar demand patterns over time in European countries? Of these would you expect a country's past demand to provide a better basis for predicting demand than analogies with other countries at a more advanced stage?

5. Give your own definition of the market saturation point for a consumer durable, such as washing machines, and explain why the level may vary from country to country.

6. "Comparison of either total demand or per capita demand for different countries may be misleading for the purposes of formulating a global strategy, particularly if major variations occur within countries." Elaborate on this statement and suggest how the problem might be overcome.

7. You would expect to find some relationship between a country's demand for medical drugs and the numbers of doctors and hospital beds in the country. What other indicators might be used for forecasting the level of drug purchases? As the basis for a global marketing, plan how would you go about predicting a country's spending on drugs five years hence?

8. Explain how demand for the output of a primary industry might be forecast using an input-output table. What are the limitations inherent in the input-output method?

14

THE LEGAL
ENVIRONMENT

INTERNATIONAL BUSINESS must function to a considerable degree in a legal no-man's land. No comprehensive system of international law exists for guiding business transactions across national boundaries. No system of international courts is available for resolving legal conflicts in the field of international business.

The legal environment for international business consists primarily of a multiplicity of national legal systems which differ significantly in basic legal philosophy, procedures, and practices. Each nation-state maintains its own set of courts in complete independence of every other nation. Each nation-state has its own set of laws, written and unwritten. Each national system includes principles and procedures for resolving conflicts of domestic laws. But there is no final international legal authority for handling conflicts of national laws in the way that a supreme or highest judicial body does for a nation-state.

Some legal aspects of business transactions across national boundaries have been simplified through treaties, as discussed in Chapter 6, in which nations assume an obligation to deal with selected legal matters in an agreed-upon way. Some attempts at harmonization of business laws among nations have been occurring through the continuing work of the International Law Commission established by the United Nations, particularly the U.N. Commission for International Trade Law (UNCITRAL), and among member countries in the European Common Market. Yet, the legal environment for international business must still be characterized as a maze of overlapping national systems, institutions, and rules, with only the rudimentary beginnings of enforceable agreements and effective institutions at the international level.

International business activities in the traditional fields of international trade and international financial transactions do not encounter unusually difficult legal problems because the national systems have had adequate flexibility and time for adaptation. But in the case of the multinational enterprise, the changing realities are considerably ahead of legal adaptation.

This chapter will not attempt to present a how-to-do-it manual. As lawyers of all nationalities are quick to agree, the international manager needs legal specialists to guide him. Instead, this chapter has the modest goal of providing the international manager with some background on the legal framework and an awareness of some of the principal legal issues characteristic of international business operations.

INTERNATIONAL LAW AND INTERNATIONAL BUSINESS

Although contrary to the facts, there is a widely held impression that a rather precise system of international law exists for guiding business transactions across national boundaries. This impression is particularly strong as related to the protection of foreign-owned private property. It is common to hear businessmen and government officials declare that the expropriation of foreign property without prompt and adequate compensation is a violation of international law. Such wistful views have long been popular in the economically advanced investor countries, but they are not generally accepted around the world. In order for rules and principles to become international law, nation-states must consider such rules and principles legally binding upon them.

What is normally called international law is more accurately described as *international public law*. It consists of a body of rules and principles which states consider legally binding upon them. It can be enforced through the International Court of Justice, international arbitration, or the internal courts of the nation-states, which lawyers refer to as municipal courts.

Until the late nineteenth century, international law was mainly concerned with the relationships between states and the delimitation of their jurisdictions. A synonym for international law was the law of nations and control of war was long its primary function. In more recent decades, emphasis has been shifting toward an increased concern with the protection of fundamental human rights of the individual even against his own state. Through the proliferation of treaty law and specialized international organizations, the substance of the law has expanded to include cross-frontier relationships of individuals and corporate bodies.

In order to be operationally meaningful for the multinational enterprise, international law must have a system for adjudication of legal disputes and for enforcement of legal decisions. Here is where the gap exists. The only international court is the International Court of Justice at The Hague. It is the principal judicial organ of the United Nations, and all members of the United Nations are *ipso facto* parties to the statute establishing the court. The function of the court is to pass judgment upon disputes between states, and only states which have submitted to its jurisdiction are parties in cases before the court. Private persons or corporations do not have direct access to the International Court.

In order for private issues to be adjudicated by the International Court, they must be espoused by one of the member states. In some countries, business firms have had reasonable success in securing official government support. In most situations, however, this has not been easy to achieve because the political interests of governments must be the guiding rule. Furthermore, the governments representing both sides of a dispute must agree to accept the court's jurisdiction. Even if private issues reach the court and are decided, the problem still remains as to how the legal judgment will be enforced, given the relatively weak form of world government.

In some cases, international law is applied by the municipal courts of a country. For example, the international law providing that foreign sovereigns and their diplomatic representatives enjoy certain immunities from municipal jurisdiction requires the cooperation of municipal courts for its realization. Interestingly enough, where governments trade through state corporations incorporated in a foreign country, such as the USSR trading company Amtorg incorporated in New York, an important unsettled issue persists as to whether the state corporation has diplomatic immunity.

Treaties and Conventions

From the standpoint of international business, the nearest approximation to international law is the growing number of treaties and conventions covering commercial and economic matters. According to modern diplomatic usage, the more important international agreements are referred to as treaties. Those of lesser importance are called conventions, agreements, protocols, and acts. All of these forms are agreements between two or more nation-states which normally become legally enforceable through the municipal courts of the participating countries. In some countries like the United States, the constitutions make treaties automatically the law of the land. In certain other countries like the United Kingdom, the legislature must act to give domestic force to the provisions of a treaty. In either case, the path for judicial action becomes the municipal courts and an international court is not essential. The principal multilateral treaties and conventions of importance to international business have been discussed in Chapter 6, as part of the framework for international transactions.

Regional Harmonization of Laws

A new force that promises to reshape the legal environment for international business has emerged from the regional economic integration movements, particularly the European Common Market. Through the Treaty of Rome, the EEC came into existence to provide for an economic union in which goods, manpower, capital, and services could move freely among the member countries. To achieve these economic goals, the member countries have established common policies in agriculture and transportation and are harmonizing their laws in certain fields such as taxation and social welfare.

The Treaty of Rome considered company law merely a side issue since the main objective was to establish a common market. Nevertheless, the treaty provides more or less adequately for a company to work from a base in a single member country through branches in the other Common Market countries. A convention on mutual recognition of companies signed in 1968 further facilitates this working pattern.

An even better situation is anticipated if the proposal for a European Company Law, submitted in 1970 to the EEC Council of Ministers, is adopted. The European company statute will not replace national rules regarding companies, but rather it will complement the rules by facilitating mergers and the formation of holding companies and joint subsidiaries by companies from different member states. The EEC already has effective judicial and administrative machinery, and the European companies will be under the jurisdiction of the Community's Court of Justice. An interesting feature of the proposal is that worker representatives are required to be on the boards of directors of the European Companies, unless workers or unions object by a two-thirds margin.

In an important sense, the move toward a European Company Law is favorable recognition of the multinational business trend. It has been argued by a high EEC official that a "single company law throughout the Common Market countries . . . would make it possible for companies to combine to achieve optimum size, move freely to the best production location, rationalize their research and distribution networks through common efforts, and have access to available sources of finance in the country of their choice."[1]

To be sure, the European Company Law is not a reality at this writing, and it may to a degree complicate as well as simplify the legal

---

[1] Raffaello Fornasier, "Toward a European Company," *Columbia Journal of World Business,* September–October 1969, p. 52.

environment. Yet, the proposal merits attention as a potentially significant new force in the legal environment.

National Legal Systems

A multiplicity of national legal systems constitute the legal environment for international business, except where legal issues are covered
by treaties and conventions or by regional laws. Great diversity exists
in national legal systems because each has been molded to conform
to the special interests and features of the specific country. Yet in fundamental legal approach, most national legal systems are based on either
the common law or civil law system. In some countries, Islamic law
may also exert a major influence.

The civil law system has traditionally been the legal system for most
of continental Europe. From there, it spread to a number of Asian and
African countries which decided to Westernize their laws: for example,
Japan (1890–98), China (1929–31), Thailand (1925), Turkey (1926),
and Ethiopia (1958–60). The civil law system, supplemented by religious
laws or native customs, also prevails in the former colonies of France,
Belgium, the Netherlands, Portugal, and Italy. Supplemented by Islamic
law, civil law has come to predominate in the Near Eastern countries.

The common law system, developed in England during the Middle
Ages, has been adopted by most of the countries where the English
settled or have governed. The United Kingdom, the United States,
Canada, Australia, New Zealand, Ghana, Nigeria, India, and other
present and former British colonies are all common law countries.

Civil law countries embody their main rules of law in a' legislative
code. In common law countries, the judge is normally guided not by
a code but by principles declared in the reports of previous decisions
in similar or analogous cases. In practice, however, the distinction between common and civil law is not clear-cut. It would be erroneous
to identify civil law with codified or even statutory law and common
law with judge-made or case law. Large parts of Anglo-American law
are contained in statutes and codes. In civil law countries, large parts
of the law have never been reduced to statutes or codes but have been
developed by the courts.

The most significant difference between common law and civil law
countries is in the role of the judiciary. In common law countries, the
responsibility for adapting the law to changing conditions has traditionally been the task of judges. In the United States, the judiciary is the
ultimate decision maker in the legal system. The powers of the court
system range from that of annulling enactments of the legislative bodies
to that of compelling performance by public officers under the threat
of fine or imprisonment. As a political fact of life, the U.S. courts are

accepted as the final interpreters of the Constitution and of legislative acts.

In the civil law countries, the judiciary plays a lesser role than in common law countries. In Latin America, it is not the court decision which gives life to the statute, but rather the implementation of the legislative act by government executives through the *reglamento,* which specifies the detailed working rules. Under the French system, the general pattern is to deny law courts the power to pass on executive action and to maintain separate administrative courts. The German system places great emphasis on review of legal questions by government departments. The general result in many civil law countries is that great reliance is placed on the prestige of a career civil service as a counterpart to the judicial power in the Anglo-American system.

Differences in the formal structure of national legal systems are important. Equally crucial can be national differences in the legal process for resolving legal problems and in the infrastructure of attitudes, beliefs, and customs. The gap between the developed legal system and effective administration of justice will vary greatly among nations. In some countries, even the most advanced laws remain dead letters on the books because of a limited capacity to implement the laws or because an underdeveloped judicial system does not have the capability for an expeditious handling of litigation.

The American society probably goes further than any other in translating issues into legal questions and expecting courts and lawyers to resolve them. By way of contrast, Chinese and Japanese societies go to the other extreme: abhorrence of lawyers, laws, and above all, litigation. "It is better to be vexed to death than to bring a lawsuit," says a Chinese proverb. The Chinese and Japanese prefer conciliation and mediation to litigation. The aversion to litigation reflects a fear that legal rules are too impersonal and rigid to accommodate the realities of particular cases and a desire to avoid the disruptions of friendly relations attending a clear-cut victory and defeat in litigation.[2]

The role of lawyers differs greatly from country to country. In the United States, lawyers frequently serve on the boards of directors of corporations. In France, a lawyer (*avocat*) cannot be a member of the board of directors by the rules of his own profession, which reflect a different concept of professional relationship to the business community than is held in the United States. In the United States, one of the attractive areas of legal practice is taxation. In many other countries, tax problems are handled exclusively by the accounting profession.

One important legal practice that is often a surprise to American international managers is the prominent role of the notary public. In

---

[2] Henry J. Steiner and Detlev F. Vagts, *Transnational Legal Problems* (Mineola, N.Y.: The Foundation Press, 1968), p. 141.

the United States, there are many notary publics but they perform only a minor function. In civil law countries, the notary is a key figure. He is trained as a lawyer. By virtue of his office, he gives conclusiveness in a legal sense to contractual instruments. The legal necessity to have virtually all legal instruments notarized requires time and may be considered excessive red tape by the American businessman. But in Latin American, Western European, and other countries, the businessman considers it absolutely essential that a transaction is adequately recorded, preserved, and made firm and certain through being recorded with a notary. The importance of the notary may be illustrated by the case of at least one Latin American country, where the privilege of being a notary is granted only by the president of the Republic and is considered to be the most lucrative of all political grants.

SELECTED LEGAL PROBLEMS IN INTERNATIONAL BUSINESS

Even an abbreviated introduction to the ambiguities and complexities of the legal environment for transnational business activities should persuade the international manager to rely upon specialized assistance for legal matters. He does need, however, some awareness of the major types of legal problems likely to arise in international business.

In the traditional field of international trade, legal practices are well established and potential legal problems are rather well defined. In contrast, in multinational business operations the enterprise will encounter a wide range of legal problems to which legal systems and legal practices have not yet fully adapted. Legal questions may arise such as the choice of legal form for affiliates or subsidiaries, the status of foreign enterprises, legal protection of persons and property in foreign jurisdictions, the extension across national boundaries of domestic laws regulating business restrictive practices and antitrust matters, and the legal access of foreign firms to domestic capital markets. Other important legal problems may relate to concession agreements between a national government and a foreign private enterprise.

Legal Problems in International Trade

International trade is based chiefly on the use of standardized forms and practices. The standardized instruments contain most of the rules governing the parties. Sales memoranda, brokers' notes, bills of lading, charter parties, marine insurance policies, and letters of credit all embody familiar clauses which shipping clerks and bank tellers are trained to follow. Also, the import or export of goods can be, and usually is, arranged so as to involve the law of a single country.

The field of law associated with the movement of goods and the financing of trade is predominantly that of contracts. The standard expression in international trade, CIF, actually describes three contracts. "Cost" refers to the main sales contract. "Insurance" refers to the insurance coverage or contract arranged by either party. "Freight" means the transportation contract.

By including a "choice-of-law" clause in the contract, the parties can select the law that will govern their obligations on issues that lie within their contractual capacity—such as sufficiency of performance and excuse for nonperformance. But even with a choice-of-law clause, issues may arise that are outside the contractual capacity of the parties and on which the governing law is uncertain. In the absence of such a clause, what law governs the validity of a contract is somewhat confused. Because of uncertainties as to which law applies, the parties may choose to follow the rule that the law of the place of acceptance, that is, the location where the contract becomes final, governs the transaction. But where agreements are negotiated in telephone conversations between New York and Paris, for example, such a procedure is not helpful.

Another common legal issue in international trade is whether to include a clause in the contract prescribing the method of arbitration if future disputes arise. If arbitration is to take place in the United States, the normal clause provides that the rules of the American Arbitration Association will be followed.[3] If arbitration is to take place in Europe, the usual pattern is to follow rules developed by the International Chamber of Commerce. Where trade is with Eastern European countries, the agreement may be to submit disputes to the Moscow Foreign Trade Arbitration Commission.

Many lawyers are suspicious of arbitration procedures and prefer the expertise of courts. They feel that the tendency in arbitration is to split the difference between the parties rather than resolve the issue of liability. Nevertheless, where the amounts at issue are small, arbitration may be a more sensible and less costly approach than court proceedings.

A unique source of legal difficulties in the international business field is the problem of languages and translation. The problem is present in the drafting of contracts, in the preparation of corporate documents, in negotiation and settlement of disputes by arbitration or court proceedings, and in any reference to foreign laws or concepts. To the businessman, a contract is essentially a set of operating rules to be observed in arranging details of delivery, payment, and similar matters. But as a legal instrument, the contract must also be drafted with a view toward its meaning to a judge or arbitrator when foreign legal elements are involved.

---

[3] See American Arbitration Association, *New Strategies For Peaceful Resolution of International Business Disputes* (Dobbs Ferry, N.Y.: Oceana, 1972).

To facilitate performance, the contract must be understandable in the language of the personnel to be guided by it. For settlement of disputes, the same contract must also be accurately understandable in the formal language of the deciding body. The translation problem expands the area of uncertainty not only because of the normal difficulties of translating the meanings of words from one language to another. The translation of legal language also involves a transfer of concepts rather than a mechanical matching of words. Furthermore, courts differ in their procedures for accepting documents into evidence. U.S. courts emphasize oral testimony as a means of presenting foreign language documents. In many foreign courts, oral testimony is not allowed, and translations are admitted only when made by official translators.

The vital issue for the international manager, according to one distinguished legal authority, is to make sure that the matter of translation is properly worked out during the period when the instrument is drafted.[4] From the point of view of potential litigation, legal instruments should be written in the language of the decisional body which will settle the disputes arising in connection with the instrument. At the same time, it has been emphasized that there is no simple solution to the language barrier in legal documents.

Legal Factors in Multinational Operations

In the present international legal environment, the business enterprise engaged in multinational operations cannot become an international corporation in a legal sense. No international agency has yet been created with the authority to grant international incorporation. Consequently, the multinational business enterprise must content itself with stringing together a series of corporations created by the laws of different nation-states. The legal complexities arising out of such a situation are immense. The presence of the same enterprise in many countries necessarily subjects it to different laws and legal climates which in many situations may conflict.

Whose Law Determines "Inc."?   In setting up multinational operations, one of the first considerations is to determine which country's laws will be applied to give life and motion to the component parts of the multinational enterprise. This issue has been posed by one legal authority as "Whose Law Determines 'Inc.'?"[5]

The legal test of nationality varies among countries. Like an individual, a corporation can have dual nationality. It can also be "stateless,"

---

[4] Henry P. de Vries, "The Language Barrier," *Columbia Journal of World Business,* July–August, 1969, pp. 79–80.

[5] Henry P. de Vries, "The Problem of Identity: Whose Law Determines 'Inc.'?" *Columbia Journal of World Business,* March–April 1969, pp. 76–78.

thereby exposing the members of the corporation to individual liability. The question of nationality may have significant tax consequences. It may also determine whether an enterprise can benefit from government subsidy programs or engage in certain strategic businesses.

In the United States, it is not strictly correct to speak of the nationality of an enterprise. Corporations are created under the laws of the individual states and are identified with the specific state where organized. A Delaware corporation is one organized pursuant to Delaware law even though the activities of the corporation are completely outside of the state and the owners are nonresident. Nevertheless, the underlying U.S. view for all corporations is that a corporation secures its life and existence from a grant of the sovereign, and the nationality of the corporation is that of the sovereign power making the grant.

In many other countries, particularly civil law countries, a corporation is considered to be created by the contractual intent of its members rather than by a grant from the sovereign. The nationality of such a corporation is not necessarily that of the country in which it is constituted. In determining the law applicable to a corporation's existence and internal relations, several countries like the United Kingdom and Brazil follow the U.S. pattern and look at the place of incorporation. On the other hand, France, Belgium, and Greece look to the center of management. Italy and Egypt use the test of main business activity. Still others, such as Morocco, look to the place of the registered head office. As a result of these variations, multiple incorporation in various countries may be necessary to protect stockholders from personal liability.

The problems and risks arising from different concepts of nationality can be illustrated by a recent case brought before the German courts. A suit was filed against the U.S. stockholders of a corporation organized in the State of Washington to conduct mining operations in Mexico but with the central management of the corporation meeting in Hamburg. Since the corporation was administered in Germany but not constituted pursuant to German law, the court held that it was an unincorporated association in Germany and that the stockholders were personally liable for corporate liabilities.

Choosing the Form of Business Organization. Another major legal consideration is the form of business organization to be used in different legal jurisdictions. Tax considerations both at home and abroad may play a key role in the choice of legal form. The principal objective, however, normally will be that of insulating the parent organization or the investor from direct liability for obligations incurred in local operations.

In the choice of legal form, a clear distinction exists between common law countries and civil law countries. As noted previously, in common law countries a grant from the public authority gives life to the corporation. In civil law countries, the corporation is created by a contract between two or more persons, and the root concept is that of *société* or *Gesellschaft*. Thus, the one man corporation is a contradiction in terms, and most civil law countries tend to reject the one-man corporation and the wholly owned subsidiary. In some countries, the acquisition by one individual or legal entity of all the shares of a corporation may lead to its automatic dissolution and to personal liability of the stockholder for the corporation's liabilities.

In most countries, the choice of foreign business organization to operate as a subsidiary or affiliate will be between two forms, both similar to the U.S. corporation. The two forms are a *société anonyme* (S.A.) or a *société à responsibilité limitée* (S.A.R.L.). In German-speaking countries the similar forms are the *Aktiengesellschaft* (A.G.) or the *Gesellschaft mit beschrankter Haftung* (GmbH). The S.A. or A.G. is the most common form of business organization for medium- and large-scale businesses outside of the United States and British Commonwealth countries. However, the S.A.R.L., often referred to as Limitada in Latin American practice, has gained in favor as the form for foreign subsidiaries.[6] Several features of the S.A.R.L. explain its growing attractiveness to international enterprises. As compared to the S.A., it requires fewer formalities for formation and operation. It can afford considerable flexibility through contractual details inserted into the charter, whereas the S.A. must conform to more cumbersome mandatory provision of law. This flexibility is of particular importance for controlled companies, as well as for joint ventures with local interests. The S.A.R.L. can have a simple structure with management often centered in a single person and without a board of directors or other supervisory bodies required of an S.A. In each country, however, the S.A.R.L. will have distinctive features which vary as much as do the laws in different countries relating to the S.A.

The establishment of a joint venture creates special legal problems because the stresses and strains of the normal business operations may result in discord. In the choice of business form for a joint venture, the international enterprise should be alert to the problem of eventual liquidation and dissolution. The divorce may be far more complicated than the marriage, particularly where patents, trademarks, and the use of an internationally known firm name is involved.

Concession Agreements. The right of a multinational enterprise to engage in certain activities in a host country may be based on so-called concession agreements, sometimes referred to as economic-development

---

[6] Henry P. de Vries, "Legal Aspects of World Business," in *World Business,* ed. Courtney C. Brown (New York: Macmillan Co., 1970), pp. 289–93.

agreements. In its most common form, the concession agreement involves an extractive or public utility enterprise, although there are examples of such agreements in the field of manufacturing.[7] The provisions of the agreements, which specify a series of rights and obligations for both the enterprise and the government, vary widely among countries and industries, generally reflecting the relative bargaining power of the government and the investor.

Unlike traditional examples of contracts between a government and an alien such as debt instruments or purchase and sale contracts, the concession agreement is apt to be a unique instrument tailored to meet special needs. Furthermore, it may involve mineral rights or other interests controlled by the government and arrangements on matters, such as taxation, which are within a legislature's competence. These agreements often resemble special legislation governing relationships between the country and the international enterprise.

For a variety of reasons, concession agreements are likely to generate disputes between the parties. Problems will turn up for which no solutions or analogies can be found in legislation or in previous legal decisions. When such problems emerge or when governments breach a concession agreement, purely legal considerations have not been of great significance, even though the agreement is a legal instrument. The vast majority of disputes over concession agreements have been settled by direct negotiation between the parties, with the investor's government sometimes involved. The positions taken by the parties have generally been more influenced by economic issues, political factors, and equity considerations than by legal aspects of the situation.

The long-run trends in many concession contracts proceed through several identifiable stages.[8] The first stage begins when a country suspects that it has natural resource possibilities that might attract foreign investors, but the existence of such resources, as in the case of petroleum, or the economic feasibility of production is not known. In this stage, the host government is negotiating from weakness because the risks as seen through the eyes of both parties are high.

A second stage begins when the investments have been made and the projects are successful. As judged by hindsight, the host government reviews the original concession agreement as excessively favorable to the foreign investor and begin to raise its sights regarding its share of the returns from the concession activities. With its bargaining power greatly strengthened, the host government tends to increase its demands

---

[7] Steiner and Vagts, *Transnational Legal Problems,* p. 371.

[8] See Raymond Vernon, "Long-Run Trends in Concession Contracts," *Proceedings of the American Society of International Law at its Sixty-First Annual Meeting,* 27–29 April 1967 (Washington, D.C., 1967), pp. 81–89.

in the form of taxation, requirements for foreign enterprise to provide educational and other public facilities, and in a number of other ways.

At a third stage, the government presses for greater linkage of the concessionaire's activities with the economic-development aspirations for the local economy. For example, the foreign firm may be required to develop local sources of supplies for many types of equipment and services.

At a fourth stage, local governments become interested in sharing in the ownership of the foreign enterprise or in the process of decision making or both. As concession agreements move through these stages, it is the relative bargaining power of the parties, generally economic but sometimes political, that influences the patterns of conflict and resolution rather than conventional legal considerations.

Legal Protection of Property in Foreign Jurisdictions

International business operations which involve the ownership of property in many different nations are subject to the risk of expropriation without adequate compensation. To a large extent, the security of alien-owned property depends on nonlegal factors and, in particular, the long-term community of interest between the multinational enterprise and the foreign government.

Yet the international enterprise must plan its strategy so as to maximize whatever legal protection might be available against such noncommercial risks. Depending upon the kind of risk, the possibilities for legal protection may be (a) under local law, (b) under international law, (c) under bilateral or multilateral treaties, and (d) under home-country law.

Legal Protection under Local Law. Many governments have attempted to encourage inflows of private investment by issuing policy statements aimed at reassuring investors of the security of their property. Some nations have also embodied property protection provisions in domestic legislation and constitutions. For example, under its Law of Investment by Foreign Nations, Nationalist China (Taiwan) offers a complete guarantee for 20 years against expropriation or nationalization of all approved investments with at least 51 percent foreign ownership. Constitutional provisions, where they exist, specify the intent or reason for which an expropriation measure can be taken and require that compensation must be paid to the owner of property. However, mention may or may not be made of the adequacy or effectiveness of compensation.

The general conclusion of leading legal authorities, however, is that local legislation and constitutional instruments have limited value in the protection of foreign investment and that apparent rights under local laws, may in some cases prove largely illusory.[9] Foreign firms may have great difficulty enforcing their rights, because in many countries actions against the state before local courts are allowed only in exceptional cases, under the principle of sovereign immunity. Furthermore, parliamentary sovereignty implies that one parliament cannot bind its successor so far as the legislative functions are concerned. Government policies, local laws, and even constitutional provisions may be altered unilaterally at some future date. No rule of international law makes such changes illegal.

Legal Protection under International Law. The subject of responsibility by a state for injuries to aliens has been the focus of intensive study and debate in international law. But the views held by the capital-exporting countries, the communist-bloc nations, and the capital-importing countries of the less developed world are so divergent that no wide agreement exists on meaningful substantive principles of international law.

The United States adheres to the position that under customary international law, compensation must be prompt, adequate, and effective when an alien's property is taken by a foreign state. But even where this view is recognized, there is large room for argument over the precise operational meaning of "prompt," "adequate," and "effective," in a concrete situation.

Many of the less developed countries do not recognize the compensation rule as usually asserted. They believe that where the taking is pursuant to a broad program of economic and social reform, the requirement for immediate and full payment would deny to poorer countries the right to undertake reform programs they desire and need. In their view, "social" considerations may be paramount to the rights of the property owner. In the communist nations, expropriation without compensation has been justified as the means of implementing a philosophy opposed in principle to private property.

Where international law is relied upon for protection of property, the basic question again becomes one of enforcement. As previously noted, the International Court of Justice only receives for adjudication disputes between governments and in which both parties consent. Thus, a crucial issue for the international enterprise is whether its home-base government is willing to assert a claim under international law. Furthermore, before it may call upon its home government to espouse its claim, the international enterprise must, in most cases, exhaust its local remedies without obtaining redress.

---

[9] E. I. Nwogugu, *The Legal Problems of Foreign Investment in Developing Countries* (Dobbs Ferry, N.Y.: Oceana, 1965); Walter S. Surrey and Crawford Shaw, eds., *A Lawyer's Guide to International Business Transactions* (Philadelphia, Pa.: American Law Institute, 1963), p. 311.

Even after this prerequisite is fulfilled, the home country is under no obligation to assert the claim, if for any reason it is not desirous of doing so. If the home government does press the claim, the realities of international negotiations are such that the international firm is unlikely to receive what it considers to be fair reparation.[10]

In a number of Latin American countries, access to diplomatic protection of aliens by their governments and consequently to international law is specifically rejected by the Calvo doctrine, named for an Argentine jurist. The doctrine asserts that a foreigner doing business in a country is entitled only to nondiscriminatory treatment, and that by entering the country he implicitly consents to be treated as a national.[11] The Mexican Constitution includes a Calvo clause which requires aliens who acquire land or concessions for working mines or for the use of water or mineral fuel to agree "to consider themselves as Mexicans in respect to such property, and bind themselves not to invoke the protection of their governments in matters relating thereto; under penalty, in case of noncompliance, of forfeiture to the nation of property so acquired."

The Calvo doctrine was a response to the unhappy experience of South American countries during the nineteenth century with diplomatic and military intervention on behalf of foreign investors. Calvo clauses appear not only in statutes and constitutions but also in contracts. The doctrine continues to be used in certain countries but its importance has been diminished by new trends, such as investment guarantee treaties. A recent codification of international law would validate the Calvo clause if the interests affected are economic, if the investor in fact receives national treatment, and if there is a bona fide remedy in the national courts that satisfies the requirement of procedural justice.[12]

Legal Protection under Treaties.   Since the end of World War II, some investor countries such as the United States have placed great emphasis on negotiating a network of bilateral treaties of Friendship, Commerce, and Navigation, designed primarily to protect private investment abroad. These agreements, as discussed in Chapter 6, cover the rights of nationals of each of the contracting parties to trade, invest, or establish and operate a business in the other country. Some legal scholars argue that FCN treaties have greatly improved the investment climate for international enterprise.[13] One reason for this optimistic view

[10] Surrey and Shaw, *Lawyer's Guide,* p. 331; Seymour J. Rubin, "International Law and National Policy," in *Private Foreign Investment* (Baltimore: The Johns Hopkins Press, 1956), pp. 1–28.

[11] Steiner and Vagts, *Transnational Legal Problems,* pp. 419–25; Donald R. Shea, *The Calvo Clause* (Minneapolis: University of Minnesota Press, 1955), pp. 269–81.

[12] American Law Institute, *Restatement (Second) of Foreign Relations Law of the United States* section 202 (St. Paul, Minn.: American Law Institute, 1965), pp. 599–605.

[13] Nwogugu, *Legal Problems of Foreign Investment,* p. 134.

is that the treaties provide for resolution of disputes ultimately by recourse to the International Court of Justice, if other means of settlement fail. On the other hand, each of the treaties contains an escape clause permitting the parties to abrogate the provisions if necessary to protect essential security interests. Furthermore, the broad and often ambiguous phraseology of treaty provisions, the omitted items and other weaknesses lead still other legal authorities to conclude that the FCN treaties are likely to offer only a limited measure of effective legal protection.[14] In any event, relatively few of the less developed countries of Africa, Asia, and Latin America, where the need may be the greatest, have signed FCN treaties.

The idea of a multilateral investment convention for protecting private capital has gained support over the years in many legal, business, and political quarters. The Havana Charter for the aborted International Trade Organization contained some weak provisions on foreign investment which dealt mainly with the rights of the capital-importing countries and the avoidance of discrimination. Many subsequent efforts were made to formulate and secure regional or international agreement on investment codes. The International Chamber of Commerce approved in 1949 an "International Code of Fair Treatment" for foreign investments. The Council of Europe worked on the preparation of an Investment Statute in 1959. In addition to many other similar attempts, the OECD prepared a Draft Convention on the Protection of Foreign Property in 1967. The most recent efforts are the convention creating the International Center for Settlement of Investment Disputes, which operates under the wing of the World Bank and the "Guidelines for International Investment" proposed in late 1972 by the International Chamber of Commerce.

Investor nations and the international business community have dedicated considerable energy and resources in attempting to formulate and secure acceptance for a multilateral treaty or convention establishing a code for fair treatment and protection of private foreign investment. But the goal has not been achieved. One reason has been that the less developed countries have generally not participated in the formulation of such draft proposals. Furthermore, many of the newly independent countries of Asia and Africa are not prepared to participate because of a lingering fear of both economic and political domination by the rich countries.

Many of the newly emerged states are not anxious to assume any commitments which may impede some future decision to try out any political experiment in socialism.[15] For these reasons, multilateral agreement on a code for "fair" treatment of foreign private investment appears to be only a long-term possibility at best.

[14] Surrey and Shaw, *Lawyer's Guide,* p. 330.

[15] Nwogugu, *Legal Problems of Foreign Investment,* p. 157.

Legal Protection by Home Country. The inadequacies of legal protection for international business transactions under international and local law has resulted in the adoption of measures by several of the capital-exporting countries to fill at least part of the gap. The principal device has been to offer investment insurance or guarantees. As a means of stimulating exports, many of the industrialized countries have instituted programs of export credit insurance, covering short- and medium-term export credit.

The United States Investment Guaranty Program came into existence in 1948 as part of the European Recovery Plan. Other countries have cautiously followed the U.S. lead. At present, investors from virtually all of the industrialized countries can cover some of the risks involved in foreign investments through home-country guaranty programs. The plans vary widely, as shown in Table 9.1.

Another form of home-country protection is diplomatic intervention. States are in the habit of intervening diplomatically to protect property situated abroad which belongs either to the government or its nationals and which is threatened by or facing actual injury at the hands of a foreign government. It has not been unusual in the past for states to intervene with armed forces. Between 1899 and 1927, the United States intervened on at least 24 occasions with armed forces to protect American lives and property abroad.[16] However, under the United Nations Charter, unilateral threat or resort to armed forces either to enforce international law or to obtain satisfaction is illegal except for self-defense.

Summary. Legal protection against risk to property, industrial property rights, and other components of international business operations is quite limited under international law, international treaties, and host-country laws. Yet the risk arising because of limited legal protection should not be overemphasized. International enterprises have been expanding their commitments on a large scale, even after taking full account of such noncommercial risks. This suggests that prospective gains are sufficiently attractive to outweigh the noncommercial risk element and that means other than legal protection for minimizing risk may be reasonably effective.

The basic problem encountered in relying upon legal protection has been well summarized by a leading authority as follows:

World War II let loose forces of nationalism whose reactions to earlier conceptions of property and its protection are far different from those of a world in which colonialism and mercantilism held sway.[17]

---

[16] Offut, *The Protection of Citizens Abroad by the Armed Forces of the United States,* 1928, cited by Nwogugu in *Legal Problems of Foreign Investment,* p. 272.

[17] Preface by James Landis in Seymour J. Rubin, *Private Foreign Investment,* p. x.

As emphasized previously, the security of a particular foreign transaction or investment, as a practical matter, will depend largely on nonlegal factors. The best protection arises from a long-term community of interest between the international enterprise and the foreign government. The risk of losing future inflows of foreign investment and the benefits of international business operations can be a powerful deterrent against the taking of property by a foreign government. The economic pressures that can be exerted by the international enterprise itself can also be a significant source of protection.

Transnational Reach of Economic Regulation

The transnational reach of national laws regulating domestic business behavior can present vexatious problems for the international enterprise, particularly in the fields of antitrust and securities regulation. Such laws are intended to govern business behavior within the specific nation and are not directed specifically toward business transactions that cross national boundaries. But in their application they can have an extraterritorial reach when foreign-based conduct has a significant impact on the domestic scene.

In many respects, the international enterprise can adjust its global strategy and operating policies to differences in national laws. But the effects of certain business actions or policies are not coterminous with the national boundaries within which such actions are taken or policies decided upon. Certain practices may be legal in one jurisdiction, but the same action may be considered in violation of the laws in another country in which the enterprise is operating. Such a situation raises the difficult problem of extraterritoriality, because legal action in one jurisdiction can have significant effects on activities in another area where the law being applied does not have legal jurisdiction. In this way, the international enterprise can be the vehicle through which conflicts between nations arise.[18]

Antitrust Laws and Restrictive Business Practices. Restrictive business agreements are agreements among enterprises to fix prices, limit production, allocate markets, restrain the application of technology, or engage in similar schemes likely to reduce competition. Such practices have been illegal in the United States for many decades under various antitrust laws, but, until World War II, they were either permitted or positively encouraged in most countries outside of North America. The situation changed drastically after World War II when many other

---

[18] For an assessment of the resentment by other countries to the extraterritorial application of U.S. antitrust laws, see Jack N. Behrman, *National Interests and the Multinational Enterprise* (Englewood Cliffs, N.J.: Prentice-Hall, 1970), pp. 114–27.

nations followed generally the American pattern and adopted laws designed to curb restrictive business practices. Presently, at least 24 countries—13 in Europe, 4 in Latin America, and 7 others—have national antitrust laws.[19] National laws in the European Economic Community countries have been supplemented with Articles 85 and 86 of the Rome Treaty, which are directed toward regulating competition in the Common Market area.

Some significant differences in national laws exist. In its domestic application, the U.S. law looks at the *act* of conspiracy, or of monopolizing, whereas the European laws look at the *effects*. The basic philosophy of antitrust laws in the United States is that competition per se is good and that any acts to restrain competition are illegal. The basic philosophy of European antimonopoly law is that some anticompetitive agreements may be beneficial and others may be harmful. It takes the position that certain types of cooperation or mergers can lead to increased productivity, economic growth, technological advance, and price reductions.

The Sherman Act of 1890 passed by the U.S. Congress at a time when few American firms had foreign subsidiaries holds in Section 1 that:

Every contract, combination in the form of trust or otherwise, or conspiracy, in restraint of trade or commerce among the several states, or with foreign nations, is hereby declared to be illegal.

The Sherman Act and subsequent legislation extends the U.S. laws to actions abroad which "substantially affect" the commerce of the United States and competition in the U.S. markets. To do otherwise, it is argued, and to make enforcement turn on nationality or physical events, would open the door to widespread evasion and abuse.

The non–U.S. antitrust laws are relatively recent, and the applications are still limited in number. Yet indications are that they will also have a transnational reach. West Germany and Austria, for example, expressly extend their laws to include restrictive business practices abroad having "effects" within their territory. The Canadian Restrictive Practices Commission has similarly interpreted Canadian law.

As a practical matter, a nation must be able to assert jurisdiction over the international enterprise in order to enforce its laws. The legal test of jurisdiction by U.S. courts is whether the foreign corporation is transacting business "of a substantial character," and the test governing service or process is whether the corporation is *found* in the jurisdiction. The wide reach exercised by the U.S. laws is illustrated by the Swiss Watchmakers Case. Two Swiss trade associations in the watch industry were held subject to local jurisdiction because of the activities

[19] See **Corwin D. Edwards,** *Control of Cartels and Monopolies: An International Comparison* (Dobbs Ferry, N.Y.: Oceana, 1967).

of a jointly owned New York corporation doing advertising and promotional work and acting as a liason agency in servicing the American market with repair parts.[20]

The U.S. courts found the defendants guilty of conspiracy to restrain the commerce of the United States and ordered them to stop all restraints on exports to the United States and to change industry practices developed in Switzerland with the active support and participation of the Swiss government. The decree imposed wide prohibitions on contracts made in Switzerland and on agreements made between the Swiss industry and manufacturers in Great Britain, France, and Germany. It also ordered sweeping changes in certain bylaws of the Swiss Watch Federation which were considered restrictive of U.S. commerce. After the Swiss government intervened directly with the U.S. government, important changes were made in the final judgment, including the insertion of a provision that nothing in it would limit or circumscribe the sovereign right and power of the Swiss government.

Foreign mergers and acquisitions have been challenged under U.S. antitrust laws. A suit was brought against the Gillette Company in 1968 to prevent its acquisition of Braun, A.G., a German concern, on the grounds that the acquisition would eliminate a potential competitor in the domestic shaving-instrument industry. Through the threat of court action, the U.S. Department of Justice delayed and reshaped a merger of two foreign firms: Ciba and Geigy. These two major Swiss pharmaceutical companies postponed a merger and revised their merger plans in 1970 when officially informed that the merger as planned might be in violation of U.S. law. The alleged grounds were that the combining of the U.S. operations of both companies would reduce competition in the American dyestuff market.

The transnational reach of enforcement techniques of one government can be interpreted as interference by another government with the international enterprise in the middle. For example, U.S. courts have ordered U.S. banks to turn over bank records on foreign companies held in the bank's foreign affiliates. As a result, a number of governments have passed laws prohibiting companies located in their jurisdiction from complying with the orders of foreign courts to produce documents.

Still another aspect of the transnational reach of antitrust laws has been the concern expressed by foreign firms interested in establishing operations in the United States that U.S. authorities may seek to apply U.S. laws to their activities outside of the United States.[21]

[20] United States v. Watchmakers of Switzerland Information Center, 133 F. Supp. 40, SDNY (1955).

[21] J. J. A. Ellis, "The Legal Aspects of European Direct Investment in the United States," in *The Multinational Corporation in the World Economy,* ed. Sidney E. Rolfe and Walter Damm (New York: Praeger Publishers, Inc., 1970).

Laws Relating to Access to Capital Markets. In the field of securities exchange legislation, the United States has established broad requirements for registration with the Securities Exchange Commission and for disclosure of business information by companies whose securities are traded on the organized exchanges and over-the-counter market in the United States. The problem faced by foreign companies that would like to have their securities traded in U.S. markets is that U.S. disclosure and reporting requirements generally go far beyond the requirements of the home-base country.[22]

Although the Congressional history of the U.S. law makes it clear that Congress intended the requirements to apply to foreign issuers of securities, the SEC was given authority to grant exemptions to foreign issuers where it found that such exemptions were in the public interest and consistent with the protection of investors. Based on this authority, and after considering the objections of several foreign governments to proposed rules, the SEC modified the transnational reach of the regulation of securities so as to minimize the difficulties of foreign companies in having access to U.S. capital markets.

The rules adopted in 1967 permit foreign companies to be exempt from SEC registration if they, or an official of their government, furnish to the commission substantially the same information as they (1) would have to make pursuant to the laws of the country of their incorporation, (2) would have to file with a foreign stock exchange on which securities are traded and which was made public by such exchanges, or (3) would have distributed to their security holders.

FUTURE TRENDS

Clearly the legal environment is in a transitional stage of adaptation to new international business patterns, and the international enterprise must be sensitive to future trends in the legal framework. In traditional international trade activities, the adaptation of national legal systems has been substantial and new legal problems are likely to be minimal. In the case of securing legal protection for foreign investment and industrial property rights (such as patents, know-how, and trademarks), adaptation has been only partial despite a long history of legal concern over such matters. With regard to multinational business enterprises operating transnationally with global strategies and integrated operations, the legal response is only in a beginning stage, and the legal framework is likely to change most in the future. Furthermore, as previously independent foreign investments increasingly become part of an integrated system of multinational business operations, many long-standing issues related

---

[22] Steiner and Vagts, *Transnational Legal Problems,* pp. 962–76.

to legal protection of foreign investment and industrial property rights have also become more complex.

Although the multinational enterprise phenomenon is frequently described as a private international government, in the present world of nation-states the key to forecasting future legal trends is a clear recognition that nations make laws or agree to multinational treaties. Consequently, future trends at both the national and international levels are certain to reflect the concerns and aspirations of the individual nations vis-a-vis multinational enterprise. And the emerging patterns for legal change and adaptation in investor countries differ sharply from those in predominantly host nations.

Investor nations are adapting their national legal systems to facilitate international business activities and to extend the transnational reach of domestic laws so as to maximize home-country benefits and minimize home-country negative effects. The advanced countries of the European Common Market are working at the regional level to create a legal environment that facilitates the international business expansion of national firms, even though the rhetoric often suggests that the primary concern is for legal measures to control foreign investment inflows.

In nations which are predominantly hosts to multinational enterprise, the legal trends are in the direction of controlling the domestic expansion and operations of foreign firms. Where host countries are able to work cooperatively at the regional levels, such as the case of the Andean-bloc nations in South America, the trend is toward treaties of a defensive nature that will harmonize domestic control measures so that the foreign enterprise is less able to dilute national benefits by playing one country off against the other.

Given the highly divergent national interests in the international business field, the consensus needed to establish an international legal system for simplifying and harmonizing the legal environment for international business has not emerged and is unlikely to emerge in the near future. If, for political reasons, the nations of the world move toward a strong world government, a comprehensive system of world law would be created which could include broad coverage of international business matters. But as of the early 1970s, the political route toward an international legal framework for international business does not appear promising.

One possibility at the international level, short of a comprehensive system of world law, is the "Cosmocorp" proposal to permit multinational enterprises to become truly international or nonnational autonomous entities.[23] This could be achieved through agreement by members of the United Nations to create an organization that could grant international incorporation. Another way might be for companies to incorporate

---

[23] George W. Ball, "Cosmocorp: The Importance of Being Stateless," *Columbia Journal of World Business,* March–April 1968.

in places like Luxembourg or Bermuda, with general recognition that such incorporation is a *de facto* declaration of independence from all significant relationships to a home country.[24]

The Cosmocorp proposal emerged from legal circles and has attracted academic support in the investor countries. But despite the appealing logic of having an international companies law for international business enterprises, neither business firms nor nations have urgently pressed for action on the Cosmocorp proposal. The multinational enterprise apparently recognizes that having a nationality may have advantages over statelessness. In a world of nation-states, the business firm would be giving up access to national investment-guarantee and incentive programs as well as the potential support that a home government could give the business interests of the firm in international tariff negotiations and in the resolution of conflicts concerning such matters as taxes and the taking of property. Furthermore, the enterprise would still be considered as a foreign company by any nation so long as its home base is not in that specific country. The lack of interest by nations in the Cosmocorp proposal may result from the nations' greater concern for expanding rather than reducing their control over foreign business activities in their countries.

A more certain trend is toward expanded coverage of international business matters through partial international regulation. A recent proposal in this direction is for the creation of a GATT type of international organization that would be concerned with five problem areas: taxation, balances of payments, export controls or trading with the enemy, antitrust, and the issuance of securities.[25] It is anticipated that the less developed countries as primarily host nations would be unwilling to join such an organization in the first stages. The proposal is that participating countries would only agree on a few simple rules but be willing to establish the organizational machinery for resolving specific cases in the selected fields put to it by governments or by corporations.

Partial international regulation may also be expanded through the extension of the activities of existing international organizations such as the IMF, GATT, UNCTAD, and the OECD. When these agencies were created, the multinational enterprise was not an explicit matter of their concern. Yet the work of these organizations has facilitated the expansion of international business, and the operations of multinational enterprises are having an increasing impact on the goals and programs of the agencies. In lieu of or as a complement to a new interna-

---

[24] Detlev F. Vagts, "The Multinational Enterprise: A New Challenge for Transnational Law," *Harvard Law Review* 83, 1 (February 1970): 787–89.

[25] Paul M. Goldberg and Charles P. Kindleberger, "Toward a GATT for Investment: A Proposal for Supervision of the International Corporation," *Law and Policy in International Business* 2, no. 2, Summer 1970: 295–325.

tional organization, an extension of existing organizations into international business matters appears logical and inevitable.

The trend toward reducing legal difficulties through bilateral treaties is likely to continue and to be of major importance in reducing conflicts of laws. Bilateral treaties have been successful in resolving issues of double taxation and tax evasion. In connection with investment guarantees, the less developed countries have been willing to enter into bilateral treaties with the United States and Germany, whereas they have been loath to sign traditional treaties of friendship, navigation, and commerce. The investment-guarantee treaties give the host countries reasonable assurance that investment projects will conform to their priorities and include some motivations for the country to fulfill its obligation.

In the antitrust field, the trend favored by most U.S. international firms is a simple formula of having the jurisdiction of antitrust laws stop at the country's border. But the simplicity of this solution is deceptive. In its nature, international business, whether in the form of trade or multinational business operations, involves the jurisdictions of more than one country. Any country that would adopt a self-denying policy to disregard restraint of trade conspiracies entered into outside of the country would simply be giving away the right to protect itself against foreign arrangements that it thought harmful to its national interest.[26]

Another possible future trend would be for the many nations with antitrust legislation to adopt uniform trade regulation laws and policies. One legal authority claims that there has been some harmonization of law and policy by others moving in the direction of U.S. practices.[27] Yet as the new laws become more systematic and as interpretations in each country harden into precedents, complete uniformity in trade regulation policies becomes increasingly difficult.[28] Aside from some harmonization, the most likely trend appears to be an increasing use of bilateral agreements and diplomatic negotiations to handle conflict issues arising in the antitrust field.

Summary

Although the paths are uncertain, the prospect is that a sizeable number of countries will begin to evolve more comprehensive legal principles to govern the international corporation. There will also be forward movement by groups of countries—either by multilateral international

---

[26] Raymond Vernon, "Antitrust and International Business," *Harvard Business Review,* September–October 1968, p. 86.

[27] Seymour J. Rubin, "The International Firm and the National Jurisdiction," in *International Corporation,* ed. Charles P. Kindleberger (Cambridge, Mass.: The M.I.T. Press, 1970), pp. 194–95.

[28] Corwin D. Edwards, "The World of Antitrust," *Columbia Journal of World Business,* July–August 1969, p. 24.

treaties, the adoption of a uniform business law, or by some less formal and more unconventional approach—to evolve codes of legal principles for dealing better with the international business phenomenon. Progress will be uneven and novel approaches will have to be devised. But there are certain to be important changes in the legal environment. International business has become such an important component of the world economy that the legal environment will have to adjust to this reality.

EXERCISES AND DISCUSSION QUESTIONS

1. "When a foreign firm does business in our country its local affiliate must legally become a national enterprise," explained the official of a host government. "As a national enterprise the affiliate is entitled to the full legal protection of our laws in case of expropriation, alleged breach of concession contract, etc. in the same way as any other national enterprise. Why should the investor countries and the international business firms be insisting on additional legal protection for foreign investment through international investment codes or international organizations to arbitrate what are essentially national legal issues? Such proposals violate our national sovereignty and discriminate against purely national companies." Discuss

2. The legal doctrine, *rebus sic stantibus,* relates to the presumption in contracts that things will remain in the same condition as they were at the date of agreement. There is a difference of opinion among the authorities as to whether the principle of *rebus sic stantibus* is a recognized rule of international law. To what extent do you think that the principle should be clearly recognized in the settlement of disputes concerning concession contracts?

3. If national laws on antitrust and restrictive business practices were harmonized, as an international manager would you prefer the U.S. version which looks at the act or the European version which looks at the effects? Why?

4. If the United Nations were prepared to establish a new specialized agency with limited powers to improve the international legal environment for multinational business operations, as a representative of the international business sector what specific activities would you recommend that this agency undertake? To what extent would you expect that your recommendations would be acceptable to host countries as well as investor countries?

15

POLITICAL RISK

POLITICAL RISK has long been a familiar term in the lexicon of international business. International enterprises are increasingly recognizing the importance of political-risk elements in many investment and operating decisions. Yet, a recent survey of major U.S. multinational enterprises concludes that few companies undertake a systematic evaluation of political risks, "involving their identification, their likely incidence, and their specific consequences for company operations."[1] Thus, one of the challenges facing the international manager is to develop techniques for evaluating and forecasting political risk so that political-risk elements can be included in decision making on a more objective basis.

The mention of political risk is most likely to bring to mind the business environment characteristic of the newly independent and less developed nations (LDCs). With two thirds of the world's population, these areas are not insignificant for international business even though they are relatively low-income areas. But political risk is a much more pervasive issue for the multinational enterprise. It can be encountered by investors in industrialized countries such as France and Canada, as well as in the LDCs, and even in the home countries of investors like Sweden and the United States.

U.S. companies doing business in South Africa have experienced political boycotts and harassment in the United States from groups opposed to the racial policies of South Africa. In 1965, the Firestone Tire and Rubber Company terminated negotiations for a contract to design and equip a synthetic rubber plant in Romania because of unanticipated

---

[1] Franklin R. Root, "U.S. Business Abroad and the Political Risks," *MSU Business Topics,* Winter 1968.

political pressure from a conservative youth organization vigorously opposed to expanded U.S. business relations with Soviet-bloc countries.

In Sweden the big electrical firm, ASEA, became the target for intense leftist criticism for its proposed participation in an international power-plant project in the Portuguese colony of Mozambique. The political opposition in Sweden argued that the project would serve the objectionable Portuguese colonial power and weaken opposition movements.[2]

Political risk usually connotes the possibility of losses. Yet, as in the case of other types of risk, political risk can result in gains as well as losses. Political considerations were responsible for the 1962 restrictions by Brazil on profit remittances, but opposing political forces caused a change in the government in 1964, one result of which was a liberalization of profit remittances and of other policies relating to foreign private investment. Similarly, drastic political changes in Indonesia in 1966 and in Argentina during the same year had the effect of improving the international business environment.

DEFINING POLITICAL RISK

To assess and forecast the likely influence of political risk in international business decisions, one must start with an operational definition—political risk in international business exists (1) when discontinuities occur in the business environment, (2) when they are difficult to anticipate, and (3) when they result from political change. To constitute a "risk" these changes in the business environment must have a potential for significantly affecting the profit or other goals of a particular enterprise.

It follows, therefore, that political fluctuations which do not change the business environment significantly do not represent political risk for international business. It follows, also, that what is political risk for one firm may not be political risk for another. Abrupt changes in concession agreements are political risk for petroleum companies but not for soft-drink producers.

To be sure, political considerations are continually modifying the business environment at home and abroad, but not all such changes can properly be considered as political risk. Where change is gradual and progressive, and when it reflects continuity in government policies and political forces, future trends are neither unexpected nor difficult to anticipate. In such "normal" circumstances, the decision maker's task is to recognize the evolutionary path along which change is occurring, identify the principal motivating forces behind the change, and make judgments as to timing. For example, tax laws and tax burdens are constantly

---

[2] Sven Ersman and Torsten Gardlund, "In Sweden, Investment Abroad Is a Moral Issue," *Columbia Journal of World Business*, January–February 1970.

changing, but much, if not most, of the change does not represent a radical departure from past trends nor is it difficult to anticipate.

It would be convenient if the international manager could look to the political scientists for an understanding of the sources of political risk for international business operations. Political scientists have done considerable research on the subject of "political instability" in the form of revolutions. But they still disagree significantly on how to define political stability or instability, on how to measure the phenomenon, and on what are the causal forces. Furthermore, the political scientists' principal focus of interest is not likely to produce the answers needed for international business. For one thing, the discontinuities that might affect international business do not necessarily require a revolution.[3] Another consideration is that political instability, depending on how it is defined, is a separate, although related phenomenon from that of political risk.

A conceptual framework is presented in Figure 15.1 showing the sources of political risk, the political groups through which political risk can be generated, and the types of influences that political-risk elements can have on international business activities. It should be noted that several of the specific effects shown in the far right column are not exclusively associated with political risk. Taxation policies, transfer freedom, market restrictions, and pressures for local sharing of ownership can change in relatively stable political situations and as a result of reasonably predictable nonpolitical forces. In such cases the difference between normal business risk and political risk is a matter of degree. It becomes difficult to draw the line between continuity and discontinuity, between certainty and uncertainty, and to determine that political forces are in fact dominant.

A particularly difficult problem at times may be to separate political and economic risk. Although government decisions are always political—by definition—the forces dictating the decisions may be purely economic. For example, the political-risk insurance offered by the U.S. government to domestic firms investing abroad includes inconvertibility of currency as a political risk. Yet currency inconvertibility can occur for predominantly economic reasons in politically stable nations and at times when political systems and political leadership are not changing.

In some situations, political forces may be the dominant factor in inconvertibility. Political uncertainties in some nations have stimulated large outflows of flight capital, which in turn caused a balance-of-pay-

---

[3] Anthony Leeds, *Latin American Research Review*, Spring 1968, p. 83. Leeds defines "revolution" as a "system-wide disturbance characterized by organized fighting flowing out of conflict in a social situation where one or more major *classes* is fundamentally unrepresented in the decision-making and reward-allocating operations of the state."

FIGURE 15.1
Political Risk: A Conceptual Framework

Sources of Political Risk	Groups through Which Political Risk Can Be Generated	Political Risk Effects: Types of Influence on International Business Operations
Competing political philosophies (nationalism, socialism, communism)	Government in power and its operating agencies	Confiscation: loss of assets without compensation
Social unrest and disorder	Parliamentary opposition groups	Expropriation with compensation: loss of freedom to operate
Vested interests of local business groups	Nonparliamentary opposition groups (Algerian "FLN," guerrilla movements working from within or outside of country)	Operational restrictions: market shares, product characteristics, employment policies, locally shared ownership, and so forth.
Recent and impending political independence	Nonorganized common interest groups: students, workers, peasants, minorities, and so forth.	Loss of transfer freedom: financial (for example, dividends, interest payments), goods, personnel, or ownership rights
Armed conflicts and internal rebellions for political power	Foreign governments or intergovernmental agencies such as the EEC	Breaches or unilateral revisions in contracts and agreements
New international alliances	Foreign governments willing to enter into armed conflict or to support internal rebellion	Discrimination such as taxes, compulsory subcontracting
		Damage to property or personnel from riots, insurrections, revolutions, and wars

ments crisis. Or internal political forces in opposition to foreign enterprise have compelled governments to limit the repatriation of profits and other financial transfers by foreign firms. For example, the restrictive Brazilian Capital Remittance Law, adopted in 1962 by the Goulart regime, was motivated primarily by antagonism to foreign enterprise and a conviction by powerful political forces that foreign firms were draining too much foreign exchange from the country.

The international manager must be aware of the potential intermingling of political and economic motivations. Even where considerable intermingling of motivations exists, the decision maker may get useful results by trying to separate the political factors from the others.

Macro Political Risk

The international business enterprise may encounter both macro and micro types of political risk. The risk is of a macro nature when politically motivated environmental changes affect all foreign enterprise. The risk is of a micro nature when the environmental changes are intended to affect only selected fields of business activity or foreign enterprises with specific characteristics.

Macro political risk can be indirect and spasmodic. At times of political turmoil, foreign companies are tempting targets for political factions of just about every stripe. Harassment or physical damage can occur to embarrass the political regime in power. An example of this indirect type of political risk occurred in 1969, when a large number of U.S.-owned supermarkets in Argentina were bombed on the occasion of Governor Nelson Rockefeller's visit to Buenos Aires as a special envoy of President Richard Nixon. The supermarkets were owned by the International Basic Economy Corporation, which Nelson Rockefeller had founded.

Direct and relatively permanent macro risk can be illustrated by the take-over of private enterprise in 1959–60 by the Castro government in Cuba. Foreign enterprises were seized along with domestic firms. In part, the broad-sweep confiscation of foreign investment has been explained by a basic change in political philosophy brought about by the Cuban revolution—a shift from a private enterprise to a socialist or communist system. And in part, the large size and the specific composition of foreign investment in Cuba may have played a significant role in shaping the policies to expropriate all foreign private investment.[4]

The Cuban experience deserves special attention. It suggests that specific business projects may be subjected to political risk because the

[4] See Leland L. Johnson, U.S. Private Investment in Latin America: Some Questions of National Policy, Memorandum RM-4092 ISA (Santa Monica, Calif.: The Rand Corporation, July 1964).

overall size of the foreign-owned business sector is large relative to the total size of a country's business sector; or because foreign firms dominate several strategic and politically sensitive fields of activity. In such situations, revolutionary political changes are likely to be accompanied or even supported by political pressures to end the "economic colonial" status of a country by reducing or eliminating the influence of all types of foreign business.

The Cuban case is not an isolated example of macro risk. In recent years, international enterprises have felt the impact of broadside actions—frequently along with domestic private enterprise—in Algeria, Burma, Chile, Egypt, Ghana, Indonesia, Uganda, and Southern Yemen. These are in addition to the communist expropriations in Eastern Europe and China following World War II.

Macro-risk situations can also occur where broad action is taken against foreign enterprise as a political boycott. In the Middle East, various Arab countries began in 1955 to boycott any companies that had branches in Israel or allowed the use of their trade name there. The Arabs ignored direct trade with Israel, but any permanent investment in that country, or any long-term agreements, such as licensing arrangements or technical assistance, earned the company a place on the blacklist. The implementation of such policies has been sporadic, but after the 1967 war with Israel, the boycott was tightened.

An even more comprehensive boycott was announced in 1970 by Mainland China. The Chinese prime minister told visiting Japanese traders that China would not do business with Japanese companies that gave credits to or invested in Taiwan and South Korea or with firms which entered joint ventures with U.S. companies or otherwise assisted in the Vietnam war. In retaliation, Nationalist China (Taiwan) announced its own list of Japanese companies which it was banning for doing business with Mainland China.

Micro Risks and Product Vulnerability

Macro political risk is dramatic. Micro political risk is more prevalent. With considerable frequency, the international manager is likely to encounter abrupt and politically motivated changes in the business environment that are selectively directed toward specific fields of business activity. But the types of business operations with a high vulnerability to micro risk will vary from nation to nation and over time in the same nation.

At a particular point of time and for a specific country, it should be possible to rank types of business activities according to their degree of political-risk vulnerability. However, such rankings constantly change. The forecaster of political risk must do more than look at a snapshot to identify and assess the sources of political risk for specific business activities and to understand the rationale for radical shifts. He must analyze a continually evolving situation over time.

In a current ranking of industries, public utilities have the highest degree of political-risk vulnerability. A few decades ago, public-utility investments by foreigners were politically and economically popular with both host countries and investors. But styles change, and recent world-wide trends have been toward domestic, usually government, ownership of public-utility enterprises because of national-security and develop-mental goals. As a result, international enterprises have not been expand-ing in these fields, and the high political-risk ranking is relevant only to such operations as still exist, mainly in less developed countries, as holdovers from a previous era.

The extractive industries, particularly petroleum and mining, also have a high degree of political risk because of growing nationalistic feelings and a conviction that natural resource endowments should be exploited for the welfare of all people in a nation rather than for private profit. As the recent Gordon Report in Canada explains, Financial insti-tutions are also vulnerable because of "their pervasiveness and their potential as bases for influence and control."[5]

Two factors can change the political-risk vulnerability of an industry over time. One is the dominance of foreign enterprise in a major industry sector. If the share of the automobile industry controlled by foreign countries is relatively low, as in the case of West Germany, political risk also tends to be low. If foreign companies completely dominate the industry, as was the case in Peru during the early 1970s, political risk is likely to be high.

A second factor that may affect or compound the risk is the capacity of nationals to operate a business successfully. At an early stage in a nation's development, foreign enterprises may be welcomed because they provide scarce capital, management know-how, and technical skills not locally available. Over time, countries manage to accumulate capital and nationals who have learned the techniques of management and be-come skilled in the technology of the foreign enterprise. To the extent that local personnel have been trained for copper mining, running a tea plantation, or managing some other type of business initiated by foreign firms, the political pressures for curtailing or eliminating foreign enterprises are likely to increase. To the extent that an enterprise is dependent upon a continuing import of new technology in a technologi-cally dynamic industry, local political-risk elements are likely to be weak.

If one were to judge by the fee schedule for political-risk insurance

---

[5] *Foreign Ownership and the Structure of Canadian Industry: Report of the Task Force on the Structure of Canadian Industry* (Ottawa, Canada: Information Canada, 1970), p. 389.

offered by many governments, one would have to conclude that the degree of political risk is similar for all types of business activities and for investments in all countries. Insurance fees are at the same rate for all projects. Yet the implication of the fee schedule is not consistent with historical experience.

Sources of Political Risk

From the standpoint of international business, the six general sources of political risk shown in Figure 15.1 are of particular importance. The most comprehensive is the existence of political forces hostile toward foreign enterprise in general, or toward foreign participation in selected business fields, for philosophical reasons that diverge sharply from prevailing government policies. Others are social unrest and disorder, the private-vested interests of local business groups, recent or impending independence, new international alliances, and armed conflicts. Less predictable, and political only in the sense that it is a tool of politicians, is the exposure of corruption or scandal. It is often linked to a government official who might well have provided influence for a foreign firm.

Latent Philosophies. Some latent hostility to foreign enterprises is present in most nations, including the United States. The potential strength of such hostile forces determines the degree of political risk. The avenues available for making such political strength effective in changing government policies are numerous. The basic form of government can be changed, as happened in Cuba. The leadership of government can change but the political system remains the same, as happened when Pompidou succeeded de Gaulle in France. Or concessions can be exacted from the political parties and leaders in power without changes in the form or leadership of the existing government.

A drastic change in policy without a change in political leadership can be illustrated by events in Zambia and in Trinidad. The Zambian case was described by the *Economist* in its August 30, 1969, issue: "For some time internal strife in Unip, the ruling party, has threatened to bring down the whole government. It was partly to prevent this happening that President Kaunda announced at the Unip national council meeting earlier this month the 51 percent nationalization of the copper mines." The Trinidad case followed a similar pattern. According to the *Economist* in its August 29, 1970 issue: "Trinidad's Dr. Eric Williams has pulled off a major coup to regain the confidence of his electorate and to disprove his critics who maintain that he is a mere puppet of foreign capitalists. At the beginning of this month he announced that the government will buy 51 percent of the island's largest sugar producer, Caroni, a subsidiary of the British Tate & Lyle group."

The hostility of strong internal factions of a country to foreign enterprise may arise out of adherence to such philosophies as socialism and nationalism. They may also spring from concepts of national security, national welfare, and appropriate economic-development goals.

Socialism commonly means government rather than private ownership of the means of production. Yet political labels can be misleading. "Socialism" as a label has been extremely popular in many parts of the world in recent decades. But the specific goals of political forces banded together under the socialism label vary greatly. For example, government leaders in India have declared that India's guiding political philosophy is socialism. Although the public-enterprise sector is large in India, a substantial share of the business activity has been reserved for private enterprise, much of which is foreign. Likewise, Yugoslavia calls itself a communist or socialist country, yet numerous joint ventures with foreign private enterprise have been negotiated in recent years. Thus, the international enterprise must look behind labels for the specific goals of political groups in different countries.

The nationalistic philosophy generally asserts that control over a nation's economic destiny should be in the hands of nationals and that nationals should have preference over foreigners in benefiting from economic and business opportunities in the country. Both of these views can generate political risk for international business enterprises.

An example of national-welfare concepts that can create political risk is the persistent pressure in many countries of the world for land reform. If land-reform measures are suddenly accelerated, as occurred in 1969 when a military junta took control of the government in Peru, foreign as well as domestic business firms with landholdings are likely to be expropriated.

National aspirations for economic development can create political risk for international business when the nation believes that the ultimate goal of development is to enlarge the domestic capacity for *self-generating* growth. This view implies that a country does not want to increase its dependence on outside forces any more than is necessary. This philosophy underlies the stated policy of the government of India that private foreign investment is not allowed in industries where indigenous capital, talent, and know-how are available.[6]

Other Sources of Risk. Social unrest and disorder may create political risk, not because of specific hostility to foreign enterprise, but because of general disruption of business activities. The causes of social unrest may range from the existence of extreme economic hardships to racial disorders as experienced in the United States and religious disputes such as have occurred in India, and even student riots.

Ineffective law enforcement can also be included in this category.

---

[6] Indian Investment Center, *Seminar on International Investment in India* (New Delhi, 1968).

It can result in risk to property and to persons and can greatly influence the costs of doing business and the efficiency of production, transportation, and communications.

The risk that can result from the political influence of local business interests that consider themselves threatened by foreign enterprises should never be underestimated. In Japan, local business interests have been extremely active and successful in influencing government policies or decisions that have restricted the activities of foreign enterprise. It was an open secret in Brazil that conservative indigenous business interests allied themselves with radical left-wing political groups in 1962 to influence President Goulart and the congress to adopt highly restrictive policies on the remittances of profits by foreign firms.

Nations recently attaining independence, or about to do so, are likely to face great political uncertainty. In many cases, a nation secures widespread political cohesion on the issue of gaining independence but not on what policies should be followed after independence. In addition, new nations frequently lack experienced political leadership and undergo considerable turmoil while experience is gained and the policies and political power of various groups are tested.

The role to be played by private enterprise and the attitudes toward foreign investment are not always clarified in the early stages of organizing a new nation. Political power may swing from one party to another, and great uncertainty may exist as to what national policies toward international business are likely to emerge.

Internal rebellion may be an extreme stage of social unrest and disorder. The situation in the late 1960s between the central government of Nigeria and Biafra illustrates the kind of political risk that can occur. The effects on foreign business may be similar to those on domestic business or they may be accentuated because of the leverage that the opposing groups think they have in gaining support by putting pressure on foreign firms.

Armed conflicts between nations such as the ones that have occurred between India and Pakistan and Israel and the Arab states can greatly affect the feasibility and profitability of foreign business operations.

An extreme case of political risk arising out of new alliances by a nation would be a situation in which a previously noncommunist nation establishes close relations with a communist country. Such was the case in Indonesia during the early 1960s. New pressures were placed on foreign enterprise, and the alliance offered Indonesia the possibility of alternatives to foreign enterprise.

New international alliances would also include the case where a country joins a common market or free-trade area and in the process agrees to give preference in certain ways to business activities of common market nationality. Or, as in the case of the Andean Common Market in

Latin America, the member countries agree to harmonize their policies toward foreign private investment. When such intergovernmental agreements are concluded, some national policies under which international enterprises are operating may drastically change. Still another example is the action taken in 1970 by the European Economic Commission to reconsider its association agreement with Greece because the commission disapproved of the political behavior of the Greek military regime.

Political Risk Effects

The principal ways that political risk are likely to influence international business operations are shown in Figure 15.1. They fall into two general categories. New operational restrictions, loss of transfer freedom, contract breaches and revisions, tax policies, damage to property and personnel will change the operating environment for the international enterprise, usually in a negative way. Confiscation, expropriation, and, in some cases, contract breaches eliminate completely the feasibility of foreign operations.

Confiscation and Expropriation. In the case of both confiscation and expropriation, a government takes over a business activity. The owners are compensated in an expropriation but not in a confiscation. An example of the former is the Congolese expropriation of the mining properties of Union Minière, S.A. in 1967. The Cuban takeover of foreign investment in 1960 was a confiscation.

Expropriation is the recognized legal right of any sovereign government. Normally, however, the taking of private foreign-owned property must be for the public interest, and the private owners must be given "prompt, adequate, and effective compensation." Expropriation under the right of eminent domain is a not uncommon occurrence even in the United States, where the government appropriates private land for highway construction and urban renewal projects and where local and state governments take over electric-power companies and other public-utility services from private owners. If voluntary agreement cannot be reached between the parties as to compensation, legal procedures exist for adjudicating the issue.

When discussing the subject of expropriation as related to international business, some clarification as to definitions is necessary.[7] Strictly speaking, the term expropriation refers to a governmental action to dispossess someone of his property. In a loose manner, the term has been used to cover a continuum of government actions which interfere with normal management rights. Along this continuum is so-called creeping

---

[7] For an examination of the law and practice of expropriation in Argentina, Brazil, Chile, Mexico, Peru, Venezuela, and the United States, see Andreas F. Lowenfeld, ed., *Expropriation in the Americas: A Comparative Law Study* (New York: The Dunellen Co., 1971).

expropriation—restrictive government actions that steadily and gradually curtail the freedom of management in operating a business. But the intent of acts likely to be described as creeping expropriation is generally that of increasing a nation's share of the benefits from international enterprise while allowing the firm to continue its operations.

Another clarification should be made between expropriation and nationalization. Expropriation normally refers to the taking of a single property or business activity by the state. Nationalization usually means the taking of all activities or properties in a certain field—such as the nationalization of the steel industry in Great Britain, of the banks in Tanzania, and petroleum distribution in Ceylon. Nationalization may involve a number of expropriations.

The number of expropriations and nationalizations since World War II has been significant, though only a relatively small share of international business activity has been affected. And this form of political risk continues to be important in selected areas and selected fields of business activity. The techniques for achieving the goals of expropriation and nationalization have become more varied and ingenious, but as one scholar has recently observed, "the straightforward, standard form of expropriation and nationalization is not yet extinct and not really significantly diminishing in frequency or magnitude—it is alive and well in South America, Africa, and the Middle East."[8]

Some selected cases of major expropriations of U.S. and British private foreign investment are shown in Figure 15.2. Geographically, British losses have been concentrated in former colonies. For U.S. firms, the bulk of the expropriations were concentrated in Latin America. As measured by the number of individual firms deprived, insurance has been the most vulnerable British foreign investment, with export-import trade, commercial banking, and petroleum product distribution next in order of popularity. In contrast, expropriations of U.S. firms have been concentrated in petroleum, especially distribution, followed by public utilities and manufacturing. The manufacturing cases involved the production and distribution of detergents in Iraq and Algeria and a textile manufacturing joint venture with the government in Nigeria.

A recent study by the U.S. government identified 70 current situations in noncommunist countries of nationalizations, expropriations, negotiated sales, or contract disputes involving property in which U.S. corporations have a majority or minority interest.[9] Of the total situations, 16 were in Chile alone. The large majority of the cases are resource industries and banking and insurance operations. Aside from several situations

---

[8] J. F. Truitt, "Expropriation of Foreign Investment: Summary of the Post–World War II Experience of American and British Investors in the Less Developed Countries," *Journal of International Business Studies,* Fall 1970, pp. 21–34.

[9] *Nationalization, Expropriation, and Other Takings of United States and Certain Foreign Property Since 1960,* Bureau of Intelligence and Research, U.S. Department of State, November 30, 1971.

FIGURE 15.2
Expropriations of U.S. and British Private Foreign
Investment: Selected Cases

U.S. Direct Private Foreign Investment
  Bolivia, 1952, tin and petroleum
  Guatemala, 1953, land
  Argentina, 1958, utilities
  Brazil, 1959–60, utilities
  Indonesia, 1960–65, petroleum and rubber plantations
  Ceylon, 1962, petroleum distribution
  Iraq, 1965, bank facilities
  Algeria, 1966–67, insurance and detergent manufacture
  Chile, 1967, utilities

British Direct Private Foreign Investment
  Burma, 1948 collectivization of agriculture, forestry,
    river transport, and petroleum
  Ceylon, 1948, rubber plantations and tea estates
  Iran, 1951, petroleum
  India, 1955, banking
  Egypt, 1956–64, Suez Maritime Canal Company,
    banking, agriculture, commerce, and manufacturing
  Burma, 1963, banking and commerce
  Tanzania, 1967, banking, manufacturing, and trade

Source: J. F. Truitt, "Expropriation of Private Foreign Investment," (Ph.D. diss., Indiana University, 1969).

in Chile, virtually no manufacturing industries have been affected. Another interesting result of the study is the extent to which settlements have eventually been worked out. Of some 51 actions initiated in the period 1961–68, 40 have been settled and 11 were still unresolved at the time of the study. The study also reports that efforts at settlement are underway in all current situations and an agreed settlement is considered likely in most cases.

To the sophisticated international enterprise, expropriation risk is not a bar to investment but an element to be weighed against prospective gains. Over time, the risk may increase. Nevertheless, the international enterprise may conclude that the profit possibilities up to the time when the risk of expropriation is high are sufficiently attractive to make the project of interest. Such an approach has been characteristic of the international petroleum industry.

Recent experience with expropriations also suggests that companies can gain as well as lose by expropriation, even though the international enterprise may be more interested in the right to continue to do business than in the payment for assets. In 1970, the government of Peru took over the 51 percent interest that Chase Manhattan Bank held in the Peruvian Banco Continental. The government reportedly paid Chase more than twice the price Chase originally paid for its stock in 1964, and roughly three times the quoted market value of the shares.

Unilateral Acts. The international manager, conditioned by the legal norms of the advanced Western countries, may suffer considerable emotional as well as business shock when he is informed by a nation that it is unilaterally altering the terms of its contract or agreement with his enterprise. In his home environment, the manager was most likely indoctrinated with the philosophy that contracts are morally and legally sacred, that both parties to an agreement must agree on revisions, that disagreements are adjudicated through courts, and that penalties are imposed upon the party violating a contract. To his consternation, the manager discovers that familiar norms are not universally accepted and that no effective international legal system exists to enforce his norms.

The prevailing philosophy in many countries, particularly the newly independent nations, is that concessions or agreements can be revoked or revised at the discretion of the host country if the national interests are no longer being adequately served. In practice such revisions are likely to occur when the goals of national governments change, when a new political regime feels that contract revisions will strengthen its domestic political support, and when key circumstances surrounding an agreement change.

In September 1969, for example, a group of young military officers seized control of Libya, sweeping aside the monarchy of King Idris I, and established a "socialist republic." The announced goal of the new regime was to reduce foreign influences in the country.

Shortly after the 1969 change in government, Libya began to revise its agreements with the international oil companies. One of the reported motivations was the need felt by the new regime to prove its toughness to the people by standing up to the oil companies, and the oil companies were blamed for corrupting the previous government with bribes.

Concessions negotiated with colonial governments or with newly independent regimes when the bargaining power of the governments was weak, and when few foreign investors were attracted, have been vulnerable to revocation and renegotiation after a change in government. This is especially so when the success of the pioneering foreign investors has stimulated other investors to come forward with more attractive offers. Many new governments feel that they are not obliged to suffer under the terms of the original agreement. In the absence of international legal constraints, such governments are likely to invoke their maximum degree of bargaining power for unilateral revision of concession contracts.

Political Instability and Political Risk

To what extent is "political instability" a reliable index to political risk? The question deserves special attention because political instability is so frequently cited as an obstacle to flows of private foreign investment.

In a broad study of investors from the 12 major capital-exporting countries—Belgium, Canada, Denmark, France, Germany, Italy, Japan, the Netherlands, Sweden, Switzerland, United Kingdom, and United States—many investors reported that they had eliminated countries and even whole geographical regions from their investment considerations for political reasons. By far the most frequently cited political obstacle was political uncertainty or political instability.[10]

With such a high sensitivity to political instability, it is quite possible that inexperienced international enterprises have missed business opportunities because they have perceived more political risk than actually existed. When the international manager with limited background and experience perceives political risk, it often means that he is not familiar with the political patterns and styles of a foreign country. He would feel insecure trying to operate in a strange environment. In such cases, the problem is to come to terms with an unfamiliar rather than hostile situation.

Another possibility is that the international manager is applying ethnocentric standards, based on political systems with which he is familiar, which are not appropriate to the country being considered. As one study of international business experience notes, "Governments reject many charges of political instability as due to lack of knowledge or unfounded fears on the part of the foreign businessman. There is evidence, they say, that political differences that would pass at home as 'natural discord' become 'disturbing imbalances' when viewed by investors in a distant country. 'The political struggles that take place within a parliamentary regime,' says one government spokesman, 'should not be mistaken for political instability.' "[11] In other words, the criteria for political instability are different for each political system.

An approach to political instability that can be highly misleading is to interpret frequent changes in the leadership of governments as political instability. France, after World War II, had many different heads of government until the return of de Gaulle. Yet continuity in governmental policies was maintained by a strong professional civil service with considerable stability and strong institutional norms, characteristics of the French political system.

From 1947 to 1970, Brazil had 11 presidents of the Republic. It is not surprising that the flamboyant political style of that country was widely interpreted by international managers as presenting a high degree

---

[10] National Industrial Conference Board, *Obstacles and Incentives to Private Foreign Investment, 1967–1968*, 1 (New York, 1969).

[11] National Industrial Conference Board, *Obstacles and Incentives to Private Foreign Investment, 1962–1964* (New York, 1965).

of political instability. But an analysis of the links between political events and two principal indexes of the business environment, namely economic-growth trends and rates of inflation, suggests that such links were not strong except for the three-year period from 1961 to 1964 of the Goulart administration. The growth rate of Brazil fluctuated during a few of the years, but the declines can be explained by the effect of a serious drought in one period and the collapse of the international coffee market in another period. Inflation has been generally high, but the sharpest rise in inflation prior to the Goulart regime occurred in 1959 during the Kubitschek regime, one of Brazil's most stable political periods. President Kubitschek was determined to push the construction of a new capital city at Brasilia to the "point of no return" so that the project could not be abandoned after his term of office. And to accomplish this big push, measures were taken that resulted in a major increase in inflation.

A reasonable presumption for international business operations may be that frequent and unexpected changes in government leadership should not be interpreted per se as political instability. The more fundamental question is whether strong factions are present with divergent views from those of the government on policies toward foreign business. Furthermore, the potential for political instability and political risk in countries with centralized political control, sometimes headed by a military dictator, can also be great. One-man governments can often behave erratically and generate underlying tensions. Considerable uncertainty may exist as to how an orderly transition to a successor will be possible.

FORECASTING POLITICAL RISK

As international corporations are becoming more experienced and more widely involved, they are beginning to establish political forecasting staffs on more or less the same level as economic forecasting staffs.

The task of political forecasting involves four basic steps: First, an understanding of the type of government presently in power, its patterns of political behavior, and its norms for stability; second, an analysis of the multinational enterprise's own product or operations to identify the kind of political risk likely to be involved in particular areas, for example, is the problem one of macro or micro risk; third, a determination of the source of the potential risk. If the risk is expropriation, is the source that of socialistic or nationalistic philosophy? If the risk is on operational restrictions, is the source that of local businessmen? Having developed a familiarity with the political system of a country, having identified the kinds of political risk to which the business operation can be vulnerable, having determined the political force or group that may be the source of that risk, the fourth step is to project into the future the possibility of political risk in terms of probability and time horizons.

Throughout the process, the emphasis must be on political forces that are difficult to anticipate and can cause abrupt changes in the environment for the business firm. To repeat, changes in governments, in parties, and in leaders may or may not involve political risk.

The necessary background information on the political environment of a country goes far beyond a knowledge of the attitudes and policies of the present administration to foreign private enterprise. The need is to understand within a nation's historical context its type of government, its political parties and forces and their philosophies.[12] The challenge is to understand the path along which all policies and attitudes have been travelling, particularly those of the political groups that are not shaping the policies of the present administration but are likely to do so.

The second step in evaluating the vulnerability of a company to political risk is to analyze its operations, with the following questions in mind:

1. Are periodic external inputs of new technology required?
2. Will the project be competing strongly with local nationals who are in, or trying to enter, the same field?
3. Is the operation dependent on natural resources, particularly minerals or oil?
4. Does the investment put pressure on balance of payments?
5. Does the enterprise have a strong monopoly position in the local market?
6. Is the product socially essential and acceptable?

In general, projects or products that contribute strongly to national goals are likely to receive favorable political attention when first initiated. But as the projects become taken for granted over time and a local capacity is developed to operate such projects, political favoritism may shift to new fields.

The third step is the most difficult. Once the types of risk to which a company is especially vulnerable have been analyzed, how can the sources of these risks and their strength be identified and evaluated? The easiest situation is that of a parliamentary democracy where the opposition views can be determined from parliamentary debates or political platforms. At the other extreme is the difficult task of determining views and weighing the political strength of antagonistic opposition

---

[12] See Lee C. Nehrt, *The Political Climate For Foreign Private Investment* (New York: Praeger Publishers, Inc., 1970) for an excellent analysis of political risk in North Africa. Nehrt suggests a model for political analysis and applies it to Tunisia, Algeria, and Morocco.

forces in a dictatorship where considerable censorship occurs. In such cases, the task of political forecasting should include an examination of the views of political exiles. This final step of forecasting the specific environmental risks may result in a considerable amount of error and uncertainty. But over time, skill can be developed to accomplish this task within limits of probability. In retrospect, it appears quite certain that many expropriations of minerals and petroleum operations could have been forecast with reasonable certainty. The same is true with changes in contract conditions and the nationalization of the various public utility companies.

How One Company Forecasts

Political-risk forecasting as practiced by one major international company calls first for two projections: one on the chances of a particular political group being in power during discrete forecast periods, and another on the types of government interference to be expected from each of the political groups. From these data, probability estimates of the political risks likely to arise during specific time periods can be calculated. Finally, the present value of expected cash flows, or the internal rate of return from the investment project under consideration can be adjusted to reflect the timing and magnitude of the risk probabilities.[13]

The following over-simplified example shows how the first projection can be arrived at. It assumes that there are only two political parties concerned—the Conservatives and the Radicals. The Conservatives are in power in 1970. The next election will come in 1971, and the following one in 1976. It assumes that the elected party will stay in power for a 5-year period.

The consensus of the political analysts, shown in Figure 15.3, is that the probability of being elected in 1971 is 70 percent for the Conservatives and 30 percent for the Radicals. If elected in 1971, the Conservatives are estimated to have a 70 percent probability of being reelected in 1976. Thus, following only the left half of the probability tree, the probability of a Conservative government from 1976 through 1980 is 49 percent (70 percent of 70 percent).

Now turning to the right half of the probability tree in Figure 15.3, if the Radicals are elected in 1971, for which there is a 30 percent chance, the probability of the Conservatives regaining power in 1976 has been estimated at 50 percent. Thus the weighted probability through this chain of future events is an additional 15 percent probability in

---

[13] This section is based on unpublished research carried out by a major international company. The procedure follows the general outline suggested by Robert B. Stobaugh, Jr., "How to Analyze Foreign Investment Climates," *Harvard Business Review,* September–October, 1969.

FIGURE 15.3
Quantitative Political Forecast for a Hypothetical Country, 1971–80

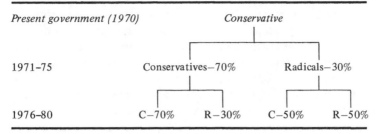

1976 for the Conservatives (50 percent of 30 percent). By joining the political chances of the Conservatives through both of the possible paths, the combined probability of the Conservatives coming to power in 1976 is 64 percent—the 49 percent chance of staying in power throughout the period plus the 15 percent chance of regaining power following a Radical victory. This leaves a 36 percent probability of a Radical government coming to power in 1976.

The next step is to assess the probabilities of risk associated with each political group. To simplify the illustration, only one type of risk is dealt with—confiscation. In this case the consensus of political analysts is that the Conservatives present virtually no risk of confiscation in either period. But if the Radicals come to power, there will be a 50 percent probability of confiscation in the first period, and a 60 percent probability in the second.

Finally, the probabilities of being in power, and the propensity to confiscation of each political group are weighted to give an average risk of confiscation during each time period. In the case of the example, the results, in Figure 15.4, show a 15 percent probability of confiscation in 1971–75 and a 22 percent probability in 1976–80.

Confiscation is, of course, only one of many types of risk likely to

FIGURE 15.4
Probability of Confiscation

	1971–75	1976–80
Conservative Party		
a. Probability of being in power	70%	64%
b. Risk of confiscation	0	0
Radical Party		
c. Probability of being in power	30	36
d. Risk of confiscation	50	60
Weighted average risk of confiscation		
(b × a) + (d × c)	15	22

be encountered. Additional types of risk can be incorporated into the overall forecast by the same method.

Using only three types of possible interference: no interference, confiscation, and expropriation, the hypothetical example could have 10 different possible outcomes over a 15-year period, ranging from early confiscation at one extreme (a 15 percent probability) to no interference over the entire period (a 10.7 percent probability).

The final step is to adjust the anticipated cash flow pattern according to each of the possible 10 outcomes and calculate the present values of the adjusted cash flows. If three of the possible outcomes, for example, show negative values and their combined probability totals 33.3 percent, the project has one chance in three of a loss due to political risk. Also the adjusted present values of all the outcomes can be averaged after weighting each outcome by its probability of occurrence. If the result is negative, the political-risk analysis favors a negative decision on the project even though there is only one chance in three of a losing outcome.

If different political assumptions appear to be reasonable possibilities, additional political-risk appraisals can be made on the basis of the new assumptions. Or the analysis can be extended to consider the effect of changes in the timing and form of the project.

MINIMIZING POLITICAL RISK

It is obvious that political-risk forecasting can be crucial to the international enterprise in reaching a "go" or "no go" decision on a particular project. It may be less obvious that risk identification and evaluation can guide the firm in reshaping a project so that a "no go" can become a modified "go." The international enterprise is not helpless in the face of political risk. To the contrary, it has a significant range of options for minimizing the magnitude and effects of such risks.[14] Some of the possibilities have already been discussed in Chapter 10.

Summary

The international manager operates in many sovereign political units whose systems differ radically in form and philosophy from those of his own country. Lack of familiarity with foreign political environments and lack of a process for systematic evaluation of political risks increases the probability that the mutinational enterprise will invest in countries when it should not or refrain from investing when it should.

Some sophisticated international enterprises are beginning to establish forecasting staff units to improve the techniques for assessing, forecast-

---

[14] See Jean Boddewyn and Etienne F. Cracco, "The Political Game in World Business," *Columbia Journal of World Business,* January–February 1972, pp. 45–56.

ing, and minimizing political risk; and to make more objective the political-risk elements included in decision making. Such enterprises will be in a far better position to deal successfully with the uncertainties and challenges of the international business environment.

EXERCISES AND DISCUSSION QUESTIONS

1. How would you define political risk? Would you consider a political risk the "Inability to convert into dollars foreign currency representing earnings on, or return of, the investment or compensation for sale or disposition of the investment," one of the items included as political risk in the U.S. risk-guaranty program?

2. "Political stability is equated with democracy, with elections, with modernization, with a broad-income distribution, with consensus, with participation, and so forth. This conception is derived from an ideologized model of what the American type of democracy is supposed to be like, projected on to other societies." Evaluate and discuss.

3. "When Castro came to power in Cuba, the total book value of U.S. business enterprise in Cuba was greater than in any other Latin American country except Venezuela. On a per capita basis, U.S. investment in Cuba was over three times the average for the rest of Latin America. One third of the U.S. investment in 1959 was in public utilities. Another large share was in agriculture, particularly sugar production. Seven of the ten largest latifundios (agricultural estates) were owned by U.S. interests." How would you have assessed the macro political risk in Cuba prior to the revolution?

4. How would you rank types of business activities as to their political-risk vulnerability? What is the basis for your ranking?

5. What is the relationship between political instability and political risk for international business? What criteria would you use to identify political instability?

6. What steps are required for political-risk forecasting? Why is the time dimension important?

7. How can a business project be modified so as to reduce political risk?

16

NATIONAL-CONTROL
FORECASTING

ANOTHER IMPORTANT CLASS OF RISKS arises from the attempts of different governments to control international business activities within and beyond their boundaries. Controls imposed by governments can make a considerable difference to a firm's profit and growth performance and can be as important as market and competitive considerations in the allocation of a firm's resources.[1] The controls of even the most stable countries, moreover, will be far from immutable in the face of the increasing importance of international business.

As defined in Chapter 9, controls are used here in a particular sense to cover anything done by a government directly or indirectly to influence or regulate international business, whether through its operations, ownership, or existence. Controls include incentives as well as disincentives, controls over multinational firms of local origin as well as foreign firms, controls aimed *primarily* at international business activities even if purely local firms could be affected, and all controls which have a differential effect between local and international activities.

---

[1] National Industrial Conference Board, *Obstacles and Incentives to Private Foreign Investment, 1967–1968* Studies in Business Policy 1, no. 130 (1969) : 2. Comparing results of their 1962–64 and 1967–68 studies of obstacles and incentives to private foreign investment, the National Industrial Conference Board stated: "Only one trend stands out clearly from a comparison of the two studies. Investors cooperating in the current study cite governmental restrictions on the operations of their subsidiaries with much greater frequency than did cooperators in the 1962–1964 study. Government pressures for local participation, local content requirements, price controls, and restrictions on the entry of expatriate managers and technicians are now cited as obstacles to investment about twice as often as they were before. General charges of government interference with business are also about twice as common."

To make predictions of the changing pattern of controls requires an underlying theory. Classification of countries as more or less risky solely on the basis of a general review of their individual situation is not adequate. Without a sound underlying theory, predictions are almost certain to be excessively influenced by immediate past conditions. Important determinants of change may be given inadequate weight, and predictions are likely to be inconsistent as between countries. Many businessmen, for example, relate the risk of controls to the economic and political stability of a country and completely ignore signs pointing to additional major controls from such stable countries as Canada or Australia.

In Part III the different classes of controls that governments have used were described, and the need for a predictive theory of controls was introduced. This chapter presents one attempt to develop such a theory of controls. Working from objectives and decision rules of representative firms and representative countries, predictions are made of the overall pattern of controls over international business and of control strategies for countries in similar strategic positions with respect to international business. Readers should regard this as only one example of possible theories and use it as a datum against which to test and refine their own theories. The field of control prediction is not yet well developed, but that does not mean that the international businessman can ignore the need to base his decisions on some prediction of how controls will affect the various alternatives open to him.

INTERNATIONAL BUSINESS AS A GAME

The imposition of controls over international business can be depicted as a vast international game. There are players, moves, strategies, and payoffs. The players are firms and countries, and the moves are changes in location of business investment and location of operations on the side of firms, while countries may change the nature and level of controls. The moves of the players interact to determine the payoff to each. For purposes of this theory the players are depicted as representative firms and representative countries acting to achieve payoffs of return on investment for firms and national benefits for countries.

Although multinational firms in the real world aim for return to the firm rather than return to the economies in which they operate, neither firms nor countries are motivated solely by rational economic calculation. The limitations to rationality in firms have been shown clearly in many studies.[2] Few people would attempt to argue that countries act rationally.

---

[2] Yair Aharoni, *The Foreign Investment Decision Process* (Boston, Mass.: Division of Research, Harvard Graduate School of Business Administration, 1966); Richard M. Cyert and James G. March, *A Behavioral Theory of the Firm* (Englewood Cliffs, N.J.: Prentice-Hall, 1963).

Pressure groups, coalitions, selective perception, and a range of other behavioral phenomena better explain particular decisions. Real-world objectives, however, would produce descriptions so complicated that any simple prediction would be impossible. Nor is it necessary for a theory to be based on completely realistic assumptions. Assumptions need only be sufficiently good approximations of reality for the purpose in hand in order to yield sufficiently accurate predictions. A useful theory should be simple and efficient, explaining a lot with a little.[3] The success of simplifications must then be judged by the success of the predictions and not by the theory's correspondence with reality.

An assumption of rationality seems to provide an efficient basis for predictions when applied to an aggregation of countries and firms over time. It can predict an unfolding pattern of controls over international business very similar to that which has actually emerged, as evidenced with footnotes throughout the chapter. For any individual firm, however, the investment pattern may not approximate a profit maximizing one, and for any individual country, the pressures influencing its policies at any point in time may produce controls quite contrary to the maximization of national benefits.

The international business game proposed here is a non-zero-sum game. Rewards to any one of the players do not necessarily reduce total rewards to the opposing players by the same amount. But there is definite conflict between the objectives of the different players. A control which increases the benefits to one country will usually reduce the payoff to firms in some way. The same control may also decrease the benefits to some other country. For example, the main effect might be to switch the firm's productive activity from one country to another, with a secondary effect of decreasing the firm's profits. The players are thus not arranged simply with countries on one side and firms on the other. Countries also compete with countries, and firms compete with firms. It is the competition among countries for shares of a virtually independent total of business activity globally that plays the major role in determining the pattern of controls. This idea moves well away from a common assumption in international business that controls may be explained from an examination of the conflict between firms and individual countries independently of other countries.[4]

The game is sequential and dynamic with continually evolving action and reaction. Players do not all disclose their hands at the same time

---

[3] Milton J. Friedman, *Essays in Positive Economics* (Chicago, Ill.: University of Chicago Press, 1953), Part I.

[4] See Charles P. Kindleberger, *American Business Abroad* (New Haven: Yale University Press, 1969), p. 150 et seq.; Raymond Vernon, "Conflict and Resolution Between Foreign Direct Investors and Less Developed Countries," *Public Policy* Fall 1968, pp. 333–51.

before knowing their opponents' moves. With a large number of players competing under these conditions it is not feasible to extend the formal presentation of the game to the point of proving optimum strategies. The prediction of strategies is based instead on the following simplified sequence of play:

1.   International firms locate business activity for a "practical maximization" of expected return on capital subject to allowances for the risk of potential controls.

2.   Countries alter controls to maximize national benefits, bearing in mind the likely reactions of firms and ultimate reactions of other countries.

3.   Firms realign existing operations and redirect new investment in the light of the changed controls.

4.   Other countries feel indirect effects of the changed controls and move to alter their own controls.

The prime focus of this chapter is the prediction of step 2 in the sequence—the strategies of countries. Step 4, of course, will be covered by the same prediction. This prediction is itself made against the backdrop prediction of where firms locate their activity with an existing set of controls and how they react to changes in controls. Firms' objectives are therefore the starting point for the analysis.

OBJECTIVES AND DECISION RULES
OF THE REPRESENTATIVE FIRM

The representative international firm is defined as motivated toward a "practical maximization" of the present value of expected net cash flows from its activities. While it would be theoretically possible for the representative firm to calculate for any point in time the location of further investment and the relocation of production activity that would maximize the present value of future profits, the practical difficulties in making such a calculation are legion. Not the least would be the impossibility of collecting adequate data on costs and demand to choose between a large number of alternatives. Instead of representing the decision process of the representative firm by the impracticable programming calculation that would be needed, it is replaced by a 12-step approximation to maximization. This is summarized in Table 16.1. Many of the steps incorporated in this decision process coincide with what is widely regarded as good practice in international business decision making. Only the salient points will be outlined at this stage, however, as the individual steps are examined in more detail in the next chapter, which covers the building of a global strategy.

The horizon year is the target year which the firm chooses as the basis for setting sales targets and building an optimum location of production activity to meet those targets. A four- or five-year horizon is

TABLE 16.1

The Representative Firm's Decision Process for Practical Maximization

1. Select an horizon year.
2. Predict country demands for products supplied by firm, annually up to the horizon year.
3. Decide marketing emphasis to be placed on each country, for example, full development, distributorship, agency.
4. Set annual target sales for each country to horizon year.
5. List countries where operations *must* be located to meet targets in horizon year.
6. List countries where operation in horizon year is not required but probably economic.
7. Estimate costs of investment and operation for the set of alternative sites, and the transport and tariff costs from these into alternative markets.
8. Calculate an optimum location and logistics pattern for horizon year.
9. Prepare schedules of annual additions to investment that meet the annual targets and the horizon patterns.
10. Calculate the expected cash flow and return on proposed investments.
11. Calculate limits to available investment.
12. Align investment plans and sales targets.

common in the real world.[5] An earlier horizon may produce a pattern of investment location that is far from optimum for the subsequent pattern of market demand, while a later horizon may produce a pattern in which the profits are well below what they might be for some time.

The dominant role of marketing in the modern firm is emphasized by the next three steps. Market potential is taken as the basis for allocating the firm's effort.[6] From a prediction of country demands the representative firm decides the marketing emphasis to be placed on each country and sets annual sales targets to the horizon year. These decisions will usually be based on broad indicators of the profit potential from supplying a market and the competitive vulnerability from not doing so.

With market targets established, the next stage is the calculation of the investment in additional capacity required to meet the targets. There will be some countries where controls make it imperative to locate production if the targets for their markets are to be met. A set of alternative production investments to meet the remaining capacity needed for the total horizon target can then be generated. These alternatives will again be based on broad indicators of what are likely to be the most economic sites; for example, low resource cost, low outward transport, low entry barriers to other markets. From these, the alternative with the lowest cost of meeting the sales targets in the horizon year is calculated.[7]

[5] George A. Steiner and Warren M. Cannon, *Multinational Corporate Planning* (New York: Macmillan Co., 1966), pp. 85, 97, 107.

[6] Judd Polk, Irene W. Meister, and Lawrence A. Veit, *U.S. Production Abroad and the Balance of Payments* (New York: National Industrial Conference Board, 1966), pp. 59–61.

[7] Robert E. McGarrah, "Logistics for the International Manufacturer," *Harvard Business Review,* March–April 1966.

This horizon investment alternative is next translated into annual investment schedules over the intervening years. A practical decision rule would be to invest each year in those additions needed to achieve the horizon objective that would give the lowest cost of meeting the next year's targets. The procedure next moves to return-on-investment calculation. For each proposed addition the calculation would be based on the incremental net cash flow accruing from it, estimated as far into the future as practicable and reduced by the expected effects of controls and other risks. Any limit the firm's resources may place on investment is now calculated and projects accepted in decreasing order of return on capital, so long as the return is above the return from other alternatives open to the firm. Finally, if the investment limit is operative, the whole process will be repeated with lowered sales targets. If there is surplus investment capacity then sales targets will have to be raised.

FIRM'S INITIAL STRATEGIES

What is the likely pattern to emerge from the strategies of representative international firms? The starting point for the prediction is the schedule of the firm's market targets. For many products it is the markets of the developed countries in which the demand will build up first. Higher levels of disposable income generally lead to faster adoption of new consumer goods and higher wages rates to faster adoption of labor-saving industrial goods.[8] The firms that supply these more advanced markets gain the advantage of the earliest experience and hence a higher position on the learning curve and also the earliest economies of scale.[9] It follows then that a rational global strategy would be to move into these markets early and from these to successively less attractive markets for the products in which the firm has established a lead.

Using this schedule of market targets, the representative firm will locate production through the process already described. For new products this is likely to mean location of as much production as possible close to the more advanced markets where the managers of the international enterprise are already located. At this stage, speedy adjustment of the marketing mix carries greater weight for profits than siting for minimum production cost.[10] But as the product matures, design tends to become less flexible and production costs more important. In step with this, the demand in other markets will grow to justify production on an economic scale and transport and tariff costs add a further incen-

---

[8] Raymond Vernon, "International Investment and International Trade in the Product Cycle," *Quarterly Journal of Economics*, May 1966, pp. 190–207.

[9] Louis T. Wells, "A Product Life Cycle for International Trade," *Journal of Marketing*, July 1968, pp. 1–16.

[10] Vernon, "International Investment and International Trade in the Product Cycle."

tive to relocate production away from the initial base. Production will then tend to move to the lowest cost sites taking into account the cost of transport, tariffs, and other controls—actual and expected. This trend, though, will be conditioned by the sequence in which markets develop. Established plants, because they represent sunk costs, may be retained when later market expansion might suggest relocation at otherwise lower cost sites.

Relocation may also be hindered by internal management rules of the firm. Exports to other countries are frequently discouraged or prohibited for subsidiaries as a matter of policy.[11] It is not difficult to show that a profit-maximizing production and distribution pattern for an international corporation as a whole would not allow free competition between units of the same firm. Subsidiaries developing in the same field as a strong international parent can be confronted with an established network of foreign activity by the parent and its other subsidiaries in what could otherwise be potential export markets for an independent firm.

There are exceptions, of course, to the general pattern suggested by the "product cycle" approach. One exception relates to investments in raw materials extraction and certain stages of raw materials processing which can only be located economically near the source of raw materials. Other exceptions occur when new products are developed to meet culturally conditioned demands specific to one market.

The firm's organizational evolution as it expands internationally will influence the location of top management functions. A likely pattern is a "hen-and-chickens" approach with a large home base in a developed market on which strategic decisions are centralized, while subsidiaries are established elsewhere and local management is expected to introduce products and experience from the parent rather than initiate new areas of activity.[12] Such a pattern can foster a caretaker type of subsidiary management not required to use great entrepreneurial skill in forming and shaping the firm.[13] Promotion to headquarters would be needed to exercise such skill, and this would further remove expertise from the country in which the subsidiary is located.

Following the same sequence of development, a rational business strategy with regard to research and development would be to concentrate on producing innovations first for the markets of developed countries. The worldwide expansion of the international corporation would provide

[11] Donald T. Brash, *American Investment in Australian Industry* (Canberra: Australian National University Press, 1966), p. 228; A. E. Safarian, *Foreign Ownership of Canadian Industry* (Toronto: McGraw-Hill Book Co., 1966), p. 133.

[12] Gilbert H. Clee and Alfred di Scipio, "Creating a World Enterprise," *Harvard Business Review,* November–December 1959.

[13] Kenneth Simmonds, "Multinational? Well, Not Quite," *Columbia Journal of World Business,* Fall 1966.

a bigger market against which to justify expenditure, and reinforce research activity in the developed countries with little incentive to duplicate research facilities elsewhere.[14] The establishment of research facilities in many less developed countries would be limited—perhaps only adaptation centers. This would mean little support and feedback from industry for universities and advanced research institutions in such countries and fewer opportunities locally for top graduates—all of which would reinforce a brain drain.[15]

It also follows from the profit objectives of representative firms that they will arrange their investment so that it is protected against a future control when the cost of protection is less than the resulting reduction in the expected cost of the control. The expected cost of a control is the loss of profits that would result from its imposition, multiplied by the probability that the control will be imposed. In the real world, firms may seek local associates or raise debt finance. There is an incentive to those providing local finance or productive services to act as a buffer against local pressures for increases in controls. The retention of marketing, management, or research expertise in the hands of expatriates can also limit the risk of expropriation.[16]

Where the international firm supplies market demand in one country with raw materials or products produced in another country, reduction of risk may take the additional form of developing alternative sources of supply. Alternative sources would lower the level of controls of maximum benefit to the current supplier country because of the increased likelihood of business being transferred to other sources. International corporations in the oil, mineral, rubber, and produce fields have resorted to such strategies in the past.[17]

FIRMS' REACTIONS TO CHANGES IN CONTROLS

A change in any control may alter the optimum location pattern for a firm's existing operations and possibly the ranking of alternatives on its investment schedule. For every control change that increases profitability of local production in a particular country there are likely to be some representative firms for which the change leads to an investment being made in that country that would otherwise fall outside their

[14] Brash, *American Investment in Australian Industry,* p. 150; Safarian, *Canadian Industry,* p. 174.

[15] Committee on Government Operations, House of Representatives, *The Brain Drain into the United States of Scientists, Engineers, and Physicians* (Washington D.C.: U.S. Government Printing Office, July 1967).

[16] Richard D. Robinson, "Conflicting Interest in International Business," *Business Review,* Boston University, Spring 1960, pp. 3–13.

[17] For example, see S. May and G. Plaza, "The Case Study of the United Fruit Company in Latin America," (Washington, D.C.: National Planning Association, 1959).

investment limits. Conversely, a change in controls that reduces profit-ability is likely to shift some existing operations to other countries and lower some alternatives on investment schedules so that they no longer fall within the investment limits. As a general rule, then, at the margin, foreign-business activity and investment will be discouraged when con-trols that decrease profitability are extended and encouraged when such controls are reduced.

But this is not the full story. There are classes of controls with other effects. Tariffs and local component requirements, for example, discrimi-nate among the production sites open to a firm for supplying a market. Their imposition will usually increase the cost of supplying a market from outside sources and, even though the cost of local production is likely to be increased too, lead to the transfer of more production activity into the local market. Another class of controls places restrictions on the transferability of resources. This class includes capital controls, in-ward or outward pricing rules, royalty, and dividend-remittance re-straints. These may also reduce the firm's after-tax profitability, which would discourage investment, yet the desire to make use of locally re-tained resources may induce more firms to expand local production.

OBJECTIVES AND DECISION RULES
OF REPRESENTATIVE COUNTRIES

We now turn to the objectives of countries. A representative country for this theory is motivated toward maximization of net national benefits. And national benefits embrace all those tangible and intangible objec-tives, already discussed in Part III, which countries consider as a basis for governmental action, such as contribution to development, expanded foreign exchange earnings, monetary stability, defense, economic inde-pendence, and national prestige. To specify a national-benefit function in full, together with measures for the achievement of each objective, would require a study of its own. For the purposes of this chapter, however, the general notion of national benefit is sufficient. Others have introduced similar omnibus concepts in referring to maximization of "net social benefits,"[18] "a social-welfare function,"[19] or adjusted "social yields."[20] In Chapter 7 it was explained that costs to the country must be balanced against the gains to calculate net benefits. Moreover, only the incremental benefits over domestic or international alternatives open to the country should be included. It is also assumed here that controls

---

[18] John H. Dunning, "The Multinational Enterprise," *Lloyd's Bank Review,* July 1970, p. 29.

[19] Kindleberger, *American Business Abroad,* p. 192.

[20] Vernon, "Conflict and Resolution Between Foreign Direct Investors and Less Developed Countries," p. 334.

are independent and their individual benefits additive. Country-control strategies can then be expressed in terms of a collection of separate controls.

The representative country acting rationally to maximize national benefit will set each individual control at its *control optimum* which is defined as the level at which the control brings maximum net national benefit. The national benefit from adjustment of any control is the incremental benefit accruing as a result of the adjustment. An increased control, for example, may increase the national benefit from investment and business activity which remains in the country as well as from that which comes on the new terms. But there may be an opportunity loss of the benefit from lost investment and business activity that would otherwise have come or remained. If a control is increased beyond its control optimum the loss of national benefit from discouraged international investment or business activity outweighs the gain from imposing the control.

Implicit in this definition of the control optimum for any control is an allowance for reactions by other countries, and reaction may be expected when alteration in controls will alter the control optimum of another country. The greater and the more immediate the effects on another country's business activity, the more likely the other country is to take matching action. For example, with a fixed supply of international business investment the lowering of controls by a less developed nation might siphon off a large proportion of the investment that another marginal recipient of such investment would have received. This second country might then move very quickly to offer the same or greater incentives. In many cases, however, countries will be unable to predict what reactions their actions will produce from individual competitor countries. There are too many countries, too many investors, and too many controls for individual effects to be assessed very accurately. The reaction of many other countries to change by one country is, moreover, likely to be a gradual process over time and best predicted as a decay in the benefit gained from a control as a function of time. Where it is clearly apparent that competition among countries can weaken each country's bargaining position and the number of such competing countries is relatively small, as in the case of the oil-producing countries, a possible strategy is to form a cartel and bargain as a group. This possibility, however, is limited to countries in an oligopoly situation as suppliers of raw materials.

GENERAL FEATURES OF COUNTRY STRATEGIES

The theory has now reached a stage where it is possible to derive some general features of country-control strategies from the juxtaposition of country objectives and decision rules against the prediction of strategies for representative firms.

Controls for which the control optima are likely to be high are those for which a given gain in national benefit would come with the smallest reduction in expected profits of investors or, what amounts to the same thing, where a given reduction in expected profits would be accompanied by large increments in national benefit. This may occur where a control:

a. results in a contribution to the country that is crucial to continued development;
b. was anticipated by firms and its imposition does not therefore alter the expected cash flow to firms or its position on the firms' investment schedules;
c. takes effect a considerable time in the future;
d. is not reflected in return-on-investment calculations;
e. restricts access to the local market to gain power over location of production.

An example of a control that might produce a major contribution to development with a small cost to firms is the requirement to use local nationals in the management of local activity. While it may impose some immediate costs, it can bring offsetting benefits.[21] A local top executive reduces the foreign image, cuts the cost of expatriate staff, introduces someone attuned to the local culture and influence network, and adds a local ally. For the country, the move contributes to the pool of trained management which is essential for continuing development.[22]

The controls anticipated by firms will depend very much on the firm's forecasting assumptions and on the messages countries have themselves relayed about future controls or the implications of their ideology. Cash flows will be heavily discounted for opportunities in countries with an image of opposition to capitalist ownership if it seems likely to lead to costly controls or expropriation.[23] The situation can be created where there is nothing to be lost from increased controls because they have already been discounted.

The further in the future increases in controls begin to take effect, the less the current discouragement. The effect is discounted by the rates used in the investment calculations of the investing firms. Any control affecting an investor's cash flow after the first 10 years is likely

---

[21] John C. Shearer, *High-Level Manpower in Overseas Subsidiaries* (Princeton, N.J.: Industrial Relations Section, Princeton University, 1960), Chapter 3.

[22] Peter P. Gabriel, *The International Transfer of Corporate Skills* (Boston: Graduate School of Business Administration, Harvard University, 1967); Harry G. Johnson, "The Multinational Corporation as a Development Agent," *Columbia Journal of World Business*, May–June 1970, pp. 25–30; Frederick Harbison and Charles A. Myers, *Industrialism and Industrial Man: The Problems of Labor and Management in Industrial Growth* (Cambridge, Mass.: Harvard University Press, 1960).

[23] National Industrial Conference Board, *Obstacles and Incentives to Private Foreign Investment 1967–1968*, pp. 9–10.

to carry little weight in the investment decision, because its discounted cost would be infinitesimal given the discounting rates commonly used for assessing international opportunities. A country that guaranteed income for the first 10 years, but required a renewal of license after that time, might actually increase its attraction to investors.

Regulations which do not affect cash-flow calculations and which do not show up in return-on-capital calculations are also potentially very significant. The right to expand into further areas of business within a country, for example, is unlikely to be highly weighted in a return-on-investment calculation for any investment that by itself is worth undertaking. Yet by removing this right, a country can retain opportunities for national firms, and it can protect itself against the international corporation expanding without bargaining separately for further access to the market. Controls that limit the share of foreign ownership also reduce foreign participation in a country's markets without reducing the return on investment to investing firms. If such controls are coupled with restricted access to local loan capital, then the investment inflow to the country may be unaffected yet obtained on reduced ownership terms. Finally, controls on transferring funds out of a country are also likely to create minimal discouragement to further initial investments if return on investment remains high and there are opportunities for profitable reinvestment locally.

Controls that restrict access to the local market to gain power over the location of production are also likely to have high control optima. Production for the home markets of many countries will not be located locally in the absence of controls, and production that has been located locally will tend for some to move to lower cost locations. Controls such as tariffs, import licensing, or local component requirements that would change firms' location decisions are thus likely to bring high national benefits, particularly for countries with large, advanced markets. While many economic studies have investigated the conditions under which reaction by other countries will eliminate any gains, the imperfections of the multilateral international business game are likely to mean that for individual countries the national benefits are not always eliminated.[24] And on the firms' side of the game it may well be that investment required to supply the market from within the restricted areas remains profitable, further supporting the argument that the optimum level for these controls will be high for some countries. This argument conflicts with Professor Kindleberger's view of the future of tariff controls:

The nation-state is just about through as an economic unit . . . Tariff policy is virtually useless, despite the last-gasp struggles of the protectionists to keep out Japanese steels, Danish cheese, Middle East oil, Brazilian powdered coffee,

---

[24] Harry G. Johnson, "Optimum Tariffs and Retaliation," *Review of Economic Studies* 21, no. 55 (1953–54): 142–53.

and of the Johnson administration to get the American public to stop going abroad.[25]

Some statements can also be made about the sort of controls with low optimum-control levels. First, anything which threatens assets is likely to produce much greater reaction than other equally effective controls aimed at operations. To those identified with a firm's performance, the removal of the right to capital which is clearly recorded in the firm's books is more drastic than an equivalent reduction in potential earning capacity.[26] The crude concept of expropriation gives way then to more refined actions to restrict the profits taken from the market, for example, compulsory selling through a government marketing organization.

Nor will controls be common that can be avoided through an international firm's foreign ramifications. Attempts by the United States to prevent foreign subsidiaries of U.S. firms from trading with the communist bloc were not very successful. Countries have also been generally unsuccessful at enforcing retention of export markets when a local production base has been taken over by the subsidiary of an international corporation. French attempts to prevent the expansion of United States ownership in some industries have similarly been thwarted by the ease with which the same firms can locate in other EEC countries and then export to France.

COUNTRY STRATEGIES OVER TIME

It can be argued that optimum control levels, and hence controls, will rise with the level of development of a country relative to other countries. This happens because the national benefit from business operations or investment lost as a result of increased controls is likely to be lower and because the growth of the country's market is likely to raise the country's position on firms' investment schedules. The reduction in potential national benefit occurs for two main reasons. First, with development there will be lower incremental benefits from additional international business because the country can do more from its own resources. Its local alternatives will have increased because it will be better able to provide skills in management, production or technology, and necessary capital. Second, rising incomes and wage rates are likely to mean for some types of manufacturing that countries with lower labor costs may become increasingly attractive, and controls will not

---

[25] Kindleberger, *American Business Abroad*, p. 207.

[26] National Industrial Conference Board, *Obstacles and Incentives to Private Foreign Investment 1967–1968,* p. 9. "An act of expropriation lingers long in the minds of potential foreign investors, swaying investment decisions for many years after the event."

so much discourage new investment and activity as they will prevent investment and business activity from leaving. As a corollary, then, the more advanced a country's market relative to other countries the more likely that certain important types of production will move elsewhere and the more it will pay to use controls to retain production locally. Exceptions will occur, though, where the increasing demand brings economies of scale from local production that outweigh the cost advantages of other locations when transport costs are included.

For any given set of conditions for supply from outside, a country's bargaining power in setting the conditions on which it is supplied increases with the size of its local demand. One reason is that with bigger volume it is less costly to produce locally. Ultimately, control of the market demand dominates ownership of resources—because value of resources stems from their use in the market. Suppose the country with a market increases controls over business to the extent that at the previous cost of supplying the market it becomes no longer economic to supply. Yet suppose in addition the previous cost included the cost of controls, say local taxation, imposed by the resource-owning countries. Then these latter controls could be forced down, particularly if resource-owning countries competed among themselves.[27]

With optimum control levels changing over time and besides the fact that they are difficult to measure without information about firms' other investment opportunities, countries will be reduced to experimentation and adjustment as results are fed back. Over time, countries' control strategies should come nearer to their control optima—by definition, their best strategies.

There may come a time for some countries when the strategies of international firms would lead to extraction of earnings and little further investment. Markets important to an expansion strategy at one point can become saturated and no longer included on investment schedules. In such situations, control optima could become infinite and economically justify controls up to and including expropriation. But this would be a special case for a country with very little growth.

This process of adjustment over time raises the question as to whether initial strategies will undervalue or overvalue the optimum control levels. One likely hypothesis is that the greater the gap between a country and the most advanced country, the higher its unfilled aspirations, and the greater the likelihood it will increase controls beyond the control optima.[28] As national benefits from additional business investment are

---

[27] For one example, see J. E. Hartshorn, *Oil Companies and Governments* (London: Faber & Faber, 1967), Part 3.

[28] Ragnar Nurske, *Problems of Capital Formation in Underdeveloped Countries* (Oxford: Basil Blackwell, 1953), p. 61; Hadley Cantril, "A Study of Aspirations," *Scientific American,* February 1963, pp. 41–45.

high for relatively backward countries, there will be a tendency to add controls to achieve the maximum from international firms—only to produce the opposite effect. Conversely, more highly developed countries are likely to underestimate their control optima in the absence of a major lag in their development, particularly when their own international firms dominate the market.

It seems generally clear that the stronger hand in the international business game lies with the more developed country. The weaker a country's attraction to firms, the less it will find it worthwhile to impose controls to increase national benefits. While countries' strategic positions with respect to international business will vary markedly with such factors as population, business capabilities, agreements with other countries, ownership of international business, and level of gross national product, the strategies of countries in similar positions under these headings should have major similarities. The strategies of five such country groupings can be sketched. They are (1) less developed countries, (2) smaller, more advanced countries, (3) countries with their own foreign investment as well as foreign-owned local activity, (4) minority partner countries, and (5) countries prohibiting majority foreign ownership of local activity.

Less Developed Countries

This grouping covers the great number of countries for which foreign investment is deemed to be of outstanding national benefit because of the contribution it can make to further development.[29] Foreign investment contributes to development by providing capital and know-how to mobilize local resources that would otherwise not be mobilized—or, at least releases foreign exchange available to a country to do the same thing. If foreign investment is developing production for the local market, it contributes to the circular flow of demand and supply and also saves foreign exchange through import substitution. If, on the other hand, foreign investment is to provide local production or resource extraction to meet foreign market demands, it will add to export revenue.

Not only are the national benefits and hence the opportunity cost of foreign investment high for these countries, but elasticity of investment in response to controls is likely to be high. Except for investments in extractive resources, there will be many other countries almost as attractive to international investors and ready to replace those countries in which profitability is impaired in any way.

Countries in this situation are likely to avoid high controls because there will always be some other country not invoking equivalent restric-

---

[29] See Isaiah Frank, "The Role of Trade in Economic Development," *International Organization* 22, no. 1 (1968) : 44–71.

tion which would gain the investment. A good initial strategy for the least developed countries would be to present an environment as attractive as possible to international business with no hints of national animosity. On the other hand, nationalistic pressures against foreign ownership will frequently build up to produce controls in excess of these very low control levels. When this happens, the inflow of investment will slacken, and if the controls are high enough, or the nationalistic pressures seem likely to produce such controls, the inflow may dry up altogether. Interests from within the country that realize that investment is being forgone are then likely to begin advocating policies that will bring the country back towards its control optima, pointing out the national benefits from doing so.

Indonesia and India are examples of countries that exceeded their control optima in this way. In Indonesia's case, an increasing antipathy towards foreign business under the Sukarno regime discouraged investment, and confiscation of properties completed the process. This extract comes from a statement by the Government of Indonesia made at the time.

At present, foreign investment in the traditional classic form is not acceptable. Indonesia does not deem it compatible with its economic philosophy if foreigners establish enterprise in Indonesia, owned and run by them, and then claim the right to transfer profits for an indefinite period and insist as well on the transfer of depreciation and salaries.[30]

The inevitable result was a complete cessation of foreign investment. The new regime after 1966, however, reversed the policies, handed back expropriated property, and took active steps to encourage foreign investment. The reversal seems to have brought Indonesia back below its optimum control levels, as illustrated by the growing investment figures and this statement from a U.S. company three years later:

Events in Indonesia make it necessary to revise our 1964 remarks to the point where they are nearly reversed. Indonesia has done a great deal in the intervening years to restore confidence in Indonesia both as a market and as a place to invest. The Indonesian Government seems to be making genuine efforts towards curtailing rapid inflation, stabilizing their currency, and (by means of worthwhile incentives) making Indonesia generally a market worthy of investigation. We plan a detailed survey of that market with the ultimate aim of manufacturing there in the reasonably near future.[31]

Statements by firms also indicate that controls eliminated much activity that would otherwise locate in India, leaving it with a negligible

---

[30] National Industrial Conference Board, *Obstacles and Incentives to Private Foreign Investment, 1962–1964,* Studies in Business Policy, no. 115 (New York, 1965), p. 83.

[31] National Industrial Conference Board, *Obstacles and Incentives to Private Foreign Investment, 1969,* p. 76.

share of private foreign investment.[32] Unlike Indonesia the relaxation of controls in recent years has been minor, for example, some relaxation of local component requirements and loosening of import controls over materials. Given its great need for foreign exchange to spur its development, India has almost certainly retained many controls above the control optima.

The gradual raising of control optima as a country develops and an accompanying policy of creeping controls has already been mentioned. The more developed a country, the more likely it is to avoid drastically exceeding its control optima. In striking contrast to the experience of Indonesia and India and its own expropriations of past eras has been Mexico's ability to increase controls and yet successfully maintain capital inflow. Rapid and sustained growth, political and monetary stability, greater infrastructure to support local production activity, and less open hostility to foreign investment have all contributed to higher sanction limits. Moreover, the high controls on foreign ownership, foreign personnel, and local content with Mexico has imposed may discourage less investment than controls over capital and profit repatriation, which have been largely avoided.

There may be exceptions to the general pattern of strategy predicted here when foreign capital is not a major limiting factor to development. In Libya, for example, high petroleum revenues and an abundance of foreign exchange changed the strategy to one of resource conservation.

Smaller, More Advanced Countries

Quite different strategies can be predicted for the smaller, more developed countries which have not developed much international activity of their own. Countries in this group include Australia, New Zealand, South Africa, Finland, Austria, and Norway, but exclude the smaller EEC countries. These countries have sustained reasonable growth and can normally expect to have a fairly high ranking as market targets for international firms with their small size offset by high incomes and high purchase rates. They also tend to have policies of encouraging local industry through tariffs and subsidies and, in addition to their ranking as market targets, appear well up on international firms' investment schedules.

It is unusual, on the other hand, for these markets to attract investment that will engage in worldwide exporting, or support much development of new products. With high income levels these are not low labor-cost locations, and the scale of local production is generally limited. International business, therefore, is likely to develop only subsidiary activities in these countries aimed solely at the local market. It is also

---

[32] Ibid., pp. 66–73.

likely that as one international competitor makes a move into one of these markets it will be matched by others also feeling that the market is ready for increased attention and not wishing a competitor to gain an advantage. For a particular industry the result may well be a collection of small subsidiaries none of which would be large enough to justify exporting. From the viewpoint of international business these countries become permanent subsidiary countries.

Another effect of this pattern of expansion by international firms is for existing local firms to be circumscribed by international competitors either with a cost advantage or with newer products or techniques. Firms operating on a global scale with a larger sales base can afford more rapid product innovation and support a wider range of development. This extends to service industries as well as manufacturers. Bank, stockbrokers, equipment lessors, insurance firms, and business consultants, for example, have all been following the international expansion of their customers into this group of countries. They bring little capital with them, yet operate with a competitive advantage because they have developed to fit the international corporation. Moreover, with an international network behind them they facilitate centralized management from New York or Brussels reinforcing the advantages a multinational firm may have over local firms.

Countries in this grouping, then, have a high attraction for international firms but also strong reasons for controlling international operations. Yet, with the exception of tariffs, they tend to have few protective controls against international business, and little international business of their own against which others might retaliate if controls were extended. These conditions sum to high control optima relative to existing controls. An increasing awareness that they can play the international business game to much greater advantage may be expected of these countries. Turning this around to the viewpoint of international business, the expected cost of controls may be much higher for these countries than for more aggressively nationalistic underdeveloped countries.

The strategy likely to emerge is one of increasing selectivity for further foreign investment with home markets used as a lever to extend the international activity centered on these countries. Permission for entry will become harder to obtain where the investment might threaten local firms who are not so much inefficient as behind in global-market percentage. For international units that are permitted, efforts will be directed at increasing their local autonomy and, hopefully, their incentive to export. Controls likely to emerge will be limitation of foreign ownership percentages, pressure to offer equity on local stock markets, and more official approvals that favor foreign-debt capital over equity capital.

A range of new control combinations can also be expected. These countries just beginning to realize the potential in controls have the capability to design and to administer quite sophisticated strategies. For example, it might be fruitful to couple tariff protection with a selection policy for incoming investment that gave preference to investment which would develop exports. Differentiation between investment according to the country ultimately controlling the activity might also be attempted. This would dilute the influence of any one country. Furthermore, investment from smaller investing countries can bring with it a greater possibility of expansion from the local base to supply leading markets not covered by the parent organization. With such policies, for example, Australia might have developed a strong research and even export center in the chemical field. As it is, the Australian market is sliced between half a dozen or more subsidiaries of established giants in the chemical field.

These countries are also likely to develop a range of positive encouragements to expand outwards across their borders, for both their own firms and local international subsidiaries, as the awareness grows of what is necessary to avoid permanent subsidiary status. The external growth of any local unit will become strongly identified with national benefit. In the long run, these efforts should produce international operations of a significant size and this very success begin to modify control strategies in a way similar to that for countries already having substantial international businesses, which make our next grouping.

Countries with Their Own Foreign Investment As Well As Foreign-Owned Local Activity

For countries with significant foreign investment of their own, either direct or portfolio, their dual capacity as investor as well as recipient of foreign investment will influence their decisions concerning controls. The perception of national benefits by such countries as the United States, United Kingdom, Germany, France, Canada, and Switzerland is likely to embrace benefits from foreign investments by firms with their home base in the country as well as those from foreign investments of firms based in other countries. To the extent that this is so, investor countries will avoid controls on inbound investment for which the national benefits might be offset by controls affecting their own foreign investments, either in direct retaliation or because the legislation provides an example for other countries of what can be achieved. The potential cost of retaliation can be very high if other countries were prepared to escalate their response, and even a small amount of investment in another country will give that country scope for escalation.[33]

---

[33] Thomas C. Schelling, *The Strategy of Conflict* (Cambridge, Mass.: Harvard University, 1966), Chapter 1.

To avoid specific retaliation, then, controls in this grouping of countries are more likely to be proposed as positive encouragment of desired characteristics and of local ownership than as negative restrictions on foreign ownership. Canada, for example, has a reduced taxation rate for companies with at least 25 percent local ownership and has published a set of 12 guiding principles for foreign companies, designed to minimize the disbenefits of foreign control.[34] There is also likely to be more informal administration of controls than formal published regulation. Foreign-owned operations are required to obtain permission before they can be set up in France, although published rules that discriminate against foreign investment have been generally avoided.

A natural extension of these elements of strategy is the development of positive steps to strengthen a country's own international business operations. Simply to protect the home market for local producers is inadequate when the local market base is too small to provide research, production, and management economies to match the largest international operations. And if indigenous international corporations of the strength needed fail to emerge on their own, governments will increasingly give them a hand through forced merger, government aid, and protected home markets. The idea is not new. The United Kingdom successfully created the Imperial Tobacco Company in 1902 to oppose the American Tobacco Company and between the wars created ICI to meet German and United States competition. Methods of using attack as a means of defense seem to have grown in popularity in Europe and Japan in the late 1960s. Perhaps it owed something to Servan-Schreiber's advocacy of this means of countering what he diagnosed as an American challenge.[35]

A further stage of this sort of strategy is to develop controls that will strengthen a country's multinational firms in their foreign operations. The United States went farthest in this direction. For example, under the "Cooley Loan" amendment to Public Law 480, U.S. government holdings of foreign currencies received in payment of agricultural surpluses were permitted to be lent to United States firms for trade expansion in the foreign country, but under no condition were the funds to be used for production that would be exported to the United States in competition with U.S.-made products or marketed to compete with U.S. agricultural exports.

The Foreign Assistance Act of 1961 also followed this pattern by

---

[34] Department of Trade and Commerce, *Foreign-Owned Subsidiaries in Canada* (Ottawa: Queen's Printer, 1967), pp. 40–41.

[35] J. J. Servan-Schreiber, *The American Challenge* (New York: Atheneum, 1968); Stephen Hymer and Robert Rowthorn, "Multinational Corporations and International Oligopoly: The Non-American Challenge," in *The International Corporation,* ed. Charles B. Kindleberger (Cambridge, Mass.: The M.I.T. Press, 1970).

limiting loan guarantees and insurance to what it euphemistically called "friendly" countries. A friendly country was one that would sign guarantees not to expropriate. Germany also established in 1960 an investment-guarantee program limited to countries having signed bilateral agreements. This statement recorded in 1965 illustrates the strength of the U.S. legislation:

It has generally been a policy of the Government of India to insist that in the case of all new industrial companies in the private sector, at least 51 percent of equity capital is held by Indians. The American Mission that was visiting India a few months ago informed the Finance Minister quite definitely that unless he was prepared to allow American control, there would be no further private American investment in India. The reason for this is that the United States Government appears to have introduced an insurance scheme for overseas investment in developing countries, but projects will only qualify for cover provided American control is assured.[36]

The strategy of countries with their own foreign investment, however, is not likely to continue along a straight progression of increasing influence over foreign operations of locally based firms. What is good for the foreign performance of local corporations is not necessarily good for the home country. The possibilities for divergence between maximum performance of firms and what is seen as maximizing national benefit are very many indeed.

Investing countries pushing for lower controls over their own firms' operations in other countries are finding that with lower optimum control levels in these countries they help to create a double standard of high controls at home and low controls overseas. Relaxation of investing countries' local controls such as the United States Webb Pomerene Act, which relaxes the antitrust requirements for operations outside the United States, compound this. Supported by such parent-country government backing, the snowballing of international business activity is producing major antipathy towards the investing countries—bringing a high foreign policy cost to the investing countries.[37] Awareness that a country's interest diverges from maximum foreign performance of its international firms should lead eventually to strategies that are less punitive to weaker countries.

For countries also involved in direct aid to developing countries it may be argued that a greater benefit to such countries for less cost might be controls over their own firms that direct them to make a greater contribution to development. Then again, investing countries may feel much more is to be gained from protecting home production than from

---

[36] National Industrial Conference Board, *Obstacles and Incentives to Private Foreign Investment, 1965*, p. 81.

[37] Leo Model, "The Politics of Private Foreign Investment," *Foreign Affairs*, June 1967, p. 648.

facilitating their firms' movement of production to lower cost foreign sites.

The strategy for this class of countries then might be summarized as cautious unpublicized discouragement of others' international activities, positive encouragment of desirable locally owned activities, and initially an active stimulation of international expansion by local firms. Ultimately though, the identification with locally based multinational firms will decrease as their interests diverge.

Minority Partner Countries

These are countries which are partners to trade agreements for which permitted tariffs plus transport costs do not deter imports from partners, yet which, by reason of their size, will be less preferred for major investment than their larger partners. The outstanding examples are the smaller EEC partners of Belgium and Holland. Controls leading foreign investment to locate outside a minority partner's boundaries would in these circumstances hinder export opportunities for any local plant that could be developed and might, instead, produce imports into the local market. Conversely, foreign investment that does come in is likely to lead to exports to the partner countries.

When there are a number of such countries competing against themselves, or where the advantages of their larger partners appear large to foreign investors, competition to de-escalate controls is likely, even to the extent of positive encouragements. Such a strategy has emerged in Belgium, somewhat to the detriment of France. Low-cost sites, capital and interest subsidies, and various types of taxation remission have been offered.[38] An EEC study that has been circulated but not published has reportedly argued for EEC countries to eliminate competition on these fronts and increase the optimum control levels for the community as a whole.[39] Agreement to avoid competition through controls is not a foregone conclusion, though, with such divergent interests.

**Countries Prohibiting Majority Foreign Ownership
of Local Activity**

A fifth type of strategy is appropriate for the communist-bloc countries and Japan—countries that have achieved a significant measure of development while virtually excluding capital that places majority ownership in foreign hands. These countries have strong central control which shows in an equally strong strategy towards foreign investment.

---

[38] National Industrial Conference Board, *Obstacles and Incentives to Private Foreign Investment, 1967–1968*, pp. 10–12.

[39] *Economist*, 27 June 1970, p. 73.

They have evolved a strategy of attracting technological gains while retaining control of their own markets and preserving access to export markets. The limitations on foreign ownership, however, may delay the inflow of the latest technological advances from international corporations, but on the other hand, the multinational firm is still likely to protect its technological supremacy by withholding the latest advances even when it fully owns a subsidiary.

Once international corporations accept that they cannot gain majority ownership and that the direct threat to their own operations is not immediate, they have shown that they will settle for whatever participation they can get on the principle that something is better than nothing. U.S. national policy for a long time restrained U.S. firms in deals with communist countries, but the speed with which the Firestone-Goodyear competition built up for the Romanian market in 1964 following relaxation of the U.S. embargo was a good example of how competing capitalist units react when faced with limited access and centralized purchasing.[40]

A corollary to this sort of strategy is that these countries will develop their own strong local operations able to move into international attack. In the initial stages this attack is likely to aim at building export markets and outgoing investment should be largely to acquire outlets and market position. As the international attack meets with success, however, the strategy is likely to change into something very like the global planning of our representative international firm.

Pressure to relax the restrictions placed on international investment capital in the home markets of these countries is unlikely to make much of an impression until reverse investments and exports can be used as a lever. But when a significant lever does develop, the countries affected are more likely to be concerned with protection from the attack than relaxation of controls in the home market of the attackers.

Despite repeated pressure, particularly from OECD countries, Japan has not significantly reduced controls on inward investment.[41] Approval must be obtained for branch operations and royalty agreements. In addition, there are laws preventing foreigners owning real estate or mineral rights, and regulations on entry of foreign personnel are rigorous. Some investors complain of long delays in approving applications and instances of particulars communicated to local competitors who then move to close the opportunity. Recent moves relaxing investment restrictions are more apparent than real. They mainly cover industries in which the Japanese have already developed world eminence and others, like

---

[40] See Frances Sheridan and R. W. Bareness, *Firestone and Trade with Rumania (A) and (B)*, Northwestern University, School of Business (Boston, Mass.: Intercollegiate Case Clearing House) no. 10G73, 10G74.

[41] Herbert Glazer, "Japan Unbars a Door," *Columbia Journal of World Business,* July–August 1967.

tourism, for which investment would bring additional foreign earnings. Alongside this liberalization, moreover, the Ministry of International Trade and Industry is reported to be developing further measures to strengthen local firms against foreign interests, such as empowering the Japan Development Bank to advance loans and guarantee obligations for industries needing support.

In comparison to Japan, the communist countries are behind in their international expansion, but as they move outward they, too, begin to play the international game to maximize benefits. They have recorded notable success in pitting western suppliers against one another to obtain technological expertise at the lowest competitive rates. In a number of cases, Russia and other bloc countries have obtained as much as 12 years' credit from international firms competing on narrow margins to supply what amounts to pure technological input, while unskilled labor and materials are largely supplied from local sources. On the export side their producing units show evidence of rational strategies, with products such as Polish hams aiming for strong positions in the leading markets.

In summary, the pattern of strategy of this class of countries is predicted as limitation of foreign ownership with maximum acquisition of technological know-how, followed by international expansion that shapes them as investing countries.

Conclusion

The emphasis of this chapter has been entirely away from the popular concern for the decaying power of the nation-state in face of the rise of multinational firms. The emphasis has been on prediction of the pattern of controls that will emerge as countries adjust to competition through these changed intermediaries. Countries have been taken as the ultimate competing powers endeavoring via their controls over international business to alter the allocation of activities for their national benefit.

Several conclusions stand out. Countries are not in equal strategic positions with respect to international business and the poorer nations have the weaker hands. Moreover, they cannot find an easy way out through unilateral nationalistic action. Such action is a quick way to decrease the national payoff from the international game. Their best strategy lies with gradually creeping controls. On the other hand, the most costly controls from the viewpoint of international business are likely to be imposed by the smaller, more developed countries who have less to lose and are likely to lose less from strict control policies. There will also be major differences in the effectiveness of controls because of the way they affect the performance of multinational firms. Tariffs will remain strong because they tie the attraction of the local market to local activity, and controls not reflected in return of investment calculations or taking effect some time in the future will be widely employed. In particular, limitation of foreign equity ownership will be more widespread.

Given the concept of the international business game and an embryo terminology for approaching its analysis, the international businessman should be able to develop cost and benefit calculations as the basis for his decisions. Such calculations will be limited by the assumptions made about the various interacting strategies, but control risk will be quantifiable. For any investment the cash flow can be reduced by the cost of controls multiplied by the expectation (probability) they will occur.

EXERCISES AND DISCUSSION QUESTIONS

1. Numerous writers have observed an "inevitable tension" between multinational companies and nation-states and proposed ways for governments to control the operations of these firms. Is the conflict really between firms and countries, or simply between countries just as it has always been? What are the implications of this distinction for the sort of controls that might be recommended?

2. In recent years the Canadian government has been introducing more and more controls over the Canadian operations of foreign firms. What would you expect will be the characteristics of further controls to be imposed in the foreseeable future, and why?

3. Do you think managements of tomorrow's multinational corporations will generally act to minimize the effects of controls on their firms' performance? Should they? If not, what exceptions would you wish to see?

4. Select one country and, as a consultant to its current government, prepare an overall strategy for control of international business activities that fall within its jurisdiction.

5. What types of controls will be most likely to affect the performance of international firms as against simply being passed on by the firm to its customers? Does it make any difference?

6. Criticize the assumptions of the model for forecasting controls that has been proposed in this chapter.

PART V

Managing the Multinational Enterprise

THIS SECTION OF THE BOOK concentrates on international business from the viewpoint of the decision maker within the firm and is prescriptive rather than descriptive. Only those managerial issues which bear a uniquely international slant and require new and different approaches by decision makers will be dealt with at any length here. They are legion, however, and the analytical and decision-making approaches can only be introduced rather than exhaustively treated in the chapters that follow.

The first chapter in this part of the book sets out a framework for the overall planning of a firm's international activities. Subsequent chapters then fit onto this framework, examining particular aspects in more detail. Global strategy deals with the planning, timing, and location of a firm's expansions as well as the strategies for entry, ownership, and management of a global operation. Organizational patterns for the multinational enterprise constitute an area of managerial responsibility where a growing amount of analysis is beginning to define the principal options and the criteria for choice. Managing the international product mix deals with the question of choice of products, distribution channels, and marketing strategies, while financial management involves some of the more complex new variables resulting from crossing national boundaries into a number of currency areas and financial environments. The final topic covered is managing human resources, both managerial and work force.

Throughout the managerial function, conventional analytical and decision-making approaches may require considerable modification to allow for national interest. Decisions concerning internal pricing, location of research, production, and financial resources can be of critical importance to the individual nations in which the firm operates. Also differences in the objectives of different nationalities represented within firms can be a significant constraint.

All of the earlier parts of the book are background for the international manager. He must understand the framework for international transactions, the common interests and conflicts between the multinational enterprise and the nation-state, and the control environment in which he must operate. And he must assess and forecast the international environment in performing the decision-making function in the multinational enterprise.

17

BUILDING A GLOBAL
STRATEGY

MOST BUSINESS FIRMS BECOME INTERNATIONAL by a process of creeping "incrementalism" rather than by strategy choice. Some firms are first attracted to foreign markets by unsolicited export orders and, after discovering new opportunities, move through a series of stages to the establishment of foreign-production facilities. Other firms initiate international activities in response to threats to an oligopoly position. Still others respond to specific opportunities for developing supplies of resources or achieving greater production efficiency through foreign operations. But rarely are these early moves part of a comprehensive global strategy. And in some stage of becoming a global enterprise, the international activities of many firms could be best characterized as a portfolio of diverse and separate country companies tied together by a network of ad hoc relationships.

In fact, a recent survey of many major American and European international companies reveals that in many enterprises, "the strategy (if it can be called that) has been to put an operation wherever it was feasible . . . and then let things shake out later."[1] And even in the late 1960s formalized global strategic and long-range planning was still in a stage of infancy in most companies.

Increased competition, growing environmental pressures, and a keener awareness of the synergistic benefits of a multinational enterprise are moving international companies to adopt global strategies and global planning. European companies began their formalized global planning in the late 1960s, while U.S. companies began earlier in that decade.

---

[1] John S. Schwendiman, "International Strategic Planning: Still in Its Infancy?" *Worldwide P & I Planning,* September–October 1971, p. 52.

WHAT IS A GLOBAL STRATEGY?

What is a global strategy? It is simply a plan whereby an enterprise makes its major business decisions by taking into account global opportunities, global alternatives, and future global consequences. A global strategy means that the decision maker frees himself of any national blinders and considers world markets and world-resource locations and not simply the markets or resources of a particular country in isolation. A global strategy aims to maximize results on a multinational basis rather than treating international activities as a portfolio of diverse and separate country companies. And a global strategy generally requires that the enterprise engage in a formal process of strategic and long-range planning.

Consider the large U.S. chemical company with plants in over 20 countries whose chief executive proudly asserts:

I don't like to be too explicit in telling my division managers what I think we should be doing around the globe. They just might take me too literally—and then they might not do enough of their own thinking . . .[2]

Such a management philosophy, where the president does not assume a leadership role in developing global goals and strategy, runs the risk that the enterprise will go in so many directions that the advantages of being a multinational enterprise are missed.

Without some form of global strategy, the timing and location of a firm's expansion would become merely a reaction to perceived opportunities and threats with no basis for evaluating their enterprise-wide significance. The new plant acquired in London by a corporation from Midwest America because the president's wife found the "Beefeaters and all that" so fascinating may turn out to be a profitable venture. Yet to make such major decisions with no analytical model for evaluation is inviting poor performance. The other extreme of tying a firm's international business development rigidly to a prethought strategy can be equally unfortunate. The world is too complex for flexibility to be completely discarded.

It is not necessary for a firm to be engaged internationally or to be on the point of outrunning its national market before global planning becomes desirable. If competitors within its national market extend their horizons to include a broader sales base, the firm could find itself less able to maintain the same pace of research or product development given its smaller sales base. There are few businesses in which there are no economies of scale extending beyond the size of national markets, even if it be only in marketing or management expertise. Even where the immediate domestic competition is not moving rapidly to other mar-

---

[2] Ibid., p. 25.

kets, there may be foreign firms which will ultimately pose a threat. European firms that disregarded the higher growth rates of American or Japanese firms in a number of industries were largely unprepared for the competitive challenge when these firms broke into their own national markets. Other firms have been left behind in the competitive race because they failed to go to the cheapest sources of supply.

On a strictly rational basis, no firm should automatically limit its horizon to its home market. For example, with its large population, high-wage rates, high discretionary spending power, and high propensity to innovate, the U.S. market has been the leader in adoption and growth rates for many products. This has placed U.S. firms at an advantage. They did not need to think globally in the early stages of a product's life, because the strategy coincided with achievement in the U.S. market. But many firms outside the United States needed to plan globally from the beginning. A United Kingdom firm introducing a technological advance was likely to find that after the very early stages the U.S. market took off more rapidly. If U.S. demand was left to U.S. competitors, the sales and experience of American competitors soon outpaced that of the United Kingdom firm.

Many European firms failed to enter the U.S. market in the 1950s when they were throwing off the shackles of reconstruction and in a position to develop an optimum global strategy. The British Imperial Chemical Industries (ICI) is a good example. At a time when W. R. Grace, for example, was building itself from virtually no strength in chemicals into one of the world leaders, ICI placed its main emphasis on the British Commonwealth. Needless to say, its growth rate and performance were not as high as that of its American competitors.

Another reason for thinking globally is to avoid actions which might create obstacles to a firm's expansion at a later stage. If a global strategy indicated that there would be advantages in separating production activity from marketing activity, then an arrangement that sets up a combined production and marketing unit with outside ownership interests in one country would clearly be undesirable.

INTERNATIONAL STRATEGIC AND LONG-RANGE PLANNING

Corporate planning is an essential task in virtually every enterprise, but in no other organization is it of more vital importance than in a multinational firm that follows a global business approach.[3] The "ideal" international corporate-planning process shown in Figure 17.1 indicates the four major elements in the formal planning of global strategies: (1) environmental assessment, (2) internal company assessment, (3) the strategic objective setting, and (4) formulation of long-range

---

[3] See George A. Steiner and Warren M. Cannon, *Multinational Corporate Planning* (New York: Macmillan Co., 1966).

FIGURE 17.1

An Ideal International Corporate Planning Process

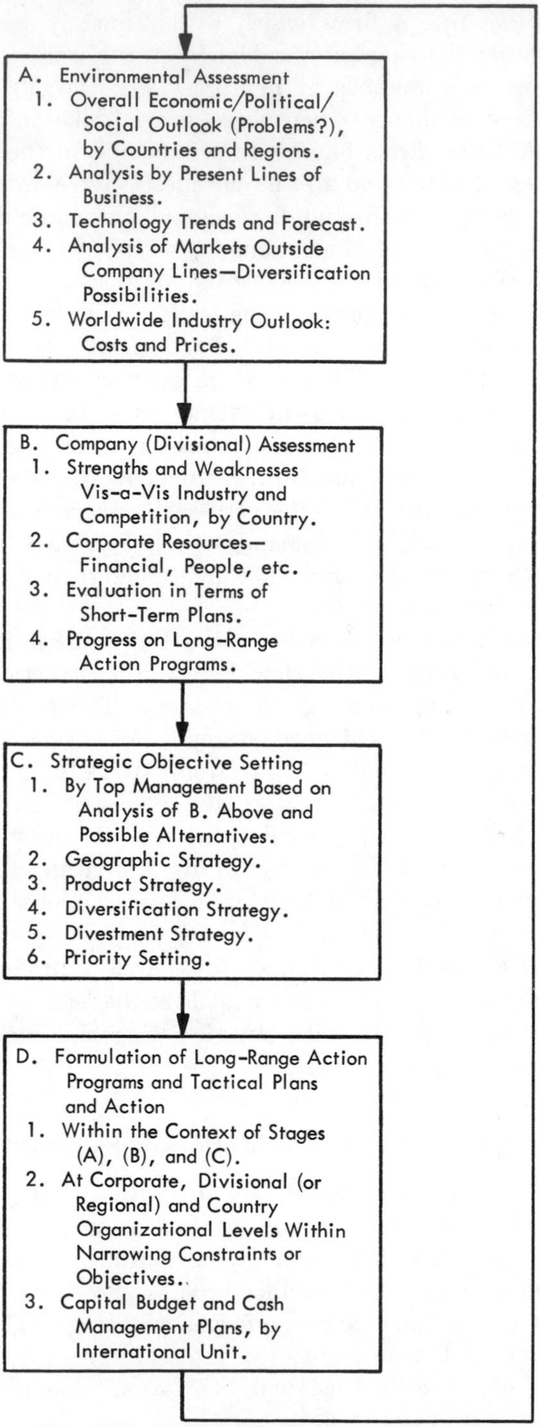

A. Environmental Assessment
  1. Overall Economic/Political/
     Social Outlook (Problems?),
     by Countries and Regions.
  2. Analysis by Present Lines of
     Business.
  3. Technology Trends and Forecast.
  4. Analysis of Markets Outside
     Company Lines—Diversification
     Possibilities.
  5. Worldwide Industry Outlook:
     Costs and Prices.

B. Company (Divisional) Assessment
  1. Strengths and Weaknesses
     Vis-a-Vis Industry and
     Competition, by Country.
  2. Corporate Resources—
     Financial, People, etc.
  3. Evaluation in Terms of
     Short-Term Plans.
  4. Progress on Long-Range
     Action Programs.

C. Strategic Objective Setting
  1. By Top Management Based on
     Analysis of B. Above and
     Possible Alternatives.
  2. Geographic Strategy.
  3. Product Strategy.
  4. Diversification Strategy.
  5. Divestment Strategy.
  6. Priority Setting.

D. Formulation of Long-Range Action
   Programs and Tactical Plans
   and Action
  1. Within the Context of Stages
     (A), (B), and (C).
  2. At Corporate, Divisional (or
     Regional) and Country
     Organizational Levels Within
     Narrowing Constraints or
     Objectives..
  3. Capital Budget and Cash
     Management Plans, by
     International Unit.

Source: John S. Schwendiman, "Long-Range and Strategic Planning in the International Firm," Ph.D. diss., Alfred P. Sloan School of Management, Massachusetts Institute of Management, Cambridge, Mass., 1971).

action programs.[4] International planning, as indicated, should be a multi-level activity, with integration both in a "top-down" and "bottom-up" context. But global strategies must be thought out at the top, not arrived at by simply totaling plans from individual countries where local bias may conceal important data needed for global planning. Furthermore, decisions for expansion into new areas must necessarily be made at the top.

The analysis of the anticipated internal and external operating conditions provides a foundation for the realistic determination of long-range objectives: what markets to serve with what products, sales, profits, and return-on-investment targets, social commitments, and so forth. As will be discussed in Chapter 20, the financial objectives should reflect different levels of risk, such as political and foreign exchange risks in the countries in which the company operates. A clear set of objectives leads to a consideration of alternative courses of action that might be used to accomplish them and to the adoption of a specific set of strategic programs. These include the choice of countries for expansion, the location of supply and production, and coordinated long-range plans for each of the major management areas.[5] Strategic planning relates to the basic directions of an enterprise and the way in which it uses its resources. It provides a framework into which each functional plan can be integrated, resulting in a global plan for the entire company.

An Example of an International Strategic Planning System

After examining the planning systems of 22 major American and European multinational companies, Schwendiman selected *Company W,* a European chemical company, as having the best system.[6] In *Company W,* the executive committee of the management board takes the lead in plotting corporate strategy. It is primarily concerned with how to allocate corporate resources and how to influence company growth and responsibility. The company has six phases in its planning process.

1.   The executive committee decides on corporate policies, objectives, and worldwide strategies, making substantial use of inputs by product division managers.

2.   Concurrently, a "planning data base" is prepared throughout the company. Major components are environmental assessments around the

---

[4] For a related approach, see Hans Schollhammer, "Long-Range Planning in Multinational Corporations," *Columbia Journal of World Business,* September–October 1971, pp. 79–86.

[5] Richard D. Robinson, *International Management* (New York: Holt, Rhinehart & Winston, 1967), p. 6. Robinson has divided the total international management field into eight subsets of strategies: marketing, supply, labor, management personnel, ownership, financial, legal, and control.

[6] Schwendiman, "International Strategic Planning," p. 61.

world and analyses of the company's strengths and weaknesses vis-a-vis competitors. The competitive evaluation covers the current situation and a five-year future period. It includes R & D capabilities and manufacturing capacities for the company and its competitors. The planning data base is up-dated each year. After the data base is analyzed, tentative conclusions are reached for possible strategies.

3. Five-year plans are prepared by the different "planning units," generally country subsidiaries. As guidelines for this planning step, management distributes to all divisions and subsidiaries a statement of corporate objectives and policies and suggestions as to how the subsidiary should plan in order to integrate well into total corporate strategies. Fitting the strategies of the subsidiaries into the total corporate plan receives a lot of attention in the dialogue between different planning levels, and alternative strategies are thoroughly considered. As plans are developed and written up, they generally follow the format shown in Figure 17.2.

FIGURE 17.2
Company W's Written Plan Format (prepared by each "planning unit")

Chapter 1 Introduction (1–2 pages)
Chapter 2 Assumptions (1–2 pages)
Chapter 3 Opportunities and problems, with objectives and strategies (10–15 pages)
Chapter 4 Time schedule for strategies (1–2 pages)
Chapter 5 Personnel and resource requirements (3–5 pages)
Chapter 6 Five-year budget (3–5 pages)
Chapter 7 Problems for higher management attention (1 page)

Source: John S. Schwendiman, "International Strategic Planning: Still in Its Infancy?" *Worldwide P & I Planning*, September–October 1971, p. 61.

4. As a fourth phase, the written plans are integrated into a corporate framework and presented to top management for decision on final plans. Generally, conflicts between planning units or among the divisions are arbitrated before the final integration. The plans are reviewed carefully by top management with particular attention to assumptions, possible inconsistent objectives, and action plans. The final product of this phase is a planning letter approved by top management that contains (a) top management's decisions and priorities, (b) emphasis on actions in the next year, and (c) details on corporate decisions which will affect the longer-range planning horizon.

5 and 6. The fifth and sixth phases are the preparation of one year plans, budgets, and the financial integration of all budgets.

A PRESCRIPTIVE APPROACH TO GLOBAL PLANNING

In practice, many firms expand and operate without a global strategy, and do so profitably. Others plan only part of their operations or build decision rules for measuring opportunities when they arise, without making any effort to search for opportunities or bring them about. But the purpose of studying international business is not to describe what firms do. It is to decide what they could do to improve decisions. The better the underlying model against which decisions are made, the better the decisions might be.

Specific decisions and actions, of course, must be largely determined by environmental factors and such internal considerations as the history and structure of the organization and the objectives of the individuals and groups of which it is composed. Thus the value of any prescriptive model that can be presented here must lie in producing a framework that gives those within a firm a basis for arranging their thinking and guiding their organizational participation. A rigid procedure would be of little value.

There are other limits to rational decision models. It might be theoretically possible to calculate for any firm a global profit-maximizing allocation of investment, production, and marketing activity over a specified period. But there are many practical difficulties in making such a calculation. Invariably, many approximations must be made in collecting data and the number of possible alternatives for comparison must be kept to a manageable number.

Within these constraints, the decision model presented here for developing and implementing a global strategy has been prepared to meet four major objectives.

1. It should be a general model that can be adapted to different types of activity and organizational settings.
2. It should make specific provision for considering variables known to have a significant effect on international business performance.
3. It should specify how the variables should be weighted and decisions arrived at. It should be a model with decision rules, not merely a list of considerations.
4. It should be as simple as possible, adding complexity only when the additional value in improved decision making outweighs its cost.

The decision model follows the 12-step procedure shown in Chapter 16 as Table 16.1.

Market Assessment as the Starting Point

The formulation of a global strategy starts from global markets and works backwards towards the location of activity and investment to achieve best performance in these markets. Although the prime objective may be to obtain the greatest return on invested capital, the way to reach it is not to take country after country and calculate what rate of return would be obtained from investing in a plant in that country.

This would be a replication of national thinking many times over. It is not global strategy. Global strategy requires that the investment location be decided against the global pattern of market targets.

This in turn requires some prediction of demand and competition in the different markets. With different rates and patterns of growth in different markets, any simple extrapolation of the current situation would be inappropriate. A more refined prediction of market growth is needed. In making such predictions, a whole range of forecasting methods can be used as discussed in Chapter 13, ranging from multiple-correlation techniques for developing relationships between demand and independent variables that can be predicted to input-output analysis for estimating demand derived from other industries. And the international businessman should be well prepared to use the best methodology available.

Whatever the methodology, the basic data required will involve past measurements of actual demand and of likely indicators or determinants of demand and then estimates of how indicators or determinants will behave in the future. In the initial stages of building a global strategy, the fastest and most effective approach for analyzing market potentials may be to centralize this responsibility in headquarters staff and rely on data sources centrally available, such as from international agencies. As the firm develops an international planning system, it can begin to rely on its foreign subsidiaries for much of this information. But in the initial stages, the decentralized approach will be extremely slow because of the time required to receive information from around the world. Also, the communication problem of specifying what figures and estimates are required will be extremely difficult if at the time of the request the subsidiaries have had no experience with the practical aspects of the planning process for which the data are required. And lastly, consistent forecasts are probably more important than accurate forecasts when they are to be used for allocating emphasis between markets. To call for estimates from a wide range of sources is to invite major inconsistencies. Different individuals will have different biases in assessing future market growth for their areas.

The analysis of market potentials provides part of the information needed for building a global strategy, but management's investigation of foreign-business opportunities should go beyond judgments of market growth if it is to recognize the opportunities before they become obvious to the world at large. For promising markets, it will want to appraise the competitive situation by making a financial, economic, and operational analysis of competing companies. This broader type of evaluation has been labeled "opportunity analysis."[7]

---

[7] Raphael W. Hodgson and Hugo E. R. Uyterhoeven, "Analyzing Foreign Opportunities," *Harvard Business Review,* March–April 1962, pp. 60–72.

How far into the future should market opportunities be predicted? This will depend on the time horizon of the decision maker. Given the inflexibility of an investment once it has been committed, an early horizon may produce a supply pattern that is far from optimum for the subsequent market pattern. On the other hand, if the horizon is set far in the future, intermediate profits will be more likely to suffer, the market pattern more likely to vary from the prediction, and current management less likely to see the full fruits of its decisions. In practice, a four- or five-year horizon is common.[8]

Allocation Rules

Once these market opportunities have been established, the next and most important step in building a global strategy is to select a set of decision rules against which the firm should allocate its efforts to the different markets. These rules are chosen with a view to producing the highest present value of profits from the allocation, but are a compromise on building a full decision model to arrive at a mathematically provable optimum. Such a model would contain too many alternatives and would collapse under its own weight, and some set of rules for reducing the alternatives is unavoidable.

Such rules might be conceived as simple choices between participation or nonparticipation in a market, but they are more likely to emerge as guidelines for determining the emphasis to be placed on achievement; in other words, what the sales budgets should be. The sort of rules that are commonly found in policy documents are as follows:

1. Enter all markets for which the absolute size is over a certain level and competitive entry conditions are favorable.
2. Expand as fast as possible without losses in all markets above a certain size for which the growth rates exceed a given figure.
3. Reduce margins where competitor market shares are high, the company's market shares low, and margins are above a specified figure.
4. Enter new markets only if necessary to match a competitor who would otherwise build up a strong position unchallenged.

These rules will depend on the products involved. As for all business decisions, actions must be reasoned back from the characteristics of the marketplace in which their effectiveness will ultimately be tested. The way in which potential customers make their purchasing decisions will determine the type of outlets and sales forces that are needed and, in turn, determine the speed and manner in which activities can be built up in individual countries. Suppose, for example, the product range

---

[8] Steiner and Cannon, *Multinational Corporate Planning,* Part I.

covers industrial capital goods sold largely to industrial organizations who purchase against bids from competing suppliers. Involvement in individual countries might then require only local agents to obtain enquiries for bids and maintain a continuing local base for customer service of one sort or another. In contrast, a branded food manufacturer might decide on local production, warehousing, merchandising to retail outlets, and heavy consumer advertising, based on knowledge of how customer decisions to purchase a particular type of food are made.

Some writers on global strategy recommend that instead of setting targets directly for individual markets, the markets be first classified according to some definition of importance which, in turn, would indicate the appropriate entry strategy. Such a classification might be:

a. Markets requiring immediate, direct, and full-scale development by the firm.
b. Markets for major development in the next five years, or immediately if entered by significant competitors. Develop distribution outlets and build image through promotion.
c. Markets to be covered through resident distributors.
d. Markets to be covered through export agents or periodic sales trips.
e. Markets warranting no particular attention.

Other groupings have been suggested frequently, in particular that based on Rostow's classification of stages of development.[9] Whatever the intermediate steps introduced, however, the ultimate result must be the selection of targets for individual markets.

Location of Supply and Production

While alternative sources of supply may have been loosely considered in setting the market targets, detailed planning of the sourcing of supplies must wait until after targets and market-entry strategies have been set. It is then possible to design a supply system from raw material through to final delivery to the customer that would minimize costs of achieving the targets. There can be few firms that could determine supply independently for each market without throwing away significant economies from coordinating supply.

While it is theoretically possible to calculate a profit-maximizing pattern of supply and the consequent investment needed to meet market targets up to the horizon year, such calculations would invariably be too complicated for practical application. The number of alternative supply patterns is infinite. The ownership-strategy options are many and will influence the investment required. And the introduction of a

---

[9] W. W. Rostow, *The Stages of Economic Growth* (Cambridge, England: Cambridge University Press, 1960).

sequence of changing targets for each market further complicates the issue. Here again it is necessary to simplify the calculation by adopting a set of rules that limit the alternatives considered without moving the result too far away from a best solution.[10] Where, for example, there is no major impediment to separating out the decision as to the best location of manufacturing activity, the decision rules that might be used would be:

1. Retention of existing locations as against new locations where fixed costs are high and an experienced labor force a valuable asset.
2. Consideration of new sites when the local market is above a certain size, resource costs are below a certain figure, or tariffs exceed a certain level.

In some cases, too, the adoption of targets for particular markets will require local production because of the local regulations concerning access to the market.

With the reduced number of required and potential siting alternatives determined, the next step is to estimate the costs of investment and operation at alternative sites and from each the transport and tariff costs into alternative markets. For each possible alternative the lowest cost of supplying the market targets in the horizon year might then be calculated. The alternative with the overall lowest cost would then be selected. The methodology involved in such calculations can become very advanced, but it is possible to reduce it to a linear-programming calculation.

Subject to the accuracy of the assumptions, estimates, and decision rules the lowest cost combination should approach that which maximizes the firm's cash flow in the horizon year. But it does not follow that the firm immediately extends to the locations indicated. The horizon objective must be translated into annual investment schedules over the period up to the horizon year, and each year's schedule submitted to return-on-investment analysis and limited to the firm's resource availability. A practical decision rule for deriving the annual schedules would be to invest each year in the additions needed to achieve the horizon objective that would minimize the cost of meeting the next year's targets—although it would be possible to calculate an optimum over the full period. The return-on-investment calculation for each item would then be based on the incremental net cash flow accruing from the expansion, estimated as far into the future as practical and reduced by

[10] Robert E. McGarrah, "Logistics for the International Manufacturer," *Harvard Business Review*, March–April 1966; David P. Rutenberg, *Stochastic Programming with Recourse for Planning Optimal Flexibility in Multinational Corporations* (Ph.D. diss., University of California, Berkeley, 1967); Richard H. Ballon, "Dynamic Warehouse Location Analysis," *Journal of Marketing Research*, August 1968, pp. 271–76.

FIGURE 17.3

A Simplified Application of the Prescriptive Model for Global Planning (given: demand, sales, and cost data)

	Seven County Markets							
	A	B	C	D	E	F	G	Total
Market projection and sales targets in 00's units:								
Year 1 Market	260	400	320	800	250	470	510	3010
(Target)	(60)	(90)	(80)	(160)	(100)	(80)	(110)	680
Year 2 Market	280	420	350	840	260	480	510	3140
(Target)	(65)	(95)	(90)	(165)	(100)	(80)	(105)	700
Year 3 Market	310	420	390	880	270	490	480	3240
(Target)	(70)	(100)	(110)	(175)	(100)	(90)	(105)	750
Year 4 Market	360	420	430	930	280	510	460	3390
(Target)	(90)	(105)	(130)	(185)	(100)	(100)	(100)	810
Year 5 Market	410	440	470	930	290	560	460	3560
(Target)	(110)	(105)	(150)	(195)	(100)	(110)	(100)	870
Market price per unit	$85	$100	$100	$90	$90	$95	$85	
Current annual production capacity in 00's units	—	90	—	300	200	—	140	730
Production cost per unit with existing plant	—	$ 70	—	$65	$60	—	$60	
Cost of standard plant extension of 5,000 units annual capacity— $250,000								
Production cost per unit from a new extension	—	$ 65	$ 75	$65	$55	$70	$55	
Transfer cost per unit (including transport and duty, in dollars)								
From A to:								
" B	15	—	20	10	15	15	20	
" C	20	25	—	10	15	15	5	
" D	25	25	10	—	15	10	5	
" E	20	25	15	20	—	10	5	
" F	20	25	15	20	15	—	5	
" G	25	25	15	15	15	15	—	

Simplifying Assumptions

1. Five-year horizon with plant extensions possible for year 3.
2. No change expected in sales prices.
3. Production cost per unit excludes plant cost and is taken as directly variable.
4. All transfer costs directly variable and no possibility of customs duty saving through manipulation of transfer prices.
5. Production strategy to be determined independently of corporation tax considerations.

Decision Analysis

Inspection of the following table shows that all expansion should be located at E to supply A's requirements and the balance of F. (Where one alternative is not so dominant a linear-program calculation would be needed to establish profits of the alternatives.) Extensions should be completed to increase capacity by a further 5,000 units in each of years 3, 4, and 5.

Return on capital can be based on the profit that would be forgone if the extension were not available. If this meant simply the elimination of sales to the least profitable market given the reduced supply system, it would be solely sales to A in years 3 and 4, but in year 5 production would be reallocated and 1,500 sales forgone in B, 1,000 in C, and 500 in F for a total revenue lost of $262,500.

Profits Per Unit from Alternative Location of Plant Extensions (in dollars)

Source	Destination						
	A	B	C	D	E	F	G
A	–	–	–	–	–	–	–
B	5	35	15	15	10	15	–
C	–5	5	25	10	5	10	10
D	–5	20	25	25	10	20	15
E	10	20	30	15	35	30	25
F	–5	5	15	–	5	25	10
G	5	20	30	25	10	25	30

the expected effects of changes in controls and other risks that might affect the flow.

Finally, each year's investment schedule will be subject to a cutoff limit determined by the firm's capacity to expand. The representative firm can be assumed to operate under capital rationing with a specified expansion capacity determined by management's ability to cope with expansion. This capacity might be expressed as a maximum investment sum for any year which together with reinvestment funds is available to meet the schedule of investment opportunities. The firm then accepts these opportunities in decreasing order of return on capital until the investment sum is fully committed. It is assumed that this sum is committed to projects for which the least profitable would show an expected return well above the cost of raising capital, hence the firm's capacity to handle expansion is what limits investment and not the cost of capital. Finally, if the available investment is not used up, then the firm will raise its market targets and repeat the process. Conversely, targets that cannot be met will have to be lowered.

Thus, the prescriptive approach to global planning would follow the process described above. To make the approach more concrete, an illustrative example is presented in Figure 17.3.

Entry Strategies

The entry strategies adopted by a firm are an important consideration in building the total global strategy and warrant a little more attention than was given in the prescriptive approach. The firm has a choice of alternative approaches for penetrating new markets and for establishing new sources of supply. These alternatives imply different levels of commitment for the financial and other resources of the firm. They also have a time dimension and can operate as a building block or an obstacle to the achievement of long-term goals.

Moving from a minimum to a maximum commitment of company resources, entry strategies can be grouped into the following five categories: (1) licensing, (2) exporting, (3) local warehousing with direct sales staff, (4) local packaging and/or assembling operations, or (5) full-scale local production and marketing.

Within the categories, additional options may exist. Exporting, for example, can be done through an export merchant who buys products from domestic companies in the country of origin and sells abroad at his own risk. Or a company may engage a selling agent as a complete and exclusive marketing arm. Or a company can have its own export department and engage in direct exporting.[11] In the case of entering

---

[11] See Endel J. Kolde, *International Business Enterprise,* 2nd ed. (Englewood Cliffs, N.J.: Prentice-Hall, 1973), pp. 454–69.

a market by establishing a full-scale production and marketing subsidiary, the company may have the option of acquiring a local concern or of establishing a completely new operation.

A similar set of entry strategies is available for initiating projects that are primarily a source of supply for the multinational enterprise. A minimum commitment of resources would be involved in establishing only a buying office in a foreign location. A maximum commitment of resources would be to invest in company-operated production facilities and in supporting infrastructure such as transportation, electric power, or housing, health, and educational facilities for employees. Many alternatives are available between these two extremes.

During the 1960s, Japanese firms made extensive use of loan-purchase agreements whereby they assisted in the establishment of foreign supply sources, by making loans, and by agreeing to buy a given share of the output from the new project. In this way, Japanese companies expanded the availability of needed resources without taking an equity position and without assuming any managerial responsibility for new projects. Another interesting strategy used by some textile companies operating in Southeast Asia has been to establish local warehouses for raw materials and finished goods but to subcontract the manufacturing function to independent local companies. The international firm does the purchasing of supplies, the design and fashion work, and the international marketing but not the actual manufacturing. Other strategies previously mentioned are to establish producing facilities in free port or border industry areas, primarily to make use of lower labor costs in a foreign country.

Given these many alternative entry strategies, what are the variables that determine the best choice for a company? Returning to the case of a market seeker, the decision variables will be both external and internal to the firm. Most of the decision variables apply also to the entry decision for supply projects.

External factors
  Host-country policies and controls
  Size and attractiveness of markets
  Competitive conditions in the foreign market
  Availability of local supply sources in the country
Internal factors
  Characteristics of technology and products
  Enterprise-wide availability of productive capacity
  Minimum economic size for producing units
  Locational characteristics of production
  Availability of capital and managerial resources
  Company's willingness to assume risk
  Long-term corporate goals

In many cases, one or a few of the decision variables will dominate the decision on entry strategy and, in effect, reduce sharply the available options. Japan has followed policies of prohibiting foreign direct investment in designated fields so that the only options available to an international company for entering the Japanese market may be licensing and exporting. And in some cases, quota or tariff restrictions may still further reduce the option to that of licensing. This assumes, of course, that the international company controls patents, technology, or trademarks that have licensing value. Or a less developed country attempting to encourage foreign direct investment may have such prohibitive import restrictions that the only realistic option for entering its market is to establish a foreign-production subsidiary. Or the size of the market may be so small in relation to the minimum economic size required for efficient production that exporting is the only sensible initial-entry strategy.

For each project, the feasible alternatives will have to be sorted out and compared as to profitability and consequences for achieving the firm's long-term goals. Licensing and exporting provide relatively low-risk entry strategies but frequently are not the optimum means for maximizing the gains from a company's competitive advantage.[12] But in all cases, the firm should make sure that its initial entry strategy will not create future obstacles for achieving long-run objectives. An essential characteristic of global planning is that interim moves should be designed to achieve long-term goals. A licensing arrangement may have immediate attractiveness to a neophyte international company because it is an inexpensive and profitable way of becoming educated on foreign markets and international business operations. But when the company later matures and wants to become a multinational enterprise, it may discover that the once-attractive licensing arrangement has become a barrier to the establishment of the company's own production facilities in a promising foreign market.

Ownership Strategies

Ownership strategies are another important component of overall global strategy. Should foreign subsidiaries be wholly owned by the multinational enterprise? Or should the firm follow the joint-venture approach of sharing ownership in its foreign subsidiaries with local interests, either private or government? If the joint-venture approach is adopted, should the international firm seek a majority or minority participation? Ownership policies change investment requirements and other resource commitments for new projects and can significantly affect the extent to which individual subsidiaries participate in an enterprise-wide global strategy.

---

[12] See David B. Zenoff, "Licensing As a Means of Penetrating Foreign Markets," *IDEA*, Summer 1970, pp. 292–308.

In a number of countries, ownership policies for foreign firms are prescribed by national-control policies or laws. Mexico, India, and Japan are examples of countries that require joint ventures, generally on a minority-participation basis. Some bargaining has been possible in such countries, and a few firms which control a product or technology keenly desired by the host country have been able to get permission for establishing a wholly owned subsidiary or securing majority participation. But in general the ownership-strategy alternatives are limited in these countries. For a wide range of other countries, however, the multinational firm has considerable choice.

Of the 170 major U.S. international enterprises, less than 25 have never entered into a joint venture. But the remaining companies have been involved in roughly 1,100 joint ventures in countries where they could have legally chosen to have wholly owned operations.[13] There has been a widely held view, particularly in Europe, that preference for wholly owned or majority-owned subsidiaries is a peculiarly American trait. Yet, one recent investigation concludes that any great difference in ownership policies between American and European companies, either in attitude or in fact, has been difficult to substantiate on the basis of available information.[14]

The benefits to be gained by joint ventures fall into three areas: technical resources, financial advantage, and political considerations. Where competitive conditions make speed an important factor in entering a foreign market, a joint venture with an established local enterprise may be the means of acquiring local marketing know-how or other managerial skills at substantial savings in time and expense as compared to the alternative of creating an entirely new organization. In many cases, later events have shown that creating a new enterprise would have been a better solution. Yet, the apparent advantages offered by joining with a local enterprise have led many foreign firms into joint ventures. Frequently, the small firm trying to expand internationally at a rapid pace to keep up with its larger competitors may have little choice because of its limited managerial resources. But actual benefits will depend upon whether the local partner in fact has the complementary abilities needed for the kind of local operations desired by the international enterprise.

The joint venture that Xerox Corporation entered into with the Rank Organization of the United Kingdom to produce and market its copying machines outside the United States has been explained by the rapid

[13] Lawrence G. Franko, "Joint-Venture Divorce in the Multinational Company," *Columbia Journal of World Business,* May–June, 1971, p. 14; Franko, *Joint-Venture Survival in Multinational Corporations* (New York: Praeger Publications, Inc., 1971).

[14] Michael Z. Brooke and H. Lee Remmers, *The Strategy of Multinational Enterprise* (New York: American Elsevier Publishing Co., 1970), p. 262.

growth in the U.S. market for Xerox machines.[15] Domestic business expanded at such a rate that all available managerial resources of Xerox were being absorbed at home. Rather than lose out in the vast potential that foreign markets promised, Xerox opted for a partner and a joint venture.

The financial advantages of joint ventures may also permit an international enterprise to enter into more foreign projects when its financial resources are limited or its home country is imposing restrictions on the export of capital. In some cases, the foreign investor may be able to find local partners who are willing to accept the technological know-how, patent rights, or even the trade name of the international enterprise as a substitute for capital in payment for a share of the subsidiary's equity. Economizing on capital has been one of the motivations for many firms entering into joint ventures, but it has been less important for American firms than for companies of Japanese and European nationality.[16] Besides enabling a foreign investor to stretch his financial resources, joint ventures also provide a hedge against political risks by reducing the amount of investment at stake. The local sharing of ownership can also lessen the risk of foreign exchange losses.

Political considerations have probably been the most important motivation for joint ventures in many countries. Sharing ownership with nationals can encourage national identification and reduce the appearance of foreignness. Furthermore, local partners may in some cases be able to contribute political influence and protection against the possibility of increasingly severe national controls. The maximum of local protection could be achieved by a joint venture with the national government, although where governments change with frequency, even this strategy cannot be a complete defense. In terms of public-relations benefits, a wide distribution of shares among the investing public may be the best strategy.

Studies of the joint-venture experience of the principal American multinational firms suggest that a company's long-run tolerance for joint ventures is closely related to its product strategy.[17] Firms following a strategy of foreign product diversification, directed toward ever enlarging their offerings of products and services and their coverage of foreign markets, as contrasted to specializing in selling one particular function to similar countries worldwide, have found joint ventures positively use-

---

[15] Ibid., p. 362.

[16] W. G. Friedmann and G. Kalmanoff, eds., *Joint International Business Ventures* (New York: Columbia University Press, 1961).

[17] Franko, "Joint-Venture Divorce in the Multinational Company," *Columbia Journal of World Business,* May–June, 1971, pp. 20–21; John M. Stopford and Louis T. Wells, Jr., *Managing the Multinational Enterprise* (New York: Basic Books, 1972), pp. 99–168.

ful in both the short- and long-run. In such firms, marketing and production decisions are largely taken at the subsidiary level, and marketing policies are relatively unstandardized across a number of countries.

The disadvantages of joint ventures revolve largely around the desire and need of the multinational enterprise to retain control over the decisions of foreign subsidiaries. Other disadvantages relate to the reluctance to disclose information to outsiders and an unwillingness to share the earnings of the subsidiary. The control issue can be the source of many conflicts between the international firm and its local partners. Where the special advantages of the multinational enterprise inhere in a unification of markets and the rationalization of production, financial, and other functions on a regional or global basis, the interests of any subunit and the local partners owning shares in that subunit are likely to conflict with global objectives and opportunities. As one example, for tax reasons the firm may prefer to show its profits in one subsidiary rather than another and adopt transfer-pricing policies to implement this goal. Or local partners may prefer dividends rather than retaining earnings as a source of financing expansion. In such cases, conflicts with local partners may be inevitable.

In the past, many international enterprises have followed strongly fixed attitudes which insisted on having 100 percent ownership at all times and under all circumstances.[18] Such policies have been justified as the need for complete control or by the attitude expressed by one executive who said, "We do all the work and take all the risk; if it's a success why should we let the locals in on it? If it's a flop, they won't be interested. Either way, I can't see the point."[19] Other strong opponents of sharing ownership locally have argued that nationals can share in the operations of a subsidiary by purchasing shares in the parent company, either in the home-base country or when listed on local exchanges.

But with a growing body of experience and greatly increased pressures by host countries in the developed as well as the less developed countries, multinational enterprises have been moving toward more flexible and pragmatic views on joint ventures. Again, the degree to which multinational enterprises can tolerate joint ventures is closely related to the product strategy of the firm. Product-concentrating firms, specializing in providing one product or one service to their customers, find it most difficult to succeed with joint ventures.[20] In such firms, marketing and production-output decisions need to be relatively centralized on a supranational or regional levels. Marketing policies tend to be standardized

---

[18] See Robinson, *International Business Policy* (New York: Holt, Rinehart & Winston, 1964), pp. 147–74 for results of a 1956–59 study of 172 American firms.

[19] Brooke & Remmers, *Strategy of Multinational Enterprise*, p. 269.

[20] Franko, *Joint-Venture Survival*, pp. 15–16.

across borders and expenditures on product-differentiation tend to be high. A coordinated export strategy is required so that the firm avoids meeting itself in many export markets. And under these circumstances, a high potential exists for conflicts between the parent company and the local partners over market decision making.

The issue of ownership strategy has a time dimension. The point has been made that the stream of benefits of the foreign investment to the host country may decrease over time. Such a maturing of benefits and an increase in the alternatives open to a country can reduce the bargaining power of the foreign enterprise for maintaining 100 percent or even majority ownership.[21] And in a growing number of countries, the international firm may encounter national policies which require gradual divestment of foreign ownership over time, or what has been called a fade-out policy.[22] Or the enterprise itself may want to change ownership patterns over time. A joint venture may have served the purpose of helping a firm acquire local experience in the initial entry stage but no longer serves this need at a later stage. For this and other reasons, the joint-venture divorce rate has been relatively high where divorce has been legal.

As in the case of entry strategies, the decision criteria that should influence ownership strategies will be a mixture of factors internal and external to the firm. The internal factors will be the product strategy of the firm, the availability of adequate financial and other managerial resources, the degree of operating experience it can command for new and different situations, and the speed with which it desires to initiate new projects for competitive or other reasons. The external factors will be the control policies of the host countries,[23] the availability of local partners or of adequate financial markets where widely shared local ownership is desired, and the local competitive situation, which may require that entry be made through acquiring a local firm that desires to retain an ownership interest.

Home-country policies may be another important external factor. U.S. tax policies, for example, limit foreign tax credits for the parent company to situations where a specified minimum of ownership is held. Or antitrust liability may arise where agreements exist between the parent company and jointly owned subsidiaries, whereas the same arrangements with a wholly owned subsidiary would not be challenged. Or home-coun-

---

[21] Peter Gabriel, "The Investment in the LDC: Assets With a Fixed Maturity," *Columbia Journal of World Business,* Summer 1966, pp. 109–19.

[22] Albert O. Hirschman, *How to Divest in Latin America, and Why* (Princeton, N.J.: International Finance Section, Princeton University, November 1969).

[23] It is significant that the United Nations in 1971 published a *Manual on the Establishment of Industrial Joint-Venture Agreements in Developing Countries* (New York: United Nations, 1971) in response to the growing desire of LDCs to secure joint ventures.

try investment-guarantee programs may not be available for foreign projects where less than a certain minimum ownership exists.

A GLOBAL HABIT OF MIND

In the last analysis, developing a global strategy depends upon the way executives think about doing business around the world. The design and implementation of a global strategy requires that managers in both headquarters and subsidiaries follow a worldwide approach which considers subsidiaries as neither satellites nor independent city-states but as parts of a whole the focus of which is on worldwide as well as local objectives. And each part of the system makes its unique contribution with its unique competence. This approach which Perlmutter has popularized as "geocentrism" involves a collaborative effort between subsidiaries and headquarters to establish universal standards and permissible local variations on the basis of which key decisions are made.[24] However, geocentrism requires a reward system for subsidiary managers which motivates them to work for worldwide goals and not just defend country objectives.

Three general types of headquarters orientation toward subsidiaries in international enterprise have been described by Perlmutter. While they never appear in pure form, and there is some degree of each philosophy in most firms, they are clearly distinguishable as ethnocentric (or home-country oriented), polycentric (or host-country oriented), and geocentric (or world-oriented).

The ethnocentric attitude can be characterized as "We the home country nationals are superior to, more trustworthy, and more reliable than any foreigners in headquarters or the subsidiaries." In such firms, performance criteria and decision rules are generally based on home-country standards. Ethnocentrism works against a global strategy because of a lack of good feedback and because the experience and views of managers familiar with local conditions in the areas of operation do not carry appropriate weight in decision making.

Polycentric firms go to the other extreme by assuming that local people always know what is best for them and that the unit of the multinational enterprise located in a host country should be as local in identity and behavior as possible. A polycentric firm is more akin to a confederation of quasi-independent subsidiaries. And a polycentric-management philosophy is likely to sacrifice most of the unification and synergistic potential benefits of multinational operation. The costs of polycentrism are the waste due to duplication, to decisions to make products for local use which could be but are not sold worldwide, and

[24] Howard V. Perlmutter, "The Tortuous Evolution of the Multinational Corporation," *Columbia Journal of World Business*, January–February 1969, pp. 9–18.

to inefficient use of home-country experience. The approach has the advantage of making intensive use of local resources and personnel but at a cost of global growth and efficiency.

Geocentrism also has costs, largely related to communication and travel expense, time spent in decision making because of the desire to educate personnel as to global objectives and secure consensus, and the expense of a relatively large headquarter's bureaucracy. But the payoffs are a more objective total enterprise performance, worldwide utilization of best resources, improvement of local company management, a greater sense of commitment to worldwide goals and last, but not least, more profit. A globally oriented enterprise, of course, depends on having an adequate supply of managers who are globally oriented.

Summary

Few, if any, companies are born with a global philosophy and a worldwide view. They normally become international by a process of creeping incrementalism, adding a series of international units to the parent company as isolated reactions to perceived opportunities or competitive threats. But at some stage of internationalization, either as a result of growing experience or competitive pressures, the firm becomes aware of the need for a global strategy and a global decision model in order to benefit from the synergy potential of multinational operations and to maximize results on a worldwide basis. At this stage, if not before, the truly multinational enterprise engages in a system of international strategic and long-range planning. A case study of an actual international planning system has been briefly described.

The formulation of a global strategy starts from the identification of global markets and works back to determine the location of supply and production activities and investments to achieve optimum performance in these markets. It requires decisions as to the best entry strategies for securing access to markets and foreign locations of resources or production. Another sub-component of a global strategy is a company's decisions concerning ownership and joint ventures. Above all, the formulation and implementation of a global strategy requires managers with a global, or geocentric, habit of mind.

The nature and necessity of a global strategy has been well expressed in a study of Massey-Ferguson, a leading Canadian multinational farm machinery company as follows:

It seems that the essence of a sophisticated international industrial corporation is that it, at all times, is prepared and in a position to develop markets for its products wherever on earth such opportunities exist and seeks to deploy its manufacturing and engineering facilities internationally in a way that will minimize its global production and development costs and will assist in the development of particular markets. Arbitrary rules guiding asset deployment can only do harm to such a corporation. Rational judgments relating to prospective rates of return, based on detailed knowledge of local social, political, and economic conditions must lie at the heart of its international asset deployment decisions. Emotional attachments to the "home base" and misconceptions about conditions and opportunities abroad have no place.[25]

EXERCISES AND DISCUSSION QUESTIONS

1. If a global strategy is required to maximize the special advantages and synergistic benefits of multinational operations, why have so many firms been successful in their international operations by responding to perceived opportunities and competitive threats without international strategic planning and global decision models?

2. How can an enterprise simplify the complexities of international possibilities and reduce the variables it includes in its decision making to manageable proportions?

3. Under what circumstances would global planning be desirable, even if the firm's international involvement is minor?

4. What decision rules other than those mentioned in the chapter might be used for choosing among alternative sources of supply?

5. "Entering a new market through licensing is generally the best strategy because market potentials can be tested with little or no investment." Comment.

6. "A multinational firm needs to have complete control over its subsidiaries in order to make optimum use of its resources and compete most effectively. This generally means 100 percent ownership." Comment.

---

[25] E. P. Neufeld, *A Global Corporation: A History of the International Development of Massey-Ferguson Limited* (Toronto, Canada: University of Toronto Press, 1969), p. 385.

18

ORGANIZATION FOR MULTINATIONAL OPERATIONS

AN ENTERPRISE THAT BEGINS OPERATING in more than one national market normally finds that this leads to new organizational problems that require changes in its organizational structure. The multinational firm must cope with geographically dispersed operations, personnel from many cultures, diverse political and economic environments, and divergent trends in different countries. A firm operating in a single market does not have these challenges. Clearly, an organizational structure designed for purely domestic business is not likely to be suitable for multinational operations.

The array of different organization structures being used by international firms is as diverse as the strategies they have been following in achieving growth abroad.[1] Few, if any, are identical and no simple criteria exist for selecting the best organizational form. Yet, looked at from the level of senior managers who make strategic decisions, the number of general types of structural alternatives are relatively small. Despite the diversity that exists within the broad organizational categories, a number of useful guidelines exist for resolving the organization problems as a firm develops from a domestic to a multinational enterprise.

Each of the broad structural designs through which the enterprise can be administered has advantages and disadvantages, but for any specific company the net advantages will depend upon a large number of variables, many of which are unique to the products, markets, re-

---

[1] For example see, Harold Stieglitz, *Organization Structures of International Companies* (New York: National Industrial Conference Board, 1965); Business International, *Organizing the Worldwide Corporation* (New York, 1970).

sources, or personalities of that firm. Organizational questions, however, are rarely resolved in a rational or a definitive way. Firms usually choose a solution by a process of bargaining among advocates of different alternatives.[2] As changes occur in operating strategies and in bargaining strength among internal groups, pressures are created for reopening negotiations. Also, because of the different characteristics and sizes of their respective markets and wide variations in attitude and in national and corporate history, U.S. and European companies have had quite different approaches to the problem of organization.[3] Thus, the international manager must look upon the organizational question as an issue that will be continually under review.

STATUTORY AND MANAGERIAL ORGANIZATIONS

The international enterprise encompasses two distinct but interwoven component structures: the statutory, or legal, organization, and the managerial organization.[4] The statutory organization exists on paper only. It is designed to conform to legal requirements while best meeting the objectives of the firm, for example, minimization of commercial restrictions or taxation. The managerial organization may cut right across the statutory structure and is concerned with the authority and responsibility of each executive and the lines of communication among these executives. It is also concerned with the information that flows along these lines of communication and the procedures for channeling and processing the information.

The statutory organization defines the legal and ownership structure that links the parent company with its various units. Each unit may have a different statutory status—branch, subsidiary, holding company, and so forth—depending in part of the legal requirements of the jurisdiction in which it is established. Holding companies in low-tax areas have often been used for the statutory organization and the statutory center is rarely the operating center. In fact, some statutory centers may consist of only a part-time local lawyer and a mail clerk. Thus, the statutory and managerial structures must be considered as separate entites. The lawyers and tax experts will be primarily responsible for designing the statutory structure. The international manager will be mainly involved in the design and functioning of the managerial structure—the subject of the rest of this chapter.

---

[2] John M. Stopford and Louis T. Wells, Jr., *Managing the Multinational Enterprise,* (New York: Basic Books, 1972), pp. 13–18.

[3] *Organizing For European Operations* (Geneva, Switzerland: Business International, 1967). See Chapter 3 on the European experience in organizing for worldwide operations.

[4] John G. McDonald, "New Organizational Concept of the World Enterprise," *Management International* 1, no. 5/6, 1961.

EVOLUTIONARY STAGES OF ORGANIZATION

The evolution of the organizational structure of an enterprise can be viewed as a series of stages, with each stage a modification or adaptation of the structure in the previous stage. A description of the detailed organization structure at any specific stage is something like a snapshot, or still picture from a film, that shows isolated, but typical, moments in a continuing process of organizational change. The speed of the process varies from company to company. Some tread cautiously and take one step at a time, whereas others rush through certain stages and bypass others. In general, the evolutionary process of U.S. firms going international has closely paralleled the structural developments that accompanied growth and diversification at home.[5] As yet, less research is available on the evolutionary process of non–U.S. firms.

In the early stages of entering foreign markets through exports, a company may assign the export responsibility to an independent trading company. As foreign sales increase in importance, the typical organizational response of the large enterprise is to establish an export department with some medium-level company official designated as export manager. Still concentrating on exports, the firm may go further and set up its own sales, service, and warehousing facilities abroad.[6] In the early stages, the basic organizational structure of the firm is left undisturbed.

A statutory organizational response available at this stage to U.S. companies is to assign responsibility for Western Hemisphere exports to a Western Hemisphere Trade Corporation (WHTC) to reap the tax advantages given to such units. More recently, many U.S. companies have organized a Domestic International Sales Corporation (DISC) for exports to gain tax benefits authorized by the Revenue Act of 1971 intended to encourage export expansion.[7] However, the WHTC and DISC are generally statutory organizations and unlikely to affect the managerial organization structure.

The Japanese firm typically follows a different pattern in entering foreign markets through exports because they have been able to rely on the services available from the giant Japanese trading companies instead of forming their own export departments. The Japanese general trading firms have no comparable counterpart in other countries. Their basic business is foreign trade and they handle many of the international business functions that American and European companies normally perform for themselves. Of the several thousand trading companies, six

---

[5] Stopford and Wells, *Managing the Multinational Enterprise,* p. 11.

[6] See James Greene, *Organizing For Exporting* (New York: National Industrial Conference Board, 1968); Endel J. Kolde, *International Business Enterprise* (Englewood Cliffs, N.J.: Prentice-Hall, 1968), pp. 242–45.

[7] See Chapter 8.

are giants: Mitsubishi, Mitsui, Marubeni–Ida, C. Itoh, Nissho–Iwai and Sumitomo. In 1971, these six had a total volume of \$57 billion and handled about 40 percent of Japan's imports and about 50 percent of its exports, through an overseas marketing and information network of over 500 offices employing over 12,000 people.[8] Some Japanese firms, however, have followed an evolutionary pattern similar to that of American companies in order to secure more specialized attention for their export business than the giant trading companies could provide.

As the nature of international operations changes from exporting to a mix of exporting, licensing, and foreign production, and as the scale of international sales becomes of more than incidental importance to the firm, conflicts of interest arise between internal units of the firm that are not easily handled by an export department type of organization. Where a need has emerged to fortify the firm's foreign market position by establishing production-facilities in areas served by its export department, an export department structure is particularly inadequate. The export department may fail to recognize the need or prefer to continue with exports because foreign-production facilities may mean a loss of export sales attributed to the department. The usual organizational response by American companies to such conflicting interests has been to create a full international division which includes the previously independent unit for handling exports.[9]

Before moving to an international-division structure, some companies pass through an intermediate stage where the firm acts only as a holding company for largely autonomous foreign subsidiaries. The autonomous foreign-subsidiary pattern can be adopted without making any significant changes in the organizational structure of the remainder of the company. It occurs where foreign ventures are first established, not as a result of planning but in response to a specific threat or opportunity. Because such first ventures are small and not critical to the success of the organization, and because the parent firm has insufficient international experience to make much of a contribution to the new foreign ventures, foreign managers are allowed virtually unlimited powers of decision and action. As one study explains, "The need for learning exceeds the desire for control."[10] The subsidiary will have rather loose financial ties to the senior financial officer of the parent company, but its operating freedom will be great so long as the financial results of the venture are satisfactory.

[8] *Forbes*, 1 May 1972, p. 26; Morihisa Emori, *The Japanese Trading Company* (Tokyo: Mitsubishi Shoji Kaisha, 1969); Leon Hollerman, *Japan's Dependence on the World Economy* (Princeton, N.J.: Princeton University Press, 1967), pp. 239–44.

[9] Cedric L. Suzman, "Whatever Happened to the Export Manager?" *Worldwide P & I Planning*, pp. 16–25.

[10] Stopford and Wells, *Managing the Multinational Enterprise*, p. 20.

For American companies, the autonomous-subsidiary phase may have a short life. If the foreign units grow rapidly and accumulate significant resources, pressures will arise within the parent company to introduce management controls. The success of the foreign venture makes it significant to the total enterprise. The international experience that ownership of the subsidiary has brought to the parent firm enables it to approach the design and implementation of controls with more assurance. The possibility of economic gain from coordinating its foreign subsidiaries will generate pressures for organizational change to permit a greater degree of central control over the subsidiaries decision making.

The establishment of an international division, generally of equal status to other major divisions, normally results from four factors. First is the matter of size. The international commitment of the firm has reached an absolute size and a relative importance within the enterprise to justify an organizational unit headed by a manager with a senior level of authority. Second, the complexity of international operations requires a single organizational unit that can resolve within it such conflicts as the best means for entering foreign areas on the basis of a broad view of the firm's international opportunities. Third, the firm has recognized the need for a group of specialists within the enterprise who can deal with the special features of international operations. And finally, the enterprise wants to develop an affirmative capability for scanning the global horizon for opportunities or competitive threats rather than simply responding to situations that are presented to the company.

By the early 1960s, the international-division organizational approach was the most common type of structure of large U.S. enterprises with foreign operations. However, the continued growth of these divisions sowed the seeds of their destruction by enlarging the interest of top management in the international opportunities. By the mid-1960s, a growing number of firms had abandoned their international divisions in favor of a global-organizational structure.[11] As Clee and Sachtjen have observed, "The really decisive point in the transition to world enterprise is top management recognition that, to function effectively, the ultimate control of strategic planning and policy decisions must shift from decentralized subsidiaries or division locations to corporate headquarters, where a worldwide perspective can be brought to bear on the interests of the total enterprise."[12]

At the global stage, responsibility for both foreign and domestic is moved to the top echelons and new subdivisions are specified on either a functional, geographic, or product basis. The choice among the func-

---

[11] Stopford and Wells, *Managing the Multinational Enterprise,* p. 25.

[12] Gilbert H. Clee and Wilbur M. Sachtjen, "Organizing a Worldwide Enterprise," *Harvard Business Review,* November–December 1964, p. 67.

tional, geographic, or product-division structures depends primarily on the business strategy of the enterprise.

The global structure, however, is not the final stage in the development of organizational structures capable of providing effective administration for a multinational enterprise. Most global structures are based on the management principle of unity of command: one man having sole responsibility for a specified part of the business, either subdivided by function, product, or geographical areas, and accountable to a single superior officer. But the conflicting need for coordinating all three dimensions can still remain a serious problem. Some firms have attempted to build new structures where managers have dual or multiple reporting relationships and where area, function, and product responsibilities overlap. Experimentation is underway with various types of "grid" structures and an evolution to organizational forms beyond the global structure is already underway.

European multinational firms appear to follow a somewhat different evolutionary pattern from that of American companies. Unencumbered by huge domestic markets, European firms tend to move directly to a global form of organization without passing through the international division stage.[13] A company based in a small country knows from the beginning that it can never grow large without expanding into foreign markets. Its export-marketing operations may be placed in a special export unit. But its domestic and foreign operations develop together under a top management that is committed to international business. This integrated approach does not necessarily mean that the foreign company has become a global firm in the sense that it has a global strategy and attempts to maximize the potential gains from worldwide operations. It simply accepts the need to do business across national lines as a normal condition of growth and structures its organization accordingly. By necessity, the greater dependence of European firms on exports and foreign production has emphasized worldwide organizational forms rather than a separation between foreign and domestic activities through the creation of an international division.

THE INTERNATIONAL DIVISION

For the firm extending its activities internationally from a large domestic market like the United States that has dominated the company's attention, the international division provides an organizational umbrella

---

[13] See Hans Schollhammer, "Organizational Structures of Multinational Corporations," *Academy of Management Journal*, September 1971, pp. 345–65; Andrew J. Lombard, Jr., "How European Companies Organize Their International Operations," *European Business*, July 1969, p. 37; Lawrence G. Franko, "Strategy + Structure — Frustration = The Experience of European Firms in America," *European Business*, Autumn 1971, pp. 29–42.

for all the foreign activities of the enterprise and a focus for learning about the management of international operations. It permits centralized direction over a company's foreign operations, particularly during the developmental and expansion stages of the international program. It concentrates international know-how and skills in a separate unit detached from domestic responsibilities and makes possible a concentrated drive on market expansion and investment overseas. It places a champion of foreign activities and a strong voice in the top-management echelons for allocating the necessary resources to new foreign activities.

The international division is usually headed by a vice president who reports directly to the president or chief executive of the company. Some enterprises form an international company headed by a president that plays essentially the same role as an international division. In most cases, the international division is responsible for policy and global-strategic planning for international operations. But in some situations, this responsibility has shifted to executives at the corporate level without significant change in the formal structure. And there is considerable variation in the administrative practices for maintaining links between the international activities and the domestic side of the enterprise.

A representative organization diagram for a firm using an international-division structure is shown in Figure 18.1. At an early stage, the corporate staff groups, except for finance and control, are likely to continue to be domestically oriented. The international division will rely mainly on its own divisional staff. As policy and strategic planning shifts to the corporate level, the marketing, manufacturing, research, personnel, and other staff will become internationally oriented. As mentioned previously, both patterns can occur while maintaining the international division or international company structure.

The international division usually has direct responsibility for all export and licensing activities of the parent company and is accountable, directly or indirectly, for the operations of overseas manufacturing and sales units. Its task is to coordinate all the international activities so as to raise the level of performance above that likely where subsidiaries are autonomous and other international functions such as exporting and licensing are dispersed within the firm. The division may be able to reduce the cost of capital for a subsidiary by borrowing in some other area or in international capital markets. It can be the channel for the transfer of experience among subsidiaries. It may be able to reduce tax liability through transfer-pricing policies. In brief, it has responsibility for improving total performance through the unification or synergy potentials of multinational operations.

The international division has constraints on its ability to assist the foreign subsidiaries. As a division, it normally does not have the resources to develop detailed knowledge on the environments and characteristics

FIGURE 18.1

An International-Division Structure

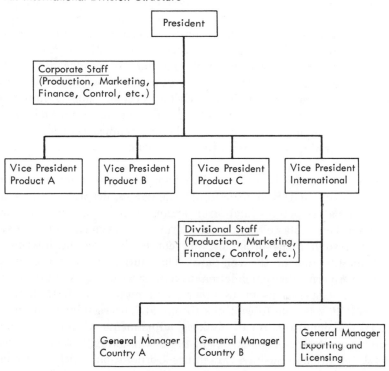

of large numbers of local areas and must heavily delegate direct operating responsibilities to the foreign subsidiaries. It cannot centralize many decisions because the competitive position of the subsidiary may be reduced by the time lag involved in securing decisions from the international division. In general, the amount of decentralization will vary with the particular functions involved, product characteristics, the degree of expertise accumulated at the divisional level, and the time taken to refer matters to the division. Firms engaged in the production and sale of a narrow line of mature goods with relatively stable technologies and markets, for example, tend to move farther in the direction of centralization than firms expanding into many different markets with diversified lines of new products involving rapidly changing technologies.

Where the products manufactured or sold abroad are the products developed at home, as is normally the case, the international division is heavily dependent on the domestic-product divisions. In this respect the international division has less autonomy than the product divisions and depends upon their assistance more than they depend on each other. The international division normally does not have its own product development, engineering, and research and development staff, and the domestic divisions controlling these important components of the overseas operations are frequently reluctant to give priority to foreign needs because they are measured solely by their domestic performance. Thus the international division depends heavily on the communication and cooperation procedures that are worked out with the domestic-product divisions for making the specialized skills of the domestic units available to the international operations. As product divisions become more familiar with international needs, the effectiveness of the communication and cooperation devices can improve. But the inherent conflict between the goals of the domestic and international divisions is never completely eliminated.

The fact that the international-division structure remains dominant in the majority of U.S. multinational companies, despite a strong move toward global structures and grid arrangements, suggests that many firms have been able to work out informal arrangements or formal devices for resolving the problems inherent in dividing the international unit from the rest of the company. One authority cites the example of a giant American automobile manufacturer with plants in 20 countries, its own sales operations in 18 others, and more than 100,000 workers overseas that was able to continue to operate successfully with an international-division structure by making adjustments within the structure for altering patterns of management decision making.[14] Another example is the International Business Machines Corporation which continues to handle its extensive and rapidly growing international operations through its separate IBM World Trade Corporation while integrating basic research, product development, and manufacturing activities on a worldwide basis.[15]

GLOBAL STRUCTURES

As the international division increases in size relative to the total enterprise, the same forces that led to its creation begin to work toward its dissolution. Top management becomes aware that there are gains to be realized by coordinating production, for example, on a worldwide scale by taking advantage of economies of scale. Unless all components of the enterprise are judged on their performance worldwide, they will not be motivated to act in accordance with the worldwide interests of the enterprise.

The alternative to the international-division structure is the global structure which eliminates the domestic-international dichotomy and

---

[14] Clee and Sachtjen, "Organizing a Worldwide Enterprise," pp. 57–59.

[15] Business International, *Organizing the Worldwide Corporation,* January 1970, pp. 12–13.

pays no more attention to national boundaries than the realities of time and place require. No single national market draws greater interest or attention than its contribution to overall corporate objectives. The global company may be structured along functional, product, or regional lines, and if a functional or product basis is used, divisional managers have worldwide responsibilities. The global or world corporation concept, of course, requires a global management philosophy and an integrated management team at the top level that thinks in terms of the worldwide commitments of the firm.

The Functional Structure

The functional-organizational structure for international operations has been the dominant form used by European companies. The division of responsibility at headquarters is organized by functions such as marketing, manufacturing, finance, and so forth, and the heads of these divisions have worldwide responsibilities as line executives (See Figure 18.2.) The marketing or sales division, for example, has worldwide mar-

FIGURE 18.2
Functional-Organization Structure

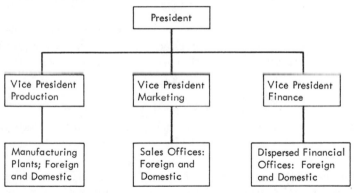

keting responsibility, with direct control over all sales companies and distributors, wherever located. In addition, the division normally has staff responsibility for coordinating the marketing of manufacturing subsidiaries, which usually control sales of the goods they produce, except for exports which are handled directly by the marketing division. The manufacturing division usually has line control over domestic plants, staff responsibility for worldwide product standardization, product development, quality control and R & D, and a mixture of line and staff responsibility over the foreign-manufacturing subsidiaries.

As long as companies remain comparatively small and have a fairly narrow range of products, the functional structure usually works rather well. Even in large international companies like SKF of Sweden, with a limited product line—ball bearings—that is not heavily dependent on the vagaries of regional markets, the functional structure is used with great effectiveness.[16] Some European firms, however, that have grown rapidly have experienced difficulties with the somewhat hazy responsibility assignments of this organizational form and with breakdowns in the informal lines of communication and reporting.[17]

The functional structure has the advantage of tight control over specific functions such as production, marketing, and finance.[18] It allows a relatively small group of officers to maintain line control over operations without much duplication. But the functional approach also has three basic weaknesses. Sales and production tend to become separated in their operations and objectives. Managers of subsidiaries normally have to report to more than one person. Finally, the structure results in tremendous duplication with regard to environmental inputs. Each of the functional divisions may need its own regional specialists and could be making different assumptions about future trends in the several areas of operations.

The Geographical Structure

Under a geographical structure, the primary operational responsibility is assigned to area managers each of whom is made responsible for a specific geographic area of the world. Corporate headquarters retains responsibility for worldwide strategic planning and control. Where the geographic form of organization has replaced the international division in U.S. companies, the United States becomes simply one of a number of world markets. Each area division has responsibility for all functions within its area and is able to coordinate marketing, production, finance, and so forth within its region.

Companies successfully using the geographical structure are ones with a narrow range of products whose end-use markets, local marketing requirements, technological base, and methods of manufacture tend to be similar, if not identical. The major oil companies generally employ a variant of the geographic structure. Key decisions on concessions, re-

---

[16] Ibid., pp. 45–46.

[17] Lombard, "How European Companies Organize their International Operations," p. 38.

[18] See Michael Z. Brooke and H. Lee Remmers, *The Strategy of Multinational Enterprise* (New York: American Elsevier Publishing Co., 1970). Brooke and Remmers call this a *Type A* company. For an example of the decision-making process in an actual *Type A* company see Figure 2.2, p. 30. By their designation, *Type B* has a geographical structure, *Type C* is organized worldwide by product groups, and *Type D* is a complicated mixture which has also been called a grid structure.

finery scheduling, and tanker-fleet management are logically made on a centralized basis. Within this framework, the area manager exercises true line responsibility or functions as a coordinator for all operations in his particular geographic area. The geographic form permits handling variations from market to market which require modest levels of technological skills. It works well also where the product is highly standardized, but techniques for penetrating markets differ, as in the case of soft-drink companies.

The principal difficulties of the geographical organization arise when the firm has a diverse product range. The structure does not easily handle the tasks of coordinating product variations, transferring new product ideas and production techniques from one country to another, and optimizing the flow of product from source to worldwide markets. One organizational response has been to create a global-product manager at the corporate level who is assigned worldwide responsibilities for particular products or product lines. His principal tasks are to mold a global-product strategy and to facilitate the transfer of experience from one area to another. But his operating relationships with the area managers who have line responsibility are likely to be ambiguous.

A geographical structure usually requires a large number of internationally experienced executives to staff the various regional headquar-

FIGURE 18.3
Geographic Structure

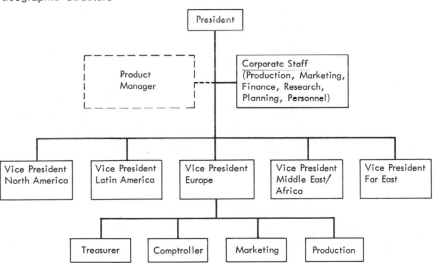

ters. It may result in too much information being screened from corporate headquarters and undue focus placed on the performance of the specific regions as opposed to the company's worldwide interest. It may also require considerable duplication of product specialists within the enterprise.

Product Structure

The product-structure organization assigns worldwide product responsibility to product-group executives as the primary line managers, and coordinates activity for all products in a given geographical area by having area specialists at the corporate staff level. (See Figure 18.4.)

FIGURE 18.4
Product Structure

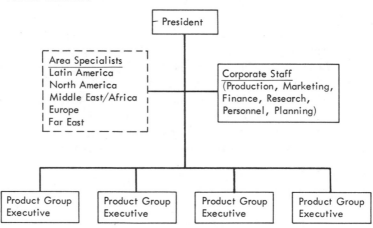

Overall goals and strategies for the company are set at corporate headquarters and within these corporate guidelines, the plans of each product group are reviewed and approved by top management. Each product group, however, has primary responsibility for planning and controlling all activities for its products on a worldwide basis.

The product structure works best when a company's product line is widely diversified, when products go into a variety of end-use markets, and when a relatively high technological capability is required. It is also advantageous when high shipping-costs, tariffs, or other considerations dictate local manufacture of the product.

The most important problem with the product structure is that worldwide responsibility is frequently assigned to managers with great product expertise whose experience has been largely domestic. Similar problems can arise at all levels when the personnel assigned are selected because of their product expertise and may have little experience and capability for dealing with the new kinds of problems that arise out of international operations.

Another problem inherent in the product structure is the difficulty of coordinating the activity of different product divisions in any given area. Suppose, for example, that *Product Division A* wanted to license a European company to manufacture *Product A* while *Product B*'s European plant was operating below capacity and could only avoid a loss by taking on an additional product. Without someone on the local scene responsible for the success of the enterprise as a whole, the two divisions might be unaware of each other's needs. *Product Division A* would incur the unnecessary expense of licensing the European plant. *Product Division B* would take a loss. The company as a whole would suffer.

The General Electric Company preserved an overlapping geographical responsibility to avoid these problems. The firm centered its foreign activities for many years in an international division that was organized as a separate company—International General Electric Company. Under pressure from changing internal and external forces, the company gradually moved to a structure which assigned worldwide responsibility to its domestic product groups. A reorganized International Group, however, continued to operate along with the product groups, as one company executive explained, "to provide a mechanism that would avoid the risk that 50 to 60 General Managers might start at a furious pace reinventing the wheel, competing with each other in committing the same blunders instead of learning from each other's experience."[19] The International Group has four overseas area managers who are responsible in their areas for governmental and business relations, and whose staff experts assist operating departments on entry strategy and environmental assessment.

Through a form of grid arrangement, G.E. has assigned heavy international responsibility to units that contain product expertise while still trying to achieve coordination on a geographical area basis. The difficulties of finding a perfect organizational structure are demonstrated by the fact that a product-organizational structure adopted by G.E. in 1964 was restructured within only five years by creating a strong International Group to review and coordinate all international operations of the company. Probably G.E.s costly experience in assigning managers with product expertise but with little international experience to head its computer operations in France after the acquisition of Machines Bull had more than a little to do with the reorganization move to dilute the responsibility of product divisions. The G.E.–Machines Bull project caused a loss to the company of many millions over the period.[20]

---

[19] W. D. Dance, "An Evolving Structure For Multinational Operations," *Columbia Journal of World Business,* November–December 1969, p. 29.

[20] Gregory H. Wierzynski, "G.E.'s $200 Million Ticket to France," *Fortune,* 1 June 1967, pp. 92–95, 159–62.

CHOOSING AMONG ALTERNATIVE
ORGANIZATIONAL STRUCTURES

The basic organization problem common to all firms operating internationally can be summed up in three questions:

1. Should the corporation be divided into domestic and international divisions?
2. Should line responsibility be subdivided for management purposes according to major functions, major product lines, or major geographic areas?
3. What is the best way to provide for needed specialization and co-ordination according to the other two variables, or how should the three necessary inputs—functional, product, and geographical—be meshed?

Clearly, there is no one right way to organize, no perfect organizational structure, and no organization form that can remain static when once adopted. Successful companies are using various organizational patterns to manage their international business operations effectively.

Although there are no standard requirements, the choice of organizational pattern has generally been determined by a relatively small number of variables. The variables which help to choose an organizational form that best fits the needs of a given firm in a given set of circumstances are the following:

1. The relative importance in the present and future of foreign and domestic markets as perceived by top management.
2. The historical background of a firm and its evolutionary stage in international operations.
3. The nature of a firm's business and its product strategy.
4. The management traits and management philosophy of the firm.
5. The availability of and willingness to invest in internationally experienced management personnel.
6. The capacity of an enterprise to adjust to major organizational changes.

The absolute size of international sales will determine the desirability of moving from an export-manager form of organization to an international division for most American companies. The choice between an international division and a global structure will be influenced by the relative importance of international and domestic markets as perceived by top management. The benefits of having all senior managers experienced in the diversities of international business may be great. But when a company's future is likely to be dominated by a large domestic market like the United States, the investment needed to man a global organization with internationally experienced personnel may not be warranted. Also, so long as domestic activities promise to continue to be much larger than international operations, separate attention may continue to be required for international activities so that they do not become subordinated to domestic considerations. At the other extreme, European companies have quickly adopted global structures, because foreign markets are invariably of major importance relative to domestic markets.

The choice of organization structure is inevitably influenced by a company's history and past experience. A company that has operated internationally for decades and possesses a top management experienced in dealing with worldwide problems will approach organizational change differently from a company which is a comparative neophyte on the international scene. During a firm's early stages of growth abroad, its organizational decisions are likely to be influenced by the need to encourage a concentrated drive on international opportunity by separating foreign from domestic activities. At a more advanced stage, organizational decisions will be increasingly motivated by the potential gains to be realized by coordinating all components of the enterprise on a worldwide scale.

As a firm's international activities become large relative to domestic business, the choice of organizational structure is closely related to the nature of the company's business and its product strategy. Where there is little product diversity, and where the success of the firm is not heavily dependent on diverse trends in different geographical markets, a functional structure can be effective. Where there is a limited product line, great similarity in end-user markets and in marketing techniques and distribution channels, but where area expertise plays a major role, a regional, or geographic, structure operates well. In such cases, it is less costly to duplicate product and functional expertise than area expertise. Where product lines are diverse, have a high-technology component, serve different end-user markets, and where production and sourcing can be advantageously rationalized on a worldwide basis, the product structure for organization has major advantages. The product structure facilitates the transfer of technology and sales support from producing divisions to international operations and can accelerate growth by forcing domestic divisions to become more aware of the markets and potentials of foreign areas.

Management traits and management philosophies can be another key variable determining the organizational structure of a firm. Some managements are bold and willing to make frequent organizational changes. Others are cautious and make changes only when absolutely necessary. The management philosophies and heritage of executive experience of European-based multinational companies favor structures which facilitate a potentially more centralized control over the totality of corporate operations by a few key executives, thus giving preference to functionally oriented organization structures. The management philosophy of U.S. firms is more likely to favor structures which provide greater opportunities for decentralized decision making, but with formal control devices like the profit center concept which allow for a more strict supervision, control, and coordination within the product-oriented or regionally oriented divisional activities.[21]

Another dimension of a firm's management philosophy is its orientation toward foreign people, ideas, and resources in headquarters and subsidiaries, and in host and home environments, which Perlmutter has described as ethnocentric (or home-country oriented), polycentric (or host-country oriented), and geocentric (or world oriented).[22] A polycentric firm would have something akin to a holding company structure with loose connections to quasi-independent subsidiaries. A geocentric philosophy leads to a global structure that permits a worldwide approach in both headquarters and subsidiaries.

But, even if a firm can determine the merits of one organizational form over another, the question arises of finding qualified managers. All global structures require an increase in the number of internationally experienced managers, and a shortage of such managers can be a serious barrier toward adopting a global structure. As noted previously, the investment required to expand the international experience of the numerous managers needed for a global structure would have to be justified in terms of the future relative importance of international activities as compared to domestic business.

A final variable, related in part to management traits, is the capacity and willingness of an enterprise to adjust to organizational changes. Major organizational realignments are likely to disrupt delicate working relationships. Executives of domestic divisions may be unwilling to accept new managerial roles until there is overwhelming evidence of the need for change. Or a forceful manager of a successful international division is likely to use his record of success to resist reorganization pressures that would dilute his responsibility and authority over international activities. Where the capacity and willingness of an enterprise to adjust to organizational change is limited, informal arrangements and devices other than a major organization change may have to be adopted to secure some of the prospective benefits of a major change.

Organizational structures normally cannot be changed and operated effectively when they are imposed unilaterally by top management. The choice of structure must emerge out of a political process of group bar-

---

[21] Schollhammer, "Organizational Structures of Multinational Corporations," pp. 352–53.

[22] See Chapter 17.

gaining in which decisions are frequently reached by coalitions of groups. As one study of the process of structural change in multinational corporations emphasizes, "Although the choice of structure is ultimately the responsibility of top managers, they have the role of identifying a workable solution, persuading each group of its logic, and implementing the reorganization."[23]

RELATIONSHIPS BETWEEN CORPORATE HEADQUARTERS AND FOREIGN SUBSIDIARIES

One of the crucial issues facing multinational corporations is the organizational relationship to be maintained between corporate headquarters and operating units. The ideal relationship for implementing a global strategy is for corporate management to determine overall corporate objectives, to specify organization-wide strategies and policy guidelines, to decide on the allocation of corporate resources to the various operating divisions, and to institute effective systems of communications, coordination, and control. Within this framework, managers of individual units are supposed to be free to determine a specific course of action for achieving the expected contribution to corporate objectives.

As one example, the policy of Massey–Ferguson Limited of Canada, a large, multinational farm-machinery company, is to give maximum responsibility and authority to its local operating units for achieving the defined objectives of the parent company. Its philosophy stresses the maximum separation of corporate or parent company executives from line responsibilities in local operations, even to the extent of avoiding the temptation of sending executives from the "home base" to manage operations abroad.[24]

But whatever the stated ideology and intentions of the company, complicated and contradictory pressures cause relationships to oscillate between varying levels of centralization. Among factors that determine the degree of centralization or decentralization are the age, size, and profitability of a specific subsidiary. Large, long established, and profitable subsidiaries are likely to have a maximum degree of autonomy.[25] Another important factor is the amount of confidence placed in subsidiary management. Still another force that can press for local autonomy is an environment with strong national governmental controls

---

[23] Stopford and Wells, *Managing the Multinational Enterprise*, p. 75.

[24] E. P. Neufeld, *A Global Corporation* (Toronto, Canada: University of Toronto Press, 1969), pp. 389–90.

[25] For extended discussion and case studies of the "Relationships With Foreign Subsidiaries and Affiliates," see Enid Baird Lovell, *The Changing Role of the International Executive* (New York: National Industrial Conference Board, 1966), pp. 140–48.

which requires frequent and unique local decisions. Factors that work toward centralization are an increasing integration of multinational operations, an increasing speed of technological change, and the rapid development of global techniques, strategies, and communications. Brooke and Remmers, after studying in depth the organization of subsidiaries and the power and control systems operating between the head office and foreign subsidiaries of a large number of multinational companies of nine different nationalities, concluded "that a decentralizing ideology masks a centralizing reality."[26]

In virtually all cases, however, the relationship will vary by function. Corporate control will be strongest in those functional areas in which the suboptimization problem is likely to arise and where important economies of scale can be achieved by the joint utilization of high-cost specialized personnel.[27] Depending, of course, on a firm's product strategy, the opportunities to optimize for the entire system may be in a regional or worldwide rationalization of production, in the field of purchasing or in research and development activities. Such functions tend to be centralized, whereas the marketing function tends to be most decentralized.

An important piece of geographical organization that some companies have developed between corporate headquarters and the subsidiary is a regional office. This is designed to coordinate the activities of local companies in a group of countries and is normally regarded as a part of the corporate headquarters that has been moved physically nearer to the operations it controls. The number of companies actually having regional offices has been increasing, particularly among American firms. The advantage of a regional office is that it brings some part of the head office into closer contact with local operations. It meets the lack of local knowledge at headquarters and the lack of expertise in the subsidiary. The disadvantage of the regional unit is that it lengthens the lines of communication and tends to reduce the autonomy of the national operation.[28]

An Illustration: The International Financial Function

A recent study of U.S. practices in organizing and managing the international-financial function illustrates how organizational patterns and the allocation of responsibility between headquarters and the subsidiaries vary over time and with the possibilities for optimization and with the relative capabilities of staff at headquarters and in the subsidiaries.

---

[26] Brooke and Remmers, *The Strategy of Multinational Enterprise,* p. 285.

[27] Richard D. Robinson, *International Management* (New York: Holt, Rinehart & Winston, 1967), pp. 151–53.

[28] Brooke and Remmers, *The Strategy of Multinational Enterprise,* pp. 43–47.

In the early stages of foreign operations, the domestic financial staff at headquarters generally copes with the new problems, ignoring at times some of the more sophisticated approaches to foreign financing and planning. At later stages, many companies decide to employ full-time specialists in international financial management or to designate one of their financial staff for the handling of foreign financial matters. A few companies feel that their extensive international operations are best served when every senior financial executive develops equal expertise in both the international and domestic aspects of his particular function.

The principal American international companies follow no single master plan in organizing the management of the international financial function. In broad terms, however, three basic patterns exist.[29] The international functions of both policy making and performance of financial services may be:

a. Centralized at corporate headquarters.
b. Centralized at the headquarters of the international management unit with only overall guidance from corporate headquarters.
c. Split between corporate headquarters and some subordinate headquarters (that is, central international unit, regional headquarters, product-division headquarters, and so forth.

The important determinants of organizational patterns and the resulting financial behavior have been the size of an international company and its degree of international involvement. The small firms, defined as having foreign sales of about $50,000,000, typically run a decentralized operation with an "every tub on its own bottom" policy. Headquarters provides little direction and few decision rules and makes little effort to move towards optimum financing for the entire system. Medium-sized firms, with foreign sales of about $200 million, typically run a centralized operation with strong direction from headquarters and substantial concern for the net cost of an action to the total system. Large firms, with foreign sales of about $1 billion, typically run a decentralized operation, but with guidelines issued from the headquarters staff, which also performs a coordination function.[30]

The large multinational enterprises strongly favor system-wide optimization but are too large and too complex to attempt an overall system approach. A computer optimization model of a multinational enterprise with subsidiaries operating in as many as 100 countries and

[29] Irene W. Meister, *Managing the International Financial Function* (New York: National Industrial Conference Board, 1970), p. 5.

[30] This section is a summary of Robert B. Stobaugh, Jr., "Financing Foreign Subsidiaries of U.S.-Controlled Multinational Enterprises," *Journal of International Business Studies,* Summer 1970, pp. 43–64.

with numerous interconnecting flows of goods and money, would be well beyond the capabilities of today's most advanced high-speed computer system. As a result of this complexity, headquarter's management uses a variety of rules of thumb to assist them in decision making, for example, setting equity equal to fixed assets in forming a new subsidiary. Even if the large multinational enterprise were capable of calculating some crude overall systems optimum, it could not take actions that might jeopardize its position in a foreign country.

The medium-sized firms have a greater tendency than other enterprises to attempt an overall systems optimization and more nearly approach the economists' concept of one "economic man" running the enterprise from headquarters. Small firms, on the other hand, typically lack international experience and tend to have decentralized operations without close control from headquarters or coordination among subsidiaries. In fact, each subsidiary may be viewed as an "independent" operation, and little attempt is made to take the overall system into account in financing one subsidiary.

The different patterns of organization and of financial policy behavior which prevail among U.S. international firms undoubtedly represent different stages of evolution along the path toward following global strategies and integrated management policies. They also reflect the state of knowledge in optimizing complex systems and the likely constraints on such optimization because of potential conflicts between optimization on a world basis and the interests of nation-states. As increasingly sophisticated organization and management techniques emerge, organizational patterns for the international financial function will continue to change.

Control over the financial function is a key element in achieving global-corporate goals, and pressure usually builds up for strong central guidance from corporate headquarters and system-wide optimization. Ideally, the financial management function of a multinational enterprise would have three goals. One would be to take advantage of the potentials in multinational operations for reducing financial costs and increasing efficiency. A second would be to adapt to environmental constraints at the national and regional levels. A third would be to protect the value of assets and revenues so that the benefits of multinational operations are not eroded through financial risks. The efficiency contribution can occur through the ability of the multinational enterprise to secure capital at a lower cost since it has access to many different sources and can achieve economies of scale and skills in financing. The adaptation responsibility is one of meeting national constraints on remittances of funds across national boundaries both in the home and in host countries. The protective function is to avoid losses through foreign exchange devaluations or revaluations or through differential rates of inflation.

Summary

An international commitment by a business enterprise normally requires significant changes in a firm's organizational structure. There is no one organizational structure that is ideal for multinational operations, and any structure once adopted must be continually reviewed and revised as internal and external factors keep changing. At the senior management level, the broad types of organization options for assigning responsibility and authority are relatively limited. But within the broad patterns, considerable diversity is possible.

The organizational structure of most international enterprises evolves over time in a series of stages. American companies have typically moved from an export-unit structure to a separate international division or international company as operations are extended to foreign areas. As top management becomes increasingly interested in international opportunities, a global-organization structure may be adopted. International companies based in Europe and Canada tend to skip the international-division stage and move directly to a global structure because domestic markets are smaller and less important to their overall success. Global structures can be organized with primary emphasis on function, product, or geography. Some firms have attempted to build complex "grid" structures where managers have multiple reporting relationships, and function, product, and area responsibilities overlap.

The choice among alternative structures depends on a small number of variables. The key problem is the inherent conflict between three dimensions of a firm's activities—functional, product, and geographical. A functional structure has the benefits of integrating marketing, finance, and production, but at the cost of area coordination and difficulties in transferring product and technological expertise from the parent company to the subsidiaries and among foreign operations. The product structure reduces problems of transferring technology and new products among locations, but it incurs the costs of duplication in functional tasks and of coordinating all the interests of an enterprise in a foreign area. The area structure gives good coordination geographically but at the cost of product coordination among areas and duplication in functional expertise. In the final analysis, the choice of organization structure will reflect management's choice between sets of problems.

The relationships between corporate headquarters and the foreign subsidiaries present another difficult organizational problem—namely, the centralization versus decentralization issue. In general, the preference is for headquarters to be responsible for strategy and the final decisions on long-range goals and for the subsidiaries to have maximum responsibility and authority for operations. Here again, a firm's product strategy becomes a key determinant. Where the product strategy may result in suboptimization by not taking advantage of enterprise-wide unification possibilities, such functions as manufacturing, research and development, and financial management are likely to be closely controlled or coordinated at the center. At the other extreme, where great diversity in products and in end-use markets exists, marketing is particularly likely to be decentralized.

EXERCISES AND DISCUSSION QUESTIONS

1. What are the principal considerations that make organizational structures that work well for domestic operations less suitable for multinational operations?

2. "There is no single best structure for all international companies. Each company's operations are different, and each company has an almost unique set of needs to be served by its organizational structure." Discuss.

3. Why do you think one of the major U.S. automobile companies retains an international-division structure whereas a company like General Electric has a global structure that emphasizes product groups?

4. "Within a tendency toward greater centralization of decision making, there is yet a discernible trend to greater individual independence for managers in multinational enterprises. Increased independence can accompany a reduction in the area of decision making by subsidiary managers." Discuss.

5. One of the major advantages of multinational operations is the possibility of optimizing the financial function on a worldwide basis. Why do many large and small companies fail to do so?

19

MANAGING THE INTERNATIONAL PRODUCT MIX

MARKETING IS THE PROCESS of identifying consumer needs and preferences, matching the capabilities of the firm to these needs and preferences, and directing the flow of products to the consumer or user. The specific marketing functions include market research and demand analysis; the development of policies and programs on product design, pricing, distribution, service, and advertising; and the planning and control of the overall marketing effort. These functions cover the so-called controllable variables in marketing. The uncontrollable variables are competitive forces and environmental factors—cultural, economic, and political. The task of the marketing manager is to mold the controllable elements of his decision, or the product mix, in light of the uncontrollable elements to support performance in specific markets that will achieve the marketing objectives of the enterprise.

The only difference between domestic and international marketing is that in international marketing these activities take place in relation to more than one country and are performed across national boundaries. The basic functions are the same in both markets but the implementation of marketing programs can be quite different. The applicability of marketing technology depends on the circumstances of the environment in which it is applied, and the behavioral aspects of markets—reflecting mainly cultural, societal, and social circumstances—differ widely among countries. In addition, the interests of national governments, individually and collectively, create an international environment in which marketers operate. There is generally no equivalent to these factors within the national or domestic economy.[1] But as is true in all aspects

---
[1] See Robert Bartels, "Are Domestic and International Marketing Dissimilar?" *Journal of Marketing* 32 (July 1968): 56–61.

of international business management, the crucial management need is to know when and where environmental differences require changes in marketing practices.

At its simplest, international marketing may require adjusting only one or two of the product-mix variables. A small firm whose exporting activities are incidental to predominantly domestic activities may be concerned solely with distribution channels. At a more complex level, a globally oriented enterprise will be concerned with planning, coordinating, and controlling all of the product-mix variables as required for the simultaneous conduct of marketing programs in a number of different national environments.

International marketing should be differentiated from foreign marketing and comparative marketing. As discussed in Chapter 1, the three fields are interrelated but different. Foreign marketing is national marketing conducted without regard to international considerations. The multinational firm needs to be aware of domestic practices in the countries in which it sells. Likewise, knowledge of comparative marketing can be applied to international marketing.[2] But the major focus of international marketing is the special responses required for conducting business activities across national boundaries and simultaneously in a number of different national markets.

RESPONSIBILITY FOR STRATEGIC DECISIONS

The global planning of a multinational firm rests upon a geographical selection of markets in which it hopes to compete, but before this stage is reached the firm must decide the customer needs at which it is aiming. This involves much more than geographical selection. It may mean entirely new types of product activity. Strategic decisions do not begin and end with existing products. The firm usually seeks to identify demand areas where its capability for performance against competitors is greatest, even though the specific customer needs to be filled are different from those the firm has been filling in the past. This approach to strategic decisions requires a prediction of the demand environment and a matching of the firm's and competitor's profiles of competence against it.[3]

For the multinational firm it is an important issue whether the firm adopts a central-market focus or a decentralized approach for its stra-

---

[2] For studies in comparative marketing, see Jean Boddewyn, *Comparative Management and Marketing* (Glenview, Ill.: Scott, Foresman and Co., 1969); David Carson, *International Marketing: A Comparative Systems Approach* (New York: John Wiley and Sons, 1967); Montrose S. Sommers and Jerome B. Kernan, eds., *Comparative Marketing System*s (New York: Appleton-Century-Crofts, 1968).

[3] Kenneth Simmonds, "Removing the Chains From Product Strategy," *Journal of Management Studies,* February 1968.

tegic decision making. In the central-market approach, the firm selects its area of concern, or mission, based on one central national market, establishes a marketing mix, and later moves its activity outwards to other national markets. The central national market normally is the firm's home market but does not need to be so. At the other extreme, decentralized strategy development, the firm identifies its best opportunities worldwide, and where there is already an international organization, each unit develops its own strategy. As will be discussed below, most firms follow a path between these two extremes.

By choosing against one geographical market, decision problems are reduced and subsequent geographical broadening of coverage with an established product can bring high profits. If the firm, however, does not develop its new activities against the market with the largest demand for them, some other firm will presumably do so and gain an advantage. The largest market is likely to be that in which customers adopt the product earlier than in other markets. So long as product diffusion remains ahead of other markets, the largest market will continue to retain its size advantage.

As has been argued in the product-cycle literature, the U.S. market develops first for many products. Because of the size and advanced nature of the U.S. market, American firms have been able to concentrate on their home market for the choice of new areas of activity and from this base they have been able to match or excel non–U.S. firms that begin to build internationally from other home markets. Furthermore, American companies have frequently been able to expand internationally without doing early global planning. For firms with home bases in other smaller and less advanced markets, the argument for planning global expansion to maintain market leadership applies much earlier.

In some cases, Japanese and European firms have selected the U.S. market rather than their home market as their central focus for selected product lines. But while a number of European companies have introduced new products in the high-income, sophisticated U.S. market before doing so in Europe or other markets, such a policy has generally not been followed on a continual basis. Many Europeans see the cost of communications and coordination efforts in such a large market as the American one as a deterrent to producing products first in the United States as part of their world product strategy.[4]

The international product cycle does not apply in all fields, and the comparative advantage that supports an international firm in a foreign market may depend upon a mixture of business capabilities other than advanced product technology or design. In such cases, particularly where the economies of large-scale production are not important, the firm might

---

[4] Business International, *European Business Strategies in the United States* (Geneva, Switzerland, 1971), p. 24.

aim first for those markets in which the cost of obtaining each percentage share of increased sales is lowest. And where local conditions require particular products, such as agricultural fertilizers and pesticides, the argument is strong for a decentralized approach which gives a great deal of independence to subsidiaries. But as we shall see, the choice among alternative strategies involves the central issue of international standardization versus product differentiation.

INTERNATIONAL STANDARDIZATION VERSUS DIFFERENTIATION

Within a firm's general-market focus, marketing is concerned with identifying which segments should be treated differently, that is, those for which the marketing mix should differ. There is a continual conflict, however, between differentiation to meet the needs of smaller segments of the market and standardization to reduce unit costs.[5] For the international firm, standardization across national barriers gives it its greatest advantages. These advantages are not confined to production economies. A broader sales base, drawing on the same research and development, advertising and promotion, and general management skills, may permit substantial cost savings and greater consistency in dealings with customers. Links across national boundaries outside the firm can also provide the basis for international economies. International magazine readership, for example, can build up international awareness of a brand from continued exposure to the advertisements—as can international travel or migration. It is likely, then, that an international firm's best strategy should be to avoid detailed adjustment of its product to a local environment, wherever possible, and to act as a change agent transplanting its culture around the world in a not entirely receptive environment.

The stresses in the other direction, however, are great. International business invariably uses countries as the basic building blocks for its organization, and identification with a particular country market can lead to adjustments to fit that market. The whole emphasis of good marketing is to do just this. Given a demarcated country market, the good executive will move to adjust his marketing mix against his assessment of the market characteristics. As marketing decisions must be highly subjective, though, any selection of executives would be likely to come up with different recommendations even for the same market. The difficulty confronting the international firm is to identify when there are market differences sufficient to justify the loss of standardization.

Against an international canvas there is the further complication of identifying segments which could profitably be given separate treatment

---

[5] See Robert D. Buzzell, "Can You Standardize Multinational Marketing?" *Harvard Business Review,* November–December 1968, pp. 102–13.

across national boundaries. Small market segments in individual countries may be regarded as insufficient for any one country unit to justify
development of an appropriate product. Worldwide, however, such a
segment may readily justify the expense.

The case for standardization or differentiation of products and marketing practices across national boundaries will rest upon differences
in both consumer characteristics and the institutional framework within
which the firm must operate. Approaches towards the assessment of
these differences have already been introduced in Part III. The other
necessary decision elements are estimates of the impact of standardization or diversification on total revenues and costs.

The physical attributes of products and product titles are the elements
most costly to adjust separately. If products are to be marketed globally,
it is important for the initial choice to avoid building in major impedi-
ments to performance in individual markets. The importance of different
features will depend on the physical environment in which the product
is to be used as well as on behavior, attitudes, and preferences of the
customers. Thus, if a piece of agricultural equipment were designed to
be marketed across a wide geographical area, it must be tested to with-
stand extremes of heat and not simply built for performance in one
particular climate. Taking cultural differences into account, variations
in attitudes regarding repair and maintenance of machinery and technical
ability to do may be so great that design against the market of a relatively developed country would produce equipment unusable in less
developed areas.

This is not an area of marketing in which generalizations are likely
to be very useful. The aspects of culture impinging on the use of a
product will be so particular to that product that generalized knowledge
about the patterns of particular cultures will provide little guidance
in designing products for international performance. Of more value is
an approach that examines the ways in which the product is purchased
and used within each cultural setting, developing from this a list of
important criteria for design. If test samples can be made physically
available to those concerned with selling in different countries and shown
to outlets and users, even more tangible reactions can be obtained.

Despite the potential costs of failure to develop products in this way,
consideration of the global suitability of different features is not very
common at design stage. At that time there is generally more concern
for establishing a product that will become viable in just one market—let
alone on a global scale. The implication for later expansion of sales
is that management should avoid being dogmatic concerning a product's
suitability without adjustment when entering new markets. The head-
office mentality can be unwisely reinforced by success in the one market.

As opposed to physical features of a product, the product title is more easily changed. But it can involve greater costs if it means losing the spillover from advertising in other areas and establishing new brand loyalty. Coca–Cola stands out as an example here. While the flavor can be easily adjusted to local palates, a change of name in any market would lose most of the marketing value. Where there would be a large loss from inability to build on an established brand name it becomes important to choose the name in the first place so that it does not have any unfortunate clash of meaning in any of the major languages.

ALTERNATIVE PRODUCT STRATEGIES

The product strategy of an international firm generally falls somewhere between the extremes of central-market focus and decentralized development and between the extremes of product-mix standardization or diversification. The choices available can be illustrated by the five alternative strategies summarized in Figure 19.1.[6]

FIGURE ˙9.1
Multinational Product-Communications Mix: Strategic Alternatives

Strat-egy	Product Function or Need Satisfied	Conditions of Product Use	Ability to Buy Product	Recom-mended Product Strategy	Recom-mended Communi-cations Strategy	Relative Cost of Adjust-ments	Product Examples
1	Same	Same	Yes	Extension	Extension	1	Soft drinks
2	Different	Same	Yes	Extension	Adaptation	2	Bicycles, Motor-scooters
3	Same	Different	Yes	Adaptation	Extension	3	Gasoline, Detergents
4	Different	Different	Yes	Adaptation	Adaptation	4	Clothing, Greeting cards
5	Same	—	No	Invention	Develop new communica-tions	5	Motor vehicles

Source: Warren J. Keegan, "Multinational Product Planning: Strategic Alternatives," *Journal of Marketing,* January 1969, p. 59.

Strategy One: One Product, One Message—Worldwide

The easiest and most profitable strategy is that of product and communications extension. The same product is sold worldwide using the same sales message. In every country in which it operates, Pepsico sells

---

[6] This section is based largely on Warren J. Keegan, "Multinational Product Planning: Strategic Alternatives," *Journal of Marketing,* January 1969, pp. 58–62.

the same product and does it with the same advertising and promotional appeals that it uses in its central market—the United States. The product-communications-extension strategy has great appeal to most international companies because of the enormous cost savings associated with this approach. Important among these are the substantial economies resulting from the standardization of marketing communications. For a company with worldwide operations, the cost of preparing separate print and TV-cinema films for each market would be extremely high.

This strategy is widely used in the marketing of advanced-technology producer goods. As Holton has noted, "The world of advanced technology is more nearly a single world than is the world of consumer goods."[7] A firm selling equipment to commercial television stations, for example, normally does not find specifications varying as much across markets as is likely to occur in the case of consumer goods. Furthermore, advanced technology firms often find themselves selling to the same multinational firms in different parts of the world that want equipment specifications standardized. Even in the less developed countries, the technological specifications for producers' goods generally follow those developed in the advanced countries.

Unfortunately, the product-communications-extension strategy does not work for all products. When Campbell soup tried to sell its U.S. tomato soup formulation to the British, it discovered after considerable losses that the English prefer a more bitter taste. Numerous other examples can be cited of cases where consumer preferences in new markets do not favor a product developed for the central market, and where the extension strategy will fail. In such cases, the goal of maximum profit performance may require the use of an adjustment or innovation strategy.

Strategy Two: Product Extension—Communications Adaptation

When a product fills a different need or serves a different function under use conditions identical to or similar to those in the central market, the only adjustment required is in marketing communications. Bicycles, for example, satisfy needs mainly for recreation in the United States but provide basic transportation in countries like India. In this approach, the same physical product ends up serving a different function or use than that for which it was originally designed. The appeal of the product-extension-communications—adaptation strategy is that savings in manufacturing, research and development, and inventory costs can still result. The only additional costs are in identifying the different product functions the product will service in foreign markets and in reformulating

[7] Richard H. Holton, "Marketing Policies in Multinational Corporations," *Journal of International Business Studies,* Summer 1970, p. 18.

advertising, sales promotion, and other dimensions of market communications around the newly identified function.

Strategy Three: Product Adaptation—Communications Extension

A third approach to an international product strategy is to extend
without change the basic communications strategy developed for the
central market but to adapt the product to different use conditions.
The product-adaptation-communications-extension strategy assumes that
the product will serve the same function in foreign markets under different use conditions. Esso followed this approach when it adapted the
physical characteristics of its gasoline to the different climatic and user
conditions of different countries while continuing to use on a worldwide
basis the invitation to "Put a tiger in your tank." International companies in the soap and detergent fields have adjusted their product
formulation to meet local water conditions and the characteristics of
local washing machines, with no change in the companies' basic communications approach. Likewise, a European chemical company entering
the U.S. market had to modify its line of U.S.-produced dyestuffs to
adjust to the habits of U.S. housewives in washing clothes.

Strategy Four: Dual Adaptation

Strategy four is to adapt both the product and the communications
approach when differences exist in environmental conditions of use and
in the function which a product serves. In essence, this is a combination
of strategies two and three. U.S. greeting-card companies have faced
these circumstances in Europe, where the occasions for using greeting
cards differ from those in the United States. Also, in Europe the function
of a greeting card has been to provide a space for the sender to write
his own message, in contrast to the U.S. situation where cards contain
prepared messages.

Strategy Five: Product Invention

A final strategy is that of product invention. When potential customers
cannot afford one of the firm's products, an opportunity may exist to
invent or design an entirely new product that satisfies the identified
need or function at a price that the consumer can afford. If product-de-
velopment costs are not excessive, this may be a potentially rewarding
product strategy for the mass markets in the less developed countries.

As an example of this approach, both Ford and General Motors developed entirely new motor vehicles designed specifically for markets in
the underdeveloped countries, including, hopefully, markets in Mainland

China. The vehicles are small, inexpensive, easily assembled, and designed with emphasis on utility and durability rather than style and comfort. The Ford vehicle is built in the Philippines for sale throughout Asia. The GM vehicle is designed to be assembled by company-owned or independent distributors in the developing countries. GM supplies essential components from its subsidiary in England but up to 50 percent of the components, those not requiring heavy tooling expense, can be manufactured locally. The product strategy not only attempts to meet the low price requirements of the less developed countries but is also designed to satisfy the pressure of the countries for a high degree of local content. The engineering requirements are relatively unsophisticated so that with blueprints and instructions supplied by the multinational company, "any sheet-metal shop in any country can be used to build this car," according to a GM executive.[8] The companies see their product as a replacement for the animal cart, bicycle, motor scooter, and even three-wheel vehicles in the developing countries.

The best product strategy—the one which optimizes company profits over the long term—will depend upon the specific product-market-company mix. Some products demand adaptation, others lend themselves to adaptations, and still others are best left unchanged. The same is true of markets. Also, companies differ not only in their manufacturing costs but in their capability to identify and produce profitable product adaptations. Thus the choice of product and communications strategy in international marketing is a function of three key factors. The first is the need to define the product itself in terms of the function or need it serves. The second factor is the definition of the market in terms of the conditions under which the product is used, including the preferences of potential customers and their ability to buy the product in question. Finally, the costs of adaptation and manufacture to the company must be considered. Only after analyzing the product-market fit, the company's capabilities, and costs, can managers choose the most profitable international product strategy.

INTERNATIONAL MARKETING AND ORGANIZATION

The marketing function was previously mentioned as the activity most likely to be decentralized. More so than any other function, marketing has been viewed by many international companies as a local problem. The organizational implication of this view is demonstrated by the statement of a top executive of the Singer Company only a few years ago who wrote, "Marketing is conspicuous by its absence from the functions which can be planned at the corporate headquarters level. . . . The op-

---

[8] *Business Week,* 27 May 1972, p. 15.

erating experience of many international firms appears to confirm the desirability of assigning long-range planning of market activities to local managers."[9] More recently, however, the trend toward designing marketing strategies with a multinational perspective has resulted in a clear move among leading companies toward establishing marketing coordinators, international committees, and other mechanisms for a greater participation by headquarters in marketing management.[10]

A recent study of the marketing policies of U.S. appliance and photographic manufacturers in Europe underlines the degree of decentralization in marketing decisions in these consumer goods industries. In the cases studied, local management was primarily responsible for 86 percent of the advertising decisions, 74 percent of the pricing decisions, and 61 percent of the distribution channel decisions. Only product-design decisions were imposed upon local management in 55 percent of the cases observed.[11]

The absence at corporate headquarters of responsibility for managing the marketing function reflects a conviction that a multinational approach is not realistic because of the great differences that still exist, and probably will always exist, among nations. And the limited role of headquarters has been characteristic of both extremes of product strategies. Where products and marketing approaches have been extended from the center market to foreign areas with little or no adaptation, a major contribution to the marketing function from headquarters was considered unnecessary. At the other extreme, where market differences were so great that major adaptations were required, the prevailing view was that the strategies and the implementation had to be handled at the local level.[12]

The trend toward an increased role by headquarters has been called "inter-active market planning," which recognizes both differences and similarities in national markets. Although there are many obstacles to the application of common marketing policies in different countries, the tangible benefits from doing so, as previously noted, can be substantial. The relative importance of the pros and cons will, of course, vary from industry to industry, from company to company, and over time. But in most cases the benefits are sufficiently universal and important to warrant a significant role by headquarters in standardizing some parts of the marketing strategy while leaving the subsidiaries with principal

---

[9] Millard H. Pryor, Jr., "Planning in a Worldwide Business," *Harvard Business Review,* January–February 1965, p. 137.

[10] Buzzell, "Can You Standardize Multinational Marketing?" p. 112.

[11] R. J. Aylmer, "Who Makes Marketing Decisions in the Multinational Firm?" *Journal of Marketing,* October 1970, pp. 26–27.

[12] Warren J. Keegan, "Multinational Marketing: The Headquarters Role," *Columbia Journal of World Business,* January–February 1971.

responsibility for handling the differences and unique factors. Finding the right balance between local autonomy and central coordination is not an easy task, any more than is balancing the gains of standardized marketing strategy against the needs of heterogeneous national markets.

What guidelines are appropriate for defining the role of headquarters and for organizing the marketing-management function? First, headquarters must be adequately informed concerning markets to carry its responsibility for strategic planning. Market research is an important source of information and, therefore, should be monitored by headquarters. Second, headquarters should be able to make international comparisons on marketing performance and country potentials, and certain market measures can be standardized so that such comparisons can be made. Third, headquarters' involvement should insure that no country or area unknowingly duplicates market research on marketing experimentation that has already been undertaken somewhere in the international system. Fourth, the benefits from headquarters' involvement must be related to the cost of such involvement in terms of personnel, information flows, and standardization of the research formats.

The principal justification of the headquarters' participation in the marketing function along the lines just considered is that headquarters can better fulfill its roles of strategic planning and controlling performance. But to make the process inter-active, headquarters must be alert and aggressive in making affirmative contributions in the marketing field to the local subsidiaries. Such contributions can be in the form of making experience from one country available to other countries where comparable conditions prevail. If good ideas are scarce, and if some of them have universal appeal, they should be used as widely as possible. It can supervise experimentation in marketing and make the results of different experiments available to all units in the system. If a manager questions the relative effectiveness of advertising versus personal selling, instead of splitting the communications budget between these two activities, he could run 75 percent advertising and 25 percent personal selling in *Country A* and reverse these proportions in *Country B*, where both countries were preselected as most nearly comparable in other marketing dimensions.

Headquarters can also perform certain functions that cannot be easily accomplished at the subsidiary level. For example, as previously mentioned, it may discover opportunities that consist of a number of small market segments in different countries which country subsidiaries might regard as too small to warrant development. Other arguments favoring central-market control stem from the need to allocate limited resources according to a global strategy. Development of individual markets must be started in ways that fit the total development pattern laid out for the enterprise and arranged so that individual markets can fit without problems into later stages of the plan. It may be necessary, for example, to choose outlets or sign distribution agreements not initially the best for a smaller range of products selling in lower volumes than will be the case later on. The brand image might also be important for carrying future lines and require special attention when products are first introduced. In pricing, too, central guidance is frequently necessary if the advantages of an international scale are to be realized.

One of the more common ways of placing responsibility at the level of those closest to the customer, yet still retaining overall control over the marketing diagnosis, is through the use of a standard annual plan and review routine. Plans are requested in a standard format working from an assessment of the market environment towards specific action proposals and budgeted profit performance and resource requirements. These are then subjected to careful scrutiny and related to the overall plan for global performance. Any clashes or omissions discovered can then be raised before actions are taken.

This method of central control also acts as a major implement in educating the international organization in the use of marketing. A good grasp of marketing cannot be assumed to exist throughout any international organization. The ideas are alien to many cultures and frequently opposed to the message of the programs under which many international executives have been educated. The discipline of the marketplace, however, is clearly demanded in any planning system that works from an assessment of the market through to recommendations for action in that market. When the central executives are seen to check for consistency and completeness in both the analysis and the planned actions and each year to raise the quality of market assessment and analysis they expect, the message of marketing control is carried much more concretely than it would be through a less direct educational program.

The decisive question is not where ultimate control of strategic planning should lie, for this inevitably must rest with top management. The real question is the extent to which headquarters executives should be involved in the strategic-planning process. In the absence of headquarters' involvement in the individual subsidiary-planning processes, it is difficult, indeed impossible, for headquarters to impose global considerations in the strategic-planning process effectively. In the absence of subsidiary involvement, on the other hand, the local adaptation requirements of a market may be overlooked.

As a general rule, headquarters should be involved in subsidiary-planning processes to the extent necessary to keep informed of the nature of basic opportunities and threats globally. Also, headquarters involvement should be measured against the degree to which it stimulates or contributes to subsidiary-planning efforts. Alternatively, a check should be kept on the extent to which it may detract from initiative and enterprise on the part of subsidiary managers. The organizational form must facilitate the task of international marketing, particularly where marketing skills are important as a key element in the competitive advantage of the international company. As Terpstra has pointed out, marketing skills and orientation were critical components of the competitive advantage on which many American companies based their expansion into European markets.[13]

The marketing relationship between the parent firm and its subsidiaries can vary, of course, among different activities. When Pechiney of France acquired a majority interest in its U.S. affiliate, Howmet Corporation, Howmet was already well established in a product area in which Pechiney had no previous experience. Thus, Howmet Corporation enjoys full autonomy and exercises full responsibility for the marketing abroad, even in France, of superalloy investment castings made by one of its groups. For its other products which are completely outside Pechiney's experience, sales and licensing of technology are handled almost 100 percent at the group level in Howmet. On the other hand, for the international marketing of certain Howmet-produced special alloys and other metal products, the Howmet divisions concerned rely on certain Pechiney resources and coordinate sales through Pechiney marketing and distribution channels.[14]

INTERNATIONAL PRICING

Pricing decisions present many complex problems to the international company From the marketing standpoint, price is only one of the variables of the marketing mix to be considered along with many other variables. But from the standpoint of the total enterprise, prices determine the total revenue available for all functions and to a large degree the profitability of the enterprise. Thus, pricing decisions must take into account the interests of many groups within the enterprise and frequently conflicting price objectives.[15]

The director of international marketing seeks prices that will be competitive in the marketplace. The divisional vice president is concerned with the effect of pricing on divisional profits. Regional managers are concerned about profitability at the regional level. The managers of foreign subsidiaries are concerned with the effect on profitability at the country level of policy limitations on intercorporate transfer, export,

[13] Vern Terpstra, *American Marketing in the Common Market* (New York: Praeger Publishers, Inc., 1967).

[14] *European Business Strategies in the United States* (Geneva: Business International, 1971), p. 38.

[15] This section draws heavily on the Business International report, *Solving International Pricing Problems* (New York: Business International, 1965).

and local market pricing. The controller and financial vice president want prices that are profitable. The manufacturing vice president wants prices that will permit longer production runs and maximum manufacturing efficiency. The tax manager is concerned with the implications of pricing decisions to the total tax liability of the corporation, tax-deferral opportunities, and governmental regulations on transfer pricing. The legal counsel is concerned with antitrust implications. Even the domestic-product managers have an interest in the prices at which their products are transferred to the international division or overseas units. With so many sectors of the enterprise crucially dependent on pricing decisions, top management invariably assumes major responsibility for formulating pricing policies and strategies. The implementation of these policies, however, may be widely diffused throughout the organization.[16]

The role of pricing differs considerably for different types of goods and from market to market. In the case of standardized or relatively undifferentiated products, the market sets the price and the seller has little control over the level of prices. The same will be true of situations where government price controls prevail or prices are fixed through patent-licensing agreements. But for differentiated products selling in nonregulated markets, the producer has genuine alternatives in setting his prices. And much of the international business activity is based on differentiated products and oligopoly elements.

In setting its pricing policies, two basic choices are available to a company. Prices may be used as an active instrument for accomplishing market objectives. Or prices may be considered as a static element in business decisions. American companies generally regard price as an important variable in their marketing decisions. In other countries, a more passive attitude toward the strategic role of pricing is likely to exist. For example, a study of marketing practices in the European Common Market countries reached the conclusion that "among those manufacturers who had reasonable latitude in setting their prices, there was generally a tendency to disregard pricing as an important element in the marketing strategy."[17]

In setting its prices for any single market, both cost and market considerations are important. Costs set the price floor, and competitive prices for comparable products set the price ceiling. Between the floor and the ceiling there is an optimum price which is a function of the demand for the product and the cost of sourcing the product. The inter-

---

[16] For an example of how the responsibility for pricing is distributed among the various units of an international company in the pharmaceuticals and chemicals field, see Enid Baird Lovell, *The Changing Role of the International Executive* (New York: National Industrial Conference Board, 1966), p. 52.

[17] Bertil Liander, *Marketing Development in the European Economic Community* (New York: McGraw-Hill Book Co., 1964), p. 49.

national company that uses pricing as part of the strategic-product mix will develop a pricing system and pricing policies which recognize the diversity of national markets in three basic dimensions—cost, competition, and demand. In addition, pricing policies will have to be consistent with a number of international constraints such as tax policies, dumping legislation, resale price-maintenance legislation, and governmental price controls where they exist. Another constraint may be multinational accounts that demand equal price treatment regardless of location.

The cost considerations which set the lower limit for prices may not be easy to define. Firms must decide whether they are going to use variable costs or full costs in their pricing decisions. In variable cost pricing, the company is concerned only with the marginal or incremental cost of producing the goods sold in foreign markets. The logic for using variable costs may be that foreign sales are incidental to a company's main operations and any returns over the marginal costs are a bonus contribution to net profit, or that the firm has to price more competitively to enter a foreign market or to meet local competition. But companies selling products in foreign markets at lower prices than in domestic markets are subject to charges of "dumping," which may subject the company to antidumping tariffs or penalties.

The firm that regards itself as a global enterprise is more likely to think in terms of full-cost pricing for all markets.[18] Full costs do not have to be covered in every market, and occasions may arise where the firm should price below full cost. But as previously mentioned, the determination of full costs may not be an easy matter. How much of general administrative, research and development costs, and other overhead items should be included in intra-corporate transfer prices? What share of marketing, sales, and advertising costs incurred in the domestic market but which generate marketing approaches that can be extended abroad should be included in the cost to foreign subsidiaries? Where capital is tied up for longer periods because of the time lags inherent in international transactions, and where foreign exchange risks are involved, how should these financing and risk costs be incorporated into the pricing decisions? And innumerable other cost uncertainties exist, depending on the market, the product, and the situation, including differential bribery costs.

The cost-plus pricing strategy results in relatively uniform prices worldwide, except for variations in such costs as freight and import duties. It has the advantage of simplicity since information on competitive or market conditions is not required for its implementation. It is widely used for export pricing and can be designed with some flexibility for adjusting the markup over costs to fit different market conditions.

---

[18] Philip R. Cateora and John M. Hess, *International Marketing*, rev. ed. (Homewood, Ill.: Richard D. Irwin, Inc., 1971), p. 672.

But it has the serious disadvantage that it is not directed toward maximizing the company's sales and revenues or profits in each national market.

Without ignoring the realities of cost, a market-pricing strategy gives principal emphasis to the demand and supply conditions of each market and the state of competition. The example in the Appendix to this chapter shows how different demand elasticities in different markets can result in advantages from different price policies for subsidiaries in each market. Through the separate adjustment of prices for each market, a greater profit can be achieved for the total system than by any choice of a common price for both markets. It should be noted, however, that in situations where national markets are not separated from each other, a common, final price policy may be necessary in order to minimize country-to-country arbitrage through companies other than those controlled by the international firm.

INTRACOMPANY TRANSFER PRICING

When a company is engaged solely in exporting, its pricing task is normally limited to the setting of export prices and terms at which goods are sold to customers outside the firm. Once the company expands its involvement beyond exporting and begins to establish foreign subsidiaries, the matter of intracompany transfer prices becomes an important and complex dimension of pricing strategies. Transfer pricing refers to the prices charged for goods and services exchanged within the corporate family. When transactions between units of the same enterprise take place across national frontiers, a host of environmental factors become important, such as variations in custom duties, tax rates, rules of competition, and business practices. These environmental differences impose on each buying and selling unit, though parts of the same company, the need to meet the requirements of different jurisdictions. They also create opportunities for increasing profits to the company as a whole through adjustments in transfer prices.[19]

In a world characterized by differential rates of income taxation, a multicountry enterprise can reduce its taxes by charging higher transfer prices to units in high-tax countries and thereby shifting earnings to low-tax environments. Duty costs can be lowered by shipping goods into high-tariff countries at a minimum transfer price so that the duty base and duty will be low. Dividend repatriation can be facilitated by transferring income in the form of higher prices for products shipped to subsidiaries in countries where dividend repatriation is being curtailed. Or where governments impose deposit requirements when import permission is granted there is clearly an incentive to minimize the price of

---

[19] See *Solving International Pricing Problems* (New York: Business International, 1966).

imported goods. Unusually low transfer prices can be used to provide finance to a new subsidiary or to help it show profit during a start-up period and thereby improve its ability to get local credit.[20] Another purpose of transfer-pricing policies might be to understate profits in a situation where high profits might encourage customers or local authorities to ask for price reductions or labor unions to ask for wage increases. And the transfer-price mechanism can be an important element in the managing of liquid assets and in reducing foreign exchange risk— topics that will be considered in Chapter 20.

As is generally true for pricing decisions, numerous internal and external pressures exist that push the firm toward different transfer-pricing policies. Executives in home-country producing units want to push up transfer prices and service charges to foreign affiliates. Buying units abroad want to reduce them. Outside the company, home-country tax authorities and custom officials abroad press for high transfer prices; foreign tax officials pressure the local company to buy cheap. From an enterprise-wide perspective, optimum transfer-pricing decisions would be based on where and when it is most advantageous to take the profit on a transaction without regard to national boundaries, and on the real role of intercompany transactions in improving the corporation's total profitability over a time horizon that usually extends beyond the current accounting period.

Given the opportunities to shift funds and profits by the transfer-pricing mechanism, how extensively is the instrument used by multinational companies? Because of its attractiveness as a subject for applying operation research techniques, transfer pricing has attracted considerable academic attention.[21] But despite the intriguing theoretical possibilities developed by model builders, several recent studies suggest that transfer pricing, particularly as a means of avoiding taxes, is no longer widely used by U.S. companies for operations in Europe and North America.[22] In practice, most American firms claim that they apply arm's length standards to their transactions with overseas controlled subsidiaries.[23]

---

[20] James Shulman, "When the Price is Wrong—By Design," *Columbia Journal of World Business,* May–June 1967, pp. 69–76.

[21] For example see David P. Rutenberg, "Maneuvering Liquid Assets in a Multinational Company: Formulation and Deterministic Solution Procedures," *Management Science,* June 1970, pp. B-671 to B-674. As an interesting sidelight, this research project funded by a government agency was publicly attacked by an American legislator as an improper use of government funds to assist multinational companies in evading U.S. taxes.

[22] Michael Z. Brooke and H. Lee Remmers, *The Strategy of Multinational Enterprise* (New York: American Elsevier Publishing Company, 1970), p. 176; Jeffrey S. Arpan, *International Intracorporate Pricing: Non-American Systems and Views* (New York: Praeger Publishers, Inc., 1972).

[23] James Greene and Michael G. Duerr, *Intercompany Transactions in the Multinational Company* (New York: National Industrial Conference Board, 1970), pp. 22–23.

If the buying unit can buy the product from external sources, the parent companies usually negotiate transfer prices with their subsidiaries as though the subsidiaries were an unrelated party. If the material can only be purchased within the company, as would be the case for components containing patented technology, then goods are usually offered on a cost-plus basis. The principal exceptions were for transactions with certain of the less developed countries whose tax rates were extremely high. India and Pakistan, where tax rates on distributed profits were 70 percent or more, were frequently mentioned by U.S. firms. Among British companies, few executives admitted that they used transfer pricing to shift profits between various units of the group.[24]

A principal constraint on transfer-pricing policies is the popularity of the profit-center concept as a means of monitoring and evaluating the performance of foreign units and as an overall financial incentive to the managers of the controlled unit. The use of the profit-center concept which makes foreign units responsible for the profitability of their operations requires that goods be transferred at competitive prices that are relatively uniform as between units in the system whose performance is being compared. In effect, this means treating foreign units of the company on roughly the same basis as an unrelated firm. When transfer prices are manipulated, the profits of a subsidiary are frequently meaningless as a measure of its performance. And the tax and other gains may not be worth the trouble caused. As Brooke and Remmers point out, ". . . in order to produce any real tax savings, there would have to be an optimum combination of substantial tax differentials between countries, adequate profit margins, and perhaps low customs duties."[25]

Several techniques can be used to maximize total system profits through manipulating transfer prices while still retaining the profit-center concept. One method is to share the total realized profits of the company between the parent and foreign subsidiary on the basis of assets employed, costs incurred, or on a more subjective basis of equitable treatment.[26] Another way is to keep two sets of accounts—official accounts for tax and other local purposes and another set for management control purposes. Still another is to take account of transfer-price manipulations in the budget and measure performance against planned results, even if a loss were intended. But each of these techniques has drawbacks and the critical question becomes one of whether the gains from manipulating transfer prices more than offset the resulting cost and complexity of judging performance.

[24] Brooke & Remmers, *Strategy of Multinational Enterprise,* p. 176.

[25] Ibid., p. 176.

[26] Greene and Duerr, *Intercompany Transactions in the Multinational Company,* p. 10.

A second major constraint on transfer-pricing policies has been the rapidly expanding role that tax and customs authorities have come to play.[27] Governments have become aware of the possibilities of tax minimization by international companies and most nations have been increasing their supervision of multinational business operations so as to maximize their tax revenues or to assure equitable treatment. In this respect, the transfer-price review program of the U.S. Treasury is perhaps the most advanced in the world today. It includes not only the sale of tangible property but also the pricing of money, services, the use of tangible property, and the transfer of intangible property such as patents and trademarks. From the viewpoint of the U.S. treasury, Section 482 of the Internal Revenue Code (1954) and the regulations promulgated by the Treasury in 1968 to govern international pricing practices are intended to insure that the U.S. government gets its fair share of the taxes on income earned by the multinational corporated system.[28]

The general rule governing pricing of controlled intra-company transfers is what is called the "arm's length" formula and several methods are prescribed by the Treasury to conform to the "arm's length" formula. The general principle is that transfer pricing should be set at the level comparable to prices where the two parties are relatively independent and bargaining at arms length. As might be expected, the application of these methods still involves considerable ambiguity, and the regulations are still in process of being interpreted and tested in the courts.

Increasingly, governmental tax and customs regulations in home and host countries have set limits on transfer-pricing policies. But within these limits there is frequently latitude for pricing to meet market and competitive factors. Even the U.S. regulations appear to leave an opening for a company to lower its transfer price for the purposes of entering a new market or meeting competition in an existing market.[29] Consequently, for most companies, the opportunity to support marketing goals and to increase system-wide profits by alternative transfer-pricing strategies should not be disregarded.

With all of these counterbalancing and conflicting forces to be considered, how does a multinational enterprise establish its international pricing policies? The international complications, added to those that always arise, whether or not national boundaries are crossed, clearly point to the impossibility of having fixed rules for pricing in the international

[27] Brooke and Remmers, *Strategy of Multinational Enterprise*, p. 175 report that international companies have experienced many disputes with customs authorities even though avoidance of duties is one of the lesser reasons for manipulating prices.

[28] See Warren J. Keegan, "Multinational Pricing: How Far is Arm's Length?" *Columbia Journal of World Business*, May–June 1969, pp. 57–66.

[29] Ibid., p. 65.

corporation. They equally point to the need for central monitoring of price strategy and an open-minded approach to the possibility of significant gains from central action to alter patterns that otherwise emerge. Naive calculations of the profit in individual units should not be accepted without measurement of the ultimate effect on the system, and the effects on the enterprise as a whole can be complex. Nor should pricing decisions be imposed without a realization of offsetting costs. In sum, to get the most out of pricing decisions within a multinational corporation requires a mapping of the entire system and a calculation for any potential change of the net effects across all units.[30]

INTERNATIONAL CHANNEL MANAGEMENT

In the marketing literature dealing with the choice of distribution channels, the message is clear that the product mix to reach the consumer must be carefully matched against the channels that are available or can be built.[31] Channels cannot be changed frequently and moves are usually not reversible. Alternatives forgone may not remain open and outlets that have been dropped in the past may not be again willing to carry the line.

At the international level the same approach applies. The policy problem areas are similar to those in domestic distribution but the answers are likely to differ because of the added complexities of many different market environments and institutional patterns. The firm will have to decide on the best channel pattern for each of a number of countries. And for each market it will have to assess the significance of the channel choice not only for immediate marketing goals but for future development. The national firm through the early stages of its existence is usually constrained by its past history and limited resources as to how it might mold its channel structure. But when an established firm moves into global expansion, it generally has much greater flexibility in choosing its channel structure in new markets.

If the firm's products follow a fairly well-defined diffusion pattern through different classes of consumers and the channels of distribution should change as the products mature, then it may be important to select the channel pattern so that it is flexible or at least does not place later restrictions on the firm's expansion. If, for example, large inventories and widespread distribution would be required as the product became established, an exclusive arrangement with a local importer who

---

[30] See Thomas Horst, "The Theory of the Multinational Firm: Optimal Behavior Under Different Tariff and Tax Rates," *Journal of Political Economy,* September–October 1971, pp. 1059–72.

[31] John A. Howard, *Marketing Management,* rev. ed. (Homewood, Ill.: Richard D. Irwin, Inc., 1963).

would never have the resources to offer such coverage would be a mistake, even though he might do the best job in the earliest stages.

International channel management is intimately related with many other dimensions of marketing management and global strategy. If the best strategy for entering a given market appears to be through licensing, the primary responsibility for developing and managing distribution channels becomes that of the licensee. Likewise, if the indicated strategy is to serve a market through exports, the channel decision may be limited to a choice between exporting indirectly through one of several types of domestic export merchants or middlemen or exporting directly to an importer in the market area. But even for an export strategy, the alternatives are more numerous than a simple choice between a domestic export agent or a foreign importer. An international firm may conclude that a given market potential warrants a major commitment and consider the possibilities of overseas sales branches on subsidiaries or foreign storage or warehouse facilities.[32] If the entry strategy is through foreign production as a joint venture or wholly owned subsidiary, then the channel management problem is largely a domestic business question.

No matter what the initial entry strategy, the choice of channels must be evaluated against the longer-range goals of the company in the specific market. Will the channels be sufficiently effective to develop the scale of sales in the country that will permit the company to move at a later stage to local production? Or will the channels be a barrier to the expansion of direct selling activities in the area when such a channel strategy becomes economic and desirable? Or will the channels be an efficient transmitter of information to the producer that will help it to match its product policies to changing consumer demands? As a first step after identifying attractive markets and their potentials, the marketing manager should specify the functions that the channel system is expected to accomplish.[33] These functions will be determined both by the nature of the product mix and by the environmental characteristics of the markets. As producers of automobiles exporting to the U.S. market or producers of construction machinery exporting to less developed markets have discovered, a necessary function that must be performed by the channels of distribution is the provision of after-sales service and repairs. Or in other types of products, an essential function may be the carrying of an adequate inventory in order to stimulate sales or the provision of consumer financing.

---

[32] See Franklin R. Root, *Strategic Planning For Export Marketing* (Scranton, Pa.: International Textbook Co., 1964), pp. 72–88.

[33] For more detailed discussions of international channel management, see Gordon E. Miracle and Gerald S. Albaum, *International Marketing Management* (Homewood, Ill.: Richard D. Irwin, Inc., 1970), pp. 313–416; Philip R. Cateora and John M. Hess, *International Marketing*, rev. ed. (Homewood, Ill.: Richard D. Irwin, Inc., 1971), pp. 751–90, 815–58.

The next step is to understand the channel alternatives available and the environmental characteristics of the institutions. In this respect, much detailed information on many countries has become available through comparative market research that can help the enterprise to develop its distribution strategy and select its channels. Again, it should be emphasized that in most areas the structure of the distribution system is in process of change, and the changes are as important to the marketing managers as the differences. The formulation of a strategy and the selection of channels must take into account the evolutionary changes underway and must fit into the process of change. Retailers and wholesalers are middlemen, not only in the flow of goods, but in the whole process of satisfying the material needs and desires of a society. Their effectiveness is largely determined, therefore, by the changing environment in which they stand.

The key elements in decisions as to a distribution system are (a) the availability of middlemen, (b) the ability and effectiveness of the alternatives in performing the necessary functions, (c) the cost of their services, and (d) the extent of control which the multinational enterprise can exert over the middlemen's activities. The preferred system is the one that will provide the optimum patterns of function, cost, and control. However, variations among nations may indicate different solutions to channel distribution needs for various market areas.

The alternatives available for exporting fall into three primary categories: agent middlemen, merchant middlemen, or a company's own sales and distribution system. In many instances, the enterprise will use more than one of these methods at the same time. The principal differences between the agent and the merchant is that merchant middlemen purchase for their own account and bear the majority of the trading risks for the products handled. Agents do not take title to the merchandise but work on a commission basis. In general, the firm has more control over prices and other aspects of the distribution function through agents. It has even more control by establishing its own distribution system, but the prospective scale of operations in a given market may not justify in terms of cost the establishment of a company's own system.

The wholesale distribution function can be handled by foreign importers, by the companies own overseas facilities, or by independent wholesalers.[34] A wholesaler is a middleman who sells to retailers or industrial users. His chief functions are negotiating for the buyer.[35] buying,

---

[34] See Robert Bartels, ed., *Comparative Marketing: Wholesaling in Fifteen Countries* (Homewood, Illinois: Richard D. Irwin, Inc., 1963); Sommers and Kernan, eds., *Comparative Marketing Systems*.

[35] See John Fayerweather, *International Marketing*, 2nd. ed. (Englewood Cliffs, N.J.: Prentice-Hall, 1970) pp. 73–74. "Negotiation for the buyer" refers to investigating sources of supply, checking the quality of products offered, and working out reasonable prices. Much of the negotiation on behalf of the buyer is performed by the channels of distribution.

selling, and storing. He may also offer a host of other services such as financing or servicing. The distribution system for industrial goods in advanced countries is generally quite similar. In the less developed countries, because a large share of industrial goods is imported and the volume of any one item may be small, the distribution of industrial goods is generally handled by importers who deal in a wide range of products in order to generate enough sales to support their operations. The smaller the market, the wider the range of products the wholesaler must carry. This feature reduces the choice of alternatives and frequently means that a distributor handles goods of several competing firms in the same field.

The retail distribution systems vary greatly among countries in the size of distribution units, in the services they perform, and in the assortment of goods they handle. In the Middle East, for example, "retail distribution is characterized by large numbers of little shops with small capital investments, much imitation, low turnovers, high margins, and high mortality."[36] Generally, as we go up the economic scale, the sizes of retail units increase, the amount of personal attention given to customers decreases—moving toward self-service—and the assortment of goods handled changes from a high degree of specialization to a wide variety of goods in one retail unit. Again, many comparative studies of retailing patterns are available for the marketing manager to secure essential information for deciding on his channel choices for a specific country.

In summary, international channel management requires the design of a structure of distribution units that will perform the physical distribution task, provide service and other functions, and provide an effective transmission system for returning necessary market information to the company. The alternatives vary tremendously with the environment and are in a process of change around the world. Starting from its market targets and an understanding of the functions that the distribution system must perform for each product or group of products, the marketing manager must design a system that not only serves present needs but that will have the flexibility to permit changes in the channel structure over time.

How is the international channel-management responsibility shared between headquarters and the subsidiaries in a multinational company? Obviously, in the case of foreign production, the responsibility must be highly decentralized. But headquarters has a need, under all circumstances, for keeping informed and for appraising the effectiveness of distribution channel experience. Some of the experience might be profitably transferred from one area to another. Some of the experience may indicate changes that should be made in the product mix in order to

---

[36] Charles F. Stewart, "The Changing Middle-East Market," *Journal of Marketing,* January 1961, p. 50.

permit distribution channels to be more effective. Where distribution channels are having great difficulty in providing post-sales service, for example, product redesigns that reduce or simplify the service requirement add to the effectiveness of the available channels.

The need to develop working relationships with outside channels working in a different cultural background presents further problems in the international firm. Not only will the firm face problems in seeking to transmit its past experience to these channels but also in communicating with them about current questions. Particular concepts will often not be directly translatable, and the approach to market assessment is likely to have many cultural biases.

One way of overcoming some of the problems is to develop representatives with preparation in both liaison with channels and the peculiarities of particular cultures. Caterpillar, for example, developed a range of international representatives with language and area courses and special training for aiding distributors in solving inventory, financial, and merchandising problems.

INTERNATIONAL ADVERTISING

International standardization versus differentiation has long been debated in the advertising field around the question of whether advertising themes and advertisements should be uniform internationally or developed specifically for individual national markets. Increasingly, advertising experts have been accepting the view that the advertising task is essentially the same in most markets—namely, to communicate information and persuasive appeals effectively. Therefore, the same approach to communication can be used in every country but the specific advertising messages and media strategy sometimes must be changed from country to country.[37]

Any component in the set of components making up an advertisement—the words used, the symbols, the illustrations and so on—might be changed to produce an improved impact when the culture of the audience changes. The age of a product user depicted in an illustration might appear just right to one culture yet young and immature to another. The overall message that an advertisement conveys might also be changed for different cultures. The product image that would most influence purchasing will differ in many ways from country to country. Finally media characteristics vary from country to country.

For these reasons there is an initial bias in favor of separate advertising in each country. Good advertising campaigns, however, are expensive to produce. When they have proven effective in one culture, it seems

---

[37] See Gordon E. Miracle, "International Advertising Principles and Strategies," *MSU Business Topics,* Autumn 1968, pp. 29–36.

worthwhile testing them in others before starting at the beginning again to develop separate campaigns for each culture. As the head of a Swedish advertising agency has said, "Why should three artists in three different countries sit drawing the same electric iron and three copywriters write about what after all is largely the same copy for the same iron."[38] The economic arguments for using a standard appeal in international media are great, particularly in new markets that do not warrant the cost involved in developing entirely new material.

Advertising strategy will depend, of course, on the product strategy. When a product fits a different need or serves a different function in a foreign market than in the central market, adjustments are required in the market communications. The same is true for a product strategy based on developing new products designed specifically for foreign markets.

There can be no doubt that good advertising built specifically for one culture will be superior to that built for another. One comparison of the relative effectiveness of American and British television commercials within the British market concluded as follows:

From this particular study, there emerges the conclusion that current or fairly recent American commercials, even of the highest creative caliber, are less likely than current British commercials to be effective in the British market and that the reasons for this are either (a) that despite a common language, the social, cultural, and marketing differences between the two countries are so great that a commercial which is successful in one country is unlikely to be very successful in the other, or (b) that in marketing and advertising terms, Britain is five years behind the United States, exemplified possibly by the fact that the successful British commercials for Coca-Cola and Excedrin were, perhaps, similar in style to American commercials for those same products of a few years ago. It may be that both of these factors apply in some measure.[39]

While the nature and motives of men are more or less universal, the way in which men satisfy their needs are not. Cultural and socioeconomic environmental differences play an important part in shaping the demand for specific types of goods and services and in determining what promotional appeals are best. Thus the appeals, illustrations, and other advertising features used to sell them often must differ from market to market. But this may be only a matter of changing specific advertising messages rather than the basic advertising approach. Esso was able to use its advertising theme, "Put a tiger in your tank" with considerable success in most countries of the world. In French, however, the word

[38] Eric Elinder, "International Advertisers Must Devise Universal Ads, Dump Separate National Ones, Swedish Adman Avers," *Advertising Age,* 27 November 1961, p. 91.

[39] John Caffyn and Nigel Rogers, "British Reactions to T.V. Commercials," *Journal of Advertising Research* 10, no. 3 (June 1970) : p. 27.

tank is *reservoir* which in the context of the phrase could be highly suggestive, so the word *moteur* was substituted. And in Thailand, where the tiger is not a symbol of strength, the campaign was not understood.[40] In England, an American-designed advertising campaign built on the slogan "Don't spend a penny until you've tried . . ." had to be modified because the phrase "spend a penny" in Britain is the equivalent of "got to see a man about a dog" in the United States.[41]

Because of cultural differences, the advertiser must choose with care the symbols used in advertisement for a market. Colors as one form of visual symbol may have a different significance in one culture as compared to another. In China, yellow has always been the imperial color and is not used extensively except for religious purposes. Advertising symbols must be in harmony with the prevailing mentality of a market. In some countries, the use of a certain brand of lipstick by a well-known fashion model may enhance the appeal of the product to working girls. But, "In Belgium (for example) it doesn't. Models are scarce and their trade is hardly considered honorable."[42] Illustrations for the same product may have to differ from country to country. In Germany an advertisement for cheese might show a large, foaming glass of beer, but in France the advertisement would substitute a glass of red wine.

In the area of media selection, considerable deviation from home-country patterns may be required, particularly for American companies. In many countries, ownership of radio and television media is in the hands of the government and no commercials are allowed. The barring of radio to advertisers in much of Europe has been evaded to some extent by using commercial stations in locations such as Luxembourg and Monte Carlo to reach European audiences. Several imaginative entrepreneurs have even established "pirate ships" as broadcasting stations outside the three-mile limit to bypass the laws against commercial radio in the Scandinavian countries. Except for these media restrictions, the availability and capability of media in foreign countries are similar to the United States. But the coverage and relative economic cost of foreign media are different and require adaptation.[43]

One special feature of international advertising deserves to be mentioned. Most of the principal American advertising firms have gone inter-

---

[40] "Put a Tiger in Your Tank," *Marketing Insights,* 28 November 1966, p. v.

[41] *Business Week,* 12 September 1970, p. 49.

[42] Dan E. G. Rosseals, "Consumer Habits and Consumer Advertising in the Benelux Countries," *Export Trade and Shipper,* 28 January 1957, p. 17.

[43] C. D. Philips, "Radio Broadcasting in the Sudan," *NAEB Journal* 23, July–August 1964, p. 59. In Sudan, radio ownership was found to be out of proportion to the incomes of people. A radio is a status symbol and even the lowest paid laborer has a personal transistor portable.

national. They are particularly well represented in Europe. With many U.S. domestic advertisers expanding overseas, U.S. advertising agencies have expanded internationally as a defensive measure, required in some cases in order to keep the domestic business. This trend has increased the capability of advertising agencies that work with headquarters of multinational firms to develop advertising programs that have international appeal from the beginning.

In summary, the principles underlying communication by advertising are the same in all nations. It is only the specific methods, techniques, and symbols which sometimes must be varied to take account of diverse environmental conditions. Uniform advertising for various market segments, whether national or international, have tremendous economic advantages for the firm. The critical questions for the multinational firm are *when* and *when not* to make adjustments. The best strategy is to try to take into account the international differences when preparing an advertising campaign and to export the same advertising approach to as many different markets as possible. But final decisions on copy or media should be handled by personnel who have intimate knowledge of foreign markets.

EXPORT MARKETING AND EAST-WEST TRADE

Export marketing deserves separate mention even though most aspects of reaching foreign markets through exports have already been touched upon [44] Where production is restricted to the home country for reasons of company strategy or the economics of location, the principal issue in export marketing is whether the firm should engage in indirect exporting where no special activity is carried on in the firm, or in direct international marketing. In most of the indirect approaches, foreign sales are handled in essentially the same way as domestic sales, and a minimum of international marketing know-how is required by the firm. For American firms, the indirect approach generally means that the enterprise is small and that its international commitment and potential is limited. For a Japanese company, on the other hand, the use of the indirect approach may be explained by the availability of large and experienced international trading firms which have a significant comparative advantage in foreign selling even over direct operations by large enterprises.

In direct exporting, the responsibility for identifying markets, physical distribution, export documentation, pricing, and so on all become the responsibility of the export department or the export manager. Where exporting is only part of the activities of a multinational firm, and

---

[44] For a specialized study on export marketing, see Franklin R. Root, *Strategic Planning for Export Marketing* (Scranton, Pa.: International Textbook Co., 1966).

sales are mainly to foreign subsidiaries as components or inputs to foreign production or to sales subsidiaries of the enterprise itself, many of the marketing functions such as market research, promotion, and pricing are assumed in whole or in part by the subsidiary. But where export sales are directed primarily to independent foreign buyers, export pricing in particular becomes a critical issue. Decisions have to be made as to whether exports should be at full-cost or marginal-cost pricing, whether prices should be quoted as f.o.b. (free on board) or c.i.f. (cost, insurance, freight) to foreign ports, in home-country currencies or in the currency of the market being served, and on how to use export credit.

Exporting has received intense attention by the less developed countries because of the need to earn foreign exchange for financing their development efforts.[45] More recently, the United States has given new emphasis to the encouragement of exporting because of its balance-of-payments problems. As a result, an extensive amount of literature has emerged on the how-to-do-it of export promotion, and governments have adopted incentive programs and developed facilities for offering technical assistance to exporters with which international managers need to become familiar.

A specialized area of export marketing is that of selling to centrally planned economies of the Soviet Union, Mainland China, and Eastern Europe. Over the last decade, these markets have begun to open up to international companies of Western nationality. But unlike the usual business experience of selling directly to consumers or users, sales to the centrally planned countries are arranged through government trade ministries.[46] Imports are planned along with domestic production in both annual and five-year plans, but these requirements are never published. The currencies of these countries are not freely convertible. Barter or special financial arrangements are generally required. Because of long-standing U.S. restrictions on East-West trade, American multinational companies have developed much less experience in trading with the Sino-Soviet-bloc countries than have international companies of European and Japanese nationality. However, some American companies have gained expertise by doing business through their European subsidiaries. Also, a number of U.S. trading companies now specialize in trading with the Soviet Union, Eastern Europe, and Mainland China because of the unique features of this type of exporting.

---

[45] For example, see Amicus Most, *Expanding Exports: A Case Study of the Korean Experience* (Washington, D.C.: Agency for International Development, June 1969).

[46] For example, see, Lyman E. Ostlund and Kjell M. Halversen, "The Russian Decision Process Governing Trade," *Journal of Marketing* 36, no. 2 (April 1972): 3–11.

Summary

The basic functions involved in managing the product mix and the marketing activity are the same for both domestic and international markets, but the implementation can be quite different because of environmental differences. Consequently, the international firm faces many special problems in selecting its marketing mission and in adjusting its mix of marketing actions. Throughout most dimensions of the marketing function, there is a conflict between differentiation to meet the needs of market segments and international standardization to reduce costs. The conflict relates to product strategies, pricing, advertising, and the way in which the marketing activity is organized. Unfortunately, there are no general or fixed rules for resolving this conflict. The international marketing manager must therefore be constantly alert to the impact of decisions for any unit in the multinational system on the corporation as a whole.

APPENDIX

Table 19.1 illustrates how different price elasticities will lead to different price policies for subsidiaries in different markets where each obtains its supplies at the same unit cost and acts to maximize its profit. At

TABLE 19.1

				Price (in £)				
	100	95	90	85	80	75	70	65
Sales Volume That Would Result								
Country A (units). . . .	900	1400	2000	2600	3300	4000	4500	5000
Country B (units). . . .	1200	1400	1600	1800	2000	2200	2400	2600
Total Revenue								
Country A (£000s). . .	90	133	180	221	264	300	315	325
Country B (£000s). . .	120	133	144	153	160	165	168	169
Contribution When Transfer Price =								
£50								
Country A (£000s). .	45	63	80	91	99	100*	90	75
Country B (£000s). .	60	63	64*	63	60	55	48	39
£60								
Country A (£000s). .	36	49	60	65	66*	60	45	25
Country B (£000s). .	48	49*	48	45	40	33	24	13
£70								
Country A (£000s). .	27	35	40*	39	33	20	–	–
Country B (£000s). .	36*	35	32	27	20	11	–	–

* Indicates greatest contribution for a given transfer price.

a transfer price of £50 from the supplying unit, *Country A* would sell at £75 and *Country B* at £90. An increased transfer price, however, would lead to increased prices in both countries.

Given that the selling subsidiaries are motivated to maximize their profits, they will price so that their marginal revenue just equals the marginal cost to them. The greatest system profit will then emerge if a unit is charged a transfer price equal to the cost of supplying a unit which in most cases can be taken to be the variable cost of production and distribution. The nearer the transfer price is to this variable cost the closer a subsidiary's pricing policy will bring the firm to maximizing its contribution over and above this variable cost. Table 19.2 illustrates how the system profits increase as the transfer price is brought down to variable cost in this way.

Suppose now that the firm were to fix the final market price in order to maintain uniform world prices. Inevitably this would lead to a decreased system contribution because, in this case, one subsidiary or both

TABLE 19.2

	Sales Volume to Maximize Contr.				System Contribution When Variable Cost =		
Transfer Price	Country A (units)	Country B (units)	Total Units	Total Revenue (£000s)	£40 (£000s)	£50 (£000s)	£60 (£000s)
£40	4000	1800	5800	453	221*	–	–
£50	4000	1600	5600	444	220	164*	–
£60	3300	1400	4700	397	209	162	115*
£70	2000	1200	3200	300	172	140	108

*Indicates transfer price bringing greatest contribution for a given variable cost.

TABLE 19.3

Common Market Price (£s)	Combined Volume Country A + B (units)	Contribution When Variable Cost =		
		£40 (£000s)	£50 (£000s)	£60 (£000s)
100	2100	126	105	84
95	2800	154	126	98
90	3600	180	144	108
85	4400	198	154	110*
80	5300	212	159*	106
75	6200	217*	154	93
70	6900	207	138	69
65	7600	190	114	38

*Indicates price bringing greatest contribution for a given variable cost.

would be forced away from an optimal adjustment to the particular situation ruling in its market. Comparing Table 19.3 with Table 19.2 it can be seen that no choice of common price level for the two markets would produce a contribution for any given variable cost that is as high as that possible when the prices are adjusted separately.

EXERCISES AND DISCUSSION QUESTIONS

1. In what ways does a strategy of joint ventures rather than wholly owned subsidiaries place constraints on the task of managing the international product mix?

2. "There is a movement on the part of European companies for greater standardization and guidance of marketing policies in U.S. operations, particularly in relatively low-technology, high-market-saturation product areas such as petroleum, paper, and various sorts of consumer goods." In what ways do you think the type of product influences the degree of centralization and standardization?

3. Examine Tables 19.2 and 19.3 and explain why no choice of a common price level for the two markets will contribute as much to profits as is possible when prices are adjusted separately.

4. What are the main advantages and disadvantages of manipulating intracompany transfer prices?

5. "Until we achieve One World, there is no such thing as international marketing—only local marketing around the world." Do you agree or disagree and why?

6. Why do national differences in distribution channels frequently result in gaps in market coverage?

7. Do products sold primarily on the basis of objective physical characteristics, such as razor blades and automobile tires, lend themselves to uniform international advertising strategies more than products such as foods or dress clothing? If so, why?

20

INTERNATIONAL
FINANCIAL
MANAGEMENT

WHAT NEW DIMENSIONS are added to the financial management function as an enterprise expands its international commitment? At a minimum level of international business involvement such as incidental importing and exporting activities, the financial manager will only have to deal with a few international elements such as multiple currencies and alternative sources and techniques of import-export credit. But as a firm becomes a global enterprise, the series of new complexities not encountered domestically increases dramatically.

In the multinational enterprise, the financial manager must deal with a number of different currencies. He must deal with units in the system that are organized and are operating under different local legal and tax systems. He must take into account the variations in inflation trends, interest rates, tax burdens, and the availability and costs of capital in the many domestic environments in which units of the system operate. In addition, he must recognize the impact of national controls on financial flows across national boundaries.

In brief, international as compared to domestic financial management involves new environmental considerations, new sources of risk, and new opportunities for economies and efficiencies from an integrated global financial system. To deal with the environmental differences, the international financial manager must be familiar with the international financial framework and many national situations and have an effective global intelligence system that keeps such information current. The new risks such as foreign exchange risk and changes in tax liability that arise because of movements of funds across national borders require a considerable forecasting input into international financial management. The new opportunities arising out of access to many capital markets and the potentials for achieving indirect benefits in one part of the system from activities in another part require the development of complex management tools for optimizing financial goals on a system-wide basis. By taking a systems approach, the criterion for any particular financial decision should be the potential contribution of this decision to the entire system at the margin.

The international financial elements have already been introduced in Part II as components of the environmental framework. In this chapter, the same elements will be recast into a managerial framework and related to capital and budgeting decisions, continuing financial operations, and the control function. As information flows are the basic material for performing the financial management function, the subject of accounting in international business will be considered first. It should be noted, however, that this chapter is limited to the international financial function in industrial and commercial firms. Financial intermediaries, such as banks and insurance companies, have their own financial problems which will not be considered here.

ACCOUNTING ISSUES FOR INTERNATIONAL BUSINESS

Effective financial management requires a continuing flow of meaningful financial reports. This is especially true in international business, where top management must rely even more than usual on a financial information system because of the impossibility of supervising and coordinating widely dispersed units through continuous personal contacts. Thus, in international business the demands on the financial information system are greatly increased. Yet at the same time, the difficulties encountered in meeting these demands are also magnified because of the multiple currency problem and major variations in the accounting systems that must be used by different units of the system.

An accounting system for multinational enterprises has to satisfy several requirements simultaneously.[1] It must provide financial data for information and decision purposes that are understandable both in the country in which a particular unit of the system is operating and in the headquarters country where decisions involving more than one country have to be made. In addition, the accounting system must provide financial statements that can be consolidated on an enterprise-wide basis. To fulfill the consolidation requirements, the labeling and content of accounts must be uniform throughout the system and major difficulties inherent in translating values from one currency to another must be resolved.

---

[1] This section draws heavily upon Hanns-Martin Schoenfeld, "Some Special Accounting Problems of Multinational Enterprises," *Management International Review* 9, nos. 4–5 (1969): 3–11.

At the subsidiary level, understandability must be guaranteed within the national environment. National accounting principles and procedures, either prescribed by law or by local professional organizations, must be followed in order that financial reports can be understood by tax and other government officials. And national accounting systems will vary with the legal, tax, and other features of the environment that are decided independently by each national government.[2] Adherence to national accounting standards also permits each local manager to manage on the basis of data and concepts with which he is familiar, lets him compare his performance with that of local competitors, and permits evaluation of his results against local rather than parent-company standards. Furthermore, many managerial decisions are dependent on national environmental constraints and have to be based on pertinent relevant data. For example, price-level adjustments for company expenses or sales for different time periods may be locally essential because of inflationary conditions even though such accounting practices are not typical in the country of the parent. Other examples of differences from U.S. practice are shown in Figure 20.1.

To secure understandability of accounting data in the decision center of the home office presents many difficult problems. Because the financial information system must be based on data retaining their various local characteristics, the accounting data that flow from the units within the system to headquarters normally contain only part of the pertinent variables and may be based on different environmental decision parameters. Understandability thus requires that top management cultivate a multiple currency consciousness, a facility with multiple report forms and multiple analysis devices, and a general awareness of the assumptions, biases, or other distortions which may be inherent in the different national accounting systems. In many situations, the decision center may need several parallel financial-information systems to provide the information required for divergent purposes.

An obvious solution is to develop internationally accepted accounting principles or move national regulations toward this goal. But as Mueller concludes, "Despite great intellectual and operational appeal, uniform international accounting standards do not seem to be a reasonable goal at present."[3] Nevertheless, many diversities among national accounting practices are likely to be reduced over time. The barriers to a single set of generally accepted accounting principles are not primarily the

---

[2] For example see, *Professional Accounting in 25 Countries* (New York: American Institute of Certified Public Accountants, 1964); Stephen A. Zeff, *Forging Accounting Principles in Five Countries: A History and an Analysis of Trends* (Champaign, Ill.: Stipes Publishing Co., 1972).

[3] Gerhard G. Mueller, "Accounting For Multinational Companies," *Cost and Management,* July–August 1971, p. 7.

FIGURE 20.1

Accounting Principles and Practices That Are Different from Those Generally Accepted in the United States (some examples)

Accounting	Explanation of Difference	Selected Countries Following Different Practice
Exchange losses	Exchange losses arising on foreign currency liabilities incurred for importation of items of inventories are added to the cost of inventories if the corresponding items are unsold when the exchange losses arise. (A lower cost or market test is applied to the inventory after the exchange losses, if any, are added to the inventories.)	Argentina, Chile, India, Mexico, Peru, Philippines
Surplus entries	Capital reserves generally include items constituting capital gains which are carried to equity reserves without passing through (crediting) income.	Australia, Belgium, Ireland, New Zealand, Peru, Spain, United Kingdom
Disclosure		
Rental commitments	Material rental commitments on long-term leases (say, over one year) are seldom disclosed.	Argentina, Australia, Belgium, Brazil, Chile, Colombia, France, Germany, Italy, Japan
Consolidation of financial statements	In the case of a parent company having subsidiaries, consolidated (or group) accounts are not included in local statutory financial statements. Further, the parent's equity in subsidiaries, carried at cost, is not disclosed.	Colombia, Germany, Italy, Japan, Spain, Switzerland, Venezuela

Source: Price, Waterhouse and Co., USA, *Guide For the Readers of Foreign Financial Statements*, June 1971.

difficulties of securing agreement by representatives of many different nations. The basic difficulty is that accounting systems must be consistent with the economic and business systems prevailing in different countries. Only where environments are similar can a particular single body of accounting principles give meaningful results.[4] As one example, in the United States with a highly developed capital market, accounting practices must recognize the special needs of security analysts and the disclosure requirements of government regulatory agencies.

Even though a trend toward greater uniformity in accounting standards may eventually reduce some of the complexities of international financial management, the problem of multiple currencies is likely to

---

[4] Mueller, "Accounting Principles Generally Accepted in the United States Versus Those Generally Accepted Elsewhere," *The International Journal of Accounting, Education, and Research,* Spring 1968, pp. 91–103.

remain for some time. Transactions are conducted and records kept in one currency and the parent company must ultimately see the results in its own currency. Over any given time period, the relationship of the two standards to each other may change because of differential rates of inflation and devaluations or revaluations. The operations of a foreign subsidiary may be highly successful when measured in local currency but may actually involve losses to the multinational enterprise system because of devaluation. Action taken to reduce potential devaluation losses to the system may also reduce the income of the subsidiary in local currency. Consequently, the currency problem produces complications in using the financial information system for appraising operation results and may require that performance responsibility be assigned in each of the two standards. The manager of the subsidiary, for example, may be expected to maximize profits in the local currency and the financial office of the parent company be responsible for minimizing losses through devaluation.

The process of restating financial accounts from one currency to another is referred to as "translation." The actual sale of one currency for another is called "conversion." When foreign currency financial reports are transmitted for combination or consolidation at headquarters, the typical sequence would be to adjust them for home-country accounting principles and procedures. After such adjustments, local currencies are translated into home-country currency amounts by way of a translation procedure consistent with practices in the home country.[5] Revenues and expenses for the period in which devaluation or revaluation occurs are usually translated at an average rate for the period, but for balance sheet items four alternative methods are used in varying degrees.

The first and most commonly used method is to translate current assets (for example, cash, receivables, and inventories) and current liabilities at the current rate of exchange and all other assets and liabilities at the historical rate prevailing when assets were acquired and liabilities incurred. A second method is to apply the current exchange rate to all financial assets and liabilities and translate physical assets at historical rates. The third method varies this by extending the current rate to all current assets. Finally, under the fourth method, known as the net assets method, all items except capital and retained surplus are translated at the current exchange rate. Capital is translated at the historical rate under all four methods, and surplus represents the remaining balancing item. These four alternative methods are illustrated in Figure 20.2. Note that in this figure the retained surplus account

---

[5] The authoritative recommendations of professional accountancy organizations for translation procedures are being published in a research study of the American Institute of CPAs entitled "Reporting Foreign Operations of U.S. Companies in U.S. Dollars."

FIGURE 20.2

Translating a Foreign Subsidiary's Accounts: Four Alternative Methods

	Subsidiary's Balance Sheet in Local Currency	Translation into U.S. Dollar Equivalent			
		Method	*2*	*3*	*4*
		At Current Rate ($1 = 20 pesos)	*Financial Assets and All Liabilities*	*Current Assets and All Liabilities*	*All Assets and Liabilities*
		1			
		Current Assets and Liabilities			
		At Historical Rate ($1 = 15 pesos)	*Physical Assets and Net Worth*	*Fixed Assets and Net Worth*	*Net Worth*
		Fixed Assets, Long-Term Liabilities, and Net Worth			
	(000 pesos)	*($000)*	*($000)*	*($000)*	*($000)*
Cash	50 ⎫	45	45	45	45
Accounts receivable . . .	850 ⎭				
Inventories	700	35	47	35	35
Current assets	1600	80	92	80	80
Current liabilities	1100	55	55	55	55
Working capital	500	25	37	25	25
Fixed assets	600	40	40	40	30
	1100	65	77	65	55
Long-term liabilities (local) . .	300	20	15	15	15
Net worth	800	45	62	50	40
Capital	600	40	40	40	40
Retained surplus					
Beginning of year . . .	100	7	7	7	7
Profit for year	100 (at av. rate of 17%)	6	6	6	6
Exchange adjustment . . .		-8	+9	-3	-13

is broken into three separate elements in order to show the exchange adjustments separately.

The different methods can result in significantly different indications of performance and may influence the actions management takes.[6] Under the current-asset method, there is no inherent advantage under devaluation in holding inventory in preference to cash or receivables, nor in financing by local long-term borrowing. It implies that on devaluation, assets held as inventory will suffer the same degree of foreign exchange loss as the holding of cash and receivables; an assumption that generally is not valid. By way of contrast, the second method encourages the holding of physical assets, carrying with it the implication that physical assets will appreciate in local currency to the extent that the foreign exchange value of the currency depreciates. The third method, though, reverses this for current physical assets. By translating local long-term debt at the current exchange rate, both the second and third methods encourage the use of local debt where devaluation is likely. Although these first three methods are most commonly used, the net-asset method has become increasingly preferred by many accounting experts. While its use of the current rate throughout ignores the idea that there will be appreciation in assets to offset currency devaluation—or depreciation to offset revaluation—in fact it seldom follows that depreciation is directly in step with devaluation. By combining the use of the current rate with a policy of price-level revaluations of physical assets, however, a more accurate indication of real performance can be obtained.

Another major accounting issue is whether reports should be consolidated. A parent corporation can treat its investments in foreign subsidiaries as it would portfolio investments. Such investments are carried at cost, and income is shown only when actually received in the form of dividends, interest, or service charges. Consolidated statements which include the foreign subsidiaries give much more information about the operations over a period and the situation at a balance sheet date. For companies with a substantial fraction of their activities conducted through foreign subsidiaries, consolidation seems desirable for informing both management and the public about the true state of affairs.

Yet, the process of consolidating accounts for multinational operations has many technical hazards. The financial statements to be consolidated have a domicile in terms of an underlying set of accounting principles and such domicile orientation cannot be easily changed through restatements or adjustments of the financial statements themselves. For example, financial statements prepared according to good accounting practices in Argentina and then restated somehow to a Canadian basis would differ markedly from those resulting if the Argentine operation had taken

---

[6] For illustrations of the differing implications of the three methods, see David B. Zenoff and Jack Zwick, *International Financial Management* (Englewood Cliffs, N.J.: Prentice-Hall, 1969), pp. 494–502.

place in Canada and been accounted for originally in terms of Canadian practices. Consolidation raises such problems as the treatment of reserves for future taxes on repatriated profits. A conservative accounting approach that includes such reserves in a consolidation even though it is unlikely that the taxes will be paid, can be misleading as to the profitability of a foreign operation. A similar problem can arise in the treatment of depreciation expenses. To secure comparability among subsidiaries, a uniform rate of depreciation may be used. But to reduce current taxes and increase cash flows, the most rapid rate of depreciation allowed for local tax purposes should be taken. Faster depreciation for a subsidiary in a country where tax laws permit it, will increase cash flows but decrease net income in the short run. To consolidate the accounts of foreign subsidiaries, the financial manager may thus face a two-stage exercise: first, restatement according to home-country accounting and then, translation of accounts into the home-currency conventions. This two-stage process is illustrated in Figure 20.3.

Other accounting problems arise with transfer pricing, service charges of various sorts, and the allocation of headquarters and research expenses to the subsidiaries. Generally, the parent-company management reserves final authority in such decisions and attempts to make them in terms of system-wide optimization. Thus, financial comparisons and evaluations of local operating companies may be determined as much by parent-company decisions as by the actual operating results of the subsidiaries. In many cases, therefore, it is extremely difficult to make the necessary adjustments for a fair evaluation of the profitability of individual units of the enterprise.

Given the multiple purposes that must be served simultaneously by financial reporting and the variations in accounting principles, multinational enterprises are finding it necessary to use three or four different sets of financial statements. National financial statements are prepared on the basis of nationally accepted accounting principles. A second set of financial statements are prepared by each unit of the system which comply with the accounting principles and the translation methods that are accepted in the country of the home office. Still another set may be prepared to comply with the regulations of the various tax authorities involved. And finally, separate financial statements may be prepared which present a picture for management of the enterprise. In such a statement, for example, uniform valuation methods for assets of all subsidiaries might be used, regardless of the different legal regulations or locally accepted accounting practices.

INVESTMENT DECISIONS AND CAPITAL BUDGETING

Investment decisions represent ultimate control over the operating subsidiaries and a principal means of implementing the global strategy

FIGURE 20.3

Restatement and Translation of a Subsidiary's Accounts for Consolidation Purposes

	Subsidiary's Accounts Before Adjustment (000 ps)	Adjust- ments (000 ps)	Restate- ment (000 ps)	Translation into U.S. $ Using Method 3 (see Figure 20.2) ($000)
Revenue Account				
Sales	3,600	—	3,600	180
Less cost of sales	2,400	−120	2,280	114
Gross margin	1,200	+120	1,320	66
Less expenses	1,075	− 80	995	50
Profit before tax	125	+200	325	16
Taxation provision	25	+137	162	8
Net profit	100	+ 63	163	8
Assets and Liabilities				
Cash	50		50	3
Accounts receivable	850		850	42
Inventories	700		700	35
Current assets	1,600		1,600	80
Current liabilities	1,100	+137	1,237	62
Working capital	500	−137	363	18
Fixed assets	600	+ 80	680	45
	1,100	− 57	1,043	63
Long-term liabilities	300	—	300	15
Net worth	800	− 57	743	48
Capital	600	—	600	40
Retained Surplus:				
Beginning of year	100	−120	−20	−1
Profit for year	100	+ 63	163	8
Exchange adjustment	—	—	—	1

Adjustments are required as follows:
a) Reduce Cost of Sales by 120,000 pesos representing parent-company margin eliminated from last year's consolidation.
b) Reduce Depreciation 80,000 pesos to express it at standard rates used by parent company.
c) Increase taxation provision from 20 percent to 50 percent to allow for tax on future profit remittances.

of a multinational enterprise. Although decisions to establish new operations or expand existing ones are based on many considerations, the financial manager invariably plays a key role through his responsibility for analyzing and comparing the expected returns and other financial features of alternative proposals. This financial management activity is normally performed within a capital-budgeting framework, that is, through a process of matching advantages from possible uses of funds against the cost of alternative ways to obtain the needed resources.

In domestic business, capital budgeting has become highly developed with sophisticated analytical approaches available for investment decisions.[7] In the international field, however, the use of capital-budgeting techniques is still in an early stage because of the additional complications and uncertainties that must be handled once national boundaries are crossed. As Brooke and Remmers have reported from their survey of multinational firms, the usual difficulties in applying capital-budgeting techniques for the appraisal of investment projects in foreign operations, "are compounded by the generally poor quality of information that is obtainable, the added risks, and the different costs of capital which arise from operating in a multiple business environment."[8] Another survey of 92 American and 18 foreign multinational corporations concluded that financial investment criteria were used most often in evaluating relatively small projects which fell under the purview of local managers. "For relatively large or strategic investments, however, financial investment criteria were used only as a rough screening device to prevent obviously unprofitable projects from wasting the time of the board of directors."[9]

Another prevailing pattern has been for foreign-investment decisions to be made on a country-by-country basis.[10] Each country is considered as a separate entity and investments in that country have been justified largely in terms of the potential size and profitability of operations within the country. New operations, therefore, are proposed when conditions in a single national market seem justified, without evaluation of possible alternative schemes for supplying that market and without basing investment decisions on the return to the total multinational system. Increasingly, however, companies have been recognizing that investment decisions should be based on the net benefits that any additional investment will bring to the multinational system as a whole rather than to any unit of the system taken separately. Chapter 17 on global planning shows one way this might be done. Beyond this, financial evaluation techniques are being developed for taking a systems approach, as illustrated in Figure 20.4, about financial decisions that allow for tax and financial cost variations among countries as well as tariff differences.[11]

[7] For a standard reference on capital budgeting, see Harold Bierman, Jr. and Seymour Smidt, *The Capital Budgeting Decision*, 2nd ed. (New York: Macmillan Co., 1966).

[8] Michael Z. Brooke and H. Lee Remmers, *The Strategy of Multinational Enterprise* (New York: American Elsevier Publishing Co., 1970), p. 102.

[9] Arthur Stonehill and Leonard Nathanson, "Capital Budgeting and the Multinational Corporation," *California Management Review*, Summer 1968, p. 40.

[10] Jack Zwick, "Models for Multicountry Investments," *Business Horizons*, Winter 1967, p. 73.

[11] A pioneering study emphasizing the systems approach is Sidney M. Robbins and Robert B. Stobaugh, *Money in the Multinational Enterprise* (New York: Basic Books, 1973).

FIGURE 20.4
A Systems Approach to Financial Optimization (an example)

Characteristics of the Multinational System (by country)

3 fully owned system companies	A	B	C
Local corporation tax rates	50%	20%	40%
Import duty rates for system transfers	10%	30%	80%
Local interest rates	9%	7%	8%

Each company transfers some production to the other two
Each company has local profits and incurs corporation tax.

Possibilities for System Savings over Independent Operation

a) *Alter source of capital*

Independent decision: Raise capital from cheapest source and pay local taxes. Net cost = (A) 3.5% (B) 5.6% (C) 4.2%

System decision: Company with highest tax rate (A) to raise capital from cheapest source and advance interest free to others. Net cost = (A, B, C) 3.5%.

b) *Alter transfer prices*

Independent decision: Price somewhere between supplier company cost and receiving company revenue.

System decision: Adjust prices as indicated on the table below. Gains would continue until lowered prices reached zero and increased prices eliminated all the profits of the receiving company, but there will be practical limitations in the real world.

Gains from $100 Change

Goods Transferred From:	Direction of Price Change	Source Country Tax $	Destination Country Tax $	Import Duty $	Net System Gain $
A to B	lower	+50	−20	+30	+60
B to C	lower	+20	−40	+80	+60
C to A	Adjust to give desired company profits				0
A to C	lower	+50	−40	+80	+90
C to B	lower	+40	−20	+30	+50
B to A	raise	−20	+50	−10	+20

c) *Alter royalty charges and transfer prices*

Independent decision: Combined total to fall between supplier company cost and receiving company revenue.

System decision: Lower *all* transfer prices to minimize import duties, and charge royalties from lowest taxed company to minimize corporation tax.

The return-on-investment analysis for an international project follows essentially the same general form used for domestic business but with several additional international elements to be considered. These arise at each of three stages in the analysis. In the first stage, the estimated receipts and disbursements for the project are analyzed by including problems of exchange rates, financial costs, and risk measurement. In the second stage, the analysis moves from the subsidiary to the headquarters' level. This requires estimating (a) what amounts will be transferred, at what time, and in what form from the subsidiary to the parent company, (b) what taxes and other expenses will be incurred due to these transfers, and (c) what incremental revenues and costs will result elsewhere in the system. In a third and last stage, the project is evaluated and compared with other investment projects on the basis of incremental net cash flow accruing to the system as a return on the investment.

The projection of receipts and disbursements begins, of course, from the market forecasts, including export possibilities from the project. A unique aspect of projecting receipts and disbursements for a foreign project is the need to develop schedules of relevant, anticipated exchange rates for each type of transaction involved. This task goes beyond the general requirement for foreign exchange forecasting. Some countries will have both an official and a free rate of exchange, each applying to different transactions. Many transactions involving foreign exchange are subject to duties, special taxes, and exemptions. Equipment exports, for example, may be exempted or receive exchange rate concessions. In some instances, foreign exchange rates are subject to negotiations between the government and the international enterprise. Consequently, the international financial manager may need separate projections over time of exchange rates for equipment imports, raw material imports, and export sales, and he will have to evaluate the importance of such rates to the revenues and costs of the project.

A second international consideration may be the need to consider alternative financial structures for the proposed project, which in turn will affect projected receipts and disbursements. Local debt financing, for example, tends to reduce both foreign exchange and inflation risk. But the availability of local credit for international enterprises varies greatly among countries for national policy or other reasons. In certain countries, the international firm may be required to finance up to certain limits by local sales of equity. Or the country may offer special incentives, if external rather than local financing is used for imported equipment, in order to encourage foreign investment inflows. By considering such matters, the firm may want to develop separate receipts and disbursement forecasts for several alternative financial plans that are feasible for a particular national situation.

Still another international consideration is the need to include risk elements of a political- or national-controls nature in the investment analysis. As an extreme example, high probabilities of expropriation or confiscation can markedly change the projections of receipts and disbursements. These risks have been discussed in Chapters 15 and 16, where techniques for handling such risk elements have been suggested. In addition to their impact on projected receipts and disbursements for a project analyzed at a national level, these risk elements must be considered at the headquarters level from the standpoint of how they might affect income flows such as dividend remittances and royalty payments available to the parent and the rest of the system.

In the second stage, where the analysis moves to the headquarters' level, the principal additional issues become the availability to head-quarters of income flows from the project and the net incremental bene-fits, if any, to the system. Operations within the same country can rea-sonably assume that cash flows from one unit of an enterprise are freely available to another unit. In many countries, the repatriation of cash flows above a certain percentage return are not allowed or are heavily taxed and forecasts of remittance policies are required in such cases. Profits which are freely available to the parent concern have a different value than profits which must be reinvested. Forced reinvestment may, however, have desirable and beneficial results in cases where opportuni-ties are growing or where the firm has initially set up a new venture on a narrow financial base to minimize its exposure. In any event, the firm will have to decide whether it should assign lower values to project flows that cannot be converted into home-country currency or transferred freely to other countries, or whether all earnings from the project should be considered as available inflows to the parent company. It will also have to take into account the tax and other costs of transferring income to the parent companies. The estimated inflows must also be translated into home-country currency units on the basis of foreign exchange fore-casts over the planning period.

The incremental benefits to the rest of the system should be imputed as additional available income from the proposed project. These can be profits from increased export sales from the parent company; pay-ments of license fees, royalties, or management services; or even transfers of technological or marketing know-how available to the rest of the system from the activities of the new venture.

At the third and last stage, the alternative investment projects are compared with each other and ranked on the basis of expected return on investment, in which order they will be accepted up to the limit of the investment sums considered available for the capital budgeting period. One of the issues at this stage may be the method used for comparing projects. Another will be the criterion used for the cost of capital.

The "net present value" method has become most widely used for evaluating investments. The method takes into account earnings over the life of a project. It discounts the expected future net cash flows, using the cost of capital as the discount rate, and then deducts the original cost of capital to determine the present net value of the project.[12]

Policies on cost of capital may range from a pool-of-funds concept with a presumed single pool of corporate funds and a single target rate

---

[12] See Bierman and Smidt, *Capital Budgeting Decision,* pp. 18–38 for a discussion of alternative techniques such as the payback method and average rate of return method, and for an explanation of the way in which to apply the alternative methods.

to the use of separate costs of capital for each country of operation or each project.[13] The pool-of-funds approach assumes that funds are raised on a worldwide basis with debt incurred where the terms are most favorable and transferred to the places where funds are most desired. This concept, obviously does not apply where a philosophy of "every tub on its own bottom" is being followed and a subsidiary is responsible for its own financing after the initial phase. In such cases, the cost of capital must be estimated separately for each project. Also, where special sources of financing are available for specific projects, such as through financial incentives uniquely available to projects located in the depressed region of Southern Italy, such special costs would most likely be taken into account by using separate target rates for the cost of capital. Ordinarily, however, a single, company-wide cost of capital measure should be used as the discount factor in evaluating foreign-investment projects.[14]

The principal international risk elements—foreign exchange, national controls, and political risk—have already been incorporated into the analysis. The recommended risk-adjustment procedures are to analyze the specific sources of risk and through the use of subjective probabilities to estimate the specific impact of the possible outcomes to produce an expected return on the investment. In making a final selection, the enterprise will have its estimates of the net present value of available inflows and a measure of risk for each alternative. The alternatives may consist of different projects or the same projects financed in different ways. The final choices from the financial point of view will then depend upon the firm's attitudes towards taking risks.[15]

FINANCIAL STRUCTURES AND FINANCING TECHNIQUES

The choice among alternative financial structures and financing plans for affiliates, as previously noted, may influence significantly the attractiveness of new projects and expansions. The choice can also affect the degree of foreign exchange and political risk incurred in multinational operations. The options will differ, of course, in the case of a wholly owned subsidiary from those related to a joint venture.

In choosing optimal financing plans for foreign affiliates, the financial manager will have to decide such questions as the appropriate mix of debt and equity and the extent to which debt should be local or imported.

[13] Dan T. Smith, "Financial Variables in International Business," *Harvard Business Review,* January–February, 1966, pp. 97–98.

[14] Zenoff and Zwick, *International Financial Management,* pp. 186–203.

[15] For an example of the large amount of literature on portfolio selection covering this point, see Alexander A. Robichek and Stewart C. Myers, *Optimal Financing Decisions* (Englewood Cliffs, N.J.: Prentice-Hall, 1965).

The alternatives will depend on the local and foreign sources of capital available for financing projects in specific countries, national governmental regulations regarding financing and ownership arrangements, relative costs of the various options, and other factors.[16]

What constitutes an appropriate mix of debt and equity has long been debated by financial experts. Debt constitutes a fixed obligation to pay interest and repay principal regardless of business conditions. Because the cost of debt is generally fixed and tax deductible, it gives the suppliers of equity leverage for maximizing their earnings. There are limits to the amount of debt that can be used, however, because as the proportion of debt increases both lenders and purchasers of new equity may demand a higher return because of the risk that the firm may not meet its fixed obligations in periods of bad business conditions. But the tolerable limits of debt will vary from country to country. A study of 463 corporate financial structures in nine selected industries shows that the average debt to total assets in each of the industries is consistently higher in Japan, Italy, Sweden, and West Germany than it is in the United States or France.[17] In Japan, for example, steel companies have debt/equity ratios on the order of 4:1 (80 percent debt to 20 percent equity), whereas U.S. steel companies have debt ratios on the order of 3 to 1. Or to take a more extreme case, the share of equity in the total capital structure of major Japanese trading companies ranges from 3 to 7 percent as compared to 45 percent for Sears, Roebuck in the U.S. and 71 percent for A & P, the large food distributor.[18]

Also, the international manager must consider the effect of the financial structure of the affiliate on the total enterprise where the parent's and affiliates financial statements will be consolidated. High-debt ratios may be acceptable in the country of the subsidiary, but the consolidated balance sheet may show a higher debt ratio than is considered appropriate in the country of the parent. The result may be that the cost of financing for the parent company may be increased because the optimal financing plan for the affiliate is suboptimal for the total enterprise. Such a problem would be less common for Japanese than for U.S. multinational enterprises.

In international business, a high-debt ratio for a foreign subsidiary has important advantages beyond the usual benefit from leverage. Local debt financing in weak currency countries tends to reduce both devalua-

---

[16] For an analysis of the external financing experience of 115 subsidiaries over the period 1960 to 1967, see Brooke and Remmers, *Strategy of Multinational Enterprise,* pp. 179–210; also see Zenoff and Zwick, *International Financial Management,* pp. 185–204 on criteria for selection of affiliate financial structures.

[17] Arthur Stonehill and Thomas Stitzel, "Financial Structure and Multinational Corporations," *California Management Review,* Fall 1969, pp. 257–61.

[18] James C. Abegglen, ed., *Business Strategies for Japan* (Tokyo, Japan: Sophia University, 1970), pp. 57–68.

tion and inflation risk. When devaluations occur, servicing requirements on debts denominated in outside currencies increase. In a sense, outside debts grow as larger amounts of local currency are required to meet interest payments and retire principal. In contrast, the servicing requirements on local debt are not affected by devaluation. For this reason, firms are frequently willing to borrow locally even though the cost is higher than imported funds and the additional cost is considered as an insurance payment against devaluation risk. With revaluations, as occurred in Germany and Japan in the early 1970s, the ability to meet external obligations will, of course, increase.

The advantage of local debt in reducing inflation risk is that repayment obligations may remain fixed in local currency while revenues and profits rise along with inflation. In other words, debt is being paid off with "cheaper money." The inflation advantage of local debt, however, has been eliminated in some countries with traditionally high rates of inflation. Brazil, for example, has widely adopted the device of "monetary correction" in order to make long-term financing available in a country with continuing inflation. Under this system, debts are readjusted upward on an annual basis by the amount of inflation as determined by an official index. The practice is followed in the case of mortgages and even government bonds.

Debt imported from strong currency countries has the disadvantage already mentioned that the amount of local currency required to meet interest and repayment obligations will increase in the case of devaluation. But even where devaluations are anticipated, nonlocal debt may have advantages from the standpoint of providing greater freedom for foreign remittances where exchange controls prevail. The policy of most countries is to give preference in the allocation of foreign exchange to remittances of interest and debt repayment over the remittance of dividends on equity.

Many companies prefer high-debt ratios and a minimum of equity capital for their foreign subsidiaries for still other reasons. The parent company may feel that local managers will be more highly motivated to meet repayment obligations than to earn profit on equity. Debt obligations exert greater pressure than equity which is sometimes classified more in the category of a "free" good.

It is important for the enterprise to determine its financial structure preferences for affiliates, but it should also be recognized that in some countries these preferences cannot be implemented. Companies prefer to use locally borrowed funds in areas that appear to be politically and economically unstable. Yet it is the risky areas that chronically lack loan capital. Furthermore, certain countries will restrict foreign companies in their local borrowing on the grounds that one of the justifications for admitting foreign firms is that they can increase the total amount of local investment by bringing in capital. Another reason is that the growth of local enterprise should not be stunted by having to compete for scarce funds with large, profitable, and well-known international enterprises which have easier access to outside capital markets. Some of the less developed countries which are greatly concerned with their balance-of-payments situation will object to high-debt proportions when it appears that such a financial structure is intended to support high levels of foreign exchange remittances to the parent companies.

The preference for minimizing the amount of equity capital supplied to the affiliate by the parent company frequently leads to the subsidiaries being seriously undercapitalized. This problem has been met in many cases by open account inventory financing. The parent company sells merchandise to the subsidiary but does not require payment until much later even though the goods have been sold by the subsidiary. This method allows the parent company to increase and develop its foreign operations without actually sending either additional equity capital or formal cash loans. Furthermore, the length of the credit is flexible.

The desire to minimize equity is not characteristic of the large and internationally committed multinational enterprises. They typically use a guideline such as "let equity equal fixed assets" in order that the host country does not become concerned about excessive local borrowing or unduly high dividend remittances. This strong equity base facilitates local borrowing after the subsidiary has become established and permits it to have greater independence in the future from the parent's central source of funds.

The decision to enter into a joint-venture arrangement with a group of local partners or to sell equity shares in the subsidiary locally can also reduce the financial burden on the multinational enterprise and increase access to other local sources of capital. If the outside ownership groups have similar expectations, equity costs would be unaffected, but where expectations are dissimilar among the participants, equity costs of the financial plan can be increased. Outside shareholders, for example, may expect to receive larger dividends than are traditional for the international enterprise. If so, the larger (or smaller) return expectations should be included explicitly in the flow projections used to appraise the desirability of a project.

Business firms operating internationally differ greatly in their knowledge of and willingness to use the numerous sources of funds available to multinational enterprises. The more highly developed capital markets of the United States were for many decades the best source for both large quantities of capital and low cost of capital. U.S. firms, in particular, generally limited their source of funds alternatives to the United States, the local country in which a project was being established, or foreign funds generated by the company in other foreign projects.[19] But the international situation has been changing rapidly as to availability and comparative cost of capital, and many international firms have become accustomed to considering an ever-wider variety of capital sources and financing techniques in their decisions as to financial structures for affiliates.[20]

To the extent that local financing is undertaken in the country in which a subsidiary is operating, the principal requirement at the headquarters level is for the international financial manager to become familiar with and expert in a number of domestic financing patterns. He must become informed on patterns of commercial banking, the functioning of securities markets, and government policies and controls which may vary greatly from country to country. The American firm when going international will have to learn about overdraft lending by commercial banks which permit a customer to write checks in excess of amounts he has deposited, up to some previously agreed upon limit. The American firm will have to become familiar with government financing institutions such as Nacional Financiera in Mexico and Kreditanstalt fur Wiederaufbau (KFW) in Germany, which are major sources for local financing and for which there is no American counterpart. Likewise, Shell, the Anglo-Dutch international oil enterprise, had to develop special skills for using the highly regulated U.S. securities markets in providing local financing for its U.S. subsidiary, Shell Oil Company.

The financing function becomes much more complex when cross-border financing is required, that is, when funds are secured in one country and transferred to another, because of the national controls over capital transfers that exist in many countries. Where controls are placed on direct investment outflow, only a limited range of devices such as short-term loans, open inventory financing, or swap loans can be used for cross-border financing from the home country beyond the limits set by controls.

But aside from capital sources in the home country and in the country in which an affiliate is operating, multinational firms can also look to international institutions, private and public regional financing agencies, and international capital markets—particularly the Euro-currency markets.[21]

[19] Stefan H. Robock, "Overseas Financing For U.S. International Business," *Journal of Finance*, May 1966, pp. 297–307.

[20] For detailed current information on financing techniques, sources for cross-border financing, and the domestic financing situation in a large number of countries, see the monthly service, *Financing Foreign Operations* of Business International or other similar services.

[21] See Chapter 4 above on "Sources of Finance for International Business"; also Gunter Dufey, "The Eurobond Market: Its Significance For International Financial Managements," *Journal of International Business Studies*, Summer 1970, pp. 65–77.

The future of the Euro-currency market, as mentioned in Chapter 4, may be affected negatively by reforms in the international monetary system. Nevertheless, the market offers great attractions to both borrowers and investors which have become strong motives for its continuance. Euro-bonds are always issued in such a way that interest is paid free of withholding tax. When they are issued in bearer form, the holder has additional means to defer or avoid income taxes. The freedom from taxation, the diversification opportunities both as to borrowers and currencies, and the absence of interference by national governments are features of the Euro-bond market that appeal to investors. From the standpoint of the borrower, many of the attractive features are similar. In addition to offering a choice of currencies, interest rates in the Euro-bond market have generally been at levels little different from the prevailing rates in the home country of the currency.

In summary, the financial structure of affiliates will depend first on the willingness of the parent company to assume equity risk. Although many companies prefer to minimize their equity commitments, for new foreign projects or expansions the hard-core financing will have to come from within the multinational enterprise. It must show a willingness to risk its own funds in order to tap external sources. A common pattern has been to finance fixed assets with company funds and long-term loan capital, and for working capital to use local borrowings to the maximum extent. The mix between local and imported debt depends on local availability, the relative costs of alternative sources, the degree of operating freedom associated with funds from different sources, and local government constraints on excessive debt ratios. Where local money costs exceed imported costs, a company will have to decide how much it wants to pay for risk avoidance. Tax factors and the effect of the financing plan on the financial situation of the parent company and the total system will be additional considerations.

INTERNATIONAL MONEY MANAGEMENT

Given a multinational enterprise as it exists at any point of time, the international financial manager also plays a major role in the management of short-term assets and liabilities so as to optimize financial goals on a system-wide basis. This function, referred to as international money management, has gone undeveloped in many small firms with limited international experience. The survey presented in Chapter 18 of recent patterns followed by U.S. multinational companies in organizing and managing the international function revealed that many firms view each subsidiary as an independent operation and make little or no attempt to optimize the financial function on a system-wide basis. But a strong trend is clearly in the direction of adopting a systems view and using relatively sophisticated international financial management techniques.

In international money-management practices this trend has been supported by three factors. First, the relatively new international business companies have been accumulating the necessary international experience which they previously lacked. Second, the relatively calm and stable international financial environment that characterized the post–World War II period was irrevocably disrupted by the world monetary crises of the early 1970s. As a result, international firms became more keenly aware of the need and opportunities for more rational and efficient responses to rapidly changing conditions in national and international financial markets. A third factor has been the rapid development of improved techniques for financial management on a global basis.

A Systems Approach

The more advanced approaches to international money management that have been emerging are all systems approaches. The system consists of units in different countries each of which operates in a different environment and has an accounting system of its own. The units are connected to each other through a series of links through which assets and liabilities can be shuttled. Inter-unit flows around this system are subject to policy control within certain limits, and the challenge is to make use of the policy tools to produce the best results for the system as a whole.[22]

This section summarizes the results of one pioneering study by Robbins and Stobaugh. The primary links between the different units are equity flows, generally from the parent to the subsidiary. Dividends are a flow in the opposite direction. Other links are the provision of services and technology by the parent to the subsidiary which result in return flows in the form of management fees, royalty payments, and the sale of goods, which result in payments for merchandise received. Finally, the units have credit links in the form of inter-company short- and long-term loans, accounts payable, and interest flows.

Matching each of these links are financial policy tools which can be adjusted to set the level at which the link will operate. Dividend policy, for example, is the tool associated with the equity link and the amount and timing of dividends to be paid can be adjusted. The relationships between links, tools, and the variables they control can be seen in Figure 20.5.

Limitations to the use of these policy tools arise out of government regulations, different patterns and mores of different financial markets,

---

[22] Robbins and Stobaugh, *Money in the Multinational Enterprise.*

FIGURE 20.5

Financial Links, Associated Policy Tools, and Affected Variables

Link	Policy Tool	Variables Controlled
1. Equity	Dividend policy	Amount of dividends accruing
2. Services		
Management	Management fee policy	Amount (or rate and specified base) of fees accruing
Know-how	Royalty policy	Amount (or rate and specified base) of royalties accruing
3. Merchandise	Transfer-pricing policy	Intra-system's sales price or deviation of intra-system price from arm's-length price
4. Credit		
a. Accounts Payable		
b. Mgt. Fees Payable		
c. Royalties Payable	Payables policy	Amount outstanding, terms, and interest charged
d. Dividends Payable		
e. Interest Payable		
f. Short-Term Lending . .	Short-term lending policy	Amount outstanding, terms, and interest charged
g. Long-Term Lending . .	Long-term lending policy	

Source: Will appear in forthcoming book by Sidney M. Robbins and Robert B. Stobaugh, *Money in the Multinational Enterprise* (New York: Basic Books, 1973).

and internal constraints such as a desire to avoid disrupting the system of performance evaluation. Other limitations are the cost of having complete information at the optimization center, the difficulties of securing accurate information, and the need to make forecasts that handle the uncertainties of future events such as foreign exchange risks.

A complex strategy under a systems approach would synchronize all the policy tools available to the various units of the multinational enterprise to maximize after tax profits for the system as a whole. Although the use of complex strategies through a systems approach has not yet become common, exploratory work in this field has demonstrated that significant gains might be achieved as compared to a situation where units function as a collection of unrelated enterprises dealing with each other at arm's length. In a hypothetical case, for example, the systems approach has been demonstrated to produce consolidated profits after taxes of 15 percent higher than when the strict rules of arm's-length behavior are followed.[23]

In applying a strategy in practice, modifications may be needed to reduce conflicts between the subgoals of the various units and also to allow for international factors difficult to introduce into a systems calculation. For example, a higher interest rate source of credit to one unit may be preferred because it gives more protection against devaluation and is better for the system as a whole.

---

[23] Ibid.

Although the use of a full systems approach is yet in the future, a series of less comprehensive techniques that focus on certain subgoals in international money management are in wide use.[24]

International Cash Management

International cash management is concerned with the mechanics of money transfers, collections, and disbursements. Systems have been developed for accelerating the collection of receipts arising from exports, rationalizing transfers between affiliates, and netting certain inter-company payments. Allowing for mail time and processing at the several banks in a collection chain, delays of one or two weeks are common for payments via international mail transfers between two European countries, or between Europe and the United States. As one example of accelerating the payment process where large sums or very lengthy delays are involved, the payer may be requested to remit payments by cable directly to the exporter's bank account in the country of the currency involved. By accelerating payments, less working capital is required and sizeable savings can be realized.

The availability of funds to the multinational corporation can also be increased through the rationalization of internal transfers. Techniques range from the use of cable transfers to obtain immediate value on payments to the development of elaborate netting programs. Given the delays and expense incurred in making international payments, netting systems attempt to offset transactions among units of the enterprise on either a bilateral or multilateral basis. By analyzing the transactions of every affiliate with other units in the system, it is possible to arrange for the participants to remit or receive only their net debit or credit positions under the directions of a central control point. The volume of actual transfers is cut sharply, with a consequent reduction in working capital requirements and foreign exchange costs and commissions. These savings are commonly estimated at up to ½ percent of the amount of the transfers eliminated.

Management of Working Capital and Liquidity

The control of liquidity—liquid assets and short-term debt or credit facilities—is based in large part on the concept of pooling, which aims at offsetting liquidity differences between affiliates so that the cash deficit of one is financed by the cash surplus of another, thus minimizing aggregate interest costs. Any net surplus or deficit for the pool as a whole

---

[24] See "Developments in International Money Management," *World Financial Markets* (New York: Morgan Guaranty Trust Co., 24 June 1971).

can then either be directed into short-term investments or financed by drawing on central credit facilities. When pooling is attempted on a multicountry, multicurrency basis, tax considerations and exchange controls may preclude the actual pooling of funds in communal accounts. The same constraints may also limit direct inter-company lending. However, indirect financing between affiliates can be achieved through the leading and lagging of inter-company payments—usually trade, but sometimes dividends, royalties, fees, and loan payments. Cash-poor affiliates are allowed to lag on payments to a cash-rich affiliate; or cash-rich affiliates are directed by the central control point to prepay or lead their obligations to the others. In some cases, affiliates may be directed to draw funds available to them under low-cost credit facilities, and to prepay their obligations to those affiliates with higher-cost borrowings outstanding. In order to determine the optimum course of action, the international financial manager must be appraised of all inter-company transactions, as well as each affiliate's liquidity position and its local money market conditions.[25]

Protection against Inflation

In managing working capital and controlling liquidity, the international manager will be particularly concerned with the problem of protecting assets in countries with high rates of inflation. The physical assets such as property, plant, and equipment generally maintain their value in real terms during inflation. But the value of working capital, particularly cash and receivables, is highly vulnerable to erosion through inflation. And the international financial manager is concerned about profits and the value of assets as measured in the home-country currency or some other strong convertible currency.

The traditional local strategy for protecting working capital in an inflationary situation is to operate with a minimum amount of liquidity by minimizing cash balances, reducing receivables, lagging in the payment of local expenses and maximizing local borrowing. Where the penalties for tax delinquency are low, some companies try to lag as much as possible in local tax payments. The value of inventories, particularly imported goods, is less likely to suffer from inflation. Where a local unit is part of a multinational system, it has additional possibilities for protecting assets by accelerating cash remittances to the parent company or elsewhere in the system where inflation rates are lower and

---

[25] Ibid., pp. 3–4. Also, for two model building approaches, see Dileep Mehta and Isik Inselbag, "Working Capital Management of a Multinational Firm," in *Multinational Business Operations,* ed. S. Prakash Sethi and J. N. Sheth (Pacific Palisades, Calif.: Goodyear Publishing Company, 1972); David P. Rutenberg, "Maneuvering Liquid Assets in a Multinational Company," *Management Science,* June 1970, pp. B671–B684.

by delaying the receipt of payments from low inflation countries. Such policies of taking advantage of leads and lags is similar to the strategy for protection against devaluation to be discussed below.

Traditional anti-inflation strategy, however, has shortcomings which result from treating individual components of working capital in isolation whereas they are in fact interrelated. For example, when credit and receivables are treated in isolation, the usual policy is to restrict credit to reduce the holding of monetary assets that lose buying power. But an optimal policy under a systems approach which recognizes the inter-relationships may be to increase rather than reduce credit. Inflation adds to the attraction of credit as part of the marketing mix and, by continuing to offer credit, the firm may generate a substantial increase in sales. The increase in profit margins that can result where large-scale economies can be exploited and where costs lag behind prices may more than offset the additional costs of increasing credit in an inflationary situation.[26]

MANAGING FOREIGN EXCHANGE RISK

In many international corporations, the financial manager's greatest concern is due to fluctuations in the value of foreign currencies. And some companies have paid a high price to learn about managing foreign exchange risk. For example, in 1969, International Telephone and Telegraph reported "extraordinary losses on the devaluation of the French franc, amounting to $2,317,000 after net gain on forward exchange contracts, which has been charged to the reserve for foreign operations." Or the case of Eastman Kodak can be cited, where losses resulting from "foreign currency devaluation . . . amounted to $2.5 million in 1968, as against $9.5 million in 1967—of which $8.0 million resulted from the devaluation of the British pound and related currencies."

Changes in the value of currencies, generally devaluations but sometimes revaluations, have been frequent and significant in amount. But statistics on the number and extent of changes understate the frequency with which the financial manager must be concerned with foreign exchange risk. The number of devaluations or revaluations have been much fewer than the number of false alarms which must be considered and dealt with.

The risk of foreign exchange loss is run not only by companies with foreign operations, but also by any company with a receivable or payable to be collected or paid in a foreign currency. The problem can be illustrated most simply in the case of importing and exporting. The

---

[26] Lee A. Tavis, "The Management of Short-Term Funds Under Conditions of Inflation: A Systems Approach" (D.B.A. diss., Graduate School of Business, Indiana University, 1969).

trader is "exposed" to the risk of a loss from the depreciation in value of a foreign currency he has contracted to receive in the future or a loss from the appreciation in value of a foreign currency he has contracted to deliver in the future. If a U.S. exporter had sold merchandise to a French buyer and agreed to accept payment in francs and if the French devaluation in 1969 occurred between the time of the sale and the time the exporter collects for the sale, the exporter would receive 11 percent less in U.S. dollars than he had expected. He would suffer an exchange loss of 11 percent of the sale.

The "exposure" of the trader is limited to foreign currency receivable or payable. The exposure of the multinational enterprise is far more complex.[27] The firm has a range of assets and liabilities that are exposed in the sense that a currency fluctuation will change their value in the yardstick currency of the company. For U.S. companies, the U.S. dollar has normally been the yardstick because it is U.S. dollars that are to be maximized, not foreign currency profits. A hypothetical truly multinational company, however, would logically consider the strongest world currency as its yardstick, such as the Swiss franc, and try to manage foreign exchange risk so as to protect values in that currency.

Several approaches are used by accountants and financial analysts for measuring exposure and they have a high degree of overlap. Accounts receivable in foreign currencies are the most obvious kind of exposed assets, but cash, bank deposits, and other current assets expressed in local currency are also vulnerable. As a general rule, current assets are separated into "exposed" and "not exposed" classifications according to whether or not their currency denomination is "softer" than the yardstick currency. One of the most difficult items to classify is inventories. Local source or paid-up imported inventory amounts are not affected because their dollar replacement or dollar market values are not likely to change in the event of devaluation. Fixed assets should be counted entirely as nonexposed, because the real value of a fixed asset is the present value of the future stream of income it will generate.

On the liability side, there can also be exposure. All accounts and notes payable in a foreign currency constitute exposed liabilities. Devaluation has the opposite effect on an exposed liability. Fewer dollars, for example, would be required to repay a bank loan in French francs after a devaluation of the franc, and a company might realize a foreign exchange profit in such a situation.

The difference between a company's exposed assets and its exposed liabilities is its "net exposure," and net exposure is the key variable

---

[27] The principle sources for this section are R. B. Shulman, "Are Foreign Exchange Risks Measurable?" *Columbia Journal of World Business,* May–June 1970, pp. 55–60; Bernard A. Lietaer, "Managing Risks in Foreign Exchange," *Harvard Business Review,* March–April 1970, pp. 127–38.

for the financial manager in planning and implementing a hedging policy. The object of the hedging policy is to reduce net exposure to as close to zero as possible so that what the company loses on devalued assets it makes up on revalued liabilities. At times the manager may be able to arrange his hedges so that the company has a *negative* net exposure. In such a situation, the gain from revalued liabilities will exceed the loss on devalued assets, and the company will make a profit on devaluation.

The key to managing foreign exchange risk through a "hedging policy" is to have an "early warning system" such as was suggested in Chapter 12, for forecasting the amount, the timing, and the probability of changes in foreign exchange rates. The less difficult task is to measure the exposure and develop a strategy based on the available protection alternatives, comparing potential loss with the cost of protection. Timing is of great importance so that the available means of protection can be used before they become too costly.

Given the analysis of the firm's exposure and the forecast of foreign exchange risk, the financial manager can work out a protection strategy. Computer models have been developed for formulating a hedging strategy and considerable additional work of a model building and quantitative nature is available on managing foreign exchange risk.[28] Many means of minimizing foreign exchange losses are available to the financial manager, including financing alternatives and foreign exchange contracts. He can accelerate payments of accounts and remittances to hard-currency countries. He can delay dollar inflows and try to delay obligations such as accounts payable, loans, and taxes due in local currency. He can try to accelerate local currency receivables through intensive collection efforts, reduction of credit terms, and offering generous discounts. He can use currency or credit swaps when local financing cannot be arranged. For a short list of international financing instruments commonly used and their hedging implications, see Figure 20.6.

After calculating net exposure and working out financing alternatives and reduction of exposure, the financial manager will try to use the forward exchange market to cover the rest of the exposure, providing the cost of such cover compares favorably with the prospective loss. In some cases the cost of insurance will be too high or nonfinancial considerations such as local goodwill are involved so that the company will prepare to absorb the foreign exchange loss itself. To use a simple example, suppose that the forecaster gives an estimated devaluation size of 20 percent, a probability of occurrence of 75 percent, and suppose

[28] For example, see Bernard A. Lietaer, *Financial Management of Foreign Exchange* (Cambridge, Mass.: The M.I.T. Press, 1971); Alan Shapiro, "Management Science Models for Multicurrency Cash Development" (Ph.D. diss., Carnegie-Mellon University, 1971).

FIGURE 20.6
Typical International Transactions and Their Financing and Hedging
Implications

Dollar financing: Credits repayable in U.S. dollars.

Foreign currency credits: Financing repayable in foreign currency, such as foreign bank loans, overdrafts, or other lines of credit.

Discounting or factoring of foreign bills or promissory notes: The borrowing technique by which the company draws a bill or note on its commercial bank (discounting); alternatively, the sale of receivables to a factor (factoring), which accelerates the conversion of foreign currency claims into cash.

Forward exchange contracts: The purchase of foreign currency at a given rate, for future delivery.

Financial swaps: Transactions in which equivalent amounts of dollars and foreign currencies are swapped for a given period, at the end of which both parties return the original amounts of each currency.

Arbi loans (International Interest Arbitrage Loans): Transactions that enable a company to increase financing in a scarce currency by supplementing it with capital from a country where money is abundant and cheap. (money is borrowed in the cheap money market and simultaneously transferred to the tight money country, and a forward exchange contract is arranged that bears the same maturity as the loan itself.)

Here is a summary of the effects that these various transactions have:

	Cash availability	*Net exposure*
Dollar financing	increases	no effect
Foreign currency credits	increases	decreases
Discounting or factoring	increases	decreases
Forward exchange contracts.	no effect	decreases
Financial swaps	increases	decreases
Arbi loans	increases	decreases

---

Source: Bernard A. Lietaer, "Managing Risks in Foreign Exchange," *Harvard Business Review*, March–April 1970, p. 128.

the forecaster on his record has been wrong 10 percent of the time.[29] These three factors multiplied together ($.20 \times .75 \times 1.10$) equal 16.5 percent. This result is multiplied by the company treasurer's safety factor which reflects the company's willingness to accept risk, say a 15 percent safety factor. Then, 16.5 percent multiplied by 1.15 equals 18.98 percent. This number can be compared with the market cost of cover to reach a decision. Suppose the annual market discount rate on forward contracts is 15 percent. The treasurer would spin off the risk because the cover cost is less than the expected loss indicated by the analysis. If the market price of cover is 22 percent the company would self-insure because the cost of the cover would be more expensive than the probable loss.

---

[29] Shulman, "Are Foreign Exchange Risks Measurable?" pp. 59–60.

REMITTANCE POLICIES

The management of international remittances has already been discussed in relation to international money management and foreign exchange risk. The subject of remittance policies, however, deserves some additional comment. The actual practice of many multinational companies in the recent past has been to make their decisions on dividend remittances separately from the decisions regarding other remittances or flows from royalties, management fees, interest on intercompany loans, and repayments of such loans.[30]

One dominant consideration has been to have subsidiaries help the parent company meet its dividend payments to stockholders by remitting a fixed percentage of their earnings after foreign taxes. Another important consideration has been to establish a record of regular remittances in the operating country in order to improve the company's chances for continuing to remit during difficult balance-of-payments periods for the country. Still another motivation for having local managers remit substantial amounts on a regular basis to the parent company is a feeling that local managers need to be reminded that the parent company supplied the capital and that the controlling objectives are set by headquarters. Where a company does not consolidate its accounts, only the remittances from the affiliates are recorded as income by the parent company and dividend remittances policies can be used to influence the profits reported by the parent.

When the local subsidiary is a joint venture with local shareholders, the problem of remittances becomes more complicated. When dividends are declared by local subsidiaries, local shareholders, as well as the parent company, share in the payments. While funds remitted to headquarters may still be available wholly or net of taxation to the multinational enterprise, dividends paid locally will generally leave the system and come back only through new financing. Also, it is not uncommon for local shareholders to expect high dividends, whereas the multinational enterprise may prefer to reinvest a large share of earnings and declare only modest dividends.

THE TAX VARIABLE

In a world of independent taxing authorities, the enterprise conducting business within many nations and across national boundaries faces an almost infinite variety of types of taxes, levels of tax burdens, tax incentives, patterns of tax administration, and possible overlaps in tax sys-

---

[30] See David B. Zenoff, "Profitable, Fast Growing, But Still the Stepchild," *Columbia Journal of World Business,* July–August, 1967; and "Remitting Funds from Foreign Affiliates," *Financial Executive,* March 1968, pp. 46–63.

tems.[31] Because of the pervasive importance of the tax variable in financial management and because of the diversity and complexity of taxes, the multinational enterprise requires great expertise to anticipate tax burdens with accuracy and to minimize tax obligations within legal limits. As has already been noted, taxes are an important variable in capital budgeting decisions, in the choice of business form for foreign operations (for example, branch versus subsidiary), in selecting the financing strategy for an affiliate, in working capital management, and in the formulation of remittance policies.

At the subsidiary level, differential tax burdens can change greatly the profitability of similar operations in different countries. The United States relies heavily at the federal level on direct taxes, mainly personal and corporate income taxes. In contrast, European countries depend mainly on indirect or turnover taxes such as the tax on value added (TVA). Corporation income tax rates differ somewhat among countries both in statutory and effective rates. The differences in effective rates reflect the varying treatment of depreciation and other expenses, investment allowances and credits, and undistributed profits. The way in which such differences can alter the profitability and financial management practices of a subsidiary can be illustrated by the case of Germany. Profits not distributed to shareholders but retained by the corporation are taxed at 51 percent. Profits distributed to shareholders are taxed at only 15 percent. Under such a system, the pressures are to distribute profits to shareholders and meet needs for additional capital through new financing rather than through retained earnings.

The tax issue at the local level is mainly one of becoming fully informed on the characteristics of the system and its administration and adapting accordingly. In some cases, though, a special problem may arise through discrimination against foreign enterprises under the tax laws or through the administration of such laws. At the second stage of the multinational level the tax variable becomes increasingly complex. When profits are transferred from the subsidiary to the parent company or to other units of the multinational enterprise, the firm must cope with overlaping tax jurisdictions and possible double taxation. Also, additional local tax obligations are frequently imposed when profits are remitted out of a country.

The international firm must recognize and adjust to the attempts of different taxing authorities to collect taxes from activities that take place outside their territory. The policies of the major industrial coun-

---

[31] Various tax guides are published periodically by some international accounting firms such as Price, Waterhouse and Co. and Arthur Anderson and Co. These give detailed information on the tax treatment of foreign income and related matters and are available for most countries where international business is a significant activity.

tries toward foreign income that is repatriated range from complete exemption to full taxation at domestic rates, with a range from full credit down to no deduction for taxes paid to a foreign jurisdiction. The Netherlands, Belgium, and France, for example, may exempt foreign earnings from income tax or tax them at a reduced rate, under certain specified or negotiated conditions. In contrast, the United States goes beyond the policy of any other country and even taxes the parent company for certain undistributed profits of some foreign-based companies.

In a practical sense, the different national policies reflect the potential importance of foreign-earned income as a source of taxation and the inevitable desire of taxing authorities to maximize their tax revenues. Such taxation of foreign-earned income has been justified as necessary for securing an equitable division of tax revenues among taxing authorities and on the grounds that the total corporate enterprise, rather than the corporation as a legal entity, should be the unit subject to tax. In the debate over the tax changes adopted in the Internal Revenue Act of 1962, the U.S. government argued that history shows that U.S. parent companies are willing to overlook the nationality of a subsidiary when it is advantageous to do so and yet expect the U.S. government to protect their foreign interests in whatever form they may be in case of confiscation or expropriation by a foreign government.

Since the adoption of its Federal Income Tax law in 1913, the policy of the United States has been to impose its income taxes both on income arising within its boundaries, regardless of the nationality or residence of the earner, and on income received from foreign sources by resident individuals and corporations chartered within the United States. Initially, foreign taxes were deductible from taxable income. Later, the policy was changed to permit income taxes paid abroad to be deductible from income taxes due the U.S. government.

A few countries known as "tax havens" have exceptionally low tax rates and liberal interpretations of taxable income. Income "sourced" in tax-haven countries could until 1962 avoid the U.S. tax and that of other relatively high-taxing authorities by being retained in the low-rate country and by not being paid out as dividends to owners in the United States. The Internal Revenue Act of 1962, however, sharply reduced the importance of tax havens.

In the tax field, as previously discussed in Chapter 6, governments have taken steps to avoid double taxation through bilateral treaties. Under such treaties, a country agrees to share with another on a prearranged basis the taxes imposed on business operations in the territory of one country by nationals of another country. Tax treaties may also provide for information exchanges between the governments that will aid each other in tax collection. The negotiation of a network of tax treaties has resulted in more tax uniformity among countries.

Another tax topic that deserves mention is the matter of "tax sparing." Some countries offer special tax incentives to attract foreign investment. Such incentives may temporarily spare the multinational enterprise the imposition of part or all of certain taxes which it would otherwise have to pay. Tax sparing in a foreign country offers little advantage to the business enterprise if the income is taxable at the same or higher rate in the home country of the parent company. Some countries permit a tax credit for taxes which have been spared in a foreign country. But others, particularly the United States, do not. The effect of policies such as that of the United States is to reduce or cancel the attractiveness of foreign tax incentives in influencing the investment decisions of U.S. multinational enterprises.

IMPORT AND EXPORT FINANCING

In the traditional field of importing and exporting, an extensive range of financial services has been developed for financing international transactions. Whether for transactions within an international firm or with suppliers or customers, these offer the international manager important opportunities for extending the funds available to him.

There are two broad categories of credits. "Supplier" credit is extended by the exporter to the foreign importer from his own funds, and the exporter in turn is refinanced with credit from external sources. "Buyer" credit is granted directly to the foreign buyer to be used by him for stipulated imports. Supplier credit generally covers short-term credits and some medium-term transactions. Buyer credit is usually available only for medium-term and long-term credits of large amounts, normally for purchasing capital goods.

In extending supplier credit, the seller is primarily concerned with credit risk, the protection of export proceeds against currency fluctuations, and political risk. In recent years, many countries have developed export credit insurance-guarantee programs to expand the country's export earnings by reducing these risks. Export-guaranteed paper may then be financed more easily and at a lower financing cost.

Financing may be with or without recourse. If the importer fails to pay the note or the bill when due, the financing institution may or may not have recourse to the exporter for the amount due. Most export credit is granted with recourse to the exporter. However, an insurance policy or guarantee issued by a government export credit insurance agency makes the financing without recourse to the extent that risks and losses are covered by the insurance.

Commercial banks are the principal source of short-term export financing. Private commercial finance firms are also important in export financing but the growth of export guarantees has encouraged the use of commercial banks because the private finance houses usually charge more than banks. Traditionally, commercial banks have been reluctant to grant medium-term financing, but as a result of government export promotion programs, sponsorship of new institutions, and guarantee programs, commercial banks and other private sources for medium-term financing have been increasing rapidly.

For long-term financing, public sources, and lending agencies are the most important. The U.S. Export-Import Bank is the biggest and most diversified export-credit institution in the world. It offers programs of long-term project financing, direct medium-term export financing, medium-term guarantees, short-term insurance through the affiliated FCIA, a banking program for export financing, and a rediscount facility.

A special form of payment increasingly used in trade with communist and some developing countries is the use of clearing currencies within the framework of currency clearing arrangements between two countries. In the case of an export switch, the importer in a communist or developing market pays the exporter from a clearing balance held against a third country. The exporter then has the possibility, with the assistance of specialized agents (mainly in Austria, Germany, the Netherlands, and Switzerland) to use the clearing funds in the country holding the balance or to sell the bilateral funds at a discount.

Summary

International financial management is primarily concerned with the maximization of profits after taxes for the multinational system as a whole, within the framework of a wider pursuit of corporate objectives. International operations adds many complexities to the financial management function, ranging from the difficulties of developing an adequate financial information system, where the initial data input into the system must necessarily be shaped by varying patterns in national accounting systems, to the problems of dealing in multiple currencies and managing foreign exchange risks. At the same time, a multinational system affords opportunities to minimize interest costs, tax liabilities, the effects of differential inflation rates among countries, and to reduce working capital needs through pooling liquidity among affiliates.

Thus, the major challenge and opportunity in international financial management is to optimize on a system-wide basis. Toward this end, major progress has been achieved in the development of concepts and tools for complex strategies that reveal profit-taking opportunities that normally do not become apparent under simple strategies focused on subgoals of financial management. But the use of complex and sophisticated techniques can be expensive in terms of required data, personnel, and experience. Given these cost and other limitations, many international firms deal with each subsidiary as an independent operation and make little or no effort to optimize the financial function on a system-wide basis.

Under most circumstances, however, the investment and capital-budgeting decisions above certain financial limits are a centralized responsibility for the multinational firm. The international financial manager has also become increasingly involved in decisions on financial structures of affiliates, financing techniques, and on managing foreign exchange risk. The management of cash flows and liquidity on an international basis has been growing rapidly as an international financial management function.

EXERCISES AND DISCUSSION QUESTIONS

1. What are the special accounting problems of multinational operations? Why is it unlikely that uniform international accounting standards will be adopted?

2. Why might a multinational firm decide to invest in a project that shows a low expected rate of return on the basis of the first level analysis at the local country level?

3. Which source of funds would be the cheapest? A loan in the United Kingdom at 7 percent annually on an overdraft basis or a loan from an American bank at 6 percent annually but with the requirement of a 20 percent compensating balance?

4. An American multinational enterprise has three subsidiaries each located in a different European country. The British subsidiary imports semifinished products from its Dutch affiliate for further processing and distribution. Part of the British subsidiary's output is exported to its German affiliate, and the rest is sold in the British home market. Normal trade credit terms on all transactions is 60 days.

   In anticipation of the 1967 devaluation of British sterling, the British subsidiary was directed to give its German affiliate 110 days to pay and to reduce its liabilities to the Dutch affiliate to zero, that is, to pay for its imports C.O.D. How can such tactics provide a hedge against one-time exchange losses?

21

MULTINATIONAL MANAGEMENT OF HUMAN RESOURCES

THE QUALITY OF A FIRM'S EXECUTIVES is almost certain to be the single, most important determinant of its success in international business. An aggressive global strategy implies managerial resources of a caliber to think out and implement such policies. More broadly, as one international executive has observed, ". . . virtually any type of international problem, in the final analysis, is either created by people or must be solved by people. Hence, having the right people in the right place at the right time emerges as the key to a company's international growth. If we are successful in solving that problem, I am confident we can cope with all others . . ."[1]

Multinational business brings with it many new and unique problems in the management of human resources, the most fundamental of which is the necessity for managers raised and experienced in one culture to play bicultural or multicultural roles. The managers of foreign subsidiaries must know the culture and language of the nation in which they work. They must also understand the foreign cultural assumptions underlying the technology and business practices being introduced into the national environment and be able to adapt foreign patterns to the national environment without serious loss to the global objectives of the international enterprise. Thus, managers at the country level, whether nationals or expatriates, need to deal with at least two sets of cultural patterns.[2] Management personnel at the headquarters or regional level have an even more complex set of responsibilities. They must integrate

---

[1] Michael G. Duerr, "International Business Management: Its Four Tasks," *Conference Board Record,* October 1968, p. 43.

[2] See Chapter 11.

and coordinate activities taking place in many cultural environments that are being directed by managers with diverse cultural orientations. Furthermore, the natural tendency of personnel to identify themselves with the particular interests of a national unit can result in major conflicts within an international firm.

Any international firm operating against a background of cultural differences and national conflicts must inevitably transfer some of its employees across cultural and national boundaries. These transfers introduce a further range of management problems not arising in the national firm. The selection of those who are to be transferred involves choice among the various nationalities involved, raises questions concerning desirable characteristics, education, and renumeration, and requires procedures to facilitate the adjustment of those who switch cultures and residence.

Finally, the international extension of a firm changes the situation in labor-management terms and opens the whole question of international unions and international bargaining.

GENERAL POLICY ON INTERNATIONAL EXECUTIVES

At an early stage, the international firm should decide on its general policy for the recruitment and development of international executives. It should decide on the employment pattern it wishes to achieve over the long term in the managerial positions of the subsidiaries and at regional and world headquarters. Implicitly, the general policy will comprehend the firm's specific policy on cross-national employment. In the absence of a policy, a firm's employment patterns can easily evolve in ways that hinder its longer-run performance.

Essentially, the international firm can choose from among three alternative policies for staffing management positions, or design some combination of the three. It can fill key positions everywhere in the world with personnel from the home country of the parent company—an ethnocentric policy. It can use local nationals to manage foreign subsidiaries and home-country nationals as headquarters' managers—a polycentric policy. Or it can recruit and develop the best men without regard to nationality for key positions anywhere in the multinational system—a geocentric policy. Each of the alternatives has advantages and disadvantages.

The most common policy followed by international firms, particularly American companies, has been to favor the hiring of local nationals for foreign subsidiaries and home-country nationals for management posts at the headquarters level.[3] Within this general policy, actual prac-

---

[3] Michael G. Duerr and James Greene, *Foreign Nationals in International Management* (New York: National Industrial Conference Board, 1968), p. 3.

tices have varied to fit specific situations. For example, when a subsidiary is newly established, it is common to fill the top posts with personnel from the parent country but later replace them with local nationals as they are recruited and trained for the positions. For example, when Ford Motor Company started its Mexican operations in 1963 and 1964, top management sent a team of about 100 key men from the United States. Three years later, the team was reduced to 50 and plans were made to transfer still others back to the United States and replace them with local managers.[4] Or in countries where chronic local shortages of management personnel exist, home-country or "third-country nationals," that is, personnel from a country other than that of the parent or the subsidiary, might be posted indefinitely to manage a subsidiary.

At first glance, the most rational and effective policy would appear to be a geocentric one, where the best man is sought for the best job, regardless of the man's nationality and the location of the job. Such a policy would be consistent with the unique strength and the *raison d'etre* of multinational business. The competitive advantage of multinational enterprise and its social contribution arises out of its ability to rationalize on an international basis the use of natural resources, financial resources, and technology. Why shouldn't it also rationalize on an international basis the use of managerial resources by stimulating a flow of international managers throughout the whole structure of the multinational organization. To some degree and for a period of time, the managers of foreign subsidiaries might be handicapped by not being local nationals who are fully immersed in the national cultural, political, and economic situation. But these disadvantages would be more than offset by his superior ability and experience. Even more important, the tendency of national identification of managers with units of the system will be reduced so that the firm will be better able to realize its multinational potentials.

Yet there have been only modest beginnings by a relatively few international firms toward developing a truly international executive force. The factors explaining the limited popularity of a geocentric policy are numerous and indicate the disadvantages of this alternative.

First, host countries are strongly desirous of having foreign subsidiaries staffed by their local nationals and have frequently adopted national controls to achieve their goal. Second, an international executive policy can be expensive. It is expensive because it requires widespread recruitment, a substantial investment in language training and cultural orientation programs for managers and their families, substantial costs in transferring executives and their families into and away from foreign posts, and a willingness to pay international salary levels which are sig-

---

[4] Dimitri N. Chorafas, *The Communication Barrier in International Management* (New York: American Management Association, 1969), p. 62.

nificantly higher than national levels in many countries. Third, to achieve such a pattern would require a high degree of centralization in the control of personnel and their career patterns and undercut the cherished prerogative of local managers to choose their own personnel. A fourth reason is that the policy would take a long time to implement. Finally, firms have discovered that adaptations to an undiluted policy of using nationals can achieve many of the advantages of a truly international executive policy.

Foreign Nationals for Managing Subsidiaries

A policy of hiring nationals has many obvious advantages which are mainly the obverse of the disadvantages of an international executive-career policy. Nationals in both foreign countries and at headquarters come equipped with a built-in understanding of the local environment and local language, which costs both time and money to impart to a foreigner. Hiring nationals largely eliminates the language barriers and expensive training periods and reduces the cross-cultural adjustment problems of managers and their families. In foreign countries, it lowers the profile of a foreign firm in sensitive political situations. It permits the firm to take advantage of lower national salary levels, while still paying a premium over local norms to attract high-quality personnel. And since the career of nationals will be in their home country, they will give continuity to the management of foreign subsidiaries and at headquarters.

Nevertheless, there is a price to be paid in following a policy of hiring nationals. At the overseas subsidiary level, nationals will adapt well to the local environment, but they are likely to have difficulties in bridging the gap between the subsidiary and the rest of the system. The education, business experience, and cultural environment to which they have been exposed all their lives may not have prepared them to work as part of a multinational enterprise. They may experience cross-cultural problems because of different concepts as to business practices, differences in personal values such as a reluctance to "dirty one's hands," and many other cultural variables. They may identify with their country as against the spirit and advantages of multinationalism. They are not likely to be fully knowledgeable about the management techniques, products, and technology developed in the parent firm's home country on which the firm's international expansion is based. There is an inbuilt immobility. Once a foreign manager reaches the top position in the overseas subsidiary, he has nowhere to go. The narrow focus of his career can affect his own morale and block the promotion of those underneath him. In turn, some of the most promising foreign nationals may be difficult to recruit and to retain because of the limited promotion possibilities within the total enterprise.

Headquarters Managers

Discussions of executive employment policies have generally focused on the management of overseas subsidiaries, with only relatively minor attention devoted to the implications of alternative policies to the filling of management positions at headquarters. Just as local nationals in foreign subsidiaries will have cross-cultural problems in communicating and dealing with headquarters, home-country nationals at headquarters will have even larger problems in cross-cultural dealings with a large number of foreign countries. A study of the communication barrier in 55 companies of U.S. and non–U.S. nationality concluded that two major causes of communication problems in international management were (1) the lack of multinational working experience by the corporate top executives who are assigned to run the international operations, and (2) the limited number of experienced international executives on the boards of directors of these companies.[5]

A policy of employing nationals makes it difficult for young executives from headquarters to get experience working outside of their home country and to develop their capacity to communicate, coordinate, and effectively supervise in a multicultural setting. Such a policy is unlikely to create a body of international executives able to switch between units of the multinational firm as the need arises. It also reinforces the dominance of home-country executives, frequently with little actual foreign working experience, in the higher corporate posts dealing with strategy and capital allocations decisions between subsidiary units dominated by local nationals. The almost complete domination of top-management echelons of American international companies by U.S. personnel in the middle 1960s was demonstrated by a study showing that out of almost 4,000 top managers of the 150 largest U.S. industrial corporations, only 59, or 1.6 percent, were foreigners, and half of this foreign group was Canadian.[6] Although the situation has changed somewhat since the time of the study, the general pattern still persists.

It can be claimed that retention of top corporate management at headquarters in the hands of nationals of the parent country has a number of advantages. The executives will come from a reasonably similar cultural background and have little trouble in communicating with each other. They are likely to have experienced the build-up of the parent unit and to have developed skills and evolved a working pattern in the management of an international operation. In the longer run, however, a firm with this sort of management pattern can become a grouping of virtually independent national units with the prime responsibility for transfer of ideas and for general cohesion falling on executives

---

[5] Ibid., p. 63.

[6] Kenneth Simmonds, "Multinational? Well, Not Quite," *Columbia Journal of World Business,* Fall 1966, pp. 115–22.

of the parent unit. Many of the advantages of the international corporation will be in jeopardy and the interests of the national units placed above the interests of the corporation as a whole.

Criteria for Choosing a Policy

Clearly, none of the alternative policies—including the use of home-country personnel around the world—provide a perfect or complete answer to the complexities of managing multinational enterprises. But subprograms which complement or modify a basic policy of favoring nationals can go a long way toward giving the firm the "best of both worlds." One of the techniques is to identify replacement candidates for key executives throughout the system and arrange at least one cross-cultural assignment of generally two years' duration as part of their international career plan. This will expose headquarters executives to the challenges of their field operations and expand the experience of foreign nationals, while still keeping them in a career path toward top management in their home country. Another approach is to hire local nationals for foreign subsidiaries who have had academic training in the country of the parent company. Many foreign students graduating from U.S. business schools have become a significant source of management personnel for American multinational companies. Still another practice that has been followed by only a few advanced companies is to develop a small group of truly international career managers who will have several cross-cultural assignments and be considered for assignments throughout the enterprise.[7] In addition, most companies carry on training or management-development programs designed to transfer technical and managerial skills to promising local national managers and other candidates for middle- and upper-management positions.

But even when a policy of employing nationals is supplemented by cross-cultural training assignments and other programs, some companies still feel that they must have a home country "presence" in each foreign subsidiary. In practice, this "presence" for American firms which follow such a policy is the local general manager or chief finance officer. Some companies go even further in insisting on home country personnel as essential for transferring technological strength from the parent company and feedback from the subsidiaries. As one manager of a European company claimed, "There should be a European at the head of the U.S.

---

[7] For examples of two of the most advanced programs for internationalizing management personnel, see Charles K. Campbell, *Cross Cultural and Cross Functional Development of Personnel in IBM World Trade Corporation,* mimeographed (New York: National Foreign Trade Council, February 1970), NFTC ref. no. M–9292; Donald N. Leich, *Transnational Executive Development in the Royal Dutch Shell Group of Companies,* mimeographed (New York: National Foreign Trade Council, February 1970), NFTC ref. no. M–9293.

operation. I have a rapport with our parent that dates back over 33 years. This rapport is terribly useful for communication back and forth. How could an American develop such a rapport . . . particularly with a French mother company?"[8] Or when Olivetti bought the Underwood company, an old typewriter manufacturer in the United States, its first step was to replace top American management with company men from Italy. Olivetti expected to compete in the United States on the basis of a particular product concept, and a particular manufacturing technique and marketing strategy, which were the basis for its success in Europe. The Olivetti touch, it was felt, could be more effectively implemented and the worldwide Olivetti operations most successfully served by having Olivetti men as top management for the U.S. subsidiary.

Given the various alternatives, how does an international company decide on its policy for international executives? Its choice depends heavily on an evaluation of the following five factors.

1. The constraints that it faces in national controls and policies favoring the hiring of local nationals.
2. The supply of managerial personnel in the countries of operations.
3. The costs of alternative policies, including the cost of remedying the deficiencies of the policies.
4. The difficulties and importance of cross-national communications, coordination, and supervision for the type of business activity in which the firm is engaged.
5. The mobility of management personnel.

Whatever policy or combination of policies is adopted, the international firm must have a long-range and continuing program of management recruitment and development. It needs to work constantly toward internationalizing the experience and outlook of all executive personnel, including the higher echelons of corporate power. Promising managerial talent must be discovered early so that young managers can secure cross-national experience and be moved in the middle of their careers either to regional or global headquarters where they can make the jump from a "functional" to a "general" manager. Any strategies directed toward greater internationalism of managerial resources will, of course, be constrained by national laws. However, within this framework, much can be done. The most compelling argument for developing multinational executives is that it will avoid inbreeding and narrowness at the top. For the firm of the future, truly international management will have greater sensitivity to changes in the world environment and flexibility in adapting to them.

---

[8] *European Strategies in the United States* (Geneva, Switzerland: Business International, S.A., 1971), p. 42.

PROBLEMS OF CROSS-NATIONAL TRANSFERS

All international firms transfer employees across cultural or national boundaries to some extent. Cross-national transfers may be part of an international career-development program, a result of a borrowing and lending concept between countries, or a means of supplying experienced personnel for a new subsidiary while local nationals are being trained. Or cross-national transfers may result from a combination of various management policies. In any event, managers who are assigned to foreign posts for extended periods are likely to encounter special problems of working in a foreign environment, living in a different culture, and maintaining satisfactory relations with the parent company.

New Working Relationships

The executive transferred will, of course, have to establish new working relationships. He may have to do this within a cultural environment vastly different from the one to which he is accustomed. He will have to be aware of the cultural variations discussed in Chapter 11 as they affect local patterns of decision making, of issuing and accepting instructions, and of conducting many other day-to-day aspects of management and business operations. He must deal with local foreign personnel with backgrounds, languages, attitudes, values, and points of view different from his own. He must learn how to adapt his technical and managerial know-how to an unfamiliar environment. He must cope with economic and political environments that are unfamiliar and often more complicated than those he encountered at home.[9]

A number of studies have investigated the kinds of problems encountered in cross-national assignments, mainly of Americans in less developed country settings.[10] Anecdotes and case examples abound. European and Japanese expatriate managers undoubtedly face numerous similar problems in cross-national transfers, although their experiences have not yet been well documented. However, one study reports that a number of European managers transferred to the United States discovered that dealing with American labor unions was too traumatic for them and that this task was best left to Americans.[11] But the emphasis on prob-

---

[9] See Wickham Skinner, *American Industry in Developing Economies* (New York: John Wiley and Sons, 1968), pp. 222–48.

[10] For example, see John Fayerweather, *The Executive Overseas* (Syracuse, N.Y.: Syracuse University Press, 1969); John C. Shearer, *High-Level Manpower in Overseas Subsidiaries* (Princeton, N.J.: Industrial Relations Section, Princeton University, 1960); Richard F. Gonzalez and Anant R. Negandhi, *The United States Overseas Executive: His Orientations and Career Patterns* (East Lansing, Mich.: Michigan State University, 1967).

[11] *European Strategies in the United States*, p. 43.

lems, as Skinner cautions, "should in no sense imply that all men sent abroad fail to perform well, that most assignments abroad are unhappy ones, or that expatriate managers always present difficult and absorbing problems for executives in the home office. This is not so."[12]

Family and Social Adjustments

Outside his working situation, the foreign executive encounters environmental differences, which also involve his family, that are even more marked than the on-the-job differences. The development of social contacts may be severely curtailed, for example, if the expatriate's wife cannot speak the local language. Wives of local business and social acquaintances are unlikely to be able to speak anything other than the local language, and significant relationships are not likely to be built up across a language barrier. Wives in some countries will have several servants and with some relief from household duties have considerable free time. Boredom, excessive drinking, and high spending are not uncommon results. A broad study of almost 2,000 employees of a multinational firm on cross-national assignments, about 20 percent of whom were of American nationality, concluded that an employee's satisfaction with his foreign assignment depended mainly on his wife's adjustment to the assignment. The wife's satisfaction ranked as the most important element among the American group and only slightly lower than job-related elements in the total group.[13]

Cross-national transfers put a great deal of stress on an executive and his family and produce a variety of behavior patterns that reflect on the manager's performance. Rejection of the new culture and glorification of the old is not uncommon. Frequently referred to as "culture shock," this can appear with the establishment of tight groups of expatriates from the home country who devote themselves to recreating the home culture and dwelling on the "weaker" points of that in which they reside. This result is part of what a Shell executive calls "those bloody people" syndrome.

The expatriate goes young and fresh to his first "new" country and he makes a big effort to integrate. He learns about local culture, he travels the country and he tries to learn the language. Then he is moved. The next country is a little more difficult. Those people in his first overseas assignment were pretty unreliable anyway. The new lot are worse. He makes some kind of effort, but it's not such a big effort. By the fourth or fifth country, he may have given up. He locks himself up with expatriate colleagues and he doesn't

---

[12] Skinner, *American Industry in Developing Economies*, p. 222.

[13] Gillian Purcer-Smith, *Studies of International Mobility (in IBM World Trade Corp.)*, mimeographed (New York: National Foreign Trade Council, 1971), NFTC ref. no. M-9936.

want to see anything of the local scene except when he is actually working. That man, I submit, is a major liability in any multinational operation . . . for him, they are only "those bloody people."[14]

Career Patterns

Still other problems raised by cross-national transfers have to do with career patterns and relationships with parent company headquarters. Unless international assignments are part of a planned cross-pollination program, that is, the process of moving high-potential professionals between foreign affiliates for management-development purposes, the executive who undertakes such an assignment may experience amplified feelings of insecurity and concern over his future career. As his distance and time away from headquarters increases, an "exile complex" may develop and he will begin to ask himself such questions as: "Will I be forgotten at the home office?" And "Where is my next assignment going to be?" Even if the manager is scheduled to return to the parent company or his home subsidiary, he may be concerned about his reentry problem.

To reduce the potential dissatisfaction of executives being transferred, the international firm should have a policy for repatriation. If the firm always repatriates the executives concerned and finds them a post with equally high status in the parent company, unhappy executives will expect to be taken care of. The cost can be high. Not only are transfer costs large, but the foreign subsidiary must find a replacement with additional transfer costs and lack of continuity in the job. It is not always easy to find a job for a returning expatriate when he is ready to return. Some firms make it clear that those going overseas do so on a career basis and will be returned only if they are asked to take another position in the firm. Other firms argue that even the more successful and experienced managers within the firm will have failures in foreign posts due to factors outside their control, and that these managers are worth retaining despite the cost of repatriation. The more important task is to minimize the failures through careful selection and prior training.

RECRUITMENT AND SELECTION OF INTERNATIONAL EXECUTIVES

If a firm is to develop a truly international management team, the best place to start is with its recruitment policies. When a firm takes its first steps toward becoming international, it normally has not had the opportunity to develop a cadre of international managers. Its middle-

---

[14] Leich, *Transnational Executive Development in the Royal Dutch Shell Group of Companies,* p. 22.

and top-level managers would have been recruited in earlier periods when selection criteria were based on domestic business needs. Its recruitment would almost certainly have been limited to persons living in the home country. Prior to going international, the firm could not offer internal opportunities for managers to gain international experience except in the exporting field. Thus at such an early stage, managers for international operations have been mainly recruited from within the organization without having had any previous experience in foreign operations.[15] Where international expansion occurred through acquisitions, some firms were able to add key executives of the acquired companies to their international-management staff. A third source may have been "buy-ins," or experienced international managers hired from outside the company.

Such makeshift methods, however, must be replaced by a continuing system of management development and career planning for international operations. Such a system, of course, is not uniquely international. It begins with a forecast of future management manpower needs on an annual basis for at least a 5-year forward period. Given the long lead time necessary to develop top and middle management within an enterprise, a company such as Royal Dutch Shell works with 15-year forecasts based on the firm's long-term planning.[16] The forecasts estimate future demand for different regions and for different functions. The forecasts are matched against an annual inventory of staff with potential to qualify for forecasted vacancies. The shortfall or deficiency then becomes the recruitment target. With a total employment in 1970 of more than 170,000 in the Royal Dutch Shell group of companies, except for the United States and Canada, the number of top- and middle-management positions with which the company's executive development program was concerned totaled about 5,000.

With recruitment targets specified as to positions to be filled, the location of these positions and the type of personnel required, the international firm can follow conventional recruitment practices, except for several additional international complications. Some of the international issues on which it must decide are as follows:

1. In what countries should the company recruit?
2. Where recruitment is planned in countries other than the home country, what new techniques and sources will have to be used?
3. To what extent should recruitment decisions and activities be cen-

---

[15] Enid Baird Lovell, *The Changing Role of the International Executive* (New York: National Industrial Conference Board, 1966), p. 26. A study of 144 U.S. companies concluded that "In a substantial proportion of the companies the incumbent (international) executive was transferred to the top executive position without having had any prior experience in its foreign operations."

[16] Leich, *Transnational Executive Development in the Royal Dutch Shell Group of Companies,* p. 4–A.

tralized in the parent company or decentralized in foreign subsidiaries?

4. What special selection criteria should be used because of the international nature of the company?

5. To what extent, if any, will the general policies on international executives assist or act as an obstacle in recruitment?

Although few international corporations are as yet following such a policy, recruitment for international managers should extend beyond the universities or business schools of the developed countries. They should include universities wherever the firm operates. Outside the United States, management training is a relatively new educational field, but the amount and quality of such academic training began to expand rapidly in most developed countries and in many less developed countries by the late 1960s.[17] Good international managers are in sufficiently short supply so that the international corporation should develop as large a recruitment network as possible. In many countries, universities have not yet developed adequate facilities for assisting firms in their recruitment. In such cases, recruitment techniques may have to rely heavily on newspaper advertising, executive recruitment companies, or special efforts to contact young people when they finish their military service.

An enterprise-wide executive development and recruitment program will necessarily be a cooperative effort between the foreign subsidiaries and regional and global headquarters. But for the larger corporation, a central inventory of international executives will be needed to assure that promising executives do not become lost in a foreign posting. This in turn will lead to some surrender of power to make appointments on the part of individual units of the organization. Without a central voice in appointments, continued career development of the international executive might be sacrificed to the interests of individual units or jeopardized by preferred promotion of those known locally.

The actual recruitment activities, however, can be decentralized and the managers of foreign subsidiaries should have a voice in the final decision on the hiring of personnel that will work under their direction. A company like Proctor and Gamble has its subsidiaries establish their recruitment needs which are then consolidated at the division level, for example, the European Division, which has responsibility for recruitment.[18] Foreign nationals studying in the United States are recruited by the parent company for the foreign subsidiaries but only up to a

---

[17] For example, for a survey of management resources and training programs in Latin America, see Robert R. Rehder, ed., *Latin American Management* (Reading, Mass.: Addison-Wesley Publishing Co., 1968).

[18] D. F. Howe, *Recruiting Overseas For International Operations,* mimeographed (New York: National Foreign Trade Council, May 1969), NFTC ref. M8979.

preselection phase. Such candidates are then interviewed by the manager of the division or the subsidiary which makes the final offer. In some cases, the prospective candidate may even be flown back to his home country at company expense so that the local manager can interview the person and make the final decision.

In selecting executives for international management and for cross-national postings, it must be borne in mind that few firms have large numbers of executives competent and available for such posts, and a highly complex and selective system for choosing international executives is likely to be unnecessary. Moreover, so little is known about measuring characteristics that make for success in cross-cultural management and foreign postings that the accuracy of such systems is questionable. One fairly reliable characteristic is previous cross-cultural experience. For this reason, many American firms aggressively recruit foreigners who have studied business administration in the States and who thereby have become familiar with much of the culture of the parent company.

Listings of the qualities needed for success in a foreign posting seem very like those needed anywhere for success as an executive. The requirements, anyway, vary from situation to situation and country to country so that no single set of standards would be adequate. Because of these difficulties in predicting success in foreign environments, the failure rate can be high and the costs so great that some care is warranted in searching for factors that are likely to lead to failures. Measurement becomes more a check for weakness than an absolute testing. As one recruitment expert has observed, "Most selection methods . . . are in effect rejection schemes."[19] Inflexibility, and insensitivity to others' views and to new political situations have been cited as frequent characteristics of failures. But failures can be equally caused by strong attachments to a family grouping left behind in the home country, health problems, or basic marital instability.

Long interviews with executives who are being considered for foreign appointments are perhaps the best means of drawing out potential problems.[20] Some firms also find it worthwhile to interview wives, given their large role in the success of an appointment. Other firms take the view that it is up to the executive himself to judge whether his family will and should be transplanted. Firms making assessments on the basis of one or more interviews with an executive's wife are not likely to be more accurate than the husband in projecting family success in foreign living. Of course, the most difficult time will be the first overseas posting,

[19] A. T. M. Wilson, "Management Recruitment for the Multinational Company," *Prospect 3, Journal of AIESEC International,* Autumn 1969, p. 25.

[20] See William Alexander, Jr., "Mobil's Four Hour Environmental Interview," *Worldwide P & I Planning,* January–February 1970, pp. 18–27. Alexander reports that Mobil has had "only 5 complete failures out of 750 employees placed abroad."

but then many executives will be younger and their pattern of life less rigidly established.

A final issue that has great relevance to the success of recruitment programs is the firm's policies on promotion. In order to secure good managers for foreign assignments, the international firm must make clear by its actions that cross-national service is of importance to the firm. And in order to recruit promising executive prospectives to work with the subsidiaries, the firm must have a policy of open career opportunities for top-management positions. The view of many ambitious and able young foreign nationals was expressed as follows by an international manager:

He must feel that if he has the ability he can aspire to any job in the company, apart perhaps from the presidency. It may be that when he is faced with the prospect of going on the main board, and so spending the rest of his working life outside his home country he will decide to reject the opportunity. If so that will be his decision. But he must feel that his nationality does not, of itself, disqualify him from aiming for the stars."[21]

TRAINING FOR THE INTERNATIONAL EXECUTIVE

Training programs have a special importance for the international firm. They can be the key to developing national managers in countries where management and technical skills are in short supply. They may be a necessary step for indoctrinating foreign employees in the products, policies and procedures of the parent company. They can be a principal means of preparing managers to deal with the special cross-cultural challenges posed by international business operations. Special training for cross-national transfers can significantly reduce the failure rates in such assignments. In recognition of these needs and opportunities, multinational firms have developed a wide range of formal and informal training approaches.[22]

The use of training programs to develop local management talent can be illustrated by the case of Celanese in Mexico.[23] When it decided in 1944 to build a synthetic fiber plant in Mexico, Celanese had to import technicians and managers from the United States. At the same time, Celanese also recruited 12 recently graduated chemical engineers from the National University of Mexico and brought this group to the company's plant in Virginia for a year's training program in handling the process technology on which the Mexican plant was based. Through this and other training programs, by 1972 Celanese Mexicana with more

---

[21] Christopher Tugendhat, *The Multinationals*, (London: Eyre & Spottiswoode, 1971), p. 197.

[22] Duerr and Greene, *Foreign Nationals in International Management*, pp. 29–43.

[23] See Richard W. Hall, *Putting Down Roots: 25 Years of Celanese in Mexico* (New York: Vantage Press, 1969).

than 6,000 employees was able to operate with only 14 foreigners, some of whom were on temporary assignments.

Even where the supply of personnel is adequate for the needs of foreign subsidiaries, the international company invariably needs to use training programs to familiarize its foreign staff with the company's products, policies, and procedures. There is no substitute for this type of training in a multinational company. It transfers knowledge; it improves communications; it helps to impart the parent company's way of operating. Frequently, this type of training is conducted at corporate headquarters so that foreign personnel and headquarters personnel can also become personally acquainted.

For all managers, whether at headquarters or working in foreign subsidiaries, training can be a valuable means of increasing their sensitivity to cultural patterns that are foreign to their own experience and values. Such training should have at least two dimensions. It should develop in the individual an awareness of his own cultural assumptions and the nature of his cultural conditioning. It should also develop a special kind of intellectual and emotional radar that will alert the manager to situations where cultural assumptions other than his own are present. If culture sensitivity could be achieved simply through intellectual awareness that cultural patterns differ, the task of developing cultural sensitivity might be accomplished through readings and lectures. But the problem is more difficult. Human reactions are likely to be emotional, visceral, or psychological motor responses. One can be fully aware in an intellectual sense that time has a different meaning and value in Latin America, and yet have unkind and unfriendly reactions when forced to wait hours rather than minutes beyond the previously fixed time for an appointment.

Foreign language training can be extremely useful for developing cultural sensitivity. Other valuable measures are sensitivity training and cross-cultural living experiences. These approaches, of course, are generally relevant for all kinds of cross-cultural work, be it as a businessman, religious missionary, a government diplomat, or technician in development-assistance work.

Although still controversial among executives, the relatively new field of sensitivity training has flowered over the last decade. This type of training—as the name implies—is designed to make a person more sensitive to his own behavior in its conscious and unconscious motivation, and to the ways that his own behavior is perceived by and affects others. Such training aims to increase the accuracy of individuals in understanding and predicting the behavior of others with whom they work. Sensitivity training has special relevance to cross-cultural relations, even though its use has not been uniquely directed toward international business.

Sensitivity training is typically undertaken through what is referred to as T-groups (training groups). A T-group may be composed of from 10 to 12 persons who are placed together in a group dynamics situation for a period that might range from a weekend to a month. The subject matter of the T-groups becomes the behavior of participants. Experiencing behavior emotionally and viscerally through face-to-face interaction in a group becomes the process through which learning occurs.[24]

The most lasting means of achieving culture sensitivity comes through a sustained experience of living and working in one or more foreign environments. Such living experience may strain a person emotionally, regardless of his adaptability and preparation. The learning process may be painful and agonizing but out of it is likely to come the behavior changes needed to deal with cultural variables.

Training for cross-national appointments will, of course, heavily emphasize language study. Even though both a husband and wife may be required to devote several months on a full-time basis to language study, the benefits to the firm invariably justify the investment. In the process of such language training, moreover, there will be a considerable amount of learning about the characteristics of the new culture. If only a short period of time is available, an executive can still develop a considerable understanding of a language through an intensive language training course. Some institutes have experimented with total immersion courses in which the student is subjected to shifts of tutors instructing him by using only the new language. As some have commented, the executive either learns a great deal and comes out "thinking" the language or rebels and fails to complete the course. Courses in the particular cultural differences of the new country can also be devised as well as training in business practice under specific environmental differences.

In addition to such orientation, training firms have also experimented with presentations of experiences by returned executives and their wives, probationary appointments of the husband alone so that he can gain experience in the environment and smooth the way for introducing his family, and, in some cases, short husband and wife visits to the new country ahead of the actual posting.

Multinational firms also use training programs to fit special needs arising out of a company's business strategy or the nature of its product. In firms which rely on a worldwide network of independent distributors, training programs have been used to develop a corps of what amounts to international consultants who can advise and service distributors in a large number of countries. In other firms where the nature of the product has led to logistically interdependent manufacturing units in

---

[24] Harold M. F. Rush, *Behavioral Science: Concepts and Management Application* (New York: National Industrial Conference Board, 1969), pp. 42–49.

a number of foreign locations, teams have been specially trained to assist in the establishment of new units and to build them into an international production network.

In designing management-training programs to fit its needs, the international firm has many alternatives available and will encounter numerous problems. Much of the training is best handled by the company itself either at corporate headquarters or in foreign locations. Companies may also rely on educational institutions in the home or foreign countries for specialized or custom-designed training programs.[25] Outside programs in which many firms participate have the advantage of exposing participants either formally or informally to the experience of other companies. Whatever the approach, the wide range of problems peculiar to international business that can be resolved through training make the training function a crucial element for achieving the benefits of multinational operations.

COMPENSATION POLICIES

Levels of wages, salaries, and other allowances can produce some of the sharpest international conflicts within an international firm. Not only do bad policies create major friction, but they can influence the entire pattern of promotion that executives seek within the corporation. Overpaid posts in peripheral foreign activity, for example, might attract good executives away from more important but lower paid posts in the mainstream of the firm's development or, worse still, discourage them from returning to mainstream jobs later on. International compensation policies thus deserve the careful attention of top management.[26]

In developing its compensation policies, the international firm must decide whether it is going to maintain different salary structures in different countries, and if so whether this will extend to all grades of employment. Average rates of pay usually differ between nations for roughly comparable positions. Competition, however, will normally make it unthinkable to raise all rates to the higher levels. The firms could end up costing itself out of the markets where lower labor costs prevail. Only at the higher executive levels is a uniform international salary scale likely to be possible.

If different rates are retained, further problems arise when executives are transferred. Executives on the higher rates will not want any reduc-

---

[25] See Nancy G. McNulty, *Training Managers: The International Guide* (New York: Harper and Row, 1969).

[26] For surveys of the practices and problems of international companies in the compensation field, see Hans Schollhammer, "The Compensation of International Executives," *MSU Business Topics*, Winter 1969, pp. 19–30; *Worldwide Executive Compensation* (New York: Business International, 1967); *Setting Up An Overseas Compensation Package* (New York: Business International, 1970).

tion when transferred. Tacit acceptance of this attitude can result in a policy of retaining an executive's national salary level when he is transferred—plus expense allowances. For executives going to higher wage-rate areas, this solution is not so easy. If they are remunerated at the high-level rate, problems arise when they return to their home country. Do they revert to their old salary scales? What happens if they find themselves working alongside colleagues of the past few years who will still get higher salaries because of their national origin? How long does it take for an executive to lose his national identification? The idea of a national salary heritage can be important in third countries. In European countries, for example, an Englishman may find himself with an increased salary working alongside a younger and less experienced American on a far higher rate. It is not uncommon to find younger Europeans without family ties trying to establish an American identification early in their careers so that they can maintain American salaries later after returning to Europe. Among non-American graduates of American business schools this idea is particularly prevalent.

Some firms adopt the attitude that after a given period national identification should disappear, and a foreign-born executive should cease to be regarded as a "temporary" expatriate. Such a policy removes any inequity toward executives from low-salary countries. But it is likely to discourage the foreign assimilation of executives from higher-salary countries. In recent years many Americans in Europe have become comfortably "assimilated" on American salary scales and have little desire to return to the United States—just as 50 years ago the British created professional expatriates who came home with their wealth only on retirement.

These fundamental questions of compensation policy have no one answer. They must be decided by executives working towards a set of objectives with a given time horizon and constraints imposed from the various interested parties. The executive wanting maximum global expansion of the firm's activity in the short term, for example, will be little concerned with the long-term implications of a salary policy he might devise to get his best men into new markets.

In addition to questions of basic salary level, there are issues of a shorter-term nature as to what premiums should be paid for overseas service and what allowances should be made for hardship and for increased costs of living in a different environment. A premium for overseas service, or a hardship allowance, is seen by many executives as a reward for the hidden costs of moving away from a familiar environment to live and work in a strange culture to which they will never really belong. Whether such payments are justified, though, depends on the situation. If good executives who are usually flexible in location will not accept certain cross-national assignments without a premium, and there is a need for them to go, then there is a case for premium payments. If these conditions do not apply, then the premium is unnecessary or too high and will create problems, not cure them. There is no need for any concept of equity in payment of premiums. They are justified solely to overcome the disadvantages of a transfer in the eyes of the executive concerned, and these will differ according to the country and the executive involved. An across-the-board premium, according to one authority, "Tends to attract the worst employees, retain the mediocre employees, (and) motivate the worst behavior in all employees."[27]

Allowances are a different matter. They are made in order to cover additional expenses arising because of the international transfer. The firm paying allowances, however, should be clear as to just what expenses it is covering and no matter what it covers realize that any general statement as to the purpose of the allowances can lead to major arguments that the purpose has not been met. The two largest items are usually taxes and housing and these are best treated separately.

With taxes, many international firms follow a policy of deducting taxes at the rate for residents in the employee's home country and then paying the actual tax assessment. This can become expensive if the tax rates of the foreign country are higher and if the country also levies a tax on tax equalization payment. Other firms follow the argument that high tax rates may mean that more services are provided out of public funds thus saving the employee what he would otherwise have to pay out of after tax income. The difference between the United States and the United Kingdom in medical costs partly makes up for the higher tax rates in the United Kingdom, for example. This second argument, however, does not hold universally, particularly in countries with steeply progressive taxes on salaries. Generally speaking, it is only worth equalizing taxes if the differences are more than marginal and the difference in benefits fails to account for most of the variation. If ever a situation of double taxation arises, this is a different matter. If the firm is responsible for this through the timing of its transfer, it should clearly reduce an employee's tax obligation to that of residence in one country or the other.

Housing allowances are less clear-cut than taxation. In many situations, the cost of housing resembling what an executive would occupy in the suburb of a developed city will be much higher than at his home base. Presumably there is then some case for making him an allowance for the difference, although this has never been widely practiced for domestic moves—except for capital city allowances–New York, Paris, or London—even though the difference in costs as between say Indianapolis and Boston could be large. With international transfer even

---

[27] John M. Vivian, "Premiums and Allowances: The Expatriate Numbers Game," *Worldwide P & I Planning,* November–December 1969, p. 27.

an allowance for differences in standard housing costs may not be adequate to cover the sort of housing the executive will be expected to occupy in his new post. Within an expatriate community the executive may be expected to entertain more, have several servants, insist on air conditioning, and so on. If the firm feels that this is really necessary, there is a case for allowances. One possibility for establishing housing allowances is to base them on outside calculations such as those used by the U.S. Department of State or the United Nations to establish housing allowances for their diplomats around the world.[28]

Apart from specific allowances such as taxation and housing there remains the general cost-of-living allowance. While it is time consuming and expensive to calculate the variations in a cost-of-living index around the world, the greatest difficulties arise in determining what the index should cover in the first place and in arguing with employees why that particular index is used.

The U.S. Department of Labor has produced the following analysis of the spending of an average U.S. family after taxes, savings, investment, housing, and child education,[29] and this is sometimes used as the basis for calculating a cost-of-living in different locations:

Item	Percent
Food at home	22.7
Clothing	11.7
Domestic service	2.7
Household operations	5.1
Household furnishings	6.1
Transportation	11.9
Medical care	7.0
Personal care	5.1
Food away from home	7.7
Recreation	5.1
Tobacco	1.8
Miscellaneous	13.1
	100.0

However, this assumes that spending patterns approximate an average, that they do not change with foreign postings, and still leaves unanswered what items are to be included under each heading. If the executive were to transfer his home-spending pattern abroad, he would most certainly be faced with an extremely high cost of living. But few family spending patterns will fail to adjust in some ways to the local living pattern. Then again, in a foreign posting there may be a requirement for more entertainment and greater medical expenses.

---

[28] State Department housing and cost-of-living allowances are published with quarterly revisions in *Labor Developments Abroad* (Washington, D.C.: U.S. Government Printing Office).

[29] Vivian, "Premiums and Allowances," p. 33.

Given the problems and expense with calculating indexes, it seems preferable to use some outside index without pretending that it is meant to approximate any particular individual's increase in living cost.[30] Or even better, avoid a cost-of-living allowance entirely. Some firms argue that a high initial allowance should be given to give employees time to adjust their spending habits but after a given period only specific additional requirements of the particular job will be met.

Whatever a firm decides to offer in the way of allowances, it should make sure they fit in with its own objectives. If the firm wants its expatriate executives to merge in with the environment and serve there for long periods, it should pay whatever salary is necessary to get the executives there and avoid allowances. Alternatively, if appointments are shorter term, flat allowances rather than reimbursements may encourage the executive to live on the local economy and save on his allowances.

LABOR RELATIONS IN THE MULTINATIONAL FIRM

The multinational firm operates in and across several or many different industrial relations environments.[31] Thus, important general characteristics of any industrial relations system, such as strike propensities and collective bargaining structures, become variables at the global planning level. In some nations, the employer may be forced into a paternalistic relationship with his employees whether he likes it or not. At the other end of the spectrum, employers are required by law to share management responsibilities with representatives of the workers, as in the codetermination system of Germany. Labor unions vary greatly in strength, in their degrees of political activism, and in the issues considered appropriate for negotiation with the employer. Furthermore, many features of national labor relations environments have been changing significantly in recent years.[32]

---

[30] For example, the Union Bank of Switzerland, *Prices and Earnings Around the Globe* (Zurich, June 1971) has a comparison of purchasing power in 31 cities, available in 5 languages. Lloyd's Register of Shipping in London, which maintains expatriate staff in over 100 countries, revises their own established budgets for ten countries each week all year round. David Young, "Executive Compensation on a Worldwide Scale," *Columbia Journal of World Business,* November–December 1970, p. 74.

[31] For a representative comparative study of industrial relations environments, see Everett M. Kassalow, *Trade Unions and Industrial Relations: An International Comparison* (New York: Random House, 1969).

[32] See Jean-Daniel Reynaud, "The Future of Industrial Relations in Western Europe," *Bulletin, International Institute for Labour Studies* (Geneva, February 1968), pp. 88–115; B. J. Widick, "The New Look in Labor Relations," *Columbia Journal of World Business,* July–August 1971, pp. 63–67; Robert W. Cox, "Approaches to a Futurology of Labor Relations," *Bulletin, International Institute for Labour Studies* (Geneva, 1971), pp. 139–64.

Work Force Management

In recognition of the unique cultural, legal, and institutional settings in different nations which affect labor relations through varying social values, psychic needs of workers, the peculiar industrial relations lore, pertinent legal intricacies, and so forth, multinational firms have generally delegated the task of work-force management to the managers of foreign subsidiaries. In the negotiation of agreements, local managers know the local situation in more detail, and as they will have to manage under the terms of the agreement, they should be responsible for its final arrangements. For international management to hold the final authority in negotiations would, moreover, tend to lower the status, authority, and efficiency of the local management. A policy of great local autonomy in labor relations, however, assumes that local managers have been competently trained for administering labor affairs.

There are strong arguments, though, for international management exercising some central coordination.[33] In new units, acquired as going concerns, local management experience in labor management may not be extensive nor up to the standard expected of a multinational corporation. Also, agreements made in one country may affect the international plans of the corporation or create precedents for negotiations in other countries. The more unions cooperate across country boundaries, the more need there will be for the firm to present a consistent front. The case for central labor relations coordination is thus strong but such coordination should involve full participation by local management and infringe as little as possible on local autonomy.

Coordination does not necessarily mean that the international firm should have common policies in all countries. A whole range of elements may differ from environment to environment leading to different arrangements in each. Any attempt to impose parent company policies on new situations where they do not fit would be wrong. To have a worldwide policy to avoid unionization simply because this had worked in the parent company would be one example. Many companies who are not unionized in the parent unit have successfully followed unionization in subsidiaries and vice versa.

In fulfilling its coordination role and in managing its own responsibilities, headquarters' staff needs to develop considerable understanding and a continuing flow of information on national labor-management patterns. Assessments and forecasts of the labor relations component of national environments are a necessary input for decisions on the location and expansion of facilities. They are also necessary for evaluating the per-

---

[33] See Duane Kujawa, *International Labor Relations Management in the Automotive Industry* (New York: Praeger Publishers, Inc., 1971).

formance of subsidiaries and local managers. Where transnational sourcing patterns have been developed and a subsidiary in one country relies on a subsidiary in another country as a source of components or as a user of its output, labor relations throughout the system become of direct importance to central management for maintaining its global-production strategy.

Transnational Labor Union Collaboration

The most urgent consideration, however, pressing for headquarter's involvement in labor-management affairs has been the move toward internationalization of the labor movement as a direct reaction to the growth of the multinational corporation. Unions around the world have felt increasingly threatened by powerful multinational employers and have made major strides in the direction of cooperation across national boundaries in organizing, bargaining, and in striking. In essence, their situation parallels that of national governments: they are national institutions facing an international challenge.

Many trade unionists are firmly convinced that multinational companies make their decisions on all important matters on a highly centralized basis, with central headquarters concerned only with global goals. Others feel seriously handicapped because of what they describe as a floating and invisible decision center for labor relations matters. Subsidiary companies, so the complaint goes, claim that decisions are made at central headquarters, and central headquarters respond that decisions are made by their subsidiaries. Another belief is that international companies can shift their investment at will and will do so if a trade union is found "unreasonable" in its demands. Still another problem they see in collective bargaining is the ability of the firm to call on plants in another country to meet production needs when there is a strike in one particular location.[34]

While the internationalization of business has been going on for many years, the response of labor union organizations has begun to crystallize only since the middle 1960s. Although strong environmental forces favor local labor-relations patterns and mitigate against the internationalization of the labor movement, transnational collaboration among unions has expanded and operated with considerable effectiveness in several areas. Four general types of union strategies have already emerged in response to the multinational corporation. These strategies are the collection and dissemination of information, international consultation, coordi-

---

[34] Harry Weiss, "The Multinational Corporation and Its Impact on Collective Bargaining," *Collective Bargaining Today* (Washington, D.C.: Bureau of National Affairs, Inc., 1971), pp. 287–312.

nation of union policies and tactics with respect to specific international firms, and a drive for controls over multinational corporations.[35]

The collection and dissemination of information has become a highly developed and widely utilized activity. The United Auto Workers, as only one example, recently developed a computer guide to collective bargaining and national social security provisions in the Latin American automobile industry which it was hoped would support the international harmonization of wages and working conditions in this industry. International consultation has occurred through worldwide meetings focusing on a specific multinational enterprise as well as through small meetings between representatives of two specific unions. In 1969, for example, the International Federation of Chemical and General Workers' Union, known as the ICF, held a precollective bargaining strategy meeting concerned with the worldwide operations of the French company, St. Gobain. This consultation led to agreements by the various unions to adopt coordinated negotiating policies. While all the unions did not follow the strategy recommendations, a number did. As an example of coordinating tactics, the International Metalworkers' Federation (IMF) has been attempting to organize procedures for a simultaneous ending of all labor agreements with a particular multinational company, thus possibly taking away from the firm the opportunity of using its subsidiaries in various countries to help break strikes elsewhere.[36] The fourth tactic, the drive for controls, has been used at the international and national level. A June 1971 meeting of the International Confederation of Free Trade Unions (ICFTU) passed a resolution urging the adoption of international and national standards for regulating international firms. On the national level, the U.S. union movement sponsored and supported legislation in 1971 that would lead to complete government regulation of the outflow of direct investment and the export of technology.[37]

Unions are basically nationalistic, and strong political and ideological cleavages exist between different national labor movements. Consequently, the degree of success that unions can achieve through international collaboration is uncertain. Nevertheless, attempts at cooperation in one form or another are bound to increase, and the management of the multinational firm must develop policies for meeting international requests, as well as partisan requests from labor in individual companies

---

[35] David H. Blake, "Corporate Structure and International Unionism," *Columbia Journal of World Business,* March–April 1972, pp. 19–26.

[36] For many specific details on the trade union response, see Tugendhat, *Multinationals,* pp. 180–92; Charles Levinson, *Capital, Inflation, and the Multinationals* (New York: Macmillan Co., 1971); International Labour Organisation, Metal Trades Committee, *General Report* (Geneva: International Labour Office, 1970), pp. 145–80.

[37] See the symposium on the "Foreign Trade and Investment Act of 1972," *Columbia Journal of World Business,* March–April 1972, pp. 11–18.

which are concerned with their position vis-a-vis employees in other countries. Local labor strategies will continue to be dominant, but supplementary global labor strategies will also be required.

Conclusions

In international business, as in most other activities, human resources are the critical elements. The peculiar problem that international firms face is that people are usually raised, educated, and indoctrinated in one culture whereas international business management requires cross-cultural communication, coordination, and supervision. The challenge is to develop managers who can think globally or at least biculturally.

The multinational firm has various options in choosing a policy that will develop international managers with this ability. It can follow a policy of hiring local nationals to manage its subsidiaries, but it will then have to rely on training programs to internationalize its personnel. It will have to invest in training programs to prepare executives and their families for cross-national transfers. One of the most perplexing problems faced by multinational companies has been the matter of compensation policies, but with increasing experience most companies have been able to work out reasonably satisfactory solutions even for handling cross-national transfers.

The management of labor relations must necessarily be delegated largely to local management because of innumerable local variations in worker attitudes, labor union roles, and the degree of governmental participation in labor-management affairs. However, the growing internationalization of the labor movement, in response to a perceived threat from the multinational enterprise, has tended to bring headquarters management increasingly into the formulation and implementation of labor strategies, and is likely to continue to do so in the future.

EXERCISES AND DISCUSSION QUESTIONS

1. What are the advantages and limitations of a policy that favors the hiring of nationals as managers of subsidiaries?

2. Many international companies recruit potential managers for their home country domestic operations and later look to this staff for their international managers, particularly at headquarters. Under what conditions, if any, would you advise a company to do specialized outside recruiting for its international management personnel?

3. You have been asked to design an orientation program for personnel being transferred on a two-year assignment to a less developed country (you select the country). The program must be completed by the participants

in three weeks of full-time study. What are the several most important subjects that should be included in the program and why?

4. How would the local labor situation affect your location decision for a new foreign plant that produced a product whose characteristics or technology would have to change rapidly to meet competitive conditions?

5. How would you answer the fear of labor unions that the multinational corporation can easily transfer its operations to a different country if it feels that the demands of labor unions in a specific area of operations are "unreasonable"?

PART VI

Cases and Problems in International Business

WORKING WITHIN THE INTERNATIONAL FRAMEWORK

Freelandia

FREELANDIA'S MAIN EXPORTS came from its primary industries and included wool, meat, butter, timber, fruit, and a variety of less advanced manufactures. For 1972 the total exported was $1,120 million.

Imports totaled $1,103 million, made up mainly of heavy manufactured goods such as machinery and transport equipment, while an additional $12 million was spent on transport and travel and $5 million on other services.

The country had recently begun to encourage foreign industry to invest in new factories and plants, provided that the output either substituted for imports or had export potential and included at least 40 percent of Freelandian content. This campaign had proven quite successful and during 1972 a total of $116 million was remitted for direct investment in Freelandia. The policy was beginning to meet resistance from the opposition political parties, however, because the considerable income these companies were earning was payable to them in overseas funds and placed a strain on the balance of payments. In 1972 a total of $66 million was repatriated by overseas companies, out of their net earnings of $98 million.

The Freelandian government had also been encouraging its major domestic producers to establish processing plants overseas to increase their receipts from primary exports. A total of $42 million was invested in this way in 1972 and was expected to add significantly to the future inflow from overseas business investments which totaled only $18 million in 1972.

There was an additional reinvested income of $22 million from these direct investments overseas during 1972, but it was still true, as the opposition argued, that foreign firms' ownership in Freelandia far outweighed Freelandia's overseas business activities—in cumulative figures at the end of 1971 a comparison of $963 million to $242 million. This comparison, moreover, was similar for holdings of investment securities. Foreign investment in Freelandian securities totaled $360 million at the end of 1971 and increased in value $44 million during 1972, while Freelandian holdings of overseas stocks and bonds were only valued at $122 million in 1971, increasing in value by $13 million over the year. Heavy restrictions permitted only $5 million to be remitted by Freelandia for further purchases during 1972, but foreigners purchased a further $42 million in comparison.

The government's policies had also led them to borrow $28 million from overseas investors during the year in order to finance new container facilities at the major ports, but their indebtedness to the IMF was reduced to $321 million with a repayment of $25 million. Total interest payments to service the government's liabilities were $56 million including the interest on government debentures floated overseas which totaled $403 million at the end of 1971. The central bank's holdings of convertible currencies overseas increased during the year by $19 million to $126 million.

Shorter-term commercial finances were less important to the Freelandian situation but local holdings of foreigners again more than offset Freelandian holdings overseas. Short-term overseas holdings by Freelandian companies were $80 million at the end of 1971 and liquid holdings $6 million, while overseas companies held $56 million short-term claims and $48 million in liquid funds within Freelandia. By the end of 1972, the net change on short-term nonliquid funds was $14 million. Overseas companies had increased their claims by $6 million, and Freelandian companies had increased their claims by $20 million. There was no change over the year in Freelandian liquid claims, but foreign banks increased their holdings by $18 million.

1. From the above particulars prepare balance-of-payments accounts for Freelandia for 1972 and show the country's international investment position at the end of 1971 and 1972.

2. What do you think might happen if Freelandia's currency were to be devalued against other currencies by 20 percent? Do you think this devaluation is likely?

Peters Brass Company*

JIM PICKED UP THE MEMO from the Buenos Aires office and glanced at it. He looked more closely, then swore softly and went into Bill Adams' office next door. Bill was comptroller for the Peters Brass Company, a young and rapidly growing casting company, and Jim was the executive vice president. The year was 1965, and it was spring.

"Bill, take a look at this—the Argentine peso just got devalued from 180 to 205 to the dollar. Sam Baxter, our manager down there, just passed on the word."

Bill looked up. "I knew we never should have gone into Argentina. What does it mean?"

"How should I know? You're the comptroller."

Bill scrambled around his crowded desk and found the financial statements from the Argentine branch. "Let's see—these were just sent in. Statements as of the 31st of last month. Hell, they're all in pesos." He smiled. "Boy do we look good—millions of pesos of profits." He paused. "But all the investments we made down there are in dollars."

"Yeah, but what does this devaluation do to us?"

"Look, Jim, I went to B-school a long time ago. I was in Argentina a week before I realized that they used something other than dollars down there. Don't ask me."

"Well, who do we ask, then?"

1. In this case, what will be the effect of devaluation on the balance sheet?
2. Peters Brass invested $2,350,000 in Argentina in 1961, when the peso was worth 1.2 cents. If the company now receives 65 percent of the affiliate's

---

* This case was written by Richard N. Farmer, professor, Graduate School of Business, Indiana University. Copyright retained by the author.

profits and brings it home at the new exchange rate, what percent return is that, in dollars, on the original investment? What percent return is it on the original investment converted at the newly declared exchange rate (205 pesos = $1)?

TABLE 1

Peters Brass Company of Argentina

Balance General al 31 marzo de 1965
(Balance Sheet, March 31, 1965)

Pesos

activos (Assets)

Caja y bancos	
(Cash on hand)	8,100,000
Deudores en cuenta	
(Accounts receivable)	32,700,000
Bienes de cambio	
(Inventories)	90,700,000
Maquinarias y accesorios	
(Machinery and equipment).	142,400,000
Immuebles (menos amortizacion)	
(Buildings, less depreciation)	253,400,000
Terreno	
(Land)	129,800,000
Total.	657,100,000

pasivos (Liabilities)

Deudas (Debts)

Comerciales	
(Accounts payable).	40,000,000
Bancarias	
(Bank overdraft)	25,000,000
Equipo hipotecarios	
(Equipment notes payable)	55,000,000
Capital, reserves y resultados	
(Shareholders' equity*)	
Suscripto	
(Common stock)	300,000,000
Reservas y utilidades	
(Capital surplus)	237,100,000
Total.	657,100,000

*65 percent owned by Peters Brass, U.S.A; 35 percent owned by Sr. Pedro Gomez y Silva, S.A. of B.A., Argentina.

TABLE 2

Peters Brass Company of Argentina

Cuadro Demostrativo de Ganancias y Perdidas al 31 de marzo de 1965
(Profit and Loss – Year Ending March 31, 1965)

Pesos

Entrada (Revenues)

Ventas menos costo de la mercaderia vendida.	220,500,000	
(Sales less cost of goods sold)		
Comision	40,000,000	
(Commissions)		
Renta	50,000,000	
(Rental income)		
Varias entrada.	30,000,000	
(Miscellaneous income)		
Total entrada (Total revenue).		340,500,000

Gastos (Expenses)

Remuneraciones al personal.	130,500,000	
(Wages and salaries)		
Gastos de operacion	40,000,000	
(Fuel, heat, and light)		
Amortizaciones	15,500,000	
(Depreciation)		
Gastos de comision y regalias	35,000,000	
(Commission expenses and royalties)		
Impuestos	50,500,000	
(Taxes)		
Total gastos (Total expenses)		271,500,000
Utilidad del Ejercicio (Net profit)		69,000,000

American Wallboard Corporation*

THE AMERICAN WALLBOARD CORPORATION has a subsidiary in Brazil, which has been operating since 1960. Financial statements for 1963–66 are shown in Table 1.

During 1963–66, the average increase in the Brazilian price level has been about 30 percent (compounded) per year. Over the past 20 years, average price increases in Brazil have averaged about 25 percent per year compounded. Thus the price index at the end of 1965 was 2,050, with 1958 equal to 100.

AWC management has been concerned for some time about low profitability of their Brazilian branch. "The statements seem to show profits," the treasurer commented, "but somehow they seem to melt away before we can remit them."

The Brazilian cruzeiro-dollar exchange rate tends to reflect the relative difference between American inflation (which has averaged about 1.5 percent per year in the past 20 years) and the Brazilian inflation rate. Often there are considerable lags in exchange-rate adjustment, in that the cruzeiro price does not fall as rapidly as inflation would suggest, but over time the two rates tend to maintain relative purchasing power parity. When AWC wants to remit profits, it does so at the prevailing rate of exchange at the time of transfer.

The local Brazilian comptroller of AWC is an American who has been in Brazil since 1964. Before that time, he spent 20 years working in various financial capacities in AWC American plants. AWC has prided itself on close financial controls of its branches for many years, and the relevant decision rules about cash handling are developed at the New York head office. Present general policies for such items as inventory levels, credit terms, and so on for Brazil are shown in Table 2. They are similar to the American rules of the company.

---

* This case was written by Richard N. Farmer, professor, Graduate School of Business, Indiana University. Copyright retained by the author.

546

TABLE 1

AWB Corporation: Brazilian Branch

Profit and Loss Statement
(billions of cruzeiros)

	1963	1964	1965	1966
Total sales	10.2	18.5	31.5	51.5
Cost of goods sold	4.1	6.2	11.8	14.1
Gross margin	6.1	12.3	19.7	37.4
Expenses.	2.2	3.1	4.0	5.5
Depreciation.	1.5	1.5	1.7	1.8
Taxes.	1.1	2.1	3.3	5.2
Net profit after taxes	1.3	5.6	10.7	24.9

Balance Sheet
(billions of cruzeiros)*

Assets	1963	1964	1965	1966
Cash on hand	1.5	1.7	1.9	2.3
Accounts receivable	3.1	5.9	12.5	33.6
Plant and equipment	5.5	5.2	5.1	4.9
(net of depreciation)				
Inventories on hand	3.3	4.1	4.4	4.7
Total assets	13.4	16.9	23.9	45.5
Liabilities				
Accounts payable.	0.9	1.2	1.7	1.9
Long-term debt	3.0	3.0	3.0	3.0
(to parent company)				
Capital stock	8.0	8.0	8.0	8.0
(wholly owned by AWC)				
Earned surplus	1.5	4.7	11.2	32.6
Total liabilities	13.4	16.9	13.9	45.5

*Exchange rates as of:
Jan. 1, 1963—$1 = CR   475
Jan. 1, 1964—$1 = CR   620
Jan. 1, 1965—$1 = CR 1,850
Jan. 1, 1966—$1 = CR 2,220

TABLE 2
American Wallboard Corporation General Cash Planning Policy

1. Cash is our most valuable asset. It should not be idle, nor should it be tied up in items which are not absolutely needed.
2. Inventories shall be kept at the minimum consistent with proper service to our customers. Tying up cash in inventory is always a waste, unless some clear benefit in terms of sales and/or profitability can be demonstrated.
3. Each branch manager shall be responsible for developing a credit-rating scheme for customers. Class A customers (best credit-rating) shall get 60-day credit; Class B (less desirable) shall get 30-day credit; Class C (doubtful) 10-day credit; and all others shall pay cash on delivery.
4. Capital equipment locks in cash for many years. Branch managers shall make every effort to minimize capital investments, consistent with necessary requirements for production and customer service.

American Level Corporation

ON GRADUATION FROM BUSINESS SCHOOL, James Bennett joined American Level Corporation in July 1971 as assistant to the corporate treasurer in the New Jersey headquarters.

American Level had two wholly owned manufacturing subsidiaries, one in Brazil and one in Germany, but apart from a quarterly review of the foreign exchange situation by the corporate finance committee, there had been no regular procedure for avoiding the foreign exchange risks arising from the international operations. The treasurer was aware of the gaps in the American Level procedures and asked Bennett as his first major assignment to outline a methodology for forecasting exchange rate changes as well as a set of decision rules to ·be followed for minimizing foreign exchange costs. The treasurer thought it would be wise to prepare the way for the procedure recommendations with a clear statement of the foreign exchange exposure of the two subsidiaries, based on their accounts to June 30. This was to be ready for the finance committee meeting on August 25, along with the usual estimate of the previous month's foreign exchange gains or losses.

The spot rate on June 30 for the German mark was DM 3.65 = U.S. $1, and for the Brazilian cruzeiro 5.20 = U.S. $1. During July, however, the German mark had been "floated" with the end of month rate quoted as D.M. 3.35 = U.S. $1. The exchange rate of the cruzeiro had also been changed to an official rate of 5.40 = $1.

The balance sheets of the two subsidiaries on June 30, 1971, are shown in Table 1. In the case of the Amel S.A. about 50 percent of the raw material and packaging material was imported from the United States, mainly from the parent company.

TABLE 1

American Level Corporation

Subsidiary Balance Sheets as of June 30, 1971

	Amel Gmbh. *(DM 000)*	*Amel S.A.* *(Cruzeiro 000)*
Assets		
Cash	4,419	415
Accounts receivable: trade other	25,134	13,078
Inventories		
Raw materials	9,807	15,972
Packaging material	744	3,221
Work in process	10,323	5,321
Finished goods	3,525	1,972
Total current assets	53,952	39,979
Fixed assets	11,246	3,106
Less depreciation	1,479	916
Net fixed assets	9,767	2,190
Deferred expenses	–	1,121
Total assets	63,719	43,290
Liabilities		
Notes payable	3,418	8,876
Accounts payable: trade and intercompany	18,259	13,808
Accrued expenses	1,369	473
Accrued taxes, miscellaneous	7,803	4,367
Total current liabilities	30,849	27,524
Reserve for patent infringement	186	–
Capital	16,508	6,527
Retained earnings	11,075	8,189
Current profit	5,101	1,050
Total net worth	32,684	15,766
Total liabilities	63,719	43,290

MEETING THE INTERESTS
OF NATION-STATES

Acme Manufacturing*

PETE JACKSON, vice president of international operations for Acme Manufacturing, swore to himself and picked up his phone. "Al, come up here as soon as you can. Boy, do we have problems!" While he waited for Al, who was vice president of production, he worked over some figures from Acme's Indonesian operation.

"What is it, Pete?" Al asked as he walked in.

"Have you seen Peraldo's Indonesian capital-budget request?"

"Sure. A lot of the spadework was done by us. He's had troubles getting some good engineers out there," Al replied.

"Al, when I was out there last year, you could hire all the men you wanted for about 50 cents to a dollar a day. Now, here Peraldo wants to buy four automatic front-end loaders for his gravel operation. Those machines cost about $47,000 each here—out there, delivered with duty paid, they'll be over $60,000 each. Boy, you can buy a lot of labor for that kind of money. And furthermore, he'll only be using the loaders about six months a year."

"He needs the four," Al replied, "because he has seasonal peaks, and he has to deliver gravel fast."

"Look, Al, I saw thousands of men with picks and shovels out there, working in tin mines and what not. Why can't he just hire some more men? It would be cheaper."

"It would be a bit cheaper, on paper at least," Al said. "But we started to figure it out. If we did it by hand, we'd need about 800 men. That means 800 houses, or beds, or something. It also means a

---

* This case was written by Richard N. Farmer, professor, Graduate School of Business, Indiana University. Copyright is retained by the author.

big personnel department, to handle payroll, grievances, vacation plans, and who knows what else. Oh, yes, we'd have to have an expanded legal staff—Indonesian labor law is complicated and tough."

"All of that still doesn't add up to that much money," Pete commented.

"Oh, there's more. We'd have to pay family allowances, and there's been a lot of labor trouble on the island in the past few years. When the communists were cleaned out a little while ago, the union got somewhat easier, but it looks like the Marxists, at least, are still in control. They agitate all the time about American imperalism. Remember last year, when they nearly tore down our expatriate camp? Of course, one short strike, and we'd probably lose our contract there—and there have been a lot of strikes recently."

"There's more?" Pete asked weakly.

"Sure," Al replied. "Indonesians are very nice, hard-working people. But on our island, they just don't get enough to eat. This sort of manual labor really is tough for them. We'd have to build a dispensary now, and probably a hospital later, to handle things like heat fatigue, exhaustion, and other things. Under the law, we're responsible for these things. That means we'd need a doctor and some nurses—and we just can't find qualified Indonesians for these posts. We'd have to hire Americans or Europeans, and it's doubtful that we could get labor visas for them too easily."

"So, we use machinery?"

Al nodded. "We use machinery. That way, we only have four new men, plus a couple of mechanics. They're hard to get, but we can find them. And of course, the government will let us import machinery. They feel that this sort of thing is the essence of industrialization." Al sighed. "You know, it's tough—here's a country with a big unemployment problem, with lots of pressure to put men to work, and then they stack the deck so we almost have to buy machinery, instead of using men. It's a shame, but then we're trying to make money, not solve the problems of the world." Al waved at the report. "Are you going to approve it?"

1. Why would a country with large supplies of low-skill labor structure its economy and laws so that the above incident could happen? What kinds of reasoning underlie this attitude?

2. Would you approve the order for front-end loaders, even if on paper a manual-labor force was a bit cheaper (say 5 percent less at present)? Why or why not?

3. Is a multinational company responsible only to itself for profits, or does it have some responsibility for solving other world problems? Why or why not?

Russell Karagosian*

WINGING SOUTH TO LATIN AMERICA aboard Pan American, Russell Karagosian had five hours flying time and an evening in his hotel room to prepare a presentation to the Minister for Industry outlining the basic characteristics of a scheme for evaluating new foreign investments.

Russell was a principal consultant for a Boston firm of business consultants. He had worked with this firm since completing his degree at a leading business school and had been mainly engaged in international market surveys and feasibility studies for multinational corporations. The current assignment stemmed from a Christmas party in 1969 at which Russell was introduced to Senor da Silva, a prominent lawyer from one of the smaller Latin American countries. On learning that Russell was an international business consultant, this gentleman had inferred that perhaps Russell's specialty was inventing ways to get higher profits out of Latin America and referred to the topical editorial from *Worldwide P & I Planning* shown in Appendix 1. Defending himself, Russell argued that any problems stemmed from the countries themselves. They had not made up their minds precisely what was in their best interests and then given a clear indication of what they wanted and how they would measure it. It was not too difficult, Russell asserted, to develop a standard set of questionnaire forms that would require potential investors to show clearly the benefits and disadvantages of any proposal from the viewpoint of the recipient country.

Three months later, after a change of government, Senor da Silva was appointed Minister for Industry of his country. Shortly thereafter, Russell Karagosian received a telephone call inviting him to meet the

* Copyright 1972 by Kenneth Simmonds.

minister the following day to discuss his ideas further with a view to a more formal assignment to develop them into operative plans. There was no time to build a careful presentation but Russell was able to put his hands on two papers in his files as he left for the airport. One of these was a set of measurements introduced in the Philippines some years previously as a guide for profit remittance, shown as Appendix 2. The other was an extract from a Council of the Americas study discussing the measurable effects of U.S. direct investment in Mexico, shown as Appendix 3.

APPENDIX 1

The Latin American Repatriation Game*

"If I were a Minister of Finance in South America, I'd get me a good tough audit staff of young guys trained in Uncle Sugar Able. Then I'd comb the books of the bigger *Yanqui* subs in my country . . . and I'd sock it to 'em, sock it to 'em, sock it to 'em."

With this malediction my international controller buddy, Chuck Mc-Gregor slid into place next to me at *Charlie Brown's* in the Pan Am Building. He certainly was more than slightly steamed (and oiled) as he flipped open a copy of the October '69 *Fortune* to the article "Threatening Weather in Latin America."

"Here's someone who says U.S. subsidiaries in Latin America contribute 20 percent of that area's tax revenues. If I had the job, I could get that up to at least 35 to 40 percent, without half trying. Hell, in some subs, my company is taking out its original investment every year or more and there are others like us."

I chastised him for being un-American, unpatriotic, and warned him, with loose talk like that he could be drummed out of the National Foreign Trade Council as well as the Council for Latin America and the International Executives Association. And, if he kept on blithering that he wanted to repatriate less money from South of the Border, he would soon talk his way out of the cushiest controller job in mid-Manhattan.

Didn't he know, I emphasized, that U.S. subs "down there" accounted for 12 percent of all Latin production? And 20 percent of that area's exports? Or didn't he care?

"Sure I know these things and I care," he sniffed. "But I'm running scared. What with the anti-*norteamericano* climate in Peru and Bolivia—and rumblings elsewhere—I don't want our five Latin plants to be expropriated. So we damn well had better come up with some

---

* *Worldwide P & I Planning,* November–December 1969.

more loot for the locals—and fast. I hate to say it, but as *Fortune* hinted, they're beginning to wise up."

But hadn't his firm done a lot for local Latin economies? I mentioned a double-page ad spread in *Time* which dramatically showed what his company's sub had done for a small Latin town "before" and "after." Money was pumped in with no promise of return. And look what happened. New schools, new roads, with illiteracy down, disease down, and employment up.

"I remember that ad," he chuckled. "Our local guys had a helluva time rounding up enough good-looking Indians for the photo. Sure we did something for them. But we're doing a lot more for us. Do you remember what the copy said? 'We are again proving our faith in _____ by reinvesting profits for our workers' future.' "

"But," Chuck went on, "do you want to know the real score? After our 'allowable' repatriation and after we took our several hundred thou' more in pre-tax 'expenses,' then we're glad to invest the little that's left. Because in weak-currency countries, we've been taking out 50 to 100 percent R.O.I. every year."

Was he intimating U.S. subsidiaries in Latin America kept two sets of books?.

"Well, it isn't two sets of books in the classic Tuscan sense. We only have one, but we make it do the work of two. Any local tax man can see we carry 'expenses' on the books. But they're just a neat device to siphon off as much pre-tax income as we can."

I cautioned him not to give away company secrets as I looked around to see if any of his competitors or Latin tax authorities were tuning in. Chuck tends to get boisterous after his third Tanquerary.

"The only trouble is," he said, ignoring my blunt warning, "that we're weakening, not shoring up, the economies of these countries by scarfing off all the foreign exchange the traffic will bear. Let's take a hypothetical case. I'll exaggerate somewhat but I'll show you how to play the Latin American repatriation game.

"Let's say our investment is $500,000 . . . and local authorities fix our repatriation ratio at 10 percent of investment. Then we quick pump in a $2 million loan from our Mexican sub at 20 percent interest for fixed asset expansion. We 'convince' Exchange Control that our fixed assets are now $2.5 million—and 10 percent of *that* begins to look pretty good. With our true return of $1 million on $6 million sales, then I can 'legitimately' get out $250,000—50 percent of our original investment—as our allowable dollar repatriation.

"But," Chuck grinned slyly, "I'm still way ahead of the game because I'm getting 400 thou' as interest on our $2 million Mexican loan. Then I work up some nifty Home Office charges such as technical management advice, special research, packaging design, etc. We figure these at 4 percent of sales, so this is a cool $240,000."

Are the charges real, I wanted to know.

"Of course not," he said spiritedly. "You sure are green. But who's to prove me wrong? And isn't our trademark and name worth something? Of course, it is," he said, answering his own question. "And I value these at 3 percent of sales which is another $180,000.

"When I have loaded on all the hard currency pre-tax expenses, I have one final fillip left. I make the local sub pay $500 a month towards the salary of our regional Latin Vice President in Coral Gables. It's a real check, but he never sees it.

"Let's total up," Chuck said briskly, writing on the bar tab with his Cross ball-point.

Home Office charges	$ 240,000
Trademark value	180,000
Share of "salary"	6,000
Interest on loan	400,000
Repatriation	250,000
Total	$1,076,000

"So here I am repatriating just over twice our original $500,000 investment! Not bad for a country boy from Indiana. By the way, we never go through with expansion. We'll cancel the loan quietly, but it's served its real purpose—to really jump our investment base. The authorities won't catch on for some time—if ever—as we'll finance expansion out of local accounts."

As I reached for the check, he made one final point. "But we just have to cut back. Most Latin countries are training some sharp M.B.A. types up here. And, remember, they have a legitimate bitch. A lot of us haven't left *that* much behind in the local economy—and I'm afraid we'll have to pay the piper and dance to the Finance Minister's tune."

How much would he pay and how fast would he dance, I asked.

"A lot more. On our Baton Rouge tank farm, we went for 10 percent R.O.I. over 10 years. I'd settle for 20 percent in five in Latin America. This should keep the wolves at bay for awhile. It's less for us, but it's better than losing everything. The good old carpetbagging days are gone."

APPENDIX 2

Central Bank of the Philippines, Manila—Memorandum to All Authorized Agents

As a result of continuing analytical studies, the system of measurements has been amended to improve the method of implementing the Central Bank's policy on investment remittance. Under this policy, which applies equally to precontrol investments as well as to approved postcontrol investment, Philippine companies and branches of foreign companies are allowed to remit profits and dividends due to their nonresident stockholders or head offices on the basis of the net contributions of the companies to (a) national income and employment or "the national income effect," (b) strengthening the balance-of-payments position of the country or "the balance-of-payments effect," and (c) supply of goods and services to serve the basic needs of the economy or "the product essentiality." The system of measurements, as amended, is indicated below.

I. NATIONAL INCOME EFFECT
    A. The national income effect is the ratio of the net domestic value added by the firm to the amount of scarce resources utilized in production and is expressed by the equation:

$$Y = (V_g/I_t) \times 100\%$$

where: Y = national income effect, percent.
        V_g = net domestic value added by the firm, pesos.
        I_t = amount of scarce resources utilized in production, pesos.

    B. Net domestic value added consists of the sum of the shares of the four factors of production in the income of the firm. This is obtained by adding the shares of:
        1. labor—consisting of salaries and wages, bonuses, and commissions received by the employees and wage earners of the firm;
        2. land—rent of land and buildings used by the firm in production;
        3. entrepreneur—profits before income tax; and
        4. capital—interest payments on loans.
    C. Scarce resources consist of:
        1. replacement of fixed assets—current amortization (depreciation) of fixed assets both of domestic and imported origin;
        2. maintenance of fixed assets—cost of spare parts, labor, supplies, and other costs incurred in maintenance; (If maintenance is done by an outside firm, the total charges of the outside firm plus the cost of spare parts and supplies provided by the firm shall be deducted.)
        3. foreign exchange utilized—the foreign exchange cost of raw materials and supplies (including fuel) directly imported and indirectly (domestically purchased) imported, salaries

of foreign personnel remitted abroad, and all other foreign exchange costs (royalties, service charges, expenses of business trips abroad, and so forth).

D. Automatic rating for firms producing intermediate products. Firms producing intermediate products necessary for the production processes of other essential industries are credited a minimum 3-point rating in the national income effect. Necessity is established if the intermediate product possesses either or both of the following characteristics:

1. it forms an integral part, physically or chemically, of the product of the other essential industry; and/or

2. it is a necessary accessory for handling or merchandising, that is, containers, of the final product.

E. The rating accruing from contribution to national income effect is obtained by the following schedule:

Schedule 1

National Income Effect (percent)	Accrued Rating* (points)
Above 300	5
251–300	4
201–250	3
151–200	2
101–150	1
100 and below	0

*Except for firms producing intermediate products which are credited a minimum 3-point rating.

II. BALANCE-OF-PAYMENTS EFFECT

A. The balance of payments effect is measured by the ratio of the net foreign exchange earned and saved to the amount of scarce resources utilized during the period and is expressed by the following equation:

$$B = (F_n/I_t) \times 100\%$$

where: B = balance-of-payments effect, percent.

F_n = net foreign exchange earned and saved, pesos.

I_t = amount of scarce resources utilized in production, pesos.

B. The net foreign exchange earned and saved is determined by subtracting the foreign exchange costs of production from the foreign exchange value of the product.

C. The foreign exchange costs consist of the foreign exchange utilized in production [I (C) (3) above] plus the current amortization of imported fixed assets. Generally, land, furniture, and buildings are considered domestic fixed assets; and all the rest, imported fixed assets.

D. The foreign exchange value is determined by:
  1. earnings—foreign exchange received for payment of exports; and
  2. savings—in the case of import substitute, the foreign exchange cost of the product if it were imported (CIF value of the product shall be used). A product shall be considered as an import substitute if it is an essential commodity or its manufacture began subsequent to the imposition of exchange control (December 9, 1949) and it displaces products imported prior to the import control.

E. The rating accruing from the strengthening of the balance of payments position of the country is given by the following schedule:

Schedule 2

Balance of Payments Effect (percent)	Accrued Rating (points)
Above 200	5
166–200	4
131–165	3
96–130	2
61– 95	1
60 and below	0

III. PRODUCT ESSENTIALITY
  A. Products are first classified according to (1) export products and (2) products for domestic consumption.
  B. Export products are further classified according to the degree of processing they have undergone as:
    1. manufactured products,
    2. semimanufactured products,
    3. raw materials.
  C. Products for domestic consumption are further classified into:
    1. highly essential products,
    2. essential producer products,
    3. essential consumer products,
    4. nonessential producer products, and
    5. nonessential consumer products.

The Central Bank Commodity Classification shall be used as the primary basis of classifying products for domestic consumption. For this purpose, the unclassified items in the Central Bank Commodity Classification shall be reclassified. The criteria to be used in the reclassification shall be "utility" of the product.

D.   The corresponding rating accruing from the essentiality of the product is determined by the following schedule:

Schedule 3

Products for Domestic Use	Export Products	Category	Accrued Rating (points)
Highly essential	Manufactured	I	5
Essential producer		II	4
Essential consumer	Semimanufactured	III	3
Nonessential producer		IV	2
Nonessential consumer	Raw materials	V	1

IV.   SCHEDULE OF ALLOWABLE REMITTANCES

A.   A straight 40 percent of the nonresident's share in the net profits shall be allowed to be remitted by the following firms:

1.   firms operating under a government franchise wherein the output is of the character of a public service; and

2.   banks and insurance companies.

B.   Beginning with profits realized for financial years ending in 1958, all other companies are allowed to remit dividends or profits to their nonresident stockholders or head offices abroad according to the following schedule of allowable annual remittances:

Schedule 4

Social Productivity Rating (SPR)	Allowable Remittances (whichever is lower)	
	Percent of the Nonresident's Share in Current Net Profit	Percent of Foreign Capital Invested*
13–15	100	60
10–12	80	50
7– 9	60	40
4– 6	40	30
1– 3	25	20

*As of the beginning of the period for which the profit is realized.

The Social Productivity Rating of a firm is the sum of the ratings accruing from the national income effect, balance-of-payments effect, and product essentiality. For non-Philippine companies, the depreciated or net book value of capital assets as at the beginning of the fiscal year for which the profit is realized will be used instead of capital invested.

C.   Withholding taxes on dividends are to be deducted from the remittable amounts as determined.

APPENDIX 3

THE IMPACT OF FOREIGN INVESTMENT IN MEXICO[1]

The Measurable Effects of United States Direct Investment on Mexico's Balance of Payments

No reliable estimate can be made about the collective effects of all foreign investment on Mexico's balance-of-payments since the necessary information is available only on U.S. direct investments. However, it is estimated that U.S. direct investments bolstered the balance-of-payments position of Mexico during 1965–68 by an annual average of about $1,552 million. U.S. manufacturing investments provided balance of payments support averaging $1,140 million per year, or almost three fourths of the total support by all U.S. direct investments. Investments by mining and smelting companies and by petroleum companies provided annual balance-of-payments support of $191 million and $13 million, respectively. The annual support provided by all other U.S. investments together averaged about $208 million.

Exports by all U.S. affiliates aggregated about $446 million in 1966. Moreover, the gross import savings derived from part of the domestic sales by U.S. affiliates that year amounted to about $1,305 million. The combined export earnings and gross import savings of the affiliates are therefore estimated at $1,751 million. However, they imported goods and services worth about $190 million to help fulfill their production requirements. Accordingly, the combined export earnings and net import savings of all U.S. affiliates amounted to about $1,561 million in 1966—a year that is assumed here to represent the average annual operational results of the affiliates for the four-year period, 1965–68.

Net new U.S. direct investment in Mexico averaged $106 million during 1965–68. Addition of the amount to the net annual balance-of-payments support provided by the affiliates through their export earnings

---

[1] Extracted from *Impact of Foreign Investment in Mexico* (New York: Council of the Americas, n.d.).

and net import savings resulted in gross balance of payments support averaging $1,667 million per year. The earnings derived by U.S. investors averaged $115 million. It is therefore estimated that the *net* support provided by all U.S. investments to the balance-of-payments of Mexico during 1965–68 averaged $1,552 million annually.

The importance of U.S. investments to Mexico's balance-of-payments may be evaluated in part by the following:

Total exports from Mexico averaged $1,180 million per year during 1965–68. Exports by U.S. affiliates amounted to about $446 million in 1966, or 37.8 percent of the average annual total.

Total imports by Mexico averaged $1,718 million per year during the same period. The additional imports necessary to meet the production needs of domestically owned enterprises and the consumption needs of the Mexican people would have averaged about $1,115 million annually—64.9 percent in excess of actual imports—if U.S. affiliates had not provided import substitutions of that amount. (The gross import savings provided by U.S. affiliates, about $1,305 million, were offset by imports of about $190 million that they effected for their own production purposes.)

Other Effects of U.S. Direct Investment

Taxes. Total tax payments to the government of Mexico by all U.S. affiliates are estimated to have amounted to 2,288 million pesos in 1966. This was 11.8 percent of the government's total tax revenues, as compared with 16.9 percent in 1957. Tax payments by the U.S. manufacturing affiliates alone amounted to 1,175 million pesos in 1966.

Employment. The estimated employment in 1966 by the U.S. manufacturing, mining and smelting, and petroleum affiliates was 104,430 people, only 685 of whom (less than 0.7 percent) were U.S. employees. The total managerial staffs numbered 1,072 people, of whom 432 (40.3 percent) were U.S. employees. The total number of technical and professional employees was 7,876, of whom 253 (3.3 percent) were U.S. employees. All the other 95,482 employees were Mexicans.

Technological and Other Effects

We have concentrated in this study on the measurable economic effects of foreign investments primarily because those effects have been important to the people of Mexico and because reliable information is available with regard to them. However, we do not wish to imply an exclusive interest in quantitative measurements or in economic or material values. Foreign investments have had important social, cultural, psychological, and political consequences. Each deserves extensive and intensive analysis by competent and dispassionate professionals in those fields, but interested as we are in these matters, we cannot claim to be such professionals. Moreover, even with regard to the "strictly economic" effects of foreign investment, it must be acknowledged that many of those effects simply cannot be demonstrated other than quantitatively, or cannot be demonstrated at all.

It is, for example, particularly difficult to *demonstrate* (rather than merely to assert or to deny) the extent to which foreign investment has been a significant medium for the transfer to Mexico of important technological and managerial expertise. Many individual examples of the effective transfer of such expertise can be cited,[2] but it is ordinarily very difficult or impossible to evaluate the full economic consequences of the separate examples. Moreover, we know of no way to determine and to evaluate the economic consequences of all, or even of most, of the infinite number of transfers of knowledge that may in fact have taken place. Nevertheless, we shall list below some of the innovations that have reportedly been introduced into Mexico by various foreign investors:

Polyester and its applications, ester gums (hydrogenated) for chewing gum, acrylic resins and their applications, chain-stopped alkyd resins, thermo-setting resins, thermo-plastic resins, chloro-benzenes, ammonium chloride, disc plows, pull-type planters and rotary cutters, commercial credit reporting, handling methods in explosives production, wire-connection techniques, aircraft loading and unloading equipment, nonferrous smelting and refining processes, automatic radiator shutters, automotive heaters, activated carbon manufacture processes, trisodium phosphate anhydrous, water repellant tube greases, low temperature soldering fluxes, cheese, butter and margarine color, aerosol cans, pull tabs for cans, powered iron cores, ferrites, grinding mills, wet milling techniques, tools and fixtures in vehicle assembly, concrete improvement techniques, coated abrasives, direct selling methods, fibre molds for round concrete columns, data processing input equipment, offset composition equipment, plastic binding methods, laminating machines, automotive wire harness, automotive and truck transmissions, forging steel, mass gear cutting, spline rolling, continuous automatically controlled heat treating, tool making, cutter grinding, gear shaving, gear honing, aspirin crystalization process, selection herbicides.

---

[2] Reference can be made, for example, to the book, *Putting Down Roots,* by Richard W. Hall, published for and by the Celanese Corporation, New York, 1969.

Anco Inc. (A)*

"ALTHOUGH IT WAS HARDLY TOTALLY UNEXPECTED," John Baker, president of Anco, Inc., commented, "President Johnson's voluntary controls on foreign investment, established early in 1965, did lead to some major changes in our company. We have over 40 major overseas operations, and we have been investing anywhere from $70 to $220 million per year net in these in the past five years. From our stockholders' standpoint, this investment has certainly been well justified—we earn more on our net equity abroad than we do here in the United States. We have not been remitting many of our foreign profits because of investment requirements abroad, but the asset position and earning power of the company is steadily being enhanced as a result of these investments.

"When we first began to move abroad in a major way in 1958, about the only official U.S. government reaction we could get was that it was a good thing. The world was short of dollars, and any outflow of them by major American corporations was highly favored.

"Over the years, our finance people got in the habit of thinking that where the funds came from made absolutely no difference. We did have problems abroad at times, say in terms of getting our pesos converted to pounds for English investment, but the dollar really was as good as gold.

"Then after 1960, the American dollar began to get into balance-of-payment difficulties," Mr. Baker went on, "And a few foreigners got

---

*This case was written by Richard N. Farmer, professor, Graduate School of Business, Indiana University. Copyright is retained by the author.

nervous. Those gold losses have been widely publicized. Of course our people kept an eye on things, which is why Johnson's move was not so totally unexpected. We don't like it, and we've argued hard against such capital controls, but of course we're going along. A 'voluntary' government program for a billion dollar company like ours is as demanding as if the Congress passed six laws about the subject. Now we have to submit our internal quarterly balance of payments for the company, showing how we're being good boys by not using too much foreign exchange. Incidentally, we've had to reorganize some of our internal reporting systems quite extensively to get the kind of currency information we now need to report. We have to show dollar uses and receipts overseas, as well as the usual kinds of data.

"Since a company like ours can't just stop projects in the middle of them, we've been forced to European capital markets for new money to finance projects also. This has been expensive—for example, we could have floated a $30.5 million bond issue in the United States at 5.5 percent in 1965 for one European project. Instead, we floated a dollar bond issue for that amount in Brussels at 7.9 percent. A few stockholders promptly sued the corporation, arguing that as long as the capital-export control was voluntary, we had no right to borrow money at higher rates when we would have got it at lower rates. But at least we did get the funds, and the capital projects in Europe went forward.

"The internal result of these capital controls has been to force us to rethink our entire capital-funds-controls system. Now we must consider the kinds of currency we have, including dollars. A new dimension has been added to our financial controls, and I don't mind saying that we feel it is a wrong and unnecessary step for our government to take."

1. If you were head of a major corporation like Anco, and such a voluntary capital-export restriction program were put into effect, would you follow the program, even if you were not required to by law? Why or why not? What obligations does a multinational corporation have here?

2. If you were a stockholder of Anco, would you have sued the corporation for floating a bond issue in a higher interest rate market, as Anco did here? Why or why not?

3. How would this sort of capital-export control affect the internal financial controls within a corporation? Give several examples of new controls the company would have to have.

4. If Anco competed with several major European companies not subject to such controls, what sort of competitive disadvantages might they face here? Why?

Anco Inc. (B)*

ANCO INC., HAS A SMALL MANUFACTURING PLANT in X (a Mediterranean country). For several years, it has operated at capacity, and backlogs of orders have on occasion been cause for serious concern by Anco's top management. But when asked why Anco did not expand the plant further, John Baker, their president, replied as follows (off the record):

"We are of course aware that our plant is too small—it just goes to show how wrong you can be about markets. When we planned the firm back in 1961, we felt that we could sell perhaps 6,000 units a year in the country, plus about 2,000 units for export to nearby countries. Now we're up to 12,000 units for domestic consumption, plus 4,500 for export. The plant runs 24 hours a day, 6 days a week. Even so, we often have backlogs of orders up to six months.

"We've decided for the moment not to expand the operation in X. Oh, we have the cash and the skilled labor, and as a matter of fact, the plant is too small for really efficient operation. If we doubled the size, we could cut our manufacturing costs by 40 percent, and we could really reduce prices. We could get much more efficient utilization from our staff specialists also, and we could reorganize the work force to be much more productive. But consider our problem. X is a highly sensitive country now, in terms of American investment. Several of our competitors have been refused permission to build plants there by the governments. The newspapers are full of talk about the new American imperialism, how we're smashing the local culture, and what not. We pay

* This case was written by Richard N. Farmer, professor, Graduate School of Business, Indiana University. Copyright is retained by the author.

about 30 percent more than local firms do for the same kinds of work, but we still are considered exploiters and imperialists.

"We are competing locally with four small, family-owned enterprises. Those families, incidentally, are among the wealthiest and most influential in the country. One of them owns a chain of newspapers that has been blasting us as tools of imperialism. But their plants are really hopeless. They only produce about 800 units a year at a maximum, and their costs are at least 25 percent above what ours are now. We price domestically so as to avoid driving them out of business, and the local economy pays the bills.

"Management in these operations is a joke—they don't have cost controls, any kind of planning, personnel practices, or anything. The families keep five sets of books, and one result is that no one knows anything about costs. In the United States, they would be out of business in six months because of competition. They squeeze their labor unmercifully—they pay well under us, and they violate the law by not providing such required amenities as restrooms and cafeterias. But they are local companies, and the pride in them is very strong. The families are careful to keep fanning the nationalist fervor, and if we tried to run them out of business, we would really be in trouble. Everybody is always talking about buying from the local companies, to be patriotic, and all that.

"The funny thing about it is that we have big order backlogs, while the local companies have to scurry around for orders. Their product has some critical quality problems, and our quality control is by far superior to anything they can offer. In fact, we deliberately try to price our product about 10 percent above theirs—and we still get a backlog of orders. Everyone talks about buying local, but when the chips are down, they come to us. We also have an after-sales-service network and servicing system in the country which is quite good, and customers know they can count on us for parts and after-sales service. When a local machine breaks, you're out of luck—the family firms have no after-sales-service organization at all. You can't even find a spare part usually.

"Already there is talk about passing a law restricting us to some fixed share of the market. Another law being suggested is to localize us by making us take a local partner, or even selling all our stock to citizens. One of these laws even got through a first reading in parliament, but it was killed before it became law—at least for now.

"Of course the local firms can't export—the product is too shoddy to sell well, even at low prices. This is about the only ace we hold. X is short of foreign exchange, and we have been consistently a good foreign exchange earner for the country. We could probably double export sales if we had the production capacity.

"What can we do in this case? We have the organization, manpower, and management to really expand, but if we do, we create a hornet's nest of local resentment about our operations."

1. Advise John Baker about his strategy here. Do you agree with his conclusions? Why or why not?
2. What alternatives might be followed by Anco in this case?
3. If you were responsible for forming public policy in X, and if you were interested in getting maximum efficiency and income for your country, what would you suggest in this case as useful legislation? Why?

GLOBAL STRATEGY

National Model Company*

THE NATIONAL MODEL COMPANY is a small company catering to serious hobbyists in the model railroad and slot-track racing fields. Until 1963 the company focused entirely on model railroad equipment, including such items as locomotives, freight and passenger cars, track, and electrical equipment. The firm has been in HO gauge since the 1930s. This scale ($1/87$th of full size) is the one used by the majority of serious adult hobbyists. After 1955 National also manufactured complete train sets to be sold to youngsters during the Christmas season. As larger trains declined in popularity, this sideline blossomed into an important part of National's business.

Slot-car racing began to boom in a major way in the United States in 1963, and National was one of the first American firms to enter this industry. As slot-car sales boomed, train-set sales fell sharply, and by 1967 slot cars represented over 60.5 percent of National's total volume. Train-set sales comprised 18.5 percent of the firm's gross sales in 1967, with sales of various model railroad components to hobbyists making up the remainder.

Sales at National have stagnated in recent years. Table 1 indicates the trend. The basic reason has been import competition. Starting in the mid-1950s, various Japanese firms began to ship model railroad equipment to the United States. American importing companies typically handle marketing of these items, usually with considerable skill. For example, all full-size Japanese railroad equipment is quite different than American, and prototypes of such equipment would sell very poorly in

---

*This case was written by Richard N. Farmer, professor, Graduate School of Business, Indiana University. Copyright retained by the author.

TABLE 1
National Model Company

	Gross Sales (thousands)			
	1964	*1965*	*1966*	*1967*
Slot cars	$424.2	$ 622.7	$ 813.6	$ 755.3
Train sets	348.5	211.5	101.5	85.5
Railroad hobby equipment . . .	215.7	212.2	211.8	215.6
Totals	$988.4	$1,046.4	$1,126.9	$1,056.4
Net profit	$100.6	$ 101.3	$ 84.4	$ 61.5

the United States. The importers arrange for Japanese firms to manufacture American prototypes of the most popular American equipment and market it efficiently through hobby shops and by mail. The Japanese models are typically handcrafted in brass, while American manufacturers, including National, stick to labor-saving methods such as high pressure injection-molded die castings. Steam locomotives are most popular among hobbyists, accounting for over 55.6 percent of total dollar sales of hobbyist railroad models.

The Japanese were not serious competitors in either the toy-train market or slot racing. The Japanese models typically sold for much higher prices than the toys. Thus a complete slot-racing set retailed for as little as $15.95 in 1967, and a complete train set for $12.95. A single Japanese locomotive (depending on size and prototype) retailed for $19.95 to $95.95, with some special models selling for as much as $195.95. About $10.2 million worth of such models (wholesale prices) were imported in 1965 (see Table 2). Japanese prices were rising at over 10 percent per year as labor costs soared in Japan. Profit margins were about 40 percent on these items in 1966.

TABLE 2
U.S. Imports of Japanese Model
Railroad Hobbyist Equipment
(millions of dollars)

1964	$ 9.3
1965	10.2
1966	11.5
1967	14.8

National's management had been seriously concerned over import competition for some years, and it had debated how it might best meet the threat. The possibilities, in their simplest form, were as follows:

1. Attempt to get tariffs raised. Protective tariffs on models had already been raised from 20 percent ad valorem to 30 percent ad valorem in 1963, but this increase had no significant effect on imports from Japan. Serious hobbyists apparently preferred Japanese equipment to American, even at higher prices. Typically the Japanese imports were of extremely high quality, particularly in attention to small details. Since these details necessarily had to be applied by hand, American labor costs (about four times the Japanese) precluded their application in American plants. Small lots of production (a typical model locomotive of one type sold perhaps 2,000 to 5,000 units in the United States) prevented any serious thoughts of mechanization or automation here.

Hobbyists in this field tended to be upper-middle-income-group individuals with very strong preferences for fidelity to detail in their equipment. They preferred to buy fewer more expensive items of high quality than more cheaper items. No American firm had yet succeeded in manufacturing locomotives which had more sales appeal than the Japanese imports—although a number had tried, including National. American locomotive kits sold from $7.95 to $49.95, depending on their type.

2. Establish a factory in Japan, or more logically, arrange a marketing deal with an existing Japanese company, and market the imports through National's American marketing system. The major difficulty here was the extreme shortage of firms in Japan available for this sort of work. Earlier American importers had helped build up four major Japanese suppliers, who now had taken a decade to accumulate skills, and no other similar firms were known to exist. Moreover, the Japanese industrial boom had made life very difficult even for existing Japanese producers. They complained that as soon as they trained a good worker, at considerable cost, a mass production electronics or TV manufacturer in Japan would lure the girls away at higher wages. This was the main reason why prices were rising so fast in Japan.

Formation of a Japanese company was impossible under Japanese law, as at least half of the company had to be Japanese owned. National knew of no Japanese firm which might be interested in this type of arrangement, and a capital investment of at least $800,000 would be required. National had $425,000 in cash in 1967, plus a credit line of $400,000.

3. Establish or help support a local firm in another low-wage, relatively high-skill country. Hong Kong was one possibility; Yugoslavia was another. Some imports of model equipment came from both countries. Again, capital costs would be high in Hong Kong, particularly in terms of training available workers. It would cost at least $600,000, and results were uncertain. The major problem here would be consumer acceptance of the product. American hobbyists are a notoriously finicky lot, and even after expenditures were made, it would not be certain

that the product would sell. If product acceptance were assured, it would be a profitable business, since sales in the hobbyist sector of this market had been very stable (and rising slightly) in recent years.

Yugoslavia, as a somewhat liberal communist country, seemed a much poorer bet, but it did offer a second choice. A state-owned Yugoslavian firm had already indicated some interest in working out a marketing arrangement, and samples of its work showed high skill at low prices. Recent currency devaluation in the country had made prices very competitive in 1967. Marketing investment here would be about $350,000.

4. Concentrate on slot cars and train sets for the low price market. This was a highly competitive field, with many American and European firms trying to gain market share. Prices were unstable, and slot-car racing in particular was quite faddish, in that sales showed signs of fluctuating erratically. No one could predict for sure whether this market would boom or collapse in the future.

5. Move into other toy lines. Again this market was highly competitive and unstable. A good item might make a firm rich overnight; a poor line in one year could quickly lead to bankruptcy. National had always avoided this line in the past, relying instead on the more stable hobby line. Several hobby-oriented firms which had turned in a major way to toys had gone broke in the period 1959–65 as fickle markets collapsed, leaving firms with overloaded inventories and low sales. National was beginning to acquire some marketing experience in this field with its slot cars, but it still felt it had much to learn.

A final point in this whole field is that patents and copyrights are of very little use to any firm. Small production runs and little investment in manufacturing facilities, combined with hundreds of firms in the industry, mean that any item of interest is quickly copied by other firms, whether or not it is patented. Attempts to sue 50 patent violators are useless in an industry where an item will surge to popularity and decline to nothing before the first patent infringement suit gets to a lower court. Also, many popular items are very old and unpatentable. The Lionel Corporation marketed slot cars as early as 1912.

1. What would you advise National's management to do in this situation? Why?
2. Lay out a five-year plan of action for National, including contingency plans, for their product line and manufacturing locations.

Dorcas International Corporation[*]

DORCAS INTERNATIONAL manufactured a line of electric razors and over the years had built a significant market position in most of the more developed countries. There had been recent signs, however, that the electric razor market had matured to a point where competition on price, and therefore cost, would be the outstanding characteristic of the industry over the next half dozen years. Recognizing the changed situation, Jorg Moroney, the Dorcas president, had established a central management services group to look into the question of concentrating further expansion of production into a smaller number of sites in order to gain greater scale economies.

In setting up this group, however, Moroney indicated that he did not intend to dispense with a policy of holding operating units to profit achievement. While profit achievement had always been applied quite loosely, each manufacturing unit had been free to set its own price for its local markets and for supply to other marketing units.

The task of proposing a plan for future plant expansion fell to Stephan Morse as head of the new management services group. He decided that the first essential in preparing his recommendations was to collect basic cost and revenue data for the Dorcas International system. This he did, and as he considered the current situation irrelevant to the problem, he projected market growth, alternative price-sales figures and cost estimates for four years ahead in current dollars. These are summarised

---

* This case was prepared by Kenneth Simmonds, professor, London Graduate School of Business Studies.

© 1972 by Kenneth Simmonds.

TABLE 1
Summary of Cost and Revenue Data for Dorcas International System

| | Unit | General | \multicolumn{6}{c}{Country} |
			A	B	C	D	E	F
1. Annual sales volume in 4 years' time for alternative average prices to wholesale	'000 units							
$9.00			50	150	250	80	250	50
8.50			55	160	320	120	300	60
8.00			60	180	340	160	350	70
7.50			65	210	370	190	500	80
7.00			75	250	400	200	600	100
2. Variable cost of local marketing, selling, and distribution per average unit	$		.50	.60	.40	.40	.20	.50
3. Corporation tax rate	%		30	50	40	20	50	40
4. Customs tariff on imports based on transfer price	%		40	60	25	25	10	25
5. Transport costs per unit of transfers								
Among A, B, C, F	$	.10						
Between D and others	$	.20						
Between E and others	$	.20						
Existing production capacity								
6. Volume limit	'000 units			400	300		400	
7. Fixed production cost per annum (including interest and depreciation)	$'000			800	1,100		1,200	
8. Variable production cost per average unit	$			3.00	2.00		2.00	
Additional production capacity								
9. Fixed production cost for plant with annual volume								
200,000 units	$'000	800						
300,000 units	$'000	1100						
400,000 units	$'000	1350						
500,000 units	$'000	1500						
10. Variable production cost per average unit from new plant	$		1.50	2.00	1.80	1.80	1.50	1.80

in Table 1. All this involved many simplifications, but Morse felt they would not materially affect a decision. For example:

1. Export duties and rebates were ignored as immaterial.
2. Any new capacity would take about two years to build and cost variations among alternative sites were unpredictable.
3. About 30 percent of fixed production cost was represented by depreciation in the first year (15 percent of plant cost). As depreciation reduced, it would be more or less offset by increased repair cost. The three existing plants could continue production at the indicated figures indefinitely. Plants would have little scrap value.
4. Tax rates applied to nonremitted funds only, but as Dorcas had large borrowings in each country no profit remittances were envisaged in the foreseeable future.

The next task seemed to be to calculate some sort of approximation to an optimum and then to mold this into reasonable management recommendations.

Rediplant[*]

EARLY IN 1971 John Bryant, owner and chairman of a successful English timber-products firm, was asked by his close friend Martin Nievelt whether he would consider becoming a commisar of Rediplant N.V.—a company being formed to exploit the new Rediplant method for packaging bulbs. Commisars of Dutch corporations are outside directors appointed by the shareholders to oversee the employee directors. They have a number of specific powers and their consent must be obtained for all borrowing by the company. Nievelt also wanted Bryant's opinion on the number of sealing machines that should be purchased in advance of the first full season of Rediplant sales. This was a particularly difficult decision as there was little guide to the volume of sales that could be expected and most of the packaging would have to be carried out during the month of August.

Martin Nievelt and Walter Praag were owners and joint managing directors of Hans Praag & Company, an old established Dutch bulb exporter based on Hillegom, Holland. Before the Rediplant development Praag had concentrated on bulb sales to France, United Kingdom, Switzerland and Germany, selling to nurserymen, wholesalers, and large retailers, as well as directly to the public through mail-order catalogs. There were two seasons each year. The larger was for spring bulbs which were lifted from the bulb fields and distributed in the autumn for planting up to mid-winter. This season represented 70 percent of the bulb market and covered tulips, crocuses, narcissi, and hyacinths.

---

* This case was prepared by Kenneth Simmonds, professor, London Graduate School of Business Studies, with the cooperation of Rediplant management.

© 1971 by Kenneth Simmonds.

Performance of many firms in the bulb business had been poor and there had been numerous failures over the previous two years. There were some 600 exporting houses and although they belonged to an industry association and argued the need to hold price levels, competition amongst them resulted in continual margin cutting. Praag had recorded losses both years mainly because of low response to their mail-order catalogs attributed by Nievelt to cold, wet weekends discouraging customers from thinking about gardening. While substantial profits could still be made in a good mail-order season the response rates had been dropping at an average rate of 8 percent per year and increased order size had not grown in step. The development of the Rediplant system therefore came at a particularly opportune time and gave Praag an opportunity to differentiate its product and increase its margins. Praag decided to withdraw from the direct mail-order side of the business and concentrate on building the broadest possible sales of Rediplant packed bulbs. Sale of the mail-order lists, moreover, would provide finance for the new effort and avoid surrender of ownership interest which was usually required in order to obtain long-term bank lending for small private companies.

The French, German, and Swiss mailing lists were sold to Beinum & Company late in 1970. Beinum was the largest Dutch bulb merchant, with a turnover of around 50 million guilders (Fl 50m.)[1] and a mailing list of five million catalogs. Praag's United Kingdom mail-order list and the United Kingdom wholesale business was sold to Sutcliffe Seeds Ltd. of Norwich. Sutcliffe were moving into the bulb market as an extension from their traditional seed activities and the agreement provided for Praag to supply all Sutcliffe's requirements for Dutch bulbs whilst retaining the right to go directly to a selected list of retail chains and large stores in the United Kingdom.

Development of the Rediplant System

The idea for Rediplant was first conceived in November 1969 by Praag, who concentrated on the engineering and production side of the business leaving the commercial side to Nievelt. Rediplant was basically a transparent plastic strip molded to hold bulbs in equally spaced blisters open at the top and bottom. It was designed as a usage container that could be planted directly in the soil without removing the bulbs, giving them protection from frost, birds, rodents, and slugs, and enabling the bulbs to be easily retrieved for planting in subsequent seasons.

Praag explained the development in this way: "I got the idea at

---

[1] The standard abbreviation for a Dutch guilder, or florin, is Fl. Exchange rates in January 1971 were: $1 (US) = Fl 3.60; £1 (Stg) = Fl 8.60; 1 deutsche mark = Fl 1.00.

the end of 1969 and aimed only to make our competitive position easier and to solve planting problems for the buyer. We ran trials and found that it made not only for easier planting but also gave protection and a better flower, though it was not invented for that purpose. We tested a great quantity with a sensitive control test and the packaged bulbs showed up better than bulbs planted by hand. We limited our tests to hyacinths, tulips, narcissi, crocuses, and gladioli because the others have extra difficulties for packaging and these are the main selling items. With gladioli we had some trouble, and I had to redesign the pack as the sprouts came out of the side of the bulb rather than the top. We make our own prototype wooden molds and have our own cabinet-maker for this. When we told people the name of our new pack was Rediplant, many remarked that it was not a very good name—but minutes later they would all use the name without any prompting. We decided it must be a very good name."

The bulbs were packed automatically into previously formed plastic strips which were then sealed and fitted into a cardboard sleeve printed with details of the bulbs and planting instructions. After considerable experimentation the new pack was ready for launching and in May 1970 a vacuum-forming machine was purchased to make quantities of the strips. At this stage the pack was comparatively crude with a single-colored cardboard sleeve which totally enclosed the plastic strip, which was in turn stapled together to hold the bulbs.

Nievelt did his own market research by asking friends, acquaintances, and the general public what they thought of the packs, and if they would buy them. On his frequent sales trips to England, for example, he asked customers in garden centers and large stores he visited whether they would buy the packs and they all said they would. The packs contained six tulips with a suggested retail price of 32½p as against a price of 25p for similar loose bulbs. Nievelt also asked retailers in England what they thought of the packaging. He recalled, "Large retail chains, Woolworths, Boots, Debenhams, and John Lewis liked it, and after a while the larger garden centers would say that they would buy it. Small centers and garden stores, however, generally said they did not like Rediplant. They gave few reasons, but they seemed worried that it would mean other types of stores would find it easier to sell bulbs." Nievelt also persuaded three different outlets to test market the strips—a store on a U.S. air force base at Woodbridge, a seed shop in Ipswich, and a garden center at Ramsey, Essex. Each received one hundred strips, without charge, and each quickly sold the entire assignment at 32½p.

Rediplant packaging was next featured in Praag mail order catalogues for spring bulbs sent out in autumn 1970. These were mailed to some 300,000 customers in England, France, and Germany at a cost, including postage, of £.05 each. Prices for a Rediplant package of six bulbs were set about 30 percent below the catalog prices for a standard quantity of 10 loose bulbs, making the price for a Rediplant bulb 15 percent higher than an equivalent loose bulb. Rediplant packaging featured on the cover and the catalog started with a two-page spread outlining the Rediplant system and offering a 200 percent guarantee to replace every nonflowering Rediplant bulb with two new bulbs. The spread also showed how Rediplant strips could be planted in evenly spaced rows or in cartwheel or zigzag patterns. Walter Praag commented that this sort of thing seemed to appeal particularly to the Germans, who were also much more concerned with rodent and insect damage than other nationalities. He thought the British tended to be keener gardeners and more knowledgeable about bulbs, while many more potential customers in France and Germany would avoid buying loose bulbs that they did not understand or else buy some and plant them upside down. With Rediplant packages these customers would find it much easier. Praag experience had been, too, that the British tended to be much more price conscious than the others, while the French tended to identify value with the price charged.

As orders began to come in during the early winter months, Praag was very encouraged by the high proportion of Rediplant sales. Final figures were as follows:

Country	Catalogs Posted	No. of Orders Received	Average Order Size	% of Total Ordered in Rediplant Packs		
				Tulips	Hyacinths	Narcissi
United Kingdom.	150,000	8,056	£3.50	18	20	10
France	101,000	5,581	£5.20	27	32	13
Germany.	50,000	2,091	£5.45	44	39	39

Examination of 160 United Kingdom orders at random showed the average order for Rediplant to be £2, representing an average 50 percent of the customer's total order.

Walter Praag continued work on the Rediplant design and at this stage employed a local firm of two young design consultants with excellent reputations in the textile and packaging markets. The cardboard sleeve was redesigned with full color pictures of the blooms and better instructions, and the strips were made narrower and extended to include seven bulbs rather than six in a new pack measuring 40 centimeters. Nievelt thought this might discourage price comparison with loose bulbs sold in dozens. These new strips can be seen on the display stand in Table 1.

TABLE 1

Assortment 180 s

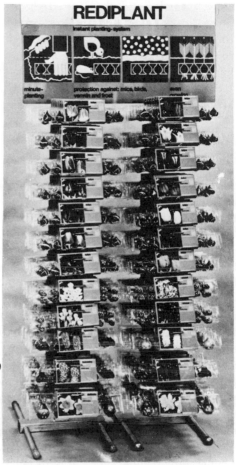

An exclusive new pre-assembled Assortment for You!

112 packs of tulips in 14 varieties 7 bulbs per pack
 24 packs of hyacinths in 4 varieties 5 bulbs per pack
 12 packs of narcissi in 2 varieties 5 bulbs per pack
 32 packs of crocus in 4 varieties 14 bulbs per pack
―――
180 packs in 24 well-chosen varieties

Floor space: 15" x 33"
Height display: 63"
Size display poster: 31½" x 18½"
Weight case: 59 lbs.

This display offers an easy and fast set-up with a minimum of floor space

Advantages:
REDIPLANT is unique (patent pending)
Honest presentation in see-through packs
Optimal ventilation preserves the quality of the bulbs
Packs are delivered on pegs, saving labour in setting up display (except assortment 180 and 90)
REDIPLANT has been successfully tested
Over a century of successful bulb-growing experience guarantees a high quality product
Your Department as well as the Dutch Dept. of Agriculture inspects all bulbs before they are exported

For sale through retail outlets special units of 90 and 180 strips were designed with wire pegs for each six strips. These pegs could be fitted onto pegboards or specially designed Rediplant display stands for floor or counter displays. The mix of varieties for the units was based on a statistical analysis of the historical proportions of bulbs sales and would not be varied for individual orders. The "180" unit contained 112 strips of tulips in 14 varieties, 24 strips of hyacinths in 4 varieties, 12 strips of narcissi in 2 varieties, and 32 strips of crocuses in 4 varieties. Large display posters illustrating the planting of Rediplant strips were designed to accompany each unit which would be boxed with or without a display stand as required.

Patents for the Rediplant system of packaging were applied for and obtained in the Benelux countries, the United Kingdom, France, Germany, Canada, and the United States. This patent was granted for a "usage" package and competitors would find it difficult to break through simply by altering the design. Moreover, anyone wishing to compete would find it essential on a cost basis to package in Holland rather than to ship, pack, and then redirect the bulbs—and Praag was sure that it would be advised by the Dutch customs if its patent was infringed.

Partnership with Van Diemen Bros.

In early 1970 when the new designs were being developed Praag was approached by Van Diemen Bros. who had seen the packages and wanted to explore ways by which they too could use the new packaging method. Discussions led to the idea of a partnership for developing the system. Van Diemen had the largest sales force in the Dutch bulb industry, owned their own bulb fields and research laboratories, and were suppliers by appointment to the Netherlands royal family. "The idea went against the mentality of the industry that it is not right to work together," said Martin Nievelt. "We had the idea but the other firm had 40 sales people against Praags' two, as well as contacts with wholesalers all round the world. A partnership would provide resources and backing at the same time as it removed one of the major sources of potential competition. Another reason was that the product had to be kept secret while patents were applied for and Van Diemen was one of the few companies with its own laboratories." Nievelt believed that the fragmented nature of the industry and the lack of product differentiation were the prime causes of low prices and small or nonexistent profits, and he hoped that the combined strength of the two firms would enable them to make a much larger impact on the bulb market and eventually claim a significant proportion of Dutch bulb sales at higher margins.

The arrangement worked out on a friendly basis with Van Diemen was that Rediplant N.V. would be formed as a limited company with Hans Praag & Co. and Van Diemen Bros. each owning 50 percent of the equity. Rediplant would lease Praag's storage and packing facilities in Hillegom and manufacture for the two sales companies, invoicing them at cost after payment of a royalty to Praag of Fl .02 per strip. Praag would retain the right to all sales anywhere in the world destined for customers via mail order and also to wholesale sales in the United Kingdom, Holland, and Switzerland. Van Diemen would cover wholesale sales in all remaining countries. This arrangement meant that there would be little change from past concentration because Praag had had very little wholesale revenue from France or Germany. The direct mail market, moreover, accounted for some 20 percent of Dutch bulb exports for dry sales. Martin Nievelt and the senior Van Diemen agreed to act as commisars for the new firm and to ask John Bryant to act as a third neutral commisar. Solicitors were asked to draw up formal agreements and as at the end of February 1971 the drafts had not yet been received.

Meanwhile, Walter Praag and Dik Van Diemen, son of the Van Diemen president, had agreed to become joint managing directors of Rediplant and had become immersed in detailed planning of the production requirements for the 1971 spring bulb season. The elder Van Diemen had also applied to the Dutch government for a grant to develop the invention—on the basis of its potential contribution to Dutch exports— and Rediplant had received a nonreturnable grant of 65,000 guilders.

Meeting the Demand

The period for selling spring bulbs to intermediate outlets ran from January through August, but delivery requirements would be very tight. Excluding mail-order business, 55 percent of all sales must be packed by August 17, the next 30 by the end of August, and the last 15 percent by the end of September. All United States sales were included in the initial 55 percent because of the need to meet shipping dates but another week could be saved by air freight, although it would increase the freight cost for a standard shipment from $6 per "180" unit to $18. After September, mail-order business could then be supplied fairly evenly until early December. Delivery commitments were regarded as very important by all the Rediplant executives. The retail buying season was concentrated, and a supplier who failed to meet his commitments would ruin his chance of repeat business. Nievelt considered it would be better to take a limited amount of Rediplant orders in the first season rather than run the risk of not being able to meet orders on time and ruining the Rediplant name.

The supply of bulbs themselves presented few problems. Most bulbs were bought from the growers on a contract basis in the spring while still in the ground. A buyer would contract to buy all the production of a given acreage at a fixed price per bulb. As he sold to his customers before he knew how many bulbs he would receive from this acreage he had to buy any additional requirements or sell any excess on the free market where the price could fluctuate wildly, depending on whether there was a glut or a poor season. Although the average price of bulbs could usually be predicted within 10 percent, a given tulip had fluctuated in price between Fl 14 and Fl 22 per hundred over the previous few years. By industry agreement, payment to growers was required promptly on November 1, and for a merchant to retain a good name amongst suppliers this could not be delayed.

The real problems in supply stemmed from the short packaging season after the bulbs were taken from the fields. Crocuses might not be ready to be packed until July 25, narcissi and hyacinths until the end of July, and tulips between July 25 and August 10, depending on the variety. Packaging, therefore, had to be very carefully planned.

When bulbs arrived for packaging, they would be inspected and sorted before being placed in the PVC strips by semiautomatic filling machines. The strips would then pass along conveyors to an automatic radio-frequency sealing machine and from there to a station where they would be fitted with the cardboard sleeve and packed into cartons. While the vacuum-forming machine making the PVC strips could produce only 900 strips per hour, stocks could be built up well before packaging began. The sorting machines worked rapidly and could take large quantities of bulbs so they did not limit the output in any way. The speed of the filling machines could also be increased, if needed. Four filling machines, moreover, had been built and these could keep at least four sealing machines busy. The limiting factor, then, seemed to be the number of sealing machines. These operated with an output of 900 strips per hour and at Fl 16,500 were the most expensive items. One machine had been specially designed for Rediplant and modified after tests. Orders for further units would have to be placed immediately as there was a three-month delivery time and orders placed after the beginning of March might not be received in time for the packaging season if there was any delay. The machines were believed to be reliable, but if an electronic component should break down, an engineer from the manufacturer would be required.

Praag and Van Diemen were annoyed that the manufacturer of the sealing machine was insisting on payment before delivery, had raised the price to Fl 16,500 from a verbally agreed figure of Fl 12,500, and would not make any effort to schedule shorter delivery. They had, therefore, investigated other methods of sealing that did not require expensive equipment. All had major disadvantages. Adhesives and stapling were much slower and stapling spoilt the look of the package while adhesives attracted the dust from the bulbs and were not 100 percent effective.

Nievelt argued that only one further sealing machine should be ordered. He pointed out that there was no guarantee that huge volumes of Rediplant could be sold in the first season when the buyers knew it to be experimental, moreover, financial difficulties could limit the opportunity to expand in later years. Hans Praag & Co had little finance available and this had been a further reason for the partnership with Van Diemen. The total requirement for subscribed capital had to be

TABLE 2
Rediplant Costings

Equipment		Fl
Vacuum-forming plant	42,000	
Transformer and electrical installation	10,000	
Molds	20,000	
Sorting machines (5,000 × 4)	20,000	
Filling machines (3,750 × 4)	15,000	
Transport lines	10,000	
Sealing machines (16,500 × 2)	33,000	150,000
Packaging Cost		
Electricity & maintenance	5,000	
Rent	20,000	
Labor (25,000 hours @ Fl 6)	150,000	
Other overheads	50,000	
Depreciation @ 20%	30,000	
Interest		
On equipment	15,000	
On materials & working capital	10,000	280,000

	Per Strip	Per Unit (180 Strips)
Packaged Cost (excluding display stands)		
Bulbs	.62	111.6
PVC	.04	7.9
Sleeve	.06	10.8
Royalties (all sales)	.02	3.6
Packaging (@ 1m. strips)	.28	50.4
Carton packaging, including labor	.04	7.0
Point-of-sale advertising (display posters and pegs)	.03	4.3
Packaged cost	1.09	195.6

kept to 200,000 guilders (see Table 2) if Praag's share in the partnership was not to fall below 50 percent. There was no chance of credit from the machinery supplier and at this stage banks would only advance capital if there was a surrender of some of the ownership equity.

During the busy season it was usual to work two shifts seven days a week, using mainly student labor. For the peak period from July 27 until August 17, Nievelt calculated that two sealing machines would enable a production of 605,000 strips—21 days × 16 hours × 900 strips × 2 machines. As this period would represent 55 percent of the season's activity, this would mean a total production limit of 1.1 million strips. To be on the safe side he set a first tentative limit of 4,750 units (855,000 strips) for the season's selling activity.

Rediplant Sales

While Walter Praag and Dik Van Diemen concentrated on the production planning, Martin Nievelt took on the task of coordinating the Rediplant sales commitments. With Van Diemen agreement, he had in January allocated the tentative target limit of 4,750 units on the following basis:

1,500	United Kingdom
1,000	United States
1,000	Germany
500	Sweden
250	France
250	Holland
250	Switzerland

Nievelt was quick to admit that these were little more than rough guesses based on what he thought the salesmen would achieve, but he felt that the overall demand figures offered even less help. These are shown in Table 3.

TABLE 3
Dutch Bulb Exports, 1969

	Total Exports (Fl millions)	Exported for Dry Sales* (%)
Germany	118	31
United States	48	70
Sweden	35	35
United Kingdom	34	64
France	31	59
Italy	21	42
Switzerland	8	68
Canada	6	64
Austria	5	55
(All other markets less than Fl 5m)		

*Dry sales refer to the proportion of the sales going to the general public either directly or through outlets. Wet sales refer to sales to nurserymen for forcing cut flowers.

By the end of February the sales force was just commencing its main effort and there was still very little sales' feedback to go on. One large order of 1,000 units without stands, however, had just been confirmed by the largest garden-supply wholesaler in Germany who had placed this initial order against a request that he be the sole German distributor next year. This firm employed a sizeable sales force calling on both garden-supply outlets and major retail chains. The price negotiated by the Van Diemen sales force was Fl 1.33 per strip net ex Praag warehouse. The retail price the wholesaler would aim for was not known, but the German retail markup was usually 35 percent on sales, and the Van Diemen sales representative had gained the impression that the wholesaler himself would take a 20 percent markup on retail price. Transport costs to be met by the wholesaler, moreover, would be small, and there was no duty into Germany.

There had also been other inquiries for large volume supplies, but Nievelt had argued against pursuing these for 1971. For example, Beinum, the mail-order house which had purchased Praag's mailing lists, had inquired about Rediplant. Beinum would supply its own bulbs and purchase only the packing—but the volumes required could be very large indeed. After initial discussions that ranged around a figure of Fl 0.6 per strip it was decided not to do anything until the following season. A very large U.S.A. mail-order firm, Henry Field Seed Nursery Company of Iowa, also showed interest but would have required delivery for September when their mail-order packing commenced. Several of the large U.S. retail chains had expressed interest. Other than arrangements for a modified test by A & P, the supermarket chain, however, these were not followed up because this one firm alone could absorb all Rediplant output in just one of its regions. Van Diemen's U.S. salesmen were instead concentrating on the suburban garden centers which mainly purchased loose bulbs. One of them had reported that by chaining the size of the Rediplant order he would accept to the amount of loose bulbs ordered he had been able to gain a substantial increase in sales of loose bulbs.

Nievelt felt that he could safely leave the Van Diemen sales effort to the Van Diemen management, which was well organized, with a worldwide sales director and four area managers. He had, however, provided sets of Rediplant brochures and price sheets drawn up in five languages. The prices Van Diemen chose were set to allow them around 20 percent on sales and meet the usual trade margins in the particular country. In the United States, for example, the wholesale price for a strip had been set at $0.46 US (Fl 1.65) to cover such a margin, 12½ percent duty, and delivery costs.

Van Diemen salesmen were paid a basic salary of Fl 12,500 plus a commission of 2 percent for the first Fl 400,000 increasing by ½ percent for each additional Fl 100,000. A detailed technical training was given and maintained on all aspects of bulb culture, although there was no special sales training. A geographical breakdown of Van Diemen's sales is shown in Table 4, together with the numbers of salesmen concentrating on each country. Scandinavia, with a 5 percent growth rate, was the fastest growing market as well as bringing Van Diemen its largest sales.

TABLE 4
Van Diemen Bros.—Geographical Performance

	Percentage of 1969 Turnover	*No. of Salesmen*
Sweden	20.1	4
West Germany	19.7	4
Finland	16.7	1 + 1 agent
France	10.7	6 + 3 agents
Italy	8.2	1
Norway	7.0	1 + 6 agents
United States	4.5	5
Denmark	3.8	1
Switzerland	3.0	1
Canada	1.4	–
Austria	1.2	1
Iran	1.1	–
England	0.9	1
Greece	0.4	–
South America	0.4	–
Belgium	0.4	–
Japan	0.1	–
Portugal	0.1	–
Hong Kong	0.1	–
Others	0.1	–

United Kingdom Market

Having reserved 1,500 units for the United Kingdom market, Nievelt was anxious to meet this figure and was awaiting news from Jan Straten, Praag's only other salesman, who was currently on a sales trip in England. Nievelt expected him to come back with some good orders for Rediplant, some of which would be test orders from the major chains.

Praag's United Kingdom bulb turnover in 1970 had been £90,000, of which £40,000 was direct mail. Nievelt had built this turnover steadily since the end of World War II, even shifting his home to England for the first few years in order to get a good start. At this level of activity Praag was sixth or seventh in the ranking of about 300 Dutch bulb exporters to the United Kingdom. It was this entire turnover that Praag had sold to Sutcliffe Seeds Ltd. at the end of 1970. As part of the agreement Sutcliffe undertook to purchase all its Dutch bulbs from Praag at an agreed formula, whether sold by direct mail or through outlets. Prices were to be set to cover packing and shipping costs and give Praag a 20 percent markup on the packaged cost. The suggested retail price would then be set at a 100 percent markup on the price to Sutcliffe (50 percent on sales). Sutcliffe would give its outlets a discount of 33.3 percent off this suggested retail price plus an additional 5 percent for payment within 30 days.

Praag's agreement with Sutcliffe had been reached at a time when

Sutcliffe was actively looking for ways of expanding its sales of bulbs. Sutcliffe had recently taken over the garden seed division of Charles Gibb & Sons and now held over 30 percent of the retail seed market in the United Kingdom. With a total United Kingdom seed market of only £6 million, however, further growth would be difficult. Against this the United Kingdom bulb market of around £10 million offered more opportunity, and Paul Duke, managing director of Sutcliffe, had set his sights on 10 percent of this market by 1975. Although Sutcliffe had bulb sales of only £40,000 at this time and there were a great number of competitors, Duke planned to develop into the quality end of the market using Sutcliffe's name and selling only the best Dutch bulbs. Local bulb growing had expanded considerably in recent years and Dutch mail-order firms had been undercut by local suppliers, but there were still many bulb varieties better provided from Holland and direct container shipment in bulk could offset almost all the location advantage.

Paul Duke had also asked if Sutcliffe could have an exclusive distributorship for Rediplant in the United Kingdom. Nievelt knew that Praag would not have the resources to set up a significant sales force and had agreed to Duke's proposal subject to Praag retaining the right to visit a number of its existing outlets and 20 of the largest chain stores and department stores in the United Kingdom. Nievelt undertook not to sell to these outlets at a price lower than Sutcliffe's net price to its outlets less 2 percent cash discount, on the understanding that Sutcliffe would use the same markups as for loose bulbs.

Nievelt was very pleased with the agreement made with Sutcliffe. He thought that in the first year Sutcliffe's sales force of 60, which called on all the garden centers and hardware and garden stores in the United Kingdom, would take orders for somewhere in the vicinity of 600 units. The top salesmen sold between £50,000 and £60,000 of merchandise each year. Sutcliffe planned, moreover, to spend £20,000 on advertising its bulbs in the ensuing year and were planning to hold a cocktail and dinner party to announce their venture, which would be widely covered in the trade papers.

With the major demands of the Rediplant development Nievelt had been unable to manage a selling visit to the major outlets he had retained for Praag, and had sent Straten in his place. Straten had started with Praag eight years ago at the age of 18 and with the exception of a two-year spell in the Dutch army had worked with them ever since. He was paid a fixed salary of Fl 12,000 and received £6.50 a day to cover his expenses while in the United Kingdom. He retained his home in Hillegom, seldom being away from home for more than a month at a time, and had sold £25,000 last year, which Nievelt thought was fairly good for a younger man.

The price at which Straten was seeking Rediplant sales in the United Kingdom was 22p per strip delivered to the customer, less 2 percent discount for payment within 10 days. This price was based on a suggested retail selling price of 33p per strip which Nievelt had decided would be necessary to give Sutcliffe the same markup as for loose bulbs and still leave a reasonable profit for Praag. Costs of packing, freight, insurance, duty (10 percent), delivery, and so forth would amount to about 20 percent of the packaged cost although this percentage might be reduced for full container deliveries. Nievelt would have preferred the retail price to be 29p, which would have about equalled the price for similar loose bulbs in garden stores, but was convinced that at 33p Straten should be able to persuade several of the chains to place orders.

Compagnie Generale Comestible*

IN MAY, 1967, John Carron, the Treasurer of Compagnie Generale Comestible (CGC), was considering a proposal to can and process fish in Gelibolu, Turkey. A report describing the prospective investment had been received in February, 1967, from Giles Donahue, managing director of the company's middle eastern division, headquartered in Istanbul. In addition to Donahue's report, Carron had obtained a critique of the report from Omar St. Jean, a headquarters' staff assistant, and a "rebuttal" of St. Jean's criticisms by Donahue. It remained for Carron to evaluate the testimony and to make a recommendation to the board of management.

Compagnie Generale Comestible was a Belgium company which manufactured cereals, canned foods, frozen foods, and confectionery·products. In 1966 CGCs total assets were in excess of 50 billion francs and the common stock plus retained earnings of the company amounted to more than 40 billion francs. Sales during 1967 were expected to reach 55 billion francs with attendant profits after taxes of almost 4 billion francs. Headquartered in Antwerp, the company had established manufacturing and distribution facilities throughout the common market, Great Britain, South Africa, and Turkey. The managing director in each country was responsible for both manufacturing and sales of all CGC products within the country. Major decisions, such as approvals of plans and budgets, required the agreement of the country managing director and the headquarters' board of management.

---

* This case was prepared by Professor Jack Zwick as the basis for class discussion rather than to illustrate either effective or ineffective handling of an administrative situation.

To assure continuous growth of company sales and income the managing directors outside of Belgium had been encouraged to identify attractive investment possibilities and, after completing a cursory analysis of the prospects, to forward related data and preliminary conclusions to corporate headquarters. It was Carron's responsibility to evaluate the various projects which flowed into headquarters and to present attractive proposals to the board of management for ultimate disposition.

The Turkish Affiliate's Proposal

In February Carron had received the following memorandum from Donahue in Istanbul.

Dear John:

For some time I have been studying the possibility of our entering the fish business in Turkey. The more I look into the subject the more convinced I become that we have a unique opportunity for profits from both domestic and export sales which can be realized within a reasonably short period of time and return our original investment many times over. As you may know, Turkey's fishing grounds rank second only to Norway's in European productive capacity. Yet Turkey is far behind the European producers because of antiquated fishing vessels, a shortage of seagoing trawlers, and insufficient facilities to can the fish or to convert fish into by-products.

It's been estimated that over 500,000 tons of fish pass between the Black Sea Straits twice a year, moving from the Black Sea to the Sea of Marmara and back: Moreover, large tonnages of a wide variety of fish are found in the Turkish waters of the Black Sea, the Aegean Sea, and the Mediterranean. Both salt water and fresh water fish are equally prevalent and include the principal varieties, for example, mullet, anchovy, turbot, swordfish, blue fish, bass, sardines, tuna, sturgeon, shad, trout, perch, and pike. Of particular significance is the availability in Turkish waters of shrimp, prawns, lobsters, oysters, and sturgeon.

The shortage of refrigeration facilities here has severely limited the local demand for fish. Even more important has been the canning problem. Of the 65 canneries in Turkey only a dozen are canning fish. The majority prefer to concentrate on fruits and vegetables. Canning costs have been high in the past because Turkey has had to import its tin-plate requirements. Yet the new steel mill constructed at Eregli recently is beginning to supply tin plate and its availability should enhance significantly the country's ability both to can and to provide end products at a price which will encourage much greater consumption than at the present time.

You might find this hard to believe, but authorities here estimate that the average Turk consumes less than one can per year of all types of canned foods at the present time. I am certain that if we use modern canning techniques and promote fish products aggressively it will be possible to provide products at a cost low enough to induce substantially higher rates of domestic consumption than at the present time. We should have a big jump on the competition since their equipment for the most part is outmoded and requires a great deal of hand operations to supplement the machinery. The local producer's high cost of production resulting from inefficient techniques will continue to be an important barrier for them. Moreover, fish canning and processing is a minor operation for existing producers (about 15 percent of their total output).

Now, let me turn to the exciting part of the marketing picture. At the present time a large proportion of the Turkish fish catch is exported even though virtually nothing has been done promotionally to induce the purchase of canned or fresh/frozen fish abroad. Right now, most of Turkey's fish exports are going to surrounding countries. An enormous and virtually untapped market consists of the European countries which CGC is ideally equipped to serve. After your recent visit, I don't need to tell you how good the native fish dishes are!! Turkey's present "associate membership agreement" with the Common Market will certainly provide a competitive advantage over other exporting countries. The well-known excellent flavor of Turkish species, together with the low and competitive price position, can be expected to strengthen our position.

Rather than drone on in this memorandum, let me show you what we think sales figures look like. I can provide a justification for the numbers later. It suffices to suggest here that both the demand and sales figures for the proposed project are conservative.

Projected Demand and Sales for Next Five Years

Year		Demand (000 metric tons)		Sales (000 kilograms)	
		Domestic	Foreign	Domestic	Foreign
1969	Fresh and frozen fish	122.0	40.0	1000	2000
	Canned fish	0.8	1.0	500	4500
1970	Fresh and frozen fish	130.0	50.0	1000	2500
	Canned fish	1.0	1.0	500	5000
1971	Fresh and frozen fish	138.0	60.0	1500	2500
	Canned fish	1.0	1.2	500	5500
1972	Fresh and frozen fish	146.0	68.0	1000	2000
	Canned fish	0.8	1.6	1000	6000
1973	Fresh and frozen fish	160.0	100.0	1000	2000
	Canned fish	0.6	2.0	1000	6000

To exploit the existing and growing demand (especially in foreign markets), I suggest that we procure fish from local suppliers and confine our activities to (a) the production of tin cans, (b) fish canning, and (c) fish processing. Since the cans produced in Turkey have been quite primitive, they would never meet European standards. Tin plate required for canned production is now available locally and the government has prohibited the importation of cans. Consequently, all companies active in canning food must now produce their own cans since there is no can producer per se. The plant should be located in Gelibolu which is the main fish supplier of the country. Water, electricity, and native labor are readily available in Gelibolu.

I think we should build a plant with a 10 million kilogram capacity and plan for initial production of 7.5 million kilograms, increasing output to 10 million kilograms by 1970. The cost of such a plant will run approximately 14 million Turkish lire (TL) and certainly would not exceed 17 million TL. The government can be expected to react favorably to the project since we will be using local labor and raw materials and generating a lot of foreign exchange by virtue of our export emphasis. In the major landing centers the fish are sold wholesale at auctions which are supervised and managed by the local municipalities. Although we could buy the fish ourselves, I suggest that we use the so-called middlemen to act as agents on a commission basis. In this way we can reduce our permanent overhead while utilizing fully the middlemen's experience and established long-time personal relations with the local fishermen. With respect to personnel, we should employ only a small permanent group of workers and supplement them during the peak seasons with an additional labor force. We will need approximately 20 skilled and 80 unskilled employees on a permanent basis, which will cost approximately 2 million TL per annum including the various required social and fringe benefits.

The projected output, costs, revenues, taxes, and profits for the first three years of operations should look something like this:

	1969	1970	1971
Projected Output *(000 kilograms)*			
Fresh and frozen fish (marketing)	3,000	3,500	4,000
Canned fish	5,000	5,500	6,000
Totals	8,000	9,000	10,000

Projected Revenues
(000 TL)

	1969	1970	1971
Net Sales[1]	25,000	29,000	33,000
Cost of fish	10,000	12,000	13,000
Packing material	1,093	1,305	1,182
Labor.	1,972	2,100	2,220
Plant overhead (10%)	457	457	457
Cost of Production.	13,422	15,862	16,859
Gross Margin	11,578	13,138	16,141
Less: Administrative Cost	1,560	1,560	1,560
Less: Contingency[2]	5,600	5,600	5,600
Profits Before Taxes	4,458	6,018	8,981
Less: Corporate tax (36%).	1,605	2,166	3,233
Profits After Taxes.	2,853	3,852	5,748

Net Return on Investment: $\dfrac{2,853}{14,000} = 20\%$ $\dfrac{3,852}{14,000} = 28\%$ $\dfrac{5,748}{14,000} = 41\%$

---

[1] Estimated sales revenue is based on "average minimum price of fish" in the Common Market countries during the last five years (=330 kurus).
[2] Contingencies for various local taxes + transportation costs + power, water, etc. + adjustments in administrative salaries and bonuses; the cost of temporary labor forces is also included in contingency.

As you can see, returns should be extremely high with return on investment in the range of 20 percent, 28 percent and 41 percent in 1969, 1970, and 1971 respectively. Therefore, I hope you will give this proposal your immediate attention.

If the board of management can approve the project by the end of 1967, it should be possible to start construction early in 1968 and have planned activities on stream by the beginning of 1969.

I am quite enthusiastic about this one and hope that we can get a reading in the not too distant future.

Best regards,
Giles Donahue (signature)

Carron turned the memo over to his assistant Omar St. Jean, who made a number of adjustments in the figures supplied by Donahue. In his report, St. Jean first determined the total investment required.

He accepted the Turkish figures for the cost of the land, building and equipment. He added, however, a 25 percent allowance for installation costs, inflation during the period of construction and also as a general reserve for underestimation. Thus, the estimated cost of the project was increased from 14 million TL to 17.5 million TL.

Next, St. Jean added an allowance of 6.125 million TL for working capital bringing the total investment up to 23.625 million TL. He did not know why Donahue had omitted cash, receivables, and inventory requirements from his memo but inquiries in Antwerp confirmed his suspicion that one could count on approximately 35 percent of assets being tied up in these categories.

Another entirely new cost factor which St. Jean added was an allowance for training expenses. In his discussions with headquarters production people St. Jean learned that it would probably be necessary to maintain three engineers on location in Gelibolu for six months to train the production crews in the tin can section, in the fish canning plant, and in the fish processing section. This would cost approximately 150,000 TL for salaries and relocation expenses. St. Jean made no further adjustments to the cost figures and the "total investment required" stood at 23.775 million TL. It was assumed that CGC would provide the necessary funds for the investment since no difficulties were anticipated in recovering dividends from Turkey.

St. Jean next turned his attention to the economic life of the fixed assets which Donahue neglected in his cost calculations. Inquiries with equipment manufacturers revealed that the average life of the building and the various types of equipment was about 15 years and, consequently an annual depreciation charge of 1.167 million was tacked on to the annual cost estimates (17.5 divided by 15).

St. Jean also noticed that the Turkish figures assumed that the relationship between cost of production and sales were the same for 1969, 1970, and 1971. This seemed to him to be overly optimistic for several reasons. Presumably, it would be necessary for the Turkish affiliate to incur above-average promotional costs and aggressive pricing policies to break into both the domestic and export markets. Also, one could anticipate higher-than-average production costs during the initial phase of operation. Moreover, it seemed logical to St. Jean that production costs would automatically be higher during the first couple of years before capacity production was reached. Recognizing that such judgments of necessity were arbitrary, St. Jean decided to assume that gross margins during 1969 and 1970 would be 9.262 million TL and 11.824 million TL respectively, or 20 percent and 10 percent below Donahue's predictions.

The staff assistant next recomputed the profits for the proposed venture using the same format as Mr. Donahue. His figures appear below:

Projected Revenues
(000 TL)

	1969	1970	1971
Gross Margin	9,262	11,824	16,141
Less: Depreciation[1]	1,167	1,167	1,167
Less: Administrative cost	1,560	1,560	1,560
Less: Contingency	5,600	5,600	5,600
Profits Before Taxes	935	3,497	7,814
Less: Corporate Taxes (47%)[2]	439	1,644	3,673
Profits After Taxes	496	1,853	4,141
Net Return on Investment	$\frac{496}{23,625^3} = 2\%$	$\frac{1,853}{23,625} = 8\%$	$\frac{4,141}{23,625} = 18\%$

[1] St. Jean added depreciation to Donahue's cost calculations.
[2] St. Jean added anticipation Belgium taxes to the 36 percent Turkish taxes which Donahue had predicted.
[3] St. Jean substituted 23625 for the 14000 in Donahue's calculations to reflect the additional investment elements.

St. Jean then calculated rates of return for the project on a time-adjusted basis. Specifically, he computed the present value of anticipated net inflows for the project at a discount rate of 20 percent. St. Jean decided that a 20 percent rate after taxes should be the cut off rate. This figure was a company goal and he had seen a number of investment proposals in recent weeks which would yield at least this amount. The results of his calculations are shown as Table 1.

On the basis of his calculations St. Jean decided that the Turkish project was not to be recommended since it failed to achieve a satisfactory rate of return on capital, for example, its net present value was negative.

Before reaching a decision on the proposal Carron decided to send St. Jean's report to the Turkish affiliate for comments. Excerpts from Donahue's reply are presented below:

Clearly, St. Jean's study uses some management techniques which we consider novel, to say the least. Naturally, I am not in a position to challenge these present value methods or their relevance to our situation. On the other hand, I do feel qualified to comment on some of St. Jean's assumptions. Skillful as St. Jean has been in bringing the various projections back to their present values, he has also shown a serious ignorance of some essential aspects as they pertain to our Turkish operations.

First, it is totally unnecessary to add 6.125 million TL of working capital to the capital investment on which you require a 20 percent return. Like other businesses here, we operate with much smaller proportions of working capital than is customary in Europe. Besides, it is a common business practice to rely on local commercial banks for working capital needs which will cost us no more than 5 percent after adjusting for taxes. Such leverage is entirely normal as well as highly desirable for us in Turkey as well as you in Antwerp.

TABLE 1

Compagnie Generale Comestible (present value analysis of Turkish project, 000 TL)

Year	Investment +	Profit after Turkish and Belgium Taxes* +	Deprecia- tion =	Cash Flow	20% PV X Factor =	PV of Cash Flow
1968	(23775)	0	0	(23775)	1.000	(23775)
1969	0	496	1167	1663	.833	1352
1970	0	1853	1167	3020	.694	2096
1971	0	4141	1167	5308	.579	3073
1972	0	4547	1167	5714	.482	2754
1973	0	4774	1167	5941	.402	2388
1974	0	5013	1167	6180	.335	2070
1975	0	5264	1167	6431	.279	1794
1976	0	5527	1167	6694	.233	1560
1977	0	5803	1167	6970	.194	1352
1978	0	6093	1167	7260	.162	1176
1979	0	6398	1167	7565	.135	1021
1980	0	6768	1167	7935	.112	889
1981	0	7106	1167	8273	.093	769
1982	0	7461	1167	8628	.078	730
1983	0	7834	1167	9001	.065	585

15 yrs. net present value = (166)

*St. Jean assumed that profits would increase at a 5 percent annual rate after 1971.

Finally, the investment in working capital will certainly not take place until 1969 and 1970, instead of in 1968 as St. Jean's analysis presumes.

Second, although we agree that depreciation should be included in the analysis, as St. Jean suggests, isn't depreciation an expense? Apparently, St. Jean's present value procedure treats depreciation as a benefit. If his procedure is valid, why then use the straight-line method? We have quite a bit of flexibility in setting our depreciation schedule here in Turkey, and it will be entirely legal to amortize the building costs in 15 years and all the equipment in 5 years. Additionally, we can obtain permission to deduct a double depreciation charge during the first year.

Third, we may be able to reduce the required investment significantly by buying the equipment on credit and constructing the building in a section of Gelibolu which comes under the program of the State Planning Organization. Under this program we can obtain long-term loans at very favorable interest rates. Although such loans would probably require a CGC guarantee, they would add to our leverage thereby substantially improving the return on investment.

Fourth, turning to the profit margin which St. Jean deflated in the interest of conservatism, I believe our margins in the original memo were quite conservative. I did not include in the original figures the effects of export incentives which the Turkish Council of Ministers has recently established. Without question this project would be eligible for significant tax refunds which are being offered to promote exports. This tax relief would increase our after-tax margins by roughly 5 percent.

While on the subject of taxes I question the validity of applying Belgium taxes to this project. Belgium taxes are not assessed unless we remit profits to CGC and, as you well know, the board of management has invariably suggested that we use our profits for expansion or new projects.

One final question: What happens to the proposed investment after 15 years? Presumably according to St. Jean's present value analysis, everything ends after 15 years. Why not 20 years instead of 15? Even if there's adequate justification for selecting 15 years for analysis, I am convinced that the fish operations will be of value to CGC after the 15 years have elapsed.

Considering all Donahue's remarks, Carron concluded that the Turkish proposal raised some significant policy dilemmas which could be expected to reoccur as other proposals were submitted to headquarters for appraisal. He decided, therefore, to give the Turkish proposal more than his usual attention in order to develop some general guidelines for dealing with these issues in the future. At the same time he hoped to obtain answers to Donahue's questions and to pass judgment on the Turkish proposal as quickly as possible in order to minimize hard feelings and misspent energies.

Bell Schönheitsprodukte GmbH*

THE MANAGEMENT OF BELL SCHÖNHEITSPRODUKTE GmbH decided in January 1972 to give serious consideration to undertaking a major plant expansion outside of Germany. The year 1971 had seen the formal revaluation of the once-floating German mark to a parity of 0.3106 U.S. dollars. This revaluation represented an increase of 13.6% in the value of the deutschmarke (DM) over the DM–dollar rate of May 1971. The year 1971 had also seen an increase in the wage bill (including social benefits) at Bell GmbH of nearly 15 percent. As Bell exported over 60 percent of its rather labor-intensive German production, these events threatened to reduce unpleasantly the firm's profitability.

Internationalizing Bell's sources of production appeared to be the most interesting route out of this predicament. A U.S.–owned competitor which had previously been producing most of its output in Germany had just opened a plant in France and had proceeded to start a price war. Wages in France were on the order of five to six francs per hour. Wages in Germany were 6 DM per hour.[1] The unanswered question, however, was "Where should Bell put the new plant?"

The Company and Its Products

Bell Schönheitsprodukte GmbH was a German, family-owned company with a total Europe-wide turnover of 22 million DM in 1971.

---

*This case is based on the experience of a company that wishes to remain anonymous. Various data have been disguised. This case was written for class discussion rather than to illustrate effective or ineffective handling of an administrative situation.

© 1972 by Dr. Lawrence G. Franko, faculty member, *Centre d'Etudes Industrielles (CEI)*, Geneva, Switzerland.

[1] One franc equalled 0.627 DM in January 1972.

The product line consisted entirely of special opening, closing, sliding, and spring packagings for the cosmetic industry. Among Bell's over 200 customers were several very large multinational companies such as Unilever, Colgate–Palmolive and L'Oreal. The single largest customer purchased 10 percent of Bell's sales.

Bell's American name derived from the fact that its product line was produced under an exclusive license of an American Company, Bell Industries, Inc. The American licensor, however, had no ownership position in Bell GmbH. Although Bell GmbH was a relatively small firm, it had already opened a plant in Great Britain in the mid-1960s. The United Kingdom plant had a capacity of 25 million units as compared to the 200 million unit capacity of the main German plant, located in Hannover. Both plants ordinarily produced at 90–95 percent of capacity. About 18.8 million DM of sales came from the German plant's production; the remaining 2.3 million were accounted for by United Kingdom production. Because of the 9.6 percent EEC common tariff, United Kingdom production went only to the United Kingdom. All other European markets (including other EFTA markets) were supplied by Germany. Indeed, the United Kingdom plant had only been set up because of the 9.6 percent *ad valorem* EFTA tariff facing German output. Thirty people were employed in the United Kingdom plant, compared to 120 in Germany. Of the German personnel, 90 were women workers who assembled and decorated packages. The remainder consisted of administrative personnel plus technicians who designed and built much of Bell GmbH's machinery and who handled the very important (indeed

TABLE 1
Market Size for Closeable
Cosmetic Packaging

	Approximate Market Size (1971) in Units (millions)
United Kingdom	150
Germany	360
France	200
Benelux	90
Greece	5
Italy	150
Scandinavia	60
Spain	25
Portugal	5
Switzerland	40
Austria	10
Yugoslavia	5
Total Europe	1,100
United States	2,400

critical) quality-control aspects of the business. None of Bell's employees were union members. According to management, "we are too small to have attracted the attention of the unions."

Sales were made in all countries of western Europe plus Yugoslavia. Under the terms of its American license, the company was restricted to selling in Europe and the socialist countries. Table 1 shows the total 1971 European and U.S. markets for the kind of special cosmetic-packaging products produced by Bell, in units. Given normal economic conditions, that is 4 to 5 percent yearly growth in GNP, management expected 20 percent per year sales growth in the more developed areas of Europe and somewhat higher growth in countries such as Greece, Portugal, and Spain.

Competition and Prices

Bell GmbH's competitors have the characteristics shown in the table below.

Competitor	Ownership	Output of Plants by Country–1971	
A (large)	U.K. group	France	80%
		U.K.	15%
		Italy	5%
B (large)	U.S. company	Germany	65%
		England	30%
		France	5%
C (small)	U.S. (recently acquired)	Germany	100%
D (small)	Italian	Italy	100%
E (small)	Italian	Italy	100%

Bell's management suspected that the two small Italian firms (*D* and *E*) were secretly backed by their government; all the more so since the Italian price level was 10–15 percent lower than that elsewhere in the EEC. *D* and *E* had tried to export a part of their production. However, their quality standards were apparently not as high as those of Bell, *A* and *B*. Moreover their plants were unionized and subject to occasional strikes. Thus, they had a poor reputation for meeting delivery dates outside of Italy. Still, they totally dominated the local market. Bell had once had 30 percent of the Italian market and was well known there. With practically nonexistent margins, however, Bell found it increasingly impossible to compete in Italy. Nevertheless, in late 1971, just as the Italian situation began to look really hopeless, the President of Bell, Herr Kahler, had received a letter from two ex-managers of

Italian competitor *E* suggesting that Bell start up a plant in Italy—under their direction, of course.

With the exception of the Italian situation, prices elsewhere in Europe were relatively uniform: Bell's ex-factory price was 100 DM per thousand in the EEC. Competitor *B*, who had started the price war that had recently pushed prices down to 95 DM from a previous higher level also billed in DM. Competitor *A*, who because of its dominant French position, billed in francs, by and large charged a similar price once value added tax adjustments were made. According to one Bell manager, "we tend to react immediately to what *A* and *B* do, and vice versa. Everyone tries to differentiate their product other than by price, but finally, one packaging is like another."

Table 2 summarizes estimates for the market share of Bell and its competitors in France, Germany, England, and the whole of Europe.

TABLE 2
Comparative Market Shares (in percent)*

	Bell	*Competitor A*	*Competitor B*	*Others*	*Total*
Europe Total	19	35	25	21	100
France	7	70	20	3	100
United Kingdom	15	30	45	10	100
Germany	22	30	30	18	100

*Rough estimates. No one in the industry publishes his sales figures.

Alternative Courses of Action

In the face of competition, unfavorable exchange rate movements, wage increases in Germany and the Italian proposal, management felt that action would be needed soon. Herr Kahler had received a phone call from competitor *A* suggesting that they try to counter *B's* price cutting by "an arrangement." The virtues of such an arrangement from Bell's point of view, however, seemed questionable. *A*, after all, was sitting with 80 percent of its productions in France, where wages were favorable and devaluation more often the rule than not.

Putting up a new plant in France, of course, seemed a most tempting possibility; all the more so since the French government offered very interesting incentives in certain parts of the country. In addition, some technical and design tasks could eventually be performed in France since indigenous skills were available. Ninety percent of the component needs would be supplied initially from Bell's usual outside suppliers in Germany. However, by the second year of operations, perhaps 30 percent could be obtained locally, and, if necessary, all materials could be obtained locally after the third year. Last, but not least, in regions such as Alsace, French technicians and workers generally were fluent in German. Thus there would be few language difficulties during the plant start-up. But management could not help wondering whether or not the French wage and exchange rate situations would remain as favorable to exports in the future as they had in the past. Moreover, the investment incentives picture had recently been altered by the EEC agreement to limit incentive grants to 20 percent of project costs as of January 1972. And what if another May 1968 were around the corner?

In some ways, adding 25 or 50 million units of capacity to the United Kingdom plant seemed about the easiest thing to do. A plant and trained people were already in existence. Incentives might be available. The pound might devalue again. And perhaps wages would not increase as fast as elsewhere in the now expanding EEC. Still, the United Kingdom might be less attractive for the time being because it would probably take five years before tariff barriers would finally disappear between the United Kingdom and the EEC. As in France, local components could eventually be substituted for German-made goods.

The request from the Italians reminded Bell management that a local plant might well help it to capture back its once 30 percent market share. Technical skills and components would be as easily available as in the United Kingdom and France. Moreover, Italy could conceivably provide a relatively low wage base for exports. And the lira had depreciated against the mark in recent times. But could any country that had taken 23 ballots to elect a president in 1971 be a stable place in which to invest?

One final alternative that appeared interesting to Herr Kahler and other members of Bell's management was that of setting up a plant in Spain. Perhaps such a move might give the company a much greater and longer lasting competitive advantage than would the other possibilities. Whether or not components could ever be obtained locally was simply unknown. Still, wage rates were thought to be low enough to easily jump the EEC common tariff. Although a 10 percent duty might have to be paid on components imported from Germany, it seemed probable that a rebate arrangement for re-exported components could be negotiated with the Spanish authorities.

The plant sizes that appeared most interesting for Italian, Spanish, United Kingdom, or French operations were either 25 million or 50 million units per year. Factory buildings could be leased for very similar yearly rentals throughout Europe. Details of the capacity and cost alternatives considered are given in Table 3. The necessary machinery would either be made at Bell's main plant or purchased in Germany. Tentatively, it was thought best to finance a foreign plant by an equity stake equal to the cost of machinery. Working capital requirements could

TABLE 3
Capacity and Cost Alternatives

	Alternative 1	Alternative 2
Annual plant capacity (million units)	25	50
Space requirements.	600 m²	1000 m²
Approximate yearly rental cost for leased plant*	28,800 DM	48,000 DM
Cost of machinery (to be purchased in Germany).	300,000 DM	500,000 DM†
Working capital requirements	100,000 DM	220,000 DM
Components cost (per million units)	46,000 DM	46,000 DM
Direct labor (per million units produced in Germany)	7,000 DM	7,000 DM
General administration and overhead (per year)	100,000 DM	150,000 DM†
Transport costs	2% sales price	2% sales price

*Similar in all countries.
†For plants above 50 million units, machinery and overhead costs are roughly proportional to capacity.

be met either by local borrowing or by the extension of account payable terms (for components) to the foreign plant.

As Bell management was preparing to draw up *pro-forma* economic forecasts and cash flow projections for the French, United Kingdom, Spanish, and Italian alternatives, Herr Kahler reminded his colleagues of a letter he had received in November 1971. He suggested that this letter should stimulate Bell to examine the German economy a bit more carefully, too. The letter was from a Yugoslavian company that was soliciting Bell's participation in a joint venture—whose aim would be to export back to Europe. Herr Kahler rejected serious consideration of such an alternative for the time being on the grounds that Bell was too small to enter into protracted negotiations with a prospective partner in a venture that might end up competing with already existing wholly-owned facilities. Still, he felt it might be useful to look at the medium term outlook for Germany and the competitiveness of the headquarters plant. If a firm in a country like Yugoslavia were to enter into the packaging business, perhaps continued German revaluations and steep wage increases could make the position of the main 200 million unit capacity plant less and less tenable over the years. Up to this point, it had been assumed that German production would still account for most of Bell's sales, even after the new plant were added. It was quite true that the German stockholders might not want to shift a lot of Bell's current production to a foreign country. But efforts at automation could only go so far. Bell had reduced the number of its women workers from 150 to 90 between 1970 and 1971 while increasing output. However, productivity increases could not be obtained at this rate in the future. Would some existing German plant capacity eventually have to be transferred elsewhere?

TABLE 4

Exchange Rates, Money Supply and Prices, Selected European Countries 1965–71*

	1965	1966	1967	1968	1969	1970	1971
Italy							
Rate of exchange (lira per dollar)	624.70	624.45	623.86	623.50	625.50	623.00	581.5
Money supply (1963 = 100)	125	142	164	184	213	273	
Cost of living index (1963 = 100)	109	112	115	117	121	128	
France							
Rate of exchange (francs per dollar)	4.902	4.952	4.908	4.948	5.558	5.520	5.116†
Money supply (1963 = 100)	118	127	133	145	146	157	
Cost of living index (1963 = 100)	105	108	112	118	124	131	
United Kingdom							
Rate of exchange (pound per dollar)	0.357	0.358	0.415	0.419	0.416	0.418	0.383
Money supply (1963 = 100)	113	118	131	140	144	157	
Cost of living index (1963 = 100)	109	114	116	123	129	139	
Germany							
Rate of exchange (mark per dollar)	4.006	3.977	3.999	4.000	3.690	3.648	3.223
Money supply (1963 = 100)	117	119	131	142	150	165	
Cost of living index (1963 = 100)	107	109	110	113	116	120	
Spain							
Rate of exchange (peseta per dollar)	59.99	60.00	69.70	69.82	70.06	69.72	64.47
Money supply (1963 = 100)	139	155	178	198	229	250	
Cost of living index (1963 = 100)	123	130	138	142	147	157	

*Year end.
†Commercial rate.
Source: IMF, *International Financial Statistics*, January 1972.

TABLE 5

International Financial Data, Selected European Countries (millions of U.S. dollars)*

	1965	1966	1967	1968	1969	1970	1971 (Nov.)
Italy							
Official reserves	4800	4911	5463	5341	5045	5352	6431
Balance on goods & services†	1883	1779	1273	2336	2013	679	
Trade (goods) balance only	646	331	-21	1048	542	-340	
France							
Official reserves	6343	6733	6994	4201	3833	4960	7494
Balance on goods & services†			732	-238	-971	1148	
Trade (goods) balance only			356	-158	-1223	726	
United Kingdom							
Official reserves	3004	3099	2695	2422	2527	2827	5572
Balance on goods and services†	378	801	-115	-118	1613	1911	
Trade (goods) balance only	-664	-204	-1446	-1543	-338	7	
Germany							
Official reserves	7430	8029	8153	9948	7129	13,610	17,371
Balance on goods and services†	-86	1593	3970	4554	3780	3225	
Trade (goods) balance only	248	1878	4116	4485	3902	4024	
Spain							
Official reserves	1422	1253	1100	1150	1282	1817	3104
Balance on goods and services†	-846	-983	-907	-709	-959		
Trade (goods) balance only	-1759	-1992	-1781	-1574	-1871		

*End of year.
†Not including transfer payments.
Source: IMF, *International Financial Statistics.*

TABLE 6
Wage Increases Related to Output Increases in Industry, Selected European Countries*

	1966	1967	1968	1969	1970	1971	(Forecast) 1972†
Italy							
Percent increase in industrial output	11.3	8.5	6.3	2.9	4.0	-2.6	8.0
Percent increase in wages§		5.2	3.6	7.5	21.4	14.5	15.0
Ratio of output to wage increases . . .		(1.64)	(1.75)	(0.36)	(0.14)	(0.19)	(0.53)
France							
Percent increase in industrial output . . .	4.3	2.6	4.1	12.7	5.6	2.5	5.0
Percent increase in wages§	5.9	6.0	12.4	11.3	10.5	11.1	10.0
Ratio of output to wage increases . . .	(1.24)	(0.43)	(0.33)	(1.13)	(0.53)	(0.22)	(0.50)
United Kingdom							
Percent increase in industrial output . . .	1.8	-0.9	5.3	3.4	1.6	0.8	3.5
Percent increase in wages§	6.7	4.0	6.8	9.2	9.6	12.1	12.0
Ratio of output to wage increases . .	(0.27)	(-0.22)	(0.78)	(0.37)	(0.17)	(0.07)	(0.29)
Germany							
Percent increase in industrial output . . .	1.8	-1.7	12.3	12.5	6.3	3.2	0
Percent increase in wages‡	7.3	3.9	4.3	9.1	12.8	13.3	6.5
Ratio of output to wage increases . . .	(0.25)	(-0.44)	(2.9)	(1.4)	(0.49)	(0.24)	(0)
Spain							
Percent increase in industrial output . . .	15.0	6.2	6.5	14.5	7.9		6.6
Percent increase in wages‡	16.0	15.0	7.0	9.0	17.0		12.0
Ratio of output to wage increases . . .	(0.94)	(0.42)	(0.93)	(1.61)	(0.47)		(0.55)

*Calculated from OECD, *Main Economic Indicators*, various issues.
†Eurofinance-Vision Projections, *Vision*, January 1972, p. 38.
‡Hourly earnings
§Hourly rates

TABLE 7
Wages in Manufacturing (All Industries) in Local Currencies, Selected European Countries

	Austria per month Schilling†	Belgium per day Male B. Franc†	Denmark per hour (M & F)* Øre†	France per hour (wage rate) Francs‡	W. Germany per hour (M & F)* D. Mark†	Italy per hour Lira†	Spain per hour pesetas†	Switzerland per hour Sw. Fr.†	U.K. per hour Male s.d.†
1965	3141	359.0	923	3.00	4.12	386	21.57	5.20	8/9
1966	3514	389.7	1040	3.18	4.42	401	25.13	5.58	9/3
1967	3781	414.2	1128	3.37	4.60	426	28.81	5.94	9/8
1968	4018	438.7	1283	3.79	4.79	445	31.16	6.24	10/4
1969	4263	474.1	1407	4.21	5.28	489	34.69	6.64	11/2
1970	5074	—	—	4.56	5.77	—	—	—	—

*Male and female.
†Earnings.
‡Rates.
Source: *ILO Yearbook of Labor Statistics, 1970.*

TABLE 8

Indices of Industrial Capacity Utilization, in Selected European Countries (in percent)*

	Belgium	*France*	*Germany*	*Italy*	*Nether-lands*	*United Kingdom*
1965	95.3	91.7	92.1	86.8	89.7	
1966	90.6	90.0	85.8	88.5	87.6	93.6
1967	90.2	87.0	86.7	89.4	86.7	
1968	90.6	96.8	93.0	90.0	91.2	96.9
1969	94.2	94.7	97.3	79.1	93.2	95.8
1970	92.8	95.6	94.0	87.3	94.0	94.5
1971 . . . . .1)	94.7	96.1	97.1	86.1	96.5	93.6
2)	92.2	93.2	95.4	82.1	94.8	94.2
3)	92.9	95.5	93.1	79.4	93.6	93.4

*Year end, 1965–70, and first three quarters, 1971.
Source: "Wharton Indices of Industrial Capacity Utilization in Europe," *Wharton Quarterly*, various issues. (Available from The Wharton School, University of Pennsylvania, Philadelphia, Pa.)

TABLE 9

Sample Cash Flow Projection for an Italian Investment*

Projected Cash Flows: Italian investment in 50 million-unit plant

Investment
Machinery	Dm. 500,000
Working capital	220,000
Total	720,000
Less: 70% debt	(504,000)
Net investment	216,000 Dm.

Annual Cash Flows	*Before devaluation*	*After 10% devaluation*
Sales revenue (Dm. 95 × 50,000)	Dm. 4,750,000	Dm. 4,750,000
Expenses†		
Building rental	48,000	43,000
Components.	2,300,000	1,970,000
Direct labor	170,000	153,000
General overhead	150,000	135,000
Transport costs	75,000	68,000
Interest (5%)	25,000	23,000
Net Cash Flow . . . . Dm. 1,982,000		Dm. 2,358,000

*Showing results assuming: (1) no devaluation and (2) a 10% devaluation.
†Major Assumptions:
  1. All components supplied locally.
  2. Income tax holiday provided by Italian government.
  3. All production is for export.
  4. Depreciation not included in overhead charges.

ORGANIZING AND MANAGING THE MULTINATIONAL ENTERPRISE

Meridian Corporation*

THE MERIDIAN CORPORATION in 1966 was a medium-sized U.S. chemical company producing a wide range of products. The company's traditional strength had been in agricultural chemicals, pesticides, and fertilizers, but in recent years the product line had expanded to encompass pharmaceuticals, chemicals for the petroleum, paper, and plastics industries, industrial catalysts, and chemically-based fusing and fixing compounds used in electronic components.

The company had a number of plants in the United States producing different articles in the product range. Sales were made through regional sales and distribution outlets, both to wholesalers and directly to final customers. The sales force specialized under product lines and made both direct selling and "missionary" calls. Meridian also had a number of fertilizer and agricultural chemical plants in South America and Canada, where the company had operated for a number of years. Some export sales had been made to Europe, Asia, and Australia, but these generally represented only a small percentage of total sales.

In the late 1950s, the top management of Meridian examined the rapid growth of markets overseas and concluded that efforts should be made to establish Meridian in these markets. Besides offering the advantages of higher sales and profits, management thought that overseas markets would allow for greater benefits to be obtained from existing research and development facilities. However, many of Meridian's prod-

---

* Case material of the Harvard Graduate School of Business Administration is prepared as a basis for class discussion. Cases are not designed to present illustrations of either effective or ineffective handling of administrative problems.

ucts used relatively high bulk, low value raw materials which meant that plants had to be established close to markets. Other products had to be modified to suit the particular requirements of customers, or to meet climatic conditions in a particular country. Still others were subject to such high tariff barriers that export sales were not feasible.

The company's resources, though considerable, were smaller than some of its U.S. and foreign competitors. Sales in 1965 were approximately $325 million and total assets exceeded $280 million. Recent expansion had put pressure on available management, and any rapid expansion overseas meant that the company had to hire experienced outside managers rather than effecting further internal reassignments.

In 1960, an International Division was organized under William Webb, with responsibility for all activities outside North America. Webb became President of Meridian in 1964 and was succeeded in the International Division by Murray Clapham. During Webb's administration of the Division, Meridian had established operations in India, South Africa, Australia, and New Zealand, as well as expanding production and marketing facilities in South America. A simplified organization chart is shown as Table 1.

TABLE 1
Meridian Corporation—Organization Chart

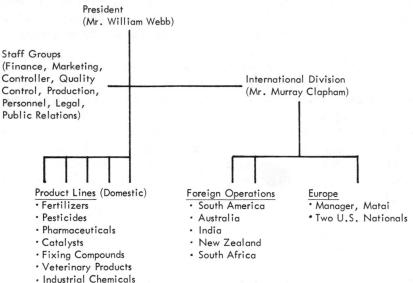

Late in 1964, just after Clapham assumed the position of International Vice President, Meridian purchased Matai SA, a small Belgian producer of pesticides. It was envisioned that this company would be the base from which penetration of the European market would be accomplished. An examination of the European market convinced Clapham that the three markets which Meridian could most profitably enter were those for pesticides, chemical fastening agents, and pharmaceuticals. The Belgian manager of Matai was regarded as very competent in the pesticide field, and in mid-1965 Meridian hired two U.S. nationals from the European subsidiaries of a U.S. electronics firm and a U.S. drug firm.

These three men were each to assume responsibility for a particular product line and develop marketing and production plans. They were to be put in charge of operations in these areas after plans had been approved. They were all to be based in Belgium. At present the two U.S. nationals who had recently been hired as managers were located in the Matai plant .They were not subordinate to the Belgian manager of Matai and all three men reported directly to Clapham.

The executive committee of Meridian had discussed at various times the most suitable method of organizing for international operations. It was thought that the International Division had acquired a considerable amount of specialized knowledge and expertise in a fairly short period of time. The new operations in India, South Africa, Australia, and New Zealand were operating profitably, but all were small and handled only basic agricultural chemicals. Local personnel had been obtained to fill most of the managerial positions in these operations, which were all headed by U.S. nationals who reported to the International Division Vice President.

Webb and Clapham were both aware of the arguments commonly advanced in favor of a product-line organization. Proponents of this type of structure held that it allowed the best use of specialized marketing and technological knowledge and enhanced the growth of a worldwide point of view. It was further argued that better strategic decisions could be made when detailed knowledge of worldwide markets for particular product lines was available, and that such information was best obtained and channeled through a product-line organization.

Since the overseas operations were small and in some countries restricted to single-product lines, they did not presently require extensive contact with the domestic divisions. Webb and Clapham were both aware that Meridian lacked product-line managers experienced in international operations. They thought that this fact, together with the problems of penetrating new markets, would mean that the International Division would have to be interposed between foreign operations and the parent company for some time, regardless of the organization structure which would ultimately be adopted.

Webb and Clapham regarded the European market as very competitive. Additional U.S. firms were entering the market, and European firms were becoming more aggressive in seeking to expand their markets. Top management of Meridian did not wish to take undue risks in entering the market. It was envisioned that expansion would take place from the Matai base both through acquisitions and through the introduction of existing product lines. The extent of resources that would be made available for these activities would be dictated by perceived market opportunities, and no formal decision had been made setting either a limit or a target for financial commitments in Europe.

Matai had sold only to a small number of customers and had been managed by one family. It did not have the range of staff functions that a similar company might have had in the United States. Clapham thought it essential to build a corporate image of Meridian in Europe. In addition, it would be necessary to have an information gathering function to survey competitive action and political and economic changes in Europe.

While he was concerned with these problems, Clapham's immediate concern was with the functions to be assigned to the three managers in Belgium and with the relations with the home organization. The shortage of experienced personnel was the main reason for Clapham's belief that adoption of a product-line structure would be premature, and that a regional office in charge of the various European activities would be needed for at least the foreseeable future. Clapham was shortly going to visit Brussels to confer with the three managers. He thought that before visiting them he should prepare a tentative scheme of organization, specifying the structure of the organization and the assignment of respective responsibilities. He proposed to discuss this structure with the three managers and with Dr. Adam, a prominent Belgian banker and educator who had undertaken to serve as chairman of Meridian's European subsidiary.

Clapham realized that there was a possibility of conflicts between the organization that might be desired by the managers in Europe and the type of organization that would best fit Meridian's total structure. Any form of organization decided upon would have to attempt to envision the conflicts which might arise and provide for their solution in the most effective manner. In particular, Clapham wondered what specific duties and responsibilities should be assigned to a regional office and how this regional office should be organized so as to best assist the managers in their respective product lines and yet maintain contact with headquarters.

He also wondered which headquarters' staff functions needed to be duplicated in the regional office. If any such duplication were undertaken, lines of authority and reporting would have to be established, and Clapham was not sure that any duplication would be necessary in the long run. The domestic operations, though organized on a product-line basis, all obtained specialized assistance and advice from a central staff. Clapham was concerned that the organization of a regional staff could introduce complications into the structure and perhaps be inconsistent with ultimate worldwide operations by product lines.

Anco Inc. (C)*

"We decided some years ago to make our European units as autonomous as possible," Mr. Baker of Anco once commented. "But now we wonder if we haven't gone too far.

"Initially we had good reasons for so doing. First, each European country has a different legal code about corporations, plus separate antitrust laws, labor laws, and so on. Second, there was considerable nationalism and pride in each country, so it made sense to structure each subsidiary with a separate manager, trademark, and product line. With few exceptions, each of our European companies now has a local citizen as manager, who pretty much runs the show the way he sees fit.

"We have also had great success with decentralized operations in the United States, and we could see no reason why this sort of operation would not work out in Europe as well. Hence each of our European managers has considerable latitude over his own operations. Really, all we want is some financial and budgetary controls, plus good operating-profit results each year. Our European managers are very capable; and after a few years of getting the system debugged, it has worked very well.

"However, now we are finding a whole new set of problems. The rapid decline in tariffs among EEC countries in the past 10 years has meant that we want to move to a much more integrated European system. In 1958, it would have been foolish for one European subsidiary to make, say, electric motors, while another made blower mechanisms, and a third completed the vacuum cleaner. By the time we paid tariffs

---

* This case was written by Richard N. Farmer, professor, Graduate School of Business, Indiana University. Copyright is retained by the author.

on all components moving between the three countries, the costs would have been prohibitive. Hence each European subsidiary made the complete unit.

"Now we are shifting to the totally integrated system. Our German plant makes motors and other electrical equipment; our Belgian plant makes other components; and our Italian plant finishes and assembles the product for sale in all EEC countries. The difficulty is in getting three previous autonomous units to cooperate properly. Our German manager can't seem to please our Italian manager—they argue all the time about delivery times and quality controls. Production has been far below expectations as we struggle with this problem. Not only have we been fighting against the usual business problems of reorganizing a complex operation, but we also have to consider the nationalities of the managers, and the views they have about the incompetence of the other managers in different countries. The basic problem is that each local manager seems to feel that he is a single, autonomous unit in a vague total system, and no amount of direct orders seemingly can change this view. As long as it persists, we will be in trouble."

1. How would you advise Anco in this situation? What actions might Anco take to correct this situation?
2. Why has the sharp reduction in tariffs in the EEC made such a difference here? What EEC rules of the game have led to this problem?
3. Do you think that a major American manufacturer with plants in Atlanta, Georgia, and Columbus, Ohio, might have the same sort of problems? Why or why not?

The Widget*

THE "WIDGET" WAS AN IMPORTANT COMPONENT in the electronics industry: its two major uses were in *Product A,* a consumer end-item, and in *Product B,* an industrial end-item. Seven European companies made the widget, which was well standardized in design. There were no duties on the widget and shipping costs were a negligible proportion of its selling price.

The largest European widget maker was Lamar Electronics, which made nearly 50 percent of the total European annual volume of 98 million units. One of the smallest widget makers was Electronic Products Incorporated (EPI), one of four European subsidiaries of Western Electronics (WE). Each of the WE houses maintained a separate profit and loss statement and balance sheet and had decentralized profit responsibility. (See Table 1 for a partial organization chart of WE and its subsidiaries.)

All four WE subsidiaries made *Product A* and three made *Product B,* but EPI was the only WE subsidiary that made the widget. The WE policy on inter-company transfers stated that the subsidiaries were free to purchase their component needs from outside the WE System if they could obtain a lower price commensurate with good quality and dependable supply. (See Table 2 for excerpts from WE's transfer policy.)

EPI had offered to supply each of the three other WE subsidiaries with their annual widget requirements, but its sister houses claimed that

---

* This case has been prepared and copyrighted, 1963, by Harbridge House, Inc., and is designed for teaching purposes only. The case does not necessarily indicate the policy or practice of any company, or corporation, and is not necessarily intended to illustrate either correct or incorrect, desirable or undesirable, management procedures.

TABLE 1
WE Partial Organization Chart

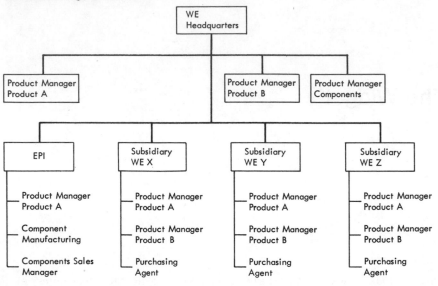

TABLE 2
Excerpts from WE's Inter-Company Transfer Policy

1. Purchases should be made from other system houses rather than from outside competitors if price, quality, delivery, and service are competitive. . . .
2. Where the parts in question are of standard design, are obtainable from outside the system, and are being used in manufacture by the buying company, they should be transferred at cost plus 10 percent, but not to exceed the lesser of market or most favored customer trade price for like quality, . . . less discount for sales and advertising expense not incurred in interhouse business.
3. As used in paragraph 2, cost is to include material, labor, and manufacturing overhead, but not administrative or marketing expenses.

they could purchase their requirements more cheaply from Lamar, and in fact they all bought from Lamar. Each of the subsidiaries admitted that EPI's quality was comparable with Lamar's.

EPI made three million widgets a year, using one million for its own production of *Product A* (these were transferred to the *Product A* division at an intrahouse price of $0.66) and selling the remainder to a variety of small manufacturers at prices averaging $0.68 per unit.

The annual widget requirements of the WE subsidiaries, the prices at which they purchased from Lamar, and the prices offered to them by EPI were as follows:

Subsidiary	Annual Purchases	Lamar Unit Price	EPI Price Offer
WE X	1 million units	$0.49	$0.55
WE Y	2 million units	0.44	0.50
WE Z	3 million units	0.42	0.49

EPI's manufacturing costs at various volumes were as follows:

Annual Volume (million units)	Total Fixed Manufacturing Cost (million dollars)	Fixed Cost/Unit ($)	Variable Cost/Unit ($)	Total Cost/Unit ($)
3	1	0.33	0.27	0.60
4	1	0.25	0.26	0.51
5	1	0.20	0.25	0.45
6	1.5	0.25	0.24	0.49
7	1.5	0.21	0.22	0.43
8	1.5	0.19	0.21	0.40
9	1.5	0.17	0.20	0.37
10	1.5	0.15	0.18	0.33

Total widget sales for the year were $2.02 million of which $1.36 million were to customers outside the WE system. EPI's marketing expenses for the year were 14 percent of widget sales to outside customers. General and administrative overhead was charged at 4 percent of total sales. Thus, the widget line operated at a before tax loss of about $60,000.

1. What is the problem here? What should be done about it and by whom?

American Oil*

A FEW LARGE AMERICAN FIRMS have dominated the local economy of a small Central American republic for 40 years. Operating in such critical fields as oil production and refining, banana growing, transportation, and so on, these companies employ thousands of local citizens, pay large taxes, and, by implication, have much to say about what kind of government exists in the country.

For many years there have been dark rumors of CIA activities in this country, and it is widely believed that the companies harbor agents and generally make efforts to maintain the status quo. Since most of the local workers in these companies have rather low-skill, low-pay jobs, it is also widely believed that the companies discriminate against local people. Protestations on the part of the companies that locals are promoted as fast as they qualify for better jobs usually are not believed.

In the past few years, Paco Gonzales, a local politician, has been attempting to generate popular support against the companies. He has usually been quite successful, since he is an effective speaker, a capable organizer, and a person who is capable of spellbinding crowds of peasants and workers.

Last year, Gonzales was elected to the senate of this country, and there are rumors that he is seriously being considered for the presidency. Although he is not exactly an establishment candidate, his violent attacks against foreign private enterprise appear to be extremely popular among the masses.

A few months ago, after a particularly fiery speech directed against

* This case was written by Richard N. Farmer, professor, Graduate School of Business, Indiana University. Copyright is retained by the author.

American oil companies, there was a small riot in the capital, which resulted in about $100,000 damage to oil company installations there. Two tanks of gasoline were fired on the outskirts of the city and the fuel and tanks were a total loss.

Last week the local president of the American oil company received a visitor who represented Gonzales. The visitor pointed out that if present trends continued, it was possible that real trouble would result, possibly even expropriation. The visitor noted that Gonzales was quite capable of inciting the country against the American companies, and unless checked, he was quite willing to do so.

But the visitor also noted that Gonzales was not a wealthy man, and that he badly needed funds to continue his political career. If the oil company, and possibly other American companies concerned would hire Gonzales as a consultant for, say, $100,000 per year, it was quite likely that the attacks on the American companies would taper off markedly.

Bibliography

BIBLIOGRAPHY

Part I
THE NATURE AND SCOPE OF INTERNATIONAL BUSINESS

Aharoni, Yair. *The Foreign Investment Decision Process*. Boston: Division of Research, Graduate School of Business Administration, Harvard University, 1966.

Behrman, Jack N. *Some Patterns in the Rise of the Multinational Enterprise* Chapel Hill, N.C.: Graduate School of Business Administration, University of North Carolina, 1969.

Brown, Courtney C. *World Business: Promise and Problems.* New York: The Macmillan Co., 1970.

Coyle, John J., and Edward J. Mock. *Readings in International Business*. Scranton, Penn.: International Textbook Company, 1965.

Donner, Frederic G. *The World Wide Industrial Enterprise: Its Challenge and Promise*. New York: McGraw-Hill Book Co., Inc., 1967.

Fayerweather, John. *International Business Management: A Conceptual Framework*. New York: McGraw-Hill Book Co., Inc., 1969.

Hays, Richard D.; Christopher M. Korth; and Manucher Roudiani. *International Business*. Englewood Cliffs, N.J.: Prentice-Hall, Inc., 1972.

Kolde, Endel J. *International Business Enterprise*. 2d ed. Englewood Cliffs, N.J.: Prentice-Hall, Inc., 1972.

Krause, Walter, and John F. Mathis. *International Economics and Business: Selected Readings*. Boston: Houghton Mifflin Co., 1968.

Madeheim, Huxley; Edward M. Mazze; and Charles S. Stein, eds. *International Business: Essays and Articles*. New York: Holt, Rinehart & Winston, Inc., 1963.

Martyn, Howe. *International Business: Principles and Problems*. New York: The Free Press of Glencoe, 1964.

————. *Multinational Business Management*. Lexington, Mass.: D. C. Heath & Co., 1970.

Rolfe, S. *The International Corporation*. Paris: International Chamber of Commerce, 1969.

Rowthorn, Robert, and Stephen Hymer. *International Big Business 1957–1967: A Study of Comparative Growth*. Cambridge: Cambridge University Press, 1971.

Salera, Virgil. *Multinational Business*. Boston: Houghton Mifflin Inc., 1969.

Stewart, Charles F., and George B. Simmons. *A Bibliography of International Business*. New York: Columbia University Press, 1964.

Vaupel, James W., and Joan P. Curhan. *The Making of Multinational Enterprise*. Boston: Division of Research, Graduate School of Business Administration, Harvard University, 1969.

Vernon, Raymond. *Manager in the International Economy*. 2d ed. Englewood Cliffs, N.J.: Prentice-Hall Inc., 1972.

Wells, Louis T., ed. *The Product Life Cycle and International Trade*. Boston: Division of Research Graduate School of Business Administration, Harvard University, 1972.

Wilkins, Mira. *The Emergence of Multinational Enterprise*. Cambridge, Mass.: Harvard University Press, 1970.

Part II
THE FRAMEWORK FOR INTERNATIONAL TRANSACTIONS

Aliber, Robert Z. *The Future of the Dollar as an International Currency*. New York: Frederick A. Praeger, Inc., 1966.

Aubrey, Henry G. *The Dollar in World Affairs*. New York: Frederick A. Praeger, Inc., 1964.

Baker, James C. *The International Finance Corporation*. New York: Frederick A. Praeger, Inc., 1968.

Balassa, Bela. *The Theory of Economic Integration*. Homewood, Ill.: Richard D. Irwin, Inc., 1961.

Baldwin, Robert E. *Nontariff Distortions of International Trade*. Washington, D.C.: Brookings Institution, 1970.

Bloomfield, Arthur I. *Monetary Policy under the International Gold Standard*. New York: Federal Reserve Bank of New York, 1959.

Blough, Roy. *International Business: Environment and Adaptation*. New York: McGraw-Hill Book Co., 1966.

Clement, M. O.; Richard L. Pfistel; and Kenneth J. Rothwell. *Theoretical Issues in International Economics*. Boston: Houghton Mifflin Co., 1967.

Einzig, Paul. *The Euro-Dollar System*. 2d ed. New York: St. Martin's Press, Inc., 1965.

————. *A Textbook on Foreign Exchange*. New York: St. Martin's Press, 1966.

Friedman, Milton. *Dollars and Deficits: Inflation, Monetary Policy and the Balance of Payments*. Englewood Cliffs, N.J.: Prentice-Hall Inc., 1968.

————. *The Balance of Payments: Free versus Fixed Exchange Rates.* Washington, D.C.: American Enterprise, Institute for Public Policy Research, 1967.

Gibbons, William. *Tax Factors in Basing International Business Abroad.* Washington, D.C.: The Brookings Institution, 1964.

Gray, Peter H. *The Dollar Deficit: Causes and Cures.* Boston: D. C. Heath & Co., 1967.

Grubel, Herbert G. *World Monetary Reform: Plans and Issues.* Stanford, Calif.: Stanford University Press, 1963.

Haberler, Gottfried. *Money in the International Economy: A Study in Balance-of-Payments Adjustments, International Liquidity and Exchange Rates.* Cambridge, Mass.: Harvard University Press, 1965.

Haberler, Gottfried, and Thomas D. Willett. *U.S. Balance of Payments Policies and International Monetary Reform.* Washington, D.C.: American Enterprise Institute for Public Policy Research, 1968.

Hinshaw, Randall, ed. *Monetary Reform and the Price of Gold.* Baltimore: The Johns Hopkins Press, 1967.

————. *The European Community and American Trade.* New York: Frederick A. Praeger, Inc., 1964.

Holmes, Alan R., and Francis H. Schott. *The New York Foreign Exchange Market.* New York: Federal Reserve Bank of New York, 1965.

Horn, Paul V., and Henry Gomez. *International Trade Principles and Practices.* 4th ed. Englewood Cliffs, N.J.: Prentice-Hall, Inc., 1959.

Humphrey, Don D. *The United States and the Common Market.* New York: Frederick A. Praeger, Inc., 1963.

Jensen, Finn B., and Ingo Walter. *Readings in International Economic Relations.* New York: Ronald Press Co., 1966.

————. *The Common Market Economic Integration in Europe.* Philadelphia: J. B. Lippincott Co., 1965.

Kenen, Peter B. *International Economics.* Englewood Cliffs, N.J.: Prentice-Hall, Inc., 1964.

Kindleberger, Charles P. *International Economics.* 4th ed. Homewood, Ill.: Richard D. Irwin, Inc., 1968.

Krause, Walter. *International Economics.* Boston: Houghton Mifflin Co., 1965.

Kreinin, Mordecai E. *International Economics.* New York: Harcourt Brace Jovanovich, Inc., 1971.

Machlup, Fritz. *International Payments, Debts and Gold.* New York: Charles Schribner's Sons, 1964.

————. *Remaking the International Monetary System: The R10 Agreement and Beyond.* Baltimore: The Johns Hopkins Press, 1968.

Maizels, Alfred. *Industrial Growth and World Trade.* Cambridge: Cambridge University Press, 1963.

Malmgrem, Harold B. *Trade for Development.* Washington, D.C.: Overseas Development Council, 1971.

Nystrom, Warren J., and Peter Malof. *The Common Market: European Community in Action.* Princeton, N.J.: D. Van Nostrand Co., Inc., 1962.

Root, Franklin R.; Roland L. Kramer; and Maurice Y. D'Arlin. *International Trade and Finance.* 2d ed. Cincinnati: South-Western Publishing Co., 1966.

Scitovsky, Tibor. *Money and the Balance of Payments.* Chicago: Rand McNally & Co., 1969.

Shannon, Ian. *International Liquidity: A Study in the Economic Functions of Gold.* Chicago: Henry Regnery Co., 1966.

Shoup, Carl S. *Fiscal Harmonization in Common Markets.* New York: Columbia University Press, 1967.

Steiner, Henry, and Detlev F. Vagts. *Transnational Legal Problems.* Mineola, N.Y.: The Foundation Press, 1968.

Stevens, Robert W. *A Primer on the Dollar in the World Economy.* New York: Random House, Inc., 1972.

Triffin, Robert. *Our International Monetary System: Yesterday, Today and Tomorrow.* New York: Random House, Inc., 1968.

Urquidi, Victor L. *Free Trade and Economic Integration in Latin America.* Berkeley: University of California Press, 1964.

Yeager, Leland. *International Monetary Relations.* New York: Harper & Row, Publishers, Inc., 1966.

———. *The International Monetary Mechanism.* New York: Holt, Rinehart & Winston, Inc., 1968.

Part III
INTERNATIONAL BUSINESS AND THE NATION STATE

Aitken, T., Jr. *Foreign Policy for American Business.* New York: Harper & Row, Publishers, Inc., 1962.

Asher, Robert E., and E. E. Hagen, et al. *Development of the Emerging Countries.* Washington, D.C.: The Brookings Institute, 1963.

Baerresen, Donald W. *The Border Industrialization Program of Mexico.* Lexington, Mass.: D. C. Heath & Co., 1971.

Baranson, Jack. *Technology for Underdeveloped Areas: An Annotated Bibliography.* London: Pergamon Press, 1967.

———. *Industrial Technologies for Developing Economies.* New York: Frederick A. Praeger, Inc., 1969.

———. *Automotive Industries in Developing Countries.* Baltimore: The Johns Hopkins Press, 1969.

Bauer, P. T., and B. Yamey. *The Economics of Underdeveloped Countries.* Chicago: The University of Chicago Press, 1957.

Bauer, R. A., et al. *American Business and Public Policy: The Politics of Foreign Trade.* New York: Atherton Press, 1963.

Behrman, Jack N. *National Interests and the Multinational Enterprise.* Englewood Cliffs, N.J.: Prentice-Hall, Inc., 1970.

———. *U.S. International Business and Governments.* New York: McGraw-Hill Book Co., Inc., 1971.

Bernstein, Marvin. *Foreign Investment in Latin America*. New York: Alfred A. Knopf, Inc., 1966.

Brash, Donald T. *American Investment in Australian Industry*. Canberra: Australian National University Press, 1966.

Cooper, Richard N. *The Economics of Interdependence: Economic Policy in the Atlantic Community*. New York: McGraw-Hill Book Co., 1968.

Curtis, Thomas B., and John R. Vastine. *The Kennedy Round and the Future of American Trade*. New York: Frederick A. Praeger, Inc., 1971.

Dunning, John H. *American Investment in British Manufacturing Industry*. London: George Allen & Unwin, Limited, 1958.

―――. *The Role of American Investment in the British Economy*. London: Political & Economic Planning, 1969.

―――. *Studies in International Investment*. London: George Allen & Unwin, Limited, 1970.

―――. *The Multinational Enterprise*. London: George Allen & Unwin, Limited, 1971.

Engler, Robert. *The Politics of Oil*. New York: The Macmillan Co., 1961.

Faith, Nicholas. *The Infiltrators*. New York: E. P. Dutton & Co., Inc., 1972.

Fatouros, A. A. *Government Guarantees to Foreign Investors*. New York: Columbia University Press, 1962.

Fayerweather, John. *Facts and Fallacies of International Business*. New York: Holt, Rinehart & Winston, Inc., 1962.

Fforde, J. S. *International Trade in Managerial Skills*. Oxford: Basil Blackwell and Mott, 1957.

Gabriel, Peter P. *The International Transfer of Corporate Skills*. Boston: Division of Research, Graduate School of Business Administration, Harvard University, 1967.

Geiger, Theodore. *The Conflicted Relationship: The West and the Transformation of Asia, Africa and Latin America*. New York: McGraw-Hill Book Co., 1967.

Gordon, Lincoln, and Englebert Grommers. *United States Manufacturing Investment in Brazil*. Boston: Division of Research, Graduate School of Business Administration, Harvard University, 1967.

Hall, Richard W. *Putting Down Roots: 25 Years of Celanese in Mexico*. New York: Vantage Press, 1969.

Hanson, A. H. *Public Enterprise and Economic Development*. 2d ed. London: Routledge and K. Paul, 1965.

Hartshorn, J. C. *Oil Companies and Governments*. London: Faber & Faber, 1967.

Hellmann, Rainer. *The Challenge to U.S. Dominance of the Multinational Corporation*. New York: Dunellen, 1970.

Hirsch, Seev. *Location of Industry and International Competitiveness*. Oxford: Clarendon Press, 1967.

Hirschman, Albert O. *A Bias for Hope.* New Haven, Conn.: Yale University Press, 1971.

Hufbauer, G. C., and F. M. Adler. *Overseas Manufacturing and the Balance of Payments.* Washington, D.C.: U.S. Treasury Department, 1968.

Industrial Policy Group. *The Case for Overseas Direct Investment.* London: Industrial Policy Group, 1970.

Johnson, Harry G. *The World Economy at the Crossroads.* New York: Oxford University Press, Inc., 1965.

————. *Economic Policies Towards Less Developed Countries.* New York: Frederick A. Praeger, Inc., 1967.

Johnstone, Allan W. *United States Direct Investment in France: An Investigation of the French Charges.* Cambridge, Mass.: M.I.T. Press, 1965.

Kamin, Alfred, ed. *Western European Labor and the American Corporation.* Washington, D.C.: The Bureau of National Affairs, 1970.

Kindleberger, Charles B. *American Business Abroad.* New Haven, Conn.: Yale University Press, 1969.

———— *The International Corporation.* Cambridge, Mass.: M.I.T. Press, 1970.

———— *Power and Money.* New York: Basic Books, Inc., 1970.

Layton, Christopher. *Trans-Atlantic Investments.* Boulogne-Sur-Seine: The Atlantic Institute, 1968.

Levinson, Charles. *Capital, Inflation and the Multinationals.* New York: The Macmillan Co., 1971.

Levitt, Kari. *Silent Surrender: The American Economic Empire in Canada.* New York: Liverwright, 1971.

Little, I. M. D., and J. M. Clifford. *International Aid.* Chicago: Aldine Publishing Co., Inc., 1966.

Litvak, Isaiah A., and Christopher J. Maule. *Foreign Investment: The Experience of Host Countries.* New York: Frederick A. Praeger, Inc., 1970.

McCreary, Edward A. *The Americanization of Europe.* Garden City, N.Y.: Doubleday & Co., 1964.

McKenzie, Fred A. *The American Invaders.* New York: Street and Smith, 1901.

May, Herbert K. *The Contributions of U.S. Private Investment to Latin America's Growth.* New York: Council of the Americas, 1970.

May, Stacy, and Galo Plaza. *The United Fruit Company in Latin America.* Washington, D.C.: National Planning Association, 1958.

Mikesell, R. F., ed. *U.S. Private and Government Investments.* Eugene, Ore.: University of Oregon Books, 1962.

————. *Foreign Investment in the Petroleum and Mineral Industries: Case Studies on Investor-Host Relations.* Baltimore: The Johns Hopkins Press, 1971.

Mummery, David R. *The Protection of International Private Investment.* New York: Frederick A. Praeger, Inc., 1968.

National Industrial Conference Board. *Obstacles and Incentives to Private Foreign Investment 1962–1964.* New York: N.I.C.B., 1965.

Nwogugu, Edwin I. *The Legal Problems of Foreign Investment in Developing Countries.* New York: Oceana Publications, 1965.

Penrose, Edith T. *The Large International Firm in Developing Countries: The International Petroleum Industry.* London: George Allen & Unwin, Limited, 1968.

―――. *The Growth of Firms, Middle East Oil and Other Essays.* London: Frank Cass & Co., Limited, 1971.

Polk, Judd; Irene W. Meister; and Lawrence A. Veit. *U.S. Production Abroad and the Balance of Payments.* New York: National Industrial Conference Board, Inc., 1966.

Reddaway, W. B.; S. J. Potter; and C. T. Taylor. *Effects of U.K. Direct Investment Overseas.* Cambridge: Cambridge University Press, 1968.

Rolfe, S. E. and W. Damm, eds. *The Multinational Corporation in the World Economy.* New York: Frederick A. Praeger, Inc., 1969.

Safarian, A. E. *Foreign Ownership of Canadian Industry.* Toronto: McGraw-Hill Book Co. of Canada Limited, 1966.

Servan-Schreiber, Jean-Jacques. *The American Challenge.* New York: Atheneum House, Inc., 1968.

Skinner, Wickham. *American Industry in Developing Economies.* New York: John Wiley & Sons, Inc., 1968.

Tugendhat, Christopher. *The Multinationals.* London: Eyre & Spottiswoode, 1971.

Vernon, Raymond. *Sovereignty at Bay.* New York: Basic Books, Inc., 1971.

―――. *The Economic and Political Consequences of Multinational Enterprise: An Anthology.* Boston: Division of Research, Graduate School of Business Administration, Harvard University, 1972.

Wasserman, Max J. *The Common Market and American Business.* New York: Simmons-Boardman Publishing Corporation, 1964.

Watkins, Melville H. et al. *Foreign Ownership and the Structure of Canadian Industry. Report of the Task Force on the Structure of Canadian Industry.* Ottawa: Queen's Printer, 1968.

Part IV

ASSESSING AND FORECASTING THE INTERNATIONAL BUSINESS ENVIRONMENT

Abegglen, James C. *The Japanese Factory.* Glencoe, Ill.: The Free Press, 1960.

Almond, Gabriel A., and J. S. Coleman, eds. *The Politics of the Developing Areas.* Princeton, N.J.: Princeton University Press, 1960.

Almond, Gabriel A., and Sydney Verba. *The Civic Culture: Political Attitudes and Democracy in Five Nations.* Princeton, N.J.: Princeton University Press, 1963.

Alsegg, Robert J. *Researching the European Market, AMA Research Study 95.* New York: American Management Association, Inc., 1969.

Arensberg, Conrad, and Arthur H. Niehoff. *Introducing Social Change*. Chicago: Aldine Publishing Co., 1964.

Edwards, Corwin, D. *Control of Cartels and Monopolies: An International Comparison*. Dobbs Ferry, N.Y.: Oceana, 1967.

Enke, Stephen. *Economics for Development*. Englewood Cliffs, N.J.: Prentice-Hall, Inc., 1963.

Farmer, Richard N., and Barry M. Richman. *Comparative Management and Economic Progress*. Homewood, Ill.: Richard D. Irwin, Inc., 1965.

Hagen, Everett E. *The Economics of Development*. Homewood, Ill.: Richard D. Irwin, Inc., 1968.

Hall, Edward T. *The Silent Language*. New York: Doubleday & Co., Inc., 1959.

Hanson, S. G. *Economic Development in Latin America*. Washington, D.C.: Inter-American Affairs Press, 1961.

Harbison, F. H., and C. A. Myers. *Management in the Industrial World*. New York: McGraw-Hill Book Co., Inc., 1959.

Heck, Harold J. *The International Business Environment: A Management Guide*. American Management Association, 1969.

Henle, Paul. *Language, Thought and Culture*. Ann Arbor: The University of Michigan Press, 1958.

Hicks, Ursula. *Development Finance, Planning and Control*. New York: Oxford University Press, Inc., 1965.

Hill, T. P. *The Measurement of Real Product*. Paris: O.E.C.D., 1971.

Hirschman, Albert O. *The Strategy of Economic Development*. New Haven, Conn.: Yale University Press, Inc., 1958.

Holt, Robert T., and John E. Turner. *The Political Basis of Economic Development*. Princeton, N.J.: D. Van Nostrand Co., Inc., 1966.

Horowitz, Irving L. *The Three Worlds of Development. The Theory and Practice of International Stratification*. New York: Oxford University Press, Inc., 1966.

Johnson, R. J., et al. *Business Environment in an Emerging Nation*. Evanston, Ill.: Northwestern University Press, 1969.

Kamarck, A. M. *The Economics of African Development*. New York: Frederick A. Praeger, Inc., 1967.

Loucks, William N. *Comparative Economic Systems*. 6th ed. New York: Harper & Brothers, 1961.

McClelland, David C. *The Achieving Society*. Princeton, N.J.: D. Van Nostrand Co., Inc., 1961.

Marris, Peter, and Anthony Somerset. *African Businessmen*. London: Routledge & Kegan Paul, Limited, 1971.

Matus, G. L. *International Stratification and Underdeveloped Countries*. Chapel Hill, N.C.: University of North Carolina Press, 1963.

Meier, Gerald M. *The International Economics of Development*. New York: Harper & Row, Publishers, Inc., 1968.

————. *Leading Issues in Economic Development*. 2d ed. New York: Oxford University Press, Inc., 1970.

Merrett, Richard L., and Stein Rokkan, eds. *Comparing Nations: The Use of Quantitative Data in Cross-National Research*. New Haven, Conn.: Yale University Press, 1966.

Mountjoy, A. B. *Industrialization and Underdeveloped Countries*. Chicago: Aldine Publishing Co., 1966.

Nurkse, Ragnar. *Problems of Capital Formation in Underdeveloped Countries*. Oxford: Basil Blackwell, 1953.

Okun, Bernard, and Richard W. Richardson. *Studies in Economic Development*. New York: Holt, Rinehart & Winston, Inc., 1964.

Pryor, Frederic L. *Public Expenditures in Communist and Capitalist Nations*. Homewood, Ill.: Richard D. Irwin, Inc., 1968.

Richman, Barry M. *Management Development and Education in the Soviet Union*. East Lansing, Mich.: Institute for International Business, Michigan State University, 1967.

Rogers, Everett M. *Diffusion of Innovations*. New York: The Free Press of Glencoe, 1962.

Rostow, Walt. W. *The Process of Economic Growth*. New York: W. W. Norton & Co., Inc., 1962.

Sommers, Montrose S., and Jerome B. Kernan, eds. *Comparative Marketing Systems*. New York: Appleton-Century-Crofts, 1968.

Urquidi, Victor L. *The Challenge of Development in Latin America*. New York: Frederick A. Praeger, Inc., 1962.

Waterston, Albert. *Development Planning: Lessons of Experience*. Baltimore: The Johns Hopkins Press, 1965.

Webber, Ross A. *Culture and Management*. Homewood, Ill.: Richard D. Irwin, Inc., 1969.

Part V
MANAGING THE MULTINATIONAL ENTERPRISE

Barlow, Edward Robert. *Management of Foreign Manufacturing Subsidiaries*. Boston: Harvard Graduate School of Business Administration, 1953.

Bartels, Robert. *Comparative Marketing: Wholesaling in Fifteen Countries*. Homewood, Ill.: Richard D. Irwin, Inc., 1963.

Basche, James R. *Measuring Profitability of Foreign Operations*. New York: National Industrial Conference Board, 1970.

Berg, Kenneth B.; Gerhard C. Mueller; and Lauren M. Walker; eds. *Readings in International Accounting*. Boston: Houghton Mifflin Co., 1969.

Bivens, Karen K., and James Greene. *Compensation of Overseas Managers Trends and Guidelines*. New York: National Industrial Conference Board, 1969.

Boddewyn, J. *Comparative Management and Marketing*. Glenview, Ill.: Scott, Foresman & Co., 1969.

Brannen, Ted, and Frank Hodgson. *Overseas Management.* New York: Mc-Graw-Hill Book Co., Inc., 1965.

Brooke, Michael Z., and H. Lee Remmers. *The Strategy of Multinational Enterprise: Organisation and Finance.* New York: American Elsevier Publishing Co., Inc., 1970.

Bryson, George D. *American Management Abroad.* New York: Harper & Row, Publishers, Inc., 1961.

Business International. *Organizing for Worldwide Operations.* New York: Business International Corporation, 1967.

Carlson, Sune. *International Financial Decisions: A Study of the Theory of International Business Finance.* Amsterdam: North-Holland Publishing, 1969.

Carson, David. *International Marketing: A Comparative Systems Approach.* New York: John Wiley & Sons, Inc., 1967.

Cateora, Philip R., and John M. Hess. *International Marketing.* Rev. ed. Homewood, Ill.: Richard D. Irwin, Inc., 1971.

Cleveland, Harlan, et al. *The Overseas Americans.* New York: McGraw-Hill Book Co., Inc., 1960.

Duerr, Michael G. *R.&D. in the Multinational Company.* New York: National Industrial Conference Board, 1970.

Duerr, Michael G., and James Greene. *Foreign Nationals in International Management.* New York: National Industrial Conference Board, 1968.

———. *Policies and Problems in Piggyback Exporting.* New York: National Industrial Conference Board, 1969.

Dymsza, William A. *Multinational Business Strategy.* New York: McGraw-Hill Book Co., Inc., 1972.

Eiteman, David K., and Arthur I. Stonehill. *Multinational Business Finance.* Reading, Mass.: Addison-Wesley Publishing Co., Inc., 1973.

Ewing, J. S., and Frank Meissner, eds. *International Business Management Readings and Cases.* Belmont, Calif.: Wadsworth Publishing Co., Inc., 1964.

Fayerweather, John. *International Marketing.* Englewood Cliffs, N.J.: Prentice-Hall, Inc., 1965.

———. *The Executive Overseas.* Syracuse: Syracuse University Press, 1959.

———. *Management of International Operations.* New York: McGraw-Hill Book Co., Inc., 1960.

Friedman, W. C., and George Kalmanoff. *Joint International Business Ventures.* New York: Columbia University Press, 1961.

Gennard, John. *Multinational Corporations and British Labour.* London: British-North American Committee, 1972.

Gonzalez, Richard F., and Anant R. Negandhi. *The United States Overseas Executive: His Orientations and Career Patterns.* East Lansing, Mich.: Michigan State University, 1967.

Granick, David. *The European Executive.* London: Wiedenfeld & Nicolson, 1962.

Greene, James, and Michael G. Duerr. *Intercompany Transactions in the Multinational Firm.* New York: National Industrial Conference Board, 1970.

Gunther, Hans, ed. *Transnational Industrial Relations.* London: The Macmillan Co., Limited, 1972.

Hirsch, L. V. *Marketing in an Underdeveloped Economy.* Chicago: The Free Press of Glencoe, 1959.

Hoghton, Charles D. *Cross-Channel Collaboration: A Study of Agreements between British and Continental Firms.* London: P.E.P., 1967.

Kassalow, Everett M. *Trade Unions and Industrial Relations: An International Comparison.* New York: Random House, Inc., 1969.

Katz, Samuel I. *Exchange Risk under Fixed and Flexible Exchange Rates.* New York: Institute of Finance, Graduate School of Business Administration, New York University, 1972.

Leighton, David S. R. *International Marketing—Text and Cases.* New York: McGraw-Hill Book Co., 1966.

Liander, Bertil. *Marketing Development in the European Economic Community.* New York: McGraw-Hill Book Co., 1964.

Lietaer, Bernard A. *Financial Management of Foreign Exchange.* Cambridge, Mass.: The M.I.T. Press, 1971.

Lovell, Enid B. *Appraising Foreign Licensing Performance.* New York: National Industrial Conference Board, 1969.

McNair, Malcom P., et al. *Distribution Costs—An International Analysis.* Boston: Harvard Business School, 1961.

McNulty, Nancy G. *Training Managers: The International Guide.* New York: Harper & Row, Publishers, Inc., 1969.

Miracle, Gordon E., and Gerald S. Albaum. *International Marketing Management.* Homewood, Ill.: Richard D. Irwin, Inc., 1970.

Mueller, Gerhard G. *International Accounting.* New York: The Macmillan Co., 1967.

Nehrt, Lee C. *International Marketing of Nuclear Power Plants.* Bloomington, Ind.: Indiana University Press, 1966.

———. *International Finance for Multinational Business.* 2d ed. Scranton, Penn.: International Textbook Co., 1971.

Neufeld, E. P. *A Global Corporation: A History of the International Development of Massey-Ferguson Limited.* Toronto: University of Toronto Press, 1969.

Prasad, S. Benjamin, ed. *Management in International Perspective.* New York: Appleton-Century-Crofts, Inc., 1963.

Richman, Barry M. and Melvyn R. Copen. *International Management and Economic Development.* New York: McGraw-Hill Book Co., 1972.

Robbins, Sydney, and Robert B. Stobaugh. *Money in the Multinational Enterprise.* New York: Basic Books, Inc., 1973.

Robinson, Richard D. *International Business Policy.* New York: Holt, Rinehart & Winston, Inc., 1964.

———. *International Management.* New York: Holt, Rinehart & Winston, Inc., 1967.

Root, Franklin, R. *Strategic Planning for Export Marketing.* Scranton, Penn.: International Textbook Co., 1966.

Ryans, John K., Jr., and James C. Baker. *World Marketing: A Multinational Approach.* New York: John Wiley & Sons, Inc., 1967.

Sethi, S. Prakash. *Advanced Cases in Multinational Business Operations,* Pacific Palisades, Calif.: Goodyear Publishing Co., Inc., 1972.

Shearer, John C. *High Level Manpower in Overseas Subsidiaries.* Princeton, N.J.: Industrial Relations Section, Princeton University, 1960.

Stanley, Alexander O. *Handbook of International Marketing.* New York: McGraw-Hill Book Co., 1963.

Steiner, George A., and Warren M. Cannon. *Multinational Corporate Planning.* New York: The Macmillan Co., 1966.

Stopford, John, and Louis T. Wells. *Managing the Multinational Enterprise.* New York: Basic Books, Inc., 1972.

Stieglitz, Harold. *Organization Structures of International Companies.* New York: National Industrial Conference Board, 1965.

Stuart, Robert D. *Penetrating the International Market.* New York: American Management Association, 1965.

Taylor, Wayne C. *The Firestone Operations in Liberia.* Washington, D.C.: National Planning Association, 1956.

Terpstra, Vern. *American Marketing in the Common Market.* New York: Frederick A. Praeger, Inc., 1967.

————. *International Marketing.* New York: Holt, Rinehart & Winston, Inc., 1972.

Thomas, Michael J., ed. *International Marketing Management: Readings in Systems and Method.* Boston: Houghton Mifflin Co., 1969.

Weintraub, Leon. *International Manpower Development.* New York: Frederick A. Praeger, Inc., 1969.

Weston, J. Fred, and Bart W. Sorge. *International Managerial Finance.* Homewood, Ill.: Richard D. Irwin, Inc., 1972.

Wigglesworth, E., ed. *Readings in Policy and Practices of International Business.* New York: Thomas Ashwell, Inc., 1960.

Wilkins, Mira, and Frank E. Hill. *American Business Abroad: Ford on Six Continents.* Detroit: Wayne State University Press, 1964.

Wilson, Charles. *The History of Unilever.* London: F. Cassell, 1954.

————. *Unilever 1945–1965.* London: F. Cassell, 1968.

Wood, Richard, and Virginia Keyser. *Sears, Roebuck de Mexico,* S.A. Washington, D.C.: National Planning Association, 1953.

Zenoff, David B. *International Business Management.* New York: The Macmillan Co., 1971.

Zenoff, David B., and Jack Zwick. *International Financial Management.* Englewood Cliffs, N.J.: Prentice-Hall, Inc., 1969.

LIST OF ABBREVIATIONS

ADELA—Atlantic Development Group for Latin America
AG—Aktiengesellschaft (German Business Structure)
AID—Agency for International Development (U.S.)
ASP—American Selling Price

BIRPI—International Bureau for the Protection of Industrial Property

CACM—Central American Common Market
CARIFTA—Caribbean Free Trade Agreement, 1968
c.i.f.—Cost, insurance, freight
COMECON—Council for Mutual Economic Assistance

DEG—German Development Company
DISC—Domestic International Sales Corporation

ECGD—Export Credit Guarantee Department
ECM—European Common Market (see European Economic Community)
ECSC—European Coal and Steel Community
EEC—European Economic Community
EFTA—European Free Trade Association
ENI—Ente Nazionale Idrocarburi (Italian State Holding Companies)
Euratom—European Atomic Energy Authority

FAO—Food & Agriculture Organization
FCIA—Foreign Credit Insurance Association
FCN—Bilateral Treaties of Friendship, Commerce, and Navigation
f.o.b.—Free on board

GATT—General Agreement on Tariffs and Trade
GDP—Gross Domestic Product
GmbH—Gesellschaft mit beschrankter Haftung
GNP—Gross National Product

IBEC—International Basic Economy Corporation

IBM—International Business Machines Corporation
IBRD—International Bank for Reconstruction & Development (World Bank)
ICAO—International Civil Aviation Organization
ICF—International Federation of Chemical & General Workers Union
ICFTU—International Confederation of Free Trade Unions
ICI—Imperial Chemical Industries
ICSID—International Center for Settlement of Investment Disputes
IDA—International Development Association
IFC—International Finance Corporation
ILO—International Labor Organization
IMF—International Metalworkers Federation
IMF—International Monetary Fund
IRGOM—International Research Groups on Management
IRI—Institute for Industrial Reconstruction, Italy
ITO—International Trade Organization
ITT—International Telephone & Telegraph Corporation
ITU—International Telecommunications Union

LACM—Latin American Common Market
LAFTA—Latin American Free Trade Area
LDC—Less developed countries

MFN—Most favored nation
MITI—Ministry of International Trade and Industry, Japan

OECD—Organization for Economic Co-operation and Development
OPEC—Organization of Petroleum Exporting Countries

PICA—Private Investment Company for Asia
S.A.—Société Anonyme
S.A.R.L.—Société à Responsibilité Limitée
SDR—Special Drawing Rights
SEC—Securities Exchange Commission
SRC—Self-reference criterion

TVA—Tax on value added

UN—United Nations
UNCITRAL—United Nations Commission for International Trade Law
UNCTAD—United Nations Conference on Trade and Development
UPU—Universal Postal Union

WHO—World Health Organization
WHTC—Western Hemisphere Trade Corporation

INDEXES

AUTHOR INDEX

SUBJECT INDEX